PURITANS
AND
PRAGMATISTS
EIGHT EMINENT
AMERICAN THINKERS

PURITANS
AND
PRAGMATISTS
EIGHT EMINENT
AMERICAN THINKERS

✠

Paul K. Conkin

INDIANA UNIVERSITY PRESS
Bloomington   London

Library of Congress Cataloging in Publication Data
Conkin, Paul Keith.
  Puritans and pragmatists.
Reprint of the ed. published by Dodd, Mead, New York.
"Midland book."
Bibliography
Includes index.
CONTENTS: The Puritan prelude.--Jonathan Edwards:
theology.--Benjamin Franklin: science and morals.
[etc.]
1. Pragmatism--History. 2. Puritans--United States.
I. Title.
B832.C6   1976   144'.3   75-34730
ISBN 0-253-34720-3
ISBN 0-253-20197-7 pbk.   1 2 3 4 5 80 79 78 77 76

PREFACE

I hope these essays reflect my enthusiasm for both the character and beliefs of these original and often brilliant men. I have no illusions about inescapable personal and arbitrary criteria either in their selection or in my interpretations. I believe these essays summarize much, but far from all, of the most penetrating thinking done by Americans. I further believe that they reflect the most distinctive and the most clearly indigenous portion of that thought, at least before our present generation.

I intend the brief, alliterative title, *Puritans and Pragmatists,* to suggest some degree of continuity, some elements of underlying unity, in the varied and always idiosyncratic thought of these men. I try to define its character in the first essay, and frequently remark it thereafter. But the continuity, however labeled, was most often a matter of striking similarities rather than of direct, causal influences. In no literal, doctrinal sense were the pragmatists also Puritans, given the doubtful assumption that anyone could give a very precise yet historically relevant definition of either term.

No technical concepts justify the grouping of these men. Neither do external circumstances, such as church (most had ties to congregationalism), geography (all were somehow related to New England), or education (many had ties with Harvard), although such environmental factors surely had some relationship to the continued re-emergence of similar modes of intellectual response. Instead of these superficial similarities, I have tried to emphasize a common moral tenor, and derivative of this an instrumental conception of knowledge and a broad, ethical conception of art. Santayana, of course, eventually rejected this moralism and affirmed an extreme intellectualism and estheticism. I conclude with his retreat from Puritanism in order more dramatically to point up the earlier continuity, to reveal by contrast what I tried to define in my introductory chapter.

But enough for the over-all plan. Even the most perceptive reader may find the unity too elusive to be convincing. Some may even resent, as distracting, my efforts to identify it. And, after all, if this book has any real merit, it has to be in the honesty, the clarity, the conviction of the individual essays, and not in any broad interpretive scheme.

I composed these essays over a period of eight years, and only with the aid and support of many people, including my students in intellectual history at the University of Maryland. Every friend became a sounding board; every serious argument a clarifying tool. Two people rendered exceptional aid: Joseph L. Brent, III, in providing indispensable insights and knowledge about Peirce, and Allen Weinstein in a perceptive critique of the chapter on Dewey. As always, my excellent typist, Miss Katherine Sampson, was patient and meticulous. A generous fellowship from the John Simon Guggenheim Memorial Foundation and two summer grants from the General Research Board of the University of Maryland enabled me to do much of the thinking and writing.

PAUL K. CONKIN

CONTENTS

vii

PURITANS
AND
PRAGMATISTS

EIGHT EMINENT
AMERICAN THINKERS

I

THE PURITAN
PRELUDE

GOD AND MAN

In the hopes and dreams of its founders, New England was to be a cleansed and moralized copy of old England. By selective emigration, by the careful establishment of uncorrupted Christian institutions, and by God's help, it could be a model republic, a Zion on a hill. Only a vast wilderness can permit such a benevolent dream of a purified community. Without its open invitation, all social vision lies exposed to visions of apocalyptic upheaval and violence. Old societies, full of error, corruption, and compromises, are difficult to purify, save in a bath of blood. But surely new societies could be born pure and clean—or so these founders hoped.

Scarcely any of the political and religious leaders of the first Puritan exodus expected any earthly perfection. A purified community entailed a correct standard, not perfect achievement. It meant a community founded on the truth, dedicated to righteousness, and strong in resistance to all overt heresy and disobedience. From a modern perspective, the main pitfall in such an undertaking would be seen as the difficulty of knowing the truth. From the perspective of the Puritans, it was the difficulty of living the truth and, beyond that, of loving and cleaving unto it. The reasonable, moderate leaders knew the subtleties and the narrow doctrinal distinctions that might still perplex even the most saintly of men. They left room for such minor differences and even expected growth in understanding. But the main outlines of truth were

1

beyond sincere doubt. The path of duty was usually clear. Such intellectual assurance eliminated the motives for sweeping philosophical inquiry and for great intellectual originality. These came later, with perplexity, intellectual threats, and a need for better rationalizations.

But such a pervasive body of doctrine did invite an intense ideological consciousness and much intramural disputation and argument. Thus, in New England no particular beliefs, including religious ones, remained static. Among the more creative individuals, particularly ministers, the prevalent world view was ever in a process of reformulation and restatement, as required by new experience or necessitated by new knowledge. For those who refused to accept the burden of reformulation or the obligation of better rationalization, old doctrines soon lost any vital tie to experience and became cold verbal abstractions maintained by habit or social convention. If Puritanism is defined in a narrow doctrinal way, then much of New England, and even American, intellectual history is a story of the decline and fall of Puritan or Calvinist doctrine. In fact, some Americans are still rebelling against Puritanism. From the perspective of many such rebels, Arminianism and rationalism, Unitarianism and transcendentalism, pragmatism and humanism mark climactic episodes in a long process of emancipation from harsh dogmas and a repressive society. The doctrinal shifts have indeed been very significant, but never as radical as each generation believed them to be. Also, when Puritanism is viewed solely as a negative though a very influential point of departure for subsequent, rebellious thought, it becomes a formal abstraction, an overly coherent model of orthodoxy fitted with great effort to the first generation of colonists.

The continuities of New England thought, even in such exact areas as theology and philosophy, have been as significant as the shifts and breaks. Intellectual habits, institutional forms, and moral and social ideals survived many changes in conceptualization and rationalization. These continuities are most easily discovered in literature—in metaphors and images. They are reasonably apparent in political forms and political theory. They are more treacherous and more difficult to define in the case of intellectual attitudes and philosophical predispositions, but even here they are manifestly present and usually illuminating. Even the various versions of pragmatism, the most technical and sophisticated products of the New England mind, are not fully comprehensible except against the backdrop of the long unraveling, if not the unwieldy sprawl, of Puritanism in America.

When Puritanism is conceived, a bit loosely, as a collection of basic attitudes rather than as a specific and static ideology, the spectacle of Puritan decline becomes the more complex story of varied Puritan development. Then the history of Puritanism, like any epic, has no specific beginning and no end. The bits and pieces that came together in English Puritanism can be traced back through the slow emergence of an English middle class with certain values and aspirations, through the whole history of English legal and political development, and, indeed, through the Reformation and the whole history of Christianity to its Hebrew and Greek progenitors. Then the elusive key to Puritanism has to be, not varied sources or varied outcomes, not originality or unique- ness in any one belief or attitude, but an enduring coherence of a group of attitudes and the character and flavor that pervades the whole. The totality alone has to be distinctive and unique.

Puritanism came to full form in a time of theological ferment, and the most characteristic Puritans, particularly in times of rapid intellectual change, continued the ferment. By the eighteenth century in America, it was the questing and originative Jonathan Edwards and the politically aware John Adams who best exhibited and continued the Puritan tradi- tion, and of necessity through major changes in the form of its state- ment. It would be unfair to identify eighteenth-century Puritanism only with the less influential provincials who still nourished a fossilized caricature of the doctrines of 1630. Likewise, the later Unitarians, who often held on to the oldest Puritan churches, were, in a new age, as authentic successors of their equally intelligent and reforming grand- parents as were the most conservative Congregationalists. In crusading zeal, in political activism, and in the sense of adventure and exhilara- tion, they were the best successors.

Briefly characterized, the typical Puritan, in 1630 or 1930, reflected ideological assurance but was, at least in most areas and when at his best, open to new ideas. He was very much a moralist, a political activist, and an often repressive reformer who believed in the possibility of progress toward an ever more righteous social order. He venerated the rule of objective laws or principles, but he just as insistently believed in congregationalism and local democracy. He usually reflected a sense

of mission, even of a peculiar destiny, and an atmosphere of seriousness
and self-importance. Yet he was, or wanted to be, pious, ever mindful of
his dependence upon an overarching but never quite fathomable reality,
which he loved even without full understanding. Although he sought
redemption above all else, he had a wholesome respect for the instrumentality of both material goods and scientific knowledge, trying always
to keep either from becoming usurping ends. He demanded a conscientious stewardship of all men and wanted all to have a useful and fulfilling calling or vocation. Finally, and contrary to most stereotypes, he was
acutely sensitive to beauty, but only beauty fully integrated with the
moral quest and with a just social order.

Other Christian sects and later secular ideologies have emphasized all
these same attitudes. Certainly none were original to the Puritans or their
exclusive property. But among Christian sects, only a few Calvinist
groups ever exhibited, together at one time, as much political and educational zeal, as great an intellectual openness, and as successful an
integration of material values into a religious framework. Even among
Calvinists, the New England Puritans were unique in their polity, both
in church and state, and it was in their polity that they made the clearest
impact upon later American history.

The difficulty of assessing the total Puritan impact on American history springs from the large areas of overlap between New England
Puritans and other colonial migrants. Apart from institutions, no claim
can be exclusive. They shared not only many of the same traditions with
other Englishmen, but a common body of religious doctrines with
Scottish Presbyterians, French Huguenots, and the Dutch Reformed.
Before the Cromwellian Revolution, Calvinism made deep inroads
within the Anglican Church. On issues like grace and election, many
Anglican clergymen were at one with Puritan ministers. In Virginia the
early Anglican churches were, to use a later term, low church and often
quite Calvinist in doctrine. Thus, it is not a great exaggeration to describe colonial religion as at least mildly Calvinistic, for the exceptions
were all small sects—Quakers, a sprinkling of free-will Baptists, and the
German Anabaptists. Of course, after the Restoration most Anglicans
adopted an Arminian or free-will position, but, without early acknowledgment, so did many influential and liberal Puritans. Even in the eighteenth century the contrasts between Southern Anglican churches and
New England Congregationalism was not primarily in theology, but in

style, organization, and public support. The Puritan churches were well supported and led and were abetted by the village form of settlement. The Anglican churches were scattered, ill-staffed, and often neglected.

Even to label early Puritans Calvinists is to invite all types of confusion, particularly since Calvinism assumed many forms and was never, even in Calvin's own writings, a fully coherent ideology. The Puritans were very concerned about correct Christian beliefs and practices, but were not at all concerned about imitating Calvin's *Institutes*. To them, both Luther and Calvin were heroes of the faith, men who launched an epochal reformation of a corrupted church, a reformation they hoped to fulfill in their own adventure into New England. By 1630 Calvin's scriptural theology, in few essentials different from that of Luther, was so fully integrated into the assumed, unreflective beliefs of Puritans that it formed, at best, only a distant backdrop. The "truths" at the heart of the *Institutes*—the omnipotence and glory of God, the proportionate hatefulness and ugliness of rebellious man, the obvious need of grace, the focal importance of conversion, the sole authority of Scripture—were too obvious for serious doubt or meaningful disputation. More focal were less basic issues of polity and the more subtle interpretations of these truths. Since the Puritans looked directly to Scripture and hence to God for their authority, they felt free to depart from Calvin and Luther on minor issues and, if Scripture and reason had dictated (they did not), on major ones.

Calvin and Luther tried to establish a purified yet moderate and reasonable form of Christianity. They tried to expound the most obvious and unquestionable interpretations of Scripture. In modern perspective, it is clear that seemingly obvious meanings concealed cultural and class assumptions.

Common to all Christians was the biblical epic. But what did it mean? It allowed a variety of doctrinal explanations. In the seventeenth century everyone still accepted the Bible's simple cosmology. God created the earth and man. From here on the Calvinist interpretation was at least distinctive in some of its emphases. Although created in God's image (with a mind or rational soul), man was permitted to rebel, to join a fallen angel (Satan) in a great and foolish charade, denying God's omnipotence and affirming human competence. But the fall was not final. Reconciliation was promised in due time. The rebellion would be crushed and God would reign in solitary splendor. The God who permitted rebellion, presumably for His greater glory, provided also for limited atonement. Some foolish men would, by a gift of special insight, by a power of perception beyond their unaided capacity, see God in his power and his glory and his overwhelming beauty; so perceiving, they would return complete love and devotion and become participants in the final splendor. The grace given, the beauty revealed, came in a visible, sudden transformation of character, a moment of rebirth or of conversion.

The concrete proof of God's redemptive grace was given in Jesus the Christ, in a mediating Logos. In his sacrificial death and glorious Resurrection, Christ illustrated the depth of God's love for the divine traits still in man and also the ecstasy of complete reconciliation with God. In Christ's spiritual kingdom, the Church, and under the supervision of his spirit (the Holy Spirit), all Christian saints could live in communion, thankfulness, and love and fellowship, awaiting the time when the earthly kingdom would be perfected, and in which all redeemed men would live eternally, one with Christ and one with God.

The central Protestant doctrine had varied wordings, such as "justification, not by works, but by faith through grace." In the most important context of the Reformation—the seeming corruptions of the Roman Church—this doctrine was clear. Today it needs translation. It could now read: "One is reconciled to God not by any human merit, not by any sacramental rite, but by absolute and total love of Christ, a love impossible, as all things are impossible, without the gracious will and consent of God." Thus, God redeems. Faith, meaning not just belief but love and full commitment, is redemptive, but faith cannot be purchased. The scales of sin, which distort the perspectives of all unredeemed men and conceal human dependence and godly glory, are removed only by the mercy of God. The transformation is so radical, so instantaneous, and so undeserved that it appears almost miraculous and calls forth fervent thanks.

The yielding, loving, redeeming God of the Incarnation was as focal to Calvin as to Luther. But Calvin, with greater emphasis than any Christian thinker since Augustine, stressed that God was God, fully sovereign, and in no way subject to human will. His love could not be coerced or won by praise. After all, God sacrificed Himself, not for the glorification of man, but for His own greater glory. Man was indeed glorified in God, but even man's just damnation contributed to His glory. To be fully aware of the wonder and power and beauty of God was to recognize one's own incompleteness and limitation, and thus to submit to Him. In a moment of self-repudiation, in the death of all self-will and prideful pretense, man glimpsed the justice of hell, of his own deserved destiny. But in that submissive moment, in the loss of one's self, man gained faith, for he then recaptured what Adam lost—the spirit and will and purpose of God. He then became a willing and loving servant in God's earthly vineyard, obedient to the limits of his imperfect body. Fully reconciled in essence, the convert had only to wait a short while until the corruptible body gave way to a fully sanctified one. Then earthly man, already by grace a citizen of a heavenly kingdom, would become a full heir to eternal bliss.

The much-maligned, largely misinterpreted doctrine of predestination reflected Calvin's profound piety and his sharply polarized view of God and man. But the doctrine of predestination coexisted with, or even complemented, a defense of human liberty and an almost exaggerated emphasis upon human responsibility. God, as the eternal ground of all being, existed as the primary cause of all things. Nothing existed apart from or in opposition to Him. In this extreme of pious respect, or self-abnegation, Calvin embraced a demanding theodicy. He did not intend any cause-effect type of determinism. The crucial demand of the doctrine of predestination was a denial of substantive evil. All things depended on God, contributed to His ends, and were redeemed in their ultimate purpose. Even Adam's fall was consistent with God's glory, although contrary to a moral code given for Adam's self-governance. The pious man had to see all history, including man's fall and partial redemption, as consistent with God's will. No thing, not even Satan, could be conceived as evil in substance or in ultimate function. Sin, or evil, was misplaced affection, pride, and with it wrong choices. It was the delusion of lower creatures, not an ultimate distortion in the scheme of things. Only with Edwards was this demanding theodicy made fully explicit.

The doctrine of predestination, first extensively developed by Augustine as a correlate of omnipotence, and implicit in mild form in all Christian orthodoxy, originated in the context of an Aristotelian rather than a mechanistic conception of causation. In this context, teleological causes took precedence over efficient ones. Truly, all things were caused by God, including all human choices. But these choices were not of necessity caused by some mechanistic, coercive past event or force, but might be irresistibly caused by man's apprehension of something supremely good. Choice could be determined by something desired, by something in the future. This was moral determinism, not physical. It required rather than excluded voluntary behavior. Love, even converting love, was voluntary or it was not love. It was freely given or it was a mockery. Grace was irresistible because the envisioned God was irresistibly lovely. Man was physically free to make efficacious choices; if not, the gospel of Christ was senseless. Yet, man's choice was so tied to his being as to be fully consistent with God's eternal will.

But there were intellectual hazards lurking within the concept of predestination. Even in an often ambivalent or ambiguous Calvin there seemed to be two quite different concepts. Predestination easily existed as a part of an ontological conception of God and with a vision of God as the supreme object of affection. But Christianity fell heir not only to Platonic subtleties but to a Hebraic cosmology and historicism. Translated into the straightforward language of the Old Testament, predestination seemed to require a rigid historical determinism, a projective plan laid down in a distant past and inevitably unfolding into a distant future. Here the determinism was temporal even if not mechanistic. It was also quite coercive. The more oppressive term, foreordination, best fit this interpretation. A type of fatalism, a resigned acceptance of plans already decided, seemed appropriate. Many perceptive Calvinists never so interpreted predestination. They were too attuned to God as eternal ground, as an all-sustaining sufficiency, or as an object of their most fervent desires. In the profundity of piety, in the soaring ecstasy of redemption, they escaped the coercive interpretation with its consequence of either fatalism or almost inevitable rebellion. Joined with deep religious conviction and authentic religious experience, predestination had a meaning totally different from its vulgarized and secularized version—virtually the only version remembered today.

The Christian epic, in its Calvinist version, provided a complex, unwieldy, but tremendously rich tool for interpreting and accounting for types of vital experience, for varied feelings and emotions that sprang from the hazards and joys of life. It was, in all the varied personal nuances that could be given it without altering its form, a powerful and viable world view for very intelligent and gifted people. Today it is easy to view the epic and all the rationalizations that surrounded and abetted it and made it plausible, but it is very difficult, if not impossible, to recapture the quality of experience that made it believable and meaningful. The Puritan wanted everyone to have these types of experience, experience that he referred to as religious. But some did not. For most men, the Puritan version of Christianity—the carefully supported and propagated orthodoxy—must have seemed abstract and remote, even when social pressure and the educational process engendered some kind of intellectual consent, or prudence indicated its social utility. There were undoubtedly less able and less outspoken Benjamin Franklins throughout New England history, men for whom the official ideology, whatever its typical form from generation to generation, had no personal meaning, since it expressed no dimension of personal experience. For them, if they thought about it, Christian doctrine became a form of myth, and Christian theology became a perverse attempt to turn myth or subjective metaphors into a form of objective knowledge.

Calvinist doctrine both expressed and supported an extreme form of piety, or a particularly self-deprecatory and submissive stance toward reality or God. Even in other, basically impious ages, most people have occasionally known frustration, self-hatred, futility, and a sense of incompleteness. The intensely religious Puritan knew these feelings daily and was constantly reminded of his worthlessness and sinfulness. In introspective scrutiny he found added support for his worst apprehensions about himself. But unlike modern children of despair, he never doubted that his insufficiency rested over against a complete sufficiency. Thus, his piety reflected his apprehension of an inescapable relationship —the all and the part, the perfect and the radically imperfect, God and man. If man probed further into himself, into the contours of insufficiency and contingency and alienation, he could only give full assent to such a plausible doctrine as original sin. Powerful as the doctrine was, it alone, or something similar to it, could account for the evident fact of an ugly human pride. Conversely, if man inquired into the nature of complete sufficiency, if he reflected on God, he was compelled to accept the idea of omnipotence and with it the doctrine of predestination. If he were to escape the terrible fate of being on the wrong side of an awesome gulf, he had somehow to become a participant in the sufficiency, and thus grace was a most congenial, almost a necessary doctrine. It was the only way out, the only hope.

Piety, in Puritanism or any other sect, denotes a humble stance toward God, or toward the totality of being or reality. It may take many forms, in part determined by the conception of its intended object. To be pious is to stand in some approved relationship to something beyond man. Thus, piety points to a ground, a source, a power that governs human destiny. Whether or not it leads to intellectual construction or philosophical description, it forces man to refer outward, to be always aware of something larger and more enduring than himself. In this sense it is ontologically pregnant. But Puritans, like all Christians, inherited no one, unambiguous object of piety. There was a vast difference between the anthropomorphic Jehovah of the Hebrews and the over-arching, immanent mind of some Neoplatonic Christians. In Edwards, and even more in Emerson, the Neoplatonic impulse overcame the Hebraic, and thus Puritan theology, at its best, always sponsored an immanent God. This immanence allowed Puritan piety to embrace the whole natural order and made easy and smooth the many metaphysical transitions in New England, including the shift from Edward's *Perfect Being* to Emerson's more romantic *Oversoul* and to Dewey's *Nature*.

Piety may lead not only to submission, obedience, and praise, but also to humble description. It may produce philosophy. Man may strive to conceptualize reality, even in its fullness. He may even do this as a type of worship. But almost as soon as he reflects he also questions. He falls prey to problems of consistency, of inferential validity, and of fact. He knows doubt even as he learns to define and to classify. The conceptual task, even though born in love, may yet destroy piety. The experiential assurance is at least vulnerable; it may be undercut and forgotten. Then abstractions reign, even in religion. Respect has no viable object except intellect, and then only one's own intellect. Man then is God, the obvious creator of his abstractions and of his world. Yet, the same reflective vocation that threatens piety and that so often rends the wholeness of life and cuts man off from the ground and source of his own attainments may occasionally celebrate and deepen piety and become a vital aspect of any fuller redemption. The Puritan, as pious Christian, accepted the obligation and challenge, as well as the danger, of reason and careful inquiry. He believed that reason could be father to more appropriate celebration rather than beget a more terrible alienation.

Typical of a people with an assured ideology, the Puritans rarely reflected and usually condemned any form of skepticism, subjectivism, and cynicism. Like the committed Hebrews of the Old Testament, they had absolutely no sense of tragedy, of ultimate futility, of inescapable conflicts of value. They granted their finite limitations, their lack of full understanding, but had no reason to despair. God, so far beyond full comprehension, had yet made available the most essential knowledge— the way of redemption. Even limited, utilitarian knowledge, so important to earthly success, could be procured by enough effort. Man was not lost in his world. By enough effort he could always find his way. Thus the Puritans rarely condemned or tampered with serious scholarship or with scientific inquiry, but welcomed them for their moral uses and for their fuller revelation of God's handiwork. Even education, most highly prized as a method of preserving undoubted truth, could be used also as a medium for inquiry and new truth.

A very humble and pious conception of knowledge remained prevalent in New England thought all the way down to the pragmatists. The Puritan affirmed the ultimate goodness of God or of reality. To curse God, to admit the substantial existence of evil, was blasphemous. Reality was infinite, awesome, and beyond full understanding, but not evil. To assay its final limits, to presume on God, was either misplaced pride or metaphysical arrogance. Reality was knowable enough for human purposes, even though man should not flatter his prideful urge to imitate God and know everything.

This attitude, with its premium on instrumental knowledge, on morality instead of sheer intellectuality, led to a typical New England stance toward epistemology—the problem of truth is not a formal, technical problem, but one of practice, of utility, of making a proper response to the demands of God or of nature. Man knows enough, or by diligent effort can find out enough, to reach correct moral choices, to attain a degree of righteousness and progress. This is all that really matters.

This intellectual piety made metaphysics a frankly speculative endeavor. Man should not assume certainty for any human scheme. Yet, God invites the human quest for understanding. Reality demands man's fullest interest and all his flattering attempts at description. The early Puritans easily mixed and blended aspects of medieval philosophy, with no concern for a final, neat system. Emerson, so typical of latter-day Puritans, was intrigued by metaphysical problems and seemed tied to far-reaching speculation as if it were a sacred duty or even a form of worship. Yet he was always tentative, fearful of falling prey to some blasphemous presumption or some ill-fated pose of omnipotence. New England's intellectuals always flirted with metaphysical issues. They never left them alone for long. They did not renounce the speculative task simply because it had so many hazards. They freely displayed their ontological yearnings as well as their ontological trust. Yet, few ever settled into a complacent marriage with any finished system. In most cases their love and awe and sense of limitation prohibited such a deadly embrace.

MORALS AND SOCIETY

The Puritan was an unabashed moralist. He still is. He was more concerned with right conduct than with contemplative truth, with useful beauty than with elegant decoration. This meant extreme activism, courage, and perseverance; he condemned relaxation, escape, and even weakness. One had to find contentment in his daily work. The Puritan tried always to keep his hand on the throttle and his eye on the rail. At his best he tried to face up to all problems and had contempt for any evasion or obscuring of issues, for easy and quick pathways, for tearful surrender, for useless techniques, for diverting amusements, for asceticism, and for consoling or escapist types of beauty. He had joy and found fulfillment in the good fight and felt lost and helpless in the absence of challenge. As a moral athlete, he required a Satan as enemy. He hated passivity and any escape from the moral battlefield. He embraced force and power and did not hesitate to use them in behalf of what he conceived as right. His sermons and daily discourse were full of the metaphors of war.

Puritan moralism was always projected outward as well as inward. It embraced a whole society and engendered his ceaseless attempts to turn the city of man into a near replica of the city of God by means of a moralized educational system, a moralized politics, and a moralized diplomacy. The Puritan expected impossible feats of man and fought any soothing substitutes of sentiment for action, of irrationalism for the hard road of reason, of tragic detachment for fervent commitment. He wanted wisdom, or the right use of knowledge. He believed that man had a sufficient degree of intellectual assurance for courageous action.

Although paradoxical to the ill-informed, Puritan moralism required a belief in almost unqualified human responsibility and in the crucial efficacy of human choice. But from his perspective it also required some degree of cosmic assurance, an assurance which he located in an omnipotent God. Instead of reversing the doctrine of predestination, this moralism reaffirmed it. Anarchic or demonic free will not only challenged God's omnipotence but denied any responsibility in human choice or any cosmic significance in man's moral struggles. Only rational or deliberate, and thus caused, acts have any moral relevance. Thus, the Puritan wanted every possible act to be considered, rational, and voluntary, and consequently subject to praise or blame. His whole conception of history rested on the efficacy of choice, beginning with Adam's. What man desires and chooses is all-important, at least to man. As a pious qualification, it is obvious that all choices are consistent with God's will, for all things depend on Him. Without God there is nothing. But His will embraces the efficacy of human choices and allows them to bear their varied fruit. The Puritan hated mechanistic necessitarianism because it exempted man from responsibility just as completely as free will or the belief in accident. This meant a characteristically balanced position between two extremes

A moralistic view of human history makes all progress conditional. It occurs only when men choose correctly. This is true even though, in a cosmic sense, all that occurs is contingent on God. If His will is translated into temporal terms, He wills all that happens. Some patterns of history, within vague boundaries, are already known because of His revelation. The future has a certain inevitability. It will come out right in the end. But even in this temporal perspective, God has only underwritten a vast drama in which the crucial proximate force is often human choice and human effort. The element of assurance—the belief in an inevitable outcome—has no other than a consoling or morale-boosting function. It does not say when any goal will be reached or identify present mistakes or present detours. It does not relieve the need for hard choices or hard work. It does give assurance that God has willed the eventual climax and that He will prevent any ultimate and tragic futility in our best choices. Instead of cosmic assurance negating effort, it may well be the crucial factor in encouraging it.

In New England this moral fervor and reform zeal led to an ambitious, doomed effort to found and maintain purified communities. The early New England towns were internally selective and exclusive, parochial and intolerant. But they were never intended as isolated refuges from an unworthy and unfriendly world. Instead, they were to be living demonstrations to the whole Christian West. In their towns, whatever the continued reliance upon traditional British institutions, the Puritans made a tremendous leap out of feudalism and, in the process, escaped some of the galling restrictions and obligations that prompted their migration.

Unlike Virginia and most other southern and middle colonies, the Massachusetts Bay Colony and its daughters originated in a carefully planned, well-considered emigration of English nonconformists. No one else came. The families were almost always of one doctrinal persuasion (or were at least sensibly silent on doctrinal issues). The men were usually able yeoman farmers or successful tradesmen, some with a degree of wealth and social standing. The extremes were excluded. Titled nobility was as absent as the impoverished or incapable. Each new town originated in a voluntary, contractual undertaking by a relatively small group of families. Each family was a tight, covenanted community governed by the father. The organized town, a confederation of family heads, controlled all unallocated land and carefully screened new arrivals. In the beginning decades, succesful emigration to New England entailed something like gaining membership in an exclusive club. One had to find his place in a family and in a town; otherwise he could not become a citizen of the colony.

The small, homogeneous New England town was not a state or a nation. It was a voluntary society, occupying a small territory granted it by the Bay Company. Confined geographically, it posed no threat to anyone who did not choose to join or who could not qualify for admission. The Puritan settlements were a small part of a large and increasingly heterogeneous British nation. In England the Puritans had been a marked, often resented and persecuted minority. They migrated to a distant and empty part of Britain, and here jealously insisted upon their charter-bestowed liberty to plan and govern their intentional communities as they saw fit. They defended an empire of liberty, or a British nation always willing to allow differences to exist and to bear their appropriate fruit. Only in such a liberal empire could they escape the uniformity of an Anglican Church and the resented disabilities of a still feudal society. In spite of horror and resentment, they were forced, by logic as well as necessity, to suffer a heretical Rhode Island at their doorstep; later they earnestly tried to get bothersome Quakers to settle in their own special colony of Pennsylvania. Any threats to the prerogatives of another colony threatened their own special privileges. Thus, their insistence upon British liberties—their defense of colonial rights— was in no way inconsistent with their exclusive and intolerant (or purified) towns. Liberty, in a large nation, meant only the right of a cooperative group of like-minded people to build a society according to their ideals and to remain secure in their achievements, safe from those who would impose external creeds, unfair taxes, or unwanted ideas.

For the Puritan, the purified community entailed more than virtue or morality. It also demanded truth. Thus it required orthodoxy. Politically, the Puritan version of Christianity functioned as a most comprehensive social ideology, demanding as complete adherence in belief and as complete outward obedience in behavior as could be secured among men and by men. The town was dedicated to an external standard of truth and excellence, even as the Christian individual was dedicated to an internal standard. The town was thus a very demanding club, full of rules, demands, prohibitions, punishments, and other social controls. It assiduously indoctrinated its youth, preached to its adults, and quarreled with its outside enemies. Yet, for a typical citizen, the town did not seem excessively repressive (he often wished it more so and was responsible for its being so). Also, the limits and rules and approved forms of belief and behavior were largely internalized and voluntary. Thus, the outward coercion, the laws and courts, the fines and punishments were notably harsh but, at least in the homogeneous beginnings, notably rare in needed application.

Many of the seeming ambivalences of New England history, of a confusing mixture of libertarian contributions and horrible repressions, of excessively democratic forms and a seeming tyranny in practice, can be dissipated by an understanding of the exact operation of the total Puritan creed.

Christianity has always laid claim to totality. It was, in theory, a whole way of life, with implications in every area of human endeavor. But as soon as Christianity grew beyond the small congregation and became the religion of an empire and, eventually, of the whole West, it developed a necessary tolerance of wide differences in practice, even while maintaining a somewhat coherent body of abstract doctrines. Medieval Catholicism, for anyone not concerned with technical issues in theology, was formally authoritarian and practically quite liberal. The authority was personal and, to an extent, arbitrary. But, partial, ineffective, lacking in fervor and fanaticism, it was rarely harsh (it became more so in the wake of the Reformation).

The Reformation led to a revived Christian commitment and, among Calvinists, to a renewed attempt to establish totally Christian communities. The Anabaptists, who often founded the most strict and homogeneous communities conceivable, also embraced passivity, separatism, and escape. They renounced politics and the world. Even the Lutheran churches soon accepted a passive political role. But Calvinists, when serious and in control, refused to leave the secular world alone. In the tradition of Augustine, they tried to redeem it as much as it would allow. They embraced politics—a very relentless, repressive politics. In fact, at times politics seemed their prime vocation. They believed that, at least in external performance, elect and nonelect alike should follow God's laws. It was the duty of the elect to see to just that. Under their collective leadership (one could call it their "dictatorship") and under the clearly expressed authority of God in Scripture and nature, the strict and pure commonwealth could be built. In New England the Puritan even felt that he had a special commission from God to achieve just this; he partook of a new national covenant. In a new land only he could be blamed for any failures. To relax, to lower the standard, to permit folly or frivolity or foolish heresy, was to betray a godly trust and lose a glorious promise of protection and progress.

Thus, for the frontier Calvinists of Salem and Boston, as much as for earlier ones in Geneva, the total Christian creed had to become operative, through gracious consent in the saved and begrudging or prudential obedience in the unsaved. But, unlike a feudal and Catholic past, the creedal authority, the governing ideology, was effectively severed from arbitrary, personal, and hierarchical authority. Much as with the Anabaptists, it was officially located in God, but operationally placed in the *consent of the redeemed community*. This democratization, this effective internalization of doctrine, had many implications, but first among them was the now possible totality of creed, both in the degree and scope of its suasion over the life of everyone. Other radical implications are rather obvious—the absolute dependence upon indoctrination or extensive education, the emphasis upon clear and usually written laws, the reliance upon internal motivation, the resentment toward personal despotism or any abuse of delegated duties and responsibilities, the vital importance of informal techniques of social control, the acceptance of at least some features of an extended family system, the stress on social scrutiny and criticism, and the hatred of diverting or frivolous forms of recreation, entertainment, or art. The listing could go on for pages. Even the special role of the minister, both as educator and ideologist, developed out of the new pattern of authority.

Both the Puritan town and Puritan congregation were thoroughly democratic and authoritarian at the same time. Both originated in a covenant or contractual agreement. Both operated by an informally obtained consensus or, rarely, by a vote of the majority. Yet, all decisions were, at least in theory, made in light of eternal principles and laws determined ultimately by God, the only real sovereign. In both congregation and town the Bible figured large, as did accepted principles drawn from English tradition, or from what seemed to be right reason. Ideologically, it was a narrow, one-party system. Democratic decision-making only operated in small, perplexing areas of slight consequence, such as who should get what land or who should be elected magistrate or selected as minister. In practice, these were major problems, dividing towns and leading to endless controversy. Yet again, in theory, land was always divided according to a clear and objective system of priorities, magistrates were elected from many able and pious men, and ministers were selected from a few devout and carefully trained candidates. The major issues were already settled by clear authority and by community agreement. Democratic techniques only applied the set standards to particular cases. Thus, as Governor John Winthrop insisted, the civil liberty of New England had no relationship to arbitrary freedom or license.

The authoritarian-democratic institutions of the Puritans have tremendously influenced American political thought. The belief that proximate sovereignty rests in the covenanted community informed the political theory of both John Adams and John C. Calhoun. The principle of consent and of compact functioned in many ways. It made clear the delegated and limited authority of magistrates and assemblies (no government is sovereign), gave objective sanction for the reserved rights of citizens, emphasized the moral ends of government, made all democratic processes subject to established principles and laws, and precluded any authority vested in rank, priestly ordination, feudal titles, or claims of divine right. The two main prongs of American constitutional theory—the reserved rights of individuals and the clear statement of delegated powers—were at least implicit in the earliest Puritan practice. It is no accident that the preponderance of modern libertarian theory— from French Huguenots, the Netherlands, Scotland, and England— came from Calvinists. But the constitutional and libertarian implications never coexisted with any anarchical tendencies or with any desire to lessen the scope or repressive role of government. Even though objective and just, political power should be quite pervasive. Men need to be governed.

The Puritan town demanded a high standard of performance. De- viance, from "unnatural" sex acts to relatively minor differences in reli- gious belief, was harshly punished. Contrary to a well-established myth, people of widely different religious persuasions were rarely a threat in New England. The irksome Quakers knew the rules in New England and should never have tried to crash the gates and take over the club. No Jews or Catholics applied for admission. They had their own clubs elsewhere. But fervent and inventive Puritans, full of theological con- cern and probing questions, often divided the community, confused simple people, and even threatened the survival of some towns. Internal heresy, or internal growth, provided the greatest challenge to the totali- tarian system. The high level of literacy, the emphasis upon education and upon individual responsibility, and the congregational system all invited innovation and local diversity. Some differences had to be toler- ated even in the beginning, and some congregations, usually under ministerial guidance, soon moved some distance from orthodoxy. But at any one time, in any one town, there were limits to change. Without the limits, the essential identity and the pervasive goals of a town would surely be compromised. To admit great diversity—to become tolerant of all types of people—would destroy the pure community and leave only an ordinary village, without a covenant, a cause, or divine justification. The idea of a mission, of a called and protected people, would die. Thus, intolerance took the form of exclusiveness: those without were not allowed in; those within were banished. But for those who were part of the community, who tacitly accepted its terms, deviance meant punish- ment. For these people law was a necessary taskmaster; it was an instrument of rationality.

The essential attribute of New England justice was not its harshness but its objectivity. The rules had to be clear and tied to the authority of

God; the procedures had to be understood and traditional. The Puritans were also Englishmen. The laws were accepted English ones or accepted biblical ones. New statutes had to be consistent with both. As a result of public demand, the laws were eventually codified and published. Likewise, trial procedures were English and thus full of protective rules and safeguards. The great crime of the Salem witch trials was not the conviction of witches, but a hysterical disregard of due process. The laws themselves were comparable to those in force in England. But almost anywhere else in the world a person had some chance of avoiding certain laws, particularly those regulating private behavior and belief. One could at least bribe authorities or flatter magistrates. This did not work in New England. Every man knew where he stood, but he had to walk a very narrow line.

The actual operation of the New England town and congregation has left a bundle of historical puzzles. Among the more intriguing of these are such questions as the scope of the franchise in early Massachusetts and the role of ministers and magistrates in all the early colonies. The franchise problem has been given undue importance. Too often modern electoral procedures have been read back into the New England town. The town meeting, as informal club meetings today, probably resorted to formal votes only on rare occasions. The same General Court order (1631) that gave the franchise only to male communicants (loss of church membership did not entail any loss of franchise) also gave every person the right to be heard in the town meeting. Then, as today, persuasive ability, community standing, and economic power probably determined the actual distribution of political power. The requirement that freemen be churchmen was not intended as a severe or arbitrary limitation and, even with the rigor by which some congregations screened their members, it never disfranchised nearly as many men as historians once assumed. Where available records exist, it seems that approximately half (and surely the more capable half) of the adult males could qualify as freemen. Finally, even before the Bay Colony lost its first charter in 1686, men of certified good character could qualify without becoming church members. Thus, in perspective, the tie between righteousness and the franchise was an idealistic, almost utopian attempt at circumventing normal and less ethical and religious channels of political power. The experiment had radical implications. Never before, and not soon again, could a poor man or a shy man claim more community power than rich and polished men who remained outside the congregation. Also, under the early conditions there seemed to be a breadth and depth of political participation never again equaled as the towns grew larger and political issues became more impersonal.

Often the exclusive franchise has been viewed in the context of a false theological interpretation. Through a distorted understanding of predestination, the system has been made out to be completely arbitrary and thus in direct violation of the central theme of Puritan politics—clear and objective authority. Historians have wrenched the idea of divine election outside its theological context and applied it to politics. Then the franchise has been pictured as a privilege; one had to await grace and with it the vote. This is nonsense. No Puritan so conceived it. Grace was a choice made and a strength of character revealed. Church membership, in the social context, was a symbol of adult responsibility accepted. It indicated good character, maturity, and wisdom. Those who chose to remain without (theologically, those who loved other things than God) were surely weak and incapable men. The franchise, as much as club membership, was a matter of qualification, of attaining a standard. Salvation was certainly never conceived as a technique by which God arbitrarily certified voters.

But by giving special secular prerogatives only to church members, the Puritans invited hypocrisy. So long as social approval reinforced the conversion experience, weak men would experience conversion, or think they did, and cynical men would falsely claim the experience as a means of attaining esteem and power. But even the misled and the hypocrites had to take on a clear role and act out a part. Religion, as a means of securing socially acceptable behavior, worked almost as well for hypocrites as for saints.

The real problem, and the loss to the community, were the few intensely persuaded Puritans who, out of fear, refused to confess what they could never be sure of—a redeeming experience. They stayed away from the communion table out of honesty. Their exclusion became even more certain as many congregations, in the burst of enthusiasm that accompanied migration, actually tightened the screening process for church membership, placing more and more weight on reports of conversion experiences and less weight on community standing and moral conduct, a development not anticipated by the early franchise provision. Eventually, the halfway covenant and an inevitable trend toward more formalized, less introspective confessions eroded the terribly difficult experiment in separating the sheep from the goats. But by then the old system was doomed. By the time of the charter repeal, the congregations were already incapable of performing this social role. Too many able and powerful men were outside, increasingly unconcerned with spiritual matters. With the new charter, the external, less idealistic, and quite objective standard of taxable goods, of at least a minimal degree of worldly success, determined the franchise in Massachusetts. In fact, it changed very little. There was no revolution in the power structure. But to some ministers, such as Increase and Cotton Mather, the new franchise provisions represented a great symbolic loss of earlier ideals and hopes. In plaintive tones they asked: What has happened to the purified community?

The political leaders of Massachusetts, from governor to village selectmen, were usually men of ability and integrity. A few statistical studies show only a normal and expected correlation between officeholding and either wealth or religious standing. Poor men often held elected office. Also, just as property was widely distributed, so was officeholding. To some extent there was surely a power elite, tied to the narrow orthodoxy of the towns. Surely there were a few outsiders, resentful and embittered. But there is little evidence of any tight, exclusive oligarchy, nor of any large or organized resistance to the system. Nor is there evidence of any clerical domination of politics. The idea of a theocracy does not fit these towns and provinces, unless theocracy entails only an attempt to follow God's will in civil affairs.

In New England the officeholder was always respected for his role and function. As a socially approved calling, a political career had few peers in the Puritan hierarchy. Able magistrates were as vital as able ministers. But respect for the vocation did not insure respect for the man. Massachusetts politics began with strife and factionalism. The towns were always jealous of their prerogatives and often ignored the rulings of General Court or governor. Elected officials were rotated rapidly; some were impeached on rather tenuous grounds. The officeholder was clearly a servant, performing only allocated duties. Within these delegated spheres, he was expected, at least in theory, to exercise real authority, following conscience and God rather than the whims and fancies of his constituency. Thus, New Englanders insisted that they did not have a democracy. Yet, in fact, they had one of the most directly responsive representative systems ever developed. Each town was represented in the General Court. Elections were held annually. Magistrates and delegates were treated to election sermons, admonitions, and frequent instructions. If anything, Massachusetts suffered from a lack of continuity (provided after 1692 by a royal governor) and from too much local jealousy. The politicians were too representative; the people too factious.

Ministers, like magistrates, were elected by their constituents. They were hired and continued at the sufferance of the congregation. Yet, unlike magistrates, in most cases the minister's tenure was secure. There were few candidates. Most earned great respect and love. In New England the minister's role was quite different than in most of Christendom. He was the foremost professional in a province with few lawyers or trained physicians. As a class, he represented the best talent and the best education. His calling commanded the most respect and prestige, and often also the highest pay. Yet, the minister had almost no ecclesiastical power. By an iron rule, he never held any political office. The minister had no control over his own congregation except by persuasion. He could not be the sole judge of even the validity of confessions. He did not control the business affairs of the church; lay elders did this, subject always to congregational approval. Yet, a minister often established the very tenor of life in a village. An able minister could dominate a town for a lifetime. He could do this through his related functions—as an educator and an ideologist.

In New England, more than anywhere else in the world, the minister was a *preacher*. The sermon dominated the two lengthy Sunday services. Small towns became famous when an able minister gained a broad reputation for his sermons. Through pamphlet publications, his sermons might be read even in England. As a preacher, the minister operated much as a village professor, teaching long and demanding classes each week. His sermons, with their moral fervor and hortatory energy, provided a continuing even if not always enjoyable education for every citizen. His topics ranged from rational and learned Bible lessons and complex even if never profound excursions in theology to pointed commentaries on politics and all the specific personal and social problems of the town, province, and world.

The minister, as expert and man of learning, usually knew more about Christian doctrine than anyone else in a town. For this reason he became the prime interpreter and custodian of the community ideology, of the generalized world view. He was the party philosopher. In this capacity he often had great influence on political decisions, especially when conscientious magistrates turned to the minister for advice. Village orthodoxy was, in large part, the minister's orthodoxy. Yet, the minister, with his education at Cambridge or Harvard, his endless theological polemics, his published tracts, his conversance with a broader world of letters, science, and scholarship, could be the source of new ideas, of new interpretations, and even of seemingly heretical doctrines. He was almost always the source of any revisionism. It was not the ministers as a class who retarded the intellectual development of New England. More than any other group, they led it. From John Cotton to William Ellery Channing and Emerson, the more able ministers were the great source of cultivation, of sophisticated ideas, of eloquence and literary output, and even of enlightened political thought. The radical congregational polity, the jealous denial of political and ecclesiastical authority to ministers, combined with their social prestige, good pay, and education, gave New England the most able clergy anywhere in Christendom. At the same time, by placing responsibility on the laity, the congregational system, as much as the democratic town, helped produce able and informed lay leaders, and by this further increased the possibility of enlightened change. The best-led and best-governed churches soon became the most deviant and heretical.

Everyone knows that New England had an established church. Few understand this unique establishment. The Puritan colonists left English villages in which political authority (legislative and judicial) was variously divided between parish and county (or borough). In many cases the vestry performed more local governmental functions than the county, and required more taxes. In a semifeudal system, the church and state were variously interwoven, with great political intervention in religious affairs. Ironically, the Puritans came to New England determined to separate church and state. In their perspective, they did just this. The congregation and town were totally separate but equally covenanted bodies. The minister and magistrate performed entirely different functions, although they shared common goals that were conceived to be both religious and political. In New England there were no church courts, no ecclesiastical hierarchy, and no direct interference by the town in the affairs of the congregation. The minister freely criticized magistrates but could not dictate to them. Towns frequently elected against ministerial advice. The magistrate could not remove a minister or in any legal way determine congregational policy (the Roger Williams case showed that there were covert and indirect ways of influencing a congregation).

The church establishment involved two things: the town paid the minister, and it used laws and police authority to support the institutions of public worship. Both were conceived as political or even welfare measures, as prime responsibilities of civil government. The church, as a social and educational as well as a religious institution, was deemed indispensable to public morals and political stability. The minister was a public servant, an indispensable official. Thus, all citizens should be responsible for his maintenance. Likewise, church attendance, respect for Scripture and for truth, for correct beliefs, and thus for legitimate authority, were necessary aspects of any stable political order. In a reciprocal relationship, the church was always politically concerned and the town religiously concerned.

In a sense, there was no church in New England. Almost all institutional paraphernalia was missing. The minister was an employee of the town even though selected by communicants. Even the Sunday services, at least in the early years, were held in a common meeting house, not in separate church buildings. Beyond the voluntary, covenanted congregation, there was no ecclesiastical system of any kind. Except when assembled in meeting, the church disappeared.

But religion and politics merged in a common goal—a redeemed society. A magistrate seeking the general welfare had to consider and make provisions for religious worship (even present American policies are predicated on this goal, as evidenced by tax exemptions for churches). Religion, it then seemed, was the most vital concern of man. How could it be separated from politics? Equally, the church, as a corporate body of redeemed and active Christians working in God's earthly vineyard, had to bear the fruits of the Holy Spirit in all areas. No Christian could escape his political duties and responsibilities. To be religious was to try to redeem a society, to make a town a truly Christian commonwealth. Thus, politics and religion were inseparable, just as morality and politics were inseparable. The collective concerns of man were as much a part of God's moral order as were the concerns of the lonely individual.

As religious heterogeneity developed in New England in the eighteenth century, the ties between church and state changed almost imperceptibly into the more basic and more enduring ties between politics and religion. With the breakdown of the dream of an exclusive and purified Puritan community, and under pressures from other, "sojourning" Englishmen, the exclusiveness gave way to freedom of conscience and then to wide institutional tolerance. Anglicans, then Baptists, and finally the minor sects were allowed to hold services, build churches, and finally even share in the church taxes. But the formal establishment remained as testimony to a public concern for viable religious institutions of at least a vague Protestant type. At the same time, even the most liberal congregationalists (and often particularly the most liberal) kept alive the Calvinist impulse to use religious vision as an instrument of social reform. They unhesitatingly used political means to implement their deepest moral and religious concerns. The broad conception of political responsibility led also to continued sumptuary legislation, to support for schools, to some lingering controls over economic activity, and even to Puritan politicians like John Adams, who wanted support for science and the arts. In the nineteenth century the first compulsory school attendance laws were enacted in New England and in spirit were close to early Puritan statutes requiring everyone to attend public worship, as were antiquated blasphemy laws and unbelievable laws governing sexual behavior.

The Puritan, in rejecting the feudal merger of church and state, repudiated the Catholic and Anglican tradition. But he just as emphatically rejected the separatist, Anabaptist tradition, which required a complete separation not only of church and state, but of religion and a secular political order. The Anabaptists wanted a church too pure to exercise any worldly power and believed true Christians had no need for external political controls. Thus, secular politics was left to the unredeemed and, at best, passively suffered by the Christian. Roger Williams, a great Puritan intellectual, always a Calvinist in theology, leaned far toward this separatist tradition. He therefore threatened the whole Puritan enterprise—a righteous commonwealth in America. In American history Williams won a small engagement but lost his war. Conditions soon necessitated the institutional separation that he advocated. But the Puritan activist bent prevailed in most American churches. As a whole, Americans have always accepted the challenge as well as the hazards of a merged religion and politics. To do less would be to divide man and confess the amoral quality of national political and diplomatic goals. Those religious groups which have completely repudiated this political activism have been the exceptions in America (Anabaptists such as the Mennonites, Amish, and the Brethren churches, certain Lutheran groups, and some fringe-area fundamentalists). Americans still crave a morally redeemed society, not a secular expedient and a divine escape.

The Puritans attempted a precarious merger of traditional church and revolutionary sectarian institutional patterns. Their exclusive, state-supported, politically and socially active church duplicated many of the state churches of Europe. But the Puritans limited membership to the spiritually strong, made membership completely voluntary, refused even the symbolic solace of infant baptism to children of the unsaved, made the self-governing congregation completely autonomous, and tried to enforce a high level of moral and doctrinal purity within the church—all distinctive attributes of European sects. The Puritan tried to achieve the best of two worlds: the dedication, fervor, and integrity of sectaries; the security, institutional strength, and stability of churches. Just as dutiful piety and soaring spirituality marked the polar magnets of individual religiosity, so sectarian integrity and churchly conservatism warred at the institutional level. Roger Williams was too much a sectary, just as Anne Hutchinson was too enthusiastic. Time, once again, worked in behalf of churchly stability, not sectarian purity. The fear of internal contamination, the almost morbid screening of new members, and the spiritual exercises gave way to lax requirements and increased for-malism and ritualism. Thus, the Puritan not only had to give up his hopes for a purified town; he could not even keep the pure congregation.

SPIRIT AND MATTER

The Puritan, like most later Americans, tried to integrate material values into his total world view. He wanted to redeem matter, not transcend it. The physical universe represented opportunity. It was a divine gift awaiting the moral transformations possible through responsible human arts. Those who saw nature as a curse, or as a form of evil instead of a blessed instrument, were blasphemous. Those who made sensual gratifi-cation the only or highest end of man were perverse and ignorant.

The Puritan hated asceticism, such as that typified by monastic vows or priestly celibacy. Useless denial was a faithless method of seeking redemption. Things may, when overloved, become idols. But even though earthly life was a period of trial, it had its intimations of later glory. In proper perspective, food, drink, sex, and all forms of secular beauty were good, awaiting responsible use and enjoyment. Life should be as free from tribulation and suffering as possible. God no more commanded needless suffering than He condemned innocent pleasures. With thanks one should eat good meals, drink good wines, cohabit in joy with a wife, beget numerous children, acquire extensive property, and build beautiful towns. One should not be content with less than his best in any area. But all should be done for God's glory. Love the whole, not the isolated part. Embrace a larger community, not just the self. In Puritanism a great zest for life and a simple acceptance of worldly pleasures joined with an equally great sense of alienation and a yearning for redemption. But redemption entailed a more balanced and even fuller affirmation and joy, not a senseless rejection of the world in behalf of some ethereal fantasies.

Certainly most Americans have joined the Puritan in finding the ideal community in a prosperous town instead of in a spiritual retreat. There has been no more pervasive theme in American history than stewardship, no more pervasive democracy than that of work, no more pervasive fulfillment than in the practical arts, no more pervasive political goal than economic opportunity, no more pervasive devil than frivolous luxury. Instead of segregating the secular from the spiritual, Americans have more often confused them.

But how can the secular world—the world of work, production, and consumption—be redeemed? Instead of the Anabaptist strategy of socializing property, the Puritan tried to socialize the fruits of property. To succeed, this strategy required an uncommonly high sense of community responsibility and a very strict, largely internalized system of moral restraints. Opportunity and responsibility, with varied levels of achievement, seemed preferable to narrowed choice, less need for personal responsibility, and a greater equality of rewards. But the Puritan as capitalist was also the Puritan as Christian. The freedom of enterprise existed within a clear context of moral authority and of redemptive types of religious experience The higher priorities were clear. Yet, wealth turned out to be a devil as often as a blessing. As in all areas, the precarious balance was difficult to maintain: the little intrinsic value of things could be magnified and their great instrumental value minimized. A constant refrain in New England thought, and in American history, has been the need to regain the original moral meaning of private property and free enterprise.

The Puritans tried to attain a proper balance between individual initiative and community welfare. The community lost in the long run. The first migrants to Massachusetts Bay abolished most feudal restrictions on land and trade, yet tried to retain enough rules to insure fairness and justice. For a time some towns kept an open-field system. But from the beginning most granted discrete plots to individual farmers, with few limitations on ownership rights. The farmer managed his own private estate, although he remained responsible to the town for proper fences, for taxes, for work on community facilities (roads, bridges), and for militia duty. The same was true for village tradesmen, except that they often had to observe some wage and price guidelines. By such economic freedom, the Puritans tried to maximize opportunity and, at the same time, preserve responsibility. They did not want economic equality. Each town had a variable, in part socially determined formula for distributing land, which led to greatly disproportionate shares. Also, much undistributed land was left for later purchases. Although there were restrictions on absentee ownership, able men could accumulate large estates. In the seaport towns, where some men entered into shipping and merchandising, great profits were possible. Some men became wealthy; others remained poor.

The Puritan, like any Christian, was committed to economic justice. The problem for him, as it is still today, was one of definition and means. Already in England they had lauded industry and condemned idleness. God commanded work. His tasks had to be done. A serious Christian could have no use for frivolity or useless luxuries, yet should be thankful for prosperity. Man was a servant in God's vineyard, responsible for the full and joyful use of his talents. Every required and socially significant task was a dignifying vocation, an important calling. Each man had to find his appropriate task in order to achieve manliness, dignity, and community respect. Every man who conscientiously pursued his calling was a professional, an artist. If faithful, he would have both intrinsic rewards (the sense of fulfillment that comes from responsible creativity) and extrinsic rewards (the respect of his fellows and the needed material goods of life). Perhaps naïvely, the Puritans assumed a rough equivalence between human talents and community tasks. They believed a religious and moral tenor, a common sense of Christian duty or community pride, could alleviate any of the jealousies and resentments that might follow from differences of talent, wealth, and social rank.

The doctrine of a calling, so vital to all Calvinists, was full of promises and pitfalls. At its best it dignified all labor, forbade all exploitation, and required an atmosphere of economic freedom. It placed the real rewards of labor outside the wealth acquired or the product created. The real ends were moral and esthetic. Consumption was only a secondary even if important goal. The great moral travesty of Europe seemed to be the separation of art and of moral purpose from labor, which had often become degrading and slavish. The Puritan tried to return social respect, community approval, and religious sanctions to the ordinary tasks of life. Perhaps this was the most significant, even the most revolutionary, social contribution of Calvinism. In celebrating work, the Puritan tried to dignify and redeem life as most men lived it. The church service was not an escape from the duties of life as much as a training for life. Too many prayers or devotional exercises could be a form of frivolity, and thus of sin. This was realistic. Any society in the seventeenth century required, for survival, a great amount of work. If even a few were permitted the "curse" of idleness, or even religious forms of nonfunctional behavior, then other men had to work even more, perhaps so much that work could only be a form of drudgery. If a hierarchy of community values placed work low and other attainments (wit, social graces, fine arts) above practical vocations, then all work might become unfulfilling and a matter of hard duty.

But work, just as worship, could easily lead to a form of idolatry. Instead of intrinsic rewards, extrinsic goals could become all-important. After all, work might lead to wealth, and wealth to social status and political power. These alone might motivate human labor, leaving it as an intrinsically unrewarding and completely instrumental interlude. Then men would lose the sense of responsibility, of God's supervening will, that went with a calling. In behalf of power, not in behalf of a redeemed community, men would seek ways to get wealth quickly and would exploit other men. They would steal and cheat and take unfair advantage of others. Then the Calvinist ideology—the stress on work and on thrift and on a willing acceptance of small and difficult tasks—

might be transformed into a tool for keeping men at work, with both small esthetic and economic returns. With a small, almost imperceptible twist, the Puritan conception of dignifying labor (their real conception of art) could become an adjunct to a non-Christian, acquisitive form of capitalism. Then, indeed, the old doctrine would become an opiate, churches would become static escape valves, and religion would turn into an elegant but false window dressing for a sick society.

There is no art without freedom. This the Puritan sensed. Rigid economic restrictions, or some form of Anabaptist communalism, does not free man, for it does not allow scope for varied and distinctive talents. Economic equality is almost as enslaving as economic exploitation. But can opportunity for differences be preserved without providing beautiful opportunities for exploitation? This question the Puritan could never answer, even as America has been unable to answer it. The early laws tried to prevent overt exploitation, even as they easily became the agent of unfair privileges. Laws to regulate prices and product quality existed side by side with laws that prevented competitive wage increases. The freedom allowed for responsible enterprise could not abide any set of arbitrary limits on wealth fairly acquired; it could only insist that wealth be responsibly used. Monopoly, which cut off opportunity, was condemned, at least in theory. Frivolous uses of wealth were condemned either by law or by social disapproval. Profits had to be reinvested in wealth-producing capital. This created the perfect moral tenor for rapid economic growth, and without overt coercion of any type. But every year of growth increased the difficulty of maintaining the moral atmosphere and the idea of community responsibility. The New Testament dilemma remained. It is more difficult for a rich man to enter the kingdom of heaven than to thread a needle with a rope (often mistranslated as camel). Yet, all honor to the man who can do it. His piety is full; his redeeming spirituality is manifest.

The Puritan did not want to secrete man from temptation, even the temptations of great wealth. This balanced their fear of any artificial props for piety, such as beautiful cathedrals or soothing music. Every man had to stand alone and be responsible. He had to live in the world and there find his redemption. Salvation, to be sure, so transformed his values that the world had only small meaning. But even for a redeemed man, it had a function and served a divine purpose. Presumably, a redeemed man worked more dutifully and more joyfully than anyone else. He just might produce more goods and glean more profits. But worldly prosperity might result from chicanery or from a completely false sense of values, as the ministers constantly warned. Yet prosperity, as with the ancient Jews, might result from righteousness and be a sign of God's favor. When wealth accompanied all the outward manifestations of piety, it was assumed to be such a sign and was thus so honored.

Nothing is more false than the accusation that any but the most crude and vulgar of Calvinists ever equated wealth with redemption. The constant complaint in New England was that economic freedom rarely led to the desired level of stewardship. Wealth was misspent. The obvious lack of moral attainment set the stage for attempted reform, either by more preaching (at its Emersonian best this became prophetic and poetic denunciation) or by institutional changes. Neither worked. Zion remained elusive.

Contrary to the stereotypes of austere and morbid Puritans smashing stained-glass windows and closing theaters (they did both), they actually had a clear conception and appreciation of beauty and expressed the dominant esthetic themes in all American philosophy up to Dewey and Santayana. For the Puritan, as for almost everyone in the West, the key esthetic themes were unity, harmony, symmetry, and reconciliation, all themes intimately connected to their religion. Beauty was the supreme adornment of life, for it was also the most compelling attribute of God. It was experienced most overwhelmingly in rare moments of insight, of ideal apprehension, as in conversion. Then the Puritan report on God, ordinarily couched in terms of awe and even fear, became one of ecstatic adoration and love, a love so profound as to provoke all types of sensual imagery.

But in their profound respect for beauty, the Puritans vehemently rejected all forms of barren estheticism. In fact, no people ever hated lower and frivolous forms of beauty more than the Puritans. As in Plato, their attacks upon conventional art forms reflected a lofty repugnance at imperfect and limiting types of beauty, all in behalf of their vision of much more encompassing and perfect forms. The higher forms took precedence. If lower forms diverted, or merely entertained, they impeded true art and thus were ruthlessly crushed.

Committed people, with a vision of truth, always display a typical attitude toward all arts—they must contribute to the cause, to the overarching goals of a society. That is, all human art must be instrumental to some larger work of art—to a redeemed man, to a reformed society, to the kingdom of heaven. The Puritan celebrated many forms of beauty. Nature, God's own magnificent work of art, was their only cathedral. They found an inspiring type of beauty in the harmonious life of the redeemed, a theme later celebrated by Edwards and Emerson. They sought a type of social harmony, or a beautiful and virtuous community, a theme later apotheosized by John Dewey. Finally, as already intimated, they sought harmony and symmetry in work, in their daily tasks.

For the Puritan, the conventional human arts, whether today classified as fine or practical (no good Puritan will accept the validity of such a distinction), had to contribute to larger moral and esthetic goals. The more practical arts or crafts clearly had a moral instrumentality; in these even a charming playfulness might be permitted. But too many fine arts (except the literary ones) seemed, at least in the seventeenth-century forms the Puritans were acquainted with, escapist, indulgent, and even licentious. They distracted rather than invigorated, amused rather than inspired, soothed rather than fortified. The dilettante, the amoral and detached esthete, was at the very lowest level of human degeneracy, lost in fragmentary bits of beauty and oblivious of all high types including the beauty of God. The Puritan would have no playthings for the idle and rich, no diverting and useless decoration, no museums of dead relics. Yet, no people ever tried harder to incorporate a simple beauty, a wholeness and unity, into every aspect of life, into town, house, furniture, and above all into their personal lives. This esthetic bent, so inseparably connected to ethics and to religion, reached brilliant expression in America's Emerson and in England's John Milton.

The moral and intellectual side of Puritan religion, the dimensions of obedience and piety, are more easily grasped than are the qualitative or phenomenological aspects, possibly because the experiential consummation was always so difficult to express. Surely the Puritan tried to communicate feeling in confessions, diaries, letters, and revealing verse. In the poetry of Edward Taylor, even in the sermons of Jonathan Edwards, there was surely the same degree of excess in celebration and ecstasy as there was in exaggerated humility or morbidity in others. Among the early Puritans, the claims of piety and moral duty were barely sufficient to balance and discipline the explosive emotions, the soaring spirituality that simmered and glowed just below the surface, waiting to burst aflame, unchecked and dangerous, in Anne Hutchinson.

The end of Puritan religion was human redemption. In vulgar terms, this was the payoff. If God the Father was the awesome creator, the source of all things, the demanding Lord, to be feared and placated, then God the Son, the beautiful Christ, was the redeemer, to be loved, passionately and overwhelmingly. As pious man, the Puritan respected God as power; in moments of spiritual exhilaration he loved and adored God as supreme beauty. When merely pious, he was humble and respectable; when spiritually moved, he knew beatitude. As a pious man he bowed before a larger dimension of being; as a redeemed saint he adored and even possessed such a larger dimension. He was a new creature, born again. In essence if not in flesh, he was already in the kingdom of heaven. All the jagged edges—the alienating pride and illusions—had been resolved into a perfect unity. All was now harmony and beauty.

Such spirituality is, of course, socially dangerous. It easily becomes irresponsible, otherworldly, and impious. In crude forms it becomes an escapist and irresponsible sensuality, an indulgent gluttony for immediately gratifying experiences. In more lofty forms, it becomes an extreme form of estheticism or mysticism, the basically aloof, amoral adoration and enjoyment of God, of pure essences, of new dimensions of being. From the cloistered meditations of medieval mystics, to the backwoods beatitude of frontier revivals, to contemporary L.S.D. cults, such exaggerated spirituality has, when taken to a certain extreme, ceased to function as the motivating and justifying goal of rational effort. Instead it has led its advocates to renounce all the mundane instrumentalities of life as insignificant or even contemptible. Hence, the spiritualist may be, at best, a parasite; at worst a destructive force. The more balanced and prudent Puritans knew the danger of spirituality and fought it from the beginning. But the danger of losing the spiritual, the experiential, the qualitative, the esthetic elements of religion was just as great a threat, and one too often ignored.

When at his best, the Puritan was both God-fearing and God-possessed. He mixed humility and a sense of beauty; consciousness of sin with a glimpse of glory. His piety, his acceptance of the ultimate goodness of things, his sense of God's sovereignty, made the doctrine of damnation intellectually tenable. Certainly, without such piety, the suffering of life on earth in itself was a sufficient refutation of any God both all-powerful and all-good. But the piety, in itself cold and abstract, could never have been maintained, whatever indoctrination techniques and social pressures were brought to bear, unless it existed in some balance with an experiential relief, a sense of attained harmony and unity. When God became only an intellectual concept and not, to use Edwardian terms, the sweetness of pure divinity or a form of ravishing beauty, then man had to reject Calvinism and almost any other form of Christian orthodoxy, for God had to be either cursed or redefined to fit new human needs. Until the nineteenth century almost no one cursed. But everyone, including most Puritans, redefined. For those who fell into the intoxication of revivals, God often became a sentimental indulgence. For those who thirsted after reason, He became a benevolent creator and a convenient insurer of their scientific method, their political ideals, and their class interests.

Few Puritans, few men of any age, are able to attain and keep in healthy tension a very demanding piety and a soaring, esthetically pregnant spirituality. Extremes of duty and bliss do not easily cohere. Some fragmented men are extremely dutiful but insensitive; others are extremely sensitive but irresponsible. The Puritan, by the drive of his overly dichotomous logic, set up almost unbridgeable polarities and extremities. Unregeneracy was painted too dark; redemption too light. The standard for sainthood was, at best, a motivating ideal, not a goal achieved. Just as was Emerson's self-reliance, it was beyond the capability of ordinary men, and heroes are scarce. But for those who could stand the strain, such an impossible standard was continuously invigorating, never permitting any sense of complacency, of full attainment. Thus, in a quite legitimate sense, Puritanism was always declining, or at least any good Puritan was almost inevitably conscious of such a decline, for he usually projected his standard back a bit and falsely adorned his forefathers with it. Even the most able and articulate of Puritans, Edwards and Emerson, could ably celebrate a harmonious and beautiful life, but never quite attain it.

Ironically, the most enduring heresy of Puritanism would not be emotional excess, but rather an experiential barrenness. It would not be a lack of intelligence and reason and humane commitment, but a lack of esthetic fulfillment. It would not be otherworldliness, but excessive absorption in the instrumentalities of the world. The seriousness, the sense of responsibility, the excessive discipline, the hard work of the new Zion too early ceased to be related to redemption, to any experienced consummation. Then all the effort became a terrible burden without moral meaning, and New England was perennially ripe for either a humane attack on the surviving and coldly abstract iconography of Calvinism or a reinvigoration of the esthetic and experiential side of Augustinian Christianity. One tangent of reform flowered in the enlightened humanism of Franklin and Adams. The other developed in the theology of Edwards, and, more distantly, in the transcendental movement.

Even today the esthetic sensitivity, the search for redemptive experience, seems the most prophetic even if most ignored legacy of Puritanism. At its best, American philosophy has come to grips with religious and esthetic themes. Edwards turned Calvinist doctrine into a lofty esthetic vision. Emerson drew out the esthetic implications of Puritan moralism and used his model of beauty and art to criticize American culture. Charles S. Peirce, the first pragmatist, floundered in logic and metaphysics before finally capping his system with an esthetic ideal. John Dewey climaxed his work in epistemology and metaphysics by a carefully developed, but essentially Puritan, view of art. Even Santayana, in his youthful phase, simply buttressed the esthetic ideals of Emerson. Later, in his retreat from practical morality and duty, from the redemptive possibilities of art, he turned inward, like an Oriental sage, to complete spirituality and an aloof estheticism. This meant a rejection of Puritanism, but in behalf of spirit, not matter. Only in the Enlightenment, in such men as Franklin or possibly John Adams, was this esthetic sensitivity and spiritual awareness either absent or unacknowledged.

PART ONE

DIVERSE PURITANS

II
JONATHAN EDWARDS: THEOLOGY

ULTIMATE CONCERNS

Jonathan Edwards was a Christian and a genius. But many of his contemporaries were so blinded by his Christian orthodoxy that they failed to recognize his genius. Edwards, a solitary figure in eighteenth-century America, observed with disgust much of the formative, adolescent period in the development of American (and also modern) thought. He was vehemently critical of his age, for in it man was slowly but decisively taking the place of God. Piety was being replaced by pride; Christianity by a benevolent humanism. Edwards' protests were quite ineffective. For the next 200 years man would at least play at being God, with only occasional moments of revulsion, or even sheer horror, at the enormity of his presumption. But today, when the horror is widespread, when so many are embracing either cynicism or some new orthodoxy, it is easy, once again, to view Jonathan Edwards as an astute prophet rather than as a curious anachronism. In any case, no one today denies his solitary brilliance. Even if he failed to provide an adequate defense of his beliefs, he certainly left a penetrating criticism of the developments of his day and, through these, of much that is contemporary.

Edwards has often been characterized, or contemptuously dismissed, as the last great American defender of a strict form of Calvinism. But even to label him a Calvinist is to invite immense semantic confusion. Edwards was as far removed from the narrow scholasticism of some of the professed Calvinists of the seventeenth century as were his closest spiritual kinsmen, the Cambridge Platonists. Yet such rigid Calvinism, with its absolute reprobation, its unrelenting decrees, and its facile rationalism, was in spirit if not in word far removed from the burning fervor of Calvin. The often ambiguous *Institutes,* as most prophetic manifestoes, suffered from too much literalistic and legalistic exegesis.

Likewise, Edwards hardly resembled those few orthodox Puritans still on exhibit in New England pulpits. He cared little for many of the doctrines of earlier Puritans. Except in sermons, he rarely used the stilted axioms of earlier ministers or even the literal language of the Bible. As a philosopher, he moved well beyond (but not away from) conventional Christian orthodoxy. In his lofty philosophical theology, he seemed to be on an entirely different plane than even Calvin. Yet, by his philosophical ideas, he tried to save the essence and spirit of Augustinian Christianity. To do this, he usually ignored the highly stylized arguments that had so long divided traditional Calvinists and humanistic Arminians (free-will advocates). Historically, the Arminians had already won this battle, for orthodox Calvinism was becoming an oddity even in New England. Thus, Edwards raised his sights and, in an original philosophical perspective, tried to do battle with the whole spirit and tenor of an Arminian age and to show the terrible emptiness of the Arminian victory. To do this, he revived, and gave conceptual respectability to, an earlier Puritan spirituality, meanwhile clarifying the esthetic and experiential aspects of any true religion. By a Neoplatonic merging of morality and esthetics and by a new, sensationalist psychology, he attacked the cold rationalism and staid propriety not only of liberal Puritans but, by implication, even of orthodox Calvinists.

As a brilliant Christian theologian, Edwards tried to use the latest and, for the time, most convincing scientific and philosophical ideas in defense of a religious faith which, for him, was vindicated by reason and even more by immediate and inescapable experience. In this, he fulfilled the perennial role of theologians. Edwards' thought grew from his own struggles with the forces of his time and place. Working in virtual intellectual isolation, with less astute critics and slavish disciples, his intellectual achievement was a highly original and very personal work of art. Neither his subjective experience nor, closely related, his basic assumptions paralleled that of a majority of his eighteenth-century contemporaries. Yet, his brilliance made him more than a match for any

American. He started with the same conceptual tools as Benjamin Franklin or John Adams, but by combining them with his unique religious experience he created a world view that seemed somewhat out of place in the age of Enlightenment. God, not man, was at its core and infused it throughout. Into a vast intellectual homage to an overwhelming God that men were ever less inclined to treat as God, Edwards poured all of himself. His biography is almost entirely a biography of the mind. All else may be quickly summarized.

Edwards was born in 1703, the fourth of eleven children and the only son of Timothy Edwards, a Harvard graduate and the capable but hardly brilliant minister of a young church at East Windsor, Connecticut. His mother, the former Esther Stoddard, was the daughter of Solomon Stoddard, the innovating minister at Northampton (just upriver in Massachusetts), who was rapidly and deservedly becoming the most famous and powerful minister in the Connecticut Valley. Young Jonathan showed precocity; he absorbed from parents and grandparents an intense but, for his day, not unusual religiosity; and he pursued his education with great zeal. Early boyhood manuscripts reveal an interest in science and an amazing ability for detailed observation. He matriculated at a new, controversy-ridden Yale College at the age of thirteen, pursuing the regular four-year course and then taking two years in divinity school. At Yale he discovered the inviting world of ideas. He read Locke's *Essay Concerning Human Understanding* and found in it a revelation. It was during these inspired college days that Edwards first composed the notes entitled *The Mind,* which was his most significant endeavor in pure philosophy, which contained the kernel of most of his later thought, and which was the most brilliant philosophical work written by any American in the colonial period.

Before he completed his work at Yale, Edwards already displayed certain distinguishing traits of character. He was austere, methodical, unrelentingly industrious, and completely humorless. Following the practice in his father's home, he was straightforward and habitually frank, both seeking and freely bestowing criticism where it was due. He never developed the requisite tact, or the willingness to compromise, that are necessary for smooth social relationships. He made impossible demands upon himself, and therefore upon others. Later, as a husband and parent, he was solicitous, loving, and above all dutiful. He drew from his children the highest respect and most sincere affection, but affection compounded with a great deal of awe and admiration. Personally, insofar as he revealed himself to others, he was the perfect Puritan type. In fact, his personal life matched the Puritan stereotype much better than his thought.

By the age of nineteen, Edwards had completed his ministerial training and had accepted a call from a Scotch Presbyterian church in New York City. A brief but happy pastorate ended when the small congregation failed to prosper, but did mark the beginning of a close relationship between Edwards and the Presbyterians, both in Scotland and the American colonies. Puritanism, as it developed in the Connecticut Valley, had slowly compromised its early, rigorous congregationalism by countenancing regional ministerial associations with much real although unofficial power over individual congregations. Edwards, who was always relatively unconcerned with such mundane aspects of religion as church organization, freely acquiesced in this trend away from·congregational autonomy. After some stormy experiences with his own congregation, he at least once expressed his preference for the more orderly Presbyterian system. His relationship to Presbyterians and thus with what was becoming the second main body of Calvinists in America contributed to his later and tragic call to the presidency of Princeton.

In 1723 Edwards returned to Connecticut, where he accepted a tutorial position at Yale. He received his M.A. in 1724 and remained as a teacher until 1726. In that year he accepted a call as assistant minister and, obviously, heir-apparent to his grandfather Stoddard at Northampton, one of the most important churches in New England. Soon after his ordination, he married Sarah Pierrepont, who was then only seventeen, but of the best lineage and a girl whose exemplary piety had been observed and celebrated in near poetry by Edwards four years earlier. The marriage was a supremely happy one, even as Edwards' early career at Northampton was obviously successful. At the death of Solomon Stoddard in 1729 Edwards became the sole minister of a congregation that sometimes numbered over 600. He was provided with a good parsonage, ample pastorage for his livestock, and a salary of 200 pounds (with later increases), which placed him among the few prosperous and aristocratic citizens of western Massachusetts. Edwards accepted this status, dressing with the best and employing the ablest servants. He remained at Northampton until 1750, when he was dismissed by the congregation because of a personal and doctrinal conflict. If he had used a minimum of tact, it is probable that he would have remained there until his death. It was at Northampton that Edwards matured his thought, and it was also there that he achieved an international reputation for the revivals, and his reports on them, which helped trigger the Great Awakening.

At Northampton, Edwards inherited a religious tradition and atmosphere that more nearly presaged nineteenth-century evangelical Christianity than it resembled the strict Puritanism of the seventeenth century. Although Stoddard had never sacrificed any basic Calvinist doctrines, he went even beyond the halfway covenant by admitting, without any required proof of conversion, everyone who so wished to the Lord's Supper and into full church fellowship. Despairing of any human judgment of who was fit, and viewing the Lord's Supper as a saving sacrament, Stoddard's "reforms" led to a series of revivals at Northampton, and to a warm, emotional religion vastly at odds with the staid and proper churches of eastern Massachusetts. This heresy in church practice, coupled with the break with congregationalism by all the valley churches, made the Northampton church somewhat of a renegade. In most ways, Edwards was a loyal disciple of Stoddard. He fully accepted the necessity of an emotional element in religion and soon had unbelievable successes as a revivalist. But he eventually broke with the Stoddard heritage by trying to reinstitute a mild confession as a minimal requirement for church membership, and by doing this lost his position when the congregation rejected such a radical innovation.

Much of Edwards' intellectual labors were devoted to a long and increasingly astute defense of his revivals, of the Great Awakening which followed, and, even more fundamentally, of an affectionate type of religion. In this defense he tried to walk a narrow line between extremes, denouncing raw enthusiasm as often as a staid rationalism. In back of his defense was his certainty that New England Puritanism had lost the fervid if disciplined zeal of its golden age and, as was customary in religious movements, had degenerated into meaningless symbols, barren words, and moral hypocrisy. In this battle Edwards was a tragic figure. His own revivals, and even more those in other churches, led to such blatant excesses that affectionate or heart religion was long embarrassed in New England. Even the continued sporadic outbursts of revivalism and the virtual explosion on the frontier after 1801 would have given small consolation to Edwards, for these revivals too often erred on the side of enthusiasm without reason.

Closely connected with the loss of real piety, and even more disturbing to Edwards, was a humanistic element that was slowly, almost imperceptibly, transforming the New England churches. God was being humanized even as man was being deified. The absolute sufficiency and perfection of God, and the absolute dependence of man, was increasingly repugnant to eighteenth-century Americans. The first point of compromise was always the doctrine of divine election, under which the individual was a completely dependent even though voluntary recipient of saving grace. Man could do absolutely nothing to earn his election, could take no credit for it, and could not even resist grace when proffered by God. Followers of the Dutch theologian, Jacobus Arminius, challenged this idea by making grace at least resistable by man. The Arminians slowly widened this slight crack within Calvinism (a radical free-will doctrine had long been held by most Anabaptists) by emphasizing the ethical side of religion, by suggesting that salvation was universally offered to all men who would qualify themselves and believe, and by emphasizing human free will. God was more and more defined in human terms and forced to accept human concepts of justice and magnanimity. Although no responsible Puritan divine had openly embraced Arminianism by 1740, the Puritan covenant theology, with its language of the contract, obscured the most rigorous idea of dependence. God, in popular concept, was obligated to fulfill his part of an inviolable covenant. If man did his part and offered faith, God had to deliver salvation. Thus, faith became a necessary cause of salvation, and faith seemed to be something which an individual could earn. To Edwards, God was no longer receiving his due respect and religion was degenerating into blasphemy.

These were the twin problems of Edwards' lifetime—defining true religion and refuting the Arminians. To cope with them, either in sermon or treatise, he had to explicate his own beliefs about God, man, and nature. In doing this, he drew from many sources, combining them in an original and cohering world view that went well beyond eclecticism. In mental bent and in the more soaring insights of his theology, he was a Neoplatonist, drawing inspiration directly from Augustine as well as the contemporary Cambridge Platonists, such as Henry More and

Ralph Cudworth. After reading John Locke, Edwards always accepted his psychology and used it to express his Neoplatonism. He also, apparently without direct influence from George Berkeley, saw the logical weakness of Locke's representationalism, and thus of his distinction between primary and secondary qualities, and made a significant jump to pure idealism. He likewise exulted in Isaac Newton's revelations about the physical universe. But while Deists were using Locke to justify a rational and unemotional religion and Newton to justify a mechanistic and self-sufficient universe, Edwards used Locke to explain the phenomenon of conversion and Newton to prove the glory of God and the moment-by-moment dependence of nature on His being.

Edwards was, first of all, an intensely religious person, and bears a kinship to almost all religious figures in history. But he was also an adherent of a particular religion, with commitments to Christianity, to a divinely inspired Bible, to Protestantism, and to a form of Calvinism conditioned by the Puritan experiences in New England. Each of these commitments involved unnoticed prejudices, glaring provincialisms, and almost unbelievable blind spots. In some ways, Edwards never rose above his environment, either intellectual or geographical. The fact that he was totally ignorant of child psychology, and thus rejoiced at the religious experiences of a four-year-old girl, or that he used the keenest logic to refute subtle errors in Arminianism and never used the same logic to analyze biblical inconsistencies may astound and disillusion contemporary readers. But these limitations of time, place, background, and temperament must not be exaggerated or falsely interpreted. For example, Edwards was not a narrow literalist or fundamentalist, to use very modern and always ambiguous terms. He did not deliberately embrace inconsistency and paradox and never refused to accept either new facts or compelling new ideas. He was as horrified at irrationalism as he was at mere emotionalism. His insistence on the ultimate rationality as well as on the immediacy and feeling of true religion linked him both to the age of reason and to scholasticism. It was the fact that he found rational and experiential support for his *particular* religion that separated him from so many of his contemporaries. If Edwards had discovered a real conflict between science and religion, between fact and value, between truth and his own experience, he would have been a tragic and a very modern figure, but even less a part of the American Enlightenment. If he had discovered (or recognized) such a conflict, he would despairingly have chosen truth and fact in place of religion and value, for such was his honesty and his commitment to a rational universe.

In the case of anything large or worthwhile, to taste is to sunder. The whole flavor is implied in the first bite, provided the whole is consistent, but other bites are almost always necessary before the whole flavor is grasped. Even the most coherent systems of thought are likewise. To apprehend them one must start somewhere and starting, sunder. With time and effort, the sundered particles are seen to fit a complete whole, and each depends upon others and all others. Such is the thought of Edwards. To try to introduce the whole is to implicate untasted and ungrasped parts. To introduce parts is to befuddle because the whole is unknown. Edwards, fortunately, does indicate one starting point. His thought included a major defense of what could be called temperamental determinism. To Edwards, all mankind could be divided into two basic categories—the spiritual- and natural-minded. The separation between the two was complete, and basic temperament was not subject to change through human agency. By his own definition, few men have ever tried to be more spiritual-minded than Edwards, but his intense consciousness of God was in part derived from an even more fundamental and less conscious temperamental bias.

Perhaps the yearning for wholeness and unity is basic to man, but it certainly is unevenly distributed in its intensity. Edwards possessed it to an extreme degree. He loved harmony and symmetry and clear categories; he always searched for the complete design, the beautiful whole. He tried to trace any experience to its foundation. He wanted to live only in a fully rational, fully ordered universe. He hated the idea of anything accidental, uncaused, or arbitrary. Always a metaphysician and an artist, he wanted to fit all loose parts into a perfect whole and into a complete unity. He wanted, in other words, to live in a universe in which nothing was left to chance, in which no loose ends or open possibilities existed. In his view, the pattern of the whole had to dominate all the parts; hence his antipathy to individual free will and what necessarily follows from it, a contingent and accidental universe.

Despite Edwards' bent for order and reason, experience does not necessarily reveal such a universe. At least when interpreted superficially, experience shows only a dangling, imperfectly ordered world equally full of good and bad, justice and injustice. Neither nature nor history gives up any ultimate secrets. The whole remains beyond immediate grasp. A universe, if such exists, exists only on the level of abstraction and is largely hypothetical. It is too cold and formal for anything like love. In such circumstances man lives in a restricted world centered on his finite self. In the absence of any meaningful relationship to infinite being, man is his own god, though frustrated and possibly headed for destruction. Of course, many arguments may sway the intellect to accept the existence of a unifying reality, of God, but the arguments (from design, causation, innate ideas, degrees of perfection) are abstract and unmoving. They also tend to place God in another, a transcendent, realm, either leaving the world isolated or, if one ascribes to God the creation, leaving God as the insulted author of what man experiences as grossly imperfect. To Edwards, such a situation actually existed for most men and was synonymous with human corruption and degeneracy. Adam's progeny were alienated from being itself. Mankind suffered from an unassuaged, and without grace an unassuageable, thirst for reconciliation and restored unity.

To Edwards, the key to man's alienation from being, and particularly his lack of love for being, was his superficial interpretation of experience. Blinded by pride, man isolated himself from the whole. Edwards was persuaded by Locke that all knowledge ultimately depends upon sense experience, but he always agreed with Augustine that a special gift of grace is necessary before this experience can reveal its full meaning. To the elect, to Christian saints, experience was a constant revelation of God, of all being, a revelation too clear to reject and a being so beautiful that consent and love was irresistible. For the elect, the reality of God, of total and infinite being, was implicated in all cognizance of lesser or created being. To them, virtually all the arguments for God's existence were convincing. Edwards variously argued from design, from a priori necessity, from a necessary first cause, and from nature as a shadow of divinity. But all arguments, however logical or persuasive, were insufficient in themselves. They might lead to rational assent but not to love. Edwards never dared to go one step beyond what he conceived as consistent with good reason, but he never once doubted reason's ultimate dependence upon experience.

The necessity of grace, which was at the heart of Edwards' thought, related him to a long tradition in Western thought. Edwards used biblical terms and a sensational psychology, but in his mentality he was a

brother to all who believe knowledge of truth and a will to virtue are
tied to a special, intuitive insight that is at least one step beyond logical
proof or isolated sense experience. Plato was the perennial symbol of
this mentality, and by way of Plotinus and Augustine, Platonism became
a central theme in Christian theology. From Plato on, the point of view
had been conducive to some type of idealism, or at least to a tendency to
view nature as only a shadow of a higher, mental reality. But occasionally, the intuitive mentality had turned to a perfectly unified natural
order as the supreme reality. In Christianity, the intuitionists usually
gravitated in the direction of pantheism or divine immanence.

Locke pointed out to Edwards a pathway to idealism and thus
somewhat simplified the problem of explaining an immanent deity.
Locke demonstrated that all knowledge is only a knowledge of various
ideas or sensations—color, hardness, loudness, smoothness, sweetness
—but he assumed that certain sensations imply qualities actually present
in outside objects. Others, which he called secondary qualities, are only
in the mind of the observer. But how could one prove the existence of
objective qualities? Edwards, like Berkeley, saw the impossibility of
such proof and rejoiced in an easy solution to what seemed a dilemma.
There is, he assumed, nothing but minds and the thoughts or content of
minds. Matter is not a substance, but only an abstraction to represent
certain sensed qualities, or ultimately one basic quality—solidity or
resistance. To view God as pervasive being does not, therefore, implicate God with materiality. The only substance is mind and all being is
ultimately one. All objects other than minds are ideas and thus depend
on consciousness for their existence. The only substance back of the
world of nature is "the infinitely exact and perfectly stable ideas in
God's mind together with His stable will that the same shall gradually be
communicated to us and to other minds according to certain fixed and
exact methods or laws. . . ." ["The Mind," in Harvey G. Townsend,
ed., *The Philosophy of Jonathan Edwards from His Private Notebooks*
(Eugene, Oregon, 1955), p. 32.] All other minds (angels and men) are
direct emanations of God's mind, to which nature is a communication.
In one burst of youthful enthusiasm, Edwards described space as nothing other than God, for it is infinite and supports all that is.

Edwards never hesitated to speculate about God's intentions and
purposes. In an almost Aristotelian sense, Edwards viewed God as a
self-sufficient and perfect being whose love had to be for Himself, or for

being in general. Of course, insofar as man shares in being, God loves man. Since outward communication is natural to such infinite and luminous perfection, God, purely for his own glory, overflowed into his creation, which is a projection of Himself. This communication, to be such, required conscious and perceivable minds, which also became part of God's self-glorification. No creature, however saintly, adds to God's glory or happiness (these are always infinite), but saintliness is not distinct from what God is Himself. God as He is in the creature responds to God as He is in Himself. A saint thus shares in the glory and is part of it. The sinner denies himself this glory, but does not hurt God, if hurt means any detraction from His perfection. Since creation is really emanation, and since all objects are really ideas, the whole world is, moment by moment, directly dependent on God. A lapse of consciousness on God's part would negate all existence. Thus, the world is a constant, moment-by-moment re-creation according to God's own intentions. It is more than dependent on God's will; it is dependent on, in fact is part of, His very being. This is only an approach to pantheism, since God is prior to and more than His communicated being.

This insight clarified, at least for Edwards, the nature of the Trinity. Since all knowledge is knowledge of ideas, and since minds and ideas make up all reality, Christ, or the Logos, is God's perfect idea of Himself. God's reflection on Himself leads to His own perfect image, or His begotten Son. Christ, as God's perfect idea of Himself, is thus the unity, the pervasive rationale, behind all created existence. Since God's perception is perfect and complete, His perfect idea is as one with Him in essence, and thus Christ is not in nature any different from God. Christ's idea of the Father (really, an idea's idea very reminiscent of Spinoza) is identical to God's idea of Himself, for the content is exactly the same, and thus Christ's idea of the Father is identical to God's idea of Himself, which is Christ. The Holy Spirit is the mutual delight that exists between Father and Son, between God and His own idea of Himself. In this consists the infinite beauty, the complete Holiness, of divinity, a beauty present wherever the Holy Spirit is present. This delight is a type of energy, or an activity on God's part. And just as it is pure and perfect delight, it also is identical in essence to the Father and Son, and thus takes its place as the third person in a perfect unity. Edwards found support for this view of the Trinity in logic and Scripture and never saw anything in it unfathomable or mysterious. He believed trinitarianism necessary to account for divinity and argued that either less or more than three persons was completely inconceivable. Once again, and typically, Edwards used his great intellect in defense of an old doctrine. Here, also, he demonstrated the peril of too glibly dismissing him as a Puritan mystic. If mysticism denotes a suprarational and intuitive insight into reality, he was a mystic. But if it denotes the willing acceptance of something beyond understanding, Edwards was as far removed from mysticism as anyone who ever lived.

Since God is in all, and all is in God, man necessarily lives in the best possible world. The essence of egocentric pride and alienation is the failure to understand and fully, wholeheartedly accept and give full consent to this fact. Edwards, within a long Christian tradition, saw all nature as good in itself. But he was certainly conscious of evil and of sin. Moral evil was endemic with man and was at least consented to by God. The inability or unwillingness to give full love to God, or to perfect being, had been man's basic handicap since Adam. But even this moral evil was part of a larger whole, and in the totality of God's creation had a positive though, from a limited perspective, an unclear purpose. Thus, it was also part of God's will. But since it directly contradicted God's revealed command to individual men, it was truly evil from the perspective of the individual. Limited, finite man, unable without grace to view and taste the glory and perfection of God, and to participate in that glory, might stumble on the problem of evil and curse God. Unenlightened and blinded by the partial and temporary, he might be unable to comprehend the justice of a God who consents to what seems to be evil, and, even more, decrees eternal punishment for what He Himself has decreed. Edwards was one of a very few men in his day who so glimpsed the perfection and beauty of being in its totality, that he could, and did, give complete and humble consent to the Calvinist scheme of things. He did it as a Puritan, not a Pollyanna. This was his beatitude, his ultimate victory. He believed that such a victory was impossible to any man unaided by God.

Edwards' idealism and his analysis of being were scarcely understood, or understandable, by most members of his congregation or even by some of his ministerial colleagues. Yet, this idealism permeated his thought even down to his more practical sermons. Perhaps his congregation would never have accepted a God who loved only Himself and who hardly fitted a fatherly image. There was in Edwards a philosophical bent that, undisciplined by his Puritan heritage and by Scripture, would have taken him beyond a literal orthodoxy and toward an absolute idealism in which God was only absolute truth, or the completely real. By reducing all reality to mind, he easily achieved a complete spiritual monism. But by eliminating matter he moved very far from the Jehovah of the Old Testament and from the loving-father idea that has been so dear to sentimental Christians in all ages. At his more philosophical moments, there was always a dominant cerebral element—a rarefied, mathematical, metaphysical type of faith—which removed him as far from the common man as Spinoza was from his seventeenth-century contemporaries. Edwards' attempt to unite his philosophy and his sincere Christian commitment had to be through the Neoplatonist stream that reached as far back as the Pauline epistles of the New Testament. But at rare moments the union was not complete. Edwards obviously questioned the vitality of his own religious experiences when contrasted to the simpler and more emotional experiences of his wife and many members of his own congregation. The gulf was never quite bridged even for himself.

One result of Edwards' conception of God was a distinctive interpretation of Newtonian physics. The whole vast system in the *Principia* was, to Edwards as well as to Newton, a beautiful revelation of God. In nature, with all its newly revealed order, symmetry, and proportion, man had an almost perfect image of being itself, or God. Illumined by grace, a saint could not but rejoice in Newton's discoveries. But Edwards was aware that the new physics, and the all-important concept of mass attracting mass according to uniform laws, was an accurate description rather than a complete explanation. What was the cause of gravity? It seemed a great mystery. By analysis in light of his idealism, Edwards concluded that bodies (being ideal) are only points of resistance in space, capable of being communicated from one part of space to another. Resistance or solidity, being the power to stop movement, is as basic and as much a type of action as gravity, or the power of originating movement. Thus both are attributable to the same cause or agent, an agent that causes effects without being acted upon or itself changed. Such an uncaused cause exhibits intelligence and consciousness (the necessary corollary of an idealistic concept of nature) and, by necessity, is God Himself. Original creation was the first causing of such resistance in space, and such lawful relations between these resisting points as

Newton had clarified. Thus, all bodies have their existence in God's self-communication, and all laws of nature are God's own methods of acting with respect to resisting space. What Newton had referred to as atoms were points of resistance (bodies) that could not be divided by any finite means. The actual size was unimportant; indivisibility was the key. Since finite power cannot divide atoms, infinite powers hold them together. God is thus responsible for the most basic energy of all, that which holds atoms together and provides the stable building blocks of the universe. What many viewed as a mechanical universe becomes completely spiritual.

Consistent with this ontology, Edwards developed a nonmechanical view of causation. Yet, he always affirmed the necessity of cause and effect. Causation was part of the way humans think and as such was essential to any meaningful understanding. He constantly denounced as completely contradictory any belief in anything being uncaused or spontaneous, and he used this insight with devastating effect on Arminians. But Edwards just as vehemently denounced the English Deists who were using causation to justify mechanism and natural self-sufficiency following an original and perfect creation. To Edwards, they ignored ontology and thus failed to see the moment-by-moment dependence of creation on God's being, and not just on some prior willing. They felt that, after the first big shove, nature was a self-operating machine, with causal chains reaching from creation down to the present. Edwards joined with David Hume in denying any mechanical necessity between a cause and its effect and in thus exposing the most vulnerable side of any mechanistic philosophy. Edwards' belief in an unending but ordered creativity by God meant that there was only one efficient cause for each event, and this was God. Every event was as much proof of God's existence as some original event. Causality, a good word when correctly interpreted, was not a matter of mechanical necessity. Neither was it a habit based on observed but possibly accidental regularities, as Hume believed. It was simply a matter of regular, God-ordained sequences of events. Within a sequence, what invariably comes before something else is referred to as a cause, and what follows is called an effect. To glimpse the regularity is not to rejoice in a good machine, but to bow in praise before a rational God.

The implications of this view of causality were revolutionary, but again too subtle for the common man. Most important to Edwards, this view wrecked any contractual interpretation of the covenant of grace. Since all causation is in God, no event in a series of events necessitates another, or is the efficient, or immediate, cause of what is subsequent. Faith, or love of God, therefore, cannot be the efficient *cause* of salvation, although according to God's plan it precedes salvation. Undoubtedly Edwards' congregation gathered to pray for rain, feeling quite sure that they were going to change God's mind if their prayers were loud and long and fervent. Useless was Edwards' insistence that God had decreed all things harmoniously and in excellent order and that earnest prayers and rain after a drought go together as part of the ordained order. To either the common man or the average intellectual who, with good common sense, argued that the continuity of events was based on the inevitable efficacy of certain causes to produce certain effects, Edwards could hardly communicate his like certainty that all continuity was simply evidence that God thinks and decrees in an orderly manner. Thus, God had decreed that diligence and industry occur with riches and prosperity, that prudence precedes success, and that preaching usually precedes the conversion of sinners. But in each case the cause is God, and to Him is due all credit. In proof of His efficient role in all events, and in behalf of a higher order than the natural, on a few occasions God had not followed the usual sequence, and thus Joshua won a victory under a stilled sun.

THE GREAT AWAKENING AND AFFECTIONATE RELIGION

Whether his parishioners understood his more subtle thought or not, Edwards was an effective preacher, using vivid imagery to stir the feelings of his congregation. He carefully wrote and read all his early sermons and never resorted either to pulpit gyrations or to a loud voice. His impact was limited to the power of words and to his evident conviction and sincerity, coupled with a meticulous and almost faultless logic. This was enough to trigger significant revivals in Northampton as early as 1734 and to raise Edwards' hopes that a new religious reformation was beginning, that the City of Zion was at last to be planted in New England. Utopia flitted into the meeting house, but so very soon was gone again. These revivals made Edwards the best-known minister in New England and pushed him into an acrimonious controversy over the merit of the revivals. From accurate, almost clinical description, he was led to a definition of true religion. In the process, he not only probed the depths of human psychology, but also translated some of his theological insights into the language of the common man.

Edwards' first successful revival began in December 1734 and flowered in the spring of 1735. It was a greater revival than any experienced under Stoddard and vitally affected not only the town of Northampton but the subsequent religious history of the United States. As the revival climaxed and declined, Edwards wrote a detailed account, which became a manual for subsequent revivals all over the country (*A Faithful Narrative of the Surprising Work of God in the Conversion of Many Hundred Souls in Northampton and the Neighboring Towns and Villages*). Yet, the account was restrained and dispassionate, replete with accurate and detailed descriptions. It was also full of concealed awe and wonder, for Edwards was the main participant in something so vast, unexpected, and potentially explosive that no one could quite comprehend it all. In his revealing language, in his great hopes and ill-concealed apprehension, he penned some of his most prophetic writings. Without intent or awareness, he was describing more than the coming Great Awakening, or even more than the revivals of the early nineteenth century; he was, in fact, and for the first time, clearly revealing what shortly became and long remained a central element in American Protestantism, and thus a major element in American life. What was spontaneous at Northampton would soon become ritualized, and Jonathan Edwards, by simply describing, did more than anyone else, save possibly George Whitefield, to establish that ritual.

The first conversions at Northampton followed the agonizing death of two young people and a controversial sermon by Edwards against incipient Arminianism and in behalf of the doctrine of complete dependence. With the conversion of a fun-loving, company-keeping young woman, the incipient awakening, particularly among young people, became a contagion, and the town became completely obsessed by religion. It was the sole subject of conversation, and secular business was pursued only as a duty. Northampton became, in Edwards' view, a Christian utopia, with an end to factions, jealousy, and frivolity. Edwards' home was besieged by those seeking the means to salvation. For one communion, Edwards received 100 new members; over 300 were converted in all. Within a few months virtually all the unredeemed adults in Northampton had been converted; church membership rose to 620, necessitating a new meeting house.

Edwards carefully noted the phenomena attending conviction and conversion. The experience in each case varied immensely, from intense fear and melancholy to rational concern; from calm assurance to exuberant ecstasy. Many were so affected that they lapsed into coma or exhibited other bodily effects. Despite an antipathy to wild enthusiasm, Edwards found no reason to doubt the authenticity of many of the most ecstatic conversions.

Although unprecedented, this early revival did not approach some of the later extremes of emotionalism. It did not create lay exhorters, was not produced by any extravagant or particularly frightening preaching, affected all classes equally, and was under the constant supervision of Edwards. Also, following the typical Puritan pattern, most of the conversions occurred during the course of daily affairs and in homes rather than in the meeting house. The group hysteria, the wailing from the mourners' bench, came later. Unfortunately for Edwards' later reputation, he selected for detailed description two of the most extraordinary and sentimental conversions, which to him were most revealing and, probably, most puzzling. One concerned the remarkable experiences and the overwhelming spiritual love of an ill and dying young lady who was, obviously, a neurotic. The other recounted the remarkable religious precocity of a four-year-old girl, who had such religious experiences that even a cautious Edwards could not doubt her authentic conversion (the next youngest convert, it should be noted, was nine years old). With the suicide of a leading man in the community, and other excesses, this early revival subsided almost as quickly as it came, leaving some despair and a great many things for Edwards to ponder.

The fuse was relit in 1739 and 1740. The champion evangelist of all time, George Whitefield, came to America, and even staid Boston was quickly at his feet. The new awakening spread through all the colonies, leaving its strangely mixed legacy of extravagant enthusiasm and vital piety, of moral excesses and lasting humanitarian reform, of ignorant exhorters and pious evangelists. Once again Jonathan Edwards was a leading figure in the revivals, hosting Whitefield when he preached in Northampton. As the hated excesses increased by 1741, as the exhorters or irresponsible fanatics threatened many established pulpits in New England, and as religious emotionalism took new and ever more esoteric forms, more and more Puritan ministers dared condemn the revivals and such defenders as Edwards. Edwards was soon left between two extremes—radical enthusiasts and the "reasonable" men who hated all emotion in religion. In a second published book on the revivals (*Some Thoughts Concerning the Present Revival of Religion in New England*), he acknowledged and condemned certain excesses, defended the authority of established ministers (he would soon have his own problems on this count), but still argued that, over-all, the awakening was a work of God. He believed this strongly enough to use all his strength to continue the revivals, traveling often to neighboring pulpits (and, on one trip, delivered the Enfield sermon, "Sinners in the Hands of an Angry God"). He was not yet so disillusioned as to give up his supreme hope—that the Great Awakening was a prediction of the millennium, of the Latter-Day Glory, which might well begin in America. With this hope, he bitterly condemned those ministers who merely ridiculed the revivals and thus, possibly, placed themselves as obstructions to the final great renewing. But even as he defended, Edwards was groping toward something more fundamental and more needful—his definition of true religion and some clear means of identifying a true conversion. With this accomplished, it would be possible to isolate the good and bad in the revivals and possibly end the controversy between the New Lights (revivalists) and Old Lights. He preached a series of sermons on this topic in 1742 and then published his final answer—and thus his ultimate wisdom gained from the Great Awakening—in his most influential book, *A Treatise Concerning Religious Affections.*

Published in the twilight of the Great Awakening, the treatise was a grand attempt to justify a middle way in religion, to disclose the Devil's wiles among enthusiasts and the cold hearts and either the error or lack of religion on the part of the Old Lights, to mediate between emotionalism and cold rationalism, to prevent either complete religious anarchy or Deism. If he could succeed, future revivals could not be so easily perverted by Satan, and hence could be enduring. By carefully defining twelve signs of gracious or holy affections, and by categorizing almost as many inconclusive signs, he tried to still critics and calm enthusiasts. The signs of true conversion were to be used by individuals to examine themselves, for no one else was capable of making such a crucial judgment. According to Edwards' careful and lengthy analysis, true religious affections came only through the direct operation of the Holy Spirit, were grounded in love of God and His moral excellence or beauty, could arise only out of an enlightened mind, always testified to the certainty of divine things and a final judgment, were accompanied by true humility and a sense of insufficiency, resulted in a radically changed human nature closely resembling the humble and dovelike spirit of Christ, were beautiful in symmetry and proportion, created an insatiable appetite for spiritual attainments, and, most emphasized, led to Christian practice. Other factors might indicate true conversion, but in themselves were never conclusive, since they might be based on something other than love of God. These included the degree of affection, bodily effects, fervent and abundant talking, involuntary behavior, sudden or vivid remembrances of scriptural verses, a large variety of feelings or passions, sudden feelings of love, visions, a certain order of feelings, and complete approval by other Christians. These listed signs, whether conclusive or inconclusive, were based upon Edwards' definition of religion as holy affection.

Edwards, to an extreme extent, viewed man as a unity, with mind and body so closely related that each unavoidably affected the other. In the same manner, he viewed the mind as a unified soul, although with varied powers or modes of operation. For convenience, he referred to the understanding and will, but never followed an older psychology into a rigid categorization of varied, almost independent mental faculties. With this approach, he affirmed that true religion involved both understanding and the will and that the essence of religion was holy affections. By affections he meant a vigorous and sensible exercise of inclination (will not associated with immediate action), with love naturally being the prime religious affection. The key word was sensible, for by this Edwards was not only showing a loyalty to Locke but was insisting upon an immediacy and a type of sensuality in religion. Sensible meant a relationship to the senses and to the intuitive certainty that accompanies direct sense experience. God, if conceived only mentally or notionally, and not directly and immediately (if not tasted, felt, seen), could never arouse real affections, although the understanding might respond to His truth.

The emphasis upon inclination and upon sensation did not mean any less degree of understanding. To Edwards, who was working within a Puritan rationalism and opposing the "hard" hearts of scoffing and allegedly rational Arminians, the emphasis had to be upon the appetitive side of religion, upon the emotions and feelings. But in brief passages, and endlessly by implication, he made holy affections directly dependent upon an enlightened understanding. He believed love of God inseparable from an understanding of God. In those cases where the appetite and inclination were purely animal, and reflected unthoughtful reactions to stimuli, Edwards used the word passion instead of affection. The passions did not spring from the mind and thus had no relation to anything spiritual.

Edwards believed that holy affections accompanied conversion and were a direct result of grace. They depended upon an added awareness, a supernatural sense, which accompanied the Holy Spirit into the heart of the newly converted. In fact, the holy affections of the elect were identical to, and shared in, the mutual affections of Father and Son in the Trinity. Edwards was most original in explaining these affections by Locke's psychology. Accepting the priority of sensation and perception, he believed that saving knowledge of, and a resultant affection for, God had to have the experiential quality of direct perception. Man must literally "have a sense of" God and not just an abstract concept. Edwards' writings were replete with sensual descriptions of divinity; one word was particularly pervasive—sweetness. Holy affections (complete love of God) depended upon an apprehension of His beauty and comeliness. The response of man to God always had an esthetic quality. It was an active response to something beautiful, to something symmetrical and well proportioned and comely. The supernatural sense (the indwelling Spirit of God), through no bodily organs, and through no added outward sensations (visions were unnecessary), added a new dimension to experience, enabling the saint to perceive divinity directly in the midst of otherwise quite ordinary experience. Edwards' greatest concern was that the experiential and sensible element be recognized in order to save religion from a sterile, unaffecting rationalism.

The principal object of religion (God) was beyond normal sense experience and, therefore, as Edwards so well understood, beyond the existential level of everyday life, at least for the average, nonconverted individual. Although he did not anticipate the near future when rational pathways to transcendence were, one by one, to fall into intellectual disrespect, he did feel that most people could not be reached by subtle arguments and that rational proofs were never in themselves productive of true religion (holy affections). Only spiritual man (one who has the

Holy Spirit) had a direct apprehension of God, as immediate and persuasive as the perception of a cow in a neighboring pasture, yet so beautiful and wondrous as to produce near ecstasy. The natural man (with only the ordinary senses) talked about God and usually believed in His existence, but the very word God only stood for a mere abstraction. But spiritual man used the word God to denote a complex image so vivid and real in the mind that, for all practical purposes, God was seen and felt and tasted.

Edwards' emphasis upon the sensual (he called it sensible) and esthetic elements in religion, and thus upon an existential immediacy, was related to his deep attachment to nature. Even as a boy his own intense religious experiences usually occurred in the fields or woods. By habit he spent time in outdoor meditation almost every day of his life. His sermons were at their best when he used natural imagery as a means of making vivid his meaning (the spider and fire in "Sinners in the Hands of an Angry God"). He spiritualized this naturalism by his stress upon emanation and immanence. To Edwards, nature contained the most immediate and persuasive revelation of God's beauty. The spiritual man saw God in all of His glorious creation. Nature was an image or shadow of divinity. Yet, as a Calvinist, he reserved this insight for the elect few and balanced it by just as ardent an allegiance to the Bible as a second revelation. His orthodoxy alone separated him from a later, transcendental view of nature.

Believing that mind and body necessarily affect each other, Edwards not only defended emotion and feeling in religion but also bodily manifestations. Strong inclination produces bodily effects, such as hunger for food produces salivation. Thus, the ecstasy of viewing divine things, or the horror of feeling or imagining hell, cannot but affect the body. The total lack of bodily changes (many of which will be invisible) might well indicate a cold and unaffected heart. Also, this view of religion justified affectionate or moving sermons. The minister must do more than logically persuade; he tries to move the affections, usually by such images as can induce a sensible grasp of the subject, whether God's glory or hell's horror. Only when the sermon can speak directly to the heart as well as to the head can it serve the interest of true religion. Edwards thus tried to justify much of the preaching in the Great Awakening and argued that a cold and lifeless religion was not religion at all, since love was never cold and lifeless. Likewise, he tried to show that religion was not morality, mere sentimentality, social or political idealism, or effective reform. It was intense love of God.

One implication of his *Treatise on Religious Affections* had immediate bearings on his own congregation. If religion consisted in holy affections, and if there were valid tests for such affections, should not church membership be limited to such as could testify to conversion and to such affections? This test would not eliminate all hypocrites or even those sincere people who misinterpreted their own experiences, but it would set up the minimal requirement for participation in the Kingdom. Edwards decided that he had to reverse his revered grandfather and tried to reintroduce a simple confession in the Northampton church. This angered some of his congregation and gave a weapon to old enemies who disliked Edwards personally, or who resented his aristocratic dress, his comfortable living standard, or his large salary. Edwards had been less than tactful in denouncing village sins, in handling the sons and daughters of the best citizens after they acquired and secretly read a handbook for midwives, and in pressing for salary raises. The common people joined with valley merchants to force an uncompromising Edwards out of his pulpit in 1750. He lingered on in Northampton for over a year, a repudiated forty-seven-year-old minister with a wife and eleven children to support. Finally, after considering pulpit offers from as far away as Scotland and Virginia, he became a missionary at an Indian mission at Stockbridge in western Massachusetts. There he assumed tiring administrative duties, won a grueling political battle with well-entrenched opponents, and yet found time to publish some long-awaited attacks on Arminianism. Disillusioned, somewhat forgotten by the outside world, he spent the last years of his life in the work of the mind.

THE BATTLE AGAINST ARMINIANISM

Except for the temporary transports of the Great Awakening, Jonathan Edwards was continually aware of a moral and religious decline in New England. He participated in a morbid awareness of a Laodicean church that had been endemic with Puritan ministers for over a century. Edwards set himself to resist the trend and tried to do this by refuting the prevalent errors of his day. In his books on the Great Awakening he had condemned a cold and lifeless religion as well as emotional excesses. Now he wanted to discover what lay behind the prevalent frigidity in religion and the deplorable absence of Christian virtue. The result of his exploration was a trilogy, with the most subtle logical arguments in his now famous work on free will, adequately supplemented by treatises on original sin and on true virtue.

Edwards did well to select free will as the crucial issue between himself and the Arminians. Here, he believed, was the crux of the related problems of moral decline, a lessening consciousness of sin and a resultant slackening of moral judgment, an accelerating and impious tendency to detract from God's greatness, and a vain, blasphemous elevation of man to the status of a God. In *Freedom of the Will* (strictly, *A Careful and Strict Enquiry into the Modern Prevailing Notions of that Freedom of Will Which Is Supposed to Be Essential to Moral Agency, Virtue and Vice, Reward and Punishment, Praise and Blame*), he furiously attacked some now forgotten and usually less astute English Arminians, writing what was easily the most brilliant philosophical polemic in American history. But too often Arminianism, as he defined it, was a useful strawman, and not fairly representative of the best libertarian thought. Edwards' attack upon free will involved some arbitrary definitions and the most meticulous logic. The result was really a median position, far short of later versions of hereditary or environmental determinism, but yet much less than a belief in either pure mental spontaneity or human self-determination. His insufficiently articulated beginning assumption was that each human possesses a certain bent, temperament, or nature that predisposes his choices and thus places him securely and neatly within the series of sequences (cause and effects if correctly understood) that constitute God's creative effulgence (nature and history).

Following Locke, Edwards defined freedom as the power to do as one wills, and thus declared man, as an active agent, to be free, for he usually can do as he wills. He certainly makes voluntary choices. But the will, the choosing part of man, is only a power or faculty and not an acting agent. Hence, by the above definition, it is not itself free, but only an essential element in man's freedom. The will, in all its choices, is determined by what it most strongly apprehends as desirable or good. But, even so, it does voluntarily choose this good. A man who has a taste for apples and despises peaches, or, even better, who is sickened by peach fuzz, will voluntarily choose an apple from a bowl of peaches and apples. The man is here free in what Edwards believed to be the only meaningful definition of freedom. But his will was bound to a certain apprehension of goodness, and, ultimately, to a basic aspect of his being (an affinity for apples or an allergy to peaches). This choice clearly exemplified what Edwards referred to as moral necessity. In the most ultimate problem, choice or rejection of God, the same situation prevails, although the choice is no longer trivial. Each sane man is again proffered alternate choices, voluntarily makes his choice, and in so doing indicates that which appears best to him. If he chooses other than God, his basic nature is corrupt and completely blameworthy, for he makes a necessary, voluntary, but a wrong and even suicidal choice. If he chooses God, he is praiseworthy, even though the choice is necessary as well as voluntary.

In areas where natural necessity nullifies voluntary choice no moral judgment is possible. If physically prevented or compelled, man is not responsible. But if the only obstacle to right behavior is of a moral nature (a defect of character, a deformed nature), then Edwards believed that men are blameworthy and subject to punishment. This is true even though, in a sense, the person cannot choose except as he chose, cannot will other than he willed. Here "cannot" means something entirely different from physical limitation or compulsion; it means a moral necessity, a stable character, a fixed quality. It is at the very heart of any Calvinist view of man, for it makes possible God's complete providence —an unbroken pattern of ordained events—and yet leaves room for moral judgment. The position never had a better advocate than Jonathan Edwards, who was able to mutilate most alternative positions.

Edwards believed that those who defended free will had to argue either for pure indifference (uncaused, contingent choice) or for self-causation. Indifferent choice was easily disposed of, both as something impossible (man is never completely disinterested when exercising volition) and as amoral even if it did exist. An uncaused act of will is a mere accident, a bit of pure chance, and thus not only irrational and nonmoral but an affront to a perfect universe and to an omnipotent God who ordered all things harmoniously. If acts of will occur without cause, then there is no valid reason why millions of other things do not also occur without a cause, and the universe is reduced to accident and man to complete solipsism. If freedom is tied to indifference, its exists only when there is no volition, or really no willing and no choice, which is a contradiction.

A self-caused will involves both contradiction and impiety. If the will is self-caused, the only freedom consists in the willing to will, and not in the final choice, which is self-caused and therefore determined. But this only puts man into an infinite regression or pushes him back toward some first determined act of will. If a person wills that he will an apple, the freedom of his prior willing is based either on indifference (and thus is amoral and accidental) or is itself self-caused (by a willing to will to will), or is determined by something, in which case it is hardly distinguishable from the secondary and determined choice of the apple. Even more distasteful to Edwards, this concept of self-causation was a direct affront to God, who alone is self-caused, but whose will is also bound to what is good. He is the immediate ground and cause for all that is. To affirm human self-causation was to deify man falsely and to sunder his ontological dependence. Either indifference or self-causation was contrary to the moral necessity involved in a moral code or legal commands, to any morality based on good habits, to a will determined by a good understanding, to actions caused by motives or ends, and, most significant, to God's omnipotence.

In blaming Arminianism for a moral decline in New England and in always associating the free-will doctrine with moral relaxation and impiety, Edwards penned a brilliant tour de force. It had been the Arminians who had constantly argued that Calvinistic necessity had negated morality and blasphemed God, and not the opposite. To them, any man given up to sin by God's consent was blameless. The only blame due man was for those acts originating in a free will. When necessity was present, whether moral or natural, moral condemnation seemed unfair for man and inconsistent for a merciful and just God. Edwards, with delightful irony, used this argument to show that, by Arminian definitions, responsibility had been abolished from the earth, for on close analysis no acts were really free and thus blameworthy. By Arminian standards, the meanest people were most completely excused, for their meanness clearly sprang from an inordinate nature which they were totally unable to change. In fact, the more difficult virtue was for a person, the more he was excused from the practice of it. Excuses always kept up with wickedness. The Arminians were using freedom of the will as an escape from the severe demands of piety and were advocating a type of pseudo-moralism that scarcely required the radical cure of grace. They expected God to be generous, to forgive man his errors, to help him, and above all, to give him a fair chance. They could not accept God's perfection and thus his necessity for self-glorification. By removing all blame from man's worst shortcomings, they in effect rejected Christ's atonement, for without guilt no atonement was needed. Without quite recognizing it, the Arminians were headed toward Unitarianism and, eventually, complete humanism. To Edwards, this escape to free will had to stop, and quickly; otherwise man would soon forget his utter sinfulness and his complete dependence on God for all righteousness. The common-sense (and Calvinist) condemnation of people with bad habits and a natural inclination to evil had to be restored. If morality were tied to an Arminian definition of freedom, all moral judgment and all morality would eventually cease to exist.

The essence of Calvinist harshness was a refusal to accept excuses. Edwards was a strict Calvinist in this respect—he would permit no relaxation, allow no weakness, pardon no inability. The Calvinist condemned nothing so much as moral inability. Not the lack of choice of God, but the moral inability to choose God was what was wrong with all men unaided by special grace. This, not the action or inaction, was prior in the scale of evil, and permitted a harsh judgment even of children. This attitude toward moral inability contrasted sharply with the Anabaptist tradition in Protestantism, which was radically free will and which placed blame directly on the evil act. To the Anabaptist, grace was given in Christ's complete atonement; conversion did not mean a completely radical alteration of character but rather a forgiveness of past sins and the gift of the Holy Spirit to help prevent future ones. The Calvinist position also differed radically from the sacramental emphasis of Roman Catholicism, in which baptism removed the blight of original sin and thus removed any necessity for a radical conversion. This Calvinist harshness was conducive to the most explosive revivalism. For any Calvinist, conversion was a single, radical, undeserved transformation wrought by God. Ordinarily, but not necessarily, conversion occurred as a step in an ordained sequence of events which included preaching, conviction, and repentance, but it was always, nonetheless, a complete gift, totally undeserved. This conversion was more significant and crucial, although not necessarily more sentimental, than the Methodist or other free-will conversions in which a continuously proffered grace was freely accepted, subject to later loss and possible repossession.

Edwards grasped the central dilemma of the indeterminists—a tendency to find everything distasteful to be determined and thus beyond judgment. Not moral relativism but a suspension of moral judgments was the danger. Edwards believed that the Calvinist position was closest to the common-sense view and that it was really less involved in metaphysical subtleties. The average man rightly condemned any deed if it was a person's own deed, obviously evil, and done by choice. In asking for one further test—is the choice free?—the Arminians confused the issue by directing attention to some cloudy, undetectable element in back of an ordinary act of volition. By seeking this obscure freedom behind a choice, they were really leaving the will under the guidance of *nothing*, making man an accidental creature lower even than an intelligently guided machine. Why not be content with the only concrete and meaningful definition of freedom—the ability to make choices guided by understanding, connected with an ability to act according to choice? That these choices were always determined by moral necessity (by apprehension of good or by basic temperament) was no excuse for giving up all moral effort, for this would be only *to choose* ease instead of virtue and therefore would provide no escape from either choice or responsibility. If a man's nature was kindly, making it impossible for him to do other than kind deeds, he was no less to be praised. If a vengeful man killed because of the compulsion of his nature, he was not to be excused but rather the more to be condemned. Only the unpremeditated murder (close to Arminian indifference) was excusable and amoral. If it was wrong to condemn sinners for their necessarily evil acts, the alternative was a complacent acceptance of evil and the status quo. If God, because of His nature, was necessarily good and holy, should all Christians withdraw their praise of God? The latter question was the most difficult for sincere, fervently Christian Arminians.

Even as Arminians attributed free will to man, they modified or rejected the doctrine of original sin, which was at the very heart of Edwards' view of conversion as an undeserved and radical operation performed by the Holy Spirit. The Arminians felt that original sin was falsely attributed to man. Edwards' keen apprehension of the moral beauty and infinite holiness of God was balanced, quite appropriately, by sheer horror at the sordid ugliness of human rebellion. One disobedient and prideful act proved the corruptness of human nature.

Sin was not, to Edwards, as much a type of behavior as a state of being, a horrible alienation from God. His awareness of this sinful state was amplified and overamplified by an intense introspection that rather dramatically separated him from his contemporaries, particularly the Deists. Being so aware of alienation and false pride, Edwards knew that sin was a fact of life, an empirical certainty, whatever its explanation. The Arminians, on the other hand, clearly identified sin with behavior, with deeds done, and usually found more good deeds than bad ones and, on balance, more good than evil in man. Thus, they rejected human depravity and original sin (as they understood it) on empirical grounds. The gulf of understanding was complete. Not even grasping his concepts, a confident age could not accept Edwards' doctrine, which seemed atrocious and unfair. Like Ben Franklin, most Americans knew not sin; they only erred.

To Edwards, evil came into the world as a type of privation, not as a substantive creation. God withdrew a favor and did not Himself commit evil. But He did permit Adam's rebellion. No matter how he struggled with it, Edwards could not exempt Adam's disobedience from the all-pervasive will of God. It too had to subserve an ultimate and good purpose. He argued that Adam and Eve were created with two natures. One, the inferior, included moral equipment (understanding and will), but also self-love, natural appetites, and a tendency toward selfish liberty. The other was a superior spiritual principle, holy and divine. This principle was in the very image of God and produced holy love and true righteousness by its dominion over the lower nature. With Adam's disobedience, God removed the superior principle, for the Holy Spirit could not dwell in a sinful and rebellious habitat. Evil, in the human sense, was thus a matter of misplaced affection and not some natural distortion.

But how, asked the Arminians, could contemporary man be blamed for Adam's past sin? What was the nature of the tie between Adam and his descendants? Edwards approached this problem with his certainty that man, as a fact, was sinful even as Adam was. Thus, to him, the problem was to justify an existing situation, not to free man of an unfair imputation. Viewing man as he did, he felt there was no unfairness in linking present disobedience to Adam's original disobedience, since there would be no greater likelihood of a better issue if each person were exposed to Adam's own temptation. All natural men, in a sense, were constantly exemplifying Adam's sinfulness.

To explain the exact tie between Adam and his descendants, Edwards utilized another concept borrowed from Locke. In trying to explain the difficult problem of human identity, Locke concluded that it was simply and only a matter of continuity of consciousness or memory, and not of essence or substance. Edwards refused to exclude the possible continuity of substance, but accepted the centrality of consciousness and built his defense of original sin upon it. By a concept of individual identity, one would feel justified in punishing a murderer apprehended a dozen years after a crime, even though a detailed chemical analysis might prove that very few atoms that were present in his body at the time of the crime were still there. In a sense, one imputes the guilt of the past atoms to the present ones, conceiving the man to be the *same* man as the one who committed the crime. Because of his constant awareness of ontological dependence, Edwards had to project even this continuity of personal consciousness beyond a law of nature to the moment-by-moment re-creation of the universe by God. Without God's sovereign pleasure, His divine establishment, there could be no remembrance of past events.

Just as there was a common identity in the individual man, justifying blame for even distant sins, so there was a similar identity for all mankind, justifying the condemnation of all individual men for sharing in Adam's alienation and false pride. Again, to be clear, one must note that Edwards had not the slightest doubt that there had been an observable, universal propensity to disobedience existing throughout human history, and that, as in all else, there also had to be some fundamental, reasonable explanation for this human condition. There was certainly something deeper at work than the voluntary choice of evil (that is, of lesser orders of good than God) by otherwise blameless individuals, or else the univeral tendency could not be explained. The answer, to Edwards, was quite simple. Mankind was one in the consciousness of God and thus had a common identity in being. As in any other species, there was in man a common nature that remained unchanged through each successive re-creation by God according to his divine constitution for the universe. In the coherence of history, each individual man was part of a unity that had its first concretion and its first apostasy in Adam and its subsequent concretions and apostasies in every person born of Adam's seed. Adam's fall was the fall of the species, and thus of all individuals in the species. God ordained that each new generation of men have the same qualities as the past generation and, ultimately, as Adam himself. There was one idea of man, one concept in God, and thus mankind stood indicted as a whole and not as several million isolated individuals. This certainly meant that all men were brothers and equal in sinfulness, but who in the eighteenth century but an Edwards would have established this brotherhood upon man's apostasy from God?

The climax of Edwards' thought came in a posthumously published and beautiful book, *A Dissertation Concerning the Nature of True Virtue*. Here he joined his earliest mysticism and idealism, his later insights into religious affections, and his pervasive estheticism. In his youth, Edwards identified excellence and beauty with proportion and harmony, or with a relationship of mutual consent between all parts. For conscious beings, excellence entailed consent to, or harmony with, other beings, with the highest excellency consisting in full consent to all being, or to being in general. Greatness was based upon the degree of being (the approach to being in general), whereas beauty and excellence depended upon the degree of consent to other beings and to being in general.

As he labored on his last writings at the isolated Indian station, a tiring and weak Edwards drew from his huge store of miscellaneous notes and from his earlier, more abstract treatment of being, to develop his definition of virtue. Although a type of beauty and excellence exists wherever there is harmony between beings, virtue exists only where the harmony is of a moral type, springing from the will and the affections. Thus it is the highest but a special and limited type of beauty. True virtue exists only when there is moral consent or, to use his key term, benevolence to being in general, or to God. His earlier definition of holy affections was a description of the qualities that go into men's saving love of God. His definition of virtue was an esthetic description of the beauty reflected by such a love. True religion and true virtue were thus inseparable aspects of the same thing—supreme love of God. Virtue could not exist when the consent was given to less than the totality of being, although Edwards constantly stressed that the virtue might result in benevolent acts to lesser beings, most notably to other men. But always there was the requirement that all love must be to God and all lesser degrees of affection held within the confines of this total love; if not, virtue and beauty do not exist. Edwards was affirming the extreme and exclusive doctrine that, apart from grace, no virtue was possible. True Christians alone were virtuous.

Edwards tried to prove that most of what was commonly defined as virtuous was really unrelated to true virtue. Most human affections and most acts springing from these affections were based not in a love of God, but in benevolence toward only a part of being—toward oneself or other beings contained in the perspective of one's private world. Here, once again, Edwards demonstrated his hatred of anything purely private, isolated, divisive, or discordant—in fact anything not fitted properly into the organic whole. Any limited benevolence toward the part instead of the whole disrupted the harmony of minds in God's universe and was therefore synonymous with ugliness. It made actions that would, with the necessary consent, be holy and virtuous into gross and ugly things. Man broke his union with being, denied his ontological dependence, and absolutized himself into a prideful, egocentric world in selfish revolt against the whole. This evil was not positive but privative. It was a matter of isolating from rather than embracing. It had no reality for God, but was real for all natural men. Harmony with being came only with grace, when natural man, by a special gift, regained the spiritual principle lost by Adam. And whether referred to as a supernatural sense, a spiritual principle, a special illumination, a holy affection, a special beauty, a saving grace, or the indwelling Spirit, Edwards was talking about what he considered the one secret of meaningful existence.

Edwards lived in an age when humanitarian sentiments had virtually captured the realm of moral philosophy. Particularly popular in the Enlightenment was a concept of a special moral sense, a principle or faculty of moral judgment implanted in all men by nature or by God. By tying virtue to grace and to the holy affections of the Christian elect, Edwards was emphatically denying that virtue consists of such a moral sense. But he did accept what amounts to such a sense as the basis of a secondary or natural type of virtue. Much that is assumed virtuous simply springs from self-love and a love of consistency that is derived from this love, or from natural instincts, such as the love of a parent for a child. But other acts spring from what amounts to an inborn love of order, harmony, and justice. This natural virtue rests on a limited and partial consent to being. In the world of nature it leads to the disinterested appreciation of symmetry and beauty, but without a recognition that the harmony of natural objects is only a shadow of the spiritual harmony of the divine universe. In human affairs, it leads to an appreciation of a well-ordered society, to a desire for justice among men, and to a type of benevolence toward other persons, but again without any recognition that this benevolence is limited and meaningless unless it is placed within the framework of a higher and more inclusive love of all being, of the encompassing whole. In fact, this natural virtue is an obstruction in the pathway of real piety, for its separates man from God by obscuring any necessity for God. In moral philosophy it occupies the same position as mechanism in natural philosophy. It was the way of the Deists and of the near future. But Edwards conceded a great deal to the Deistic viewpoint. When rightly understood as an affinity for order and harmony, a universal moral sense was rooted in the very nature of man, despite any small variation in details among various societies.

In defining true virtue, Edwards was not writing a practical moral tract. He asked for no special type of behavior, for he recognized that, in most cases, the same acts would be required by love of God, by enlightened self-interest or utilitarianism, or by an innate moral sense. Natural virtue, even as true virtue, tended to the good of mankind, restrained vice, and had to be described by the same words. Except for the individual who knew his own heart, there was no way to determine if a given act was truly virtuous. Two men might aid an unfortunate neighbor, one out of a strong sense of justice and the other because he loved God supremely and saw in the unfortunate man a partial concretion of total being and a possible instrument for the glorification of God. What Edwards was attempting to prove, here as in all other areas of his thought, was that man was completely dependent upon grace and that the Christian was radically different from the natural man despite any outward similarities. Virtue was not a matter of correct action, but of the right ground for correct action. Anticipating Kant, he found virtue only in the good will, in the right attitude and the right perspective. But unlike Kant, he tied virtue to a conscious end—the glorification of an irresistibly beautiful Deity.

In his definition of virtue, even as in his delineation of holy affections, Edwards set an almost impossibly high standard. Virtue being dependent on a constant awareness and love of God, and on a personally disinterested desire for His glorification, was an end too demanding for any but the select few. This Edwards knew and accepted. Like all good Puritans, he was constantly examining himself, searching out motives in order to exclude any private or selfish interests. Concerned with such "basic" ideas as true virtue, Edwards never gave any extended theoretical attention to social, political, or economic problems. He believed that his definition of virtue would place in proper perspective all the mundane matters of earthly life and certainly never hesitated to make a practical application in his weekly sermons, condemning village sins in too vivid detail for his own popularity. Implicit in his ethical theory, as well as in earlier Puritanism, was a strong public consciousness. In fact, Edwards made the relationship between private and public good an analogue of the relation between natural and true virtue. His organic metaphysics, his unending interest in the corporate whole, was diametrically opposed to the rampant individualism, in politics and economics, that was developing in his lifetime. He was unalterably committed to the greatest community, a community that stretched beyond either national or racial boundaries to include all mankind, and far beyond that to include the source and totality of being.

As a Puritan, Edwards shared and accepted what has been called the Protestant ethic. He demanded that all men have a responsible calling. He approved of property and even of wealth. But antecedent to this, he demanded total affection for, and total responsibility to, God. Within the totality of God's universe, each man must bestow his lesser affection according to an object's participation in being, with little affection possible for earthly goods. In this perspective, the Puritan merchant could not be a Christian and, at the same time, attach any real significance or give any real love to his wealth. In fact, the Christian mother could give precious little love to her own child, except in the larger perspective of her love for God. Edwards exhibited a strong practicality in the management of his own worldly affairs, but, like other good Puritans, tried to be fully within and yet fully apart from the world at the same time. He advocated a religion so pure, a virtue so complete, that a Christian had no need for ascetic escape. In asking for a truly responsible but private economic system, Edwards was certainly exhibiting no personal hypocrisy, but instead testifying to his impossibly noble aspirations and to an impossibly high estimation of human capability (grace, of course, was the secret). In practice, such a standard often drove men toward hypocrisy. But, increasingly, it drove most men to reject the standard itself, making do either with enlightened self-love or a universal moral sense.

In 1757 Edwards was offered the presidency of Princeton, a post vacated by the death of his son-in-law, Aaron Burr. After careful consideration, and some doubts about his capability and some concern over the future of his scholarship, he accepted. He died of a smallpox inoculation a month after taking up his new position in early 1758. At that time he was working on a huge project, which he termed a "History of the Work of Redemption," and which was to embrace the whole design of God for creation. This ambitious project, if he had been able to complete it, might have brought Edwards' work together in greater order and harmony; in fact, it might have lent his own type of beauty to his completed works. But, except for an increasing awareness of history, it probably would not have added significantly to his thought. Edwards' work had such an astounding coherence and consistency that his last books were largely further amplifications of ideas he had deposited in his own journals or in early, unpublished manuscripts. Nothing in his last work revealed any major new departure, and often indicated a decrease in mental vigor.

Edwards' thought sprang from deep personal experiences which remained vivid and valid for a moderately short but very intense lifetime. Though conditioned by his age and by parochial loyalties, much of his thought had a timeless quality that has allowed it to fare better than much of the more popular thought of his age. Much that Edwards defended is intellectually tenable in the twentieth century; even more is either emotionally or experientially persuasive. His emphasis upon immediacy and affection in religion, and his powerful description of alienation and sin, relates his theology to numerous twentieth-century and existential versions of Calvinism, although he could never have subscribed to their irrationalism. Perhaps even more important, Edwards isolated the central theme of almost all subsequent New England philosophy—the necessary subordination of both knowledge and behavior to a conjoined ethical and esthetic end, to a special type of consummatory or redemptive experience.

III
BENJAMIN FRANKLIN:
SCIENCE
AND MORALS

CAREER AND CHARACTER

Benjamin Franklin was the most imposing figure in eighteenth-century America. A child of New England, ineradicably stamped in the mold of Puritan moralism, yet fully exempt from Puritan spirituality, he became the first representative of the American intellect to the world. America could have done much worse. Franklin displayed all the possibilities of a secularized and humanized world view. Freed of all awe and fear of God, he turned his attention to the conquest as well as the celebration of natural wonders and to the realization of the fullest possible utility in common-sense Yankee virtues.

Both as an almost unbelievable reality and as a largely self-created myth, Franklin captured the imagination not only of Americans but Europeans as well. His contribution to American thought was not in any sense philosophical, but at least in science it was without comparison in the whole colonial period. Above all, Franklin contributed himself. Like Jonathan Edwards, Franklin was consistent in character. Humorously detached, extraordinarily well-adjusted, he appeared before his fellow men as open, honest, secure, and content with himself. His accomplishments, his many-faceted life, rested upon a stable and mature personality. He was an invaluable barometer of the strengths and weaknesses of the American Enlightenment, of an extremely polarized variation in the basic equation of piety and secular pride, of anxiety and self-confidence.

To even partially understand Franklin is inevitably to learn something about America, for there seems to be much of Franklin in many Americans. Yet, the various interpretations of Franklin have borne witness to the diversity of American thought and, less clearly, to the major shifts of basic concern from generation to generation. For, depending on interests or point of view, one may see only Ben Franklin, scientist, flying his famous kite or madly pursuing a whirlwind over the Pennsylvania hills; or one may see the worldly sophisticate and diplomat pursuing ladies through the *salons* of Paris. One may discover in him a somewhat frivolous dilettante and gadgeteer or an original scientific genius; a naïve provincial or the most cosmopolitan of colonial Americans. One may describe him as either delightfully or disgustingly mature and well-adjusted, as either shallow or profound, as sincerely or hypocritically religious or irreligious, as a literary artist or an insensitive Philistine, as the epitome of virtue or as a moralistic simpleton, as a wise sage or an early Andrew Carnegie, as a worldly philosopher or a typical Babbit, as a man of good taste or an incurable "lowbrow," as a wit or a cliché-monger, as a master politician or an immoral opportunist, as either the first intellectual or the premier anti-intellectual in American history. Historians may honor him as one of the chief architects of American independence and constitutional union or condemn his business opportunism and callous insensitivity toward the poor and the laboring masses.

But all these judgments probably reveal more of those who make them than of Franklin. For in back of each of them stands an imperturbable and humorously detached Ben Franklin, with an outstretched hand, willing and pleased to meet anyone, and be friends. Reluctant to censor or judge, tolerant to a fault, he invites judgment, of either himself or others. But he remains ever aloof from the subsequent confusion, from modern, often tormented efforts to gain understanding and self-assurance. And one is jealous of him, for his maturity is frightening. And one hates him because he seems aloof and insensitive. And one loves him because he is kind. And all are forced to admire him, for he is great. He may be the American Socrates. And who knows whether this is a compliment to America or a horrible indictment of it?

The broad details of Franklin's life are well-known—the more obscure early years through the deserved fame of his *Autobiography,* the later ones because of the tremendous diplomatic and political significance of his public endeavors. But the *Autobiography,* a vast parable of success and a latter-day morality play with only one character, does not even give a clue as to what ingredients in Franklin's Boston childhood contributed to his later self-confidence and his happy adjustment to his universe and to his fellow men. The fifteenth of seventeen children, Franklin did not experience the close intimacy of a smaller family. He had to share the concern of his parents with too many other children. This neglect possibly explains his later, imperturbable detachment from the most frightening experiences of life. In any case, he matured without a deep emotional dependency upon his parents, and with more respect than love for most of his brothers and sisters. His lack of closeness and intimacy, and with it his lack of personal involvement and need, marked all his social relationships. He loved sincerely but lightly. He had numerous true friends but no soul mates. He served, and asked service, of others, but never committed his all to anyone or to any one thing. He needed so little from others that he tended to give too little, particularly to those who loved him most. But with Franklin this was not so much a blighting inability to love as a freeing lack of need for intense human involvements. His dispassionate noninvolvement even carried over into his view of himself. The whimsical detachment in the *Autobiography* gives Franklin a contrived, larger-than-life quality. But in reality, it was the man and not the book that was contrived. When trying to know Franklin through his own writings, one is continuously confronted with an unbelievable image—a Franklin that was always carefully outfitted and projected according to calculated patterns. The public image of Franklin may be false, but it cannot be corrected, for he, not his disciples, created it and only it. There may have been a real Franklin, a perfect but lonely puppeteer behind the public figure, but if so he will remain perfectly hidden, for the image was perfectly manipulated.

This public image, contrived or authentic, was very useful in Franklin's vocation as a Philadelphia printer and publisher, and in his parallel and very successful quest for social status and, with appropriate modesty, political power. He moved from Boston, from the parental fold and a binding apprenticeship to a less able brother, from the penetrating concerns of Puritanism, to the Quaker city of Philadelphia, to an atmosphere of greater freedom and less intellectuality, to a growing city of opportunity, and to a culture invigorated by a group of educated,

broadly learned merchants and nearby country planters. Although awed
by the breadth of learning in people like James Logan, and always
conscious of his classical and linguistic illiteracy, Franklin found in
Philadelphia the perfect setting for America's first and greatest success
story. And it was a good one, with little that was mean or sniveling or
hypocritical. Franklin rose above his friends in part because of careful
calculation, but also in part because of superior ability and intelligence.

From any perspective, his rise was rapid. After a year of employment
by a local printer, and two more years of learning and worldly experience in London, Franklin was able to secure a partner and open his own
printing business. He soon bought out his partner and bested his competitors. An able craftsman as printer, he was an even better journalist.
A master in clear, pithy, and always concise expression, his *Pennsylvania Gazette* prospered from the beginning. His *Poor Richard's
Almanac,* which he soon launched with a deliberate and damaging joke
on his competitors, spread his fame throughout the colonies and,
eventually, even to Europe. He always knew the value of public relations, and assiduously cultivated a favorable public image. Happily, his
gregarious love of companionship, his real concern for civic betterment,
his insatiable curiosity about nature, and his ingenious and often valuable inventions and improvements, helped establish his good reputation
without requiring any insincere effusiveness on his part. The public was
soon captive.

It was in his early years as a printer that Franklin married Deborah
Read. The marriage was in part a debt for past injustices to Miss Read,
in part another venture in public relations and business success, in part
an affair of passion, and in part, within his affectional limits, a marriage
of love or at least of mutual respect. In the light of his subsequent
intellectual development and his later fame and international stature, it
was a poor match. Even in his beginning career it was a questionable
choice. A common law marriage because of an earlier but disastrous
marriage by Deborah, it led to domestic peace, produced two children
(only one, a daughter Sarah, survived), and resulted in a satisfactory
management of many of Franklin's practical affairs. But Deborah was
vastly inferior to Franklin in intelligence, lacked an education, and never
possessed the social assets befitting the wife of a world citizen. Nonetheless, she gave more in affection and loyalty than she ever received and
spent almost all of her last years alone as Franklin's "good old wife,"

capably supervising his businesses while he was in Europe. Toward her, Franklin was ever respectful and kind, but surely did not acutely miss her while in Europe.

In his *Autobiography,* Franklin justified his permanent liaison with Deborah on the basis of uncontrollable and often misdirected sexual passion, which among other things threatened disease and business embarrassment. His bachelor indiscretions led to one illegitimate son (born near the time of his marriage in 1730) and to sincere regrets over earlier examples of disloyalty to Deborah during his first trip to London. The same vulnerability to feminine wiles led, in his later life, to indiscretions and to one serious affair in Paris. Yet, his sexual errata were those of a normally sensual young (or old) man. Franklin loved dalliance and flirtation; he admired women. Possibly, though, he did not take them too seriously. Unable to love deeply and unneedful of the solace or even domination of love from others, Franklin did not put undue stress on sex, apart, that is, from its relationship to health and reputation. Many of the emotional overtones seem absent—sex was pure and enjoyable play and physical outlet.

Even before his marriage, Franklin was an active member of the Masonic Order and, more important, joined with other young Philadelphia tradesmen to form a Junto Club. It was a self-improvement society, with aspects of both later civic clubs and a Dale Carnegie course. For Franklin, it provided an outlet for his leadership ability and an opportunity for extensive education. It was the only college he ever attended. Junto members read good books, analyzed methods of attaining wealth and business success, worked at attaining private and public virtue, sought avenues of service to mankind and to their country, and took an active interest in local politics. They embraced a fraternal love for each other, a generalized love for mankind, a complete tolerance for varied religious beliefs, a higher commitment to truth, and a mission to spread enlightenment to others. They hummed a poem in unison each month and prepared individual papers to be read and criticized. The Junto can easily be either ridiculed or caricatured by those who want to debunk either Franklin or America. It can be pictured as a typically childish model of all later civic clubs, chambers of commerce, and social fraternities, or condemned for the complacent sentimentality and fraternal inanities yet associated with middle-class clubs. But for Franklin, a young man on the rise, it was a means to community recognition, to intellectual expression, and to other significant projects. The Library Company and, later, the American Philosophical Society sprang in part from the Junto. The members of the Junto remained lifelong friends and were influential in many fields of endeavor.

As a printer, Franklin used his spare moments for invention and for community improvement. His deservedly famous Pennsylvania Fireplace was perfected by 1744 and then advertised in a masterful essay. He won appointment as Postmaster for Philadelphia (with franking privileges for his newspaper), beginning what amounted to a separate career in postal work. He helped secure books for the Library Company, was elected to the Colonial Assembly, served as secretary to the assembly (thereby winning the printing contracts for the colony), and made his earliest proposals for an academy. He carried on an increasing correspondence with almost all the scholarly and scientific (philosophical in his terms) men in the colonies, as well as a few in England. The discussions ranged widely, but usually centered in attempts to better explain the operations of nature (from whirlwinds to shells on mountaintops). But his greatest scientific love, electricity, first attracted his attention in 1746, when he and interested friends began the experiments, for both pleasure and knowledge, which established Franklin's international reputation and which led to his single greatest originative contribution to American intellectual history (few would now give greater emphasis to his moral thought). In 1748 he retired from the printing business to devote his last years to public service and, hopefully, to philosophical (i.e., scientific) speculation and the pleasures of intercourse with the best minds of his day.

The importance of electrical experiments and, even more, the careful hypotheses erected upon them cannot be overemphasized in Franklin's life. They gave him his greatest pleasure, pulled heretofore inaccessible scientists and philosophers into his circle of friends, led to membership in the Royal Society and the French Academy, provided the requisite reputation and fame for successful diplomacy in France, and gave him some of the self-assurance and pride that sustained both his modesty and his magnanimity during his later years of fame and adulation. Despite his obvious talents as a diplomat and politician, Franklin's task in France during the American Revolution might have been impossible were it not for his well-known image that preceded him to Paris. This image grew out of the publication of his letters on electricity, although it certainly drew support from a romantic mystique about America. Franklin's deserved fame as a scientist was rooted in his aptitude for the type of scientific investigation (never dramatic or revolutionary) that characterized the eighteenth century. His personality —his disinterested noninvolvement—was part of his natural equipment. The other aspects of his success were bound up in his intellectual bent and in his basic beliefs about the physical universe and divine providence.

Franklin always had a fondness for the concrete and for the obvious and exhibited a growing aversion to anything abstract, obscure, or purely speculative. Flexible and more curious as a young man, he speculated rather daringly on a few philosophical and religious issues, but later regretted even this small excursion into the rarefied and insecure atmosphere of metaphysics and theology, for his logic too often conflicted with his experience. This mental aversion to abstract thought was one of his most distinctive characteristics, and by it he was most clearly segregated from his New England background. Poor Richard expressed the idea neatly: "Many a Long Dispute among Divines may be thus abridg'd, It is so: It is not so. It is so; It is not so." [*Poor Richard's Almanac,* 1743, in Leonard W. Labaree and Whitfield J. Bell, eds., *Benjamin Franklin, Papers* (New York, 1959–   ), II, 373.] Poor Richard had two great enemies—lawyers and divines, the two eternal prototypes of intellectual sophistry.

Some of the most effective critics of Franklin attack him as a anti-intellectual; they see in him a prototype of a perennial defect in the American character. Anyone who is deeply concerned with intellectual honesty and courage, who by some compulsion is forced to pursue suppositions to their foundations, who explore and unearth the crucial dilemmas in human thought, who experience the agony and frustration of floundering in unalterable contradictions—anyone, that is, who qualifies as an intellectual, will not find a kindred spirit in Franklin. He refused to join intellectuals in their quest simply because he knew its inevitable futility and disappointment. Whenever Franklin found intellectual pathways leading over the horizon, or into deep valleys clogged with fog, he assumed they were all dead ends; thus, he followed the simple, well-lighted paths of common sense. He did not have time to be waylaid in the murky byways. He knew that intellectual floundering might be caused by obscurity as often as by immense depth.

Franklin's antipathy to metaphysics, his stated lack of interest in Berkelean idealism, and his many battles against dogmatic theological positions could in themselves have been tenets of a sophisticated philosophical outlook, but they were not. He joined his avowed reliance upon experience, and his emphasis upon the effects or consequences of beliefs, with a wholehearted acceptance of many rationalistic, nonempirical, overly optimistic presuppositions current in the Enlightenment. A contemporary and friend, David Hume, shared Franklin's antipathy to mystery, obscure abstractions, and sophistic "divinity school" logic, but he accepted the burden of his empiricism and with youthful vigor pushed it far enough to challenge the whole, beautiful superstructure of enlightened rationalism. It is certainly unfair to compare Franklin with Hume, for Franklin, despite his versatility, was never a philosopher and, in our contemporary sense of the word, never aspired to be one. Thus, at least, he was never a *poor* philosopher. But if one wants all men to be philosophically self-conscious, then they must condemn Franklin. Even if they ask for unbending intellectual honesty, they will have to reject Franklin along with the vast, unphilosophic majority of mankind. But they will surely grant that there are many uses for the intellect and that all men do not share the same interest and make the same contributions.

The only extensive, although amateurish, philosophical article written by Franklin was an essay on "Liberty and Necessity," written in 1725 in London. In a vein reminiscent of Jonathan Edwards, Franklin asserted the existence of an all-wise, all-good, and all-powerful God who made our universe. He then tried to prove by good logic that our world was perfect, whatever humans believe in their limited perspective. Man is a part of God's plan and has no liberty in the great machine universe which He created. In both the natural and moral realm, all is harmony and beautiful. What humans conceive as pain is a necessary and beneficial part of the whole universe, for pain leads to a desire to be free of pain, and thus to motion and even to life itself. All action is for the purpose of avoiding pain, is universally selfish, and is neither moral nor immoral. But the escape from pain is pleasure, which is thus a result of pain, and is always exactly equal to pain escaped. In each creature there is an exact balance of pleasure and pain. Each is equally happy, and no man has any valid reasons for complaint.

These conclusions were quickly rejected by Franklin, who always felt that this excursion into logic had betrayed his better understanding of the human condition. In an essay prepared for the Junto in 1732, he still had an all-wise, all-good, and all-powerful God, but predetermination gave way to a universe that permitted free action by man and which, on occasion, needed a special intervention by God. His original doctrine was never disproved but simply forsaken. From this point on Franklin was quite content to assert accepted or common-sense doctrines with only loose arguments in their support. But this early excursion into metaphysics did reveal a characteristic love of balance that Franklin never forsook. The exact harmony between pain and pleasure, and the conservation of an equal proportion of each, were easily transferred to such physical phenomena as electricity, where pain becomes negative charge, pleasure positive, and their enduring balance the conservation of charge.

Franklin's skepticism about methaphysical reasoning marked his very misunderstood position in religion. His support of various churches, his friendship with clergymen of various faiths, and his use of religious convictions for political purposes have lent credence to accusations of religious hypocrisy. But the criticism rests on a misunderstanding—on attempts to picture Franklin either as a cowardly Deist, afraid to accept all the burdens of a public defense of an unpopular faith, or as a liberal, tolerant, and latitudinarian Christian, working toward an ecumenical faith rooted in common ethical concern and a small modicum of commonly accepted beliefs. Neither view is fully correct. Franklin had little personal concern for religious doctrine, but was curious about other people's beliefs. Religious dogma, even though based on abstract and misleading speculation, obviously had intense meaning for some people, including his mother and many of his friends. He accepted this, and, unlike the more committed Deists, never led a campaign against orthodoxy and never condemned anyone because of his belief. But believing that religious dogmas were all subjective and personal, and that none of them were true in the sense of copying reality, he had no logical basis of discrimination among beliefs, as beliefs. However, he did expect religion to lead to a more virtuous life and by observation concluded that almost any belief could lead in this direction. He found religion an important factor in maintaining public morals and had a great deal more sympathy for the simple, unsophisticated faith of the common man than for the more learned doctrines of the intellectuals.

Franklin's utilitarian blessing on religion as a source of morality and

public good gave him some strange bedfellows and dictated some misunderstood actions. His lifelong friendship with George Whitefield was
based not only on sincere admiration but also on his sympathy for the
theological simplicity and the moral emphasis of the Great Awakening.
Thus, Franklin helped the "New Light" Presbyterians build a meeting
house in Philadelphia (ironically, when the Great Awakening succumbed to a drowsy indifference, the same building housed the fledgling
Philadelphia Academy). Likewise, as a practical politician, Franklin
recognized the moving power of religious conviction and freely utilized
it for what he believed to be the public good. He tried to lure Samuel
Johnson to Philadelphia to head the new academy by emphasizing the
religious significance of teaching and by pointing to the "dire need" for a
new Anglican church in Philadelphia, which Johnson could establish.
When, in 1747, Franklin ignored the pacifist Quaker proprietors and, as
an effective tribune of the masses, formed a private association for
military training and the defense of Philadelphia against the French and
Indians, he persuaded the Council to call a day of fasting and prayer to
awaken citizens to a just sense of their condition. At this point he
borrowed from his childhood experience in Puritan Boston to furnish a
model for the proclamation, the first such in Pennsylvania. He also
rejoiced when the various ministers preached effective sermons on the
godliness of self-defense.

Franklin was acutely aware of an orderly process of events in history
and believed in the rationality of the universe. For these experienced
blessings he was always willing to render thanks. He even, at times,
sensed a guiding hand in back of the process. But he certainly had no
faith in prayer as a means of winning favor from a personal God and
delightfully ridiculed the vast number of prayers that were often credited
for the New England victory at Louisburg in 1745. Franklin wrote:
"Indeed, in attacking a strong town I should have more dependence on
Works, than on *faith.*" [*Papers,* III, 26–27.] But he knew that prayer
might induce works.

Franklin's skeptical tolerance of religious dogma turned into condemnation when dogma was directly harmful to morality, to brotherly
love, or to public good. When his religious liberalism caused his mother
deep concern, he went to great lengths to vindicate himself and relieve
her fears. To her typical New England concern over Arminianism and
Arianism, he professed ignorance of what either position implied and

deplored such distinctions when they became more important than virtue. He suggested that so long as his beliefs did not make him less virtuous, they could not be dangerous. When, in 1735, the Presbyterian ministers of Philadelphia censored and suspended a new and vigorous minister, Samuel Hemphill, on charges of heresy, Franklin rose to do battle from the pages of his *Gazette*. Hemphill leaned toward Deism and, rather clearly, rejected the distinctive doctrines of Calvin. But his sermons had been moralistic and well written (though apparently borrowed) and had almost made a churchgoer out of Franklin. The suspension of a good man for obscure doctrinal reasons horrified Franklin, who, without the slightest understanding of the significance of clearly defined and authoritarian beliefs to an orthodox Christian, battled this "new inquisition" that had invaded Philadelphia. With questionable interpretations of Scripture, he tried to refute the charges against Hemphill on the level of dogma, but could never separate the narrow doctrinal points from "The glorious Cause of Christian Liberty." He asked the members of the Presbyterian churches to fight the unfair and malicious clergy by denying them their contributions and thus preserve "Truth, Common Sense, universal Charity, and brotherly Love, Peace and Tranquility, as recommended in the Gospel of Jesus, in this our infant and growing Nation, by steadily opposing those, whose Measures tend to nothing less than utterly to subvert and destroy all. Nothing, in all Probability, can prevent our being a very flourishing and happy People, but our suffering the Clergy to get upon our Backs, and ride us, as they do their Horses, where they please." ["The Publisher to his Lay-Readers," *Papers*, II, 66–67.]

Although he often gave his vote to Christianity as the best religion, he never used the label in a doctrinal sense. He revered Jesus, but did not accept him as the Christ. He also doubted the authenticity of any claimed revelation from God to man. Possibly even more significant, he was completely lacking in personal piety. He was self-sufficient, increasingly sure of his own freedom, and unconcerned about his standing in the eyes of God. Sin was an alien concept. God had been so good to Ben Franklin that Franklin had to assume that God loved him. In a letter to Whitefield, and subsequently to other friends, Franklin grandly announced his belief in immortality based on past experiences of God's care and goodness and, thus, surely also His love. "And, if he loves me, can I doubt that he will go on to take care of me, not only here but hereafter? This to some may seem Presumption; to me it appears the best grounded Hope: Hope of the Future, built on Experience of the Past." [To Whitefield, June 19, 1764, in *The Writings of Benjamin Franklin,* ed. by Albert H. Smythe (New York, 1907), IV, 248.] Franklin was not so egotistic as to assert that he merited all his success and all God's favor (although one suspects that at times he really did think so) and, with sincerity, constantly expressed thanks for a beneficent providence.

In one sense, Franklin remained a good Puritan. He accepted the burden of Puritan secular morality, made harsh demands upon himself, worked hard, and was an incurable moralist in his approach to life. But Franklin rejected the most basic aspect of Puritanism—the profound submission to, and acceptance of, God's will. The orthodox Puritans asked for more than obedience; they wanted a love of God so complete as to negate the self. The good Puritan stood naked before Jehovah, trembling in his nothingness, humble in abject discipleship, penitent in his introverted oversensitivity to shortcomings and sin. He tried to avoid any rebellious assertion of selfish will, any unmerited pride, any self-satisfaction or glorification, and any self-praise for assumed merit or worth. Such piety was a prerequisite of salvation and a prelude for the spiritual bliss, the full reconciliation, to be attained with God. From this standpoint, from the anxiety, the spiritual hunger, and the esthetic sensitivity of a Jonathan Edwards, Franklin was the epitome of irreverence, a man of pride, self-satisfaction, and even arrogance. He was a smug little god living already in a veritable heaven. As such, he was in rebellion against God. If Franklin had accidentally met God on Market Street, he would have shook hands.

For those orthodox individuals who still placed the highest importance upon a pious, humble relationship between man and a personal God, Franklin was either incomprehensible or dangerous. To them, he seemed limited in the one most important area of human attainment. His willingness to tolerate all religions, his sophisticated refusal to join the iconoclastic Deists in stinging attacks on orthodoxy in behalf of an attenuated, atrophied, distilled Christianity, could not redeem Franklin in their eyes. Tolerant acceptance of religion in others was not the same thing as being religious, but was rather to remove oneself completely from the possibility of true piety, to commit the unpardonable sin of finding the religion of one's civilization to be no more than a myth.

Although Franklin was never interested in intensively analyzing the implications of any of his beliefs, there was in him a bit of unnoticed, well-concealed pity or contempt for the orthodox masses. Franklin had risen, on his own, to a position of fame in the community of men. He had emancipated himself from the orthodoxy of his youth. Perhaps most men, smaller than he, needed the support of revelation; Franklin did not. He was the rare individual, the superman, the uncommon Zarathustra. He saw the hypocrisy, to him, of such a basic Christian virtue as humility and even suggested that Americans should follow the Greeks and applaud their own achievements, thus removing a main source of an inverted form of self-praise that always took the form of undue criticism and demeaning of other men. He thus placed himself in a long secular or even pagan tradition that had flourished in Greece, that was reborn in the Renaissance, and that found new expression in the Enlightenment. Franklin moved into the place from whence he had removed the Christian God.

Had he been more pessimistic, more anxious, and less smug, Franklin might have been applauded by some twentieth-century existentialists, who at least agree with Franklin in attributing a Godlike freedom to man. But unlike modern irrationalists, Franklin was very much a creature of the eighteenth century. He was too blinded by a simple rationalism; he was too ignorant of many presuppositions of Christian thought; and he had too many undue expectations for science to know the tragedy of man's secular eminence in a universe believed to be without revelation or objective cosmic meaning. Thus, his rejection of religious orthodoxy was not based on courageous personal nobility, on the hard and difficult acceptance of freedom always limited by destiny, and of destiny always laboriously defined in freedom. Instead, Franklin wanted the best of two worlds—the thrill of freedom and, at the same time, the solace of a universe that always cooperated in the fulfillment of his aspirations, even including his desire for immortality. For Franklin, unknowingly, had completely inverted the Christian theme. Instead of Franklin enlisting in the humble service of Jehovah, a strangely well-disciplined and obedient God had built a universe to please Ben Franklin!

There was a positive side to Franklin's thought about religion, and this was closely related to his view of nature and influenced his achievement in science. By his definition, Franklin was religious. Even in his youthful, iconoclastic flirtation with Deism, he never doubted the existence of a God who both created and most likely governed the universe. Without question, he always accepted the idea of creation and often referred to God as a person. But God remained a person without personality, without clear outline or form—in fact, a virtually unknown God. He was wise, good, and all-powerful because nature was economical, wonderfully contrived, and beneficent. Beyond that, God apparently had been carefully instructed by Franklin, for He was kind and good and wanted everyone to be happy. This God was approached through nature, worshiped by good deeds, and might also have underwritten some eternal insurance policy to be collected at death. As a youth his speculation went further—to many subordinate gods beneath the supremely perfect Being, each governing a solar system and having personal passion and concern for man. But this anticipation of William James did not reappear, and Franklin remained loyal to his single, expert watchmaker. This distilled and humanized theism might seem an emotionally barren, drastically oversimplified religious compromise, but Franklin never put an undue emphasis upon the religious aspect of what was always, basically, more a world view than a passionate religious commitment. For Franklin, his religious views were not so much substitutes for the outdated beliefs of Christianity as verbalizations of his optimism about the natural universe.

Quite falsely, Franklin assumed that his undogmatic religion was a universal substratum, underlying all true religions but all too often obscured by speculative superstructures of theology. Because he did not need the superstructures or the ritual and beauty of historic faiths, as well as the personal emotional satisfactions that often spring from the very particular beliefs of each religion, Franklin rejected them without regret. In the language of religion, Franklin was simply asserting the sufficiency and the wonder of nature and the adequacy of a conventional, sensible morality. He never tried to speculate about the best possible world, but never doubted the wonderful reality of his own world. If he possessed any piety, it was in his feeling of wonder and awe, of finiteness and limitation, in contrast to the universe, which was not only so perfectly planned but so relevant to human concerns and human purposes. Likewise, at the moral level, he never tried to justify his much-acclaimed virtues. He did not feel burdened to ground them in eternal principles, in intuitive or a priori knowledge, or even in articulated lessons of experience. He assumed their obvious validity. Instead of explaining or justifying his view of nature (apart from attributing it to a Creator), he tried to explore it more fully. Instead of justifying his moral values (again apart from the nebulous wishes of his God), he tried to teach people how to follow them. Freed of troubling philosophical problems, he succeeded wonderfully in physical science and, for his day, had significant influence as a moral teacher and practical sage.

NATURAL SCIENCE

Franklin never doubted either the beautiful and harmonious economy and perfection of nature or its infinite utility for man. He was always a natural philosopher, with an unquenchable curiosity about the workings of his universe, with an unsurpassed brilliance in formulating ingenious explanations for its heretofore unexplained "riddles," and with a complete dedication to bettering the lot of mankind through a more rational utilization of its beneficent but too often misunderstood gifts. Here he found the most rewarding outlet for his superior intelligence, although he was never able to give as much time to science as he wished. In the study of nature, Franklin never found the frustrations, the meaningless abstractions, the unacceptable conclusions that plagued his few endeavors in theology. Here there was the unquestioned truth. As long as he speculated about the physical world, Franklin knew that he could ultimately appeal his most imaginative hypothesis to the unbiased test of experience. Here the subjective ultimately had to give way before the objective. For Franklin, quite naturally in his day and perhaps yet in ours, joined most scientists and most people in holding to a simple realism. He assumed an existent and knowable world to which we must submit our opinions if we would know truth. Unlike many of his religious contemporaries, Franklin limited the real and knowable world to the physical universe. His Creator was knowable only through it.

Contrary to many unfair criticisms, Franklin was not an early Edison, or a mere tinker and inventor. Neither was he solely or even primarily concerned with applied science or technology. Because of his determined anti-intellectualism and anti-obscurantism in religion and philosophy, it is too easy to make an erroneous judgment about his scientific work. In actuality, Franklin's greatest contribution to science, in electricity and related fields, was his highly imaginative hypotheses to explain phenomena often discovered and described as much by other people as by himself. As a scientist, his great gifts included a lucid intelligence, a vivid imagination, and enough detachment from his theories to be willing to test them and freely reject them when they proved inadequate. As much as Franklin loved to perform experiments, he loved even more to speculate about the causes of observed phenomena.

But Franklin never separated science from other aspects of his life and particularly never tried to sever it from his moral commitments. Never too concerned over immortality, never pious enough to make love of God a compelling moral motive, Franklin still felt a tremendous, a Puritan-like responsibility. The call of duty was always a clanging cymbal. He felt that life, enjoyable and wonderful as he found it to be, was not self-justifying. He lived for something above and beyond himself. Perfectly fulfilling one theme so aptly applied to the Enlightenment by Carl Becker, he lived for the betterment of mankind and struggled to win praise and honor from his contemporaries and from posterity. He wanted to leave his good mark upon his world. As much as he loved his experiments, as enjoyable as were his speculations about nature, he could never have wholeheartedly embraced science if he had not also believed, and in most cases known through tangible evidence, that science did have utility. When he could find a partner good enough to challenge him, Franklin played chess. For years he amused himself and friends with magical number squares. But these enjoyable mental exercises could only be justified as needed recreation, and both created a bit of guilt.

Franklin loved to know about things, to comprehend their workings, but he wanted to use his understanding for some improvement in the human condition. He pursued his early work in electricity out of complete fascination; despite hope and expectation, there were no early practical returns from his experiments. Rather pathetically, some of his friends tried to show that chickens killed electrically yielded a better meat, but Franklin was too skeptical to find solace in their empty hopes. But later he did find a specific use in the lightning rod and in it a balm for his demanding conscience and a new and brilliant star in posterity's crown. In terms of his ultimate commitments, here was justification for all his enjoyment and his international fame. From the perspective of today, it seems that Franklin put undue emphasis upon his lightning rod and possibly even helped obscure the greater significance of his electrical theories for later generations. But this judgment of today is based upon something Franklin could not know—the eventual practical significance of electricity itself. Thus, the contemporary evaluation is often based on his own standard of utility.

The conclusion to all this is quite clear. Franklin was a *practical* scientist. But so what? He was also, to suggest various categories, an able scientist, a speculative scientist, and an experimental scientist. There is a dangerous sophistry and a perverted type of snobbery in the tendency to give the higher value to pure philosophy, pure science, or pure art. There may be single-minded scientific investigation unrelated, in terms of motivation, to any immediate utilitarian purpose apart from the satisfaction of curiosity, or the fulfillment of a personal desire for simplicity and order. Franklin knew this type of science. But he believed the usual order—from curious investigation to personal satisfaction to social usefulness—was desirable, and was disappointed when the last step was missing. He saw, correctly, that it is logically absurd to conclude that any scientific investigation that is motivated by the hope for, or that actually leads to, practical results—to lightning rods or reactors —is somehow poor science or, at least, inferior to completely disinterested science that has no obvious practical application to human problems. Franklin sought fulfillment in science, but he sought moral as well as intellectual fulfillment. Critics in a more cynical age may, at some peril, ridicule Franklin, or Jefferson, or their colonial predecessors, for seeking a moral dimension in all areas of life. But they must realize that the condemnation is a condemnation of the men, not of their science, their art, or their political ideals. Moral commitments and practical goals underlie much, if not most, creativity and discovery. The result of creative endeavor must be evaluated in terms of some standard of beauty. The product of scientific investigation must be judged by how well it meets clear rules of verification. Neither can be fairly judged by what motivated them.

Of course, there may be valid criticisms of any undue emphasis upon applied science at the expense of theoretical science. It is unlikely that there would have been any lightning rods unless there was some understanding of electricity itself. Throughout the nineteenth century, Americans generally relied upon Europeans for their theoretical science, but gradually assumed the leadership in several areas of technology. Both

are important, but one—technology—is usually but not always dependent. In this sense, at least, Americans might rightly feel inferior.
But Franklin fulfilled both functions. He took the lead in developing a
theoretical understanding and then pointed to practical applications.

There is another possible area of confusion concerning Franklin's
scientific interest. To mention theoretical science today is to implicate
the highly technical and formalistic theorems of relativity or quantum
theory. Even in Franklin's day there was the imposing, highly technical,
and largely mathematical mechanics of the *Principia*. If by pure science,
one means the very abstract and necessarily mathematical hypotheses of
modern physics, then Franklin could not qualify. He had no training in
mathematics and could express himself exactly and symbolically only
with the simplest equations. But unless one confers literal truth upon the
formal structures of modern science, mathematics and logic have to be
regarded as very effective and exact tools for dealing with very subtle
and complex areas of experience. This is true whether experience is
related to an objective reality (as Franklin and the Enlightenment always did) or is accepted simply as experience without an assumption
about an underlying reality. If this view is accepted, the tool can only
be judged in terms of its adequacy. Franklin could not read the
Principia; he floundered completely in trying to comprehend Cadwallader Colden's attempt to outdo Newton by describing the various
powers in matter. But he had the tools he needed—a logical mind
attuned to quantitative thinking, a broad knowledge of eighteenth-
century science, and an almost perfect ability to communicate his ideas.
Electricity was a new field of scientific investigation. The first theoretical
formulations were relatively simple, yet adequate to the existing phenomena. To have wrapped his theories in needless mathematical
symbols, to have invented a new technical vocabulary, would have been
to succumb to the very obscurantism that Franklin so often deplored in
other fields.

Had Franklin attempted to do constructive work in developed scientific fields, such as in mechanics or astronomy, he would have been
forced to learn more mathematics. Similarly, he could never have coped
with later developments in his own field. His scientific speculation
remained closely tied to simple experiments. The verification was always
one step removed from the theory and required only simple types of
observation. As soon as more elaborate hypotheses were advanced,

logical bridges would have to connect the theory with possible areas of factual observation, and at that point science becomes too complex for the untrained layman, for it requires complex mathematical equations, more knowledge and training on the part of the scientist, and usually more complicated mechanical aids for the senses. If Franklin had a serious weakness in his conception of science, it was in his ambivalence about the role of mathematics. He often regretted his own lack of mathematical training. Yet, with real pride he communicated one of his experiments with this note: "If my Hypothesis is not the Truth itself it is at least as naked: For I have not with some of our learned Moderns, disguis'd my Nonsense in Greek, cloth'd it in Algebra or adorn'd it with Fluxions." [To John Perkins, Feb. 4, 1753, *Writings,* III, 121.]

Most colonial science was in the empirical tradition of Bacon and often consisted of no more than the collection and description of new natural objects or the performance of simple experiments. Only in Franklin or in a daring theorist like Colden did it reach the level of bold new explanatory hypotheses. Most eighteenth-century scientists, in England and America, were scientists by avocation and not by profession; they were scientists because of lively curiosity, not because of extensive education or training. They collected and speculated out of sheer enjoyment and cooperated because of their common interests and delightful fellowship. Science was fun and never more so than in the thrill of discovering some new object never before described or in proposing some logical explanation that could account for new phenomena and reconcile it with what was already known and with an ordered, rational universe the existence of which was beyond doubting. For gentlemen who had some leisure and who possessed either curiosity or a desire for social advancement, natural philosophy was an absorbing hobby and an excellent substitute for the divisive theological debates that had occupied earlier generations. Never again would science offer the dedicated layman, or even the dilettante, so much opportunity or pleasure. In many vast areas, man's knowledge of and control over nature was in its infancy in the eighteenth century. Only in one of these virgin areas could an untrained Franklin virtually revolutionize a whole new area of investigation and win international fame. And he did it in his spare time. Although science was his greatest love, he never made it a profession nor gave it his single-minded attention. Even here he was not irretrievably committed. He never served his greatest mistress with the devotion or the undivided attention of Isaac Newton or Albert Einstein. If he had, he would have been a much greater scientist; but possibly he would have been a lesser man.

Franklin never tried to elaborate any scientific methodology, but he did frequently express himself concerning certain requirements for establishing scientific truth. Nature was a rational entity which man experienced through his senses and comprehended by his mind. To Franklin, good science depended on careful and patient accuracy in observation and on humble, tentative, explanatory hypotheses. His great strength was his recognition that speculative hypotheses must stand the test of both logical and experimental verification. He was able to remain almost completely aloof from the unending personal jealousies and recriminations that plagued so many of his scientific colleagues. He believed that the process of experiment and reflection could lead to an ever expanding body of knowledge, to unending scientific progress. For in back of the recorded changes, the observed motions, were eternal laws, permanent and invariant. Here was the ultimate corrective of human error. A hypothesis was not a call for some scientific crusade against opposing hypotheses, but an invitation and a few preliminary directions for a voyage of discovery. A hypothesis justified itself when it launched a voyage, even when new directions had to be chosen because of the exigencies of the trip.

Franklin's scientific interests were boundless, but his contributions were somewhat restricted. He joined Peter Collinson, the English Quaker merchant and benefactor of most colonial scientists, in raising a subscription to finance the individualistic John Bartram in his far-ranging trips to collect American flora. He corresponded with Cadwallader Colden, a physician and botanist as well as an aspiring physicist, and eventually became a friend of virtually every scientist in the colonies. It was in part through the influence of Bartram that Franklin took a leading role in forming the first, abortive American Philosophical Society in 1743. His own proposals for the society were slanted toward natural history, agriculture, medicine, invention, and applied chemistry, with hardly a mention of physical science. In the early 1740's *Poor Richard* became increasingly interested in plant descriptions for medicinal purposes.

From his early work with chimneys and stoves, Franklin developed a permanent interest in problems of heat and ventilation. At various times he investigated the fascinating subject of evaporative cooling and suggested various ingenious uses for this phenomenon. Just prior to his absorption in electrical experiments he began his elaborate attempts to explain the shorter time consumed by a ship traveling from America to England than from England to America. He tried to explain this by the earth's motion, but later found the correct answer in the Gulf Stream. Some of his earliest speculations concerned geological upheavals in the past, which Franklin justified as beneficial to man because they exposed many valuable minerals. He commended the more specialized research in both geology and astronomy carried out by John Winthrop and made some of his own lay observations in astronomy. The weather continually fascinated Franklin from his earliest speculations in *Poor Richard* until his death. His speculations concerning whirlwinds, the path of hurricanes, and the causes of waterspouts led, after his identification of natural electricity in clouds, to complex but often erroneous speculations concerning all areas of climatology.

Franklin began his electrical experiments in the last months of 1746. He utilized some electrical tubes given to the library company by Peter Collinson, along with descriptions of experiments already being performed in Europe. Franklin's first letter back to Collinson revealed his early and complete absorption in the new area of research: "For my own part, I never was before engaged in any study that so totally engrossed my attention and my time as this has lately done; for what with making experiments when I can be alone, and repeating them to my Friends and Acquaintances, who, from the novelty of the thing, come continually in crowds to see them, I have, during some months past, had little leisure for any thing else." [To Collinson, Mar. 28, 1747, *Papers,* III, 118–19.] Not only did Collinson provide the first equipment, but he subsequently communicated Franklin's finding and theories to English scientists and to the Royal Society. It was also Collinson who collected the communications and had them published in book form.

Franklin's reputation in the field of electricity rests on two main achievements. He began his speculations in an area of experimental ferment and theoretical confusion and contributed simple theoretical principles that successfully explained or predicted all but one of the existing electrical phenomena. Second, by proving the electrification of clouds, he made electricity a respected branch of natural science. Formerly, it had been considered an unusual, isolated side show of physical science, conducted by faddists largely for personal amusement. These two solid achievements were timely, and they were made by an authentic American. The popular interest in electricity insured quick recognition of Franklin, while his Americanism added an extra degree of interest and curiosity. Other scientists, particularly in England, contributed significantly to the understanding of electricity, but never received a fraction of the recognition given Franklin, whose contribution was greater, but it was not so much greater as his fame soon seemed to indicate.

As he performed more and more fascinating electrical experiments, Franklin formulated tentative explanations for each observed phenomenon. Since many of the experiments were performed together with several of his interested friends, the whole endeavor had a communal flavor, with Franklin simply assuming a position of leadership. He formulated his theories within the larger framework of an economical and harmonious universe. He also worked in the shadow of Newton and among such concepts as the atomic and porous nature of matter and the probable existence of an elastic, fluid substance called ether, capable of accounting for the transmission of light. Using a simple friction machine to produce electricity, and Leyden jars, or variations of them, to hold the accumulated charge, he found only one satisfactory explanation for the mysterious effects. There must be an electrical fire or matter (later called fluid) evenly distributed throughout ponderable matter. Normally in a state of balance or equilibrium, the even distribution can be altered by friction (rubbing), and either an object or a part of an object (as the glass in a Leyden jar) can have an excess or a deficiency of electrical matter. But since there is a constant amount of electricity in the universe, every excess requires a proportionate deficiency. The most obvious (and most dangerous) electrical phenomenon, the spark that seemed to jump from one object to another, is accounted for by excess electricity jumping to fill à deficiency in another object. Franklin and his fellow experimenters used plus and minus to denominate either an excess or deficiency of electricity, and charge to designate any quantity of electrical energy.

The single-fluid theory satisfactorily explained almost all the experimental phenomena. It accounted for the attraction between plus and minus and for the great potential energy in an electrical discharge between two oppositely charged bodies. Franklin assumed that electrical matter was atomic, strongly attracted by ponderable matter, but elastic in itself, i.e., that unattached electrical atoms repelled each other. Thus was explained the mutual repulsion between two positively charged bodies. But his theory did not account for the unexpected repulsion between negatively charged bodies, a weakness in his theory that Franklin could never resolve, and which could only be rationalized later by *ad hoc* hypotheses about the elastic nature of matter, but an elasticity normally neutralized by a full portion of electricity and only visibly present when there was a deficiency of electricity. Although the flow of electrons is the reverse of what was indicated by Franklin's experiments and hence his plus and minus misleading, the single-fluid theory remains a very workable and simple explanation of electrical phenomena, particularly for the layman. Within a few years it, or a more elaborate but related two-fluid (one minus and one plus) theory, was accepted by all but a few scientists.

By submitting the first clear, workable hypothesis to account for electricity, Franklin placed himself in the tradition of all great scientists. Like Newton before him, and Darwin and Einstein later, he brought harmony, simplicity, and predictability to a confused and underdeveloped field of science. But unlike these greatest scientists, he suggested an explanatory hypothesis without working out rigorous quantitative concepts to aid in control and prediction. His was a theoretical skeleton, capable of endless elaboration by better mathematicians and more dedicated scientists than Franklin. He recognized the existence of measurable factors (charge and conductivity) in electricity and established simple ratios or proportions, but never defined an exact unit of measurement. Without the slightest awareness or comprehension, Franklin was helping open the door to a new, now all-important area of investigation. To an extent unappreciated by anyone in the eighteenth century, electricity became a means of investigating and understanding matter itself. The long journey of exploration into the microcosm was beginning, but Franklin never pushed the exploration very far. He was a Copernicus but never a Newton; he opened a door for an Alessandro Volta, a Michael Faraday, or a James Maxwell, but never uncovered much of the darkness within.

Even though the single-fluid theory became the almost universally accepted explanation of electrical phenomena, it never enhanced Franklin's reputation nearly as much as did his positive identification of natural electricity in thunder gusts, his "snatching lightning from the sky" and taming it for the use of man. Franklin was far from the first person to speculate on a common element in small, man-produced electrical sparks and the tremendous lightning stroke. But he went beyond mere speculation. In a letter presented to the Royal Society in 1749, he cited twelve points of similarity between lightning and artificially produced electrical sparks. More rewarding, Franklin proposed a simple experiment to test for electricity in clouds. Utilizing a proven but as yet inadequately explained phenomenon—the superior ability of pointed conductors to attract and draw off electricity—Franklin suggested that a twenty- or thirty-foot iron rod be attached to the top of a church steeple. A man standing on an insulated platform beneath would try, by the use of his body or, for greater safety, the use of a grounded wire coil, to draw electrical sparks from the suspended rod whenever clouds were low overhead. According to his instructions, the experiment was successfully performed at Marly, France, in May 1752, with abundant electrical effects and a clear demonstration that the electricity in clouds was identical to that produced by friction. Electricity was now more than a plaything.

The French experiment, which was carried out under the direction of Jean François d'Alibard, a French scientist and friend of the great Georges Buffon, attracted widespread attention in Europe. It helped publicize the French edition of Franklin's *Experiments and Observations on Electricity,* attracted the favorable attention of Louis XV, and led to endless repetitions of the experiment. Even Joseph Priestley described this as a "capital discovery, and possibly the greatest since the time of Newton." Even before he heard of the success in France, Franklin flew his famous kite in June 1752 and again demonstrated, in a most simple but dramatic way, the electrical nature of lightning. Standing in the dry, carefully insulated from the wet conducting string, Franklin allowed his kite, with its pointed wire top, to draw electricity from a cloud and charge a key tied to the terminus of the conducting twine. The key could be used to charge a Leyden jar even as a friction machine. Later, Franklin rigged a permanent rod on his house, so planned that its electrification would activate a clapper and gaily ring bells, giving a continuous but surely somewhat raucous indication of the amount of electricity overhead. He found that most, but not all, clouds were negatively charged and thus concluded that, contrary to appearance, the lightning bolt springs up out of the ground. But either way, a circuit is established between a charged cloud and the earth, which is an almost infinite repository of electrical fluid, freely giving or receiving according to the circumstance.

Even before there was experimental proof of the electrical nature of lightning, Franklin had conceived the lightning rod. Since pointed rods silently drew off the electricity from a charged body, grounded rods would surely draw the electricity from clouds and safely transmit the powerful charge into the earth, sparing ships and buildings. Franklin devised a practical system, determined the necessary size of the ground wires, and persuaded many people in the Philadelphia area to use his newest invention. Yet, for years, some people refused to accept the rods, while a long debate ensued over the superiority of pointed rods or balls in drawing away atmospheric electricity. Franklin was dismayed by the lack of interest in his rods in England, but was flattered when the British government hired him to plan a system of rods for arsenals. He promoted the rods, as earlier he had the Pennsylvania fireplace, by lucid description and persuasive arguments for their value. His refusal to patent them or gain personal profits helped in the promotion.

Franklin's most important scientific work was completed by 1754. A delegate to the Albany Congress and soon plunged into the military aspects of the French and Indian War, he began his almost uninterrupted career in diplomacy and public service. In 1757 he went to England for what became a five-year sojourn. Although he went as a representative of the Pennsylvania Assembly in an attempt to lessen the remaining and resented prerogatives of the Proprietors (the Penn family), he enjoyed a leisurely stay. Now famous, he could enjoy without presumption the friendship of England's greatest scientists and philosophers. His electrical work had belatedly won wide acclaim in the Royal Society, leading to a gratis, unsolicited membership and a free subscription to the Society's *Transactions*. In 1753 he had also won the Society's highest award, the Copley Medal. In England he was able to attend the sessions in person. He took residence in the home of a widow, Margaret Stevenson, became a member of the family and father and adviser to a daughter, Mary. These were undoubtedly the most satisfactory and happy years of his life. He won plaudits everywhere, honorary degrees from Edinburgh and Oxford, and saw such a pleasant side of English life that he even considered moving there from Philadelphia. All his subsequent visits to England were to be darkened by a growing rift between the mother country and the colonists.

MORAL SCIENCE

While in England, Franklin indulged an old interest in moral philosophy, a subject immensely popular among English and Scottish writers. In a visit to Scotland he met a leading British moralist, Lord Kames. Although their subsequent correspondence often involved such mundane matters as a cure for his Lordship's smoking chimney, it always came to rest on problems of virtue and morality. In commenting on Kames's books, Franklin told of a long-time plan for writing his own book on the art of virtue. Since virtue was an art like painting and architecture, and not just a matter of good will in man, he believed it dependent on correct habits, skills, and hard work. There were already books aplenty defining the good life, or inspiring people to be good, but few to tell people how to be good. As early as 1737 Franklin had deplored the absence of books that enumerated the virtues, distinguished the proper ideas that went with each, and taught individuals the all-important techniques of attaining these virtuous habits. It was time for someone to go beyond philosophy and write a usable practical handbook on morality.

Franklin never wrote his book in moral philosophy but, quite significantly, the very year that he said he first conceived it, 1732, was the year he launched *Poor Richard's Almanac*. From Franklin's many statements, there can be little doubt that the *Almanac,* aside from its success as a business venture and its attractive humor, was a highly popularized, loosely organized manual on morality, issued in annual installments for the continued instruction of its readers. But after his retirement, and his intellectual stimulation while in England, Franklin was no longer satisfied to limit his instruction to the scattered, largely borrowed homilies of Poor Richard. He was now inspired to organize and present in a coherent way his more sophisticated thoughts on morality. With the press of almost continuous practical affairs, he never achieved this goal. But in the hurried days in London, just before the American Revolution, he finally began a book on practical morality, casting it in the form of a personal parable of success and slowly adding to it until his death. Although never completed, this *Autobiography* both summarized and exemplified Franklin's moral insights. The small section containing his scheme for moral perfection was written at Passy, France, in 1784, and is now the best-known product of his pen. It was a concise summary of his art of virtue and indicated the main theme that he would have followed in a longer work—that virtue is not a matter of authority or abstract principles so much as enlightened self-interest. Virtue is the handmaiden of both happiness and business success. His life, insofar as it was successful, was an example of the rewards of virtue. In a letter of 1768, he very adequately summarized his position: "Be studious in your Profession, and you will be learned. Be industrious and frugal, and you will be rich. Be sober and temperate, and you will be healthy. Be in general virtuous, and you will be happy. At least, you will, by such Conduct, stand the best Chance for such consequences." [To John Alleyne, Aug. 9, 1768, *Writings*, V, 159.]

Franklin never tried to find the ultimate sources of morality; neither did he attempt a methodical definition of the good life. His purpose was to turn accepted moral clichés into meaningful and concrete ideas leading to good action. Morality requires right habits, is quite consistent with one's own best interests, and ultimately rests in a benevolent disposition in man. At this last point he agreed with Jonathan Edwards, but was quite willing to attribute this benevolence to most men. He assumed everyone was capable of true virtue.

Franklin's morality has been a stench in the nostrils of many, but often without good reason. It has seemed so simple, so stripped of deep intellectual probing, so smug, so mundane or purely utilitarian, and thus so superficial. And clearly, he did preach without a grain of piety, without a modicum of esthetic sensibility, and without the least bit of intellectual frills. Just as in business, he spoke with an air of authority, as one who had tried his own medicine and found it completely satisfying. But the self-satisfaction and simplicity unfortunately belied the frightful discipline, the agonizing dedication to self-improvement, that lay behind Franklin's own worldly success. Though simple to the point of being naïve, his moral thought was not undemanding.

But, of course, it was practical. He never prescribed ultimate values but rather suggested effective means. Virtue had its own rewards— success and happiness. Who opposes those? Franklin's strictures were based in part on good sense, in part on his own unrecognized prejudices. He rose from near poverty to business success and affluence. He always had an intense interest in economic problems, and with justification tended to see other values as at least dependent upon the basic economic necessities and, in many cases, upon the dearly bought leisure that comes as a reward to the successful artisan or businessman. His advice fitted the aspirations of city merchants, artisans, or farmers. He assumed a large number of lower-class laborers and servants, who he believed should have every opportunity to rise from their class, but who actually often lacked talent or virtue or both. Franklin, in one sense quite callous to the injustices of society and the problems of the poor, was offering them what he believed to be the means of salvation, the techniques for attaining wealth and any and all of the esthetic and intellectual pleasures that are dependent on wealth. He was so blinded by his success that he apparently believed *Poor Richard* was all they needed, for it could inculcate "industry and frugality, as the means of procuring wealth, and thereby securing virtue; it being more difficult for a man in want, to act always honestly, as, . . . *it is hard for an empty sack to stand upright.*" [*Autobiography of Benjamin Franklin,* Collier Books Edition (New York, 1962), p. 93.] With enough discipline, with enough hard work, with the requisite habits, with Franklin's good advice drawn from his experience, anyone could rise to the limits of his talents, and many could rise as far as Franklin.

This bias placed most problems in a personal dimension, at least in America, where neither institutions nor nature seemed to offer serious impediments to personal salvation. In Europe it was different, and here Franklin often located the source of misery and poverty in society rather than in deficiencies of character or education. In America the hope for a better world lay in virtuous individuals, even though they made up only a minority at any one time. As early as 1731, when depressed at the lack of selfless public service on the part of a generally corruptible mankind, he asked for a "united Party for Virtue," to be made up of all the "good Men of all Nations," formed into a regular body and governed by "good and wise Rulers, which good and wise Men may probably be more unanimous in their Obedience to, than common People are to Common Laws." [*Papers,* I, 192–93.]

Franklin's life had a twofold pattern: business success and then great public service in both science and government. This, he believed, was a good pattern for other men. Thus, the two invariant themes in his moral advice were success and service. Success is indispensable, but justifies itself socially in service. In a more private context, success provides access to the better pleasures—to art, discourse with the learned, comradeship—or to happiness. Virtue is the key to both—the means to success, the motivation to service. With Franklin it all sounded so simple, so easy, so lacking in subtlety, so obviously middle class, that one may see his *Autobiography* as a great caricature, or as an early satire on the gospel of wealth. But the road to success was not conceived by Franklin in terms of exploitation or of exclusive privilege, nor was his concept of service conceived as paternal philanthropy. The intellectual can sneer at the lack of reasoned justification for his thirteen virtues. The pious few can lament the total lack of a humble consciousness of limitation and of sinful pride. The romantic will deplore the simple allegiance to the rational, the concrete, and the material at the expense of the nonrational and the spiritual. The esthete will eternally hate Franklin for his seeming insensitivity to beauty and his callous oblivion to the tragic dimensions of life. Yet, his critics will still be challenged. For, will the ethical philosopher, with all his efforts, finally be able to justify a set of workable virtues significantly different from the commonly accepted ones used by Franklin, and will he be able to communicate them to the people who must, meantime, presumably lead unexamined lives? If heaven depends on it, the pious man may justify his ascetic virtues, his humility, his self-inflicted penitence, and his agonizing crucifixion of pride, but has not even the most pious often found the highest justification of their religion in what Franklin urged and personally exemplified—service? It is true that Franklin saw only obscurity where the romantic looked for man, but possibly the temperamental bias of Franklin was closer to his audience than that of the romantic. In the context of life, morality is a rather humdrum matter of habit.

Perhaps the most convincing debunking of Franklin today comes from artists. To many of them, such as D. H. Lawrence, Franklin was the eternal Philistine, the insensitive Babbit, the incurably practical and detestably utilitarian American. Franklin was not an early pragmatist. He would never have appreciated the subtlety and intellectual sophistication of philosophical pragmatism, and he accepted too many rational presuppositions to be a radical empiricist. But he did have an affinity for the realm of actual living and a distaste for any abstracted world of either pure philosophy or pure art, and in this he was equally a brother to his Puritan forebears or to such typical, morally oriented pragmatists as John Dewey. Anything that worked was not necessarily true or good, but anything that would not work, that had no utility except idle amusement, was frivolous. A poem had to preach a sermon or paint a moral, or it was relegated to the level of entertainment. Franklin wrote Lord Kames in 1762, agreeing that a good taste in the arts contributed to the improvement of morals, and thus more fervently gave his support to the arts. In a later letter to a fellow American scientist, John Bartram, Franklin discounted the value of old buildings and monuments, and added: ". . . if I could find in any Italian travels a receipt for making Parmesan cheese, it would give me more satisfaction than a transcript of any inscription from any old stone whatever." [To Bartram, July 9, 1769, *Writings*, V, 221.]

Franklin's view of art was based in a valuative system which gave the highest position to the true and the good (neither of which seemed to offer great problems) and a subordinate position to the beautiful. He was curious about the arts, speculated about problems of composition in music, invented a musical instrument, and always aspired to the cultivation of a gentleman. But when he surveyed the world critically, he focused on injustice instead of ugliness. When he tried to improve it, he perfected a fireplace or looked for a good recipe for Parmesan cheese. A work of art, if it inspired to morality, or, less important, if it provided happiness, was already justified. But art was also tied to service, to a moral imperative. Here neither orthodox Christians nor most eighteenth-century artists disagreed. Art as pure spontaneous creativity was like Franklin's magical number squares—a thing requiring apology and a moral salve for the conscience. Esthetes may truly survey an area of limitation in Franklin; he was no poet despite his many verses. But they are in danger of a one-sidedness more dangerous than his when they elevate art as the one end of life, the one value worth pursuing. True, if truth is beyond human ken, and values only a matter of whim, modern man could do no better than enlist in the honest service of taste and elevate Beauty as the new God of the West. But the very essence of the eighteenth century was the rejection of such cynicism. Certainly, one's life is far too circumscribed if he never goes beyond the practical, when practical has only a pecuniary implication. But what is the problem of one who denounces something simply because it is practical?

Franklin was much more responsive to the artist than many modern artists are to him.

In the eighteenth century moral philosophy always encompassed political and economic problems. As a moralist, Franklin never hesitated to enter the broad field of political economy. Here, as almost everywhere else, his suggestions and speculations were not only full of originality but also have had enduring influence.

Franklin's other accomplishments too often obscured his skill as a practical politician. He was a master at sensing the public mood, in carefully assuming the public pose best fitted to circumstances and to his political ends, and was invariably successful in attaining his goals. Despite frequent reservations about the intelligence and the character of the run of men, Franklin was yet opposed to formalized aristocracies and, in Pennsylvania, almost always led the masses in their battles against proprietory privilege. Most of Franklin's political writing was timely and polemical, being directed at varying practical problems. He was no political theorist. Yet he won some fame as a leading advocate of an unsuccessful unicameralism in Pennsylvania, as an effective opponent of English mercantilist control over American trade and manufacturing, and as an early abolitionist who fought against the slave trade. Before most Americans, he foresaw the inevitability of either American independence or an autonomous commonwealth under the Crown, an alternative he long preferred to independence. He was a prophet of American opportunities and its future growth and had a speculative as well as a humanitarian interest in the development of western lands. At the Albany Congress, and later, he was the leading spokesman for colonial unity, and in helping draft the Declaration of Independence and in his fatherly advice at the Constitutional Convention helped contribute to that unity. Always innovative, fervently pro-American, brilliantly provocative in his comments, he yet did not formulate any broad political doctrines and, in contrast to a John Adams or Thomas Jefferson, did not significantly influence our political institutions.

Franklin was an amateur economist before he became an amateur scientist. In 1728, at age twenty-two, he wrote a journalistic tract, "A Modest Enquiry into the Nature and Necessity of a Paper Currency," in support of paper money in Pennsylvania, and thus began an enduring campaign in support of liberal currency policies in the colonies. Because of an unfavorable trade balance and a lack of metallic gold, Franklin argued the necessity of a paper money for normal trade, lower interest, and heightened economic activity. He desired bills issued on the security of land and loaned at a low interest of 4 per cent, with the strictest supervision by the state in order to avoid depreciation. His writings, which drew largely upon the earlier economic theories of a radical English economist, Sir William Petty, helped insure a Pennsylvania paper issue in 1729, for which Franklin was awarded a lucrative printing contract.

More important than his advocacy of paper money were other theories that Franklin borrowed from Petty. He accepted a labor theory of value in all his early economic tracts, and added to this a rent theory of interest. To Franklin, any product, including even the metal in coins, was worth only the value of the labor that went into its production. Trade was simply the exchange of labor for labor. A fair, minimal interest was the rent value of land that could be purchased by the same amount of money. The wealth of a country should be measured in terms of its potential productive labor and surely not by its gold. For his labor theory of value, even though not original to him, Franklin won a later acknowledgment from Karl Marx and a brief mention in most economic textbooks.

In 1751 Franklin published an originative and influential essay entitled "Observations Concerning the Increase of Mankind, Peopling of Countries, Etc." The treatise had, as an ultimate aim, the condemnation of English restrictions on trade and manufacturing in the colonies and thus was part of his endless battle for free trade. But its population theories were most provocative. He related population increase to economic opportunity (such as available land), showed that in America earlier marriages were natural and large families inevitable, and thus predicted that the rate of population growth in the colonies would be twice that in Europe. Because of free land and open opportunities, he predicted high wages in America, and thus little manufacturing, although a prosperous agriculture and some extraction industries. Among the many reasons for population decline (conquest, loss of territory, love of luxuries, loss of trade, bad government), he found only one in America—the importation of Negro slaves and the deprivation of whites of employment, economic opportunity, and the necessary subsistence for a high birth rate. Since the expansion of territory increased population, Franklin argued for the annexation of Canada after the French and Indian War. Central in his presuppositions was the ultimate limitation of subsistence upon population. Here, without undue pessimism, Franklin directly anticipated Thomas Malthus' work on population. Not only Malthus later, but such contemporary intellectuals as Adam Smith, David Hume, and Lord Kames read and appreciated this little essay, which appeared in many editions and was even included in Franklin's *Experiments and Observations on Electricity.*

After becoming a colonial agent in England, Franklin came into contact with the writings of the French physiocrats and adopted almost all of their economic theory. Their fervent advocacy of free trade justified his own opposition to mercantilism; their agrarianism was logically compelling, complimentary to America, and increasingly persuasive to Franklin, who reacted in disgust to many aspects of an urban and manufacturing economy in England. In his earliest letter to DuPont de Nemours, a leading exponent and popularizer of physiocratic philosophy, Franklin expressed a hope that physiocracy would become "the governing philosophy of the human species, as it must be that of superior beings in better worlds." [To Nemours, July 28, 1768, *Writings*, V, 155–56.] Later, in France, he came to know most of the physiocrats, who were more than happy to count the illustrious Franklin as one of their number.

The physiocratic glorification of agricultural production, which alone adds wealth, and their antipathy to manufacturing and trade, which only changes the form or location of wealth, caused Franklin to amend his simple labor theory of value into an agricultural labor theory. The labor required to produce food for subsistence was the sole measure of economic value. The value of a manufactured product was exactly the same as the value of food that the same amount of labor would produce in agriculture. Conversely, the added value of a finished product in manufacturing was only equal to the amount of subsistence consumed by the laborers in producing it. Thus, manufacturing added no value except possibly in the added convenience of transporting the smaller product. Franklin became excessively vehement in his attack upon commerce, particularly in light of his earlier friendship and identification with merchants in Philadelphia. Ideally, trade involved only the exchange of equal values. But industrial nations used hypocrisy to exploit agricultural states. They fooled the simple and less sophisticated nation into believing that manufactured goods had far greater value than they did in fact (that is, in terms of agricultural labor value). His summary of this view has been often quoted: "Finally, there seems to be but three ways for a nation to acquire wealth. The first is by *war,* as the Romans did, in plundering their conquered neighbors. This is *robbery.* The second by *commerce,* which is generally *cheating.* The third by *agriculture,* the only *honest way,* wherein man receives a real increase of the seed thrown into the ground, in a kind of continual miracle, wrought by the hand of God in his favour, as a reward for his innocent life and his virtuous industry." The terms "innocent" and "virtuous" went beyond economic theory and revealed in Franklin a romantic and primitivistic view of agriculture, a romanticism widely shared in America.

Franklin's commitment to a laissez faire economy was consistently, almost cruelly, applied to the problems of the laborers and the poor. Franklin deplored the English poor laws and opposed any form of private or public philanthropy that in any way lessened the compulsion to labor. He assumed that the vast majority of mankind labored only from dire necessity and that they would seek any possible means of avoiding labor. The incapable should be cared for by society; all able to work should be left in complete freedom, either to starve or to find employment. He believed wages would vary according to the demand for and supply of laborers and that, generally, a man could find employment at a low enough wage. If employment did not exist, charity should take the form of public workhouses, which would be so odious as to discourage all avoidable idleness. Franklin even argued that ultimately all the income of a nation went to the laboring class. Even high profits were eventually spent for products manufactured or grown by the laboring man. Thus, "As I said at first, *our laboring poor receive annually the whole of the clear revenues of the nation,* and from us they can have no more." ["On the Laboring Poor," *Writings,* V, 126.] Here, once again, Franklin tended to smugness in his view of less gifted men. His own rise from poverty was too easily generalized into a model applicable to all who were willing to put forth the effort. But his belief that industry has to be forced by economic need represented his most pessimistic, or possibly his most realistic, view of mass man. The untypical inhumaneness of this attitude is possibly seen in fairer perspective when related to the America Franklin knew, an America where it seemed obvious that opportunity abounded, that success was largely a matter of intelligence and determination, and that impoverishment was a matter of stupidity or poor character.

In one final area—education—Franklin made a definite contribution. He had the zeal and faith in education that usually typifies the self-educated man. To him, talents useful for the education of youth were "the gift of God"; those who used them were as "strongly called as if they heard a voice from Heaven." [To Samuel Johnson, Aug. 23, 1750, *Writings,* III, 17.] His own contribution to education was in his many proposals for the Academy. He wanted a nonsectarian, moralistic, but only nebulously religious school for the training of middle- and lower-class young men (Franklin, incidentally, also favored education for women). His proposals were radical in rejecting a sectarian or even evangelical religious orientation, and in emphasizing practical arts and the English language at the partial expense of the then universal emphasis upon classical languages and on the liberal arts. Franklin wished the classical curriculum for some of the boys, but believed some would have to be satisfied with a brief education and could best use their time in mastering English and giving attention to the more immediately useful skills. He daringly suggested the same salary for the English as for the Latin Master (in practice, this was never carried out, with the Latin Master receiving much the larger salary). In a detailed and idealistic proposal for each of the six classes, Franklin suggested an interest-oriented curriculum based on history, with natural history most emphasized. Through the study of the past, with the use of available translations, the student would be naturally led into an investigation of all other areas of study. [See his "Proposals Relating to the Education of Youth in Pennsylvania," 1749, *Papers,* III, 397–421.] In his concern over educational relevance, in his emphasis upon the native tongue, in his advocacy of useful arts and skills, and in his attempt to relate the curriculum to the interests of the students, he anticipated many educational reforms in both the nineteenth and twentieth centuries, and most obviously those of John Dewey and the progressives.

After his diplomatic frustrations in England before the American Revolution, and his brilliant successes in France during and after it, Franklin returned permanently to the United States in 1785. During his years abroad he continued his various interests, particularly science, but more often as a spectator than as an active contributor. In the interim between his return and his last public service in the Constitutional Convention, he served as president of the executive council in Pennsylvania, under the unique unicameral constitution that he helped inspire. His last years were spent in true retirement, with his daughter and his grandchildren. He was universally famous and thus received the homage of all Americans. When he died in April 1790, an estimated 20,000 people attended his funeral.

There were few serious errata in Franklin's life. There were only inevitable inadequacies. Despite his versatility, he was very much a creature of an age, an age now as irrelevant in some of its assumptions as any in our American past. His practical moralism, so endemic in America, was never complemented by a clear conception of value. There seemed no redemption short of successful achievement, and no effective means of dealing with frustration. He turned too quickly from a pious and spiritual past, even as he held on too tenaciously to the pleasing assurance drawn from that past. Unlike Edwards before him, or Emerson afterwards, he failed to perceive the possibilities of natural piety, or of an experiential, esthetic reconciliation of man with the source and end of human existence. He hoped to please God but never thought to become one with Him. Thus he broke from the most consoling theme of New England thought even as he rejected the most demanding. But his own emphases, even when one-sided extrapolations from his own success, showed the fullest possibilities of a cosmically insured humanism. He never let abstract intellectuality replace common sense, petty authoritarianism replace humane concern, or a worship of obscurity replace a mature sanity. Even if not among the redeemed, he was abundantly enlightened.

IV
JOHN ADAMS:
POLITICS

PORTRAIT OF AN ENLIGHTENED
PURITAN

John Adams was both a better and a worse Puritan than he ever realized. In spite of his loyalty to the Congregational Church, his God was a world removed from that of his forebears. How much so he could never understand. But much more than he realized, his dominant character traits, his habits of thought, even his political ideals, were thoroughly Puritan. Thus, much more completely than Franklin, he was able to marry the predominant concerns of the Enlightenment to the attitudes and institutions of Puritan New England.

In 1735, the year of his birth, the first wave of revivals had barely subsided at Northampton. In a few "liberal" congregations a humane form of Calvinism was just emerging as full-blown Arminianism. Even in his childhood years at Braintree, John Adams was unable to escape the doctrinal controversy. But he soon tired of it.

His father (also named John Adams) was a prominent farmer, a church deacon, a selectman, and a believer in education. Unable to attend Harvard himself, he amassed a large enough estate to send his eldest son and namesake there. It was a fateful decision for young John and forever set him apart from his brothers. He had an opportunity to enter the professions.

Of humble origins, without social pretensions, John Adams was an appreciative and eager student. Both he and his family assumed that he would end up in the ministry. This was the normal pattern. In his whole family history only one youth, an uncle, had been privileged to attend Harvard, and he had become a minister. Upon graduation, still not twenty years old, Adams took the typical postgraduate course—he became Latin Master in a grammar school in Worcester. This was no routine interlude before beginning divinity training, for here Adams began agonizing over his choice of profession. His moral zeal and simple piety still pushed him toward the ministry, but all the doctrinal controversy appalled him and created doubts about his own orthodoxy. The minister at Braintree during his college years, Lemuel Briant, was an avowed Arminian and one of the forefathers of New England Unitarianism. Briant's humane tendencies and liberalism appealed to a moralistic but untheological Adams. But Briant provoked dissent. A doctrinal battle produced a plethora of weighty pronouncements, tedious pamphlets, and hard feelings. Repudiating such misery-producing controversy, Adams chose a new career.

Already his fervent interest in politics had warred with his concern for religion. He now chose to be a lawyer. He redirected his moral fervor to the practical task of insuring human justice and happiness. In typical Calvinist terms, he argued that his newly chosen profession was a calling of God. He made clear over and over again that a legal career was not a path to fortune but a clear path of duty. He would not commit any injustice, but always seek justice for others. In the old Massachusetts, lawyers had been suspect, but magistrates were esteemed along with ministers. In a new political context, Adams could correctly argue that the law was the pathway to politics and thus successfully gain a fuller respect for his choice.

As then typical, Adams read law in the office of an older barrister. He continued to teach until he was admitted to the bar, and to gainful practice, in 1758. He then returned to his father's home in Braintree and entered the lean years when, without fame or reputation, clients were all too scarce. But there was the farm (his father died in 1761) and, endlessly, girls. Adams could not conceal his fascination with women, nor appease his guilt over so many idle hours spent flirting with them or dreaming about them. Although passionate, he was equally circumspect. In an act of personal wisdom in 1764, he married Abigail Smith, the daughter of a neighboring minister. Her mother was a Quincy and part of a circle of very prominent New England families. Abigail was intellectually gifted, loved literature, and was able to provide intellectual as well as emotional support for Adams. All the clichés fit. It was an ideal marriage.

Adams entered politics in 1766, as a selectman in the town of Braintree. Even earlier, in 1761, he had listened to James Otis' impassioned arguments against the writs of assistance. He always viewed this speech as the beginning of the American Revolution. He joined the colonial cause in 1765, in response to the Stamp Act, placing his whole legal career in jeopardy, with trepidation but unrelenting honesty. But from 1765 on Adams never deviated. He moved steadily toward independence, with few qualms but yet with a logical acuity and a balanced reasonableness unmatched by the more emotional patriots. Although less effective than Otis and Samuel Adams in popular appeal and in propaganda, his legal knowledge and sound strategic advice soon made him the most imposing and most dangerous patriot in all New England. In a near miracle of synchronized movement, Adams seemed to be everywhere and have a hand in every important event. With his able pen he wrote the most thorough vindications of the colonial cause. As a delegate to the first and second Continental Congresses, he fought the ones tempted to retreat or seek easy compromise and early committed himself to complete independence.

John Adams was the hardest-working delegate to the Second Continental Congress. He took the lead in selecting George Washington as commander-in-chief, served on the Board of War, tenaciously fought for a strong navy (a lifelong concern), argued the cause of independence, helped draft the Declaration of Independence, and worked to gain European aid without entangling alliances. He served on a mission to get a treaty with France and later, in a year-long effort at The Hague, gained the first recognition of the United States by a country other than France. By skillful negotiation, he secured badly needed low-interest loans for the United States and finally helped draft the treaty of peace. Unbelievably, between these assignments and while on a brief trip back home, he played the major role in drafting the first copy of the influential constitution of Massachusetts (1780) and gave valuable constitutional advice to other states. In this way he contributed more to the form of government in the states and in the later federal Constitution than any other one person. In addition to all this, he remained in England until 1788 as the first American minister, finding time in the midst of endless frustration to write his three-volume *Defense of the Constitutions of the United States of America Against the Attack of M. Turgot,* the most important treatise on government that was written during the revolutionary period.

Scarcely back in the United States, Adams was elected vice-president. After years of intense activity, he was frustrated by the lack of responsibility, even though he was able to cast some decisive tie-breaking votes in the Senate. Then, from 1797 to 1801 he served well as President. Ever afterward he believed that his courageous post-XYZ negotiations with France, against the intrigues of Hamilton and his own cabinet, saved the young nation from catastrophe. His lack of political finesse, his dogged independence, and the Alien and Sedition Acts, coupled with the division in his own party, led to defeat in 1800. Embittered and hurt at public ingratitude, he retired to his growing farm in Quincy (just two miles from his birthplace) and lived there for twenty-five years until his death. His eight-room farm house, his simple tastes, and his dependence upon the farm for income belied his past fame. He rejoiced in the career of his brilliant son, carried on a large correspondence, and read as voraciously as he had from childhood. He outlived all the other early patriots, but rejoiced in the restored friendship, and in a frank and fascinating correspondence, with a younger Thomas Jefferson. In later years his interests actually broadened, his tolerance increased, and his natural optimism usually prevailed. He died with a fervent expectation of immortality and with chastened but still unbounded expectations for his country.

Adams was never as cosmopolitan, as versatile, or as clever as Franklin and Jefferson, but he was better informed, more critical and logical in his thinking, and more gifted in argument. A self-conscious son of old Massachusetts Bay, he treasured a certain provincial quality, although his pride in Massachusetts history and institutions hardly exceeded that of Jefferson for Virginia. Except for religious enthusiasms since "outgrown," Adams found no fault with the Puritan past, a historical equanimity bitterly reversed by some of his own descendants. Even in his one area of overwhelming interest—politics—he had no serious quarrel with his Calvinist predecessors. The Reformation seemed to him a great turning point in history, the dawning of an enlightened age. Even Calvin's Geneva seemed a light of liberty, despite a few mistakes. Calvin had been a man of genius, eloquence, erudition, and polished taste. The

French Huguenots were the most enlightened group in France (Adams relished their libertarian political theory). The Puritans, likewise, had been the best of Englishmen.

In Adams' view, the Puritans in Massachusetts established the ideal institutions for a good society, being grafted as they were onto the great legal tradition of England. Endlessly he heralded the town, congregation, schools, and citizen militia. If only the southern colonies could have instituted town meetings, congregational churches, public education, and training days, they would not have been so retarded and so riven by great economic and social differences. Only in New England was there the wide distribution of property, the high level of literacy, and the requisite political experience for such democratic institutions as annual elections.

As he grew to old age, Adams steadily increased the scope of his ideological tolerance. He wanted no governmental interference in private beliefs, although he always feared the moral effect of atheism and, with Jefferson, always deplored the superstition and authoritarianism he identified with Catholicism. If he had a permanent devil, it was the Jesuit Order. But tolerance of belief did not mean that government relinquished responsibility for the total welfare of its citizens. He believed that the state should foster both education and religious worship in order to produce responsible and moral citizens. As the early Puritan had argued, the magistrate had an obligation to promote the public welfare and the virtue and happiness (the two being inseparable) of its citizens. This obligation could not be separated from a rigorous concern with religion and public morals. Adams was so much a political theorist that he very often approached religion in terms of its varied political implications.

Adams supported the established church in Massachusetts. He thought it appropriate that the public be taxed for maintaining, not any set doctrine, but the paraphernalia of Protestant worship. This was only a part of a larger responsibility of government to support universities, the arts, and a free press. Laws should be framed to procure decency and dignity and good manners, to prevent folly, vice, intemperance, and even gross superstition. Even as a young lawyer he fought both for more aid to education and for a ban on most local taverns. Throughout his life he worked for more effective sumptuary legislation. Politics was the instrument of a purified community.

If possible, Adams hated theology even more than Jefferson and Franklin. But he loved the churches of his native New England. On what he always called the "Sabbath" he attended both morning and afternoon services, each of up to two hours' duration. On his trips into what is now Maine, or into western Massachusetts, in Philadelphia or even France, he went to church. His letters and diaries faithfully record the sermon topics and his critical evaluations of ministers. He was not discriminating about theological differences, but sought a bracing moral tonic. To him, as to so many New Englanders, the weekly sermon was an indispensable form of continued education, of intellectual challenge and moral scrutiny. Thus, he simply could not conceive of an enlightened society apart from free churches and learned ministers. His attitudes and his vivid reports on local churches throughout New England revealed how close, institutionally, the towns still were to their origins.

In personal habits Adams perfectly fit the Puritan stereotype. His life was full of demanding resolutions and elaborate attempts at self-improvement. A constant complaint was his wasting of precious time and his temptations to idleness. Every moment, he insisted, had to be spent at a profitable task. After college, he tried to rise before dawn and read profitably before beginning his daily teaching duties. After a prodigious amount of work always came the lament—not enough. As a young man he recorded a woeful discovery—not one new idea in a whole week. In old age, as if he had a working deadline or was on the verge of some great publication, he read endless, often ponderous multivolume books, launched endless inquiries into new subjects, and yearned for better libraries and learned companions, so that he could progress faster in his' never ceasing process of education. His intellectual wonder equaled that of Franklin. He wanted to master every subject, including mathematics and classical languages. If only he had the time, the precious time. Few men in America, and no other public figure, had ever read so much, absorbed so much knowledge, or displayed so much erudition.

Because of his seriousness, his unrivaled industry, and his moralism, Adams either openly or by clear implication placed a burden on everyone. He was a taskmaster if not a killjoy. He seemed endlessly to point out that everyone should be at the master's service. But much of the time people were not. As a youth he complained that no one could study in his town because everyone insisted on wasting precious time on that abominable social habit of card playing. The whole object of life being improvements in habits of piety and virtue, frivolity of any type, even harmless recreation, seemed sinful and degrading. In Baltimore, and elsewhere in the South, Adams found a terrible class system, for the gentlemen, instead of exhibiting decorum and virtue, showed a greed for money and land speculation, a frivolous love of cockfighting, horse racing, and card playing, but yet could not carry on an intelligent conversation. As a boyhood friend later so aptly remarked on Adams' limitations as a diplomat, he could not dance, drink, game, flatter, promise, dress, or swear with the gentlemen, or talk small talk and flirt with the ladies, all arts well developed by Franklin. Even when Adams tried to relax, to abate the struggle, he had qualms of conscience. When he traveled to some curative baths in 1771, in the midst of a generalized illness and fatigue, he felt guilty at all the loitering. Surely he could better employ his time for the benefit of his fellow men. But he did play. Every man has his games. Adams found a boyish delight in managing his farm, in planting trees, in redirecting streams, and developing a site of simple beauty and grace. In times of adversity, far away from Quincy, he turned in his imagination back to his estate and found needed consolation in dreams about future improvements.

Despite a well-entrenched reverse image, Adams was full of zest for life and never let his bad moods permanently suppress a healthy optimism. He could be brilliant in conversation and was a master of both wit and invective. He disliked long solitude and gregariously sought people for conversation and for the preening of his own ego. Temperamental to the point of explosiveness, he could nourish feelings of jealousy and resentment for years. His tremendous pride and his desire for recognition and distinction warred with his desire for intellectual clarity and his disciplined attempt at modesty and perfect honesty. He particularly resented the unfairness of a public that too easily acclaimed the superficial social graces of Franklin or the aristocratic front of Washington, but largely ignored the solid virtues of Adams. Save an eloquence in speech, Adams had none of the surface adornments of a successful politician. He was too clear-sighted, too honest, to play games with anyone. He could not be a hypocrite even when he badly needed to be one.

As so many New Englanders, Adams loved the out-of-doors. He walked miles each day as a means to good health, his wonder at nature's changing face never diminishing. His own religious emotion, variously either a sense of dependence or a sense of providential direction, most easily developed on these walks. Unlike Jonathan Edwards of a generation earlier, or Emerson two generations later, Adams missed the spiritual exaltation of an immanent deity, knowable in the very encounter with natural symbols. Instead, his God was the more prosaic, more distant designer and estate planner. He often used the now venerated watchmaker metaphor.

Although in love with his world, Adams was never as much a scientist as Franklin. He lacked Franklin's curiosity about hidden secrets and, as a Puritan, was much more willing to confess areas of mystery, of unanswerable questions: God knows; we cannot know. Man should seek useful knowledge, not answers to all the riddles. His concern was so political and moral, so much directed at the use of knowledge, that he never indulged his limited scientific interest. He even lectured Jefferson against spending undue time puzzling about Indian origins, for such knowledge had no bearing on the future happiness of mankind. Science, if directed too far from the practical concerns of men, could become as morally diverting as the abstractions of theologians and metaphysicians, or even the senseless card games of the idle. Yet, Adams read widely in scientific literature, asked sensible questions about balloons, air bubbles, and the weather, and as a youth composed a few short scientific essays. He had a great interest in new scientific discoveries, ventured into areas of mathematics and logic, and acclaimed Locke's psychology. He even offered a sophisticated conception of the scientific method. Scientific "axioms" are reasoned about deductively, and then supported by observation. Unlike the surety of internal reasoning, as in mathematics and morals, such scientific or external reasoning is never demonstrative and certain. But it is instrumental. By science, he argued in the best Puritan manner, man had acquired many curious devices to aid industry, to avert calamities, and to procure needed advantages.

Adams apologized for his lack of art. He felt that his own behavior was too blunt, too lacking in finesse and form. Perhaps this was so in part because of his determined effort to avoid the other extreme of form without substance. He eagerly condemned social graces, such as dancing ("no good men dance well, or gain anything from it"), fencing, and music. He permitted John Quincy to learn these graces, but always hoped that he would never become overly fond of any of them.

But Adams did enjoy beauty, both in nature and in human manners. He was a connoisseur of good craftsmanship, both in America and in Europe. He was less appreciative of some of the fine arts, believing that they were imitative and thus far inferior to reality. In Europe he lamented the low morals and the excess of wealth and luxury, but dutifully viewed old cathedrals and visited the museums, all the while pleading his considerable indifference and his greater love of action, passion, sentiment, and moral returns. He assiduously attended the theater in Paris and obviously enjoyed it, but always argued that he went only to better learn the language. He had no ear for music and saw an excessive interest in music as a diversion or escape from life. His own creative energies, when not directed to the supreme activity of building a just society, were directed at estate planning and farming. As a deliberate relief from a plethora of magnificent artifacts, he wrote a detailed appraisal of English manure piles and compost heaps. Here he was the better artist. Most of all, Adams loved the written word. He was one of those who began New England's long intoxication with literature. He was addicted to oratory, poetry, and even eloquent sermons. Completely consistent with his character, he found Milton to be the greatest luminary in letters, beyond comparison, and believed he had an absolute and unlimited power over the human mind. Emerson would later join him in this evaluation.

Although cognizant of his own faults, and slightly more aware of shortcomings in others, Adams was never a pessimist. As did all the great figures in the American Enlightenment, he rejected as blatant nonsense the doctrine of the perfectibility of man. There would always be obstacles, human weakness, and a need for struggle. But he hoped for progress, for limited but real improvements in all areas of society, and this without any miraculous transformation of the always selfish creature that was man. On the whole, it was a good world. He found more pleasure than pain, more comfort than distress. Despite his peevish moments, he had to admit that the good predominated. He never believed in human depravity or even in complete wickedness. He saw past progress in most areas and hoped for dramatic progress in government, and through this in moral and intellectual spheres. Not happy with the irrationality of American party politics, he died still secure in the belief that the American Revolution had launched a new era for mankind, and that, as a whole, the republican institutions which he had so laboriously defended were successful, and might become more so as education and science improved. But his optimism was more than an empirical weighing of accounts. It rested in an irrepressible belief in divine justice and human immortality. If not in life, then afterwards, virtue—indeed his virtue—would be rewarded. He died with no agony of sin but in full assurance that he had labored faithfully in the Master's vineyard.

Religion, or more specifically the authority of God, was the backbone not only of Adams' personal creed but of the whole American Enlightenment. Of this fact he was much more conscious than most of his contemporaries, and in his reiteration of it often seemed to be much more orthodox. He was not. His actual commitments were scarcely different, in any major detail, from those of Jefferson or even those of Franklin. Of the three men, Adams was by far the best informed on religious history, on varied doctrinal positions, and on non-Christian religions; Franklin was by far the least informed. On doctrinal issues, Adams was the most agnostical; on the seriousness and importance of religion, easily the most persuaded. More than either of his compatriots, Adams saw the necessity of a church, or of an institutionalized embodiment of religion. Like Jefferson, he wished to identify his religion as Christian and somehow purify the ancient faith of its dross rather than try to replace it by something new. He was afraid of popular Deism or anything that might lead toward infidelity, cynicism, and moral decadence.

By the very doctrinal labels he deplored, Adams grew up as a liberal Congregationalist, even early flirting with the three heresies of Arminianism, Arianism, and Universalism. His own church was one of the first to move toward the later Unitarian position. His early doctrinal confusion, his easy rejection of the older Calvinist themes, and his humanistic and moralistic interpretation of Christianity duplicated a path followed by many educated New England Congregationalists.

Adams knew the extreme of neither piety nor spirituality. Thus, the earlier Calvinism of Massachusetts, or the recent books of Jonathan Edwards, which he faithfully read, never made real sense except in an impossibly literal sense. So viewed, the Calvinist doctrines were obviously abominable and thus summarily rejected. And justifiably so, for when interpreted through the lens of an enlightened humanism they were so morally atrocious as to border on blasphemy. In fact, Adams could hardly reconcile his admiration of his orthodox parents or his reverence for the ministers of his childhood with the theological atrocities they seemed to believe. How could such wonderful people live with such terrible superstitions?

In the eighteenth century the earlier, Reformation-influenced sense of spiritual hunger, of alienation, of limitation, of incompleteness, and of nothingness became ever less pervasive. Fewer people were in the way of deep humility, and with it an overwhelming conviction of God's perfection and sufficiency. As man became the measure, God became the merciful parent or benevolent creator. Instead of God as the ground of being, with an attendant natural piety, He became only the creator or, at most, the repairman and regulator. God was loved, not for his non-human attributes, but for his human ones. Sin and depravity, which for a good Calvinist was a state of being, an ontological lack, became only a matter of errors and moral lapses. Redemption, which for a Calvinist was the gift of perfect love, or the attainment of God's Holy Spirit, and thus a unification with Him sufficient to share in His unutterable glory, became for men like Adams a matter of moral effort and a hope for immortality.

In Edwards, in the most perceptive Puritans, the Christian epic, including such themes as original sin, grace, redemption, as well as retribution and damnation, adequately symbolized experiential facts. The doctrines were more descriptive than hortatory. They were neither morally atrocious (being true) nor cruel. For they fit into an experiential religion that culminated in a rich, esthetic climax, in a desired spirituality that reconciled man to reality, itself irresistibly lovely and beautiful. Only as a counterpoint to this piety and spiritual vision could original sin and human depravity make sense. But unfortunately, by Adams' day, the self-acclaimed Calvinists—those who posed as orthodox and who defended their beliefs by dire warnings and by ever more elaborate confessions—lacked this spirituality. They too fell prey to a new world view and, in their incipient but repressed humanism, turned a father-like God into a revengeful and cruel dictator and original sin into an unrealistically harsh assessment of man. If seemingly innocent infants suffered damnation, they were, ipso facto, not innocent but full of concealed sins. The superficially orthodox saw heaven as a special reward for their own self-righteousness; they saw hell, not as a present reality

for the unredeemed, not as a natural end, but as a future mode of
retributive punishment for all the optimists who would not submit to
their pessimistic strictures.

Such degenerate orthodoxy, instead of reflecting Calvinism, really
vulgarized it, and in the process often lost the more distinctive political
and social commitments of earlier Puritanism. In most areas except
theology, it was the liberals, the Arminians and emerging Unitarians,
that carried on this Puritan tradition. They were the moralists, the political activists, the ardent educators, and even, in their intellectually
attenuated way, the ones closest to a vital religious experience. The
liberals had no theology of any sophistication, but if theology meant
what their opponents offered, so much the better. Even Edwards, whom
no one quite understood, had struggled so mightily against the loss of
piety, against the superficial religiosity of his day, that he had continued
the great social theme of the Puritans—a redeemed and new Israel—
only by implication. Here the liberals came to the rescue in a period
when political concerns were uppermost. Adams, in this situation, could
only choose the side of the liberals and sense that surely there were too
subtle secrets of existence hidden somewhere behind the old Puritan
creed, forever lost to modern and enlightened man.

Led by men like Adams, New England built at its political and social
Zion. It reformed its churches and its politics; it built its factories and
its colleges. But something seemed amiss. It was bountiful and enlightened, but it was ugly. Only Emerson finally had the sensitivity and the
spiritual potential to analyze the deficiency and, in the process, recapture the spiritual genius of an Edwards. He was a better Puritan than
Adams. But in the impoverished interlude between Edwards and Emerson, in the real nadir of New England philosophy, Adams was, even in
his limited and specialized concerns, the most perceptive product of New
England.

Adams left a meager repertoire of specific religious beliefs. He frequently gave simplistic summaries of his religion: a love of God and
neighbor, hope of pardon for offenses, need for contrition, a duty to
do good, the need to suffer patiently the pitfalls of life, and finally a hope
for immortality. Or, again, and much more succinctly, he said that the
Ten Commandments and the Sermon on the Mount contained all his
religion. He had no serious doubts of God's existence, a confidence
usually but not always defended by a vague design argument, and often,

even if implicitly, bolstered by an experiential sense of wonder and awe when in the midst of nature. The need for justice, and the unbearable cynicism of holding a tragic and futile view of existence, blocked any pathway toward ultimate doubt or resentful curses. He easily affirmed the goodness of the universe and thus instinctively loved its creator. Unlike both Priestley and Jefferson, who tried to defend the essential materiality of everything, God included, Adams remained a lifelong agnostic on the metaphysical mysteries of mind and matter. He endlessly rebuked reductionists on either side, believing it foolish to think that man had even begun to understand what is meant by either matter or spirit. He defended Oriental mysticism against Priestley and, when confronted with such belligerent materialism, must have had a slight feeling of forgiveness even for Plato's useless transcendental abstractions. He acknowledged a vague impression that God was a spirit, but quickly added that such a spiritual essence cannot be known. There is no point to metaphysical speculation about such ultimate questions. Whatever his essential nature, God is the author of all energy, power, activity, wisdom, and goodness. Enough said.

Adams' insistence upon his Christianity had little substance except loyalty to the past. In one revealing statement, so typical of the Enlightenment, he said all good men were Christians. Clearly, the term carried a moral rather than a doctrinal connotation. Adams accepted only two major doctrines of Christianity—a single creator-God and the promise of immortality. He ridiculed original sin; denied human depravity; saw no need of grace or special redemption; denied the divinity of Jesus; accepted the likelihood of some, but denied the religious significance of all, miracles; and hated the idea of eternal damnation for God's glory (although he accepted the idea of punishment for evil deeds). His horror at the idea of Jesus as God, at the Great Principle that produced Newton's universe coming down on this little ball to "be spit on by Jews," made him an early and emphatic Unitarian. He found very little to admire in the history of institutional Christianity. He joined Jefferson and Priestley in classifying all the cruelty and superstition, the mystification and intolerance, of both Catholicism and much of Protestantism. At times he even felt close to breaking completely with Christianity and begged Jefferson not to believe that all his complaints made him an atheist. He admired the Bible and respected the teachings of Jesus, yet saw the superficiality of such weak compromises as Jefferson's New

Bible (made up of Jesus' statements) or Priestley's uncontaminated Christianity.

All the qualifications and reservations should not minimize the indispensable role of God in Adams' life and thought. Few men ever placed greater intellectual reliance on God's existence. The concept of God, even though vaguely personal, stood testimony to a universe that had some fixed structure, some ascertainable order, some rationale. Thus, man could know things with assurance and look to the future with confidence. The order, to Adams, was not only physical but moral. Even though man had to rely on an imperfect moral faculty or on some imperfect internal form of reason (God's implant of logicality), he could be assured of a divine constitution, of eternal and immutable laws that should be obeyed (and had to be obeyed if man were to be happy). Eliminate God, the designer and lawmaker, and man would be reduced to a futile creature, possibly full of pretention, but with all assured knowledge only illusion and all precious laws only the instrument of human passion. Then, instead of Locke's moral vision of a just society, man could only hope for Thomas Hobbes's amoral vision of a peaceful one.

The French Revolution frightened Adams as no other event did, in large part because it was atheistic. The radicals in France denied God, denied an objective moral reference, and denied the infallibility of a natural order. In so doing, they opened the door to anarchic irrationalism. Willful men were about to play the role of God. Rightful authority and truth were to be trampled. Law, rooted in existence, in the way things are, was to be madly rejected. The morally inviolate freedoms of men were to be cavalierly abused. It would lead, he believed, to some capricious ideology, some fanatical and factional creed that would be even worse than Catholicism. Soon men would be as fireflies, fatherless, vulnerable, ready to become fodder for some man's fancy.

To Adams, atheism and mass democracy were equally immoral and impious, for each enthroned the only remaining authority—sheer numbers and sheer power. Surely, the moral order had to be investigated by laborious inquiry. Old superstitions should be abolished. But the path of responsible criticism was the path of humility, of a willingness to submit to the authority of fact. Adams feared a loss of respect for truth in America, and with it an exaggerated respect for personality. He cried out against all forms of superficial iconoclasm (he hated Thomas

Paine). But his last crusade, as revealed in some letters to Jefferson in 1825, was against the various blasphemy laws in America. Without hypocrisy, religion should be open to every conceivable type of critical examination. Even atheists had to be protected.

IN DEFENSE OF LIBERTY

In the scope of his contributions, in length of service and degree of personal sacrifice, and in the sophistication of his political advice, John Adams outranked all the other architects of American independence. The struggle against Britain occupied the prime years of his life (age thirty to fifty), usually kept him away from a beloved wife and children, as well as a farm and village, and never repaid him with half the public acclaim and veneration granted to Washington and Franklin. As a man of passion, incapable of Franklin's disinvolvement and detachment, Adams gave himself 100 per cent to the colonial cause. He harbored no doubts, saw no ambiguities, and wanted no compromises. But as a man of honesty and keen intelligence, he had to support his commitment by moral argument and a rational defense. His earliest intensive analysis of political theory led him to an eclectic, well-argued defense of resistance against tyranny and in behalf of God-ordained liberties. Later, when independence was won, he added his more formal and stilted defense of a republican form of government, which seemed alone fitted to preserve these liberties.

Adams opened his defense of the colonial cause in 1765. Even this early he embraced all the major principles that would later lead him to an open espousal of revolution. An expert polemicist and a clever lawyer, he was always quick to marshal historical and constitutional arguments. But from the beginning he saw the futility of such arguments unless they could be tied to the ultimate moral authority of God, the supreme sovereign. The device for this, as it had been for Locke and other supporters of the English revolutions, was the doctrine of natural rights.

In 1765 Adams wrote a "Dissertation on Canon and Feudal Law," indicting arbitrary, hierarchical obligations for church and state. For purposes of aggrandizement, priests and nobles had assumed illegal (i.e., immoral) and tyrannical power over the life and land of the common folk and had bolstered their power by superstitious doctrines and false religion. The long process of emancipation began with the growth of the English common law tradition and matured with the revolt of the Protestant reformers against the Catholic ecclesiastical system. The English revolution helped overthrow much of this confederation of tyranny and created the most enlightened government in Europe. The Puritan migrants to Massachusetts were a part of this English revolution and, in Adams' opinion, the best part. In spite of too much religious enthusiasm, the Puritans were men of science and learning who established churches and towns in direct opposition to feudal and canon law.

Here was Adams' historical perspective. Massachusetts originated in a revolution against vestiges of tyranny. The Puritans were loyal to their king and certainly respected their religious leaders. But they so formed their institutions that neither could usurp power or abuse responsibility. The congregational system forced the minister to live by talent, learning, and industry. The people appointed and removed. Yet, he was free from any civil control, free even to preach against his magistrate. At both the town and colony level, the Massachusetts form of government, with its town meetings and annual elections, eliminated feudal obligations, such as quitrents, and jealously guarded the rights of life, liberty, and property. The loyalty to the person of the king, a lingering and acceptable feudal habit, involved no secondary agents or controls. The self-governing and free citizens of Massachusetts were loyalists by consent and not by compulsion. In their towns they built their schools and created a literate, prosperous citizenry as an antidote to tyranny. Liberty, a moral right from God, had become a living possession in Massachusetts because of the wisdom and hard work of the earliest settlers.

Basic even to their continuing loyalty to the king was the principle of covenant or consent. The Puritans established their own institutions and elected their own officials, who were only trustees for the commonwealth. They demanded a responsible performance from magistrates, or else removed them in the next election. The right to revoke tyrannical authority was institutionalized not only in elections but in the right of impeachment and was maintained by public education and a free and responsible press. Indeed, the liberties of Massachusetts were often identical to those enjoyed in England under the British constitution. As a method of enlisting British sympathy, Adams often appealed to these traditional British rights. But even in 1765 he argued that, in America, these rights had been won by American efforts and expressed in such unique institutions as the town meeting. The rights had not originated in any grants of Parliament or by any gift of princes. They were the conditions of early contracts, the result of earnest covenanting. Ultimately, of course, they were inherent and essential, a part of the constitution of the intellectual and moral world.

In Adams' historical perspective, the writs of assistance, the Stamp Act, and all subsequent imposed and resented parliamentary measures represented the old feudal system in new form. An external agent, claiming power over the life and property of subjects, was, without their consent and without the legitimacy of contract or covenant, reversing a century and a half of colonial experience. Invoking the hallowed past, Adams asked the successors of the Puritans to rise up and resist the new threat of feudalism—illegitimate taxes and restrictions. By this perspective, Adams had no reason to argue the need or the merit of any English law. The method of imposition was all-important. In fact, no parliamentary law could apply to Massachusetts unless it met the approval of the people of Massachusetts and was thus legitimatized by their tacit consent. This was most true of tax laws, which deprived the people of such a basic right as property.

In constitutional terms, Adams denied the existence of a British Empire. Americans were not really colonists. Their allegiance to the king was voluntarily given to his natural person, not to his office or to him in a political capacity. Thus it never extended to Parliament as his agent. In 1768 Adams conceded as much as he ever did: that by sheer necessity, and this by a tacit and voluntary delegation of authority by colonial legislatures, Parliament had the power to legislate on questions relating to the whole kingdom or dominion. Later he compared this power, as exercised in various navigation acts, as similar to rights granted in treaties of commerce. The king was, as far as each American province was concerned, a limited monarch within a republican type of constitution. The early colonists, in a wilderness owned by savage Indians, temporarily reverted to a state of nature. No rightful sovereign existed save God and his laws in nature. By their own consent, the emigrants agreed to bind themselves to natural law, to its particularly cogent and familiar expression in English common law, and by written charter to the person of their king. The latter commitment entailed only one covenanted obligation—to make no laws repugnant to the British constitution. But the right to make all laws was clearly placed in the colonial legislatures. Affirming indivisible sovereignty, Adams located it in these separate legislatures and, behind them, in the consenting communities.

This argument, however clear or logical, was historically suspect. Certainly, Adams' ancestors had neither so conceived the founding of New England nor so viewed the relationship to king and Parliament. Adams was giving a new interpretation to events and turning the British Empire (who could deny its historical reality?) into the varied sovereign dominions of the British king. But Adams was not, at this point, overly concerned with what people had believed, or about what self-conscious considerations lay behind early colonial governments. He was instead interpreting past history in ways consistent with basic moral principles and asking Americans, possibly for the first time, to so conceive their own past. If all legitimate government is rightfully based on consent and instituted for the public good, then only such an understanding, or such a rationalization, allowed the imperative and extreme action necessary to overthrow tyranny. His argument was a work of interpretation, not the result of empirical research. It was an exercise in moral philosophy, not in history or political science. The revolution could not be justified by what had been, or even the promise of what could be, but only by what ought to be.

Eventually, and by practical necessity, the American case for independence came to rest on the doctrine of natural rights. But in 1765 Adams was almost alone in making this his principal justification. Even then he insisted that colonial rights, as well as British rights, were derivations of natural law. He preferred to turn to God's sovereignty rather than endlessly quibble about the provisions of early charters or the intent of past events.

The belief in natural rights was a somewhat disguised and modern shift of emphasis in the ancient concept of natural law. By 1776 the doctrine was so pervasive, so generally accepted, that its ablest defenders never felt burdened to explicate it in all its ramifications. Adams, perhaps better than any other American, knew the history of the doctrine and its earlier uses against real or imagined tyranny. Because of his voracious reading, he wrote and spoke within the somewhat stilted verbal context of two centuries of political theorizing. Easily, perhaps unconsciously, he fell into the language of Grotius, Hooker, Locke, Harrington, Pufendorf, and Sydney. Beyond that, he reflected not only

an intimate familiarity with classical history but also a surprisingly detailed knowledge of medieval and early modern history.

All the political arguments of Adams, like those of most of his
American and English contemporaries, were constructed as a special
emphasis in moral theory or moral philosophy. Adams wanted to make
clear the moral imperatives that *should* guide those who frame constitutions and govern states. But imperatives in terms of what? In a proximate sense, he meant that, if one wants a political system conducive to
the maximum, long-range welfare and happiness of all individuals, then
government must be based on consent, be subservient to covenanted or
contractual obligations, and never usurp the individual rights that are a
necessity for any happiness. In fact, the protection of these rights is the
prime moral justification of government. But this argument from utility
falls back on one from authority. Human welfare is achieved in an
objective and moral universe, and within the compass of God's designs.

Adams believed in the objectivity of moral law. His Puritan-like piety
still extended so far. He saw man as part of the whole order of creation,
or as part of the great design of God. Unconcerned with the intricacies
of free will, he simply accepted the unique human ability to make
choices and thus to govern events. But this ability was not an anarchic
license to direct the universe as one saw fit. It was the delightful and
hazardous ability to perceive God's order and the rationality in things,
and to adjust one's self to it and guide events in light of it. Man, in
effective choice, cooperates with the more extensive realm of nature that
surrounds him. Reasonable behavior is lawful behavior. Irrational and
capricious and unenlightened behavior is contrary to the structure in
things, and thus a matter of blindness or ignorance in conception, of
disobedience in the doing, and of ultimate misery in the result.

The Enlightenment in America never produced a sophisticated theory
of value. When Adams or Jefferson talked of happiness as the goal of
political economy, they rarely explored the experiential attributes of
such happiness or tangled with the problem of widely variant tastes and
attitudes. In other terms, they never developed an esthetic philosophy to
match their moral philosophy and perhaps ultimately even to contain it.
By implication, one can read into their vague terms many experiential
consequences, or see a veiled recognition of the intrinsic delight of
certain types of experience that they so obviously valued (such as agrar-
ian pursuits), but to extrapolate too far, to assume too much, is to make

them better philosophers than they ever were in fact. They left "happiness" and other related goals as vague symbols of what they, perhaps naïvely, believed everyone really wanted, or at least everyone would want if their basic rational and moral instincts had not been corrupted or atrophied. Thus, they could turn all too easily because all too quickly to the objective conditions for moral growth and for a more pervasive happiness in society. Despite all their reservations and qualifications, despite their realism, they still made both morality and politics seem a bit simpler than they are in fact.

Whether inherited from the fideism of the early Jews (what Jehovah commands), or from the less arbitrary natural-law tradition of the Greeks and of most Christian theory, the West always had paid lip service to the idea of God's sovereignty. The ultimate authority for man is God's revelation, either in Scripture or, much more important for the secular business of politics, in the laws of logic and of nature. In the tradition of Plato, Augustine, and Calvin, many Christians not only believed that secular government was instituted by God, that it should be obeyed, and that rulers should as a matter of Christian duty govern justly, but further insisted upon their obligation to do all possible to transform the secular world into a copy of the divine model. Medieval institutions, a respect for established authority, and a fear of revolution all helped neutralize this admittedly dangerous impulse. Even Calvin allowed only limited and constitutional action to stifle tyranny. But, stretching all the way back through the Middle Ages, the central axiom had been accepted—the state is ordained by God. It should govern in light of His will, which encompasses the welfare of those governed. If a ruler violates his calling, shirks his responsibility, he will face divine justice. The medieval church even tried to put some concrete teeth in this belief, but with ever increasing futility when its declining secular power left it only moral persuasion. Thus, in fact, a political theory involving the idea of a higher law, and commanding responsibility both to truth and to the welfare of the governed (the divinely ordained purpose of government), was part and parcel of Christian philosophy. But too often it remained only a moral stricture on rulers, not a weapon for revolution or a justification for either a degree of popular consent or for binding legal limitations. Only in England was the countervailing power of nobles and commoners able to institutionalize certain rights and privileges and set up enduring legal restraints against governmental power.

As a moral doctrine, the natural-law concept always encompassed the welfare of the governed and not any right of participation in government. It usually bolstered an organic conception of society and thus looked to the welfare of the total community and not to the special happiness of particular individuals. When the idea of a covenant, or of consent, and a heightened awareness of the importance of individual aspirations, was added to the idea of natural law, the doctrine was so changed in emphasis that it was now usually and correctly referred to as "natural rights." But it still retained all its moral flavor. It still climaxed in a higher constitution, in nature and in God, which could be understood by human reason and which, by all the suasion of logic and utility, fighting against the eternal lure of shortsighted selfishness and pride, inspired man to use it as the eternal and unimpeachable authority for his own institutions.

Paralleling and often influencing the development of natural rights, particularly among European Calvinists, were other theorists who turned from the problem of moral sanctions, from physically inoperative principles, to the practically difficult task of framing workable constitutions, to effective arts of governing (Machiavelli), and to an analysis of the realities of political power (Hobbes). Their work was not so much in conflict with natural rights as complementary to it, except that Hobbes perverted the moral sanction by making it a product of power. Admittedly, the divine constitution had never been strictly enforced, but a Western belief in divine justice, either in the afterlife or in the future unrolling of the consequences of present choice, still sustained the moral quest in politics. Thus, as Locke so well illustrated, the most thoughtful and influential theorists insisted upon a moral sanction. They placed what they believed to be God's truth above the temporal show of power. At least when circumstances were conducive, their principles seemed to determine events. They were confident that, sooner or later, power would have to bow before truth and right and that their idealism had cosmic status. This is a religious maxim. At least in America in the late eighteenth century, almost everyone believed it and used it to justify a war for independence.

In Adams the concern for individual happiness, so pervasive an aspect of his age and country, could not be easily reconciled with the demanding, self-glorifying God of his ancestors. Thus he rejected such a God. But neither could it be reconciled with the medieval use of natural law, with its sacrificial demands for individual suppression in behalf of a hierarchically ordered community. Hereditary classes, forbidden avenues of opportunity, rigidly enforced arbitrary class distinctions were foreign and distasteful to any son of Massachusetts Bay. For a farm boy who loved his landed property, who rejoiced in his opportunities for unlimited advancement, and who believed fervently in God's providence and ultimate justice, the doctrine of natural rights—the sacredness of life, the inviolability of certain liberties, and the security of hard-earned property—was a necessary corollary of everything he believed. These rights were the gift of his generous and benevolent God, even as they expressed the very thrust of his humane commitments. Only by adhering to such a demanding moralistic doctrine, but also such a promising one, could he view the science of government as a high calling and the work of a lawyer as comparable to that of a minister.

In the whole natural-rights tradition, no one ever gave a definitive definition of life, liberty, and property, the stereotyped liberties almost always tied to the doctrine. Actually, the impulse of natural rights was not toward detailed and very troublesome definitions, but toward a generalized moral atmosphere. The crucial commitment was a humanist one—to man and to his fulfillment. Government had to serve this end. It was a servant, a tool. In the political perspective, every person counted as one. The authoritarian stress—on God's will, on the lessons of logic, on the structures of nature, on the sacredness of personality—was intended to strengthen the commitment and thus place certain rights beyond political processes. The doctrine set a moral limit to any type of government, including the most democratic. Tyranny was the social counterpart of sin. No form of government was immune to usurpation, oppression, and the violation of reason and morality. Governments, like men and made up of men, had to be continuously scrutinized and checked; otherwise, they followed their natural tendency toward tyranny.

For Adams, the elementary right to life, although inseparable from property, implicated the vast procedural safeguards of English common law. By the operation of unambiguous and well-known laws, the insecurity and barbarism of personal revenge or vigilante justice had given way to civility and reason. An Englishman was alike safe from mobs and from arbitrary government agents. At times, Adams could scarcely restrain his lawyer's enthusiasm for those laws and customs that protected one's person. He first became a disciple of Otis because of his resistance to illegal search by writs of assistance. He wanted to preserve all the procedural restraints, all the safeguards against abuse of power, of Anglo-Saxon law, culminating in the right of a speedy trial by a jury of peers. He railed against admiralty courts with hireling judges and first suggested the impeachment of Massachusetts judges who accepted the bribery of royal salaries. Arbitrary criminal action or state impressment were major threats to one's person and to life itself. These could be protected only by procedures established by long usage and by careful safeguards founded in public acceptance and consent.

The right of liberty, or of varied avenues of self-expression, entailed freedom of religious conscience (not, to Adams, a complete separation of church and state), freedom of petition and assembly, freedom of self-defense, and, within certain protected limits, freedom of speech and press. The exact boundaries were not clear. As Adams grew older he saw the need for more restrictions in some areas (press) and allowed ever more leeway in others (religion). But whatever the exact context, these expressive rights were necessary to human dignity, even when their exercise presented some considerable threat to a majority, to privileged groups, or even to the whole community. In Adams, the older Puritan emphasis upon community welfare and unselfish service often warred with his enlightened concern for individual privacy and self-expression. More than Jefferson, he always honored the community. Thus, while granting hallowed rights, he still wanted a more active and far-reaching governance of human passions. At the very least, he had little tolerance for harmful expression or purely selfish private interests. Like Winthrop much earlier, he tried to distinguish liberty from license. He hated speculation, intemperance, and frivolity and saw regulation of such harmful forms of self-expression as the duty of an enlightened and somewhat paternal government.

But property was the key right. Upon it depended all prospects for human happiness. Without protected property rights, all other rights were empty abstractions. But, just as it was most vital, property was also most vulnerable. The American Revolution was fought primarily because England tried to take American property without consent and due process. Adams believed that governments existed, in large part, to protect the property of the weak against the exploitation of the strong, whether the weak be defenseless men of wealth in the face of an overpowering mob or, more often, defenseless poor men about to lose their meager property to privileged and greedy men of wealth. On the moral right of such protection, on the very sacredness of private property, Adams never deviated an inch, either to buy the favor of the rich or to win the plaudits of the poor. He never won the love of the dispossessed or the trust of the privileged.

In the tradition of Locke, Adams defined property so broadly as to encompass almost the whole scope of human aspiration. The right to property, as he conceived it, included the right of access to nature (opportunity), the right to lay a special, exclusive claim to that part of nature that one had developed or fairly acquired and now utilized for his purposes (means of production), the full right of managing such a part of nature (free enterprise), and finally the right to collect and enjoy all the products of his industry. Obviously, this is not a modern conception. Adams, almost as much as John Taylor, hated banking and finance. Paper money or bank credit was not real property, but in most cases an exploitative tax laid on property by speculators and corrupt politicians. Stocks and bonds rarely entailed managerial prerogatives and thus denied free enterprise. To him, a farm, a ship, or a shop were equally good examples of real property. Despite his love and preference for farm life, despite his capitulation to physiocratic economic theories, he never propounded a narrow agrarianism.

Adams and Jefferson believed, with Locke, in the moral benefits of property ownership and management, but they did not so carefully qualify the right of property. Locke, so close to a medieval setting, allowed exclusive claims to a part of nature not just when one mixed his labor with it and actually used it, but also only when other unused parts of nature, of *equal utility and value,* remained available to others. Adams could not accept such an unrealistic qualification. It almost necessitated socialism. He believed that there was no way of avoiding inequalities of either talent or accident. The first settlers in Massachusetts got the best land (land which required the least work to develop). Later arrivals had to take worse land, even though they often enjoyed greater social advantages. But the important thing is that they did have access to land, that nature was still open. There was as yet no exclusive monopoly, nor any complete denial of access. Each man had a real chance to work out his own destiny, to pursue his own happiness. With a vast wilderness, with a seemingly inexhaustible supply of undeveloped land, Adams and Jefferson never even insisted too much on use as a qualification of ownership, although Adams hated the use of property for purely speculative purposes and would have stopped it if possible. Speculative property was immoral property, an abuse of a privilege given by God.

Given access to nature (the minimal obligation of any society), the industrious development of land and tools and the responsible management of the means of production is the main test of a man's character and by far the most effective type of moral education. The state must keep open the opportunities, protect against arbitrary privilege, whether monopolistic or expropriative, and then let each person reap the rewards of his own initiative. In the Puritan tradition, Adams believed that man should be given both freedom and responsibility. There must be no paternal care and no unjust exploitation. Thus, human differences are respected. Some will fail and will suffer. Some will grow wealthy. Either a forced communism or a strict supervision of managerial decisions would lessen responsibility and deny freedom.

Such opportunity and freedom for the individual did not seem, to either Adams or most of his contemporaries, a threat to society. They refused to set up a false dichotomy between man and society. In fact, private property helped insure social welfare. Only propertied men, men with responsibility for managing means of production, were truly free men. Only they could be good citizens. Only they had an assured outlet for their talents. Only they could know the fulfillment of creative work. Unpropertied men were scarcely human. They usually became servants of others; they worked for others and depended upon others. As economic hirelings, they would surely become political hirelings. But men with property, or young men confidently working to get their property, had a real stake in society. They had a benefice to protect and defend. They alone would value freedom (they alone had it) and work to defend it.

Adams always desired a wide distribution of property. Massachusetts displayed such and thus easily attained stable governmental institutions of a most representative sort. Property ownership was even more important, politically, than formal education. But, in the absence of monopoly, Adams never saw the desirability of wide distribution as a justification for leveling policies in the state. Property is a protected right even if held in large quantities; otherwise it is not a secure right at all. It is, he insisted, as sacred as the "laws of God." If men like John Hancock were wealthy, yet responsibly used and managed their property, they were to be admired and emulated, not resented and taxed into penury. A tyrannical society precludes the real possibility of emulation; a just one values and uses such emulation. The unpropertied must not be excluded from nature, but must be encouraged to acquire property and assume mature responsibility. But even with the best opportunity, with inexpensive land and public education, some men will not work or will not save. They lack character. If they are numerous or have too much political power, they may violate property rights and, in effect, steal their way to greater luxuries.

Unlike some less realistic contemporaries, Adams foresaw a widening, not a lessening, of property differences in America. All European experience pointed in the direction of a propertied few and propertyless masses. Old and established societies not only accrued privileges of all sorts, but they magnified differences in talent. Like Jefferson, he most feared the effect of a proletariat. But as much as Jefferson he wanted to avoid the plutocracy that created it. He wanted to block the natural tendency toward greater privilege by men of wealth, but without destroying the just property, the superior talents, the leadership potential, the cultural contributions, of such men. His emphasis upon property as an essential right was an emphasis upon a situation that allowed an unlimited utilization of immensely varied talents, without setting arbitrary limits at the top or subsidizing irresponsibility at the bottom. His approach, more Christian than capitalist, rested on the old and increasingly remote Puritan dream of effective stewardship, of everyone using his talents freely, but in God's vineyard instead of for vulgar self-gratification or the moral travesty of mere accumulation. Like all Puritans, he wanted to socialize the function of property through a society that required personal responsibility, and not by any type of collective ownership or management.

John Adams was not just an early militant in the cause of American independence but a lifelong partisan of its goals. He wanted the colonists to rise up in defense of their freedom rather than to accept any sort of compromise. But his fervor and militancy, so typical of his personality, was not that of a social revolutionary. He wanted to preserve a way of life, not create a new one. The object of his effort was independence, not some new and more democratic and more dangerous social order. Massachusetts already had something close to an optimum set of governmental institutions, although institutions much too democratic for other colonies with less public education and less general property ownership. But the institutions of Massachusetts needed to be better understood. The informal relationships needed to be formalized and better protected by a written constitution. Through independence, and only through independence, could the great institutional labors of the puritan migrants be finally completed, and as pure a republic of virtue as possible to man be realized. Surely God willed this too.

THE REPUBLICAN IDEA

The doctrine of natural rights expressed the moral foundations of government and set the limits of governmental power. But John Adams knew that moral laws are not self-enforcing. Although sovereign, God does not rule as a dictator. He legislates in nature, in the eternal forms of logic, but gives man the challenging and awesome responsibility of reading it all aright, of establishing the best possible institutions. God provides an authoritative point of reference, but it is weak and selfish men who design governments. God's natural justice is reflected only in the ultimate verdict rendered—men suffer from their incompetence. Bills of rights, declarations of independence, constitutional restraints all quickly become inoperative moral strictures unless men really value freedom and unless they develop the institutions of government most likely to safeguard it. Even as Adams set out the justifications for a revolution, he began to formulate his theory of government. He then turned from moral philosophy to the science of government, from natural rights to the difficult task of framing constitutions.

The raw material of politics is people. Adams believed a government may often fall far short of a people's desires and expectations; it will never rise above them. Backward and crude people, even given the choice, may choose a very narrow and closed society, and thus preclude any large degree of liberty and social happiness. In their original compacting, in exercising their power to establish constitutions, the people act as gods. They do as they wish. Constitutions are human products. There is no divine inspiration, no revealed codes, no miraculous intervention. In a sense, men create what they deserve, but in their ignorance they rarely create the government they ought to have.

With the success of the War of Independence, thirteen sovereign states faced the awesome task of establishing new governments. The hazards matched the challenge. If ever men had a chance to apply the best political knowledge, it was now. Although the Lockean framework, the moral boundaries for government, seemed to be widely understood and accepted in America, almost no one seemed to know much about the science of government. Too many fell prey to the superficial axioms of Thomas Paine or to the later allures of a misunderstood French Revolution. America was blessed by its English heritage, by the continuing habits of the colonial period, but, as Adams saw it, by no developed rationale of even its most workable institutions. Without such a support of reason and theory, they might foolishly destroy the best that they had and cavort with some new and dangerous ideology. Not since the Greeks had there been any real development of the science of government (although there had been much improvement in practice of government). In America such a science was badly needed; Adams set out to supply it.

One central theme dominated all Adams' recommendations on government: a good government is a government of laws, not of men. A good republic is one so constituted as to "compel the formation, impartial execution, and faithful interpretation of good and equal laws, so that the citizen may constantly enjoy the benefit of them, and may be sure of their continuance." [*The Works of John Adams,* ed. by Charles Francis Adams (Boston, 1850–56), IV, 406.] Such a republic of law gives happiness to the greatest number and in the greatest degree. The ultimate in political virtue is the love for law, for an objective order instead of subjective whim. Adams saw various orders of law. The essential liberties are the most privileged; they are the most sacrosanct morally. Next are the terms of compact, rendered sacred by the sovereign action of a covenanted community. The compact provisions often, and rightly, rest in custom, in old and stable habits and expectations. Finally, and quite relative to the context of time and place, there are the statutes enacted by legislative authority. Only clear and enduring statutes, exempt from the selfish and arbitrary caprice of men, can make the continuing actions of a government a blessing instead of a curse, a means to greater freedom instead of a sure path to slavery.

There are few men so magnanimous as to surrender great power; few so self-effacing as to refuse it when proffered. There are few who can unendingly resist the temptation to take personal advantage of power.

They even do it without knowing it. Mankind will perish if it awaits philosopher-kings and heroes for its rulers. Those who frame constitutions are mad if they place undue reliance on the goodness or benevolence of any man, be it even a George Washington. Only law can be trusted with any unlimited confidence. Only law can secure equity among all. Magistrates are its ministers; judges its interpreters; and all men who want to be free its servants. Laws are right reason, "derived from the Divinity, commanding honesty, and forbidding inequity." They are "silent magistrates, where the magistrates are only speaking laws; which, as they are founded on eternal morals, are emanations of the Divine Mind." [*Works,* VI, 56.]

But wonderful though laws may be, they have to be enacted and enforced by imperfect men. Thus, Adams' fervent support of a balanced republican system had to begin and end with his conception of man. He wanted government to reflect the noblest principles and most generous affections of man and to so utilize as to redeem all that was irrational, greedy, and selfish. He knew that no man is totally generous or good. Enlightenment does not remove the need for law. But, to man's credit, no one is completely selfish. Therefore, the best form of government is the one that utilizes man's highest traits and screens away or effectively uses his bent for private power and gain. To determine this form requires a full understanding of human motivation.

Men are ceaselessly hungry and eternally vain. The appetite for food and sex (nature's mode of insuring self-preservation) is joined by a passion for distinction. The two impulses merge at many points. Distinction flows to those with a largess of food and mistresses. Beyond simple necessities, the desire for distinction is the main motivation for the acquisition of great wealth or even the marriage of beautiful women. Adams knew all about conspicuous consumption. The need for government arises from the necessity of protecting legitimate property, not only from hungry men but from powerful men seeking even more power and distinction. But the need parallels the solution. The very possibility of good government resides in man's vanity. Here is the source of all energy. If properly guided and checked, the craving for esteem can lead to benevolent service to society. Correct institutions can make the difference between the socially beneficent or socially harmful use of human energies. A society must reward able legislators and administrators with good pay and great respect, but at the same time check their passion for

ever greater power. Without rewards, without food and esteem, even the
most able and energetic men will renounce public service, and the more
unscrupulous will use it for graft.

Although quick to point to human failings, Adams never doubted that
men have the ability to reason, to draw correct inferences, to make
consistent their ideas, and even to make enlightened and virtuous choices.
But men never reason enough. They are pulled by blind passion or
pushed by narrow self-interest. There is no end of blindness and folly.
Everyone has a bit of the tyrant in him. Even though reason points to
the community of rights and to the irrationality of blind self-seeking, no
one always respects the rights of others. No one is fully trustworthy. All
are capable of cruelty, brutality, and injustice, either from ignorance,
laziness, or excessive passion. Thus, all are in need of external restraint.
Self-government is not adequate. Man must be governed. In moments of
rationality all confess the need. The need for government, thus anchored
in human nature, is quickly settled. The essential question remains:
What is the best form of government?

As a Puritan, Adams never desired a minimal government as a way
out of tyranny. In fact, he had no abstract fear of government. He never
wished to limit its functions arbitrarily, except for the boundaries set by
natural rights. Man needs to be fully governed, by internal restraint and
right reason if possible, by external restraint if necessary. Thus, he tried
to work out a system of balances and restraints without damaging or
seriously limiting the effectiveness and speed of governmental action.
For example, he always fought for a strong, unencumbered executive.
But such an executive, like the English king, had to obey the law or face
impeachment for serious breaches or sure electoral defeat for minor
ones. Also, he never wanted to block or stymie the legislative process.
He never saw a system of vetoes and checks as a means to block action,
but as a better technique for achieving a true consensus of interests and
for blocking the usurpation of power by tyrannical minorities or majorities. Unjust legislation was never easily remedied. People easily follow
demagogues into tyranny, but extricate themselves only with great effort.
The best medicine has to be preventive.

Adams offered his republican idea, or the idea of a balanced constitution, as the best institutional defense against tyranny. Not that he neglected other factors, such as education, traditional habits, and widespread ownership of property. But in the perspective of recent history,

he certainly seems to have given undue attention to the form. As he read political theory, as he elaborately traced the history of almost every avowed republic of the past, he always found the clue to ultimate collapse in some clear deviation from his ideal form. Too often, he came close to offering a magical panacea, a merely formal solution to the political ills of mankind. He was at his best when he dealt with practical political problems, and he was at his worst when he strayed into the formal abstractions of theory.

In his most soaring defense of republicanism, Adams alleged that even virtue was more an effect than a cause of a good constitution and that even a group of highwaymen, under a republican system of self-government, might in time become good and honest men because one rogue would be set against another. Only correct institutions can remedy the defects of our nature. There are no virtuous men to rescue us, no political saviors in prospect. He would not concede any long-term alternatives to his system. Within the republican form, the many varieties of circumstance, geography, and population could be expressed in varying laws. Outside the republican context, tyranny was inevitable.

In asking for a balanced constitution, Adams combined two types of balance through separation. First, he wanted to separate functions, providing for clearly discriminated legislative, executive, and judicial spheres. Here he followed the English model and established colonial practice. He desired a separate, appointed, life-tenured, well-paid judiciary. Although he wanted a major legislative role for the chief magistrate, he still wanted a clear distinction between his executive and legislative functions. On the other hand, he wished to deny any executive power to the legislative assemblies. The executive, as the standing power of a nation, had to be free and independent. Second, Adams wanted a balancing of interests or classes in the legislative process. Since he equated wealth and political power, and in the absence of an American hereditary nobility based on family name and on cultural and educational preeminence, his class system—his eternal gentlemen and simplemen—really amounted to little more than the endless disparity between the rich and poor. By trying to separate the two classes into two quite distinct legislative bodies, and by giving each the power to block any legislation, he hoped to avert open class conflict and either oligarchical exploitation or some type of proletarian anarchy. Both classes could concur in laws which protected the property and status of each class. But to function properly, these two assemblies, representing the many and the few, or democracy and aristocracy, had to be balanced by a strong chief magistrate representing the interest of the whole nation.

To defend this balanced constitution, Adams felt compelled to analyze the weaknesses of all simple forms of government. He argued for a European audience and for political theorists familiar with the conventional, Aristotelian classifications. Less sophisticated Americans, misled by his language, generally insisted upon misunderstanding his intentions. His stated goal in the *Defense,* for example, was a conclusive attack on simple, one-assembly democracies. Given the propensity of man for self-aggrandizement, he easily showed the tendency of each simple form—monarchy, aristocracy, democracy—to degenerate into its tyrannical extreme. But, true to Aristotle and most subsequent theorists, he saw the greatest possibilities of at least sporadic good government in an absolute monarchy, and some briefer possibilities in simple aristocracies. With only one democratic assembly, he saw none at all. If all power is given to the mass of people, then crude majorities will dispense with law and exploit minorities. The inevitable jealousy and factionalism will, as in the French Revolution, terminate in some popular dictatorship.

Adams defended his balanced form of government—a mixture of monarchy, aristocracy, and democracy—as being the only one consistent with human differences, with the inevitability of some form of nobility, and with the ever-present passion for rank and status. Any government which refuses to recognize the inequalities of talent, if not of birth, or even more any which tries to abolish such inequalities, runs against the very grain of human nature and impiously tries to redo what God has wrought. The very power behind human progress, behind heroism and statesmanship as well as chicanery and exploitation, is the desire for power. Any society will have ranks and orders, some based on natural differences (talents, virtue, beauty) and some on artificial ones (birth, wealth). Since this is a fact, the problem of good government is not how to abolish ranks, but how to control and use them for the public good. A just and fair government must protect the prerogatives of nobility, beginning with large property. It must force a degree of decorum, discipline, and even subordination among the masses. Men must know their places at any one moment. Yet, they must have a chance to change places. The desire to emulate, to rise in the social hierarchy, is a source of political energy and a possible basis for progress. But there has to be real opportunity, just as there have to be laws to prevent a senseless and anarchic attempt to take property by force or trickery.

Adams at least speculated about an ideal aristocracy, based on superior talent and virtue. But unlike Franklin, or a hopeful Jefferson, he believed such an ideal had little to do with reality. The actual gentlemen of the world, whatever their relative superiority in talent, in education, and even in virtue, are aristocrats because of more mundane, even vulgar, reasons. In his most hardheaded stance, Adams defined gentlemen as those who had power, or those who could control other men. They are respected (not necessarily loved), obeyed, imitated, and deferred to. In America, this power was based almost entirely on wealth, although bolstered by beauty or charisma and by family reputation. Adams acclaimed James Harrington's discovery that empire followed property as ranking in importance beside William Harvey's discovery of the circulation of the blood. Adams did not believe that an aristocracy based on property was necessarily wrong, particularly when property meant character-producing land rather than exploitative paper, and when extreme luxury was restrained by law and morality. But the wealthy usually reflect the general level of manners, and no better. Austere peasants mean austere lords. Puritan Massachusetts produced men of wealth who carefully disciplined their private selfishness and contributed well to public causes.

Any government that protects property rights in effect recognizes and protects orders and distinctions, just as much as one which grants titles of nobility. This was a crucial insight by Adams, and one whose full implications he recognized and accepted. An environment of freedom precludes any equality of condition. It invites industry and achievement. But unless carefully controlled by powerful moral sanctions, or politically checked through a balanced constitution, an aristocracy of wealth easily leads to a tyranny over the masses, and a very crude and vulgar tyranny. Thus, the very freedom that permits achievement stands in peril by its own success. Americans were enlightened and reasonable in abolishing such irrational props of privilege as feudal conventions, titles, pageantry, and ceremonies. They had been abused. Now the popular urge was turned toward riches, beauty, and occasionally even learning and honor. Was there a great improvement? Adams had profound doubts. Despite the arbitrary and irrational motives for giving preference to family names, this might lead to less tyranny than giving all honor to mere accumulation of wealth, particularly to wealth gained by speculation or chicanery. In any case, the changes in the symbols of aristocracy did not change man. The social distinctions remained, and would remain. The rich and learned (if necessary the rich would hire the learned) would continue to exploit the poor and ignorant. The poor and ignorant would most likely fall into a slavish attempt at emulation, or else eventually gather enough resentment to wait to rob the rich and usurp their position. Either way, a society without balanced controls to check each group still faced certain despotism.

Adams knew that class status does not change the equation of passion and reason. The rich man is both as selfish and as reasonable as the poor, although he may express his selfishness and his enlightenment in a more refined way. Gentlemen are always few in number, but they have at least an equality of power. They must not get more. The same is true for the simplemen, for the small farmers and shopkeepers. Clearly, America was a rich land. Luxuries would multiply, not decline. Liberties, if preserved at all, would have to be preserved amid luxury and great wealth, with wealth unfortunately ever tending toward greater concentration. The great and growing property of the rich, possibly ever more resented by the poor, would have to be protected. Even more difficult, everyone else would have to be protected against the ever more powerful rich. The few men of great power would try to abuse their power and thus attain exorbitant riches in the midst of a restored peasantry (or proletariat) of slavish, unpropertied common people. But, after a time, the suppressed masses would rise and destroy the rich men and, with them, legitimate property and most decorum and civility and liberty.

Clearly to Adams the most difficult task of government was maintaining a fair stance toward property. As Adams foresaw, a moral vineyard, cultivated by men of different talents, too easily degenerated into a capitalist grab bag. The easy but wrong response to the problem was to use government to attempt the impossible—to eradicate differences in talent and differences in property. To level society was to destroy freedom and thus defeat the whole strategy. A free government has to deal directly with those differences and mediate the inevitable rivalries. It must prevent exploitation by the few or appropriation by the many. The abusive possibilities of power based on wealth and of power based on number must be checked. The rich must be afforded liberty, yet denied the monopoly of effective power that might normally accrue to their wealth. The poor must be protected in their small and vulnerable property (Adams' analysis does not encompass a large class of non-propertied people) and in their opportunity for advancement, yet denied the full control of society that seems, on superficial analysis, to be their due as a numerical majority. Thus, a good government equally protects both men and property, both rational and accidental ranks and distinctions.

Although an enemy of simple democracy, Adams joined most Americans in his concern for one democratic assembly. In fact, he wanted a more directly responsive lower house than did most Americans. Much more than Jefferson, he insisted that the lower assembly be free of powerful leaders, of aristocrats of any sort, and thus be able to express the real sense of the common people. For the popular assembly, he pleaded for short terms, fair elections, broad popular participation, and small legislative districts. Without such a democratic branch no government could protect liberty. Conditioned by traditional political theory, writing for a European audience, Adams believed himself most unique in favoring such a strong, essential democratic element in government. Here was the new innovation of America: no longer would the people give only a tacit consent to a form of government; they would continuously exercise a direct voice in their legislature and maintain an absolute control over all laws and all grants of money.

But this popular control becomes a delusion unless the aristocrats are represented in a separate body, where they may intrigue among themselves and hopefully fulfill their prime function of protecting major property rights. Also, a good upper assembly provides a check on an impulsive popular body, and should represent not only property, but education, experience, and honorable family traditions. Senators could then provide a tempering force rather than an exploitative one. If appointed by the executive, or indirectly elected, they might be the most responsible, the most talented, of men. But their abilities, even their virtues, could not eliminate their ego, their vanity, and their danger to liberty.

Even if the two classes are successfully separated into two assemblies, there is still a need both for a moderating power and for further checks on the aristocrats. Thus, Adams stressed the vital importance of a strong magistrate with one-third of the legislative power. In all history the nobility had most feared monarchic power, not democratic power. Aristocrats may devise ways of winning popular support, but they will usually find an effective enemy in a strong monarch (himself a gentleman). The problem is getting such an able and strong magistrate. He represents all the people and draws his power from all groups. He often functions in a popular, democratic context, as do beloved monarchs. But this does not mean he should be chosen by popular vote. Again, Adams leaned toward indirect election or, in extreme cases, toward heredity. Even the accident of hereditary incapacity seemed less dangerous than the temptations of corrupt elections.

Adams deplored any executive role for legislators. He believed the gravest weakness of the federal constitution was the executive functions of the Senate (or even the House in declaring war). Senate involvement in treaties and appointments compromised the President's independence. Even more, the provision for overriding the presidential veto effectively destroyed the President's equality in the legislative process. He successfully fought an early battle for full rights of presidential dismissal and always urged long presidential terms.

Adams' beloved republican system, although roughly based on American constitutional experience before and after the Revolution, was all too simple. It could never work as he intended it. His two-class analysis only approximately fit the American reality. He lapsed all too easily into complete polarities (the Puritan elect and nonelect still hovered in the background). Both the social and economic gradations in America were too complex for a simple division of aristocrats and simplemen. Yet, to work as intended, his system required the isolation of all aristocratic power in the Senate. But how could men of power be exiled into an American version of the House of Lords? Short of titles and feudal privileges, would they not seek control in both branches of government? If they bought talent and controlled the intellectuals, as Adams himself suggested, would they not also buy political support among the common folk? Too disillusioned to seek benevolence or superior wisdom among men of power, Adams could only hope that a desire for eminence and prestige would cause the rich dutifully to take their place in the Senate. Thus, republican liberty seemed finally to depend upon a successful appeal to the vanity of the few. As vice-president, Adams gained only ridicule by trying to dignify senatorial office by fitting titles of address. He knew what he was about. Unless an American aristocracy of wealth could be bribed into accepting a limited political role, sufficient to protect what they had but impotent to aggrandize it, they would abuse power, accumulate more and more property, and soon destroy most opportunity and most effective freedom.

Adams could find no alternatives to his republic. If rich and poor, talented and untalented, and beautiful and plain cannot join in a balanced legislative system that insures compromise or in a broad consensus protective of all interests, then liberty in the fullest sense is impossible and government fails to secure its moral purpose. The alternative prospects are equally dismal—a narrow plutocracy or a vulgar, short-lived democracy. Both end in tyranny.

Unlike many Americans, Adams placed no great hopes in elections. He had many fears. In Massachusetts annual elections had indeed broadened and preserved freedom. But without the wide and relatively equal distribution of property, the effective schools, and the moral suasion of the churches, this would not have occurred. After 1780, he saw clear evidence that the election process was breaking down and becoming subject to all types of abuse. Thus, elections had not insured liberty in Massachusetts, but rather had reflected exceptional circumstances and a large degree of liberty.

Adams agreed with Jefferson that the mass of men would elect natural aristocrats. But to him it was obvious that the natural aristocrat was simply the person who could command other men and win their support. All too rarely, he believed, would even a literate citizenry choose legislators or governors on the basis of talent and virtue. Election more often depended on beauty, wealth, and family. Too few people use reason in their political behavior. They are drawn to charisma, to display, to pageantry. Politics becomes a circus. At worst, the masses are subject to fraud and violence.

Despite all his concern for moral philosophy and the science of government, Adams never mastered the art of politics. He hated the art too much to use it effectively. He saw that a political candidate must manipulate people, sway them by emotion, and even trick them while seeming to delight them. Adams was too honest, too open, for effective politicking. He knew that tyrants persuade and bribe their way to power, that too few people have the political maturity to resist power grabs by their betters. George Washington, had he been so minded, could have abused his position and destroyed republican safeguards even as he gleaned the plaudits of Americans. Thus, Adams wanted to frame a system of government that would bypass partisan national politics.

Fearful of the weakness and gullibility of voters, Adams wanted to limit direct election to a local geographical area and to the members of the lower assembly. In a province or town, with the aristocrats removed to their Senate, he believed that local interests could determine political choice. The people of a congressional district would elect their own kind. This was the way it had worked in Massachusetts. He did not expect talented representatives. But he did expect average men who would truly reflect the desires of the local people. They were preferable to able men who might try to manipulate and lead the local voters. But this context was threatened by large, national parties. Such parties would promote either ideologies or national policies. Soon even local elections would be structured around such national issues or, even worse, around the personality of such popular national candidates as a Jefferson or a Jackson. By this tactic, men of power would invade local politics and transform local democracy into a tool of their own careers and their own schemes for aggrandizement and even exploitation.

In his long retirement from politics, Adams watched the development of the first national parties, first with Jefferson and then with Jackson. He also watched the slow extension of the franchise. He deplored both trends. Even in Massachusetts he had always desired a minimal property qualification for voting. He could not conceive a citizenry without some stake in society being responsible. Servile men without property would be willing accomplices of demagogues. The national political parties further extended the franchise, for they soon turned the indirect election of senators and the President into popular contests. Party identification predetermined the votes in the electoral college and in state assemblies. In light of these developments, and in the wake of the French Revolution, Adams dared suggest the advantages of presidentially appointed, life-tenured senators, and even of a hereditary presidency. As his violent critics never recognized, he suggested these extreme measures in order to protect simplemen against powerful party leaders surreptitiously representing wealth and privilege.

Despite the dangers of national party politics, Adams never lost hope for his republic. He only warned of the storms ahead. Property, which makes men less vulnerable to demagoguery and bribery, would not be a permanent protection for America. In the future more and more men would not possess property. With John Taylor he lamented the early shift away from real property, from means of production, to bank notes and corporate securities. Even farmers faced a loss of power, for land could easily become captive to the power of paper, to the speculative financiers, supported as they would be by all types of political chicanery. The old devil Alexander Hamilton might finally have his way, and nothing would be so conducive to it as the irresponsible demagoguery of men like Jackson.

Adams knew as well as any American the limits of human aspiration. His republic, even as ideally conceived, was never to be a New Jerusalem. At best, it could only be a tarnished Zion on a low hill. But it was the best ideal of government that mankind had achieved, even as the American Republic was the best government mankind had achieved. As he approached the incredible day of death (both Adams and Jefferson died on July 4, 1826), old John Adams looked back fifty years and tried to recapture for young correspondents and would-be historians the exact feelings and dreams, the fears and hopes, of those who chose revolution and independence. Clearly, this had been the climax of his life. Even the presidency was anticlimactic. In old age he refought the battles with Hutchinson, reindicted the Tories and the wavering patriots, and tried to re-evaluate his own decisions. He could find no major errors. But, somewhat bitterly, he noted that it was long since settled that John Adams was a weak and vain man. He agreed. But in so doing he revealed not self-pity, but only ironically re-emphasized a long-defended truism about mankind as a whole.

In 1826 the old Puritan dream of a moralized society seemed less realistic than ever before. Like his forefathers, Adams had tried to build a republic with maximum opportunity for individual industry and creativity, yet with effective safeguards against the irresponsible abuse of power. This meant a republic of virtue. Wealth, the rightful goal and reward of successful effort, had to be dedicated to moral ends. Recognizing the temptations to excess, even the extreme moral perversion of purely acquisitive goals, Adams tried to fortify personal virtue not only by inner strength of character but by less precarious institutional props. He wanted a structure of law, of objective principle, to limit the perverse inclinations of men.

But neither the suasion of sermons nor the restraints of law seemed sufficient. As Adams never quite grasped, the maladies of man and of society, of great wealth and great ugliness, of a total moral perversion, lay deeper than institutions. As Jonathan Edwards had vainly insisted, it involved an alienation of man from nature and from reality, and with this the erection of false idols and the veneration of false gods. Such a malady required a more radical cure than republican virtue or republican institutions. The cure had to be as much philosophical as institutional, as much religious and experiential as rational. Emerson, a poet and priest, would attempt this cure.

PART
TWO
�֎

IN TRANSITION

V
RALPH WALDO
EMERSON:
POET-PRIEST

THE EARLY PILGRIMAGE

Emerson has been a great ambiguity in American history. Religious prophet, philosophic idealist, prescient pragmatist, latter-day Puritan, mystic, skeptic, evolutionist, optimist, radical, conservative, pessimist— all labels seem to have fit him in one or another of his alternating moods and stances, each authentic yet tentatively, thoughtfully, even tantalizingly advanced as if Emerson himself could neither find nor successfully communicate his correct identity. He was open to widely varied influences and was at moments so overly susceptible to even esoteric nineteenth-century ideologies as to be gullible. But then, always, came the thoughtful consideration, the last-minute "but," and the retracting, qualifying, and reversing, without a final, complete commitment. As he often suggested, and surely sometimes deeply felt, he was a refracting medium for too many currents of Western thought, too many conflicting tendencies in American life, for any complete reconciliation. In defense, he repudiated any clarifying and limiting definitions, or at times even consistency. Possibly posterity should take his own reluctance to heart and present his thought rather than summarize it. Emerson, more than any other American intellectual, begs first-hand acquaintance. Completely metaphorical, he is our most quotable writer, and suffers most when paraphrased or abbreviated in any way.

Yet, no one who would understand American thought can ignore Emerson. He stood squarely at the center of its main development, equally reflecting his own Puritan past and revealing a subsequent pragmatic development. These continuities in Emerson were only a part—though a major part—of his thought. He also reflected other, less common intellectual elements, such as Swedenborgianism, an always somewhat vague Oriental emphasis, an unusual tendency toward meditation and pure contemplation at the expense of active involvement, and an inordinate fascination with poetry that pushed him toward (but never to) a type of artistic dilettantism. He wanted to speak to America with the conviction of a priest and the eloquence and insight of the poet. To do this he gave up, first, a prosaic career in teaching and, second, a prosaic career in preaching, only to spend a poetic lifetime doing both.

Emerson was born with a considerable and quite conscious heritage. Because of the death of his father (a charming, polished, highly literate but rather innocuous Congregational minister), Emerson and his four brothers (one mentally retarded) grew up in a type of genteel poverty. The mother took boarders; the sons' education was financed by charity. Yet, the Emersons were aristocrats of a type. They were of the best families, of a limited, narrow, but quite sophisticated New England aristocracy. They knew the right people (liberal Congregationalists or new Unitarians, merchants, entrepreneurs, established farmers, ministers and professionals, Harvard graduates), had the right hopes, and shared an emerging intellectual revival, a spreading curiosity that seemed to invigorate the young men of New England. In the background, and consciously so, were two centuries of Massachusetts history, with its legacy of Calvinist thought (still orthodox in rural areas), of stress on education and, lately, on literary expression, of emphasis on a righteous society and on unremitting efforts at social reform, of cultivated manners and gentility, and of a successful industry that made a degree of affluence and of leisure a normal expectation. Poor in income, Emerson was upper class in birth, breeding, manners, expectations, education, and cultural advantages. Scarcely part of his awareness were the new families of New England (names uncommon), who were uneducated, often non-Protestant, but flocking from farm and from Europe to become workers in the growing factories or to become servants in the better homes.

As a result of his family, Emerson had access to the best education

(Harvard, of course), to broad career opportunities, to marriage into any family, to well-placed friends at every level of society, and to exceptional economic opportunities. But he also inherited expectations. Conscious of his status, he hoped to justify it. One key to Emerson was his unrelenting ambition, his desire for distinction and recognition. His youth was not happy; he suffered from feelings of inferiority in contrast to his seemingly more brilliant brothers and was continually (good Puritan) dissatisfied with his achievement. His ambition usually took a literary form, for he early recognized his limitations in scholarship, logic, or any methodical enterprise. His letters to his Aunt Mary Emerson abounded with hopes of being a poet and were often written in verse. Coupled with this, and generally a part of the intellectual atmosphere, was a running commentary on literature. The world of letters was nowhere more assiduously cultivated than in Emerson's boyhood New England. Next to the dramatic natural scenery, books were the most conspicuous part of his environment—to be read, discussed, criticized. To a young, essentially serious, often romantic, not noticeably religious Emerson, literature was pursued for self-improvement, for ideas or techniques, and not for *fun*. Not yet could a son of New England indulge himself. Yet, in letters to Aunt Mary, or even more to his most beloved brother, Charles, he strove for literary effect, and even succumbed to the intoxication of words. Serious, ambitious, eloquent in verse and letter, Emerson seemed unclear about life's goals and possibly a bit frivolous; certainly he was not pious enough for Aunt Mary.

Out of the Boston Latin School, and settled at Concord, the new family residence, Emerson was able to enter Harvard at fourteen, a bit young even in 1817. Serious, somewhat aloof, he helped finance his Freshman year by acting as the president's orderly. During vacations, he taught elementary classes, and developed an intense dislike for the teaching profession. His record at Harvard was undistinguished and even poor in some subjects. To his own deep hurt and later regret, he graduated only thirtieth in a class of 59, but was selected as class poet and received one essay prize. A bit of eloquence in expression seemed his only visible forte.

After Harvard, Emerson, out of family economic necessity, became a teacher, assisting in his brother's girls' school. To him, it was a hopeless, miserable profession. For consolation, he read history and theology and hoped soon to be able, financially, to re-enter Harvard and prepare for the ministry. Since he was on the liberal side of Congregationalism, this meant the Unitarian ministry, although the final break did not come until 1825, the year he finally entered the theological school. Meanwhile, disliking his teaching, disappointed in his achievements, he debated theology with Aunt Mary, avidly read letters from brother William, who was drinking in the new higher criticism at Göttingen, and, like many other young men, became a disciple of William Ellery Channing. The seeds of religious radicalism were planted in these years, but flowered only slowly. With family fortunes in order, he entered Harvard again in February 1825. Here he almost lost his eyesight, suffered from a sore hip and, as a student who could hardly read or write, was forced temporarily to resume teaching. Without further theological training, and already unorthodox, he was nonetheless licensed to preach in 1826 after presenting his first sermon.

Plagued by illness (possibly psychosomatic), Emerson traveled to Florida in the winter of 1826–27. Intellectually, much was in confusion. The ideas of Swedenborg, absorbed from an American disciple, seemed almost irresistible. In Florida he met a nephew of Napoleon, Achille Murat, a gentleman, and, to Emerson's surprise, a complete atheist, yet a man of nobility and virtue. His labored letters revealed in embryo such themes as compensation and self-reliance, but only as points of reference in a growing confusion. His return to Massachusetts in the summer of 1827 led to a temporary preaching job at the First Church in Boston and to the first obligation to prepare new sermons (he had been using old ones over and over at different places). In Boston he halfheartedly renewed his work at the theological school and received the M.A. degree (more an empty honor than anything else). Then, in the winter of 1827–28, as a fill-in minister at Concord, New Hampshire, he met Ellen Tucker, who was later to become his bride. Through the next year he dallied at theological subjects at Cambridge, seemed somewhat lost and lonely, continued to preach charming but noncontroversial sermons in various pulpits, and seemed likely, by the end of 1828, to secure a permanent pulpit at the Second Church in Boston. The call came eventually, with ordination in March 1829. It was a good position and well-paying, reflecting possibly as much on his family standing and his successful preaching as on any other obvious talents for either theology or the practical ministry. Yet, the more laborious tasks, not the least being a weekly sermon, were subordinated to his personal concern for

Ellen. The Second Church and Ellen were, unknown to him, to be only brief and poignant episodes in his life, leading to an almost unbearable personal crisis, but also to personal victory and to the strength and greatness of his later life.

Ellen Tucker was a girl of seventeen except to Emerson; to him she was an ideal. As such, her tuberculosis (hemorrhaging before the marriage), her fragility, her wraithlike beauty, her early and beautiful death, were all necessary but almost unbelievable parts of Emerson's one great passion. He had always yearned for an intimate friend, an ideal intellectual companion. His brother Charles came closest to being this, but no one had completely qualified. Ellen, precocious, sensitive, poetic, intelligent, independent beyond her years, with the preternatural wisdom often provoked by deadly illness, seemed to fulfill this need. Not that the relationship—so fragile, so ethereal, so circumscribed by the genteel demeanor of a twenty-five-year-old minister—was platonic or without passion. But it was soon veiled in sentiment, in romantic, often poetic exchanges. The romance, was also doomed; even Emerson must have known that Ellen could not live. They married in September 1829, after a desperate summer's journey in search of better health. Ellen touched Emerson so closely and her death left him so desolate that the subject can scarcely be treated in all its dimensions. Yet, Emerson had always a quality of detachment, of aloofness, even of calculation, which provided some strength for the ordeal. Much before the marriage, he undoubtedly (and even suggested as much) carefully considered other factors than Ellen's character or beauty. Ellen was heir to a rather large estate and brought Emerson the prospect of financial independence.

Ellen's death in 1831, after months of suffering, tended to deepen Emerson's religious sentiments, his feelings of relatedness with a transcendent first cause, and his hope of immortality. However, it did not strengthen his orthodoxy and left him increasingly lonely and dissatisfied with his ministry at the Second Church. Unhappy, trapped, still confused about himself and his own beliefs, Emerson was ambivalent, but certainly at times badly wanted to resign his pulpit. Also, he chaffed at the confinement and the formalism of even Unitarian doctrine. He already was a loner, against confining associations and organizations. His escape (perhaps more accurate than dismissal) from the Second Church came through a low-keyed, unembittered controversy over the Lord's Supper. Half defending a principle, half seeking a way out of a

church that admired him and whose membership he loved but whose
salary and living was no longer very important without Ellen, Emerson
first asked the church to discontinue the sacrament and met a firm
refusal. He then personally refused to administer it and briefly arranged
for a substitute minister on communion Sundays. To a horror-stricken
Aunt Mary, and then to his congregation, he insisted on following his
own truth and asked to be dismissed (really he resigned) from his
pastoral charge, with only friendship and concern for the congregation
and continued devotion to divine truth. He professed to find no biblical
authority for the sacrament. It began with Jesus only celebrating the
Passover, but with certain of His figurative remarks being expanded by
Paul into justification of a formal, long-since outdated rite. The sacrament clothed Jesus with authority He never claimed and never possessed. As were all forms to Emerson, it was an impediment to true
religion. The church sadly voted for dismissal, but continued his salary
for over two months. Emerson never made a formal break with the
ministry and continued giving scattered sermons for several years. But
he was free to find himself and to launch a new career.

Shaken physically and mentally by critical events, by Ellen and the
controversy at the Second Church (despite his claim, he cared deeply
about what people thought of him), Emerson succumbed to illness and
indecision. Hoping to write verse or possibly edit a literary periodical,
he instead read avidly in European literature and decided on a trip to
Europe. The trip was a crucial event in Emerson's life. Its importance
can hardly be overestimated. As he later confessed to Thomas Carlyle, it
was a mission, in fact almost a pilgrimage. Always fascinated with the
hero, with greatness, he went to Europe seeking his hero, his human
god, to bow to and to serve. Also, as so many Americans, he went
seeking a superior cultural heritage, and in it a more clear philosophy, a
more firm resolution. In one sense his mission failed; he found neither a
satisfactory hero nor heritage. In another sense, it was successful, for
Emerson found himself and his major commitment—reliance on the god
that was himself. He happily returned home, not to praise America or
condemn Europe (often he condemned both, but particularly America),
but free of any illusions about Europe. He had found his "most retired &
unuttered thought confirmed & echoed back to him by his observation of
new men & strange institutions. I am glad to recognize the same man
under a thousand different masks & hear the same commandment

spoken to me in Italian, I was wont to hear in English." [Note to George A. Sampson, Mar. 23, 1833, in Ralph L. Rusk, ed., *The Letters of Ralph Waldo Emerson* (New York, 1939), I, 371.] Seeking a hero among the venerated scribes, embellished by distance, he had possibly missed him among obscure comrades at home. There had always been more "fine society in my own little town than I could command" [To William, June 29, 1833, *ibid.*, p. 388], while he preferred his own inkstand to Paris, a "vulgar superficial unspiritual marketing community. . . ." [To Samuel and Sarah D. Ripley, July 9, 1833, *ibid.*, p. 389.]

As Emerson traveled northward through Italy and Switzerland, on to Paris and then to journey's end in England, where his greatest heroes were sought, his early, tourist-like enthusiasm for Europe steadily lessened. He came to Europe as a moralistic son of New England; so he returned to Massachusetts, and with no feeling of inferiority or need to apologize. He was no esthete, although he dutifully attended to works of art and objects of tradition. Even behind his earliest compliments, his temporary and incompetent pose as a connoisseur and man of the world, there were moments of revulsion and rejection: "how effervescent and superficial is most of that emotion which names and places, which Art or magnificence can awaken." [To Aunt Mary, April 18, 1833, *ibid.*, p. 375.] In Catholic Europe he rejoiced in the broken fragments of his own heritage in art, religion, and politics; he loved the large cathedrals, so absent, so missed in the simple church architecture of New England. But what he admired he soon recognized as largely veneer, made more lustrous to Americans by a mystique of age. Behind the façade, behind the wealth and splendor, the beauty and grandeur, were the true realities. A religion of pageantry was also a religion of idolatry; the extreme and irrational piety also produced extreme unbelief and, most appalling, unbelievably loose morals. The manners of the few, the aristocratic governments, concealed unbelievable poverty and ugliness for the many. He never valued America, or liberal Protestantism, quite so much as he did while in Europe.

If Emerson returned home with greater self-reliance and greater pride in his homeland, he also returned as a better critic. He had encountered Europe first hand and, unlike so many American intellectuals, was already equipped to utilize the experience instead of capitulate to it. The superior achievement of Europeans in several intellectual and artistic fields was too obvious for argument. Yet, as a good Puritan, Emerson was ultimately unwilling to sever these endeavors from the whole life of man and thus tip the balance in favor of Europe. To him, the works of the intellectual and of the most creative artist had to contribute to more encompassing moral imperatives, or else they were tarnished no matter how extraordinary was their isolated perfection. The good man and the good society, mutually self-supporting, were the highest goals. All artifice of man had to be judged in terms of these. He could not tolerate the sharp contrasts of Europe, yet wanted the best features of Europe for America. Unlike Tocqueville, who had just returned from an equally climactic reverse voyage of self-discovery, Emerson believed that the best features of European culture could be grafted onto the political, economic, and religious attainments of the English in America. Political independence should lead to cultural independence, which would parallel at the national level Emerson's own newly won self-reliance. Tocqueville, in the same vein, hoped that the better features of democracy as found in America could be safely merged with the superior culture of France.

Emerson came to Europe as an unsuccessful Unitarian minister. He had written nothing of significance, had no reputation in Europe, and came seeking great men to emulate if not to worship. Yet, by the time he arrived in England he had developed a surprising self-confidence, in part based on his disillusionment with men of acknowledged greatness. He found them too often one-sided, artificial, even fawning. Not that he gave up his search, but he concluded that greatness in another had to mirror one's own greatness or it passed unperceived. This turned the whole problem back to self and its plenitude of potential greatness. It led Emerson to venerate the uniqueness of men and the representative role of great men (as vehicles of the pervasive God in all), but to refuse to bow to any man, past or present. This included Jesus who, as any man, was only a partial, one-sided revelation of Spirit (also, perhaps, Emerson saw in Jesus a competitor).

In England (the previous cultural contacts made it seem less foreign), Emerson visited with Samuel Taylor Coleridge, whose interpretations of German idealism had been crucial in his development, with William Wordsworth, and, on the final and most rewarding mission of his whole pilgrimage, with Carlyle. He met each as an equal, freely criticized Coleridge and the venerable Wordsworth, and launched with Carlyle an enduring dialogue by correspondence. Yet, Emerson was not as presumptuous as he was wise. He had found himself and had discovered there the same divinity, the same God, that found alternative expression in all men, be they great or small. As happened all too rarely, an American greeted Europeans as the democrat he professed to be, not as an insecure and fawning inferior.

Back in America Emerson wandered a bit before settling down to a permanent home and way of life. He preached, but with ever less frequency, won a degree of financial security after a preliminary and partial settlement of Ellen's estate, and began his career as a lecturer, exploiting his European trip, his thoughts on natural science, and his first reflections on great men. The ideas for his first book, *Nature,* had begun developing early—during his voyage home from England. Within a year or two, many of his lasting friendships were developed, including such members of the transcendental circle as Frederic Hedge, Bronson Alcott, Elizabeth Peabody, and Margaret Fuller. But the two closest bonds of friendship were soon severed, again by the dreaded tuberculosis. His brother Edward, long seeking health in the West Indies, died in 1834. Then more unbearable, Charles, the best, the beloved friend, died in 1836. Except for the death of a son and namesake, Waldo, in 1842, this ended the tragic losses that plagued, and in part molded, the young Emerson, who, if anything, developed an affirmative, optimistic outlook in desperate self-defense against almost unbearable affliction.

Emerson, along with his mother, permanently settled in the ancestral town of Concord in late 1834. He became an accepted, even a famous citizen a year later when he gave the oration at the commemoration of Concord's Second Centennial. In contrast to most of his later writing, he carefully and meticulously compiled a history of the town and suitably embellished it with paeans of praise. Even as he prepared it, he also carried on a restrained courtship. While lecturing at Plymouth, he had met Lydia Jackson, an extraordinary, not beautiful, but exceptionally intelligent woman who was mystically inclined and rather odd or at least original in thought and habits. Both were mature adults; the courtship was brief and limited to hurried letters and short visits; and the decision to marry was less than passionate. For Emerson, his enthralldom with Ellen could not be repeated and probably should not have been. The marriage with Lydia (Emerson always called her Lidian) came in September 1835. He brought his bride back to a newly pur-

chased house and lot in Concord, which with additional purchases grew
from two acres into a small farm. Unpretentious, plain, it was to be
Emerson's lifetime home. The marriage with Lydia was happy, but after
a few years not close. Emerson grew away from, or possibly in a different direction than Lydia, who often suffered illness and lived in an
extremely private but often perceptive world of her own. But with the
marriage, Emerson had permanently settled for a life of writing and
lecturing, thinking and meditating.

At Concord, Emerson disciplined early ambitions, accepted his
limitations, and used his assets well. He dismissed meticulous scholarship (his poor eyes were only an excuse) and also earlier interests in
painting and even in science. At one level, he became an estate owner,
avid gardener, and gentleman farmer, with hired help to supervise. At
another, he became a friend and adviser to a growing group of New
England intellectuals and writers, who visited Emerson's home in an
almost unending stream. Also, he was a husband, and soon a father to
three children, but in all these close relationships of life he remained
aloof, a small god without compelling sympathy, passion, or involvement. Most important, he was a thinker and writer. A bit too poetic and
too undisciplined to be a good philosopher, he was yet too much a
philosopher and a preacher to be only a poet. His talents were combined
in poetic lecture-essays and, less often, philosophical poems. With this
combination of talents, Emerson became one of the greatest essayists in
American history.

In his essays on representative men Emerson identified his personal
ideal as the poet-priest, or a perfect blending of insight, eloquence, and
moral force. In his writings, usually tied to and even forced by the
necessities of the lecture platform, he struggled for this happy combination. In lectures and essays he was able to communicate his method of
thinking, his supreme openness to experience, his continual involvement
with conflicting, even opposite ideas, and his failure to bring perfect
logical order to his beliefs. Yet he thought and thought and, with a
greater love for the written than the spoken word, wrote and wrote, even
placing his private soliloquies in his journal.

As an essayist, Emerson rarely used a reasoned, tightly logical narrative. Instead he used metaphors and aphorisms to develop ideas that
were often little more than vague impressions. He spoke to the mass
audiences of the Lyceum and resisted any modish invention or artificial-

ity. Approving of Franklin's dictum, he tried to speak with the vulgar and think with the wise. Yet, he was never as earthy, as pungent, or nearly as humorous as Franklin; the gentility came through in spite of his esteem for common language. But he wrote with great force and always with moral passion, although softened always by an element of reserve and prudence that kept his feelings carefully disciplined. More original than brilliant, he was alert, concerned, thoughtful. For an unsophisticated audience, he was an emancipating teacher. Yet his brilliant passages do not always join to form a coherent whole. Too often they were lifted from his *Journal* and never adequately integrated into a new whole. Emerson was a man of short but memorable wisdom; of momentary but unsurpassed excellence. His careful sentences were often gems, rising to the level of the oracular. He believed proverbs were the sanctuary of the intuition and freely used them.

The total effect of Emerson's essays was often one of excess, of overwriting, of overindulgence. The food was too compact, too rich, and indigestion too likely. Climaxes came too often. To his audiences, who had to grasp his ideas from the fleeting, sincere lectures, the flood tide of beautiful language probably carried the day. The aphorisms, the everpresent ambiguities, the imprecise phrases, were unnoticed, or else served well to suggest everything and in reality to explain very little. They were more exhilarating than enlightening. The phrases were carefully formed, and quite successful from a literary standpoint. They were not intended for careful analysis.

All Emerson's essays, including a few in which he plumbed the depths of human despair, reflected his own lack of despair, his sense of assurance, his strength of character. He was a veritable prophet, speaking a divine message, a man of wisdom, unshaken by the winds of external crises. In old Calvinist terms, his faith was unswerving, impregnable. In medieval terms, he was a saint. In Buddhist terms, he was enlightened. His lectures inspired because of the authority of his own convictions. He communicated strength to the weak, courage to the cowardly, confidence to the insecure. Confused and troubled men and women, simple and profound, farmers and intellectuals, were pulled to Emerson as to a magnet, and tried to absorb some of his strength, to discover his secret. They read, memorized, quoted, vulgarized, idolized, but rarely comprehended. They could not understand until they had shared the depths of his despair and the subsequent exhilaration of his victory.

SELF-RELIANCE

Emerson's supreme assurance existed only periodically before his trip to Europe; it never seriously waned afterwards. His early sense of failure, his obviously psychosomatic illnesses, and his intellectual struggles all came to a head after Ellen's death. Emerson faced possible insanity. Life was a jigsaw puzzle; none of the pieces fit together. All meaning was elusive.

Not instantaneously, but within a few months, his life dramatically changed. He found a core of meaning sufficient to escape all cynicism and despair. He could now affirm without doubts; he could applaud existence rather than shrink from it. His jigsaw puzzle would never be complete; the jagged, unconnected edges remained; the chaotic, unused pieces stretched in all directions. Only a fool thinks he has the puzzle all together; to believe so is to commit spiritual suicide. But the center pieces were in place and made perfect sense. Who could doubt that all pieces, some still confused, some not yet examined, could be made to fit perfectly into an ever enlarging center of meaning? Emerson, working from his own self-assurance, affirmed a perfect and beautiful whole, but never knew it and could never conceptualize it. In the perspective of nineteenth-century philosophy, he could hardly doubt the ideal or mental nature of reality and thus took a particular metaphysical stance toward it, but he never embraced a metaphysical system that completely encompassed it. Even the stance was insignificant in contrast to his own experiential assurance.

Emerson's European trip did not reveal some new religion or introduce him to many unfamiliar ideas. His newfound faith, which he called self-reliance, was a compound of old ideas, fragmentarily expressed in sermons, in letters to Aunt Mary or Charles, or most directly in his *Journal*. But the old ingredients now made sense; they were grasped with new intensity and in better relationship. The same beliefs that, when fragmented, allowed confusion, denied unity, and invited a cynical cursing of a world riddled with evil, now, with new insight, reconciled Emerson to existence, pointed to an essential unity, and made evil into the product of a short-sighted illusion. Suddenly things fit. All was good. He even knew, in brief, ecstatic moments of exhilarating affirmation, what has always been called blessedness or beatitude. In Calvinist terms, he had been converted or reborn. In Edwardian terms, he had received grace or special insight that enabled him to divine aright the sensible images of God and thus escape the terrible alienation of the unredeemed. Emerson knew a new level of experience, the best attainable by man, but had not invented a new philosophy. The quality of life was for him transformed. The confused young Waldo had become the sage of Concord.

Subsequently, Emerson's central aim was the communication of his own liberating faith. He tried to share it and bring others into position to experience it. He knew that his vision could not and should not be identical in detail with that of others, but he believed the quality would be similar. Although no two ever picked up the same pieces in the same order, the puzzle was the same for all. He had already learned the absurdity of churches, of handed-down inspiration, and instinctively felt the absurdity of stagnant theological explanations for an experience that could only be conceptually suggested but never defined. Thus, much less than Jonathan Edwards did he try to rationalize, in careful logical terms, his own religious experience. He knew that he had to suggest a quality of an experience as well as, or more than, define the ultimately indescribable beauty of what was experienced. The loose conceptual structure of many of his essays was, in the light of his purposes, less an impediment than an aid to communication. The metaphors, the indefinite, suggestive, and ever changing terms, were simply the rich, poetic imagery necessary to his subject. In fact, for a prophet, he was remarkably philosophical. All parts of the puzzle of life intrigued him. Despite recognized logical weaknesses, he never stopped trying to bring as much conceptual order to his experience as he could, short of taking the terrible dialectical detour that would lead him away from vital experiencing into a hades of barren intellectuality.

A world in which men can experience beatitude is a good world. If anyone can experience it, it is the best possible world. In such a world evil has no metaphysical status; a tragic view is an uncourageous submission to ignorance. Yet, as a fact, many men do not know beatitude, but instead suffer the ravages of fate, in numb silence or open rebellion. As thoroughly as any Calvinist, Emerson believed in moral determinism. His essay on "Fate" was the most poetic defense ever penned of the central insight of predestination. Emerson saw the terrible futility, the unconscious blasphemy, of blind rebellion. He never sought a demonic free will for man, but only wanted man to share the freedom of a dynamic whole, to accept fate without becoming fatalistic and tragic in outlook. This was essentially the view of earlier Puritans, who wanted to so merge their existence by love with that of God as to participate in God's freedom rather than passively suffer His dictates or, blinded by a great illusion, follow Satan in a vast charade of rebellion. Emerson, in his self-reliant affirmation, was not a rebel, not a futile hero, not a finite god, but a lover who believed his love could reconcile him to existence and make him heir to all its wonders, even including those that, to men without love, appeared as substantial evil. Viewing existence as mind, as idea and will, and finding idea and will as man's essence, Emerson simply asked man to join himself, or be true to himself. At this point the metaphors abound. But however expressed, Emerson proclaimed a possible merging of man and all existence, a merger that eclipsed all varieties of alienation and a merger that came, if at all, only from man's own individual resources. He completely rejected the doctrine of grace. In substance, man and all being are of one nature. The Spirit of God is the spirit of man. The spirit of man is the Spirit of God. There is mind, willful and knowledgeable. There is nothing more. This view differed from that of Edwards' in two essential respects: the Christian iconography was completely rejected, and the static and legalistic conception of mind was replaced by a dynamic concept. Both innovations typified the romantic idealism of the nineteenth century.

Sainthood is a lonely profession. It is too lofty to be otherwise. Many talk about it. Some falsely claim to have attained it. Few do. The Puritan explained both the small number and his own futility in trying to identify those few by the doctrine of divine election, by a God who elected some and rejected others, bestowing the appropriate character on each. Since such a personal God was dead, Emerson needed a substitute explanation. He never found a completely satisfactory one. Like his Puritan forebears, he alternatively appeared both arrogant and humble, aristocratic and equalitarian. He never doubted the essential divinity of every man, but at times could scarcely feel other than condescending pity for the mass of mankind that denied and suppressed this divinity. The God in man was most often obscured and undiscovered. Life for most men was hopelessly discordant; alienation was the rule of life. In Calvinist terms, original sin was a synonym for this alienation, not an explanation. That had to go back to God's will. Emerson emphatically rejected such an explanation, along with any belief in a God separated from man. In fact, he found the idea of human depravity blasphemous, the height of atheism, and completely irreverent.

Emerson's tentative substitute for God-ordained depravity was a denunciation of the state of affairs, of the blinding institutions of his society. These held men captive to things and concealed the reality shimmering in and behind all nature. As summed up in his essay on "Fate," "most men and most women are merely one couple more." [*The Complete Works of Ralph Waldo Emerson,* Centenary Edition (New York, 1903–4), VI, 11.] Yet these institutions, as substitute devils, existed in Emerson's ultimately good universe. They were not insurmountable obstacles to self-reliant salvation, for, if they were, innate evil simply appeared in a new verbal guise. Why do such institutions exist? In a seeming circularity, Emerson apparently believed them products of human delusion, as well as continuing causes of such delusion. The escape from the circular prison, and any promise of a more encompassing redemption, could not begin with purified institutions; deluded men were incapable of such reform. Only self-reliant men, poets and prophets and heroes, could rise out of the midst of delusion. A good world was one in which such heroic escape was a potentiality, a world that allowed beatitude, with no hopelessly arbitrary external impediments to exclude anyone. His reputed optimism was no more than such an affirmation as this. His was a world in which nature was both the source of all evil when men adhered to the delusion of materialism, and the pathway to beatitude when self-reliant men perceived the ideal reality beyond the material shadow.

Even in admitting the institutional nature of man's alienation from his own essential being, Emerson had to reject any quick solution through institutional reform. This type of reform usually substituted one tyranny for another. Instead of radical action, Emerson advocated radical insight, and with it a good bit of confusion. Basically, he asked man to be guided by intuition or, more difficult to comprehend, by nature, instinct, or reason (itself a type of intuition). At times, in a vast ocean of roughly synonymous and suggestive terms, he referred to this ultimate insight as "poetic," and again as "genius," or most revealingly as "poetic genius." In all cases the prime responsibility was placed on the lone individual, who had to break out of the context of institutions and material possessions and soar beyond them. Possibly the emphasis upon an intuitive element was a romantic translation of what Edwards had called affection; genius to Emerson encompassed both understanding and, even more, the emotional quality of an experience.

Even though his language often suggested it, Emerson did not desire a mystic, contemplative escape from society and all its ills. Sooner or later he introduced the Kantian moral law, which was his new rendition of the Puritan sense of moral duty. Poetic insight was both a recognition of one's divine nature and a recognition that this pervasive divinity was part and parcel of a moral order. Insight into the real was also perception of the good. Like a latter-day Plato, who vastly influenced him, Emerson (with some un-American regrets) descended from the mountain. In the valley, again like Plato, he never found enough philosopher-kings to join him in any thoroughgoing reformation of society. He had no recourse but to his own unique academy; no avenue of action save the lecture, essay, and poem. Aloof, reticent, he turned vulgar reform over to those who had never ascended the mountain, and were thus doomed to pitiful endeavor ultimately signifying nothing. Emerson worked to get a few up the mountain, hoping they might share his beatitude. Possibly, a goodly number of saints might eventually reform a few institutions, and thus make the ascent of the mountain a bit easier.

For years, in order to better establish his idea of self-reliance, Emerson sought a living hero, a completely free and true man. The search was in vain; no one quite measured up. In Emerson's despairing terms: ". . . if an angel should come to chant the chorus of the moral law, he would eat too much gingerbread. . . ." ["Nominalist and Realist," *Works,* III, 227.] Yet, he kept the image of the hero as a personal ideal, as the epitome of self-reliance. As he sang the virtues of heroism, he revealed his own personal goals. The hero, like Emerson, was not a specialized scholar, philosopher, or divine. He might even be unschooled (Emerson never did well in school). But the hero was a committed person, a man of will and of instinctive vision, oblivious of petty concerns. The hero had no doubts, no fears, no qualifications, no feelings of inferiority (the very things a self-reliant Emerson had tried to overcome). The true hero was supremely moral, but oblivious to petty and conventional moral codes; he was authentic, honest, a man of deep truth, with lofty concerns and contempt for the artificial and the mundane. A complete hero was indeed a superman, but he did not exist. Emerson believed the search for such a hero had to narrow to oneself, but even here faced ultimate frustration. All men were partial men, facets of perfect men. When anyone surrendered to himself, when he reflected his unique share of divinity, he was a hero, but not a perfect one.

It is easy to lose oneself in Emerson's metaphors, and it is most easy to become lost in the confusing jungle of self-reliance. How does one get self-reliance (or, how does one know himself, rise to God, or receive the spirit)? Emerson gave many answers. As the simple Quaker, one sends one's soul soaring off to God and thus establishes direct contact (he loved the Quakers). One finds in nature the symbols or the analogue of higher laws that are personal laws (Swedenborg). Or else one, in poetic perception, finds the unity of nature and the soul. Or one rids himself of sophistication and, as the innocent child, receives again the frequencies of heaven and responds to them. Or there is a submerged instinct that, being freed, illuminates all. Always intuition, receptivity, insight were implied, and scholarship, pedantic logic, and abstract theory were clearly precluded or made secondary. With it all there was often the implication of relaxation, being simple, seeking innocence, and eschewing rigor, distinctions, and laborious inquiry by just "suffering the spirit of the hour to pass unobstructed through the mind." ["Shakespeare; or, the Poet," *Works,* IV, 191.] Each mind was a narrowly focused telescope, with its unique perspective. The right thoughts came spontaneously, ran in line with nature, and reached to primal mind.

In his most enthusiastic moments, Emerson commanded all men to eschew authority, creeds, and the confining past. Look not abroad for your gods; do not imitate past masters. God is dead. The church is irrelevant. Seek no solace in organization, or even in society. Resist the allure of sense, the sophistry of political remedies. All fail in the crisis of existence. Only by a radical turning within, by an intuitive leap, by something as drastic as Calvinist conversion does one escape alienation and despair. Self-reliance was Emerson's first shout of victory out of near insanity. He had plenty of time to learn discipline. Now he was free. The new day was bright. There was a great reformation, the dawning of a new understanding. All was excitement, wonder.

In less exhilarating moments, Emerson made his peace with existence by holding to the doctrine of compensation. His antinomian self-reliance reflected a romanticized, Neoplatonic sense of intoxication, while the more prosaic idea of compensation reflected his more prudent reflections. In compensation he stressed a mean or balance reminiscent of

Aristotle, or of the hopeful acquiesence typical of many Christians. Some of his early letters to Aunt Mary showed Emerson struggling to justify or explain all the injustice in the world, the disease, deformity, misery, cruelty, and strife of a civilization gone to rot. He could not find an intellectual answer—all answers became lost in enigma, in antinomies. He found only a partial wisdom in suspended judgment, in Montaigne's thoughtful skepticism. Neither poets nor philosophers had performed their function of giving man sufficient understanding to meet the affliction of life, to cure his distorted relationship with nature. Later his piety, expressed as self-reliance, saved him, much in the sense that grace reconciled the Puritan. The idea of God in man obliterated the problem of senseless evil and even rendered evil an illusion or a form of blindness. But at the practical day-to-day level, this form of beatific union with a perfect whole seemed to need a more prosaic helpmate. True, all suffering and grief was at a low level and an illusion of the sufferer, but it was still suffering and needed to be endured with a degree of sanity either by the nonsaint or in nonsaintly moments. Thus, the idea of compensation was the immediate prescription; self-reliance was the final solution.

Nature is made up of polarities, which Emerson believed were all neatly balanced. This belief could make one's intense grief bearable, even as it could prevent one's enjoying any unalloyed pleasure (as it did Emerson). Endlessly he repeated the theme: for every sweet a sour, for every evil a good, for every loss a gain, for every light a darkness. Emerson saw this balance as a law of nature in both physics and life. Our mistakes educate; our achievements tarnish. In adversity we can find consolation in the growth of character, even as the cold winds of spring retard and toughen the emerging flower. There was no irretrievable disaster, no complete loss, any more than there was a final or complete victory. There was no real cheating, and there were no unfair advantages.

Compensation had multiple implications, many never explored by Emerson. One he did explore. As he saw, compensation implies a radical equalitarianism. Every man has a mixture of talents and faults, and they balance out in his uniqueness. Thus every man is a distinct creation, capable of doing something better than anyone else. This seems a radical contrast to his man-God and his hero complex, as well as his continuous emphasis upon genius and intuitive insight. He feebly rescued himself from complete ambivalence by an interpretation of history. Each age requires a different talent. The hero has it. Every hero is thus the hero of the hour, in whom a quality is ripe at the time of need. Goethe was such a hero for the nineteenth century. But a higher, compensatory justice assures that there are no common men. Every "talent has its apotheosis somewhere. . . . Heaven reserves an equal scope for every creature." ["Uses of Great Men," *Works*, IV, 31.] Since each age requires a special talent, it cultivates this talent and does not provide equally for the development of others. A class system, based on temporary and artificial social values, inevitably develops. But in a time of crisis, an unsuspected man, formerly the worm in society's mud, rises to leadership. He has the requisite talent. Thus, diversity should be prized and all men honored. The disparities of power in men are superficial. "I believe it is the conviction of the purest men that the net amount of man and man does not vary much. Each is incomparably superior to his companion in some faculty. His want of skill in other directions has added to his fitness for his own work. Each seems to have some compensation yielded to him by his infirmity, and every hindrance operates as a concentration of his force." ["New England Reformers," *Works*, III, 281.] Thus, compensation could not eradicate the radical differences in men, but explained and glorified them.

PHILOSOPHY

Emerson's doctrines of self-reliance and compensation were more religious affirmations than philosophical positions. Although fascinated by technical philosophy, Emerson always viewed it in literary terms. He looked for insight, for authenticity, for general attitudes in both philosophy and literature; he never concerned himself deeply with formal arguments, technical problems, or systematic exposition. Yet, he penetrated easily to the heart themes of philosophers and was not as much a superficial philosopher as he was a preacher, seeking ideas to use for his own didactic purposes. Even as a young theological student at Harvard, he revealed some knowledge of German idealism. In a letter to Aunt Mary he emphasized the "modern" philosophic reaction against bare reason and the sympathy with feeling and sentiment. He suggested that the universe was each moment a new creation emanating from God to the mind of man and that the moral world was in the human heart, best illustrated and defined by concrete institutions. At this time Christianity was still the valued institution. By the time of his trip to Europe he was a complete convert to romantic idealism, and as he worked out his own interpretation of it, or more to the point, as he used it as a prime tool for justifying his doctrine of self-reliance, he slowly dropped all the Christian themes. The external world was phenomenal, but with manifold spiritual uses, as he tried to show in his first book-essay, *Nature*. Scientific knowledge, although completely justified by worthwhile uses, was only a type of outward understanding, a body of abstract categorizations of phenomena, of rigorous definitions of surfaces, but not a copy of reality.

Above understanding there was always reason, the direct vision of the soul. Internal instead of external and potentially perfect, reason was the pure divinity in man, the direct perception of the true and beautiful, and most of all of the supreme goodness which was always the highest beauty. From understanding, man had to strive for reason, for glorious insight. He had to find a unity beyond the rending abstractions of understanding. Throughout all his essays Emerson celebrated this double theme. His approach was always on two levels. Usually beginning with appearance, with practical understanding, with matter and science, he moved, even if only for a fleeting last, almost discordant impression, to the level of reason, of the universal, of spirit. By the interplay of the two, he analyzed all life's relations, struggling in his early years to keep his head out of effervescent clouds, and in later years above the crushing weight of practical interests.

Idealism, from Plato on, often sponsored a type of skepticism. By locating truth in the impenetrable areas of insight or intuition, and thus severing it from even the possibilities of completely adequate linguistic expression, the idealist easily accepted an epistemological skepticism embracing all concepts about the physical world, or all empirically based knowledge. The whole external world became a subjectivity, an expression of mind, an emanating shadow of reality. In his most pessimistic essay, "Illusions," Emerson showed how he could only with great difficulty escape the unending illusions of life and retain his vision of an underlying unity. Though it is easy to become lost in the phenomenal shadows, they point to the mind which produced them. When the shadows are treated, not as images or symbols of reality, but as reality, as in scientific understanding, they lose all ultimate meaning. Scientists, merchants, and small men joust with these shadows as if they were realities, never realizing their contingency, their meaninglessness, their transiency. Emerson roundly condemned Lockean empiricism and all varieties of materialism and utilitarianism. These were his strawmen, often vilified without being clearly understood. The materialist, or complete empiricist, took a small, pitiful shadow world and turned it into an attenuated reality, an impoverished and vulgar metaphysics, degrading alike to man and to Spirit. In a sense, this type of terrible illusion replaced human depravity in Emerson's revamped Calvinism. But when separated from such a huge illusion, the limited truths of understanding were highly useful, both in effecting moral purposes and as aids to the highest type of reflection. As much as any Puritan, as clearly as any pragmatist, Emerson viewed empirical knowledge as metaphysically empty, epistemologically probable, and morally useful.

Emerson always revered Kant as the most important progenitor of transcendental philosophy and also as the sublime spokesman for moral law. In some ways Kant did not really fit Emerson's picture of him. In fact, Emerson's relationship with Germanic thought as a whole can be easily exaggerated or misunderstood. The German philosophers provided the broad framework for many of Emerson's characteristic ideas or modes of speech; their ideas also helped clarify the distinctive nature of Emerson's own professed idealism.

Kant found necessary forms or categories of understanding present in mind before sense experience. These given, or a priori, categories were necessary for transforming bare sensations into perceptions and, eventually, explanatory propositions about existence. In particular, Kant saw the prime categories of space and time (transcendental esthetic) as preconditions for all knowing and thus glorified the formal, rational, or mathematical aspect of scientific knowledge. He also believed that mind contributed the necessary categories of understanding, including the all-important category of causality. In this emphasis he was an early positivist, effectively synthesizing empiricism and rationalism in a well-disciplined and metaphysically neutral theory of knowledge which lessened the skeptical import of Hume's empiricism.

As a rigorously honest man, Kant limited knowledge to rational propositions about existence, since only these combined the formal and the experiential. Although formal reason (best illustrated in mathematical reasoning) logically implied a complete universe, or some encompassing rational order (as philosophers from Plato to Spinoza had demonstrated), Kant refused to attribute existence to such formal, metaphysical concepts. Thus mind, and formal thought, contributed an element of assurance or reliability to scientific understanding, but left man, insofar as his knowledge availed, without any cognitive path to reality or God. In fact, Kant demolished the traditional arguments for God's existence, denied any possible knowledge of a substantive soul, and showed that human freedom, if it existed, could not come within the scope of knowledge.

Yet, Kant's positivism was strained. He was always a moralist and a person of deep religious piety. Although he could not know, he yet could not practically doubt the existence of an ultimate reality, or what he called a noumenal world hidden behind the phenomenal world grasped by human understanding. Here existed freedom, a moral law, and even the Christian God. The transcendental aspect of mind (the categories) only implied such a realm; a type of *pragmatic* affirmation alone could sustain belief in its existence (Kant, by way of Charles S. Peirce, thus contributed a second label to American thought). To Kant, there were never two levels of true knowledge, phenomenal and noumenal. Truth applied only to phenomenal propositions. But he did try to prove that the affirmed noumenal realm was not logically precluded by the known phenomenal realm. If his moral hopes had warred with his understanding, or if they had been irrational in a logical sense, Kant would have rejected them as illusions. But, bolstered by logical possibility, borne by great hope, he believed his subjective hopes were surely justified; otherwise life was barren and meaningless.

Emerson had none of Kant's logical rigor and never bothered with careful qualifications. Yet, Emerson sensed that, above all else, Kant was a moralist. As a trained philosopher, Kant tried to deal honestly with the leading epistemological problem of his day. Emerson, as a poet-priest, never became involved with technical problems in epistemology. From his standpoint, he had more important things to do than write abstruse and technical books. A sick society needed the inspiration of a prophet, not the difficult concepts of a specialist in abstractions. Even Kant returned, over and over again, to the realm of practical experience, to the quality of life as actually lived, to the existential level where choice, right, beauty, and beatitude were of "transcending" importance.

This was the Kant that Emerson knew and loved, the Kant that ultimately trusted his experience beyond any formal system of thought.

Kant's successors in German philosophy, notably Johann Fichte and Georg Hegel, took portions of Kant's critical philosophy and turned it into a romantic and absolute form of idealism. It was largely through this idealism, as celebrated by such literary figures as Schelling and Coleridge, that Emerson came to know Kant. Whereas Kant had only affirmed a noumenal realm, or a metaphysical ground as a postulate of practical reason, his successors proclaimed such a reality as the highest form of insight, as glorious Truth. At one point or another they fell back onto a type of intuitive grasp, which they all too easily obscured and disclaimed. (Emerson honestly admitted the intuitive foundation.) Claiming to know reality by a higher knowledge than exercised in scientific understanding, the romantics easily defined the nature of this reality. In the tradition of Plato and Berkeley, they found it to be Mind, and Mind as clarified by Kant in the *Critique of Pure Reason*. By this transformation, Kant became the father of absolute idealism. The transcendental or a priori aspects of mind as disclosed by Kant became the very characteristics of reality itself. Pure reason, apart from concomitant experience, was glorified as a higher type of truth, since it partook directly of reality or of mind. Phenomenal or scientific knowledge was demoted and rendered secondary or even suspect, since it was arbitrarily established by criterion of understanding established by reason. Correctly understood, scientific knowledge was significant only as it pointed beyond itself to legislating Reason, or to Spirit. Since Kant had stressed the synthetic or active role of pure reason, reality was necessarily now defined as active, willful, and dynamic. German idealism was thus extremely voluntaristic, setting the tenor of nineteenth-century thought. Hegel claimed to develop, for the first time, a logic that successfully revealed the inner dialectic of an evolving Spirit. To escape solipsism, Fichte and Hegel affirmed a universal or absolute mind, which either encompassed or utilized the individual human minds and which was divested of the anthropomorphic aspects of the Christian God. The earlier idealism of Berkeley was thus altered—by a dynamic element and a transformation of the Christian myth.

In a vague way, Emerson was one of the romantic idealists. He often sounded like them, for he adopted their vocabulary, either directly or from Coleridge. But the verbal identification is misleading. In the terms of his own language, he *knew* that a higher mind or spirit existed. In fact, after he developed his self-reliant doctrine, he never doubted. But when Emerson said he knew, he never meant that he had proved, or that he could prove, his deepest insight. He never tried to use the word "know" in the strict sense of a Kant or of anyone deeply involved in epistemology. He spoke as a poet, with profound distrust for both metaphysics and theology. Hegel, as the pre-eminent German idealist and surely one of the most influential men in the history of Western philosophy, was the recording secretary for the Absolute. He produced a vast, systematic philosophy to prove beyond any doubting the validity of his beliefs. Soon all the professional idealists were building their related but divergent systems.

But Emerson was horrified at such intellectual structures (almost as horrified as Kierkegaard). His terms were romantic; his commitment was practical or experiential. The romantic terminology was convenient and seemed appropriate for communicating the ultimately inexpressible quality of his own highest, nearly overwhelming experience. But on occasion he used other language, such as the soaring imagery of Neoplatonism, or the oracular proverbs of Oriental sages. Thus the type of experience, not the expressive terms, was first in importance. Without this qualification, Emerson's thought and life seem hopelessly ambivalent. With the qualification, there is a remarkable affinity between his soaring transcendentalism and his practical moralism.

With the complete assurance of an inspired prophet, Emerson proclaimed the reality of Spirit. Yet, he came no nearer to an unambiguous definition of Spirit than he ever came to defining a clear pathway to self-reliance. He preferred to point to Spirit in its partial expression in human reason or in the poetic insight of his cultural heroes. He implied at times that Spirit (or any of over twenty synonyms that he used for ultimate reality) lurked as a self-contained but always in part unknowable unity in back of its varied human expressions. In other cases he implied that the entity was no more than a compounding of individual minds and gave no special role, no added reality, to the compounded whole. Spirit lived in, and depended upon, the individual. A pantheistic but extreme individualism resulted. In both cases he always saw Spirit as active, surging, free creative will. It was not necessarily an abstract will surging into realization by the use of individual minds (Hegel), but it was free individuals creatively fulfilling their own individual destiny by the exercise of a common but divine trait.

Emerson's most soaring, and necessarily most metaphorical, idealism was expressed in his essay on "The Over-Soul," in his first series of essays (1841). His Oversoul was described in language reminiscent of Plotinus and his ineffable One and in its ecstatic quality was far removed from Hegel. As is typical of Neoplatonists, Emerson fell into the metaphor of light in a hopeless attempt to reduce the ultimate unity into adequate words. Timeless, beyond space, yet creative, the Oversoul was yet immanent, the all in all, with the web of events being only the flowing robe in which it was clothed. The soul of man was one with the Oversoul, and could share its timelessness and its power. When the individual soul rose to this level, it had genius, virtue, and love, and was one with all other souls. When describing the Oversoul, Emerson's rapturous jabs of thought related him inconclusively to many philosophers. But the relationships were not developed and, in fact, were only part of a rich and lyrical devotional tribute. He confessed overtones of spiritualism, paid tribute to Fox and Swedenborg, suggested the extremes of pure trance or possession, or even a type of insanity, and acknowledged in Kierkegaardian phrases the "shudder of awe and delight with which the individual soul always mingles with the universal soul."

Emerson's most soaring affirmations of an Oversoul were always mixed with a corollary absorption with nature. The term nature is an extremely ambiguous one in the English language, and so it was for Emerson. He used the term in at least four significant, substantive ways. In a limited context (as often in his second essay on "Nature"), he simply meant the out-of-doors, the trees and hills of New England. At this level his enthusiasm grew with age, but was never comparable to that of Henry David Thoreau. In his most comprehensive use, he capitalized nature and used it as a final term, as a synonym of Spirit, and thus as encompassing all existence, and by this usage anticipated the metaphysics of John Dewey. In a later usage, he made Nature an ultimate force or power behind the universe. But more often, and most central in his vocabulary, nature meant the whole realm of phenomena, of appearance, and thus, in conventional language, the whole physical universe.

By this last usage Emerson, much as Edwards and other earlier idealists, held nature to be the ordered ideas of a divine mind. Unfortunately, most men failed to perceive the immanent divinity displayed in nature, failed to go beyond the image to the real. Like Plato's cavemen, they were enslaved by empirical understanding and erroneously believed appearance to be reality. Thus, most of Emerson's contemporaries seemed to be materialists, with their materialism hardly relieved by the verbal clichés of a historic but dead Christianity. In his ascending treatment in the book *Nature,* Emerson granted the utilitarian and esthetic uses of nature. In his essay on "Prudence," and elsewhere, he tried to give all due respect to empirical knowledge and the utilitarian functions it performed. But he always pushed on to the higher use—the revelation of divine mind. When seen by the light of Reason, nature's phenomenal veil parted to reveal Spirit. Nature became an aid to meditation, a pathway to wisdom, an introduction to the highest truth and greatest beauty. Like many Puritan forebears, Emerson conceived nature as mankind's only adequate cathedral. But one had to perceive truly; one had to have Emerson's transparent eyeball. Such true perception was not automatic, or a gift of grace, but came through some intuitive leap. In pessimistic moments, Emerson felt that the mass of men would remain captive to the world of appearance. Then he dismissed the mob in behalf of the rare superman.

Emerson was in love with being, not with the material universe. He struggled to attain the quality of human experience that would merge the human mind with all reality, that would transcend the petty, discordant elements of sensation, that would unify and give higher meaning to the heretofore alienated and unfulfilled life. He early glimpsed the ugly, barren landscape of a commercial society and its warped, twisted lives madly pushed toward ever more senseless endeavor and consumption. In a surely agonizing spiritual pilgrimage, Emerson slowly repudiated a conventional, historical Christianity, filled with other men's prayers and the asserted authority of other men's insight. Irrelevant to each unique individual, to each distinctively personal need, the dogmas of historical religion, though clothed in the verbiage of spirit, were almost as enslaving, as inhibiting, as the lure of vulgar commerce. Insofar as they lulled one into a type of spiritual lethargy, they were more so. When men appealed to Jesus, they failed to make his appeal, to seek strength where he found it.

Yet, insofar as the historical religions incorporated the idealistic insight, they were more significant than most philosophic systems. But the insight, always a matter of experience, was authentic only in the originative prophets and mystics, and never in the doctrines or in the institutionalized forms of worship. In the West, Jesus was the most commanding example of the type of intuitive insight, in an age and context, that all men should possess. In Eastern religions, particularly in early Hinduism, Emerson found an extreme spiritualism, and for years he indulged an insatiable curiosity about the Orient. But as an incurable moralist, he could never really accept the aloof, contemplative stance of Eastern mystics. Yet, their polarity toward spirit was a needed balance for Western man's polarity toward matter. For radical critics of a commercial age, the East had manifold uses and, at times, an almost irresistible attraction.

Emerson spiritualized nature. This was his primary impulse. His early acceptance of philosophical idealism showed him the way. His hard-won doctrine of self-reliance required it. This spiritualism often led to an ecstatic voluntarism—to his God-in-man complex. It also led toward mysticism and to an occultism that could scarcely be communicated. It culminated in his yielding soul, through which surged pulses of everlasting nature, of immortal energies. But balancing this mystical inclination was a related view of nature as the womb of life. As early as the 1830's, Emerson believed in the evolution of species, although with a Lamarckian interpretation. In this evolutionary stance, he saw nature as a primordial but purposeful force or energy. In his later essay on "Nature" in 1844, as well as in his long-developed lectures on the "Natural History of the Intellect," he stressed this extremely naturalistic theme. Mind, in man, is only a product, a culmination of a process. Human consciousness brings a type of corruption, but points to a grand unity, to nature being fulfilled in man, or at least in redeemed man. Corrupt man is a terrible scar. In contrast, lower nature, from trees to higher mammals, follows a purer instinct, has greater beauty, and commands a greater rapture. This thinking led Emerson toward primitivism and a glorification of less civilized men and of prehuman nature. Yet, all lower nature points upward. All lower being aspires toward consciousness. Man is at the top, although an admixture of all his animal ancestors, with rudiments of the tiger and baboon. Even the distant plant world lies in his past. His arts and sciences are glorious from the distant perspectives of an "ox, crocodile, and fish." Thus the purpose in nature—the push—is in and toward mind. Here alone is an enveloping unity.

This evolutionary approach to nature brought Emerson closest to the later pragmatists. In it he seemed to make mind an emergent and unifying product of natural forces, moving away from his more prevalent idealism, in which mind was fully synonymous with reality. Darwinian evolution, with its absence of emergent design or any apparent teleology, came too late to influence Emerson's best thought. It seemed to challenge all forms of transcendentalism and absolute idealism and thus introduced many of the new problems to be faced by Peirce, James, and Dewey.

INTELLECT AND ART

In his youthful exuberance and soaring spirituality, Emerson was a self-acclaimed antinomian. But he also, sooner or later, paid his respects to a disciplined moralism or, at times, even to the prudent virtues of Ben Franklin. Emerson wanted the divine current to flow unobstructed through man and often suggested that spontaneous action was the best kind of action. He often viewed intellect as a product of will or emotion. Yet, as enthusiastically as any Puritan of the past, he advocated reflective intelligence as the prime tool of moral achievement.

When Emerson tried to cope with technical philosophy, with rigorous logic, with scrupulous scholarship, he reflected an equal mixture of envy and repugnance. He equally condemned the purely practical man and the metaphysician; he admitted the uselessness of chaotic ideas but never trusted highly formal systems. He asked man to worship truth and forego all things for it, even as he condemned repose and pure contemplation. He could celebrate the academy and the pure life of the intellect as man's only real interest, yet picture philosophy as a vice, scholarship as pedantry, and disinterested perception as a form of imbecility. He never tried to mold such divergent impulses into a completed and consistent harmony. As a result, he left a wealth of random ideas that could be exploited either by those who wanted to condemn the insufferable practicality of Americans or, conversely, by those who distrusted intellectuals and wanted to elevate the simple man of common sense.

Emerson, above everything else, was a moralist. He was never willing for long to desert an active, willing, struggling mankind. In the soaring, mystically inclined essay on "Circles," the steps of the ascending ladder are "actions, the new prospect is power." He never believed that the primordial impulses, the final springs of action could be encapsulated in intellectual concepts. There was always an existential level more basic than the abstractions of thought. Yet, believing so profoundly in a type of poetic genius, in an intuitive insight that gave each man a tiny but perfect glimpse of truth, he could not dismiss man as a tragically futile creature, full of sound and fury but signifying nothing. In spite of brief flirtations with pure meditation, or his tantalizing excursions into Oriental thought, Emerson always came back to the battlefield. Here intellect found its justification. He insisted that all thought is practical and thus not a type of dreaming. It takes man out of servitude into freedom only when it eventuates in action. One must possess and use ideas, not be enslaved by them. The errand of perception is not only larger perception but new action. Insight, inarticulate and unused, is worthless. Insight joined to talent, genius tied to performance, is wisdom. The heart alone is blind. Intellect without the heart is no longer subject to destiny. Americans too often valued talent and neglected thought. Europeans too often valued insight but lacked executive talent. However brilliant the insight, it was a mockery and a moral aberration unless it could be joined to the active life. Speculation and practice must not be separated.

At times Emerson came close to anti-intellectualism. Thought is beset by so many dangers. It cleaves mind and object. Unity is broken in man. The intellect that makes distinctions, that separates, is itself separated. Man thinking is alienated from the nature about which he thinks. Low things are thus gladly lost, but even the highest good can be so subverted. One who consciously loves is not love; one who reflectively grieves is not grief (Ellen surely inspired these thoughts). He felt that Goethe, the surpassing intellect of modern times, apprehended the spiritual better than any other person, yet was not spiritual. Thus Emerson could not quite trust men of thought, who indulged the vice of intelligence. He so often exalted the simple and naïve man and almost gleefully ridiculed the school rules that no mind really followed. With delight he scourged the academic retinue—the university professors who could not even state the great questions, let alone answer them. Poets did a better job. Men of fame always disappointed. Men of wit were only full of conceit and bad jokes. Scholars were worldly egotists. Scientists labored only to establish their priority to some partial truth. Philosophers mixed their private folly with public wisdom. [*Works,* XII, 5–9.]

As an idealist, Emerson saw natural laws, discovered by scientific investigation, as creations of mind. In this sense he applauded science as a method of self-revelation. But he distrusted any direct science of mind, or any scientific psychology. He granted that thought was a part of nature and believed it exhibited laws comparable to those developed in physics. In fact, physical laws, as images of divine reality, obviously contained some of the laws of intellect. But still there was mystery, and Emerson was content to leave it so. To try, through introspection, to grasp the central reality of thought, to turn mind upon itself, was, to use Emerson's own metaphor, like trying to swim upstream when the stream was Niagara. Seek the aid of intelligence. Obey its oracles. But do not spend all your time watching its mechanics. That is spying, and cold and surgical. An ode is better than such analysis. A poet's musings come closer to the whole truth.

In the same vein he condemned formal logic and probably regretted his own logical limitations. With the exact tenor of Dewey's later *Logic, Theory of Inquiry,* Emerson argued that formal logic was only a tool for the unfolding of a truth. The syllogism was an effective means of expressing or arguing a point whose truth was reached by some other process. Thus, formal logic had no justification in itself. It could not support itself, whereas instinct, even when it could give no reason, had to be trusted in the hope that it would later ripen into truth. Pure geometry had no value until it could be used to show the termini of the universe. Emerson even suggested a complete diversity of logics or methods of reasoning; each mind had its own. But unlike Dewey, he had no great desire to find one most fruitful method. He loved the diversity and never counted the cost in futility.

Pious toward existence, at times nearly ravished by its beauty and its uncharted dimensions, Emerson lambasted all comprehensive metaphysical systems. How blasphemous to expect some petty product of human reason to do justice to God. All exhaustive theories were but false and vain attempts to "analyze the Primal Thought." Metaphysics was a dangerous pursuit when carried out in single-minded desperation. He made no more revealing statement than the following: "Metaphysics must be perpetually reinforced by life; must be the observations of a working man on working men; must be biography,—the record of some law whose working was surprised by the observer in natural action." [*Works,* XII, 13.] A living metaphysics was a once-read grammar, quickly converted to its main function—use. Too often the metaphysician, in building rational defenses for a belief, destroyed belief. Emerson hoped he would one day be taught by the poet. This aversion to static systems was reinforced by his evolutionary orientation, his receptivity to ideas of growth and change. To him there was no end that was not also a beginning, no circle that could not be encompassed by a wider one.

From earliest boyhood, Emerson wanted nothing so much as to be a great poet. His life revolved around his very self-conscious courtship of the literary muse. Conceptual knowledge, a useful tool but essentially divisive, was in all ways subordinate to the apt and unifying symbol of a poet, which was not only beautiful but true. But with an inbred and almost instinctive moralism, Emerson had to bring both truth and beauty into harmony with the good. He did this by an enlarged conception of art. His thought on art was his most original and most coherent contribution to American thought. Although many of his ideas were implicit in Puritanism, and a few developed by Jonathan Edwards, Emerson still deserves the credit for articulating the first coherent esthetic philosophy in America. Never before had an American thought so deeply about art.

As the Puritans, Emerson emphasized such esthetic norms as harmony, symmetry, and proportion. In addition, true to his evolutionary perspective, he stressed movement and rhythm. These were the characteristics of ideal reality, and of man at his best. When man is open to ideal reality and intuitively grasps it, he perceives it as his own truest character. This supreme, beatific perception could be called poetic insight, for it is enveloped in feeling and is incapable of complete conceptual rendering. Reality, as perceived by the responsive person (often a simple man without artificiality), is true, beautiful, and good, with the latter the climaxing attribute. All men have the potential for such insight, and therefore all men can enjoy beauty. Esthetics, the more passive aspect of beauty, requires only a responsive stance, a type of intuition. But the true genius will not stand silent before the throne of truth and beauty. He will publish it. The active, creative attempt to embody and communicate poetic insight is art. It requires talent.

The locus of beauty is never in the object of art. Emerson, in insisting upon this, came close to the position of Plato. The art object, at the low level of sculpture all the way up to the high level of poetry (Emerson's hierarchy), is only a type of focus, or an abstraction, of the real. It abridges, selects, points up, but in either case is always derivative. The great gallery is always nature. No art object comes close to the magic of a living man. This is not to derogate art, but to glorify it and, at the same time, to escape the tyranny of isolated art objects. Emerson believed the art object was man's best symbol, capable of communicating reality most broadly, to the simple man as well or better than to the sophisticated. It educates to beauty. It reconciles man to nature (or reality) and brings him into harmony with it. Art is man's best language. But it is a growing language, changing with human history. In the hands of the true genius, who combines insight, talent, and moral zeal, it reveals the height of the human soul in each evolving hour of history. Rooted in a historical context, sharing the necessities of a historical moment, art is more revelation than striking originality.

Since the art object is an outward, symbolic expression of an ideal reality that is the essence of man, art is inseparable from the character of an artist. Beauty is best appreciated by a simple, responsive person, who honestly relies upon his own instincts or his own feelings. Such a person, with cultivated understanding, is also the best critic. With talent, he is the best artist. Without such an honesty and integrity, without such an openness or such a consent to existence, no skill in surfaces, no rules of art, no excess of talent can come close to the highest form of beauty, for "poetry was all written before time was. . . ." ["The Poet," *Works,* III, 8.] The work of art must radiate the human character behind it, must be an expression, in stone, on canvas, in sound, "of the deepest and simplest attributes of our nature." ["Art," *Works,* II, 359.] Here Emerson agreed with his Puritan forebears, and particularly with Jonathan Edwards, who always saw character, or personal holiness, as the highest form of beauty. This beauty of character is the central reality that stands before, and justifies, any individual art object. The techniques, the changing, conventional forms of execution, the infinitely varied subject matter, are all derivative or instrumental. The end purpose of art cannot be the isolated and completed object. These objects only help break down walls of circumstances, help unify life by leading men into a better understanding of their true nature. Thus, the end of all art is the supreme work of art—redeemed man, and beyond that a society in which all men are great works of art. Thus art always serves its own ends, but these ends are in all ways moral ends. The last step in art, as for Emerson in all other areas, must lead beyond the surface object until art is "practical and moral," until it "stands in connection with the conscience," and makes the "poor and uncultivated feel that it addresses them with a voice of lofty cheer." [*Ibid.*, p. 363.]

The pervasive moralism of Emerson's esthetics can be easily distorted and then dismissed as a type of moral strait jacket placed on the artist. In reality, he so joined morality and beauty that a pedantic moralist might allege just the opposite, that art now dominated the moral life. By tying insight to goodness, and viewing the person of truth and goodness as the most perfect, most beautiful work of art, the moral ends imposed upon artists were, in reality, also esthetic norms, not outside or foreign impositions. The didactic emphasis was only an attempt to push the artist toward better and higher art, the production of character in man. The best poet, it was now clear, was always a priest. Emerson dismissed sculpture as an early and low form of art—stone dolls typical of a rude and youthful people, paltry and toylike. But sculpture was a beginning education, pointing upward toward a more wise and spiritual people, and ever higher (that is, more educational and liberating) art forms. There was a moment when every gallery or museum "becomes frivolous" and was seen as counterfeit. A great man was, in every momentary attitude and stance, a far better statue. Likewise, music was an ephemeral form of art, preparatory to higher and less primitive forms. The oratorio was not nearly so sweet as the "lifetones of tenderness, truth, and courage." Emerson's famous, and often lambasted, statement that all works of art should be extemporaneous performances had meaning only in this context. If men could escape the prison and the ugliness of limiting circumstances and stand in self-reliant honesty as a revelation of the divine, then indeed every unrehearsed and authentic word and gesture would be more beautiful than any contrived work of art.

This moral, didactic emphasis provided Emerson's standards for judging past artists. It forced him, possibly against an instinctual preference for either Goethe or Shakespeare, to judge Milton as the greatest poet, with no rival in the English language or in France or Germany. Milton's style was great, but secondary to his power to inspire. He was a poet, but even more a great man who read "the laws of the moral sentiment to

the newborn race." He raised the estimate of man, threw out the challenge of manly character, and was the most inspired man in English
letters. Concerned with hope, self-reverence, piety, he was himself the
greatest poem, a man of virtue, austerity, chastity, and industry. He, like
Emerson, was a moralist, loved gardening and the out-of-doors, and was
a champion of freedom limited by virtue. In fact, he was a poet-priest,
with eloquence used to inspire. ["Milton," *Works,* XII, 248–62.]

In the same vein he praised, whether justifiably or not, the work of
Michelangelo. Goodness was at the seat of his grandeur. He realized
that "what is most real is most beautiful, and that by the contemplation
of such objects, he is taught and exalted." He knew the great truth, that
"perfect beauty and perfect goodness are one," and that they are felt or
intuited rather than known by the understanding, and thus open to all
men. He made man his central concern and used the finite form in an
ideal way to approximate the infinite inhabitant. He sought the beautiful
by "the study of the True" and thus went the highest step and sought
beauty in the "highest form, that of Goodness." In addition, like Milton,
he was a good man, hating vulgarity, loving goodness, with a platonic
love for all. Perhaps most significant, he was a great teacher, using art to
"suggest lessons of unutterable wisdom." ["Michael Angelo," *Works,*
XII, 217.]

Shakespeare and Goethe fell short of Emerson's mark. Yet he believed they were the most talented men in literature. Shakespeare had
the supreme genius of his age. The wisdom of the Renaissance, drawn
from many sources, found almost perfect expression in his drama. He
was a full man who loved to talk and to live. Supremely wise, he told all
of life, and with unsurpassed lyric power. Emerson was strongly drawn
to him and to his full-bodied, "pagan" age, even as in other moods he
was drawn toward Montaigne and his skepticism. Yet, Shakespeare was
limited. A masterful poet, he was a piddling priest. He used symbols
with complete mastery, yet he never sought the virtue in his symbols.
Playful, yet not deep, he never developed the highest wisdom, the true
piety and holiness. Swedenborg, with a near excess of moral fervor and
spiritual preachments, had the one virtue needed by Shakespeare, but
spoke in a harsh and joyless voice. If only Shakespeare could have been
a Puritan, he would have outshone Milton, and been closer to Emerson's
model.

Only with mental anguish could Emerson criticize Goethe. He was *the* poet of the nineteenth century, a giant among dwarfs. To Emerson he was also the greatest philosopher, the man of deepest insight. As no one else, he saw truth and knew what man was. He said the best things ever said about nature. In terms of poetic insight, he had no peer. No transcendentalist could do other than bow before his genius. Joined with his insight was an unsurpassed skill as a writer, holding up each object in its right relations. Such a man was so woefully missed in a practical America, where writers were ignored and ideas were subversive, and where even reformers seemed committed to action but not thought. Speculative ideas were too often excluded by the impulsive American, who never realized that great action required spiritual insight. Yet Goethe was not the complete answer, for he was not a complete man. He never ascended the highest ground. He never worshiped the highest unity (Plato's good), for he never surrendered to the moral sentiment. Less talented writers, such as Milton, were wiser and purer. Goethe sought truth for the sake of culture, not for the good. He conquered and subdued the thought of an age of mediocrities, but was never the lawgiver except for the rules of art. He knew so much about art, but was not himself a finished product of art. He was not a poem. Harsh as it had to sound, he lacked the highest type of character. He was the priest of high culture, not of mankind, of truth but not of ideals. He never learned that the "secret of genius" is not only to escape illusion, to know truth, but to realize it, and "first, last, midst and without end, to honor every truth by use." ["Thoughts on Modern Literature," *Works,* XII, 322–32; "Goethe," *Works,* IV, 261–84, 290.]

In his climactic first trip to Europe, Emerson found neither a sufficient model for his own life nor an ideal for American culture. In fact, he repudiated European culture in spite of all its wonderful artifacts. In Goethe he found continental culture at its best. His ultimate reservations undermined a plethora of effusive praise. But his criticism proved his independence and his integrity. He turned from Europe, where "art and not life seems to be the end of their efforts." ["Milton," *Works,* XII, 255–56.] He deliberately rejected the central themes of an aristocratic culture in behalf of a democratic vision. For him as for the most godly Puritans, art had to be either an integrated aspect, a glorification, of daily life, or, in spite of its compelling lures (who could be more susceptible to them than Emerson), dismissed as frivolous. It is really the pseudo artist who sees life as prosaic and creates a death which they call

poetic. It is they who dispatch the day's weary chores and fly to volup-
tuous reveries. Such art, indulgent, escapist, immoral, is decadent,
struck with death from the first. ["Art," *Works,* II, 367.] He feared this
as the consistent end of European culture and desperately wanted to
avoid it for America.

Emerson called artists back from any selfish retreat from life, from
indulgent holidays, and demanded that they embellish the daily existence of man. They had to find and serve their ideals in the functions of
life, in eating and drinking and then, if they desired and time permitted,
in painting and sculpture and literature. In words later endlessly repeated by both John Dewey and George Santayana, Emerson laid down
his challenge: "Beauty must come back to the useful arts, and the distinction between the fine and the useful arts be forgotten. If history were
truly told, if life were nobly spent, it would be no longer easy or possible
to distinguish the one from the other. In Nature, all is useful, all is
beautiful." [*Ibid.,* pp. 367–68.]

Beauty will come unannounced and spring up between the feet of
brave and earnest men. Look for real genius not in old forms or fashionable fads, but find beauty and holiness in new and necessary facts, in the
field and roadside, in the shop and mill. "Beauty should be the dowry of
every man and woman, as invariably as sensation. . . ." ["Prudence,"
Works, II, p. 231.] Art, when proceeding from a religious heart, could
raise to divine use even the railroad and the insurance company, commerce and the galvanic battery, the electric jar and the chemist's retort.
"Is not the selfish and even cruel aspect which belongs to our great
mechanical works, to mills, railroads, and machinery, the effect of the
mercenary impulse which these works obey? When its errands are noble
and adequate, a steamboat bridging the Atlantic between Old and New
England and arriving at its ports with the punctuality of a planet, is a
step of man into harmony with nature. . . . When science is learned in
love, and its powers are wielded by love, they will appear the sup-
plements and continuation of material creation." ["Art," *Works,* II,
367–68.] Here was Emerson's noblest dream, a whole society, in all its
goings and comings, in every moment, reflecting beauty and art. All that
John Dewey could do in his *Art as Experience* was elaborate upon
Emerson's vision. Here was a central impulse of his pragmatism.

From this combined moral and esthetic vantage point, Emerson was
one of the most radical of critics in nineteenth-century America. He did

not go to Brook Farm. Neither did he throw himself into many of the varied reform efforts. He saw the vulgarity and senselessness of Jacksonianism. But he gave a basic, penetrating criticism of American institutions that easily encompassed most of the varied reformers, who were simply tinkering with the pieces of a rotten system. His genteel manner, his sense of fairness, his realistic sense of possibilities, his keen analysis of the immediate pitfalls of any great crusade or revolution, and his refusal to enlist any God or inevitable historical laws to guarantee an early realization of his veiled but challenging heaven, robbed his criticism of the sheer force and energy of a more apocalyptic vision, such as gripped many of the utopian Socialists and even Karl Marx. Tremendous historic changes were triggered by Marx's metamorphosed Christian apocalypticism. But Emerson saw change as morally and esthetically meaningless in itself. In his challenges to New England reformers, he showed that reform demands reformed men, or it is doomed to be one-sided, narrow, and disgusting. However much a sense of alienation, and a humane, even esthetic impulse motivated a sensitive Marx, the political movements which grew out of his energizing vision were soon captive to the same ugly, materialistic system that Emerson decried. Marxism increasingly dealt only with alternative but essentially similar surfaces and led to the same deep futility as capitalism. It lost faith, became impious, and could never become holy. Emerson never hoped to revolutionize the world, saw the tragic element in utopianism, whether called Christian or scientific, and believed a few self-reliant men, possibly in the fields and villages of America, or the blessing of some new beauty here or there, was a realistic and quite sufficient justification for his deepest hopes. His future stretched to infinity; his hopes were tied to a few distant stars.

The same Emerson who could glorify the railroad and steamship as potential works of art constantly damned the commercial age in which he lived. In fact, no more pervasive theme ran through his writing. He glorified in technological progress and in new wealth. He knew, from unending personal experience, the value of money. He never deprecated, but rather pointedly praised the wisdom of Poor Richard, or of the shrewd Yankee. His occasional reverence for Oriental asceticism, or for the abstentious self-denial of some genius, was only because they were necessary disciplines for refining a higher luxury. He never valued denial as a self-justifying virtue. In the same way, material prosperity was

valued as a means to the good life. In an early letter to his brother
William, he discussed their financial problems, emphasizing that he
valued not money, but what money was for—ease, well-being, and fellowship. This was close to Franklin's emphasis upon success as a requisite of both honesty and humane service. But it seemed to Emerson that
a commercial devil had entered America, distorting the moral emphasis,
turning money into a new god, and enslaving a nation for its ignoble
and vulgar service. Thus the central evil of America was a new capitalism, undisciplined by spiritual ends.

In England Emerson, like Marx, analyzed an economy that was several decades ahead of America in manufacturing and applied technology. Here he glimpsed the American future, and in darkest form. England had great wealth, great resources, and an able laboring class. But
wealth was not a servant; the machine dominated the users. In horror he
exclaimed: "A man should not be a silk worm, nor a nation a tent of
caterpillars." ["English Traits," *Works,* V, 167.] The self-reliant English yeoman had become a spider and a needle. Repetitive tasks
dwarfed a man, robbing him of wit and strength and versatility. The end
of an economic system should be the culture of man. In England the
opposite prevailed. There was only falseness, sham, and a growing lack
of quality in all areas of life. Art was being driven from the human
temple. And the dragon money, the satanic finance, was worse even than
the devil machine. England did not rule her own wealth. There were
some good uses, in education and hospitals, but such welfare measures
were frightfully inadequate. The evil required a deeper cure than such
partial palliatives. All Englishmen seemed caught up in a stream of fate,
as victims in a common catastrophe. [*Ibid.,* pp. 160–70.]

In America the same fate was in the offing. In the New England past
the ends sought were good ones and spiritual ones—good sense, beauty,
conversation. The means were consecrated to these ends; even palaces,
servants, banks, and trade were so redeemed. Americans knew that
many authentic goods were unavailable to beggars, that wealth was
necessary to appease as well as to glorify animal cravings. Surely the
smoking chimneys should be cured, the creaking doors silenced, so
friends could gather in warmth and quiet to share truth and beauty. But
too soon men became so immersed in means that their thinking went no
further than the smoke and creaks of life. Soon there was only a ridicu-
lous rich who ruled a false world and a pitiful poor who wanted to be

rich and rule a false world. ["Nature," *Works,* III, 190–91.] The result was an aimless nation, almost incurable in its distortions. A deep melancholy, an inner death, was slowly breaking through all the smiles and gaiety and games of American society.

For those maladies Emerson had no ready answer. The rot was reflected in all institutions, not in one or two. The whole organism was afflicted. He approved some of the limited reforms initiated by other transcendentalists, and, except for abolition, none more than the progressive educational experiments of Bronson Alcott. He despised the new public schools, with their noneducational indoctrination based on conservative fears of the masses. He hated all opiates and diversions and bribes handed to the working classes in order to hide their tragedy or to keep them at work. At the other end of the scale, he decried a selfish scholarship. The pedant, without social conscience, pursuing knowledge for its own sake, was a profane person. He wanted to go well beyond the limits of even educational reform, although the later, broadened conception of education by Dewey would have appealed to him.

Since the whole social body was sick, patching a few parts availed but little. Most reform was addressed to symptoms or, worse, to irrelevancies. Also, American reform usually evolved into some oppressive party or association and soon demanded the sacrifice of deep personal honesty and freedom. The only salvation had to be through individuals. Their redemption could redeem a whole society by a radical change in the conception and use of existing institutions, rather than in founding new institutions. Communities do not purify men. Purified men form pure communities, founded in the ultimate unity of their individual truths. But again, and ultimately, the leverage for any progress was only in the flaming prophet, the poet-priest, a man of insight, eloquence, and moral passion. Only such a man could help uncover the genius in all men, a genius Emerson never doubted. Only in its actualization, only in divine man, could heaven exist. And for them, it exists already and always.

Emerson deserves profound respect. The respect must precede all standard classifications. As soon as he is classified as either a poet, prophet, philosopher, or social reformer, some of the respect is dissipated by his evident limitations. But by his own classification, as a poet-priest, he has no peer. No other calling demands such awesome talents. He was a pious and holy man, a truly tender-minded pragmatist. Charles

Peirce, William James, and John Dewey, the last spiritual children of Puritan New England, were all impelled by his themes, but none kept the same fruitful if fragile balance between poetic rapture, intellectual sophistication, and moral fervor. In fact, no one else in American history ever achieved it. Yet, the pragmatists tried. In them the less rapturous, the more disciplined concepts of philosophy never concealed, nor were they intended to conceal, a fervent and moral commitment to the nonconceptual richness of life as experienced. They could only explore what Emerson spent a lifetime celebrating.

PART THREE

THREE PRAGMATISTS

VI
CHARLES S. PEIRCE

LIFE

In all that he attempted, Charles S. Peirce expressed a sense of grandeur and of vastness, of soaring possibility and worldshaking significance. Perhaps the sense of grandeur fit his expectations and matched his brilliance. But it often contrasted sharply with his achievements. In every area, from personal relationships to philosophic endeavors, he did not quite live up to his promise. His personal life was a failure, dramatic and tragic in contrast to the heroic aspect of his ideals. His magnificent edifice of thought, original in so many of its details, tantalizing in its promise, remained incomplete and fragmentary.

Peirce had the ambition and many of the intellectual attributes of Jonathan Edwards. In New England, he was Edwards' first real successor, the first to reason so exactly, to probe so deeply, to seek such a complete, all-embracing system of philosophy. Like Edwards, he sought a vast, architectonic structure, encompassing all knowledge, perfectly unifying religion and science, and explaining everything, past and future. He wanted to read the cosmos aright, for he believed it to be a living symbol of a divinity that wanted to be fully comprehended. But such a grand system was more difficult in the nineteenth century than it had been in the eighteenth. It had to be evolutionary and dynamic as well as logical and experimental. It had to be built on shifting and treacherous physical sciences, on new but precarious systems of logic, on a ferment of mathematical speculation, and on an input of new psychological theory. Because of intellectual bent, Peirce first tried to ground his system on the eternal forms of thought. Later he added a phenomenology and tried to interpret the immediate, unreflective qualities of experience. Doggedly, laboriously, he kept working at his system, changing, altering, restating. More and more materials were assembled. The structure grew and became almost too vast for comprehension. But it could not be finished. Only a half-mad genius would have kept at it so long against so many odds.

Eccentricity and unconventionality, if not madness, was a tradition in the Peirce family. Fully convinced of his own bizarre and wrongheaded qualities, which he often explained by his left-handedness, Peirce rather delighted in some of his infamous forebears, including criminals, heretics, and, almost as bad in the Massachusetts setting, his proslavery father, Benajmin Peirce. Benjamin was the country's leading mathematician, a respected professor at Harvard, and prominent in the best social circles of New England. Yet, he was subject to violent outbreaks of temper, was not always circumspect in personal relationships, and apparently cultivated eccentricities in dress and behavior.

Born in 1839, Charles grew up in the midst of the transcendentalist movement as well as the less lofty political crises that preceded the Civil War. Most of the transcendentalists, including Emerson, were family friends. Yet, his father's social views and his own early bent for mathematics and physical science, provided what he later called an antiseptic against the transcendentalist virus. But after he developed his own form of idealistic philosophy, he decided that a benign form of the disease had lingered in his soul, to reappear after long incubation, modified by a new logic and by his physical inquiries. He successfully stayed aloof from the slavery issue, apparently sympathizing in part with his father's views. He deliberately avoided the Civil War draft and almost never referred to the war in his correspondence.

Charles was his father's favorite and paid dearly for it later. Benjamin responded to Charles's evident precocity and to his aptitude for mathematics and any type of abstract thought. Much too early, he led the boy into the intricacies of mathematics and philosophy and into such pastimes as chess and number games. The father's demands for exactness and precision helped create an intellectual standard, a logical ethic, that Charles never forgot but could never quite live up to. Later he moralized logic as thoroughly as any other Puritan ever tried to moralize art. Outside his world of forms, Peirce was a misfit. The father shielded a sometimes arrogant, always frightened, often rebellious Charles from a hostile, less forgiving, and more demanding world of peers and institutional authority. In practical things, he was overindulged and spoiled. His one-sided intellectual development became an escape, a compensation for social inadequacies, for a lack of self-discipline, and for an inability to assume adult responsibilities. He always remained a petulant, endearing, infuriating, overindulged child. Even his beloved father became an ambivalent figure, of near perfection and horrible domination, requiring reverence but often causing resentment. In later life, Charles continually praised his father, as if still clinging to his support. Perhaps significantly, he almost never mentioned his mild, yielding mother, who seems to have left no impression and to have commanded no great respect.

Benjamin Peirce was a fervently religious but unorthodox Christian. A Unitarian, he still fought the useless battle against real or imagined Calvinist doctrines, and thereby helped create in Charles a distaste for theology and for all Unitarian negations. Benjamin used mathematical demonstrations for religious purposes. He accepted the nebular hypothesis and thus a type of pre-Darwinian cosmic evolution. The process of development out of a primal, homogenous chaos required an exertion of force by the creator but continued by purely mechanical law. This was paralleled by a spiritual evolution and tied to it by a pre-established harmony. The discovery of reality through science was a religious duty and ultimately was destined to lead to a final truth or to the revealed order of a divine geometer. Charles would keep much of the outline, but change most of the details. He never rejected his father's faith that mathematical and scientific truth are insights into the divine plan of the world.

Charles had a poor record as a student. With some justice, he placed all the blame on the rote system of teaching. Coming from a free and near anarchic home atmosphere, Peirce could not or would not conform to the then strict requirements of both lower schools and Harvard College. He was often tardy or absent and was usually sloppy and perfunctory in his work. He did what he pleased and, with a rapier wit that marked his lifetime of controversy, usually succeeded in angering instead of impressing his teachers. His poorly prepared school exercises contrasted sharply with imaginative stories he invented for his three brothers and one sister and with an insatiable curiosity about almost any subject. According to an in part self-perpetuated legend, he began an intensive and avid study of logic at twelve, and of scientific subjects even earlier. But he never learned to write with ease and felicity.

Pushed by his father, he entered Harvard at sixteen. He finished near the bottom of his class. Had it not been for his father's position on the faculty, he might not have survived an almost constant stream of disciplinary problems. Harvard was still operated like a grammar school, and Peirce hated the restrictions. He cut benches as well as classes, missed chapel, and once had to be carried home from Boston dead drunk. A graduate in 1859, he took enough additional courses to take the then almost meaningless M.A. in 1862. More important, he also entered Harvard's new Lawrence Scientific School and, working under Louis Agassiz, Jeffries Wyman, and Asa Gray, took a chemistry B.S. *summa cum laude* in 1863. This was the basis of his later listing his profession as chemist. It also revealed to him a new type of education, which was tied to the laboratory and not to lectures and boring recitations.

As a young man, Peirce gained a family reputation as a budding Casanova. He liked beautiful women. Even more, he needed, for practical and emotional reasons, protective and long-suffering females. Not that he deserved them. He too easily shifted from dependence and child-like endearments to insufferable cruelty. But he had perfect assets for attracting certain types of women. He was dark and swarthy, of medium height, and universally accounted quite handsome. Somewhat of a dandy, he always dressed smartly. A brilliant conversationalist, he loved to entertain people. Half of his life involved some type of dramatic pose. Perhaps even more important, he was a failure and a genius. Motherly types with intellectual interests saw in him an opportunity and an obligation. They could become soulmates, guard him against his indiscretions, nurture his talents, and give him to the world, living in the glow of his greatness. He played on this theme himself, even overstressing his social inadequacies and begging for someone to like him. Harriet Melusina (Zina) Fay first responded to his appeal, becoming his wife-mother in 1862.

The Fays had long been family friends. Zina was not a beauty, but she was an intellectual and a budding feminist. Three years older than Charles, infinitely more self-possessed and mature, she easily gained the respect of the Peirce family. The marriage was premature, since Charles had no means to support a wife. This childless marriage lasted for thirteen years (legally for eighteen). Zina poured her reform zeal not only into an errant Charles but into the Episcopal Church (she helped bring Charles permanently into the church), into feminism, and into an aborted effort at cooperative housekeeping. She tried to keep Peirce out of major trouble. With her help, he attained the highest level of occupational stability of his career. She moderated his habitual extravagance and softened his illusions of grandeur. Toward him she was jealous and possessive. After all, he was her prize. She suffered him and tried to redeem him into the ornament his genius augured. He depended on her, especially when in dire straits, but seemed to resent her and kept slipping from her protective arms. Peirce could be possessed only at a dear price. He was often cruel, disloyal, suspicious, and neurotic. In the end, Zina gave up the battle and relinquished Peirce to his own unguided and demonic fate. He had not responded to her efforts at reform, and if anything had grown worse.

Even while Zina tried to cope with Peirce's erratic personality, his father continued to look after his education and career. Benjamin Peirce had long been a consulting geometer for the United States Coast and Geodetic Survey, and would become its superintendent in 1867. Thus, scientific friends in the Survey obligingly provided summer jobs for his Harvard undergraduates. As early as 1858 Charles joined a surveying party in Maine, and after taking his B.A. spent part of a year in Mississippi and Louisiana. Even as he continued part-time work for the Survey, he obtained (again his father exerted influence) part-time work as an assistant to the director of the Harvard Observatory. Here he did the work in photometrics (exact measurements by light waves) that led to his only published book, which anticipated the much more elaborate work of Albert A. Michelson. He also secured temporary Harvard lectureships in logic in 1865–66 and 1869–70.

In the midst of these varied activities, none rigid in requirements of time and attention, Peirce studied logic and philosophy, paying near exhaustive attention to Kant, to aspects of scholasticism, and to English logic and psychology. With the help of William T. Harris, he published his first philosophical articles in *The Journal of Speculative Philosophy*. Informally, and in the planned meeting of a metaphysical club, he debated with such young men as William James, Oliver W. Holmes, Jr., and Francis E. Abbot. They all drew on the wisdom, on the tough-minded criticism, of Chauncey Wright, a Socratic scientist and lay philosopher. In these Harvard years he developed the first statement of his philosophy and both stimulated and mystified his friends.

Peirce hoped for a permanent appointment at Harvard. But his field (logic and scientific philosophy), his lack of a Ph.D., and his notorious perverseness overrode his father's prestige. His less brilliant but better behaved brother later became head of Harvard's mathematics department. No other university wanted a person with Charles's ability and liabilities. Later, his separation and divorce from Zina, gossip about even more serious indiscretions, a typical quarrel with President Charles W. Eliot over the pay for his observatory work, and finally his affair with, and eventual marriage to, his second wife all combined to block any chance for a Harvard position, despite the long efforts of William James.

Peirce took the one available career opportunity. When his father became head of the Coast Survey, he made Charles his assistant. He briefly headed the Washington office and then directed a vast program of gravitational research through pendulum oscillation. His work was inventive and pace-setting. He was soon the foremost pendulum swinger in the world. He spent several years, particularly in the 1870's, traveling over the United States, living in out-of-the-way camps, and swinging pendulums under every type of physical handicap, all in behalf of an exact measurement of the earth's shape. He prepared accounts for scientific meetings in Europe as well as in America and helped establish a scientific reputation for the Survey. But he was a loose administrator, dependent on assistants for the more difficult work, totally inept in accounting for expenditures, grandly extravagant in purchases, less than fair in his work accounts, slow in compiling and reporting test results, and touchy in his dealings with both superiors and subordinates.

Zina left Peirce while he was on a scientific trip to Europe in 1875–76. On the trip Peirce not only spent more than his estimated budget (a standard procedure for him) but lost contact with Washington because of his own failure to send forwarding addresses. Thus, worried about money, deserted (his term) by his wife, and overworked and probably overindulged, he became morose and, for the first of numerous times, succumbed to a severe if brief mental breakdown. Seemingly a type of hysteria, it led to almost complete paralysis. With his father's help, and after a brief visit by Zina, he was able to return to

America. A lifetime connoisseur of fine and expensive wines, he nevertheless insisted that he had not drunk excessively. But he was at least profligate with his time and incapable of managing his own affairs. It is even possible that he met his second wife, the mysterious Madame Juliette Pourtalai, during this extended stay in France. In any case, he was corresponding with her in less than two years after his breakdown.

In 1879 President Daniel C. Gilman of the new Johns Hopkins University appointed Peirce part-time lecturer in logic. For five years he received such an annual appointment, always hoping for the professorship in philosophy, but retaining the security of his Survey post. At Hopkins Peirce did his best work in mathematics, logic, and scientific methodology. He loved teaching, effectively inspiring mathematically inclined and advanced students. He was even able to publish one group of seminar papers. But he was typically erratic in attendance and could not adhere to a normal academic calendar. As expected, he also became ensnared in controversy (over editorial procedures and scholarly precedence) with Hopkins' best mathematician. Peirce had some justice on his side, and felt aggrieved. Yet, his academic performance apparently satisfied Gilman, so much so that he was virtually assured of a professorship and bought a house. Then, by devious maneuvers and on the basis of carefully secreted, derogatory information of a moral nature, Johns Hopkins dismissed Peirce in 1884, later paying him $1,000 for losses on his house. Simon Newcomb, a pompous but respected mathematician and scientist, apparently provided the damning evidence. Peirce left without enduring bitterness. He also left with a large number of books that he had sold to the Hopkins' library but retained for his own use. Despite endless appeals, some were never returned.

Peirce married his mysterious Juliette in 1882, only a few months after his divorce from Zina. Obviously, Juliette had been his consort long before the divorce, to the scandal of family and friends. Who was Madame Pourtalai? No one knows for sure. She embellished her own past with grandiose claims about nobility and secret plots, none of which were quite believable at face value. Although listed as her second marriage, nothing is known of her first. She was youthful (about twenty-six to Peirce's forty-three), plain, sickly, and very possessive. She tended toward extravagance, posed as a person of refined taste, and could not manage Peirce's practical affairs nearly as well as Zina. But her devotion to Peirce was complete; her care was indispensable to him as he grew older. Toward her he was alternatively tender and cruel, carrying her upstairs in her illness, or berating her like a child. Intensely proud, without a good command of English, Juliette made few friends and usually seemed a meek backdrop to Peirce. But in times of crisis she worked assiduously to help her husband, and she idealized him after his death. In later years their mutual dependence was so complete as to conceal any strangeness or morbidity in the relationship.

After his dismissal from Hopkins, Peirce had only his position with the Survey, with a then quite adequate salary of $3,000 a year. A congressional inquiry in 1885 indicted the Survey for its loose policies and extravagant expenditures, some of which could be attributed to Peirce. A new superintendent, with no memories of Benjamin (who died in 1882) and no special friendship for Charles, initiated a new era of close accounting and formalized procedures. Charles was retained because of his knowledge and the large investment in his pendulum researches. But his funds were now limited, and he had to fight an unending bureaucratic war to get anything he needed. Slowly, he was restricted in his research, which was now directed by another employee. In his frustration, Peirce held on to his position out of a desperate need for money. The Survey kept him in a losing gamble to get some return from his expensive experiments, whose results had never been fully collected and prepared for publication. Peirce lost interest and endlessly failed to meet promised deadlines on manuscripts. He completed only a part of his final report, but provided the data for other men, who published the results and ended up with most of the credit. When asked to resign in 1891, he was no longer of any real value to the Survey, and had not been for some years.

In 1887 the Peirces moved to Milford, Pennsylvania, a resort town on the Delaware River, in Pike County. It was not a retirement from the world or a philosophic retreat. Juliette was not welcome in Boston; in fact, many of Peirce's old friends would not accept her socially. The old haunts were effectively closed. Peirce, as a member of the Century Club in New York City, became acquainted with several men who had vacationed at Milford. Possibly the large number of French families in the Milford area attracted Juliette. Milford was the country home of the wealthy and prominent Pinchot family. Whether or not previously acquainted with Juliette, Mrs. James W. Pinchot, the mother of Gifford, became the closest friend of the Peirces. Peirce came to Milford with illusions of wealth and fame and was so accepted locally. At least until the depression of 1893, which brought dire poverty to the Peirces, Charles and Juliette seemed to lead a gay, socially prominent life, with parties, dinners, and theater trips to New York. They were a hit at the Pinchots, where Peirce entertained by readings and by brilliant conversation. Juliette mystified people by accounts of her past and by fortune telling. She was esteemed locally for her "continental" taste.

With his mother's death in the fall of 1887, Peirce received his family inheritance. Another small bequest came from an aunt in 1888. This, added to his Survey salary and to small sums for articles in the *Nation* or for the *Century Dictionary,* plus a small annuity of Juliette's, gave him the illusion of wealth. In Juliette's name, they bought several tracts of land around Milford, totaling about 2,000 acres. Peirce found financial speculation of all types almost irresistible, and would become involved in several promotional schemes in the 1890's. Even the best of this land had to be sold later, and at a loss. On one favored plot, overlooking the Delaware River, he and Juliette erected their own country estate (the local newspaper referred to it as a French villa "a la tuxedo"), which they carefully and elaborately planned by themselves. The house was two and one-half stories, large, and luxurious in detail, at least inside. As planned, it was to contain over twenty rooms, including an entrance gallery, a large library-study for Peirce, and spacious dining and drawing rooms. It had such extras as a servants' dining room, an elaborate kitchen, full steam heat, several baths, and a fireplace in each room. Part of the second floor was never completed, but even in the midst of direst poverty Peirce found money to hire a gardener and to make needed repairs on his castle, which he named Arisbe. At times he thought of turning the house and nearby cottages into a casino for fashionable people, or perhaps into a small institute for students of logic. He even tried to sell stock, at one point when his finances were low, in a company which would make Arisbe into an institution for the pursuit of pure science and philosophy.

Peirce, with a typical lack of realism, overextended himself in the new house. He lost his salary in 1891 and, as assured income, had only irregular checks for articles. But because of the generosity of the *Nation,* of the publishers of the *Monist* and *Open Court,* and some translation work provided by the Smithsonian Institution, his average income was enough for a good livelihood and was surely well above the income of most American families. But it could not support Peirce's lavish habits. The depression that began in 1893 completely bankrupted him. Despite near desperate, at times hypocritical efforts to make money, he spent the rest of his life in debt and after 1905 was completely dependent upon charity. Most of the land had to be sold to pay off creditors. As early as 1893, Peirce threatened suicide (possibly sheer dramatics). By 1895 he had turned over all his assets to a lawyer who was to pay off debts by future royalties and earnings. Yet, in Milford, Peirce was able to keep up a pose of affluence for several years, but tax claims brought him into a series of court litigations which revealed his poverty. Peirce retained the use of Arisbe, but only by complicated legal maneuvers and large mortgage encumbrances.

His hardship came too late for any new beginnings. By 1900 Peirce was over sixty. Career opportunities seemed all in the past. Yet, he kept trying and hoping. Several universities made overtures, friends recommended him for posts, arousing false hopes. He sought government jobs and, swallowing all his pride, even tried to get back on the Coast Survey staff. He offered to teach almost any subject and even tried to trade on his religiosity. Contrary to a popular legend, he was well-known and had friends who were strategically placed in government and in the academic world. He tried to capitalize on kinship to Henry Cabot Lodge, on his brother's status at Harvard, and even on William James's friendship. His plight was almost a *cause célèbre*. Here was a genius, unsupported and neglected, awaiting an opportunity to create a great system of philosophy. Even President Theodore Roosevelt supported his last great hope, a bid for a newly created Carnegie grant. Everything failed.

He still suffered from personal scandals, but except for Harvard and Hopkins, they were fading into the distant past. More crucial, Peirce had gained a just reputation for beginning grandiose projects and never completing them. He had constantly reneged on commitments to publishers, whom he besieged with projects for texts, encyclopedias, almanacs, and scientific dictionaries. He tried to market great plans but rarely had a finished product. Two long-suffering publishers waited years for promised texts in logic and in science. He had difficulty meeting his own standards and was always reluctant to release any lengthy work. As time passed, and revisions multiplied, he lost interest and never finished them. Despite editors' efforts, he could never bring himself to turn loose even a collection of past articles. They needed more work. Meanwhile, he kept up a steady stream of planned projects— academies, institutes, summer schools, and new professional journals. He invented a new dyeing process, a new type of acetylene lighting, and even worked at a flying machine. He tried to sell his services to businessmen and even revised his pragmatism in part because he hoped for fame and, above all, some fortune.

At last, and not because he wished it, Peirce did become a recluse. He spent his last years at Arisbe revising his philosophy. Often he worked all night, without an adequate diet and, at least during a coal strike, in the bitter cold. Juliette was constantly ill, so that the expense of a New York hospital was added to everything else. Peirce suffered from mental depression and from varied bodily ills, some quite severe.

Next to the Pinchots, William James was now the Peirce's closest friend. He was able to bring Peirce, a near legendary figure to Harvard philosophy students, to Boston in 1898 to give a series of lectures in a private home, paying him more than an ample fee as an indirect means of aid. The Harvard Corporation would not even let the aging philosopher lecture on campus. But in 1903 Harvard finally relented (by then they were desperately trying to keep James from resigning) and allowed Peirce to give a lecture series, which was followed by his last Lowell lectures. These lectures, on the theme of pragmatism, forced Peirce into a final revision of his philosophy. He worked best under some pressure, such as lecture deadlines. After these public appearances, James, with the aid of the Pinchots, made up an annual Peirce fund, contributed to by numerous unnamed friends (of James as well as Peirce). This provided up to $1,300 a year after 1907. It went to Juliette and kept the Peirces eating. William James died in 1910, but the fund continued. Often Peirce had been jealous of James and had severely criticized his philosophy. But he probably loved James above all men and added Santiago to his own name in 1909. In 1911 he praised his departed friend effusively, as a man poor in logic but who loved truth and was, in practice, a wonderful psychologist. James knew Peirce and saw through all his bluff and bluster, yet loved him without taking him too seriously. No one else was so generous and forgiving.

Behind his affectations, and in spite of his tender-skinned and perverse vindictiveness, Peirce could be an appealing person. Catholic in interests, original and creative in all areas, stimulating in conversation, he could entertain and educate friends for hours on end. Although he claimed a linguistic disability, he could write sharply and cleverly. He mastered French and German sufficiently for freehand translations and as a child had learned well his Latin and Greek, both of which he used. But when he left the security of informal conversation, Peirce could be rude and insulting. Often in lectures he disingenuously played the martyr, put upon and unappreciated. He made a pretense of making greater effort and of having the capacity for far deeper thought than anyone else, and might contemptuously accuse an audience of intellectual trifling. To boost his own beleaguered ego, he loved to dismiss other philosophers as superficial or trite or illogical. Consistently, he was at his best in defending underdogs and in resurrecting the most obscure and forgotten of men. Again as a defensive measure, he repudiated all concern for popularity and dismissed fluency and good style as the antipathy of good thinking. His demeanor could shift abruptly from tearful humility and self-deprecation to unbelievable self-praise.

But his basic aims and attitudes were consistent. His philosophy grew only in order to incorporate new arguments or new data. His central task, as he early saw it, was the refutation of a morally debasing and irreligious nominalism (alias sensationalism, materialism, individualism, and determinism) and the convincing refurbishing of an extreme form of logical realism, expressed as a form of objective idealism and in the context of an evolutionary teleology. This was no mean task in the late nineteenth century; it was one which, he foresaw, would lead through the thorniest mazes of logic and metaphysics. The outcome was vital. If he could attain his objective, then men could again believe in something common and general, in the possibility of a beloved community or kingdom of heaven, and in something of greater worth, dignity, and importance than the individual's desire for survival and happiness.

Peirce found the main ingredients of a sound, realistic philosophy in Aristotle, in the classic Christian heritage, and in scholasticism. But these needed the support of a better, less static system of logic, a system inherent in modern scientific inquiry but awaiting explicit statement. On the other hand, modern science had lacked a sound metaphysics, too easily falling prey to a lame Cartesian dualism, to feigned skepticism, and to the extreme nominalism of atomistic psychology. German idealists, lost in subjectivism, shallow logic, and theological pleading, were next to useless, although correct at points. But Kant, their often misused progenitor, began the needed reconstruction and had the greatest direct impact on Peirce. Kant lacked logical finesse; Peirce had it. He would rescue Kant from obvious mistakes, improve upon his categories, but fulfill his central belief—that the correct view of reality lurked in the inescapable and universal logical forms of thought.

With defiant glee, Peirce claimed to be a disciple of Duns Scotus and the later scholastics. Here he found a subtle and sophisticated form of realism, fully consistent with modern science, but hidden behind overly formal methods of argument and an unappetizing theology. In stressing this allegiance, Peirce only roughly embraced a doctrine, but exactly proclaimed an ideal self-image. He yearned for a past age and spirit, typified not only by the selfless industry of Scotus, but by the anonymous toilers on a Gothic cathedral, or the loving scholarship of dedicated monks. Here was a perfect model of cooperative truth-seeking, paralleled, if at all, only by a few modern scientists.

Like the scholastics, Peirce wanted a philosophy that was true and not merely instrumental. To him, philosophy was a science, with a subject matter all its own—the universal phenomena of common experience. Like Spencer, he wanted philosophy to be the superscience, dealing with overarching and cosmic themes, while the special sciences dealt with isolated and unusual data. He tried to approach philosophy with the methodological rigor he identified with science, beginning with a total exclusion of personal interests. Philosophical inquiry had to be completely segregated from practical arts, from ordinary life, where custom, instinct, and private interest, not reasoned inquiry, were the necessary guidelines. The long-range welfare of mankind depended on a sound philosophy, but as a creature of habits and instincts, most of which could only be changed over generations, man gained little immediate value from either the philosophical or the special sciences. For his own life, he could excuse his aberrant behavior as the result of unsound instincts, not as the result of his philosophical theories. His ideals, which he often framed in light of his own mistakes, could only slowly be transformed into living beliefs, or into new habits, which did indeed mark the final goal of any philosophical labor.

Peirce wanted not only substance but order. His bent was ever toward complete synthesis. Like the Puritan who toiled at his systematic classification of all the arts, Peirce tried to build his philosophy into a vast, architectonic whole. He labored for years on a correct classification of all the sciences. Today, his efforts often seem arbitrary or merely clever, as if one arrangement had any but a functional advantage over another. But Peirce wanted a true classification, one that conformed to the structure of reality. He classified as an act of piety, in order to elaborate the order of creation and the intentions of God. To order, to classify correctly, was equivalent to worship. His faith in the reality of law, habit, and continuity lay behind his Atlas-like attempts to set it down aright. Even in language, he wanted order and fitness. Not only did he carry on a lifetime campaign for precision and for an ethic of nomenclature, but he also had a feeling for the natural and correct word, for the fittest language for expressing the form of an evolving universe. Thus, he was deadly serious when he talked about the principles of word formation or about the general laws of symbols. One of his first philosophical contributions was in the field of signs, or semiotic.

Peirce died in the spring of 1914. His last years were sad ones, marked by constant illness and dashed hopes. A Promethean figure for so long, Peirce finally learned resignation. The talk of great unfinished schemes slowly gave way to realistic doubts. For years he had felt it his mission, his God-appointed task, to bring the world a new system of philosophy, more comprehensive and more true than any before it. He failed to achieve his purpose and calling, and this is all the more tragic because of his failures in everything else and because of the degree of dedication and integrity that he preserved in his philosophy. His varied bodily ills (falsely attributed to cancer) were soothed by morphine, and his ever luminous mind gave out only sporadic flashes. There was now only Juliette and an English correspondent, Lady Victoria Welby, a semanticist whom Peirce had praised and who appreciated and comforted from afar. At death, the uncompleted mansion was already falling into disrepair; the grounds were overgrown. The cremated remains of Peirce were eventually buried at Milford, beside Juliette. She died in 1934, after a solitary and penurious life as an eccentric recluse, living alone in a room of the crumbling mansion, surrounded only by the artifacts and the haunting spirit of her "Professor" Peirce.

Arisbe soon lay in disarray, too grandiose to complete, too ambitious to maintain, but always impressive in the hopes and dreams that it symbolized. Peirce's philosophy was a much more enduring edifice, but was likewise uncompleted and always in need of repairs. An architect with uncompromising vision, Peirce would have nothing less than a great philosophical mansion, a dwelling place for every human concern, and a point of departure for every specialized inquiry. He wanted to provide an intellectual system comparable to that of Aristotle. And in the published fragments of a system, in the chaotic wealth of unpublished material, and in the fermenting ideas yet unarticulated, Peirce thought he had attained his goal. Maybe he did. If he could only have written it, made it clear, and given it all to the world. If! If! Peirce still lives under the haunting shadow of Philosophy's greatest "might have been."

SIGNS AND RELATIONS

For Peirce, who almost memorized the *Critique of Pure Reason,* philosophy had to begin where Kant began. The ontological validity of knowledge had to be defended against the skepticism of the English empiricists. To do this, one had to explore the thought processes in minutest detail and see what they revealed. Clearly, the problems were semantical and logical. Thought involved signs, usually of a linguistic type, related to each other in propositions and arguments. Peirce spent a lifetime classifying signs and trying to determine the exact laws or the formal principles revealed in their relationships.

From the beginning, Peirce rejected one of Kant's most controversial doctrines, the incognizable thing-in-itself. Peirce stood in horror of anything incognizable; he hated unknowns. His hatred of nominalism was in part a hatred of any gulf between experienced phenomena and some inexplicable ground of phenomena. Reality was knowable, even if in part unknown at any one time or by any and all minds. At the same time he rejected any intuitive knowledge, or any direct acquaintance with reality that bypassed normal cognition. Thus, the phenomenon of cognition had to be of the same nature as reality, and reality had to be cognizable. This meant a type of realism, but also seemed to mean an extreme idealism, beset by all types of epistemological traps. Historically, the escape from the extreme solipsism implicit in such phenomenalism lay in some form of objective mind, or in a pantheistic theism. Berkeley, much admired by Peirce, resorted to a theistic crutch, or to a fully cognizant, sustaining God. This left an intolerable intellectual gulf, but alleviated the skepticism and the deleterious moral effects of an extremely nominalistic conception of phenomena. Peirce too would spend a lifetime trying to bolster and solidify a better form of objective idealism. But all his elaborate evidence remained indicative; his best arguments enriched but did not prove the position.

Peirce began his creative work in the Civil War period; he went back to Kant and tried to improve upon his system. Working with the conventional psychology, he believed with Kant that the manifold of sense (the sensa of Berkeley) was reduced to unity by constituent elements of mind (almost the old idea of mental faculties) or by universal elementary conceptions that arise upon the occasion of experience. But since they do not come from experience, they are a priori relational concepts, which have to be discovered by formal logical analysis. Empirical psychology can discover the occasion for the introduction of such conceptions, but not their formal properties. In his own analysis, he accepted as basic the two conceptions of substance and being, corresponding closely to the subject and predicate of a proposition. Between these poles he found three other elemental conceptions: reference to a ground (quality), reference to a correlate (relation), and reference to an interpretant (representation). Thus, in publishing his new list of categories in 1867, he had reduced Kant's twelve to only five. Subsequently, he dropped substance and being and, guided by a new logic of relations, significantly transformed the other three into his famous triad of firstness, secondness, and thirdness.

In the midst of this neo-Kantian analysis, he found something more basic even than the five categories. All thinking involves representation, or signs. The standard indicative proposition is one type of sign relationship. If reality is on the same order as thought, as Peirce's early phenomenal idealism dictated, and as he would always believe, then reality itself is governed by the same relational laws that govern signs. This opened up a possibility of an objective logic on the order of Hegel's. Also, his categories, which were necessarily ontological as well as logical entities, could be derived from a careful analysis of the nature of signs. Even God and man, insofar as they are real, had to have the same mode of being as signs.

Since the structure of thought (and thus of reality) was revealed in the way signs function, then for almost all practical purposes it was also revealed in ordinary language. Here Peirce was undoubtedly influenced by Chauncey Wright, who, with no concern for ontological problems and within a biological and functional instead of an idealistic context, continuously emphasized language behavior as the key to the traditional concept of mind. Peirce's elaborate analysis of the inherent qualities of signs represented a more intensive, more formal, but often less fruitful treatment of language than the complementary studies of Wright, Dewey, and George Herbert Mead.

For Peirce there were three ways in which signs represented their object—as icons, indices, and symbols. Icons share a quality of the object that they represent. They illustrate and heighten predicated qualities. They include pictures, diagrams, images, or any other type of likeness. Icons became very important to Peirce, for he emphasized the role of icons or diagrams in all mathematical discourse.

Indices correspond to an object in fact rather than in quality. They directly relate to their object in terms of time, space, or causality, and thus denote or point to it. A weather vane, a pointing finger, and even an inflection of voice are good examples. Any existential proposition always contains an index, be it only a gesture on the part of the speaker.

But by far the most important functional type of sign is the symbol, which is the typical sign in thought and therefore in language (although a word, in addition to its symbolic function, may serve as an index by its pointing function). A symbol is related to its object only by means of an imputed character, implying that the relationship is dialogistic (it may be the dialogue between two of our selves separated by time). Without an interpreter, a symbol loses its sign status. The object referred to by the material aspect of a symbol is necessarily a matter of convention. Peirce noted the necessity of a common ground of understanding between two minds in communication and late in life referred to this as the communicational interpretant, which is remarkably similar to Dewey's definition of mind. Obviously, symbols only relate to categorical thirdness, or representation. Symbols do not identify things, but lead individuals to imagine things. The mental image so produced would be an icon. Indices lead to direct perception; symbols produce imaginary concepts.

Beyond this basic triad of signs, Peirce worked out further complex, always triadic classifications, much too involved for simple explication. He classified signs not only according to how they relate to their object, but by what they are intrinsically and by the form of representation they communicate. He subdivided symbols into terms, propositions, and arguments; divided terms into breadth, depth, and information; and divided arguments into inductive, deductive, and abductive (often called retroduction). He distinguished genuine and degenerate forms of signs, drew the rather obvious relations between signs and the categories, and tied his signs to traditional logical classifications. In all, he worked out sixty-six classes of signs and was still classifying in his last three years of life.

To Peirce, the key to all thinking and to all soliloquy and communication was the efficacy of a symbol in determining an interpretant in the mind of an interpreter or, in other words, its ability to transmit a meaning. The interpretant is not only the effect of a sign, but what makes a word, or an explosion of breath, function as a sign. In effective discourse, a word functions as a rule, determining its interpretant with some degree of precision and predictability. Peirce called the mere sound a replica of a symbol. But the living word is the true symbol and depends upon acquired interpretive habits or laws. As late as 1907, Peirce distinguished three interpretants present with any sign: an emotional (the feeling produced), a muscular (any signal effect on the body), and a logical (the meaning conveyed). All his interest centered on the logical interpretant, or the rational significance, which he often referred to as the ultimate interpretant. But, as he always insisted, this logical interpretant had, as an object, some other sign. He would allow no leap beyond symbols to some hidden substance. Only his almost incidental reference to a communicational interpretant allowed an opening into an ultimate interpretative ground, and this was also only a world of cohering signs, or a transpersonal body of meanings.

In all his early work on signs Peirce was mired in a rigid phenomenalism. He tried to escape it by a confusing and infinitely projected idea of reality, but with poor success. Without desiring it, he offered a conceptualism not unlike Kant's, or even such hated nominalists as Occam. For, if he permitted anything other than a symbol to be the object of a symbol, he slipped into a dualism between an unknowable object and its cognitive offspring. One meaning had to point to another if everything were fully cognizable. In a pure sign world one word could only be defined by another, and so on ad infinitum. There seemed no way to end the process of signification except by some unknowable substance behind the world of phenomena, a solution adopted by Kant but abhorred by Peirce.

Peirce escaped the phenomenal trap by positing, and trying to validate, a cohering world of signs, or a cosmic mind which stood as the ultimate court of appeal. The regress of signs interpreting signs properly ended in the sign which was a perfect, living symbol of the divine mind. So far, this is simply a commonplace position for an idealist, but Peirce's definition of the terminal sign was unique. By 1900 he had finally concluded that this terminal interpretant, this final and ultimate logical interpretant, is a habit, and thus made his semiotic an essential part of his pragmatism. Reality still had a sign character, since it was mind. But a living habit, itself general in nature and of the mode of being of mind, was a final interpretant of any series of purely verbal meanings. The type of causation present in habit, as in thought, was teleological or final. In both man and nature, rational action or conduct was subservient to a final goal or end, which was the end to be finally attained by a process of cosmic evolution. Thus, a habit in man or in nature was a very special type of sign, being a living symbol of God's purpose.

Peirce endlessly elaborated upon, but never finally settled, the relation of semiotic and logic and the relation of logic and mathematics. In a limited usage, Peirce's logic had dealt only with arguments, and these made up only one of three classifications of symbols. Thus, it was a development of a subcategory of a general theory of signs. Yet, in defining logic, Peirce divided the subject into three parts, beginning with speculative grammar, which included an analysis of the essential elements of assertions, or a theory of signs. To compound the contradictions, he argued at another time that logic should be founded, not on feeling or the results of some special science like psychology, but on speculative grammar and a matured semiotic. This, he argued, was undebatable. Clearly, Peirce did not always use words precisely. In a total classification of sciences, logic was, along with metaphysics, a branch of philosophy, and included speculative grammar as one division. Outside this special classification, Peirce used logic in a more limited, popular sense, to encompass only the science of reasoning, or of proper inference, which was subsidiary to his semiotic but prior to his metaphysics. Yet, his semiotic was, in large stretches, only a classificatory outline, with one small part, the three classes of argument, alone developed in great detail.

On the basis of Peirce's own analysis, mathematical thinking had to involve both the use of signs and inferential types of argument. Thus, in a classificatory scheme based on scope or on ontological status, it would fall under semiotic and logic. But when Peirce classified mathematics he always used a scale based on degree of abstractness and surety of results. Swayed by his father, awed by the self-evident nature of mathematical argument, he placed mathematics on the highest pinnacle of human thought, with every other science dependent upon it. He invited logicians to turn to mathematics, a prelogical science, for their principles, and insisted that mathematicians needed to turn to no one for support. Mathematical reasoning, as Peirce defined it, involved purely imaginary hypotheses and abstract diagrammatic reasoning. In this ideal realm of discourse there was observation and experimentation, but all under control of the imagination. Except for manipulative errors, such reasoning was infallible, yet totally unconnected with matters of fact. The diagrammatic aspect of such thought was closely tied to geometry. The necessity of using manipulative symbols to represent parts of a diagram stood as the foundation of algebra. In later work in topology, he tried to merge the two major branches of mathematics in one simple and more elementary, and therefore more abstract, subject.

Without complete consistency, Peirce made logic the highest and most regulative branch of philosophy. Like philosophy, it had to deal with common human experience, and thus with fact. Its subject area was the class of facts implied in controlled thought, or more precisely the laws governing the manipulation of signs. Unlike mathematics, logic was in no sense an imaginary science. It dealt more directly with reality than any other science, since Peirce defined reality as a universe of signs. Logic had both a methodological aspect, the control of inquiry; and an ontological one, the revelation of the structure of reality. It was a preface to metaphysics and the indispensable tool of all special sciences. But in case of confusion or uncertainty, the logician had to appeal to mathematics for a solution. This seemed to make mathematics the ultimate authority in metaphysics. Since the mathematician, by Peirce's own admission, could only appeal to the self-evident nature of his own axioms, this seemed to permit a rather vicious form of intuitionism. Or, short of this, it meant that pure formal analysis, falling back as it had to on self-evident reason, could not validate any view of reality, and thus was only a tool, and not the fount, of metaphysical truth. Possibly this was the decisive factor in Peirce's later shift to phenomenology as a direct, experiential, nonformal support for his ontology.

Peirce's all too neat relating of mathematics and logic broke down in all directions, for it involved a very narrow base. No one would deny the greater abstractness of mathematics, particularly when logic is given such a broad definition. But surely mathematical thought, the purest form of thought, reveals the structure of mind and reality as well as other types of thought. It can, in other words, be logically analyzed, and invites such analysis. In fact, Peirce finally concluded that the goal of logic was the catching in a net the soul of mathematical reasoning. Besides, there is a mathematical branch of every science, including logic. Thus, he made all purely formal, deductive logic a part of mathematics, just as a part of physics is mathematical. But in both cases the sciences also contain nonmathematical parts. His continued insistence upon the pre-eminence of mathematics was little less than filial piety, for he continually found new evidence of the interdependence of logic and mathematics. Mathematicians do not always argue by pure instinct or find self-evident solutions. They may get hypotheses from common experience, or need to clarify the logic of their operations. The appeals go in both directions.

In 1893 Peirce gave his most balanced view of the relation of the two subjects. By then he had developed a logical algebra that was prime and overarching, including within it, as special cases, all quantitative algebras. This seemed to mean that the science of quantity was a branch of logic. He uncharacteristically dismissed such a conclusion as a "mere" question of the classification of sciences. But then he made a plausible distinction. The mathematician draws necessary conclusions; logic is the science of necessary conclusions. The mathematician reasons without consciousness of his logical habit, yet instinctively reasons aright. The logician, without such aid from instinct, tries to understand such logical habits, but often flounders in error and contradiction. Then he turns to the instinctual certainty of mathematical reasoning to find his way. An algebraic logic, although embracing all mathematical forms in its principles, will normally be of no use to a practicing mathematician, who may laugh at its simplicity or ridicule its needless quibbling. The mathematician seeks the easiest way of solving problems. He represents the ultimate of practicality in the realm of pure abstractness. The logician drives his analysis into the most minute variants of thought, not in order to draw conclusions, but to illuminate the process of drawing conclusions. By process, Peirce of course did not mean psychological processes, but the strictly relational, inferential process. Also, as he stressed with greater frequency as he grew older, logic as a field of inquiry had nothing to do with epistemological problems or with the possibility of scientific knowledge. It only clarifies the inferential requirement of knowledge, provided such knowledge is possible. In this sense, logic is hypothetical, content to observe the creations of imagination in order to reveal their forms, not to glean self-evident conclusions.

Peirce was a logician, not a mathematician. That is, even his mathematical work was directed at logical and philosophical problems. But even in doing this he became deeply involved in contemporary mathematics and drew heavily upon it for philosophic ideas. Contrary to his own image of near infallibility, he was often in error in his mathematical operations, or else daringly at odds with almost everyone in the field. He did early, exploratory work in topology. He was one of the first mathematicians to appreciate an arbitrary element in geometrical systems, and he speculatively accepted a type of hyperbolic space. His whole later philosophy was tied to a debatable concept of continuity. He did early, fragmentary work on collections and multitudes. But by his last years, Peirce was well entrenched in long-cherished mathematical concepts and did not keep abreast of new developments. His occasional references to Bertrand Russell and Alfred North Whitehead indicated no real grasp of their climactic work.

Peirce wrote, but did not publish, a textbook in logic and left a multitude of manuscripts and articles. Where Emerson turned to nature as God's cathedral, Peirce turned most often to the eternal configurations of thought, or to the laws of mind. Somewhat similar to Emerson's discovery of the ascending uses of nature, Peirce found a hierarchy of uses for logic. In lengthy, brilliant attempts to solve logical paradoxes, he showed one use—amusement. He always loved abstract and diagrammatic reasoning and did much better with it than with more linguistic types of arguing. This use he rarely admitted.

For years he stressed the study of logic as a prerequisite for efficient inquiry in new areas, particularly for sciences that had moved far beyond common sense and developed instincts. This was the practical, utilitarian justification. Logic had a key role in all inquiry, but particularly in metaphysics, where it had been so notably lacking. In his Hopkins period he usually tied logic closely to scientific method. Perhaps more than coincidentally, his unimpressed Hopkins student, John Dewey, always retained a close tie between logic and methodology, even as Peirce moved on to "higher" uses. Peirce's argument was well fitted to advance his own courses at Hopkins. Everyone who reasons has a logic and believes his class of inference is logically sound. Scientific logic, as taught in college courses, subjects this *Logica Utens* to severe criticism and reveals the best methods of research in any particular science. In an age of new sciences and uncriticized logic, there was a crying need for a thorough study of logic. More intelligent methods of inquiry could, through more efficient science and better technology, save lives and hasten progress.

Above the practical use, which he later minimized, Peirce found in inductive reasoning an ethic which needed to be adopted in all areas of life. Inasmuch as inductive logic necessitates the widest possible number of samples, spread over many people and possibly many generations, it points to the unselfish, cooperative, or social aspect of inquiry. Good logical inference cannot rest on selfish, limited, or individual interests. To be logical is to be unselfish, to submit to the findings of others, to embrace the good of the whole. Also, he argued later that truth itself was but one species of the good, and thus one aspect of a general theory of ethics.

Far above all these uses, logic is a revelation of being, a pathway to ontological truth. Here he agreed with Hegel. All metaphysical conceptions spring from logic and are as good or as poor as the logic which begets them. To understand the necessary principles of inference is not merely to satisfy one's sentiment of rationality, or to procure more easily one's goals, but to see the lawfulness and rationality present in the cosmic mind and therefore at the heart of reality. The correct theory of logic, if we attain it, "is the vision and the attainment of that Reasonableness for the sake of which the Heavens and the Earth have been created." [2.122. This standard reference denotes the volume and paragraph in the *Collected Papers of Charles Sanders Peirce,* ed. by Charles Hartshorne, Paul Weiss, and Arthur Burks (Cambridge, Mass., 1958–60).]

Peirce ranked near the top of nineteenth-century logicians. His best work was original and suggestive, even if fragmentary or awkward in form. He began with classical logical problems and with the major forms of the syllogism. He found that the simple syllogism was only one very important class of deductive arguments, of a demonstrative, simple eliminative type. Other forms of argument, including induction and abduction, could be reduced to syllogistic form only by obscuring their distinctive characters. A complete inferential system would include, but not be, a syllogistic system. His great interest in inquiry led him to concentrate on the logic of induction and abduction, and these in turn helped open up the rigidity of classical logic, allowing logical status to both creative and vague mental operations.

Influenced by his mathematical interests and by an early system of logical algebra worked out by the British mathematician, George Boole, Peirce made the first American contribution to symbolic logic. For the expressed purpose of investigating the structure of thought, or for breaking up inferences into the greatest possible number of distinct steps, and not for developing a useful calculus for drawing inferences, Peirce utilized both algebraic and graphic symbolism. By extending Boole's notational system, he completed (but did not immediately publish) the first complete calculus of propositions and kept on experimenting with various and more simple systems of notation. To this he soon added notations to express quantity and climaxed his work with a logic of relations, by far the most philosophically pregnant of all his formal work.

The first relational logic was developed by another Britisher, Augustus De Morgan. As early as 1870, Peirce began improving upon it. By the 1880's he had discovered that a logic of relatives was more general and more inclusive than his earlier logic of propositions and quantifiers. As he defined it, a relative is a word or name that, according to the conjoined verbs and prepositions, requires one or more blank spaces to be filled by proper names in order to make it a complete proposition. If a single blank space (—— is a man), it is a monadic relative; if double (——— is a lover of ———), a dyad; and if multiple (——— gave ——— to ———), a polyad. Since he proved that all polyads can be analyzed into a combination of triads (but not dyads), he found only three basic modes of relation. Using the analogy of chemical valence and utilizing a type of logical graph, he developed a set of rules for expressing even the most complicated propositions. He also worked out an algebra for dyadic relatives, and finally a two-operational algebra which could express everything in his graphs. His logic of relatives opened up the possibility of varied and numerous logical operations, according *to purposes pursued*. Logic could now become a handmaiden of deliberate inquiry and not be merely a servile tool for static demonstration. More important, logic now revealed the teleological nature of being and could break the shackles of a mechanistic conception of reality. The three forms of possible relation also gave him a new, non-Kantian justification for the categories, and a new definition for them. After the necessary revisions, his categories remained the most fundamental concepts in his thought.

Peirce's logical work culminated in some curious and suggestive work on graphs. More than anyone before him, he believed necessary inference, as in mathematics, was diagrammatic in nature, and necessary only in the sense of operating within certain precise manipulative rules. These rules set limits and revealed procedures to follow, but did not predetermine the results, thus allowing an almost infinite variety of *purposeful* operations. To demonstrate this belief, he worked out a clever system of existential graphs which, under an elaborate set of conventions and permissions, allowed a wide variety of additions and erasures. By permissive cuts upon the universe, or sheet, he was able to incorporate an inverse universe of possibility, further augmenting his teleological emphasis. Not only did these graphs come closest to representing the scope and potential of the reasoning process, but they also provided a visual expression of his final metaphysical system.

Peirce's work in logic simply *paralleled* the development of his whole philosophy. From the narrow if fogless valley of syllogistic reasoning, he had moved to the vast, often hazy universe of multiple relations and open possibilities. If God's essence was, as he believed, revealed in such a study, then Peirce had moved from an early but restricted vision to one so vast as to require profound wonder and piety.

INQUIRY AND THE PRAGMATIC TEST

Peirce always placed the unselfish scientist at the top of the ranks of modern saints. He gave his own best years to physical science and ever after idealized the discipline it involved. In the years from 1870 to 1885 his dominant philosophical interests were closely related to science—to problems of cognition, meaning, and verity. Even his famous pragmatic test originated, at least in part, in his efforts to clarify scientific methodology.

In his idealization of science and scientists, Peirce tried to establish a standard rather than reveal an actuality. He loved science as a living method, as the unending search for truth, and not as a repository of knowledge, which was as yet only a "child's collection of pebbles," as nothing to the vast ocean of being lying unsounded. He revered the scientist only in his self-sacrificing devotion to inquiry. He believed that sustained inquiry, guided by a rational method, would attain such highly probable results as to be practically, if not perfectly, infallible. Also, any person, if he lived long enough, would develop, through the incessant action of experience, both the scientist's passion for truth and his required gift for exact reasoning. Ultimately, Peirce defined the highest end of man, or the *summum bonum,* as the fullest possible realization, in thought and action, of cosmic truth. He played down the immediately practical or grossly utilitarian uses of science and stressed the sublime goal of achieved rationality. To allow the practical goals any status was to degrade science to the level of potboiling, engineering, or surgery, and to besmirch the unselfish, impersonal goals of a scientist truly about "His Father's" business. For him, the precious but small steps of scientific discovery, abetted by a jealous passion for its advancement, made life worth living and the human race worth perpetuating. Thus, Peirce venerated a church of selfless inquirers, working in behalf of an ever greater incarnation of law or reason.

However sublime his task, the scientist had only one proximate goal —correct knowledge. When Peirce joined the early metaphysical club, the members were most concerned with epistemological issues. How do we know, and how well do we know? On one hand, the success of nineteenth-century scientists was almost overwhelming, especially after 1859. But the method of science, both in logical and psychological aspects, was either poorly understood or a point of controversy among widely different philosophers. Also, new logical and psychological innovations were fast eroding both the Kantian and the empirical explanations of cognitive processes. In this flux, and well before the maturation of his thinking, Peirce offered some original and even prophetic guidelines.

Peirce first developed a theory of cognition in the years when he was least concerned with metaphysics and religion. He then exhibited some of Chauncey Wright's positivistic horror of speculation and of unnecessary hypotheses. He half-rebukingly, half-approvingly noted a decline in philosophical interest about such problems as God, immortality, and freedom, and a rise in interest in scientific method and in areas of concrete consequences. For these "moderns," the validity of inductive science was the most pressing issue. Thus, Peirce began by clearing away some of the rubbish. In his earliest published papers he repudiated both Cartesian intuitionism and British sensationalism, and only in part in the name of Kant. As already indicated, he rejected Kant's thing-in-itself, or some hidden or transcendent object, either material, ideal, or unknown. He knew, with Hume, that there could be no demonstrably valid inference from our ideas to a hidden object. Although he still habitually spoke of mental faculties, he proceeded to deny most of them. Although he still thought in terms of discrete sensations, he already denied their material reference and their priority in perception. Although he left man in an inescapable world of self-representing signs, he believed this sign world was the real world and not a half-legible copy of a hidden one.

Within his world of signs, Peirce was also, and unexpectedly for so early a date and for a lifelong opponent of materialism, a complete behaviorist. Man thinks only with signs. The logical reference of one sign is to another. One cognition refers to an earlier one. Nothing is incognizable and nothing is directly or intuitively cognized. This means that a person has no immediate knowledge of self, of mental faculties or processes, or even of the difference between dreaming, imagining, or perceiving. Peirce emphatically denied any type of introspective knowledge. To him, psychology was an exclusively behavioral science, with all its content based on inference from external, observed fact. Like knowledge in any science, it was necessarily inferential. Knowledge of self, not present in small children, was inferred from the existence of error, or of behavioral incompetence. The self, as so cognized, was just another sign, or another word, which could only be interpreted by still other signs. All the so-called psychological laws, including association by similarity, contiguity, and causality, were simply types of inference, or laws governing the translation of signs. Of course such mental laws were habits, but habits in the sense that Peirce always defined them— real dispositions in things, not accidental modes of behavior.

But as his lack of a final interpretant in his theory of signs left Peirce with a seeming regress, so did this theory of cognition. How does one get the first cognition? Peirce first tried to solve this problem by an early and unsuccessful doctrine of continuity. He argued for an infinity of cognitions in both directions, in the sense of no beginning and no end. But yet the continuity of cognition had a limit outside itself. Cognition arose as a process of beginning, not in some original impression or intuition of an external object or force. This was, almost, a cosmological doctrine, a belief in the spontaneous origin of being.

In a world of mutually determining cognitions, Peirce had only the guidance of logic, or rules of correct inference, to help him escape a completely subjective view of truth and of reality. Somewhere in the conditions of inquiry itself he had to find a way to establish some degree of reliability. Thus, he turned from demonstrative and deductive logic to the problems of hypothesis formation. But the rules of the game were not enough. Thus, eventually, he also had to resort to an extrinsic test, and one tied, not to an unknown source of perception (he never gave in to this nominalistic temptation), but to the purposes served by thought, or by the habits it leads to. At this point (after 1900), he introduced a valuative system that, however much he intellectualized it or concealed it by fancy rhetoric, still fell back on felt satisfaction. But before this he had revised his whole theory of cognition.

William James paved the way. His *Principles of Psychology* (Peirce reviewed the two volumes) provided Peirce a whole bundle of new weapons. After 1890, in all major details, Peirce was in agreement with James's account of the physical and phenomenological aspects of thought. In fact, he and Santayana were both more loyal to the *Principles* than James himself. Typically, Peirce tried to improve upon James, usually falling prey to a more awkward terminology and indulging in more speculation. For example, he accepted the physical base of mental association, but tried to explain it in more detail than the facts permitted, and by this fit it to his new cosmological theories. Thus, he argued that protoplasm, unlike inorganic matter, has not hardened into such rigid habits or laws, and therefore displayed a greater instability and more chance activity. This led to a constant interruption or breakup of associative habits or neurological tracks, which in turn led to intensified feeling. The human personality was only an integrated system of feelings and habits. Consciousness was only a continuity of such feelings. In its qualitative immediacy, consciousness had no intellectual value. But it was a regulative, qualitative undertow in all reflective thought, and thus found its justification. As pure feeling, however pleasant, Peirce had no use for it, and deemed it very unimportant.

Peirce fully accepted from James an account of perception and of a type of presentational realism. The percept, itself a product of complex neurological association, and a combination of potentially inferable sensations (they are not experienced), is the ground of all deliberate and controlled thought. But the percept, itself a sheer, immediate image forced upon us by the nonego, is prereflective. Some percepts (we have no way of finding out what proportion) produce primitive forms of judgment ("That is blue"), which are also forced upon us, or almost so. This perceptual judgment, or uncontrolled abduction, is the launching point and the unifying aspect of all cognition. From here we go on to build the narrowed distinctions and abstractions which make up our more general or conceptual world. To them we of necessity turn to verify our most imaginative cognitive creations. Even the perceptual judgment depends upon a universe of signs, climaxed by a totality we refer to as the "truth." The sign reference is still there, but now it is the sheer presentation in perception that opens the door to knowledge.

The perceptual judgment, although uncontrollable, may greatly distort the pure percept. But we can do nothing about this. The perceptual judgment is final and unquestionable. It is hardly true or false, since these terms rightly apply only to controlled inference, which is itself tested against perceptual judgments. They are, at the very worst, illusionary, although Peirce tended to discount too much doubt here. Yet, the possibility of doubt is crucial, for all inference finds it premises in perceptual judgments. Once the purely formal requirements are met, the final test for their reality has to be practical. Do the perceptual judgments persist? Do other people concur? If one combines the judgment with other well-tested judgments and turns them into a tight, predicative hypothesis, does it then pay off in expected consequences? Beyond such tests, illusion has no operative meaning, and any contrived doubt is false on its surface. Inference may travel far from these perceptual judgments, but it has to be able to find its way back and rejoin the active life. He approvingly reiterated: "The elements of every concept enter into logical thought at the gate of perception and make their exit at the gate of purposive action; and whatever cannot show its passports at both these two gates is to be arrested as unauthorized by reason." [5.212.]

In the area of scientific methodology, Peirce offered many useful distinctions, but never drew his suggestions together into a single doctrine. Possibly his most famous concept—the doubt-satisfaction theory of inquiry—was repudiated by Peirce himself. His much-read but hardly representative essay, "Fixation of Belief," popularized the view that doubt or, as he subsequently defined it, perplexity and behavioral quandary, lead to appropriate action to resolve the doubt and fix belief, or to restore habitual functioning. Physiologically, doubt was an irritation of nerve, and restored belief a new electrical circuit. In this context, inquiry had but one object, the settlement of opinion, or effective organic adjustment. In the essay, Peirce tried to prove that, over the long run, the self-corrective method of science, being keyed to external permanency, led to the least disappointing beliefs. To set up his scientific model he used three arbitrary strawmen: the methods of willful tenacity, submission to institutional authority, and the satisfaction of intellectual taste. This essay, so in line with an early, biologically related instrumentalism, ran counter to Peirce's main bent in philosophy. The doubt-satisfaction theory tied science to a hated hedonism. To get away from it, he soon turned to an ideal, unselfish motivation—the attainment of truth. Instead of a preferred method for fixing belief, he could argue by 1900 that pure science had no relation to practical belief. At the immediate, practical level he urged the acceptance of tradition and custom, or something close to his earlier repudiated method of authority.

Of more enduring significance, Peirce always retained a contempt for any but real doubt, or doubt reflected in behavioral perplexity. At the same time, he tried to keep science as close to common sense as possible. All inquiry develops out of natural instincts. As a fact, all men have many indubitable (not infallible) beliefs and cognitive habits and are able to question only a few of these, meanwhile necessarily assuming the others. These indubitable beliefs are functionally innate. Just as he believed in the reality of law and thus in the likelihood that our hypothetical laws often conform to them, so he believed in the objective validity of many undoubted and possibly unprovable beliefs. He asked for only as much criticism as possible. Some near-fixed, primitive common beliefs (i.e., horror at incest; a sense of uniformity in nature) seem to be universal, but even they may have changed over a long period of time. Deliberate modification through controlled inquiry is the best mechanism of change, but it should spring from real doubt, not from a love of argument or a foolish preening of the intellect. Even controlled inquiry has to proceed on the basis of fixed beliefs and cannot in itself lead to the same fixity. The best-established hypotheses are by nature always tentative, whereas unquestioned folk beliefs are firm and sure. Peirce not only refused to sneer at common sense, but at times believed that it was more sure and reliable than anything else, since it was closer to basic instinct than more elaborate thought. At the same time, and like William James, he allowed a definite weight to subjective preference in humanly desirable and commonly accepted hypotheses (sure as the reality of human freedom), provided the weight of evidence was otherwise equal or beyond reach, and provided that such hypotheses remained open for rigorous testing.

Peirce was mainly concerned with one aspect of scientific inquiry—the development of hypotheses—and thus the one method of actually expanding knowledge through reasoning. He attended to the logic of discovery and long ignored the logic of explanation. He assumed the role of deduction and for years virtually neglected the problem of experimental verification. He talked endlessly of induction and abduction but, as he later admitted, used the two terms in a confusing way. Both were methods of arriving at postulates, not ways of testing hypotheses. Roughly, in abduction a daring and brilliant scientist, by something close to a sheer guess, or a pure mutation of intellect, invented a broad and sweeping explanatory hypothesis to encompass both known and unknown data. In induction, a cautious and careful scientist, by a rigorous and controlled process of sampling, worked out a probable hypothesis about a total universe of objects. Peirce, drawing upon and extending the already developed mathematics of probability, laid down some enduring guidelines for statistical induction, including the necessity of a predesignated quality and of an at least artificial infinity of choices. Induction, in the sense of sampling, was self-corrective, inevitably leading close to the truth in the long run. The more samples and samplers, the better. This directly supported his idealization of cooperation and his hope for an unlimited community.

Peirce never lost his fascination with abduction, or the invention of hypotheses. Because of his logic, he tried to make abduction a valid form of inference. In it, disparate subjects are subsumed under a unifying concept, but a concept which deductively implies other, nonexperienced subjects. Peirce saw the emotional impact of, and the esthetic satisfaction to be gained, from such intellectual ordering and also saw the tie with all other types of creativity. Unlike induction, which moves one toward the truth inevitably, abduction is not reliable. Yet, it is not a wild guess, since it is based upon some existing data. The weakness of abduction lies in the amount of extrapolation involved and in the deficiency of evidence for the amount of generality proposed. Peirce did not clarify the mental operations involved in abduction. He seemed to mean that a hypothesis begins as a spontaneous idea, which matures into a hypothesis through a type of inference. If so, it seems that this early inference would be deductive-inductive, i.e., a quick estimate of necessary implications and a vicarious test of these against known facts. Thus, an abduction is a mutation at conception, but has matured into a partially verified hypothesis by the time of its birth, and then awaits an endless lifetime of further testing.

But why do we often guess aright? Not by chance, Peirce effectively argued. Even if only one hypothesis in a hundred proved valid, this would still represent an unbelievable accuracy, for the number of possible guesses approaches infinity, and all the time that has passed since the earth solidified would not account for more than one or two chance guesses being right. Possibly he underestimated the guesses, since he used the term hypothesis for a relatively sophisticated mental product, not for every vague, almost instantaneous theory that flits through the mind. But his point remains—man has a tendency to guess correctly. This was the old idea of a light of reason, or the religious idea that man is born in the image of his creator. Since Peirce believed that the limited order and uniformity actually discovered by man rested upon a much greater diversity, he felt the agreement did not come from a perfect order in nature and in man. He believed the answer had to be some type of evolutionary adaptation, reflected in animal instincts and, in man, overflowing into intellectual concepts. In turn, Peirce refused to let chance account for the whole course of evolution; he thus had a motive for cosmological speculation. New hypotheses are intellectual mutations, but not accidental ones. They rear themselves out of a sea of instinct and further attest to the likely validity of common sense. Perceptual jugments are the best example of unconcious abduction, and they are so reliable that they have to be used to test all others. The mind of man, at one with nature, has the laws of nature as part of its own being, and thus easily apprehends them, particularly at the point of pressing biological need. This explanation, in line with that of John Dewey's instrumental naturalism, was transformed by Peirce's idealism. Then the world of nature became an incarnation of mind, and man's creative thought became an elaboration of divine purpose.

As Peirce revamped his theory of cognition and tied it to perceptual judgments, he also changed his early definition of induction. In later years he used the term to refer to the experimental testing of hypotheses. As a method of verification rather than as a means of developing a hypothesis, induction had a prime negative value and minimal positive value. One predicted datum may, by its absence, invalidate a sweeping hypothesis and allow another to be tried. Given a tendency to guess aright, or an instinctual basis for abduction, this speeds the process of inquiry and bypasses much tedious work. But if there were no tendency to guess correctly, and no willingness to accede to hypotheses simply because they had not yet been negated by any evidence, the only recourse would be unending sampling, and in any present moment a great deference to future results (extreme fallibilism). In almost no case can inductive checking exhaust all possible predictions. Any hypothesis, however many times verified, can be challenged as improbable, for many correct results fade into insignificance as the possibilities reach toward infinity. Thus, to Peirce, the proof of the scientific method is either purely practical or else grounded on a metaphysical assumption, not about nature's uniformity, but about an inborn tendency to conceive correctly. Given this assumption, Peirce had still to confess his fallibilism (we do not always guess correctly, and should always remain open to new inquiry), but certainly modified his earlier emphasis upon a very distant truth, discoverable only by endless sampling that could do no more than slowly minimize the vagaries of pure chance. Since man tends to guess aright, he could talk confidently of virtually indubitable hypotheses, even when these are verified by only a few sustained predictions.

The experimental verification of hypotheses requires not only deductive amplification but also crystal-clear definitions. Experiments have to be precisely controlled and carried out in behalf of the unambiguous results demanded by the hypothesis. In order to have any operative, or thoroughly testable, or negotiable meaning, scientific propositions have to indicate both the exact manipulations required and the specific perceptual consequences to be expected. This limited if obvious methodological requirement lay behind Peirce's famous "pragmatic test" of 1878. As published in "How to Make Our Idea Clear," the test had only marginal significance for Peirce. He scarcely remembered it a few years later. But after William James popularized pragmatism and celebrated Peirce as its founder, Peirce elaborately rethought his earlier statement. He read into an essentially ambiguous and confusing statement a wealth of ideas and often used pragmatism as a final unifying theme for all of his philosophy, believing that it implied or required all of his other doctrines. Thus, pragmatism was an appropriate label of Peirce's mature system, but only if it clearly embodied his vast and complex body of doctrine, some of which was of a highly speculative nature.

According to Peirce's later memory, pragmatism was born in the discussions of the metaphysical club. Intimations of it appeared in some papers of Peirce in 1868; a fairly clear statement appeared in an 1871 review of Berkeley's works. The members of the club were interested not only in scientific methodology but in semantic clarity, in the new theory of evolution, in physiology and a new psychology, and in moral and ethical problems. Peirce's essay implicated all of these areas, but climaxed in his maxim: "Consider what effects, which might conceivably have practical bearings, we conceive the object of our conception to have. Then, our conception of these effects is the whole of our conception of the object." When he later reapplied himself to pragmatism, he restated this maxim many times and, despite many alternative wordings, remained loyal to it. But he often interpreted it in the light of doctrines developed long after 1878. As a result, there is no way to make sure exactly what he meant in 1878.

He always reaffirmed one intention. The pragmatic test was a useful guideline for framing scientific hypotheses. He even argued that the test only stated the habits of laboratory scientists, and thus showed the specific requirements for a good abduction. It was applicable only to intellectual concepts or to cognitive propositions alleging knowledge of objective fact. It was another way of saying that only experimentally verifiable hypotheses were admissible in science. Thus, in one of a score of alternative definitions, he could argue that pragmatism was merely the doctrine that the inductive method was the only requirement for ascertaining the intellectual purport of a symbol (proposition or argument). The key terms, in this interpretation, were "effects" and "practical bearing." By these, Peirce apparently meant both the indicated operations to be performed in the experiment and the predicted sensual effects (or percepts) to be experienced. Thus, he meant both conduct and derivative experience. In 1902 he said as much, defining practical consequences as the conduct recommended and experiences expected, assuming the truth of the proposition. Thus, if one acts in a specified way, he will necessarily receive certain kinds of experience. Meaning, in these terms, is a prelude to actual verification, or a prior conception of the conduct and experience necessary to verify a proposition. By requiring this degree of specificity, or of operational guidelines and perceptual expectations, Peirce could eliminate verbal ambiguities in science and more easily maintain a type of objective, public discourse unburdened by unclear subjective and individualistic verbal meanings.

But the pragmatic test, as first formulated in the 1876 article, surely meant more than a restricted rule for scientific inquiry. The content of his original essay, its title ("How to Make Our Ideas Clear"), and the very wording of the test indicated a broader logical and semantical purpose. It was indeed to be a way for making all ideas clear or, as he succinctly put it later, an attempt to define the word definition. William James introduced his pragmatism as a philosophical razor to cut away verbal abstractions and to settle obscure metaphysical disputes. Peirce gladly acceded to this use. He was always trying to get rid of unclear concepts and verbal traps. Thus, in addition to a narrow scientific tool, the pragmatic test was also a semantical weapon. As such, it came directly from his study of signs and clarified the role of interpretants.

It was clear to Peirce that any word or concept is interpreted or defined by still another word. But in all meaningful propositions about existence, an index accompanies the symbols. The index goes beyond any verbal meanings and points to something directly encountered or to some memory of such an encounter. Any word with existential reference has to be defined, ultimately, by indexual reference, or by seeing, touching, or hearing. Even relational symbols have to be defined by diagrammatic demonstration. Any general term reduces to a conditional "if you do this, you will experience that." The final or terminal meaning is the actual habit formed, which involves sensual expectation and a disposition to appropriate action. To illustrate: the concept snake, if clearly defined, means that, if one encountered such a denominated object, he would experience certain perceptions and act in a certain way. If the word snake conveys any meaning, it actually calls forth images matching or approximating those that would be had by an encounter with a snake as well as images of the conduct that would arise on that occasion. In

Peirce's language, the word-symbol creates an interpretant in the hearer that stands in the same relation to its object, and creates the same effects in the imagination, as the symbol has created in the mind of the speaker. But if the word "snake" does not convey any meaning (in which case it is just a mere sound), it can be defined by other signs which stand for the several perceptual qualities intended and for the conduct expected. This is a dictionary definition. But if these words also fail to convey the meaning with any exactitude, the only recourse is to point out a snake and let the person learn an appropriate response by experience. In this way, even a word is made explicit in the same sense as a hypothesis. This semantical or definitional use of the pragmatic test is, if anything, even more fundamental than the abductive use, for it involves the very use of language and the function of signs.

One of the acknowledged origins of pragmatism, for both Peirce and James, was a theory developed by the English psychologist, Alexander Bain, and much discussed in the metaphysical club. Bain defined belief as that upon which a man is prepared to act; this would be habit in Peirce's vocabulary. Peirce introduced the pragmatic test in a series of articles in large part devoted to the doubt-belief theory of inquiry. Seen in this functional context, alternatively psychological and moral, the test was quite general. The meaning of a proposition is the conduct for which it disposes us. Here the reference is not to the specified operations of a laboratory, or to the eventual indexual reduction of a definition, but to one's behavior in general. When he most emphasized this meaning, Peirce completely dropped sense effects from pragmatism and even argued that he had never intended anything but conduct by "practical effects." In line with this, he emphasized an evolutionary, biological view of mind. Thinking, if effective, leads to adaptive conduct. This is what the intellect is for—the regulation and rational modification of conduct. Not that Peirce made conduct itself the final end, for it was in turn a means to the final incarnation of reason. But it is the actual conduct, for which one takes responsibility, that makes up the meaning of any proposition. The literal meaning of "A rattlesnake is poisonous" translates as "If I confront a rattlesnake, I will run," assuming certain conditions. To clarify meaning in this sense is to try to live rationally, or in behalf of chosen ends. It is to conceive the effects of our beliefs and to criticize and modify our beliefs in light of these anticipated effects.

Thus, he had a related threefold test: of meaning in semantics, of belief in hypotheses, and of moral use in the conduct of life.

Each of these three related emphases were present in Peirce's attempt after 1902 to explicate pragmatism. It is difficult to weigh their importance or even to make a complete separation among them. Peirce obviously thought that he had only one pragmatic test and that all his elaborations fit it. Undoubtedly, the pragmatic test was a means of clarifying the meaning of something. But what? Peirce used many terms —word, concept, expression, symbol, sign, proposition, belief, doctrine, and others. Yet, the varied emphases can be partially unified. In the most narrow sense, he developed an experiential reference for defining words and concepts. At a second level, he achieved a means of clarifying propositions, statements, or hypotheses (each compounded out of already clearly defined words) in such a way that they could be experimentally verified. Finally, he constructed a valuative framework for judging how propositions, or vast systems of propositions, function in life as beliefs and doctrines, and thus govern our behavior. To live rationally we must control our conduct and thus see the consequences of our beliefs. The first two steps subserve this teleological purpose, for clarity of language and experimental knowledge are the means for a rational life. Possibly, he could have stated his maxim as follows: "The meaning of an existential concept or proposition, in order to be unambiguous, must be expressed in terms of all the conceivable sensible effects, and all conceivable modifications of conduct, which would result if it were a true belief."

Finally, Peirce's pragmatism cannot be effectively compared to the pragmatism of other avowed converts. Whatever the verbal comparisons, Peirce did not develop a more rigorous definition of pragmatism than William James. Both fell into ambiguities. James believed that he added a test of truth to Peirce's test of meaning. This was hardly true, since the verification aspect was implicit in Peirce's own scientific application. But, more than James, Peirce did recognize that pragmatism, as a word, was being used as a loose label for quite varied philosophical positions, including many of great scope and many that he admired. In an excellent attempt at discrimination, Peirce applauded the general pragmatic distaste for necessitarianism and for any substantiative consciousness, and its favoritism to relations and real generals, and to conduct or habit as the final interpretant of concepts and hypotheses. He lamented a general reluctance to accept his own ideas on a real infinity or continuity, a loose tendency to make truth mutable, a habitual disregard for strict logic, and a pervasive voluntarism. Always seeking precise labels, he suggested that the word pragmaticism be used for his early and restricted test of meaning, leaving pragmatism as a more generic term for an international philosophical movement. He continued to use pragmatism for his own broader philosophy.

More out of jealousy than anything else, Peirce complained about the popular style of James and the resultant lack of precision in many of his lectures and essays. Nothing so readable, he believed, could be of any philosophic value. Impoverished, isolated, desperately seeking both an audience and a market, Peirce usually welcomed fellow pragmatists and, instead of quibbling, often read his own ideas into any statement that seemed to relate to his own. Also, and contrary to a generally accepted thesis, it was Peirce, not James or Schiller or Dewey, who loaded pragmatism (not pragmaticism) with such a metaphysical load that it could not long bear the burden of criticism. No one else tried to make pragmatism encompass so much or claimed so much for it. Most of the ideas of James and Dewey lurk in Peirce's papers. But they rest along with a great deal more.

THE CATEGORIES AND REALISM

Next to his pragmatic test, Peirce has been most often remembered for his categories of firstness, secondness, and thirdness. They were the framework for a philosophy more replete with triads than that of Hegel's. But the categories, as Peirce often admitted, were always loose and vague. They also changed with time. The essential category was always thirdness, for it was the indispensable support for Peirce's form of realism and his main weapon against nominalism.

Peirce's original list of categories (1867) was derived from an analysis of propositions and contained the seemingly universal concepts of quality, relation, and representation necessary to unify a manifold of substance (subject) into the unity of being (predicate). Here firstness, or quality, was complete generality or abstractness; in many ways it was close to his later thirdness. Secondness was the necessary correlate, or comparative reference, required to isolate a pure abstraction on the way to joining it to substance, or making it a predicate. The representation that he also saw as necessarily involved in subject-predicate sentences was the most enduring aspect of his early categories. He saw even in the limited context of a proposition that the relational aspect of thought required a relating or mediating term and thus anticipated the later attempt, in his logic of relations, to prove the irreducible aspect of combinatorial or triadic relations, and his later attempt in metaphysics to justify generality or continuity as the most prominent feature of reality.

From the early 1870's until the end of his Hopkins period, Peirce gave almost all of his time to physical science, to teaching, and to methodology, logic, and psychology. Only in the late 1880's did he return to the categories, and by then with new weapons. In his first revision he drew from his logic of relations. Then, in his most complete development of them in the 1890's he also applied his new theory of cognition, which he borrowed from James. Finally, he added a phenomenology and integrated his categories with a whole complex of metaphysical speculation.

The logic of relatives disclosed three, and only three, types of relation. This provided a purely formal derivation and definition of three categories. But by 1885 Peirce was after major metaphysical game, not just another classificatory trilogy to add to his growing repertory (three types of signs, of terms, of arguments, of syllogistic figures). He wrote to James that he was finally developing a vast metaphysical system, of which the categories were a part. As such, they were not only possible modes of relation, but irreducible constituents of reality and the most primitive features of experience. In experience in general and in each area of experience, the three categories always lurked, awaiting discovery and elaboration. A clever Peirce looked for them and found them in evolution, physics, physiology, psychology, and other areas, often with a bit of forcing or some equivocation about exact definition.

The final, and most crucial, source of the categories was a radical phenomenology, or "all that in any sense appears." When Peirce turned to immediate experience, he characteristically did it with a vengeance and went all the way. He tried the confessedly difficult task of looking with his mental eyes at all phenomena forced upon his attention by either outward or inward experience, and totally without interpretation or association. In its purity, this phenomenology did not represent a new form of introspective psychology, for it had no bearing on scientific explanation. It rather resembled the pure observational power of an artist, who alone is able to drink in phenomena without interpretative distortion. The pure phenomena were present in immediate perception, unalloyed by reflection, judgment, or any type of discursive thought. But thinking would be one of the phenomena which appeared. This qualification is vital; otherwise phenomenology could never get beyond pure quality, or firstness. Peirce called the totality of appearance the *phaneron,* the description of its features the science of *phaneroscopy.* He assumed that the main features of the phaneron were present to any mind. After the purest vision, after really seeing what stared him in the face, Peirce wanted to back away and reflect upon its elemental features. Perhaps to no one's surprise, there were only three essential features, and these were the same old categories. They were all present in the phaneron, but so mutually involved and inseparable as to have vague boundaries and to preclude absolutely precise definition.

The following attempt at brief definitions of the three categories, in their final form, has to exclude suggestive qualifications and the more elaborate definitions. But it will also mute internal inconsistencies and smooth overlapping definitions.

Firstness is either feeling, that which is predominant in feeling, or the quality present in feeling. In phenomenology, firstness is the suffusing qualitative aspect of perception, but not perception itself. Firstness enters the phaneron through sense experience, but firstness is not sensation. In fact, the experienced qualities do not at all depend on the senses, but rather the sense organs adapt to the qualities. Also, a quality does not depend on the material objects which possess it. It is pure possibility, awaiting accidental or purposeful actuality. Firstness is pure being, but still unrealized and nonexistent. It is perfectly self-contained. Metaphysically considered, firstness is pure, unembodied quality or essence. Existentially, it is nothing, or sheer might-be-ness. Since it pervades feeling, it involves a type of consciousness, but a type of consciousness prior to any analysis or comparison. It is immediate, unthinkable in its purity, and unknowable. To talk about it is to leave it or to transform it. Firstness is so elusive that Peirce almost conceded that it was only an inference from perceptual judgments, or from secondness. Its apprehension befits a poet. But as degenerate forms of secondness and thirdness, quality becomes a sign (icon) and functions in thought. It is a pervasive, almost subliminal firstness that allows association by similarity of quality and that permits a community of sympathy among people. Finally, there is a firstness present in all consciousness, or in all phenomena. A quality pervades the categories of secondness and thirdness. The firstness of secondness is a quality of existence; the firstness of thirdness is a quality of thought.

Secondness, from a logical standpoint, is simple dyadic relationship. It is experience as action and reaction, involving shock, struggle, force, and volition. It reflects the factuality, the sheer irrational existence, of phenomena. In secondness, ego meets nonego, in an arena of force and opposition. Secondness is not being-in-itself, like firstness, but being-over-against. It is predominant in causation, in perception, and in will. Both external impact and internal desire involve reaction. Without the governance of law (thirdness), secondness is accidental, contingent, even coincidental. A world without thirdness would be a world with irreducible and inexplicable entities, without ultimate rationality, and thus the world of materialism. Secondness is the only *existent* category (all categories are *real*), and existence necessarily implies that which is reactive and relational. Secondness includes bodies, matter, and all externality. It alone includes all the arbitrary, nongeneral traits that make anything distinctively individual. It is manifested in sheer non-rational or nonpurposeful desire, which is the equivalent of arbitrary free will. Peirce saw secondness as an antidote for romantic fancy and, in inquiry, as an indispensable test for the reality of hypothetical thirds. He denounced Hegel and other idealists for ignoring it. But Peirce did not like it. In itself it stood for irrationality, for a shallow materialism, for nominalism. Secondness is an irremovable aspect of experience and of reality, but it best functions as a pointer, or index, of the lawful and intelligible thirdness which governs it.

Thirdness is representation and mediation in logic. It is experienced as meaning, habit, purpose, and continuity. For thirdness, Peirce usually turned to semantic and logical examples. It is experientially present in language behavior and in the sense of intelligibility, of duration, and of lawfulness. The perfect example of thirdness is a concept or a meaning. The necessity of an interpretant in communication and the irreducibility of triadic relations in logic precluded any rational attempt to reduce experienced thirdness to a form of secondness. Meaning, or the whole world of mind, cannot be explained away by some reductionist materialism. Metaphysically considered, thirdness is the nonexistent but very real world of habit. Generality, intelligence, law, and growth are as much a part of experience as sheer existence. In thirdness, the negative or merely possible generality of pure firstness becomes the positive, living generality of law, which determines future facts, while the irrational "thisness" of fact becomes the content of living rationality. Genuine thirdness is symbolic, as is a word. Fact and quality are mediated by meaning or otherwise stand unrelated. But in one degenerate form of thirdness, logically considered, the sign functions only as an index (as in a word that serves as a signal), with the relationship not a matter of meaning but of existence. In a second, extremely degenerate form, represented best by random images or pure fancy, the sign is only an icon, not a symbol, and only relates other images. Here the interpretant brings neither a governing law nor even a semblance of actuality.

Peirce's whole philosophic endeavor could be reduced to one goal— to affirm and validate thirdness and all it implied. Yet, he could not understand how anyone could doubt any of the categories. They each seemed so obvious. Perhaps too many people confused reality with existence and therefore assumed that secondness, the only existent category, was alone real. Each category involves the others, but no one can swallow or absorb another. If one is real, Peirce believed they all were. He had no truck for complete skepticism and thus felt as sure of thirdness as he felt sure of anything. Of course, pure and separate thirdness would be empty abstractness. But pure existence, without law, would be blind reaction. Pure possibility, unrelated to actuality and law, would be sheer nothingness. Too many idealists tried to eliminate secondness. Too many nominalists denied real thirdness, concluding that human thought was a near miraculous and inexplicable phenomenon.

Much thinking involves degenerate forms of thirdness, or much unrecognized illusion and fancy. Our thoughts about reality may be incorrect. They may attribute law where none exists. But through the inductive testing of pragmatic or predictive propositions, we can move toward truth, or to a coherence of our beliefs, of our living habits, with the laws operative in the whole universe. Peirce always argued that pragmatism was senseless without the ontologic reality of law, for the predictable aspect of meaning falls back upon form and structure in things. Any pragmatist is, therefore, a realist. Yet, the inductive test is only negatively conclusive. Even the practical fruitfulness of scientific inquiry is only highly indicative of cosmic thirdness; it is not final proof. Yet, backed up with the evidence of immediate experience, or of phenomenology, who can really doubt the reality of law? Peirce contemptuously dismissed feigned skepticism. No one acts on the basis of it.

The category of thirdness related Peirce to both James and Dewey. James, in trying to broaden empiricism to embrace all types of relationship was trying to certify the reality of law or habit. Dewey, both in his belief in the reality of mind as a mode of organization in nature, and in his attempt to define the elements of enduring order and structure in nature, came very close to what Peirce was trying to justify by his category of thirdness. But both Dewey and James were willing to stop at the *fact* of law and mind. Their realism stopped at the portals of the unfathomable. Peirce would not stop there. Even though part of reality, as attested by experience and suggested by logic, thirdness might still be a product of chance, and thus ultimately if not proximately as inexplicable and as accidental as pure secondness. Thus he had to back up his prime category and account for its being; otherwise we might still live either in a world full of mystery and hidden secrets or in an accidental world. Here he again displayed his search for the security of a final and complete intelligibility. Much like Jonathan Edwards, he wanted to master all the secrets. His highly speculative cosmology was an attempt to discover the thirdness of thirdness, or the law of laws, and at the same time, by the possible sophistry of a new mathematical concept of continuity, avoid any infinite regress. Governing habits, so pervasively present, have to be themselves the result of an overarching habit, which is the tendency to take habits. The rationality of the limited human perspective had to share in an infinite rationality, and in this find its fullest explanation.

Even before the fullest development of his categories, Peirce had insisted upon his realism, but had never been able to explain or justify it satisfactorily. Later, he claimed that all his early years were unbearably tainted by nominalism. Yet, he never completely escaped some problems of definition and proof. His philosophy constantly ran aground on an almost impossible attempt to repudiate an incognizable ground of cognition without falling into a hopeless subjectivism, a type of voluntarism, or a lean and agnostical positivism, all of which he hated. He liked to pose as the modern Duns Scotus, battling against an almost universal host of devilish nominalists. From Occam on, the individual human mind had been given the power of originating general ideas the like of which

God had failed to create as real objects, and which were entirely wanting in either the mind of God or in heaven and earth. With ideas stripped of anything except a ghostly existence in the fleeting and mysterious human psyche, all real power, as well as all real existence, was attributed to matter. Or, in worse blasphemy, a God-complex was assumed by man, and in a false humanism and individualism he fell into the illusion that he ruled the world. Nominalists, as is quite evident, were then identical to Edwards' Arminians. Peirce, as an avowed rebel in the ranks of modern science, was reasserting a mode of influence or power—i.e., law, habit, purpose—upon external events which could not be resolved into mechanical action. This meant a reaffirmation of the reality, although not the existence, of universals or of general terms. In this sense, he renewed the medieval controversy.

Peirce's insistence upon a cognizable reality meant that real generals (all human thought is general but not necessarily all consistent with real generality) were coterminous with the irreducibly common elements of human experience, or of experience in general. The collective mind alone has a ticket for truth. This view was early stated in what was always a puzzling, and too often seemed a pseudo-regulative definition of reality—the final outcome of all inquiry. To back up this definition, Peirce seemed to assume an intriguing form of nonreductionist, semi-pluralistic idealism, as opposed to the prevailing reductionist varieties. Rejecting the idealism of Berkeley because of its false sensational psychology, rejecting any Hegelian idealism because of its reductionist denial of secondness, and following out his and James's newer ideas on cognition, he seemed to posit an omnipresent but not omnipotent mind, fully involved in, and controlling, but never absorbing the world of matter. Real thirdness was the thought of such a mind, as well as the developing laws of nature and the common, overlapping content of individual cognitive experiences, or "experience in general." But Peirce only gave hints about such an idealism. When he developed his own cosmology, he moved on to a more confusing and treacherous absolute idealism which absorbed all the categories into a broad conception of mind.

Peirce always made clear that he was defending the reality and not the existence of universals. By their reality, he meant their nondependence upon any individual thought. Degenerate thirdness, on the other hand, may represent only individual fancy. True generals, as habits or controlling predispositions, are what they are even when no one thinks them. They constrain individual thought rather than the other way around, as a conceptualist would have it. But though independent of individual cognition, they are still cognizable. This suggests something like mind stuff. But in rejecting Berkeley on this point, he seemed to reveal why he would have rejected a mind-stuff theory. He believed Berkeley was a Platonist and a nominalist. For Berkeley the independent reality of cognitive objects depended on archetypes in God's mind, not on their connection with experience in general. God's mind was apart from, and prior to, individual minds. Also, Berkeley made the cause of sensations real but not sensible or cognizable entities. Thus, his idealism was a ghostly rendition of materialism and had a Platonic variant of things-in-themselves. Similarly, any ground of thought, such as a vague mind stuff, would introduce all over again the incognizable unknown.

After the development of his final concept of thirdness (in the 1890's), Peirce believed that, however ignorant we now are, thirdness still reigns supreme in the present and that it does not await any final determination of it or any final experience in general. It is simply what such a final determination will disclose, or what such final experience will include. It is the principle of omniscience, which provides a sense of assurance in our fragmented search for truth. As such, it may spur us on to greater effort and dedication, like the religion of Duns Scotus.

It may be a good morale booster, but such a belief apparently has no explanatory role in inquiry. We have no way of conclusively demonstrating the identity of our knowledge and reality. The inescapable forms of knowledge, or the categories, may help us get a prophetic view of the form or outline of any final reality, but they do not magically produce it or reveal it in totality. Peirce at first seemed to believe that logical formalism might reveal it, but he later gave up on any such neat bypass. Experience, even in the form of careful inductive verification, only leads to a practical certainty; it leads one beyond significant doubt. An element of hope or faith, possibly translated into metaphysical speculation, seemed inescapable. Peirce, more than most pragmatists, tried to attain more than this and even as death loomed seemed intent on finding new ways of bolstering a confident hope. But his philosophy could not move beyond a practical faith and a fallibilistic view of human intelligence. His bent for finality warred constantly with his fallibilism and with his realistic estimation of human incompetence. Why should a Charles S. Peirce read it all aright? Was he a special prophet? Surely not. In an evolutionary setting, even the best of systems would have to grow and change. Thus, he could only project his concept of reality into the future and relate it to the common content of any finished inquiry. It was a social idea, not a personal one. To him, reality was a living force in the present, essentially knowable, but never fully known by any one person or, as yet, by all persons.

When pressed for a definition of reality, Peirce could never give but one answer, which had to be a variant of the following composite: "Being as assured of the reality of thirdness as I am assured of anything, and having not the slightest doubt of everything, I must define reality as that which is never disturbed by what anyone may believe about it, but which is best approximated in the present by the most widely accepted results of rigorous scientific inquiry, and as that which will be ever more approximated as the process of inquiry continues, leading toward an ideal, final agreement." His emphasis upon the inability of our thinking to affect reality was not a denial of the effectual role of thought, since he saw thought as the most determinant factor in reality, but rather was an affirmation of the fallacious and fanciful element in individual reasoning, or the lack of agreement or concurrence in results between our private thinking and thought in general (omniscience).

Peirce further complicated his concept of reality by making it evolutionary. The real grows and develops. Signs develop new meanings; ideas accrue new content. The constant mutation and development of our own ideas is analogous to a growth of over-all meaning in the universe. Thirdness increases. Deliberate, controlled, rational thinking, or scientific inquiry, is the very way in which new habits develop in the larger universe, or in a cosmic mind. The final causation present in our inquiry parallels the final causes operative in reality. We do not make truth as much as truth makes us. We belong to thought, and not thought to us.

Peirce's elusive definition of reality as that which will result from an infinitely prolonged inquiry seemed completely empty to his critics. In the most rigorous form of the pragmatic test, it was even a meaningless concept. Perhaps real, operative thirdness, like the old idea of natural uniformity, is an implicit or even necessary assumption in inquiry, but it does not aid in explanation. The most wary positivist will reach the same verified conclusions without it and usually with a belligerent refusal even to speculate about it. If law and structure are real, and not just convenient but arbitrary classificatory concepts, they do, as Pierce believed, predetermine the final result of inquiry. This is a consoling thought. But even though it insures that true opinions hold in the long run, we do not have any ready measure to determine the long run, and thus to eliminate the perversity of thought in whole generations (look how long a perverse nominalism survived). Refurbished to fit scientific aspirations, Peirce's reality was remarkably similar to the old Christian adage—God will make things right in the long run. It was the "blessed assurance" of believers.

The final agreement, after the elusive long run had elapsed, was to be more than verbal knowledge. By his final semantic distinction, and by his pragmatism, he made abundantly clear that the final truth would also be a living belief or habit. It would not be a verbal agreement among exhausted scientists, but a full conformity of everyone's thought and conduct to the generality, or thirdness, in the world. It would be a living rationality, a truth merged with the power of the good. It would be the kingdom of heaven or the blessed community. How close are we to it? Here Peirce vacillated. At times he believed we were close, that our scientific knowledge was partial but very accurate. If we could fully integrate that knowledge, in the sense of making it living belief, we would be close to the kingdom. More often, he had profound doubts. We had made only a slight, selfishly selective beginning.

Practically, Peirce ended up very close to Dewey, and merits a comparison. Dewey believed in real thirdness. As a speculative and tentative task, he tried to clarify the sort of structure necessitated or at least clearly implied by the success of scientific inquiry. With Peirce, he decried the refusal of positivists to look at these metaphysical problems; they acted as if these problems would go away if they turned their heads. But Dewey, much more than Peirce, believed that such a speculative ontology was methodologically meaningless, except in the moral and religious sense of giving courage and inspiring effort.

Peirce was also reluctant to admit what was all too obvious. In the living present, he too accepted a pragmatic and contextual truth. Dewey said this was the only "truth" that we have. Peirce and also Santayana, both close to Dewey in their epistemology, still kept the old "Truth," and both loved to think about it. It was so nice, so appealing, so far removed from the vulgar present. But whatever its methodological role, if any, Peirce at least failed to discriminate between ontology as a tool of inquiry and as an essentially religious ideal. His real thirdness was, as he conceived it, operative in the world; otherwise there would be no real purpose, and no room for any optimism. But in the perplexities of the present, it was simply an appealing unknown or, at best, an appealing "almost known." Peirce could not redeem its obscurity by all his advertisements of a future unveiling.

SCIENTIFIC METAPHYSICS

Peirce wanted to be a modern Aristotle and rescue science from its nominalistic, deterministic, and materialistic errors. Trained in logic, versed in mathematics, and acquainted with almost all the special sciences, he seemed uniquely qualified for this task. He would work out a new metaphysics which could account for all the laws of nature and provide a guide to further inquiry. Not incidentally, such a metaphysics, grounded not in selfish subjectivism but in logic and empirical fact, could provide an antidote to selfish social theories, open the doors to unbelievable progress, and even restore the prestige of common sense and of anthropomorphic religion.

In Peirce's age, and among his friends, the term metaphysics had come to mean useless speculation, without experimental foundations and hence without meaning. He believed the ill repute well deserved, for philosophers had fallen prey to German subjectivism or had prostituted themselves to the self-serving demands of theology. Existing metaphysical theories contained almost everything but good inference and hard fact. The working scientist had rightly repudiated the varied and irrelevant systems, but out of operating necessity had adopted a crude, superficial, but in the short run a functional materialism, based not on broad and general experience but on the interim hypotheses of physical science. In the long run it was proving a disastrous choice, for its doctrines were inadequate to guide further inquiry, were contrary to common experience, and were destructive of higher sentiments when extended to the social realm.

Fortunately, the great mass of men, and even most scientists most of the time, ignored the conventional materialism and followed more healthy instincts. But this still left man divided with himself. All human endeavor, and particularly all inquiry, needed to be conducted on a unitary basis. A much-needed metaphysics would have to be developed along scientific lines, meeting the rigors of the pragmatic test and being submitted, with humble piety, to experience as its final test. His system would be an offering to "the Great Power which, no doubt, penetrates his [man's] own being, but is yet all but wholly external to him and beyond anything that his poor present notion could ever, of itself, develop unfructified," for "whoever shall choose to seek his own purpose and idea shall miss it, and whoever shall abandon his own purpose and idea to adopt the purpose and idea of the author of nature shall accomplish that, and his own long-abandoned purpose and idea along with it." [8.1180.]

For what he believed were good and abundant reasons, Peirce rejected the doctrine of rigid mechanical determinism. With great enthusiasm he applauded William James's essay, "The Dilemma of Determinism," with its emphasis upon common sense and upon the moral dilemmas presented by a "block" universe. Peirce wanted to tangle, in greater detail, with the logical objections to the determinist doctrine. With analytical finesse he began by reversing a common notion. Despite what most people thought, strict determinism had nothing to do with causation, at least as the word was ordinarily used. Peirce never questioned the causal element in all events. The word cause grew out of the human experience of volition. By the modern period it generally meant what Aristotle called efficient causation. This type of causation assumes an agent (typically man), existing before the effect and not being transformed into the effect. Thus, causation is dynamic, unidirectional, and irreversible, and not nondirectional and transformative. Also, any designated cause might exist alongside other causes and allow overlapping layers of causal explanation. More important, and as too many people had forgotten in spite of Aristotle, efficient causation implies an agent's purpose, desire, or intent; it thus cannot be totally separated from final causation. An element of teleology permeates any unidirectional, progressive causation, even when general, impersonal agents are involved. If gravity really causes objects to fall, rather than being an arbitrary term to stand for the fact of their falling, it is an agent or power or law working in behalf of an end or a final state of things. Instead of following the conventional wisdom, and emphatically rejecting such an interpretation as a nonrigorous and illegitimate importation of subjective human elements into science, Peirce applauded it, and not as a devious device for sending science back to the Middle Ages. The common-sense, anthropomorphic understanding of gravity, with the implied teleology, was correct, for final causation, or a power working toward ends, was real not only in the limited area of human effort but in the universe at large. Reason was objective, not subjective, and was, by nature, teleological.

But modern science, with its conservation laws, supported a different type of determinism (one almost forgotten for centuries after it was advocated by Democritus and the Stoics), and one totally opposed to causation. By it, there was only a relative transformation of positions of particles. There was no agency, no determinate direction, no purpose, no principle of generation and growth. In every respect, it contrasted with human effort. By its use, the whole past and future could be charted by knowledge of any two instances of things, together with the laws of force. In this context, it is as true to say that the future determines the past as vice versa, since no external agent is involved. The time element is added as a law of thought, not of things, for all that is present is a fully necessary relational tie between states of the same thing. Without denying the explanatory value of this mechanical model, Peirce still rejected it as a guide to metaphysics or as a full explanation of reality. He wanted to go back to Aristotle's governing teleology, which was manifest both in man and in nature.

The sophisticated revival of teleology, or of future or final causation, was possibly the most distinctive feature of the whole pragmatic movement in philosophy. Both James and Dewey embraced it. But neither took it so far. Peirce wanted not only to justify the seeming efficacy of human purpose but even more to join man to, or even lose him in, a more general purposefulness, much like Jonathan Edwards or even Emerson. Thus, human purpose had merit, and efficacy, only as it corresponded with the purpose of God, or the true governing power in the universe. James, always the heretical Arminian, tried to go the other way and deify human purpose, with any common purpose only at best a pooling of individuals. Dewey took a middle ground. He could find the sustaining elements of purpose in the nonhuman parts of nature, but found teleology only where nature manifested not only structure but meaning, and this seemed largely limited to man. Since purpose existed only in mind and was a social product, it had a nonindividualistic but yet a noncosmic status.

Peirce launched a multifaceted attack on determinism. He granted that existence, or matter, cannot be directly influenced by other than mechanical constraint. If secondness alone were real, then mechanical explanatory models would apply to everything, including thought. But thirdness, as he defined it, involved final causes, and in some indirect way regulated matter. The material world exhibits not just brute force, but law and purpose, or at least direction. How does law interact with brute force? How do the final goals of thought become the ruling habits of things? This was the old mind-body problem stated in new, cosmic terms. In a completely static context, Benjamin Peirce's idea of some pre-established harmony might resolve the problem without any interaction. But in an evolutionary context, there was no harmony between the static world of mechanism and the growing world of habits or reason. Parallelism died with Darwin, if not with Kant and Hegel. Thus, the steady increase of a governing rationality in the world demanded two things: an element of chance or of plasticity in existence, and some indirect mechanism by which the ends of thought could be translated into new habits in matter.

To clear the way for chance, Peirce felt that he had to demolish the claimed infallibility or complete generality of scientific laws. In doing this he became, perhaps incidentally, a prophet of a scientific revolution which was just beginning in the late nineteenth century. Negatively, we never know anything for sure (fallibilism), for induction never allows more than a high probability. Informationally, if not substantially, the future is contingent and open to possibility. Any absolute, all-inclusive mechanical model can only be an unprovable hypothesis, supported by a hope for some final explanation. All that we can verify is a large degree of regularity in certain parts of nature and probably only in a few areas that concern or interest us (we never look for nonregular features). Even in certain well-developed areas of physics, such as the states of gases and the behavior of electromagnetic phenomena, Peirce observed great prerelativity theoretical confusion and the evident insufficiency of existing explanatory hypotheses. Before Max Planck first introduced the quantum, he believed that mechanical principles would not hold at the atomic level. The breakdown of Euclidean geometry challenged the whole idea of absolute exactitude, and should have long since sent all complete determinisms to the grave. More important, large bodies of phenomena were not encompassed by necessitarian formulas. Quality was generally left out, and with it feeling and the more distinctive elements of consciousness. Any full explanatory system had to be able to account for feeling as well as for diversity, spontaneity, specificity, and growth. Thus, instead of physical laws being ultimate, Peirce found them so partial and incomplete as to be in need of some explanation themselves. His attack on determinism was not an attempt to undermine scientific explanation, but to clear the way for more encompassing explanations.

Peirce not only denied the full scope of mechanistic explanation, a position quite easily defended and soon to seem almost obvious, but he also denied the absolute inviolability of any law. No law is obeyed precisely; some facts always swerve from any definite formula. Here he has had few followers. He called this doctrine *tychism* and used it to defend an all-pervasive and absolute chance. The position had to be speculative in nature, for the deviation from law was always too slight for any observation. Tychism expressed an ontological principle—there is some lawlessness everywhere and in everything. On the basis of his study of mathematical probability, Peirce believed any absolute regularity, unless in the purely imaginary realm of mathematics, was so suspect, so improbable, as to be unbelievable. Dewey, who also emphasized the contingency in events, never went so far. He believed that law was complete within limiting contexts of time and space and that the effectiveness of rational control depended upon this assurance as much as upon the contingency which kept the total of nature open to direction and management. Practically, there was no difference, since pure chance was unprovable. Peirce found tychism in harmony with the mathematics of probability and necessary for his larger ontology. Only an undiscoverable, infinitesimal lawlessness allowed him to define matter as an effete form of mind.

Peirce did not mean that chance is in any sense a dynamic force. It does not *cause* anything. It is the absence of determining law and of any form of original, coercive determination. But it still explains certain effects. A purely fortuitous distribution of molecules in space, at a given point, will retain a fortuitous element in all subsequent states, even though conservative laws are fully upheld in the interim. Thus, any individual event in a series may have a determinate cause, and the series may seem wholly under the sway of a rigid law, yet still contain an element of chance. Also, even a chance distribution (the roll of dice) is subject to statistical laws, for even a departure from law is subject to the general law of probability. In fact, some of our most certain laws may be only statistical in nature, involving immense numbers of atoms or molecules.

The net effect of these qualifications is a very elusive element of chance, pervasively sensed in ordinary experience, in spontaneity, mutation, growth, but almost impossible to locate by any careful inquiry, which will always reveal some law and some form of causation. Chance does not require the violation of law, but only infinitesimal lawlessness. It is invisible in any investigation of matter and may be largely the lingering effects of some distant state of affairs. Tychism has only one scientific role—to rid science of a superficial metaphysical doctrine. But it is a vindication of common experience, where chance pours in at every avenue of sense. It also allows the vital input of new and exceptional phenomena, or mutations of all kinds. The advance of rational purpose requires such exceptional events. This, he believed, was a good defense of miracles, one that did not resort to superhuman power or actual violations of natural laws as explanations.

Tychism has nothing to do with free will. It does make possible human freedom. At this point Peirce agreed completely with his Calvinist forebears. The laws of thought, which are inferred from external facts, are even less absolute than those of physics. This indicates that there is a greater amount of chance in brain protoplasm than in inorganic matter. But even here, in terms of physiology, the deviation from law is still too minute for observation. Yet it explains the constant breakdown of old habits (or associative tracts in the brain) and the accompanying feelings. Since feeling is the distinctive attribute of consciousness, chance again explains a great deal. Here, once again, Peirce anticipated a well-developed idea of Dewey's—that consciousness exists only at the point where thought-habits, or meanings, are undergoing change. Feeling plays a key role in deliberate or purposeful action, since it guides the thinking process. If free will stood only for the instability or plasticity of mental habits, then Peirce acclaimed it. But he never desired spontaneous choices and action, but rather rational choices determined by final causes, and causes in turn rooted in cosmic purpose (or what the Calvinists called God's will in their doctrine of predestination). Chance, or the absence of rigid law, allows habits to break down and yield to new ones. It permits reason to work its way. But chance behavior is not reasonable or lawful behavior; it is the exact opposite, as Jonathan Edwards had long since demonstrated.

With all the assurance of an old-fashioned Calvinist, Peirce argued that freedom could only mean the liberty to make choices and to take responsibility for one's character and conduct. As a fact, men effectively criticize their own conduct and redirect it in behalf of preconceived objectives. It seemed the height of absurdity to deny that a student could not learn a new principle of logic and then use it to criticize his thinking, or that a person could not get up and raise a window because of an anticipated cool breeze. This type of self-control was a fact, however it interacted with other types of causal explanation. Its reality was experimentally more sure than the result of any laboratory experiment. Mechanistic theories, faced with the necessity of doing something with intelligence, classified it as mere feeling and denied its essence—purposeful action or final causation. But short of such a suicide of common sense, men knew that they were on the stage side of the footlights, and at one with the poet of the piece.

Peirce's lifelong defense of human freedom was never an attempt to elevate man or turn him into a controlling deity. Peirce reflected few elements of individualistic humanism and almost none of voluntarism. He rebuked nominalists for so elevating the individual human mind as to make it alone the arbitrary creator of general ideas, for which there was no living counterpart in the world. To Peirce, individual reasonableness and end-directed conduct was possible only because the same reason, the same mind, was the essence of the world. To defend human freedom was not to defend anarchic willfulness, but to recognize that man's glory was only in what he shared with all reality. If thirdness, if law, if teleology did not correctly characterize, reality, then Peirce would have been inconsolable. He never had the personal confidence, the self-respect, or the courage to rely on either individual man, or on unredeemed groups of men. Only the possibility of selfless man, redeemed by a vision of truth, self-sacrificed on the altar to a future but coming kingdom of reason, and sustained by a living God, could give him the courage to face his own dismal world and his own dismal self. Peirce was a sinner and desperately needed the assurance of salvation. Few

Puritans, and no other pragmatist, so well understood what this meant
—the sacrifice of pride, of ego, of self.

But all that tychism does is open up things, and break down rigid,
deterministic hypotheses. With tychism, purpose has room enough to
operate. But does it operate? How can secondness, the world of existence, of brute forces, be governed by thought, or by such nonexistent
realities as habits and laws? His ultimate answer was speculative and
cosmological—dynamic objects spring from the stock of reason and are
naturally inclined to obey it. But he still had an obligation to show the
exact relation of mind and matter.

Since mind is final causation, it exists only where genuine triadic
relationships exist, and thus only where life and thought exist. This is
true whether mind is used in a cosmic sense or in the limited sense of a
human mind. In either case, mind has one pre-eminent and distinguishing attribute—feeling or consciousness. Any general idea has the unified, living feeling of a person. Human personality involves the closely
integrated feelings which accompany the behavior of a physical body. In
rare cases, two or more distinct personalities alternatively share the
same body. To an extent, there are collective personalities, or the integrated, sympathetic feelings of a group, such as a church. Thus, the
human personality is only loosely tied to the body; human thought
seems only accidentally joined to a brain. More correctly, the brain,
with its physiological peculiarities, is the pre-eminent form taken by the
material content or secondness of the human mind. Peirce loved to
shock people by making the tongue as much a seat of the mind as any
other organ. But in any case, there is no separation in experience of
thought and matter, any more than there is a complete separation of the
three categories. The dyadic element, formally present in dyadic relations of thought, and existent in matter, can be explicated by either
logical or mechanical principles. Physiology is always one half of psychology. Thinking requires existential acts, but is more than any purely
mechanical action. The physical substratum of thought does not lower
its dignity, its superior station, any more than the necessary servants and
agents of a king lower his status or limit his freedom. He acts for future
goals; they act at his command. Although psychical laws are inferred
from their operation in things, this does not make them similar to
mechanical laws, for they are laws of association instead of laws of

dynamic sequence. Thus, psychical laws govern only psychical processes, and physical laws govern only material processes. Seemingly,
there is still no way for the twain to meet.

Peirce brought them together by metaphysical magic. In some bold
speculation, he denied any absolute distinction between mind and matter. Mechanical explanation is, by itself, only a partial explanation,
functionally adequate for many purposes, but ignorant of all truly causal
and triadic relations. Any phenomenon, viewed alone in terms of action
and reaction, or relations of force, can be explained by mechanical law.
The same phenomenon, viewed in terms of inner feeling, has to be
explained by psychical laws. Thinking can be explained as a mechanical process, given a certain perspective and intent. The purest of
physical forces can be explained by psychical laws. He often referred
to an inner and outer classification, meaning by inner a psychological
perspective based on feeling, will, and associative habit, and by external
a physical perspective in which reaction, existence, and quantitative laws
were focal. If he had stopped here, Peirce would have joined James in a
radical empiricism, or a neutral monism of experience stuff. He rightly
insisted, when first reading James's essay, "Does Consciousness Exist?"
that he had for years believed in a similar functional distinction between
mind and matter, and by then believed such a position quite commonplace. But he went further and argued that matter possessed habit, that
habit was generalization, and that generalization was mind, or the
spreading out of feeling (firstness) into operative law (thirdness). Thus,
matter was a variety of mind, but a peculiar type of mind no longer
plastic to new habits, and therefore almost entirely lacking in feeling and
in consciousness. By this peculiar form of panpsychism, the duality of
mind and matter was transformed into a duality of highly conscious
mind and nearly unconscious mind. This resolution, though, still left
unexplained the exact manner of influence from one to the other.

This key task Peirce could not perform, even though it is at the crux
of his whole system. He confessed his failure. But, he believed the
problem was empirical, and thus he could be excused as a philosopher
for being a poor psychologist, and therefore waiting for others to do the
research. He believed he had done enough in loosening the horrible
chain of mechanism, in showing the metaphysical unity of mind and
matter, and, through a doctrine of chance, in clearing the way for
purposeful action. But he still speculated about the actual mechanism.

In his work with pendulums, he found that a differential equation for the interactive movements of two conjoined pendulums could be so mathematically transformed into two separate equations as to express all the physical facts without any conception of interaction. There were parallel ways of stating facts originally stated interactively. Perhaps the parallel statement of psychical and physical laws could be transformed into an interactive statement without logical conflict. This he tried, drawing upon the mathematics of continuity and of transfinite multitudes. He believed an *endless* series of mental events could be directly followed by a *beginningless* series of physical transformations, or vice versa. This meant a type of interaction or influence, but without direct interaction of a dyadic type, and without any transfer of force. This explanation, if it was such, required some farfetched hypotheses about vortices of ether, but was introduced not to explain but to show the possibility of explanation.

Peirce unified all his metaphysical ideas by an elaborate evolutionary cosmology. Essentially, he took human inquiry, or the deliberate quest of greater law or reasonableness, as an analogue of a cosmic process. The path for man lay from the nothingness that preceded thought, to primitive ignorance, and on to ever greater knowledge and possibilities for self-control. Surely this was in form similar to a cosmic ascent from lawlessness toward perfect rationality, or from chaos and nothingness in the infinite past to complete lawfulness, or death (no feeling, consciousness, or new habits) in the infinite future. This cosmology seemed necessary to account for other speculative beliefs of Peirce and, at the same time, often suggested others. Outside the context of his total philosophy, it seemed impossibly arbitrary. Inside it, it seemed a plausible resolution of problems or a clever synthesis of ideas. Peirce took it very seriously, although he never claimed any final proof for something so remote from empirical verification.

He had a terrible time getting his evolution going. He would allow no inexplicable first event with the suggestion of some unknown cause behind it. Yet, he was not satisfied with the inexplicable and irrational nature of an unending regress. Thus, he again resorted to a mathematical model, or to a beginningless series, in which there was a process of beginning and not an original event. He had to start by describing what preceded anything ("precede" is incorrect, for before events there was no time). To do so, he talked of an original zero fully as elusive as

Plotinus' One. A pure negation or nothingness preceded all the categories. It (one has to refer to an "it") was not death (a second to life, and the final form of nothingness) but a never-bornness that was somehow germinal. As nothing, Peirce insisted that it contained all possibility of being. It was the all-potential. With a Hegelian twist, he argued that pure nothingness annuls itself and, in a dialectic leap, attains not actuality, but some limitation of possibility, or a chaos of pure quality and feeling. It becomes pure firstness.

But this "powder of feeling" is still chaos and no-thing, yet now a nothingness with some specificity. There is still no interaction or events. Since quality and feeling distinguish consciousness, this pure firstness is also pure consciousness. In this ungoverned, relationless chaos, feeling is more intense than ever again, since Peirce always made feeling the inverse of habit. But, as always, pure firstness is too elusive for understanding. The consciousness is not of anything. It involves no awareness, no reflection. It is a sleeping consciousness, a quale consciousness, or the sheer tinge of feeling that precedes any identification of anything. This primitive feeling is unitary, whole, without conflict. It compares with Dewey's later emphasis upon the underlying qualitative unity of any experience. In man such pure firstness briefly reoccurs when, in the brain, a bit of protoplasm throws off a habit and momentarily escapes the force of all law. Whenever diversity is on the increase and habitual patterns of thought and behavior are loosening their hold, man meets pure firstness, and has a sense of how it was before there was anything.

Out of this pure feeling, by sport or chance, there develop arbitrary pairs of qualities, coming together and moving apart. Peirce was never more vague than here. But with any interaction, a form of secondness is born. Certain chance encounters repeat. The chance encounter creates a probability of more encounters. A track is laid down. A habit forms. Thirdness becomes operative. The first tendency to repeat reveals the universal law of evolution—the tendency to take on habits. This law explains all subsequent development. Chaos becomes ever less pervasive; habit ever more pervasive. Yet, the original nothingness or lawlessness remains a part of the universe, breaking out in mutations, in abductions, in all manner of instability. At first it was so pervasive that events were discontinuous and without a complete temporal and spatial setting. But soon there was enough regularity for a metrical time and space and for approximately exact measurements.

This evolutionary scheme looks toward a time when all remaining chance will disappear, and with it all possibility of life and thought. Somewhat paradoxically, the achievement of rationality means the end of rational development. When habit finally becomes omnipotent, ruling everything absolutely, there can be no more feeling and consciousness. The loving God of the present becomes the aloof and cold abstraction of an Aristotle. The psychological difficulty of such a view was never remarked by Peirce. Some men would object to furthering a reason that terminated in such a cold perfection. Apparently, Peirce would not have felt the force of such an objection. He seemed to want to lose himself in a perfect whole. A loving God was a necessity for a sinner, not for a saint. Thus one willingly enlisted in God's cause, looking toward a time when God would be perfected, impersonal, and uncaring. By then man would be totally one with God.

In any case, the present was not bleak. God's love was the motive force for evolutionary change. This doctrine he called *agapism*. As was made obvious by his teleological theories, Peirce could not accept an unaltered Darwinian view of evolution. Because of his distrust of capricious individualism, he projected purpose to a cosmic dimension. In brilliant speculation, he merged a tychistic or accidental type of change, a Hegelian or necessitarian type, and a teleological type. The Darwinian doctrine of accidental or unexplained variations, plus the progressive principle of natural selection, corresponded closely with the logic of probability. It paralleled the logic of an eliminative dice game, in which a few become more fit (or wealthy) and others are eliminated. This type of evolution, always at work in nature, is a prelude and even a necessity for any purposeful change. Whether God or pure chance lies behind it, effective human purpose awaits the spontaneous breakdown of old habits. Without chance, no new growth is possible. Without mutation and eliminative selection, minds capable of loving purpose would never have developed. At the same time, the deterministic view of Hegel, which has evolution leading inevitably and necessarily toward a foreordained end, correctly interprets the elements of lawful habit that are indeed present in all physical change. Such a view ignores chance, effectively denies freedom, but is an understandable if partial retrospective view and points up the amount of rationality already achieved in the process.

But neither of these two types include the purposeful change so familiar to common experience. In it, we anticipate goals and take on new habits. Psychical purpose, not mechanical coercion, is uppermost, although existing habits support the process and make it possible. In this type of evolution the motive force is love for something. Peirce believed the final goal, or *summum bonum,* is loved, not because of a full intellectual grasp (indeed, this is impossible), but because of the power of sympathy, a sympathy in turn based on the ultimate unity of mind and the continuity of individual minds. The vision is basically esthetic, involving feeling and will as well as intellect. In agapistic evolution, the final purpose has to embrace the good of all, or of a complete community. Such evolution conforms to cosmic or divine purpose and reflects God's love for His purposes. Individual goals, when not united to other minds and to all-mind by sympathy and love, are blind and selfish goals, essentially hateful and in the long run futile. Peirce hated the emphasis upon greed and selfishness in nineteenth-century social theory, in the practices of the new industrialists, and in so many neo-Darwinian interpretations of evolution. His hatred was embittered by his own sins of greed. Thus, he advocated a Lamarckian interpretation of evolution and an organic conception of the social order.

Agapism, in registering the ultimate purposefulness in evolution, was Peirce's mountaintop doctrine. But his whole metaphysical system was best summarized in his pervasive doctrine of continuity, or by what he called *synechism.* This doctrine culminated in a cosmic mind, wholly divisible neither into discrete thoughts nor into isolated personalities. Reality is indivisible in any complete fashion. All things are related, and individuals are never completely real. Any arbitrarily isolated thing shades into other things in every direction. By his doctrine of continuity, Peirce made time an entity, never rent, never perfectly divided. Any moment is divisible into other infinitesimal moments. By it he insisted upon the ongoing, nondiscrete nature of perception, or the stream of consciousness. By it he denounced atomistic individualism and mechanistic explanations in all areas, from physics to psychology. By it he affirmed the reality of community. Reality is a continuity of mind, or the unified personality of God. Just as a human personality is one, whatever the checkered history, the variety of experiences, so reality has the form of a living personality. It is a vast complex of ideas and memories, all related to each other, all united by the overarching quality of feeling, and all directed toward a common goal.

His doctrine of continuity, defined in mathematical terms, supported by a deliberately anthropomorphic interpretation of experience, was the theory that best resolved the problems of his life. It seemed to offer a redemptive meaning to his suffering. His highest metaphysical doctrine was always a religious affirmation. It appropriately ended in a theodicy.

In Henry James, Sr., and in the Gospel of John, Peirce found a conception of a loving God who was not only a cosmic mind developing toward greater rationality but also a personality, with feelings and compassion. God stands to man much as man stands to his own ideas. A man creates an idea, loves it, sinks himself into it, whatever its imperfections and its irrelevance to fact. Like a scientific hypothesis, he tries to nourish it toward perfection, at which point he probably takes it for granted and appropriately forgets it. Thus God, as creator, or in his incarnation, sacrificed a rigid and uncaring perfection in behalf of chaos, chance, and selfishness. He consented to a station far beneath any lofty omnipotence, a station in which he, like a parent, needed man. He loves His children, not because they are perfect or holy, but in their weakness and need. He freely bestows His love and compassion upon imperfection and evil. God loves, not Himself, not His perfect image in man, but rather evil man, man selfish and so full of pride that he may not love in return. And God, once incarnate in a creation, needs man as the proper object of His love and the proper instrument of His purposes. Thus, God's need and His love redeems and justifies man's evil and suffering. The evolutionary process is a process of reconciliation. It reveals God's unending sacrifice of Himself in behalf of His beloved, and in furtherance of man's deliverance from sin and disharmony. Man's redemption is God's greater perfection. Through love, there is growth, for love, "recognizing germs of loveliness in the hateful, gradually warms it into life, and makes it lovely." [6.289.]

AXIOLOGY AND RELIGION

In both ethics and religion, Peirce erected a largely false façade of irrationalism behind which he concealed a rather imposing body of theory. But nowhere else did internal conflicts so clearly lead him into ambivalence and irresolution. He flirted with a consistent theory of value, yet never acknowledged it for what it was. In religion he always seemed to be on the verge of a major theological offering, yet he stopped at tantalizing suggestions. Not only did these subjects reflect the over-all incompleteness of Peirce's philosophy but also some inhibiting attitudes, springing either from the bias of an age or from personal peculiarities.

Peirce occasionally fell prey to an appealing half-truth widely believed in the late nineteenth century. In extreme form, it asserted the complete incompatibility of reason or science and the emotion-laden, involved concerns of practical life. The dualism, often lamely stereotyped as the objective versus the subjective, could hardly be complete, for clearly some practical interests did motivate some successful inquiry, and knowledge did on occasion influence practical interests. But in either case the interaction was assumed to be extrinsic or even incidental. The practical man, looking out for personal interests, had no real concern with truth, but only a desire for what was immediately useful. The scientist or scholar had no concern with utility or with the pressing concerns of a busy world. In monastic seclusion, in objectivity and detachment, he gave his all for truth. Generally, this dualism was sharply weighted on the side of the truth-seeker. In a gilded age, science and scholarship could offer a new, nonvulgar basis for snobbery. But an undertow of sentimentality bolstered a compensatory alternative: the more instinctive types of behavior, such as that of a mother toward her child, or the simple worship of common folk, were most ennobling and far above the abstract and artificial concerns of intellectuals. Finally, there were those who tried to merge the two areas and let careful inquiry inform behavior and criticize belief. Pragmatism is a good word for one such effort.

Peirce, at varying moments, supported all of these positions. He could be a pompous ass, dismissing the immediate and pressing concerns of life as the veriest trifles, or seeing the individual as only a mere cell in a social organism. He often ridiculed practical and active men and an Americanism which increasingly meant a worship of business. But very often his contempt for "practicality" was only a repugnance at greed and vulgarity. Thus, he could embrace a conservative sentimentalism and venerate the instinctive habits and beliefs of common people. They were more true than any new scientific concoction. Finally, his pragmatism seemed to be the basis of a long-range and rational reconstruction of knowledge and action. Only when traditional beliefs underwent a long process of criticism could they rightly serve as a basis of action.

His most representative attitude was roughly this: live by instinct but commit yourself to the furtherance of reason. For most problems, common sense, in the form of established habits and rules, provided the best alternative. Science could rarely compete with the traditional wisdom. In contrast to our most compelling desires and needs, the latest scientific discoveries are mere trifles. Even the laborious search for truth is not important to most people. In any case, it cannot substitute for the duty of fulfilling one's calling, of doing what conscience dictates, of expressing a religion of the heart. These vital interests are real and important, even too important to entrust to reason.

Yet, even though reason be a thousand times as fallible as instinct, it is the best means we have for investigating new areas and revising antiquated beliefs. It is the prime secret of purposeful progress. Thus, Peirce's emphasis upon the disinterested nature of science and philosophy was, ultimately, only an attempt to keep both fair and honest, not because they were worthless, but because, over the long run, their results were so vital. Instead of really retiring from life, the scientist was life's greatest servant, too busy at his task to be diverted by the short-range concerns of the moment, or by the selfish machinations of vulgar businessmen and politicians. Since terms like "utility" meant something selfish and contemptible, Peirce tried to find a higher purpose for science. But, tyranny of words, all he ended up saying was that, because it was self-controlled and directed toward a long-range goal, it had more utility, or a higher utility, or a more ennobling utility, than custom or instinct.

Peirce never recognized this and almost always tried to keep an artificial wall between inquiry and practice. He believed philosophy had to be segregated from life or else become infected with selfishness and error. At the very minimum, he wanted a rigid separation of tasks, with "pure" science carried on by a group of saints, and "applied" science carried out by a group of ordinary men. He always believed that any motivation, save a pure desire for truth, would spoil the results of research, and came close to arguing that only a lofty aloofness befitted the laboratory. Thus, he not only unrealistically idealized the scientist, but, as one who should have known better, confused the psychological problem of motivation with the methodological and logical problems of correct procedure and valid confirmation. The same confusion carried over into his social attitudes, leading to snobbish attempts at ego-boosting (his pose as a persecuted saint on the battlefront of pure truth) and to evidence of contempt for a lower, selfishly motivated humanity. These attitudes did not match his own ethical position, his religion, or his pragmatism.

But the same attitudes and the same confusion kept him from making an honest statement of his theory of value. He could not honestly deal with such terms as utilitarianism and hedonism. He tried to avoid any pleasure-pain principle. Just as a scientist cannot seek a cure for a disease or the means to a new technology, so a moral man must not be motivated by something so crass as happiness. Value has to rest on something more sublime. This something sublime turned out to be an esthetic quality present in experience. But the word esthetic, carefully segregated from such terms as pleasure, and almost resentfully tied to feeling, was only a camouflage for a theory of value rooted in the intrinsic, experiential value or the felt satisfaction of certain types of experience.

In his final pragmatism of 1903, Peirce offered a quite elaborate theory of value. This was consistent with his increasing emphasis upon final causation as the dominant force in the universe. By a new classification of sciences, he placed three normative sciences, esthetics, ethics, and logic (conforming to firstness, secondness, and thirdness) at the apex of philosophy. Although logic, concerned with correct thought, was the most general of the three, it was also the most dependent, falling back on ethics, or a general theory of conduct. But ethics, in turn, seemed incapable of answering its one most crucial question: What is supremely good, not as a means to something else, but in itself? Although he was exceedingly tentative, Peirce believed the answer to this question would be found in intrinsic or experienced quality, and thus in the area of esthetics. Almost to his own surprise, it seemed, he had to make a seldom-investigated subject the key to his whole philosophy.

In projecting a teleological view of reality it is very important to be able to identify the final end, or at least to be able to detail some of its attributes. Since Peirce assumed an identity between God's purpose and man's highest purpose, he committed himelf to the furtherance of reason, or of generality and habit. This unifying ideal, or *summum bonum,* gave meaning to both ethics and logic. But the furtherance of reason, as a mere concept or statement, is vague and unmoving. It is like preaching the love of God without, in any way, demonstrating God's incomparable loveliness. Even as did Jonathan Edwards, Peirce wanted to merge an intellectual belief with an emotional and sympathetic fervor.

True belief, in the pragmatic sense, involved feeling as well as intellect, volition as well as verbal symbols. The experiential value, the attractiveness of anything, including an idea, resides in the felt quality that accompanies it. Thus, the problem for an esthetic science is the definition of the quality that gives vitality and life and power to the idea of rationality. Its full experience would be beatitude.

What is supremely good in itself? Not, Peirce insisted, mere pleasure, or even what is generally known as feeling. Would it not be catastrophic if his whole elaborate system of philosophy could be reduced to a pursuit of mere feeling? But if the supreme good is a form of beauty, it at least escapes the ordinary connotation of feeling. This highest good is an experience in which multiple and chaotic qualities are so realized and harmonized as to become one positive, simple, immediate quality. It is the icon of complete thirdness, or of being itself. It is the quality, or firstness, of reason. It is the feeling that accompanies successful cognitive activity and that particularly suffuses more encompassing generalizations. This feeling or quality, as befits the act of generalization, of bringing intellectual order out of chaos, is one of harmony, unity, and symmetry, which are Peirce's key esthetic norms, as they had been for Edwards and most Puritans. The experiential aspect of ideality is only the vital, moving side of cognitive activity, or intellectual synthesis, which is only the abstract expression of habit-forming, or the purposeful rationalization of conduct. Logic, ethics, and esthetics thus merge, as do intelligence, action, and feeling, or truth, goodness, and beauty. Value is experienced; it is still a variety of feeling, but it has almost nothing to do with ordinary eating and drinking and loving, or any very limited and self-serving pursuit. It relates to, and permeates, both the practical and fine arts only when they embody intellectual qualities and live up to the selfless ethic demanded by the pursuit of reason.

The ethical and logical import is quite clear—to act and think reasonably in all areas where thought and conduct are self-controllable. In other areas we do what we must. Mankind must give full and gracious consent, and its best efforts, to the working out of cosmic purpose, or evolution, or God's will. The beauty and harmony of a living rationality is experienceable by an individual, but the experienced rationality is independent and objective. The loveliness is an attribute of God. The normative sciences are not how-to-do-it disciplines, although they have a practical bearing; they are true sciences, depicting the real laws that relate phenomena to final ends. Morality is, in a sense, a matter of taste, of what we like and desire and therefore of necessity embrace. But it is also a matter of grace. If the scales of self-love fall in moments of humility, we may escape our own self-created hells and glimpse the *summum bonum,* the living purpose of our creator, and find it irresistibly lovable. God, working through history for our redemption, expressing His love in the law of laws, the ever progressive rationality of evolution, will finally redeem everything. Now, lonely man, in his isolation, in his awful alienation, in his divided and disharmonious and self-defeating individual goals, can only aspire to redemption and, like Peirce, take consolation in God's love, and at least half-believe that human suffering is conducive to His final purpose and all men's eventual glory.

This strange litany is unique in American history. It is the selfless requirements of logic that first convicts us of sin. It is the willing and fully cooperative pursuit of truth, symbolized by scientific inquiry, that stands testimony to our partial redemption and to the strength of our hopes for an eventual complete reconciliation. It is the process of inquiry that prefigures the holy church, or the coming kingdom. Thought, sacrificially directed at truth, realizes itself in act, and ends in bliss. This, Peirce affirmed, was the ultimate meaning of pragmatism.

Ever seeking to do God's will, ever anxious about his own salvation, Peirce remained in large part aloof from practical political and social issues. Like Jonathan Edwards, he wanted to get at the root of all modern ills and only on occasion noted the surface symptoms. Even more than Emerson, he developed a prophetic message, and this in the language of logic instead of poetry. He hoped to save the world, not by proximate reforms, but by a radical incision of all nominalistic heresy and by a radical implantation of a logically reformed, neoclassical realism. In a sense, he was the true conservative, trying to bolster and retain common sense and ancient virtues. He desired only cautious and careful change and always deplored blind and careless innovation. Part of the tragic quality of his life as well as of its at times almost ludicrous, quixotic quality, was his naïve hope that, by a new logic, through the ramifying effects of a few students, or with a twelve-volume explication of his philosophy, he could save the world and reverse many of the major trends of modernity. Like Edwards in the eighteenth century, Peirce wanted to turn things around. Then, out of all the suffering and failures of his demon-possessed life, would come a glorious vindication, and he would have fulfilled his own special calling for which God had created him. The last years were filled with the echo of such hopes and sorrowful intimations of a final failure. Although Peirce made no major contribution to social thought, he left a philosophical outline which, if fully grasped, pointed to the renovation of a whole society, away from greed, rampant individualism, social dislocation, individual alienation, and all varieties of cynical subjectivism and skepticism, and back to an organic community, with cooperation, common beliefs and ideals, and a dedication to seek new truth and greater achieved rationality.

He did take some part in religious debate. His synechism, even more than most forms of idealism, constituted a philosophical theology, although he always insisted that it was in no sense developed for that purpose. He never completely lost a youthful interest in religion, but in the Harvard-Hopkins years moved far away from Christian orthodoxy and came close to making a creedless religion out of science, or out of some vague search for truth. With the development of his metaphysics, and with advancing age, he moved back toward Christian orthodoxy and gave much attention to traditional doctrines.

Peirce defined the religious person as one who had a sentiment for, or obsessive perception of, the *summum bonum,* and of the force in the world that worked for it. To be religious was to be duly pious, to recognize one's relative being and lowly status, and to have awe for the circumambient All that sustained us. Religious goals were public and social and were supreme in their demands. Religion looked toward a creative power or force as well as toward an ideal end. Peirce usually united those in his conception of God, or of a reason at work and a reason to be attained.

At least as an ideal, Peirce loved the church, but claimed to hate all creeds, theologies, and institutional forms. Like Henry James, Sr., he believed that religion had an inborn tendency to stagnate instead of grow, moving toward a final credal dead end. But he generously attributed this tendency, not to the essence of religion, but to the selfishness of man. Drawing inspiration from his friend, Francis E. Abbot, he argued that true religion grew much in the spirit of science and counted each conquest of reason as its own triumph. But few individual churches, and no denomination, quite lived up to this openness.

With a heavy burden of ignorance and the blindness that typified his age and his best friends, Peirce hated theology. It was reason prostituted—the nemesis of true religion. He never bothered to read any or try to understand it. Throughout life he unmercifully ridiculed the theologians, the despoilers of metaphysics, the propagators of senseless and tyrannical creeds, and the masters of empty disputation. Religion, grounded in experience, in instinct, in feeling, in sentiment, required no proof. It was false and hypocritical when it had to depend on the rationalizations of crafty and interest-serving theologians. Their reasons were suspect and irrelevant; as if philosophy could validate religion, or a mouse protect a lion. Likewise, he ignored rational attacks on religion. Why should one drop the religious beliefs of youth because of some hypothesis not subjected to centuries of criticism? This was as silly as leaving the church, losing the sense of community, the common joy of Easter and Christmas, simply because one could not accept the narrow doctrines of those "professionals" who guarded the mysteries of worship. The theologians might force many people into atheism but not him. If it had not been for the air of apologetics, the system of obedience, and absurd doctrines taken as absolute truth, Peirce would have joined the Church of Rome. He wanted to be part of an ancient and catholic Church, but also of one vibrant and growing. He found his own Episcopal Church an imperfect median between two ideals.

The very word church had a magical appeal for Peirce. It stood for medieval scholarship, for the revival of learning, even for the ethic of scientists. It stood for the love of truth as well as the law of love. It stood for a more lofty life, a pathway out of egotism and alienation. He wanted to merge his own partiality and incompleteness in a larger organism, traditionally expressed by the idea of the body of Christ. Here, through the power of love, there might be real communion, with ideals celebrated and realized. In the divine community one could grow toward true virtue and come closer to a direct perception of the divine being. But this idealized, invisible church, made up of all men who had recognized their sinfulness, and who had been called back toward harmony with God, was remote from reality, or from a lonely, embittered, possibly penitent Peirce, sitting each Sunday on the back pew of the Milford church.

Peirce's idealization of religion and the church often led him close to the empty sentimentality of so many nontheological "liberals." He so often appealed to vague instincts, to open sentiment, or to a nebulous love that religion almost seemed to be the soft underside of serious pursuits. His hatred of theology often seemed to degenerate into a religion bereft of intellectual content. He could define Christianity as a "way of life," or as a simple attempt to follow the morals of Jesus. Love was the only commandment and the only creed. Such naïve views were at odds with his own philosophy, which he would have seen as a complex system of theology if he could have conquered his fear of the word.

From his youth on, Peirce professed a belief in God's reality. No doctrine, he confessed, could be nearer the truth than theism, and a theism that required a *personal* God. To define God in other than human terms would make the concept meaningless. But he confessed an element of vagueness in the concept. Often he used God in the sense of creator, or the reigning necessity or force behind evolution. God was the cause, the unified feeling, the will that sustained teleological progress. The known universe was an image of his developing purpose. God was necessarily infinite because reality is a continuum without beginning and end. God was necessarily timeless, for He was responsible for time. God was necessarily nonexistent, for He created the dyadic world of existence and was constantly molding it to His purposes. Thus, his God was only a personalized and popularized version of his synechism. The greatest problem was how to conceive God apart from his incarnation in the existing world and in human minds. Presumably, outside such a temporal setting, God is nothing, or unlimited potentiality, or pure firstness, with consciousness, rich feelings, and the potentiality of all things. He is thus prior to, and more than, his particular creation. Creation is an image of God, contains his essence, yet is not God. Pantheism is avoided. Man is not a facet of God, or a necessary constituent of God, but a separate identity loved by and needed by God.

This definition of God left no room for personal immortality. In fact, Peirce never wanted to preserve the separated individual, but instead wanted to merge him into the whole. Typical of his Neoplatonic orientation, he believed any literal heaven to be a discontinuous break in reality and almost inconceivable. A person is immortal only in the sense of merging with, and surviving in, the realized purposes of God. A great man, who tremendously advances the reign of reason, has a larger place in the final scheme of things. Not only does man face the extinction of personality, but so does God, for He moves toward a final apotheosis in

perfect habit. A selfish desire for individual immortality or future rewards is only one side of the selfish mentality of a good banker. Because
of psychic research, he was tempted toward a spiritualistic view of mind,
but still believed any mind required some nerve matter. He wanted to
explain psychic phenomena by nonconscious action and feeling. Like
James, he felt that there were great depths of dimness, great expanses of
memory lying beneath the shallow upper layer of the bottomless pit that
was consciousness. But in 1908 he finally granted that there might be
some unexplained and fragmentary life after death for some people.
Clearly, he disliked the idea.

In one of his last articles, "A Neglected Argument for the Reality of
God," in the *Hibbert Journal* (1908), Peirce tried to refashion the
arguments of William James's famous essay, "The Will to Believe." The
article, as his letters reveal, was carefully calculated for a popular audience and revealed some slight concessions to their views. In it, he went
as far as one could go in advocating belief in an unprovable hypothesis,
yet tried to avoid some of the logical traps that ensnared James. He did
not want to violate the methodological rigor of the pragmatic test. Without his realization, this last public defense of his religious ideas was also
an acute and revealing defense of his whole metaphysical edifice.

Peirce presented belief in God's existence as a peculiar abduction. It
was too vague a hypothesis for deductive-inductive verification, but was
such an irresistibly beautiful idea that, even without proof, it functioned
effectively as a living belief. Like any abduction, it arose in a creative
situation of intellectual openness, not out of a critical set of mind. In
moments of reverie, of esthetic appreciation, of wonder, or what he
called musement, the hypothesis offered itself to the imagination. The
normal emotional response to it, the most unifying of ideas, was intense.
It seemed to be a full and beautiful explanation of variety and growth
and purpose. In other words, it solved the age-old problem of design,
although Peirce had already demonstrated the impossibility of making
an absolutely valid inference about a designer, since chance could
account for all experienced order. But any but the most critical scientific
mind would be content with the hypothesis of God. The common man
accepted God as real, or even as the most obvious thing in the world,
and acted accordingly. On this crucial issue Peirce voted with the common man and tried to vote pragmatism also (Dewey protested).

The main force of Peirce's argument came from his long-established belief that abduction was not a mere random guess, but to some extent an instinctive insight into the objective mind which fathered the human mind. Ordinarily, this instinctive aspect of abduction only lessened the chance of error, leaving a manageable number of hypotheses for experimental testing. But the hypothesis of God's existence seemed a special case, since it was so simple, so intrinsically beautiful, and so universal (Peirce's argument, like James's, loses much of its force if any "normal" person is not attracted to the hypothesis). If really irresistible, as Peirce believed, it must represent a special case of exceptional divinatory power, or of a basic instinct reared into the light of consciousness. In this one case an idea, by its very appearing, is most likely true (a weak version of the old ontological argument). Since we must rely on some hypothesis (James's argument) and act in some manner, we can do no better than follow the natural bent and acknowledge our theism without intellectual qualms. Here, he believed, the usually critical pragmatist should not question common sense. But he carefully noted that the belief, in itself, was neither completely clear nor established as true in any scientific sense.

Despite his caution and his qualifications, Peirce still slipped into an untypical and hated voluntarism, for in essence he let a belief be true because it was appealing. He finally justified belief in God because of the conduct such a belief led to. This meant a detour around Peirce's objective standard, for the justifying conduct did not involve any specific sensible effects, any tangible or public data required by the hypothesis, but only conduct that, in terms of Peirce's cosmology and his concept of the *summum bonum,* furthered the development of concrete reasonableness. He thus tried to escape James's subjectivism by making the verifying conduct other than personal satisfaction. But, since the cosmic standard to be furthered by the living belief was really God's will, Peirce fell into an obvious circularity, a circularity that plagued his whole philosophy. He in effect said only that one who believes in God, or in the reality of a cosmic design, will behave consistently with such a belief, or act "as if" it were true. This is all but obvious. The reality of God and the standard, inseparably tied to each other, both remain an open issue. One can not be used to establish the other.

Clearly, Peirce's God was only a symbol for the heart themes of his metaphysics. In admitting vagueness and an irreducible element of faith or hope, he acknowledged a speculative element in his system, an element which, at best, he could lamely hide behind some universal and infallible instinct. His metaphysical system, in all its subtlety, was born out of his own hours of lonely musement. It reflected a lively and original imaginative bent and also the tremendous scope of his knowledge and interests (compare with Whitehead). He assumed, quite falsely, that he only elaborated upon a universal common sense, that the main bearing of his system was obvious and rooted in common instincts. He wanted, not to be different or original, but to clarify the obvious. Since he could not abide any degree of mystery, he pursued for a lifetime the elusive snare of full intelligibility. He did not want an element of risk in his faith. To avoid it, he kept looking for some trick of mathematical reasoning, or some universal consensus of human experience, to pin it all down. But in this endeavor he could not succeed. He fell prey to the arbitrary elements of any pure formalism. He remained too long captive to a dated Victorian optimism. His system had to be repaired with every major shift in mathematical thought; it could not survive the breakdown of an evolutionary faith in inevitable progress, or in the inevitable realization of all possibilities.

But however arbitrary, however dated, his philosophy was a beautiful and appealing creation. Gothic but modern, grandiose but impressionistic, it has to be seen in its total plan, in its over-all harmony, to be fully appreciated. When fully understood, his ideas still have and will long have tremendous appeal for many people; they will seem to articulate almost perfectly their own beliefs and feelings. This may be the fairest standard for evaluating such an architectonic system. In a more narrow and technical perspective, his arbitrary but intriguing use of the categories, his emphasis upon the realistic underpinnings of science, his sophisticated and rich defense of personalism and anthropomorphism, and, most significant of all, his reintroduction and elaborate defense of final causation remain as major monuments to his philosophic genius. They join his less significant, fragmentary, and at times incidental contributions to a philosophy of science, to semiotic, and to logic.

Peirce had a unitary vision, a feeling for the continuity of all things, that has been rivaled in American philosophy only by Edwards and Dewey. It is with those two men that his thought has to be constantly compared. He was closer to Edwards in his idealism, in his eventual correlation of his ontology with a relatively orthodox conception of God, and in his emphasis upon the need for grace and salvation. He was closer to Dewey in his evolutionary emphasis, his scientific methodology, his emphasis upon teleology, his relating of value and fact, and his merger of structure and contingency. In his moral zeal, his synthetic bent, his conception of freedom, his emphasis upon the esthetic nature of beatitude, he agreed with both men. In all American thought he was unique in his greater response to forms of thought than to nature, in his personal weakness and travail, and in the scope of his cosmic optimism about human history.

VII
WILLIAM JAMES

THE COURAGEOUS PILGRIMAGE

William James wrestled with almost all the problems of contemporary philosophy. He gave final answers to very few of them. But he suggested more possible answers and confessed more irresolvable issues than any other American. His luxuriously varied critique of pure experience ended an epoch begun by Locke and Kant. Neither rationalism nor traditional empiricism could withstand the newly revealed facts of careful psychological inquiry. But the new philosophical formulations were not carried within the bosom of scientific psychology, or any other science. They sprang, by esthetic and moral necessity, from the bosom of man— of man often troubled and confused. James worked at a mighty transformation; he died with a sense of and a feeling for a new era, but his feeling never gave birth to a coherent and total conceptual statement.

James could not resist the lure of philosophic speculation. He tried. Few major philosophers so often felt the hollowness of abstract theorizing. All conceptual thought seemed derivative, and justifiable, if at all, only by use. No formula about the universe could ruffle its majesty. The common-sense world, with all its gifts and duties, was the eternally real world. James's excursions into abstraction represented a hard road to personal sanity and affirmation, not a joyful retreat from life; a means of straightening the crooks of life, not a blessed consolation. Like Emerson, he always affirmed the ultimacy of concrete and immediate experience. Nothing horrified him more than a rationalistic inversion by which man became a servant of reason. His own personal crises, his unending involvement with moral and religious dilemmas, defined his intellectual questions, and in many cases dictated his most enduring answers, as he frankly admitted and defended. Thus, in an even more open and obvious sense than is usual, the pressing concerns of his life were also the issues of his philosophy.

Born early in 1842, William James was the eldest child of a family of five. Family experiences, intense and stimulating, provided by far the most important educative influences until his college years. His equally famous brother, Henry, Jr., his equally brilliant but more eccentric father, Henry, Sr., and his equally sensitive but invalided sister, Alice, provided most of the intellectual fare. A calmly efficient mother and two younger brothers lacked both eccentricity and effective talent. Both parents came largely from Scotch and Scotch-Irish progenitors. William's grandfather and namesake immigrated from Scotland to New York State, where he was noted for both his rigid Calvinism and his business sagacity. His fortune subsidized the dilettantish spiritual pursuits of Henry, Sr., and even provided a partial livelihood for each member of the third generation.

Under the sway of Henry, Sr., the James household combined a tender intimacy with near intellectual anarchy. The home, blessed by leisure, literacy, and love, became a somewhat chaotic school, with maximum freedom but such a lofty seriousness and spirituality as to create inordinate expectations and standards. Always on the move, forever inviting new experiences and acceptable schools, Henry, Sr., denied his children a constant environment, a clear sense of identity, or even a settled vocation. Both Henry, Jr., and William agonized their way into an adult calling, with frequent detours and dead ends. Even their father's unswerving religion failed to provide an anchor, since the children never quite grasped its deepest meaning or had the requisite experiences for feeling its inner truth. When challenged by other, more normal children, they were somewhat embarrassed by their father's lack of a business and by their lack of a nameable religion or church. As a result, the family fell back on an internal and often quite soaring dialogue, as full and rich in ideas and strong but divergent personalities as ever graced a single family. In his first long absence, homesick on the distant banks of the Amazon, William, with typical exuberance and playful exaggeration, recalled the family scene, with everyone swarming about, "killing themselves with thinking about things that have no connection with their merely external circumstances, studying themselves into fevers, going mad about religion, philosophy, love and *sich,* breathing perpetual heated gas and excitement, turning night into day. . . ." [Ralph Barton Perry, *The Thought and Character of William James* (Boston, 1936), I, 225.]

William James would always be open to other people's influence. Every compelling belief half-converted him for an interval. But only his father left an ineradicable imprint. Henry, Sr., was a perfect antinomian, intoxicated by his own highly personal religious beliefs and by his own sense of redemption, which followed an earlier conversion experience. A completely confident, full-bodied believer, Henry loved friendly controversy and excelled at a florid, visceral, biting, epigrammatic style. In a constant stream of brilliant polemics to newspapers and in a long series of theological books, he fulfilled his one vocation—preaching a rarefied spirituality that raised redeemed man to a plateau of understanding far above the level of earthly vanity, with its egotistic pride, moral strictures, and mundane pursuits. He believed in a working God, who labored to rescue man from his finite limitations, and to bind all men together in total unity. The path to such salvation lay through the dark valley of humiliation, where all worldly pretense, all claims to merit, all human art, all moral systems, all finite consciousness, all self-assertion and self-love were finally renounced in behalf of divine truth. This world-weary faith mixed elements of Swedenborgianism, Neoplatonism, and New England transcendentalism. In a monistic system, it eliminated both evil and all human conceptions of good. Uniquely for an American of his generation, Henry dwelled on the pessimistic themes in religion. His beliefs exhibited elements of morbidity and were comparable on many points with the philosophic resignation of the later Santayana. Needless to say, he was in no sense an orthodox Christian and delighted in attacks upon the barbaric vanities of conventional churches.

William James, the pre-eminent Arminian in modern America, could never feel the validity of his father's worldly pessimism and escapist spiritualism. Later, he denounced a somewhat similar escapism in Santayana. The gulf between father and son was wide enough to cause feelings of guilt on William's part. In long letters from Europe, where William was struggling with the enigmas that seemed to lurk behind modern scientific thought, he showed his difficulty in understanding his father, but at the same time he also revealed his desperate search for both understanding and solace. In a nontheological age, his father's very language seemed archaic and untranslatable. Eventually, in his *Varieties of Religious Experience,* he would be able to characterize and justify the "sick-minded" of the world, but he clearly rejected their solution to the problem of evil. Yet, he valued much that his father exemplified—his expression of heroic commitment, his hatred of orthodoxy of any form, his individualism, his love of freedom, his zest for self-expression and correspondence, his sense of the priority of being to knowing, his distaste for the pretensions of science, and much of his sympathy for mysticism. In a farewell letter, he offered profound thanks to his dying father: "All my intellectual life I derive from you. . . ." [Francis O. Matthiessen, *The James Family* (New York, 1947), p. 132.] To Henry, Jr., he wrote: "Father's cry was the single one that religion is real. The thing is so to 'voice' it that others shall hear,—no easy task, but a worthy one, which in some shape I shall attempt." [*Ibid.,* p. 133.] As he struggled with his own skepticism, he kept looking for a "glimpse through the ontological window" and kept his father's sense that religion was the most important thing in life. Long after the commanding presence of his father was gone, he still heeded its call to duty. As his own babes arrived, he only desired to transmit to them his father's humanity, his faith in the divine, and his sense of his inviolate right to have his own say about the deepest problems of the universe.

After two years in the ancestral city of Albany, William moved with his parents to New York City. It was, at least, a launching point for summer vacations in New England, visits to uncles and aunts in upstate New York, and long trips to Europe. In his New York home, Henry, Sr., entertained famous guests, including Emerson, and carried on a correspondence with eminent men around the world. He preached a personalized version of Fourier's socialism and followed with interest and astute criticism the transcendentalist movement. Surrounded, in fact almost inundated, by books and ideas, William received only fragmentary schooling from tutors and, after age nine, in three private schools in New York. None of these met his father's exacting standards. Thus, in 1855 Henry, Sr., moved the family to Europe for three years, hoping thereby to provide the boys with language skills and a better education. William, then thirteen, briefly attended a private school in Geneva, picked up an excellent command of French, and began his study of German. But this was only a beginning; he had other schoolmasters in London and Paris, and did his beginning college work in

Boulogne, where he first began serious work in science. From France, in 1858, the family returned to Newport, R.I., where William attended a good private academy. In 1860, after a brief stay in Bonn, Germany (with the inevitable tutor), William entered an ill-chosen apprenticeship in painting. In 1861, as the Civil War began, William, much too frail to enlist, entered the Lawrence Scientific School at Harvard, in what began a permanent connection with that institution. The family moved to Boston in 1864, and soon on to Cambridge. The uncertainty was almost over. Science was to be William's profession; Cambridge his home.

The travel, the varied contacts, and the linguistic tools all justified William James's long educational pilgrimage. He lacked the methodical habits of German scholars and never acquired a thorough background in mathematics and physics or in classical history and philosophy. But he had a more cosmopolitan orientation and a greater interdisciplinary curiosity than any of the young American pedants who specialized in one subject and traveled to Germany for their Ph.D. No other American professor ever achieved his degree of confident cosmopolitanism, and no other American philosopher ever made such a direct and significant impact upon Europeans. Over half of his close professional friends, including those who influenced him the most, were Europeans. He corresponded in German and French, wrote and gave professional lectures in French, and managed to learn some Italian. Often his ideas were better known in Europe than in America. He gave both the Gifford and Hibbert lectures in Britain and would have lectured for a year in France had his health permitted. For him, the Atlantic Ocean was nonexistent in any intellectual sense.

As an adult, James made twelve extended trips to Europe, in two cases for two-year periods. He and Henry, Jr., carried on an endless dialogue on the respective virtues of America and Europe. William embraced both, and for different reasons. Unlike Henry, he loved the raw and primitive aspects of America. Almost as much as Henry, he deplored the ugly defacement of America by man and turned in delight to the more trim and neat face of Europe. At times, particularly on returning home from Europe, he experienced feelings of revulsion, and then lamented the psychic effect of travel abroad, revealing the terrible suffering of a divided soul. But at other times, such as during the Dreyfus affair, he felt an even greater revulsion toward Europe, with its stagnant and unfair institutions. Then he welcomed the freer and less fettered air of America. The net effect: an ever generous and tolerant William never gave, or felt called upon to give, a final verdict. At times in America he yearned for Europe. Always, after a while in Europe, he yearned for home. And since America was home, he cultivated pride in its virtues and took responsibility for its injustices.

While his two youngest brothers fought and suffered in the Civil War, a half-guilty, highly nervous William agonized over a vocation. His brief flirtation with painting convinced him that he had more ability in science than art. Personal doubts, religious confusion, and a haunting pessimism and skepticism provoked philosophical interests, but he scarcely envisioned philosophy as a profession, believing that he lacked the emotional maturity for full-time philosophic efforts. Almost by accident he drifted into a specialty at Harvard. After a year of work in chemistry, with frequent excursions into other fields and less than single-minded devotion to tedious laboratory work, he changed in 1863 to anatomy and physiology, working under Jeffries Wyman and Louis Agassiz. Both professors, but particularly the famous and almost heroic Agassiz, won his full interest, in part by allowing his darting mind to roam the whole field of biological sciences and, even more, by encouraging his interest in related philosophical issues. In the wake of Darwin, these issues were momentous and exciting. He entered Harvard Medical School in 1863, continuing the same generalized physiological interests, without having definite plans to become a practicing physician. He finally received his M.D. (his only earned degree) in 1869, after two interruptions.

In the first of these interruptions, in 1865–66, he accompanied Agassiz and a group of young scientists on the Thayer expedition to Brazil. He was plagued by ill health in the first part of the trip, and he exhibited a notable lack of zeal for detailed zoological collection and classification. However, as his attachment to Agassiz deepened, he exulted in tropical beauties and began agonizing on philosophical issues. Back at Harvard in 1866–67 he sank into greater mental depression with attendant physical complaints. His intellectual companions both stimulated his thinking and challenged his veneer of personal confidence. A cynical Oliver W. Holmes, Jr., just back from the war, persuasively argued for skepticism and materialism. Charles S. Peirce, gifted in logic and intellectually more mature than James, and Chauncey Wright, a wonderfully tough-minded positivist foe of all sentimentality and metaphysics, completed a circle of intimate friends, and gave James a brief but sophisticated introduction to philosophy. They converted him to a Darwinian conception of evolution and planted many of the seeds of pragmatism. But the delightful intellectual excursions left him personally insecure and depressed. He needed a prophet more than a teacher.

In 1867 James went on a pilgrimage to Europe, seeking health and hope. His spiritual crisis, which would plague him for another five years, never led to a threatened mental breakdown, nor did it provoke any sudden conversion. But all alone, vainly seeking cures at German baths, and spending too many hours in brooding introspection, James came close to suicide in 1867. A moral activist, without the resignation (or the grace) required for a full and joyful consent to the universe as it existed, James floundered on the old problems of evil and determinism. He yearned for salvation, but could not accept the terms offered by existence. Evil was as pervasive as good. If a God was responsible for it all, He did not deserve any love. In fact, one could take consolation only in intense hatred of such a God. The alternatives seemed bleak. A moralistic crusade against evident evils seemed a hopeful, humanistic alternative. But here James faced the second ogre, a then convincing materialism that seemed to preclude any moral freedom. He would not follow his father and proclaim all to be vanity, or a Santayana in a cavalier resignation from the moral battlefield. He was too ardent and too sensitive to ignore evil, and he was too moralistic to tolerate it.

The parallels with Emerson are remarkable. After the death of his first wife, Emerson also suffered the same intellectual confusion and doubt and had the same psychosomatic complaints, even including eye problems. He too went to Europe in search of salvation and there slowly developed his doctrine of self-reliance. James never found quite so satisfactory an answer, but he at least discovered free will. Even if irrational, he resolved, as a first act of will, to believe in the freedom of his will. But even when he became confident of freedom and of moral possibilities, James was often too weak to battle alone. Humanism might preserve his sanity, but it left good to the hazards of future accidents. He wanted some help and, above all, some assurance of final victory. He needed a God to battle with him, to console him in adversity, and to maintain the struggle beyond his own lifetime. He never stopped searching for such a God.

But in Germany he had to be content with a humanistic expedient. He read the Bible, Browning, Wordsworth, and a French philosopher, Charles Renouvier. From Renouvier he adopted a very simple definition of free will—the ability to sustain an idea by choice. Later he would weave such a concept into his *Psychology* and labor to bolster it by physiological data. If true, this ability to sustain an idea should enable a person to overthrow evil moods by sheer force of will. Exertion and moral discipline might work. This was James's professed consolation when on the verge of suicide. God and final purposes are hidden, but our active life can add to the welfare of the race and lessen the burden of evil. He bade temporary farewell to transcendental dreams, to any hope of communion with the soul of the world, and resolved to find the good in man. He bravely asserted his own worth and cultivated feelings of moral freedom. In a sense, he tried positive thinking and found that it worked.

Germany meant more to James than healing baths. He read widely in literature, developed lasting friendships, and indulged his love of art galleries. More significant, he tried to study both physiology and psychology. In Germany he found that psychology was being studied in a new way. Experimental techniques and physiological data were transforming a highly speculative discipline into a science. James had a background in physiology. His own emotional travail had created an intense interest in mental phenomena. Here seemed a new and pregnant area, where he could apply the exacting scientific method which he so admired in Wyman and Agassiz, and in the process find concrete answers to many of his philosophical dilemmas. The new psychology became his vocation, with the more laborious scientific inquiry necessarily taking an early precedence, and the philosophical application dominating his last years. But he had to postpone his training. Hopes of working at Heidelberg with the two recognized masters—Herman Helmholtz and Wilhelm Wundt—gave way to illness and a trip back home in 1869.

Although he received his M.D. in 1869, James remained idle and sickly for three more years. He read extensively and thought too much. By 1872 he was thirty years old, unmarried, and had never made any contributions to mankind. Although leery of his health and doubtful of his ability, he accepted a temporary instructorship at Harvard for 1872–73, teaching a course in comparative anatomy and physiology. It proved a wonderful step. Activity routed his despair and helped cure his physical complaints. He proved a stimulating lecturer and was an ever loyal friend to his students. In 1873–74 he gave in to illness and spent another year in Europe, largely Italy. But then he went back to teaching and to years of stability. He added courses in psychology, established a small psychological laboratory (one of the first in the world), in ten years climbed the academic ladder to full professorship, and began a steady stream of reviews and journal articles. By 1880 he had bridged the still indistinct boundary between psychology and philosophy and had moved into the latter department. At the advanced age of thirty-six, he finally married and established a home. His bride, Alice Gibbons, who had been introduced to him by a close friend, proved a sympathetic wife. In the same year, 1878, he signed a contract with Henry Holt and Company for a small book in psychology, which was to be completed by 1880. After twelve long years, it grew into the two-volume *Principles of Psychology,* the greatest achievement of James's life and possibly the greatest achievement in American scholarship. By 1882, when James used a sabbatical to return to Europe for extra study and research, he found that he was as fully abreast of psychology as any European and that Harvard compared favorably with any European university.

Of medium build, agile, bearded, and intensely masculine, Professor James exuded nervous energy and boundless enthusiasm. Easily bored, he hated elaborate detail and all types of pedantry. He easily identified with and loved people, tolerated great differences, and prized eccentricity above orthodoxy. His bent toward reconciliation and his openness to new ideas made him a peacemaker; he had good friends in every ideological camp except that of complete cynicism. Typically, his beloved friends were often the bitterest of enemies among themselves. James could not be dogmatic, at least for very long, and risked gullibility in dealing with cranks and crackpots. They might, he thought, turn out to be right. He described himself as an activist, who welcomed a bit of tension, a stinging pain in the breastbone. He tried to rise above his own physical weakness and possibly overstressed the element of struggle and competition. He always castigated anything limp, stagnant, flabby, or self-satisfied. He often glorified righteous struggle above noble ends, for in the struggle was the thrill, danger, intensity, ardor, or, in one of his favorite terms, life *in extremis.* He loved to goad anything overly dignified, pompous, or secure. Thus, he tempted city dwellers with the virtues of the farm, chided scientists about the limitations of science, told educators about the virtue of action, exposed fellow pacifists to the benefits of war, and joked fellow professors about the pretensions of a Ph.D.

James lived simply but well. He constantly resorted to the hills and mountains for rejuvenation. Eventually, he built his own large home in Cambridge, bought and restored a large farm house at Chocorua, New Hampshire, and owned part interest in a camp at Keene, New York, in the Adirondacks. His Chocorua home provided a summer and vacation retreat for his growing family (two boys and two girls). With a legacy from his father, eventual book royalties, and a large lecture income, all added to his Harvard salary, James was able to afford frequent European excursions, gracious entertainment, private schools for his children, plenty of household help, and even a hired hand at Chocorua. Although democratic to a fault, in the sense of accepting differences and quirks and in resenting any special privileges, he nonetheless reflected the standards of a middle-class Victorian gentleman. A moralist in the most conventional sense, he never tired of his little sermons against vice, alcohol, and indolence. He had a sense of *noblesse oblige,* lectured students on the responsibilities of college men, and showed contempt for lower-class reformers, for the "falsest views and tastes somehow in a man of fashion are truer than the truest in a plebeian cad." He absorbed some of the evangelical themes of his youth and too often fell prey to newer nostrums—inner strength, hidden meanings, higher insight, or anything "to make life worth living."

In 1879, in the rhetoric of an Emerson, James asked for a new prophet, one who could demonstrate "that all our different motives, rightly interpreted, pull one way." [*Collected Essays and Reviews* (New York, 1920), p. 140.] The scientific and philosophic fashions of the late nineteenth century seemed to divide man, either denying the validity of his ideals and his feelings of worth and purpose, or else enthroning those at the expense of logic, fact, and freedom. The more rigorous scientists seemed to shame faith and deny all hopes. Evolutionary ethics, with bare survival enthroned, soon ran into physical laws that guaranteed the eventual doom of all life. Even art, instead of unlocking divine secrets, was falling into sensuality. The search for recognition and for a sense of individual worth soon perished in the mechanistic denial of independent personality. Thus, James had to clutch partial beliefs out of the moral chaos and depend upon his animal spirits for sustenance. A new, theoretic synthesis, with justice to all the facets of life, would require a deeper philosophic analysis and discrimination than any yet made. In his radical empiricism, pluralism, and pragmatism James later felt that he had a hold on such a synthesis, if only he would have the time and the ability to weave it into a coherent whole and the rhetorical ability to publicize it. In his last years, particularly in his almost evangelical defense of pragmatism, he reflected the confidence of a Luther and verily claimed a philosophical reformation. The careful analysis was in the past, in the *Psychology*. Minor differences, nuances of detail, were not worth all the controversy. Why not get on with the redemption and risk early excesses. Prophets always invite excess even when they establish a new truth.

James conceded the strength of his emotional enemies—the positivists and naturalists. He wanted to preserve the analytical rigor and the metaphysical economy of a Chauncey Wright, but he wanted to combine it with a tender-minded defense of moral and religious insight. He commended the lofty elevation of his philosophic enemies, the idealists, but wanted to be rid of their meaningless abstractions and their monistic absolutism. The solvent for all the differences seemed to be a new, psychologically informed understanding of the prime reality of life—direct experience. The wrecking job performed by the early empiricists—the great Locke and Hume—had abolished many needless abstractions but had still gone awry. The Kantians began their repair work with the barren, atomistic abstractions of this empiricism and built an artificial world out of artificial brick, connected by an abstract mind. Hume could be corrected and made over into a positive, optimistic, even religious philosopher; empiricism, purified and redeemed, could discipline, relate, and integrate all human concerns. Then the scientific lion could lie down beside the religious lamb.

In the perspective of his time—in the heyday of Spencerianism and popular science—James clearly saw the scientific lion as the aggressor and a meek, defensive religious lamb as the oppressed underdog. But the science which so often became the devil in his morality play was largely the insufferable product of arrogant and superficial scientists. James easily commended careful inquiry in every area and dared to bring careful techniques of inquiry into the field of religion. But he saw science, as sponsored and popularized in America, as a new church, rich in prestige, imperialistic in its claims, and intolerable in its intellectual pretensions. By unjustified metaphysical extrapolations, scientists had underwritten determinism, atheism, and cynicism, and had illegitimately cowed warm emotions, moral zeal, and religious aspiration. James accepted and commended the legitimate fruit of science, but loved to ridicule its pretension to a privileged and exclusive type of truth. The naturalism spawned by arrogant science (Dreiser's naturalism) could end only in deep sadness. Man, unable to find objective status for his values, could in old age only turn toward resignation or morbid despair. The essence of religion was the affirmation that all was not vanity, but the scientists seemed to see all as vanity. Most horrible, naïve students were driven to agnostic despair (James spoke personally) by the coercion of what purported to be absolute fact. Or, in an equally lamentable rebellion, they embraced romantic idealism with its morally repugnant type of absolute pantheism.

James wanted to discipline science, to put it in its place. In behalf of this, he leaned far toward an anarchic voluntarism, in which all concepts, abstract by necessity, competed on an equal basis and won victories by sheer emotional satisfaction. At moments of least intellectual circumspection, he rejoiced in his happy hunting ground of experience, where any conceptual scheme could find some justification, be it the most fanciful or most sublime. All might provide some type of satisfaction. Whereas science gave man technology, its proper fruit, sentimental religion yielded serenity, moral poise, and even, at times, seemed to cure diseases. The world's treasury house could be unlocked by many keys. No intellectual constructions were exhaustive or exclusive.

In philosophy, James was a child of modernity. He worked almost exclusively in the perspective of British empiricism and nineteenth-century idealism. Although capable of excellent insights about Greek philosophy or even about scholasticism and early-modern rationalism, he still seemed to think of these as remote and archaic. Unlike Peirce, Dewey, and Santayana, he never constructed a historical framework for his ideas. He considered himself a disciple of Locke, Berkeley, Hume, and Mill. Whenever possible, he generously read his own ideas into these progenitors and was particularly apt at exploiting congenial minor themes in their thought. He was less generous to Spencer, in part because he saw him as a traitor to empiricism. His debt to Peirce and Chauncey Wright was great, but can be easily overestimated. From Wright he gained a sharp razor for cutting through all types of useless abstractions. But he could not understand Wright's passionless rigor, or his universe, with its cosmic weather and lack of ultimate meaning. From Peirce he gained a feeling for an operational approach to truth and support for his concepts of pluralism and freedom.

James lived through the ascendancy of idealism and never realized how ephemeral the English and American wings of the movement were to be. His early attachment to Josiah Royce, his own inability to come to final terms with ontology, early left him an unwilling captive to Royce's Absolute. But in behalf of pluralistic freedom he had to fight his way beyond any monism. He replaced the idealist reality-for-thought with a broader reality-for-experience, and he replaced the all-mind with finite gods. But the emancipation was incomplete. In battling with Royce, he had a fatal weakness. He too wanted the consolation of a higher, divine consciousness, and therefore had a deep, moral sympathy for absolute idealism. As a typical Arminian, James wanted God as a support, but otherwise wanted to be free to work out his own destiny. Sacrifice and abnegation were never Jamesian terms. By reducing God to a finite level, he lessened the terrible demands, made grace useless, escaped the dilemma of evil, and certified the validity of his own moral preferences. But by confessing the need for and affirming the belief in God, he undercut most of his effective arguments against Royce, as he eventually acknowledged.

James often apologized for his logical deficiencies. Peirce helped further the idea that he was a terribly loose thinker. At times he certainly was. His first book on pragmatism, strictly on its own merits, was about as imprecise and confusing as any major work in the history of philosophy. But James was not always a sloppy thinker. In sheer technical ability, in the capacity for sustained and logical analysis and for incisive and clear style, he had few peers. Certain chapters in his *Psychology,* some articles, even parts of his *Essays in Radical Empiricism* abundantly certify this capacity. But he vacillated between careful analysis and near polemics. The *Principles of Psychology* was his philosophic *Das Capital; Pragmatism* his *Manifesto.* Parts of his later work were clear, even obvious, to anyone who had digested his psychology. Otherwise it could be terribly confusing.

More crucial, James was always a bit of an irrationalist. He followed logic to extremes in refuting his philosophic foes, but went beyond it when needs be in affirming his own convictions. He never relished the logical harness and accepted it only when larger purposes required it. His worst offenses against clarity came in public lectures, where he tried, like Emerson, to communicate a vital understanding and not technical arguments. With perfect justification, he ridiculed a student who used textual analysis against him. This was, in his estimation, the ultimate of plebeian vulgarity and simple-minded literalness. He felt that the totality of his message had some coherence. It did. But it also had gaps and unsolved dilemmas. His very openness to criticism helped muddy his intellectual waters and often prevented completeness and consistency.

The greatest strength of James's philosophy lay in its thorough grounding in psychology. He gave American empiricism a foundation in detailed psychological knowledge that English empiricists and European positivists never had, and scarcely have even yet. Even today philosophers with vastly more logical and semantic sophistication than James unconsciously revert to long-since invalidated nineteenth-century psychological concepts or fall prey to the metaphorical formulations of Freud. The disciplinary divorce of psychology and philosophy came at the very moment when psychology, grounded in careful inquiry, could inform philosophy and correct its more wanton abstractions. Even the impact of evolution upon American pragmatism came more through psychology than through biology. Any lasting empirical reconstruction depended upon a verified, objective understanding of how men perceive and conceive their world. This James provided. He used it effectively to cut away from the mistakes of the past. But he could not use his new tools all the time or in all areas. He could not follow Dewey in a thorough reconstruction. He was master of much of the traditional deadwood, yet captive to much of it. But in the perspective of time, his psychological theories remain as the most important contribution made to philosophy by an American. Royce and Peirce lacked his psychological grasp and had to struggle to accommodate it. Santayana and Dewey shared much of his understanding, but they gained most of it directly from James.

James died in midstream. His first book preceded his death by only twenty years. He started late and did not live to be very old. In 1899 he overexerted in the Adirondacks and permanently damaged his heart. In two years he fought back to a normal but more restricted life. But he would not slow down as much as his heart demanded. By 1907, after many earlier but repulsed overtures, he effected his final resignation

from Harvard. In early 1910, after having given the Hibbert lectures, his
health began to deteriorate at a rapid pace. A vain and hopeless summer
in Europe only left him worse. He barely managed to get back home to
Chocorua. There, in the midst of his beloved hills, he died on August
19. With him perished his hopes of a great metaphysical synthesis.
Possibly, he would never have completed it had he lived. At sixty he
responded as avidly to new ideas as he did at twenty. He could never
stop long enough to tie everything up in a neat bundle. His life was a
fast-flowing stream, with plenty of rapids and a large number of spring-
fed tributaries along the way. The flow widened and deepened but never
slowed.

PSYCHOLOGY

In germ at least, almost all of William James's distinctive philosophical
ideas appeared in his voluminous *Principles of Pscyhology*. But here
they were often muted and incompletely developed. By exerting a
speculative discipline, by holding back on his developing metaphysical
assumptions, James was able to renounce any finality, any resolution of
existing psychological and philosophical controversies. When he felt
confident, he pronounced judgment. Often he showed clearly where his
sympathies lay, yet tried to do justice to all points of view. The final
result was definitive enough to set clear boundaries to his subsequent
intellectual development. Here was his philosophical prolegomenon,
with the identified problems and the relatively safe and assured points of
departure.

The *Principles* included a tremendously complex treatment of the
varied phenomena of mental life. James tried to answer the question:
What do we now know, in precise, objective terms, about human thinking? He summarized the returns from recent research in physiology and
in both human and animal behavior. He equally relied upon introspective data. When problems still seemed ambiguous and unresolved, he
carried out his own limited research or, more often, tried to read aright
his own mental processes. As much as he appreciated some results of
experimental psychology, of Germanic fact grubbing, he never wanted to
become a slave to a laboratory. He did not enjoy detailed work. He
avowed that anyone intelligent enough to be bored could not spend all
their time patiently starving out and harassing minute details, and in

spying and scraping with deadly tenacity and diabolical cunning. He wanted to go on to a grand style and consider the most significant theoretical issues.

The end result was a near encyclopedia. He used behavioral data to judge existing theories and tried to marshal all the competing evidence before telling where "the truth lies." He stressed continuously that psychology was an infant science and that all judgments were very tentative. Beyond this central purpose—the summation of existing knowledge and theories—James also pointed to dangling metaphysical issues, provided a running bibliography, occasionally presented historical essays on crucial problems, and often pointed out the practical and moral relevance of various topics. In several detours, and in one chapter on hypnosis, he explored abnormal mental phenomena, and whenever possible offered theories to account for it. Unlike too many classic psychologists, dealing only with formal abstractions, James professed an interest in what he termed the gothic shadows and often searched the prisons and madhouses for data.

The great new factor in late nineteenth-century psychology, a solvent for many past illusions, was the successful expansion of physical science to encompass mental phenomena. If psychology lost its soul with Kant, it was now finally losing its mind. No subject matter seemed exempt from a physicalistic or behavioral explanation. Physiologists, utilizing new and delicate experimental tools, had finally explored the brain and lower nervous system. As Santayana insisted, psychology was really a subbranch of physics.

The reflex-arc concept, with its many ramifications, seemed capable of accounting for all types of animal behavior, including so-called higher types in man. In modern terms, the reflex-arc concept pictured the brain as a complex computer. Programming occurred at the senses, with a tremendous amount of data soon stored in its memory cells. The computer was tied, by complex organic circuits, to the body, and gave the directions for its operations, with self-corrective feedback again coming through the senses.

The one thing unaccounted for by this model was the mental phenomenon of consciousness, or the feelings that attended its functioning. But as far as anyone could tell, these feelings, per se, had no dynamic role, and in an explanatory science could be ignored. Perhaps they were an extra hum given off by the electronic machinery, and might disappear if the machinery reached a higher level of functioning, although they seemed to increase with its intricacy. Rabid behaviorists insisted that, being purely subjective and without effect, they should be forever abolished from psychological science.

James accepted the reflex arc, as he had to. At the same time he accepted the existence of mental phenomena, as he also had to. As a matter of belief, not yet clearly elaborated or proved, he felt that the mental phenomena accompanying the underlying physical processes had some functional role and that an automaton theory had some hidden limitations. But for the purposes of an infant science, he preferred to mute all speculative issues, including metaphysical ones, and work in terms of a naïve dualism of mind and matter, just as most physical scientists did. Whenever possible he correlated physical processes and mental states. Mind remained a substantiative entity as much as matter. Already James was working toward a radical concept of pure experience, in which both mind and matter would dissolve, being only functional classifications. In fact, even in the *Principles* physiological and mental data are clearly viewed as alternative and teleologically determined conceptualizations of what seemed to be one reality—pure experience. Thus, his movement back and forth from the physical to the introspective and mental never pointed to some Cartesian parallelism.

Do mental states accompany all neural activities? Apparently not, at least in the simple reflex behavior that bypasses the brain, and seemingly not in the most habitual responses of a cerebral type. Thus, consciousness seemingly attended only more intricate, slower, and less habitual response cycles, where large amounts of computer circuitry were involved, and where electrical energy was forcing new discharge paths in the brain, perhaps through biochemical mutation or by hidden nutritional growth. But James would not be rigid. Vague types of awareness seemed to be present even in very habitual behavior; in hypnosis memory could be extended to unbelievable minutiae of experience. In any case, new human habits originated in conjunction with acute awareness. Unlike lower animals, man developed new brain paths that were not an organic inheritance but a product of learning.

Under the influence of this physical model, James stressed habits and the means of their formation. If conscious feeling had a role, it had to be in the formation of new habits. He showed that habits are assets, simplifying life and lowering mental tension to a bearable level. His sermon on habit, written, he later said, as a moral inducement to young people, has become a classic in psychological literature.

One implication was now clear. The complex neural processes in all animals are teleological or, in biological terms, adaptive. Most of all, the process of reflective thought in man, or the restructuring of brain paths by internal stimuli and the use of elaborate codes, is a mechanism for changing the world, both within the brain and even more by the re-directed motor activity that it often leads to. When the internal pro-cesses are working properly they change the world in behalf of the organism. Even if the purely mental phenomena, the feelings, do no more than register a physical process, the process itself is an active one. Learning, in this behavioral view, is no copying of some external reality, but the perfection of the most complex regulative device in the natural world. Here, in short, was a death blow to any conception of mind that made it a camera. Whatever the role of the hum, no sensible person should ever discount the work of a computer. Mind, now tied to quite concrete physical processes, could never again become a divine spec-tator. It was a skillful worker, and as a perennial moralist James would have had it no other way.

James's most significant contribution to a physiological account of mental life was his theory of emotions, or the James-Lange theory, since he generously acknowledged a later publication of similar ideas by the German psychologist Friedrich Lange. This theory had great philosophi-cal implications, but they were never explicitly recognized by James.

Simply summarized, James gave a seemingly inverse account of cer-tain intense feelings, which he called emotions. His point was that some bodily changes, when they involved perceptual awareness or higher brain action, give rise to intense feelings that are as varied as the bodily responses. Thus, emotions never precede or cause bodily activity. We do not run because we are afraid. To dispel this idea, James almost created an opposite misapprehension—that we act and then feel. But in the context of his total psychological theory, he had to mean that all mental phenomena, including highly emotional states, accompany bodily activity. Instead of "we are afraid because we are running," James could better have said "we are afraid when we are running away from something."

James did not develop the full implications of his theory, perhaps in part because he restricted it to emotions or to particularly intense types of feeling. Since highly excited or active responses, such as running when caused by a powerful stimulus, are attended by emotional states, then obviously less frenetic responses to less powerful stimuli are also accompanied by less intense emotions or feeling, until the activity drops to the level of unconscious reflex and thus completely beyond the range of conscious feeling of any kind. Also, James seemed to make feeling an end result of a stimuli-response cycle, or at least the partner of only the response side of the arc. Therefore, he made perception the mental aspect of only the stimuli, seemingly splitting the mental life into two parts. Dewey later showed the fallacy of such a split.

Since the organism is continuously active, James would have been more consistent, even with his own later philosophy, if he had identified feeling as the essential ingredient of the perceptual continuum. The seeing of a bear, given a well-formed response habit, does indeed lead to running away. But it does not consist of percept–response–feeling. It is rather, in this case, external stimuli and physical response, with perception and feeling suffusing the whole process. Thus, when the body, by its sensory apparatus, first encountered the bear, the mental accompaniment was just certain feelings, in themselves quite inarticulate but variously pleasant or distasteful. Even the image of the bear is composed of felt qualities. The bear, as percept, is nothing other than these qualities and feelings. Then, a moment later, the emotion of fear (as reflectively identified) is a certain complex of feelings that accompany the new bodily activity. Fear is the perception of legs moving and muscles straining. It is intense because of the number of stimuli present and because the whole body is active and alert. On reflection, the feeling state may be judged painful, whereas the casual glance toward the tree in which the bear sat may have given a mildly pleasant feeling. Only a well-developed stimuli-response pattern caused such a rapid transition in movement and in the intensity of feeling.

So interpreted, the James-Lange theory marked the real advent of instrumentalism in philosophy. Dewey made much of it. An organism's active encounter with its environment leads to a skein of feeling, intense and mild, painful and pleasant. Every feeling is a counterpart of some bodily activity. Even when activity is centered in the brain, in thinking, there is still an accompaniment of feeling. In Dewey's philosophy, and implicit in much of James's thought, these feelings, and the roughly identifiable qualities present in feeling, are the source of all unity in cognition and are the only glue available to bind any concepts to the realm of existence. In his account of perception, James would show how the phenomenological becomes boss over the purely rational, requiring of it a begrudging fealty. It is discriminated and linguistically coded feelings that guide and discipline thinking and permit major adaptive changes in behavior without costly trial-and-error types of conditioning. Feeling, prematurely routed from psychology by some of the more radical behaviorists, is nonetheless the essential unifying element in their own explanatory theories, and the indispensable source of any existential verity in their conceptual schemes. To prove this, James had to analyze perceptual experience in great detail.

One major theme united both volumes of the *Principles*. Throughout James defended a more radical empiricism than that of the British associationists, from Hume to Mill to Bain. The long-accumulated facts of introspection, now bolstered by the new facts of neural physiology, completely discredited the sensationalist assumptions of the British. Kant appreciated the lack of any unity or synthesis in atomic sensationalism and tried to restore the unity by his *Critique of Pure Reason*. But surely, by 1890, all evidence precluded the complex mental machinery invented by Kant. James therefore proposed to go back to where Locke began, to make a new and better critique of pure experience in order to circumvent all the epistemological dilemmas. In summary, he denied any experiential reality to the bare sensations or atomistic ideas of the associationist school. Pure sensations are selective and useful abstractions in human thought, but they are rooted out of and isolated from a complex continuum of experience that, correctly viewed, contains all the unity and all the relations provided by either Kant's transcendental esthetic or his arbitrary categories of understanding. Instead of perceptual objects being arbitrary constructs out of sensations, sensations are arbitrary discriminations from prior perceptions. Obviously, this thesis needs careful elaboration.

James argued that our conscious experience, whatever the nature of the underlying physical processes, is not composed of tiny sensory atoms or pure sensations, strung together in various combinations. Instead, we experience the world as a continuum of feelings, as a flowing stream, with each moment imperceptibly shading into the next, and with no sharp breaks or lost connections. Consciousness is holistic and unitary, not fragmentary and discontinuous. The transitive states, the relational terms, are felt just as much as is the substantiative content. Each moment of consciousness, each feeling, is a whole, a small universe, subject of course to subsequent analysis into various elements or parts. But this subsequent analysis leads to new and equally unified states of consciousness, which know (and in knowing, fragment) only experiences that are now past. There is never, at any moment, a manifold of coexisting feelings (or of ideas, which are conceptual copies of feelings). Feelings or ideas never coexist, although an idea may be about coexisting things. Ideas only supersede.

Unfortunately, the British sensationalists applied the analogy of disparate things, or possibly the atoms of Newtonian physics, to consciousness, and thus substituted a type of anarchy for the flowing stream. They imposed a conceptual strait jacket on experience. In a great psychological fallacy, abetted by the substantiative form of our language, the manifoldness of objects thought about was confused with mental states. For simple, common-sense objects, the fallacy was excusable, for there may be at least a numerical correspondence between the conceived object and the perception. But by conceptual analysis, any object can be divided into any number of parts, and ultimately into abstract and purely conceptual fragments that are beyond direct experience. These tiny conceptual units may be correctly conceived, in a given explanatory scheme, as more real than the original perceived object, and as constituting it by a certain combination. Such analytical processes are at the heart of inferential thought and underwrite our most developed sciences. But it is absurd to fragment the mental life in such a fashion, to turn every rich feeling into a compound of tiny bits of mind stuff. Even if every brain state is really a bundle of monads, each with its own psychic aspect, the monads so combine that, experientially, we never know the parts or even any effects of them. So they are purely speculative concepts, not experienced realities. If we still insist on some atomistic explanation, James felt such a panpsychism the most respectable.

If each conscious moment consists of combinations of discrete sensa, without inherent relational qualities, then the felt unity of perception is specious, unless some spiritual agent, standing outside the experiential context, magically accounts for the unity. But such an agent is, at best, a desperate substitute for an explanation. It begs all questions and has no operational meaning. But James, ever tolerant of religious belief, refused to ridicule the ancient idea of a soul. He merely pointed to its uselessness in psychology, since empirical concepts could account for all its presumed functions. He believed the idea of a soul was preferable to traditional sensationalism, or to the pantheistic glue of idealism, and even, in its avoidance of explanatory problems, closer to common-sense experience and thus closer to reality.

What does this analysis do to the traditional gods of empiricism—sensations? In effect, James eliminated pure sensations as constituents of experience. They fit into the conceptualization of experience, but not into the immediate stream of consciousness. Always, sense impressions are intermingled and mutually modified; these in turn join numerous associated sensations, and are again modified. Physiologically, consciousness always accompanies the activation of a syndrome of habitual brain paths, even if the original stimulus was only one poor little sensation. Thus, we are conscious of things, of wholes, and not of the one or many distinct qualities impressing our peripheral nerves. For this reason, percept, either of simple or very complex things, is the correct term for our minimal units of consciousness. Indirectly, by the use of substitutional concepts, the whole world may be present in one perceptual moment. This is not to minimize sensations as physical concepts. Obviously, in much perception, there is an inflow of sense data. Sensations act as a trigger for perception, or actually for various types of physical response accompanied by a perceptual continuum. But these sensations never become the units or entities of mental life, somehow magically glued together to make up a world of complex objects.

The term sensation can be correctly used to denote a very simple percept. When a possessed quality includes a minimal of associated content, and is as discrete as redness, hotness, or loudness, it very closely parallels the physical process triggered by a single sensory stimulus. Even this simple percept, in its high degree of sensorial purity, usually results from very careful selection and discrimination, guided by conceptual thought. We have to look for such simple qualities in order to isolate them as objects of attention. We do it for a purpose, usually as a means of better guiding our action (John Dewey elaborately developed this theme in a famous critique of an oversimplified reflex-arc concept). These irreducibly simple perceptions, or, as we usually term them, sensations, represent a boundary to our conceptual thinking. They play a major, unambiguous role in verifying our beliefs about existence and provide the only clear content or meaning of any concept. They are the termini to which all conception must lead if it has existential import.

Since James believed we directly and immediately perceive objects, in all their spatial and temporal dimensions and relations, rather than have to create them mentally out of elementary sensations, he bypassed many traditional epistemological problems. After Hume, a great issue was the nature and validity of the process by which sensations were strung together to make up a universe. Associative habit, with its skeptical import, or constituent, a priori mental machinery seemed the only possible answers—one empirical, the other rational. But there was one point of agreement between them. Even extreme skeptics accepted the existence of elementary mental states. They were given, even if irrational and unexplainable. But these given data were believed to be discrete sensations. James argued for no greater starting assumption, but tried to show that elementary mental states, in their perceptual wholeness, contained within themselves all the unifying material. The world is directly present to us, and it is just as it seems to be. There is no mystery and no problem. This world of direct acquaintance can be reflectively analyzed and turned into truly discrete concepts that stand for parts of it. But the reality they stand for is an ultimate fact.

This direct acquaintance is not knowledge, at least as usually conceived. But conceptual explanatory schemes, if they have existential relevance, have to depart this perceptual realm and sooner or later return to it for verity. Without the felt qualities of experience, concepts would flutter endlessly in a dialectical void. Insofar as the problem of valid knowledge usually pertains to these conceptual schemata, James obviously did not claim truth as an ultimate, experienced fact. But the problem of truth, as he later developed it, would be a problem of methodology and not of epistemology. James could not persuade most rationalists to accept his view, for they rejected radical empiricism almost as readily as old empiricism. But he at least stole their fire. Without the residual skepticism and devious devices of the associationists, James believed he could empirically account for every cognitive operation in such a way as to leave rationalistic devices empty of content. About half of his *Psychology,* accordingly, was devoted to this task. In the most lengthy and brilliant chapters, James accounted for space, time, and identity. His long chapter on space, the work of several years, was the most masterful single product of James's career.

Unfortunately, James's detailed arguments cannot be briefly summarized. One tactic unified his various chapters. By introspection, backed up by known physiological processes, James showed that each quality or relation under consideration was built into our experience. For example, we perceive the world as extended, or in spatial terms. The quality of extensity is simply a part of our perception. What more can be said? Turning this felt extensity into a metrical space continuum is not a matter of direct experience, but of conceptual construction. But its existential worth falls back upon the experiential quality.

The same is true for time. Every conscious moment involves a sense of duration, of succession. The very immediate past lingers and contributes a suffused feeling of continuity, much as after images condition our immediate sight. This "specious present," as James called it, is very brief, but it provides the sense of time and makes consciousness the moving stream of James's most famous metaphor. Memory is entirely different, for in it, rather than an immediate past still lingering in the present, a lost past is recovered. But memory is not just the recovery of a past perception, but recovery plus an added feeling that it has been known before. Physiologically, it is more than an old brain tract reactivated.

The problem of identity has several aspects. The sense of an ego, of immediate selfhood, depends on a felt presence of something going on in the body and particularly in the head, and warm feelings of approval or disapproval, usually very intense. Everything connected with this body has this same special felt quality about it. The sense of continuing personal identity, that the person who lived yesterday is the same person as I now am, depends upon memory, upon the recognition of similar qualities. The remembered self of past glory is myself if the memory has the same quality of intensity and intimacy and animal warmth that attaches to my present self. Thus, our present experience owns or claims certain past selves, and subsequent experiences keep extending the claim. Finally, and quite important, the sense of objective identity, of enduring structures in the external world, also depends upon felt qualities of sameness in different objects or events. These allow what was for James the most distinctly human mental activity, associating by similarity.

Thus, every life-situation has an emotional tenor which gives it an identity and a wholeness. Extensity and duration are simply those feelings with the greatest conceptual uses, for they help unify everything else. Feelings do all the cementing that rationalism could ever do with souls, absolutes, and categories. But the cement is existential, not conceptual. It supports, but does not provide, the conceptual knowledge by which we turn experience into abstract and rational propositions, and by which we make all types of judgment.

In human life, percepts and concepts intermingle and so condition each other that they are almost indistinguishable. James was not very successful in keeping them distinct, for all too often he introduced conceptual content into what he called perceptions. In fact, he often, in conformity to the more usual connotation, used percept to mean a directly present but conceived (or named and defined) object, and not for the primitive, inarticulated qualities of direct encounter. It is hard to isolate a pure perception, for we are inclined to name it, and turn it into a discrete object. In perception, experienced qualities rain in on us and remain as untranslatable feelings and fleeting images. Possibly the best example of almost pure perception is the appreciation of music, or of certain paintings without nameable content. Each perception, in some small nuance, in some varying but modifying context, is different from any other, since it is a part of the moving and never-same stream of consciousness. Percepts cannot be approached except through a radical phenomenology, and this is almost impossible to sustain. Perhaps an animal remains at this level. Possibly man, if he could lose all linguistic ability, could live at the same level.

When James turned from the primitive flux to concepts and human thought, he balanced his phenomenology by a complete rationalism. Heraclitus and Plato both had their due. Only at the very end of his life did he repudiate a rigid logic of identity and dare affirm irrational propositions in the face of logical contradictions. But he clearly preferred the flux, or the existential encounter, and jealously guarded intellect against any unwarranted claims. It was derivative, not primary or especially worthy. Concepts were only instruments. He could not dwell long on them without pushing and tugging to get them into the moral harness. Santayana, so close to James in doctrines, rendered an opposite evaluation and tried to emancipate himself from the moral battlefield in order to contemplate essences.

James defined a concept as a numerically distinct and permanent subject of discourse (these are the essences of Santayana). Each concept has perfect identity and is eternal and unchangeable. A concept may be as complex and universal as pure being; as simple and as discriminate as a color. Events, feelings, relations, things—all, insofar as they figure in discourse, are conceptualized. In fact, we cannot talk about perception until we turn it into a concept. But concepts, unlike the directly experienced world, have no existence except as subjects of discourse. Unlike Santayana, James never tried to develop an implicatory ontological realm of pure essences, much less accept a Platonic ascription of separate existence to them. When not part of human thought or memory, concepts drop from existence. Even Dewey went much further, holding to a social backdrop of developed meanings, or to an overarching mind, as the emergent and climactic form of organization in nature. To Dewey, concepts or essences, developed in social intercourse, made possible a society or community of individuals united by common meanings and ideals. Also, unlike Dewey and George Herbert Mead, James tended to minimize the special role of language in conception. He never made clear whether concepts are created or determined by conventions of language, or whether they are born in air, are mutually determined by their inner connection, and are then simply designated by words. In the *Psychology* he seemed to lean toward the latter position. By *Pragmatism*, language seemed to be in the ascendancy.

The use of concepts enables man to arrest the flowing world of perception, establish its more obvious habits, and chart its main channels. Beyond this, in pure flights of conceptual invention, he can spin out his rational systems ad infinitum, linking concepts together according to formal manipulative rules. Although sense impressions are necessary to activate the mind or program the computer, James felt sure that, except for this purely genetic dependence, conceptual thought had no necessary empirical basis. It is free and in itself existentially empty. That is why he accepted universal terms and, unlike Peirce, never took them very seriously. When existentially relevant, universals simply become signs of, or substitutes in discourse for, experienced similarities at the perceptual level. Universal or class terms do not magically create existential relationships, but name them. If they were not already there, directly presented in perception, no magic could ever create them, and some form of nominalism would be imperative for an empiricist. Taken for themselves, one conceptual scheme is as good as another, except for esthetic and formal criteria. No concept duplicates any reality, for reality is the many-hued and ever varying world of pure experience. Concepts are abstract and static entities.

But concepts do stand for, or know, the real world. Here James first tangled with the problems later developed, with less logical rigor, in his pragmatism. In reflecting back upon a perception, one discriminates certain elements in it. These elements are defined, or turned from felt qualities into specific concepts. Perceptual redness, with whatever subjective peculiarities it has for an individual, becomes conceptual redness, and identical for everyone, at least in intent. In this fashion, portions of experience are named, or as Dewey would say, objectified. But this discriminatory selection obviously distorts, for it names only some small number of the endless nuances present in the perception. But these conceptualized qualities, or possibly one quality, becomes, for us, the essence of the now intellectualized object. For purposes of discourse, the other qualities are forgotten, or by rigorous positivists dismissed as hopelessly subjective. By association of similars, other experiences, however divergent in certain qualities, are seen as part of a common class of objects, for they too have this one conceptualized quality. A mental state today, as divergent as possible in some respects, is related to one yesterday, for it has a common essence and means the same thing. The green grass of yesterday noon, now colored red in the sunset glow, is still recognized as grass. The perceptions were worlds apart, as a painter would testify, but as a typical intellectual would never even notice. Thus, in the midst of the perceptual flux, we begin to discover the ever similar and the ever different. As we hold fast to our ever growing body of meanings, as we build wider bridges of relationship, we know more and more, or at least think we do.

How do we conceive rightly? Even assuming the nonhallucinatory nature of our perceptions, in reflecting back upon them we surely select only a few elements for discrimination. The essence of an object is usually the one abstracted property that is important for our immediate concerns. The essence of the moon varies for an astronaut and a lover. There is a virtual infinity of aspects to any object. The title we bestow on a perceived object characterizes us a great deal more than it does the object. Thus, the essence of a thing is teleological. It is selected in behalf of some human impulse. Propositions that relate many things, in such terms as classification or causality, rest on this selective bias, for only certain qualities are defined and related while others are ignored. Even further from concrete experience are those concepts that touch our experience only after several deductive operations. Here James firmly believed that a plurality of conceptual schemes might often equally well relate a given number of objects, in a vast plurality of partly overlapping systems. Some would not concede so much flexibility, among them John Dewey. But in James's view, concepts begin by being less than full copies of experienced objects, are necessarily arbitrary in terms of selectivity, and, finally, in their broadest sweeps, in their greatest generality, even lose their exclusive properties. Knowledge, so undoubted and direct at the perceptual level, so unified by felt qualities, seems to flounder in all manner of hazards at the conceptual level. Presentational acquaintance is so sure; representational knowledge so insecure. The first comes easily. We have to work like Satan to get the other.

In spite of all this, James did not doubt the validity of conceptual knowledge, given its limitations and purposes. There was some constancy in perception, some structure in the physical universe. In the *Psychology* he was content to beg the ontological problems here. Thus, even the most general laws may obtain in fact. But he kept insisting that the conceptual knowledge that we possess is mostly limited to those areas where we have practical and subjective concerns. We only reason here, although when the concerns become too powerful we often stop reasoning.

On the crucial issue—how do we confirm the correctness of our conceptual knowledge?—James seemed to have two answers in the *Psychology:* one tough; one soft. He was never to drop either, despite much confusion. On the one hand, he assumed that correct concepts, although never duplicating the luxurious and fluctuating world of perception, do accurately represent aspects of it. They unambiguously stand for some quite distinct qualities, qualities which have appeared, or can appear, and are thus meant by the concept. As stand-ins for appearance, the concepts serve for all types of shorthand manipulations, or for implicatory reasoning. That which represents, must represent correctly, or we live in illusion. Thus, when we rely upon a concept, or act upon it, it must be able to lead us to, or terminate in, the actual perceptual qualities for which it stands representative. The unseen tree over the hill must, when sought out, provide the specific sensations, the specific felt qualities, that the concept tree now stands for and means. The process never ends until we go, look, and experience. Only perceptual experience can verify our concept. Vast propositional systems likewise have to pay off at the level of perceptual qualities. Here, James seemed to advocate a very disciplined, rigorous conception of validity. The final test seems clearly to be the specific perceptions required by the concept. The correctness of conceptual thought is thus totally apart from the personal interest of the thinker, although it is in his personal interest to think correctly.

But no sooner said than undermined. A lifelong voluntarism would never allow James to stop at such a rigorous test. It might exclude too many things that he loved, and, in the case of God, very much *needed*. He believed our minds loved to construct conceptual systems. Unless involved in contradiction, we tend to attribute reality to all of them. Doubt springs from a lack of coherence between our concepts, and only then do we have to choose between our conceptual worlds. James conceded that, when such choice is required, we usually assign reality to things closely connected to us and generally feel that sensible qualities are real. These we then use as a test for our concepts. So far, so good. But he went further. Quite correctly, he pointed to compelling psychological reasons why people believe some concepts true and others false. Some concepts, like various ideas of God, move and excite us, and easily and uncritically become preferred beliefs. Practical import, esthetic appeal, moral compulsion, and explanatory scope all help support our favored beliefs. From these indubitable facts, he jumped to the rather unexpected conclusion that there is no "truer way to conceive, but only more serviceable ways." To conceive rightly is to conceive by the one abstract concept or proposition which explains the largest body of experience and which also leads to the sort of conclusion which it is someone's temporary intent to obtain. Possibly, he only meant that, at a high level of abstraction, variously overlapping but not exclusive theories may equally well unify a body of data and that here one rightly selects the one theory that fulfills his purpose in knowing. But he also suggests that, at least in an area of conceptual ambiguity, personal preferences of a different sort, such as a scientist's love of elegance and economy, or a religious man's need for consolation, also properly determine the choice. Here, it seems, the criterion of validity is removed from the specific demands of a proposition and placed in the personal desires of an individual. James, ever vague here, might have retorted that such subjective desires only supplement the rigorous test, and only when ambiguity allows.

Although James anticipated most of his subsequent philosophical concerns in the *Psychology,* he still reserved a great many issues for a more thorough or a more speculative treatment. He still had the difficult task of extending radical empiricism a second step, dissolving matter and mind into alternative and equally valid but purposefully distinct conceptualizations of pure experience. Then, with his hypothetical prop of naïve realism overthrown, he would have to deal with ontological problems and struggle to escape some type of solipsism. At the same time he had to deal more thoroughly with the automaton theory and somehow rescue freedom from its deterministic bias. The problem, broached in the *Psychology,* received immediate attention. In some form, the problem of free will haunted him throughout the 1880's and early 1890's.

VOLUNTARISM

To a greater extent than any other major American philosopher, William James apotheosized the human will. His voluntaristic emphasis often encouraged an extreme irrationalism and had an erosive effect on his other philosophical doctrines. However much reason may insure it, James always felt that will was the source and final arbiter of belief. For an individual, reality is what he wants it to be. If a formula for expressing the nature of the world, such as a mechanistic model, violates our moral demands, James felt free to reject it. His earliest defense for such a subjective criterion was his often repeated argument that all belief rests in part on subjective preference and that any belief finds its objective insurance in certain practical effects to which it leads. These attitudes, tied so closely to religious and moral themes, dominated a series of popular lectures that James combined and published in 1897 as *The Will to Believe and Other Essays in Popular Philosophy.*

James did not limit his voluntarism to a descriptive account of how men come to believe as they do and to the demonstrable effects of certain beliefs. He pushed on into more dangerous epistemological and metaphysical terrain and often there warred with himself. In fact, his whole voluntaristic emphasis can be dropped from his philosophy, without destroying the remainder and in some cases to its benefit. But to

drop it would be to distort James and to ignore one of his most persistent character traits.

James, with complete justification, wanted to live in a world in which
human ideals, in which man's fondest hopes, can make a difference. At
least some of the things we want to be true surely are, or may become,
true. Even our wanting may help make them true. He continuously
affirmed that our mind is an actor and not a passive mirror. Our human
needs produce beliefs, which are assumed to be true and are acted on as
if they were true. This action helps transform the world and make true,
or even more true, what we already believe. His key analogy made all
this seem plausible. A person wants to live in a harmonious world,
which requires men of good will and some magnanimity. So one affirms
as a belief the goodness of one's neighbors and acts in the trustful way
permitted by the belief. Lo and behold, our neighbors justify our belief,
in part as a result of our belief and action. However true at first, the
belief is soon even more true. Since the belief concerns a very desirable
state of affairs, disbelief in the beginning would have precluded the
enjoyed satisfaction and left the world in a much worse condition. In his
famous essay, "The Will to Believe," James applied this same argument
to belief in God's existence.

What is wrong with this argument? Actually, nothing but confusion.
Several themes are intermingled, with ambiguous terms like "truth" con-
cealing the hodgepodge. One significant theme extended a central
hypothesis of the *Psychology*. The mind (or the brain) is a very active
thing. Its thought processes help change the world, both in the restricted
area of brain circuits and, through directed muscular activity, in the
larger external world. Belief, defined rigorously as habit, as an established brain tract, or as a disposition to act in certain ways given the
correct stimuli, is a major factor in determining the future. This is
equally true whether mental phenomena are defined in physicalistic or
spiritualistic terms, as determined or to some extent spontaneous. In this
sense, one who believes in the existence of God is predisposed to certain
types of behavior, behavior which, if carried out, will change the world
by just so much. The behavior may occur without any direct contact
with the object of belief and thus have no direct role in proving the
validity of the belief. But the individual, tremendously pleased with the
results of his behavior, may attribute the result not only to his belief, but
to his God. This illustrates very well the role of belief, and, in a sense,

might be said to verify James's belief about belief. But it has nothing to do with the correctness of the belief in question, which is none other than God's existence.

Given the activist conception of mind, it is quite legitimate to say that many of our desires can be achieved, at least in part as a result of our desiring them. Some, of course, cannot be achieved. James, although he flirted with the doctrine, never really believed in miracles occasioned by sheer will. He always had a realistic belief in a natural order that placed certain limitations upon human behavior. But what has successful action to do with truth? Does it not confuse things to say that our hopes, our fondest beliefs, can become true? Not necessarily, for this implicates a subtle theme of all pragmatism. But James was unable to unravel the exact and quite intricate sense in which this may be so. In any case, a fond belief becomes true, not because of the fondness with which it is held, but when a determinate relationship is established between the belief (hypothesis) and the objects to which it refers.

When James said that truth may result from acting upon a belief, he had to mean one of two very different things. First, he could have meant that a belief, tentative and hypothetical, could be verified (and in this sense become true). This means that God, as a presently existing personage, could be known, or better known, to exist in the future, and as a direct result of certain action dictated by the present belief (read hypothesis). Or he could have meant that the belief was a belief about the future. Thus, a presently nonexistent state of affairs, it is believed, can become existent in the future as a result of certain prescribed action. Both of these possibilities, although seemingly obvious, cannot only be developed but related with great subtlety.

Since James slanted his arguments toward theistic affirmation, he must have meant that a presently existing God could be known to exist only as a result of certain action and that this action would not take place except as a result of a prior confidence in the truth of a hypothetical belief. If one thought the very idea of God the height of foolishness, obviously he would not try to verify the belief, would not act upon it. If this is what James meant, no one could quarrel with him. But this does not mean that acting upon a belief in God makes God exist; it only means, in a quite arbitrary use of words, that acting upon a belief in God makes *the belief* true. Until acted upon, until verified, the belief is neither true nor false (this entails a peculiarly pragmatic sense of the

word true). The active process of verification is additive and transformative. In the case of belief in God, it may require monumental
transformations before verity can be even tentatively assigned. But if the
belief is so framed as to assert the existence of God at a time prior to the
verifying activity, the verification process does not alter God, the subject
of the hypothesis. It does change the world. Now if God is so defined as
to be intimately involved with every single aspect of the world, He is
transformed by the very process of verification, for He is synonymous
with all reality. But even here the God of the proposition, being the
earlier existing God, is not changed by the verification process. To
multiply subtle implications, if God is further defined as a completely
static God (and reality therefore frozen), then either the verification
process could not take place at all, or God is not also eternal, for
verifying His existence at point "A" would deny the possibility of His
existence at point "B." Any action based on God's existence, but other
than that action required for verification, may for emotional reasons
lead a person to affirm God's existence with greater fervor, but with no
more justification than before. Acting "as if" does not prove anything if
the action does not directly relate to the hypothesis. Thus, leaving a
door unlocked because neighbors are believed honest cannot in itself
prove their honesty, but it may, day by uneventful day, heighten our
belief nonetheless. In a most peculiar way, unnoticed by James, this type
of action may have some relevance to truth. If it heightens the confidence in a hypothesis, it may lead to the threshold of urgency beyond
which verifying activity will be initiated. Thus, a revival in a church may
stir enough interest in the sinner to lead him to a serious inquiry into the
truth of God's existence. Assuming a clear, operational definition of
God and available verifying data, it may lead to a true belief and to all
the personal joys of such a belief.

When James transferred his voluntarism from an affirmation of
theism to purely moral affirmation, he changed its intent. But still he
kept referring to the truth of ideals, with inevitable confusion. Again he
confused existence with truth. Ideals may be realized. When they are, a
desired and future state of affairs exists. To believe that such a state of
affairs can exist as a result of certain specified action may indeed be a
true belief. As a result of my trust, my neighbors may indeed become
men of good will. In fact, multiplying the process, the world may experience brotherhood. Such a belief in future eventualities is, in fact, a belief

about certain present conditions, about certain relations between them, and about possibilities open in the future. To truly believe an ideal can be realized by specified action is to say something about the present. But still the ideal is not true in almost any sense of the word true. Here again, there are subtle distinctions. The proposition that *A* combined with *B* will give *C* is a typical hypothesis about nature. It may well be that *C* does not exist at present. Also, *C* may be an object of great desire, an ideal of great value. In this case the verification of the proposition does lead to *C,* and thus an ideal, being a certain desired state of affairs, comes into actuality. But still, all that has been proved true is the proposition, the belief. In itself, *C* is neither true nor false, but just is. But, to give credit to James, *C* would never have existed without the belief. Action in behalf of unproven beliefs is an ineradicable part of both the moral life and scientific inquiry.

Not only did James confuse truth with existence, but he also challenged the whole concept of objective truth. Since beliefs involve conceptual judgments, rather than the undoubted presentation of reality in perception, beliefs are not copies of reality but selective and abstract representations of it. The selective aspect insures that our concepts are all teleological, that they serve certain of our preferences and impulses. Like too many others of his generation, James easily jumped to the conclusion that such purposes compromised objectivity. Thus, he felt that the love of simplicity, unity, and economy—all sentiments reflected by the men who became great scientists—were no less teleological and subjective than the more analytical bent of empiricists, or the practical sentiments of common folk. Therefore, he argued, why not frankly admit the validity of interest and personal desire as a determinant of belief? They always play a role and usually the decisive role. He made famous his temperamental categories of tough- and tender-minded and rather delighted in stressing that the bias of scientists and philosophers was a narrowly distributed and comparatively rare sentiment of rationality. By shifting the focus to the psychological reasons behind the development of belief, James easily confused the crucial question: How do we verify them?

If beliefs reflect subjective bias, why not allow such bias a verifying role? Thus, even as James insisted upon submitting beliefs to the test of consequences, he refused to limit the consequences to one privileged type. Often he seemed to condone a plurality of beliefs, none of which, except in the clearly stated terms of certain goals, could claim pre-eminence. Given the interests served, James accepted a basis of discrimination—the test of practice. The best scientific theory fulfills the sentiment of rationality. The best religious ideal leads to a desired consolation. Which theorem, which god, best serves our varied interest has to be worked out in practice. When this mood possessed him, James was completely tolerant of conflicting beliefs, regardless of the lack of public data to support them. He would not fight out intellectual conflicts on the basis of some external order that permitted some and not others. Here he and Dewey parted company. James, at times at least, thought the universe so open, so unformed, or so unknowable, that it allowed a glorious anarchy of theoretic constructions, and so "on the move" that almost any strange or seemingly absurd theory might sooner or later become accepted.

In making belief in part a matter of interests served, or of ultimate preference, James opened up options of all sorts. Even as Dewey was trying to use a pragmatic test to close down all manner of options and to elevate one clear and concrete method of dealing with reality, James kept slipping away from all rigor and condoning (not accepting) absolutes, esoteric deities, sentimental hopes, mystical revelations, and even the trance reports of mediums. Over and over he tried to assure his popular audiences that their religious beliefs (whatever they happened to be in detail) had not been undermined by logic or science. They had a right to their belief even if they lacked all the evidence, or the proper arguments, needed to prove their belief. Of course they took the risk of their commitments, but stood to gain all possible benefits. But James usually urged that even religious beliefs utilize all possible intellectual supports and rely on faith only in areas where evidence was lacking. He advocated beliefs finally sustained by desire, but beliefs held in some consistent relationship with each other and to some discipline of fact.

In "The Will to Believe," one of his most controversial essays, James gave a "new" defense of religious belief. He loosely defined religion as a belief that the best things (presumably left up to the individual to define) are more true or more eternal (he left open the "than"), and he asserted that we are better off by believing this so. He also stressed that, for most people, the more eternal things are united in a "Thou," or some personal deity. But definition was not important. James always hated theological niceties. He was simply trying to be general enough to encompass all the theists in his audience. For those who had lingering beliefs in a God, but who were disturbed by scientific or philosophical challenges, James came as a consoling preacher. He handed out a broad license for belief, but a license with certain restrictions. It was to be good only for live hypotheses, or for unprovable beliefs of real, felt significance; for forced or truly disjunctive beliefs, which allowed only acceptance or rejection; and finally for momentous beliefs, where the whole tenor of one's life was vitally involved. In all other cases of unprovable beliefs, he advocated skepticism and thus hoped to assuage the scientists in his audience.

James did not realize how much his argument was slanted toward his audience. In fact, any belief is live, forced, and momentous if, because of social pressures, native endowments, careful training, or arduous thinking, it is well established in a community or in an individual. The most absurd fantasy, not disproved by evidence, could be live if someone sincerely believed in it and had structured their whole life around it. The reason James selected a vaguely Christian affirmation was social, not logical. Almost agreeing with an earlier statement of Peirce's, James argued that vital belief has to be supported on other than strictly intellectual or evidential grounds. But unlike Peirce, James often generalized this view and denied a privileged intellectual status to scientific evidence. Since all belief is rooted in temperament, in moral sentiments, even in our distinctive personal preferences, why single out religion as peculiarly but justifiably irrational and then elevate science as rational but, in terms of our deepest concerns, usually trivial?

In "The Will to Believe," as so often when defending religion, James's arguments floundered in imprecision or contradiction. In effect, he argued that no evidence fully supports or fully disproves a belief in God (or in things most eternal). Thus, if we believe at all, our passional nature casts the final and decisive vote. Since disproof is impossible, passion also casts the vote against belief. Everything is equal between the believer and nonbeliever, at least so far as evidence and logic are involved. But the disproof argument is specious, since James rejected any type of intellectual certainty on any existential issue. He earlier had defended the use of skepticism for clearing the way for a life of action based on "assumed truth." Thus, lack of conclusive proof, instead of equalizing the status of belief and nonbelief on a less-than-certain hypothesis (by definition any hypothesis), should open the issue for weighed evidence and lower and higher probabilities. It is almost meaningless to say that the disbelief of an atheist or the doubt of an agnostic (James saw correctly that suspended belief on a momentous issue is virtually equal to nonbelief) rests on no rock of certainty. Although James felt that we may know truth, he always argued that we have no a priori means of knowing infallibly when we have it. This, again, should point to the necessity of relying on evidence.

James made belief rely upon outcomes in the future. A belief leads to some practical maximum or resolve and to some concrete experiences. If, in the ongoing drift of life, these experiences continue to affirm the belief, then that is the only possible meaning of its being true. Despite similarities in language, James did not mean a self-corrective scientific march toward unanimity based on public evidence, but a lone individual's continued sense of well-being so long as he believed in God's existence and acted accordingly. Thus, without exploring the possible hazards of illusion, James therapeutically validated belief in God, but suggested no clear means of validating God. As a clinical psychologist, his recommendations may have had some merit. He looked to the beneficial effects of a certain belief, not to any effects of God. At the end as much as at the beginning, God's existence remained an open issue. James gave no evidential support for belief, or even for tentative affirmation. He acknowledged the risk of error, but found it of minimal importance compared to the risk of losing all the consoling effects of positive belief, and presumably also the even more bountiful effects of it being a true belief. Here was the woeful result of disbelief.

On such a weak skein of argument, James ended the essay with a typical Sunday School cheer—quiet your fears, your nagging doubts, and believe. As you act upon your faith it will deepen and become ever more true. Assuming a tremendous "If," James was surely correct. If there is a God working toward great future ideals, our belief in His existence, our commitment to His goals, will indeed hasten their attainment. But this not only begs all manner of questions about God's nature and our freedom, but deftly avoids the crucial issue—is there a God?

"The Will to Believe" represented a very crude type of pragmatism, even though James did not use the word. In his later essays, entitled *Pragmatism,* he still retained some of his voluntarism, mixed in with a criterion of meaning and a more disciplined test for truth. In the controversy over pragmatism, James tightened his arguments and acknowledged his most glaring confusions. He granted to Arthur O. Lovejoy that he had long confused the effects of believing with the effects of a belief being true. Without further elaboration or later fulfillment, he promised to revise his will-to-believe thesis. But his repudiation here did not mean a rejection of voluntarism. If anything, he extended it in his last years.

Intrigued by the Italian pragmatist, Giovanni Papini, sensing some of the larger implications of Dewey's instrumentalism, and vastly influenced by Henri Bergson, James gave ever greater importance to man's creative powers. In his last years he alternated between a creative humanism, with man directing processes of change in the dynamic, temporal flux of a nonrational existence, and a liberating theism, with man somehow merged with and supported by a larger, finite consciousness, and at least helping God to work out vast creative processes. In more humanistic moments, James applauded Dewey's type of naturalism and seemed to catch its moral exhilaration, although he hardly accepted its methodological rigor. In Dewey's view man was a small, severely limited god. As an emergent part of nature, he had the intellectual tools for directing events according to conceived ideals. But the task was difficult and a successful outcome hazardous. Man, instead of exulting in his power, had best work at his humble but redemptive tasks and be thankful that nature was such as to respond to some of his feeble efforts. James could hardly bow to the demands of such an uninsured idealism or look ahead to such possible frustration. He wanted a more heady view of man's creative potential.

He found it in Papini, and with an assertive vengeance. Papini wanted none of Dewey's utilitarianism or speculative discretion. He despised useful science and rejoiced that pragmatism, instead of certifying science as man's best tool, had freed man from the yoke of conceptual knowledge. To him, Dewey was both a puritan moralist and, in epistemology, a near positivist. Papini valued freedom, exuberated in speculation, and, like James, loved to poke fun at science and emphasize its limits. He was intoxicated with a creative spirit and yearned for heroic commitment. This motor or vital pragmatism, with its exaltation, its love of power and direct action, its flirtation with danger and violence, appealed to the romantic and activist side of James. He saw some possible abuses, but at least it was a vibrant and live alternative to the growing deadness of academic philosophy. Papini recognized that creativity was part and parcel of reality and that no strait jacket of rationality could take it out. Reality validated our reasons and not the other way around. It was through his relationship to the ultravoluntaristic Italian pragmatists that James exerted some influence upon Mussolini and Italian fascism.

Bergson, with his vitalism and mysticism, moved James more than any other philosopher. In a few short years the two men became fervent admirers, despite philosophical differences—differences which James typically minimized or generously attributed to misunderstanding. In fact, when James read Bergson he acceded to every idea he could understand. Coming at a time of religious perplexity, Bergson's writings converted James to a professed irrationalism and allowed him to go ahead and believe in a pluralistic God despite the veto of logic. Bergson, like James, had a compelling sense of the priority of a directly experienced world, or of the existence that preceded any conceptual rendering. James, as early as his *Psychology,* had stressed this, and thereby won Bergson's admiration. But James had tried, with desperate sincerity, to erect a logical conceptual structure upon this pure experience and thus to rationalize and objectify the world. He assumed, even as late as his *Pragmatism,* that conceptual systems could at least roughly transcribe the perceptual world. He thus merged existence and essence and believed that they fit each other.

Bergson was not so rationally inclined. He disliked the essential realm and minimized logical order. Logic only relates concepts. When tied to the world of experience, these conceptual systems help us transform the world in terms of practical interests. But they do not reveal the world. Reality lies buried, unavailable to thought. Its inwardness, its true relations, are negated by our concepts. We "know" reality only in our immediate experience, and we know it then in a concrete but limited way. Even though conceptual knowledge gives us the wings of an angel and allows us to tie all reality up in a neat system, it reveals only the abstract surface of things. Conceptual knowledge is quite superficial and really makes things less "intelligible" than they are in direct experience. Reality lies in the flux, in process and duration, or in qualities inexpressible by concepts or even by language. Metaphorical suggestion comes closer to reality than scientific concepts. Poetry may well be the best tool of ontology. Intellectual constructs are bits of retrospective patchwork or post mortem dissections. Lifeless, they reveal the horrible stillness of death.

When under Bergson's influence, James eagerly retreated to the phenomenological realm. He could not follow Bergson on to mysticism but half-wished he could. Now convinced that life, at the level closest to reality, was essentially nonrational, he determined to follow experiential promptings even in the face of logical dilemmas. By his earlier logic, the very logic that justified his pure concepts or essences, he could never reconcile a pantheistic God with human freedom. One identity had to displace the other. If God involved some merger of individuals, then man could not retain his autonomy, or else God had no autonomy. James avoided the problem of God-ordained evil by affirming a finite God (or gods), but still desired the intimacy of relationship involved in a pantheistic merging or a pooling of consciousness. This involved the same logical dilemma as absolute idealism. But in his last fully completed book, *A Pluralistic Universe,* he justified such a God in spite of logic. Bergson was his master. Life exceeds logic, overflows and surrounds it. Logical categories are justified when useful. When they threaten our deepest hopes they must give way. Then, divested of man-made abstracts, of vicious intellectualism, we fall back on existence and follow its passionate urgings. Voluntarism can go no further. It can present no better justification.

Freedom was clearly implied by James's voluntarism. After his youthful pessimism and his deliverance from materialistic determinism by the philosophy of Renouvier, he always defended what he usually called free will. But he never stuck with any one concept of free will and never found any final argument for its defense. No subject was closer to James's ultimate concerns, and no subject gave him more continuous worry. As his other doctrines developed, he had to keep returning to free will and making appropriate repairs.

In the *Psychology* James conceded that free will, at the very most, could only mean some inward power to sustain an idea in one's attention, letting fixed, organic habits take care of the external behavior. James believed that thinking of any object that terminated a habitual response cycle served to trigger the whole cycle. If outward circumstances, or internal equipment, permitted, a person no sooner thought than the act was done, with no awareness of intervening means. Thus, an idea, a merely conceived object, acts as the stimulus in voluntary behavior. Unless several ideas conflict and mutually cancel each other, thought and action are as one, even when the action is more thinking.

To have a single idea is to act upon it, whether successfully or unsuccessfully. To keep one idea before the mind to the exclusion of all others is to act in a given, usually quite habitual way. But in the midst of vital, conflicting ideas, it is hard to keep one idea before the mind. The alcoholic cannot keep his mind on his wife and children; almost in spite of himself he thinks of alcohol. Even in the most favorable environment, his attention may wander off to the forbidden subject. So often we war with ourselves. High ideals fight with low ones, and all types of incipient action are arrested at their very beginning. Thus, we experience indecision, agonize over decisions, and feel in a quandary. Whatever the explanation, we often experience what we call moral effort. We deliberately think of one object and, however difficult, force others out of our attention. Psychologically, this feeling of effort seemed to be the only possible meaning of free will. In a fully adequate conceptual explanation of mental action, the experienced freedom might be illusionary. But at the phenomenological level all "know" it and at least naïvely believe it makes the difference in our choices and in our conduct.

We may be very wrong. As Jonathan Edwards argued so effectively, the object of sustained attention may fully account for our adhering to it. There may be an affinity between our nature and the object. To escape it, therefore, requires a revolutionary transformation in our nature, or what he referred to as grace. Thus, the feeling of mental effort which indeed accompanies attention does not cause the attention. James had no way of refuting this determinant conception. The evidence was insufficient for any full explanation. But he conceded all he had to. Certainly, the exertion of mental effort, the willing, has no dynamic role in the sense of causing organic movements. At most, it triggers a self-contained process, already established as a fixed habit. If no organic habit exists, or if outward forces do not cooperate, such ideas are helpless, being merely wishful thinking. Yet, imaginative ideas, rather than being the determinant product of material forces, seem to be spontaneous in origin, to be sustained by deliberate effort, and quite often to lead to effective behavior, behavior that would otherwise not have occurred. This much James accepted as a scientist, leaving any ultimate explanation (possibly at the molecular or chemical level) for future research.

As a moralist he went further. Rather than making our ideas mechanical effects, on one hand, or sheer mutations or accidents on the other, he often took recourse to some spiritual agent. In popular talks on psychology [*Talks to Teachers on Psychology, and to Students on Some of Life's Ideals* (New York, 1899)], he suggested a purely "spiritual causation," or some star performer in the background, working through the brain. Thus, in as clear language as he ever used, he accepted a spiritual agent, or a substantiative explanation for free will, even though he had eliminated such an agency from the science of psychology, since it had no directly observable effects. But in introducing a spiritual agent, as hidden as Kant's noumenon, James also verged on a morally uninstructive conception of free will. To him it was all so confusing and so very speculative.

James much more easily turned to the implication of free will or, more often, to the effect of believing in it. He at least convinced people that without it we lived in an awful world, but in so doing often did an injustice to some of his opponents. In setting up a disjunctive situation, particularly in "Dilemma of Determinism," James refused to accept a middle ground, typified in religion by the Calvinist doctrine of predestination. To James, fatalism plagued any doctrine short of a substantiative free will. At least as late as 1900, he desired a universe with spontaneity or chance, without complete or universal law or any overarching ontological ground. Like the Arminians of old, he wanted some supernatural agency in man, some exemption from both physical and moral necessity. Only then could our desires have cosmic significance. He simply denounced as useless quibbling the middle way—that our actions are our own, that there is no internal coercion or compulsion, that our choices are efficacious, that we correctly take responsibility for them, but that this is so only because there is a lawful order which our choices exemplify. So long as such an order obtained, at least in a full and complete sense, James believed that a logical necessity underlay all events and that the obvious evil in the world could not be condemned as something that not only should not have existed, but might not have existed. He insisted upon seeing law, not only as observed uniformities, but also as a coercive ordering of events. A fully lawful world, he then believed, would force total acceptance or total rejection. The world being what it was, James clearly would have rejected it. Thus, his defense of free will was a justification of his optimism and his will to live.

Throughout his life, James professed a pluralistic view of reality. This was a more enduring and a better justified implication of his free-will doctrine than some spiritual agency. By pluralism, he meant a universe without a coimplication of all parts, or without a complete mechanism. He hated any iron-block, fixed universe. The future had to be ambiguous, however determinant within the limited reach of certain causal laws. Structure was partial, not complete. Here, for once rejecting a disjunctive position, he insisted upon something between complete flux and a full and perfect unity. On only one occasion did he suggest that this pluralistic view demanded some random or nondeterminant behavior at the molecular or atomic level. More often he suggested panpsychism, in which the experienced novelty of human experience was pushed back into the smallest particles of existence. At other times he rested his case for pluralism upon the derivative nature of conceptual explanation, including the overly influential mechanistic model of physics. Any extrapolation of such limited determinism to include all of reality had to be justified by a sentimental preference for order and uniformity. It could not be proved and was contrary to experience itself. In the absence of proof on behalf of determinism, there seemed no valid reason to depart from common sense.

In his last years James reversed himself on free will, decisively repudiating any idea of spiritual agency, supernatural causation, or even random chance. In his *Essays in Radical Empiricism* [Edited by Ralph B. Perry (New York, 1912)], James argued that he had never meant to affirm a transphenomenal principle of energy (technically true, since his earlier spiritual agent did not play a dynamic role), but only meant by free will a character of novelty in activity situations (simply untrue on the face of many earlier statements). Since novelty was an experienced fact, there was no need for a principle of free will, or for any separable agent or ontological principle. In *Pragmatism* he argued that the term free will only meant such experienced novelty and therefore the possibility of a better future. Thus, free will was a doctrine of relief or a type of spiritual food, with emotional meaning. But experienced novelty begs the issue of determinism, for, as many conceive it, determinism can account, in fact must account, for the novel features of each new situation in nature.

In his last but uncompleted book, *Some Problems of Philosophy* [New York, 1911], James let the old problem lie, seeing it as unsoluble and almost meaningless. At the level of perception, when we are directly in contact with reality, novelty is omnipresent. This novelty cannot be satisfactorily explained, for our concepts, because of their frozen, static nature, can only represent certain abstract elements squeezed out of the lode of experience. The common-sense view assumes a type of freedom but not some abstract free will. Being closer to direct experience, it is probably superior to any more sophisticated conceptual reduction. In the flux of events, new possibilities constantly appear. We are the author of some of this novelty. The new, by any human analysis, cannot be completely discovered in what is already given. Deterministic explanation is always retrospective in fact if not in theory. Even the idea of causality, of some dynamic and necessary relation between sequential events, sprang from an experienced quality of goal-directed activity, and thus like all other existential relations had its source at the subjective and perceptual level. Thus, as Hume first revealed, the idea of causality has no metaphysical import. To use causality as a defense of determinism is to fall into the worst sort of pathetic fallacy and to ascribe to all parts of nature a type of willful and completely rational action. James was often willing to accept panpsychism, but not the full rationality of each particle of being.

All that James could finally do with freedom, and perhaps all that anyone can do, was undermine the determinist position and leave freedom as a speculative position without any operational guidelines for verification. The same was true of free will, in the sense of an agent at work behind the scenes. Whether reality itself grows, or only changes its form according to some hidden rationale or law, is beyond human comprehension. Existence is begged in either case. Novelty, either absolute or apparent, is where we start and where we have to end. Beyond there was only mystery. This was James's final word.

In the more extreme statements of his voluntarism and irrationalism, James revealed how far away he could be from the mainstream of New England and Puritan thought. Revealingly, the sources of his voluntarism were almost entirely European. Even Emerson had been more cautious and circumspect. This irrationalism was only a facet of James, and it was probably not the most essential facet of either his life or his thought. But it was a disruptive facet, clearly separating him not only from other concerns of his own but from both Peirce and Dewey and from the more enduring tendencies of American pragmatism. Unfortunately, because of this voluntarism in James and in several European disciples, the very term pragmatism grew out of an ambivalent situation and, at least by superficial critics (almost all of them), was usually defined in terms of this voluntarism, its most aberrant and uncharacteristic offspring.

IN PURSUIT OF AN ONTOLOGY

Year after year, amidst teaching duties and endless lecture obligations, James professed a final philosophical goal—to work all his ideas into a new metaphysical system. His great masterpiece was never completed, or even hardly begun. He died with several metaphysical issues unresolved. But he wrought more than he thought. His essays in radical empiricism, although burdened with occasional irrelevancies, contained the most significant metaphysical innovations since Kant. Yet, despite its endless subtleties and possibilities, James never wove his radical empiricism into other portions of his thought and never turned it into an exclusive world view. In fact, in his last religious views, he frequently violated it.

The groundwork for a metaphysical version of empiricism lay in the *Psychology*. His essays in radical empiricism, posthumously collected and published but often dating from articles written in the 1890's, only represented a sequel, in which he applied his psychological doctrines to the nagging mind-body problem, thus finally eliminating the awkward dualism of his earliest book. In the *Psychology* he kept mind and body in a type of limbo. His watered-down dualism allowed him to bypass embarrassing questions. In various contexts, he moved toward materialism or toward idealism. For practical purposes, the mental states and the physical structure seemed complementary but somewhat arbitrary ways of picturing the same experience. By 1895 he was ready to formalize this view and in that year launched radical empiricism.

He suggested that selected aspects of pure experience, when reflectively analyzed, may, according to the relations traced, become either objects of an external world or moments in a stream of consciousness. Both worlds, external and internal, are reflective abstractions. Neither mind nor matter exist as substantial entities. Each equally exist as functional aspects of experience, and as valid classifications of experience. The idea was not exactly new. Both Chauncey Wright and Peirce had anticipated it. But now it was to have its first forceful statement. In

1900 James rather awkwardly summarized his view: "The problem I take to be this: Assuming no duality of material and mental substance, but starting with bits of 'pure experience,' . . . to show how this comes to figure in two ways in conception, once as streams of individual thinking, once as physical permanents, without the *immediately real* ever having been either of these disrempted things, or less than the full concrete experience or phenomenon with its two aspects." [To Shadworth Hodgson, June 10, 1900, in Perry, *Thought and Character*, I, 647.]

Radical empiricism, as sponsored by James, was supposed to be a new and revolutionary view of reality. Pure experience was the irreducible ground for any of our conceptual views of the universe. It stood behind any assumed substances, powers, egos, or souls. A moment of experience is a pure datum, and in its purity and wholeness simply is. It is neither true nor false, since it stands beyond any possible doubt. Conceptual knowledge is not a precarious perch on the riverbank of experience, but is itself within the flow. In conception, one experience knows a former experience, and knows it in a certain context or field of relations. A former experience becomes either a part of a conscious stream or an object existing in a material universe. The former experience is not re-experienced, or it would still be conceptually neutral and nonanalytical. But the past experience is now cognized by a present experience and thus classified or, as Dewey emphasized, objectified. The present, cognitive experience, however it deals with past experience, is itself a pure datum. It may figure in a subsequent experience, and then become part of an objective world. That is, we may conceptualize our cognizing experience and may think about our thinking, or doubt our doubts. But at the moment of doubting, we never doubt our doubt, or even know it as doubt. In man, large sections of pure experience may be cognitive or conceptual in nature, as subsequent reflection will testify. This is what we refer to as thought. Usually, in reflecting on it, we classify it exclusively as part of a mental field. But in physiological psychology, it is classified as part of a material field, linked to relatively stable and enduring cells, fibers, and muscles.

Pure experience, as the *Psychology* demonstrated, had all the qualitative richness needed to support all types of conceptual structuring. The most fervent rationalist, whenever disillusioned with a priori cement, could turn to James and praise him for supporting the integrity of scientific knowledge. But as his periodic voluntarism demonstrated, James could turn his radical empiricism into a support for a fervent anti-intellectualism, into a deprecatory stance toward conceptual thought. Since pure experience is fluent, it contains no paradoxes and no intellectual contradictions. It may contain plenty of pain and animal frustration, but no doubt, cynicism, or skepticism. In language modeled on that of Santayana, James adjudged reflective intelligence as the serpent in the garden. It names, disjoins, and, ever short of complete synthesis, flounders in incomprehensibility and contradiction. But some intellectual synthesis is philosophy's goal, since it seeks redemption to take the place of innocence. With his moral interests, James saw redemption in terms of practical guidance. We leave pure experience, not to enter a better and higher realm (the error of the Greeks), but to save our lives and thus broaden the range of experience and secure more and better experience. He never had any great respect for anyone who plunged into the conceptual realm and tried to stay there. This seemed a morbid escapism, a perverse Platonism, attractive only to sick souls like Santayana. Yet, he saw thinking as a type of experiencing. If pleasurable, it could be a goal as well as a means. James rarely conceded this. But as a philosopher, he exemplified it. He really did enjoy the dialectical game, if only as an occasional diversion.

James often climbed mountains only to find fog-shrouded peaks still ahead. Radical empiricism brought James face to face with inescapable ontological alternatives. Pure experience, as the irreducible ground for conceptual thought, and for all knowledge, is clear enough. But does pure experience alone exist, or does it alone bring man into contact with existence? Here was the crucial ontological question, and one James never unambiguously answered.

Most often, James tried to limit existence to pure, neutral experience. There is no further referent, no ultimate ground. But this led him into all types of solipsistic dilemmas, to several suggestive but inadequate outs, and finally to unresolved questions that haunted him until his death. These dilemmas led James away from radical empiricism. He never explicitly repudiated it, but increasingly treated it as a speculative position that could not bind him if he felt a need to go beyond it.

It is difficult to talk about pure experience without conceiving it as a mediate or middle ground between reality and human thought. Yet, as James saw so clearly, if pure experience is the full and sufficient ground for all our concepts, then any nonexperienceable reality behind experience is unknowable, and thus a seemingly quite arbitrary and highly speculative postulate. But can pure experience be dealt with conceptually without such postulates? James thought so, but never proved so even to himself. Since he confessed his failures so often, the following analysis is useful only in revealing some of his difficulties.

We cannot talk about pure experience, or anything else, except in conceptual terms. Mind and matter, the all-inclusive but polar fields of reflective analysis, cannot be excluded from conceptual thought. To say that pure experience alone is real is to invite some vague conception of a shadowy and enduring material universe behind experience, or else some ghostly intelligence to keep thinking it into existence. At the very minimum, pure experience is conceived as *my* experience, and an illicit ego is introduced into the pure ground of being. After all, the very word experience is loaded with subjective content. As commonly used, "experience" assumes an experiencer and an experienced, a subject and an object. But James wanted to escape this implication; he wanted to posit a pure, neutral perceptual continuum, which not only implied but contained subject and object, or at least all the reality in any derivatively identified subject and object. Experience is thus something that supports our logical and grammatical forms, but is yet something very different from these forms. Thus, in a sense, it is unthinkable or inconceivable. James tried to talk about it, but without a postulated conceptual framework (such as Dewey's *nature*) for expressing it. Thus, he fell into an easy trap. He too often turned pure experience, a metaphysical ground, into something similar to our own experience. He could hardly avoid this. A perceptual continuum cannot be expressed in any other way, for this is about all that we can mean by a perceptual continuum. Thus, in a maddening circularity, James conceived of pure experience as a product of a conceptual product of itself. That is, the derivative "I" or "you" has to be introduced before one can talk of pure experience. And, at that point, one has traveled so far from a pure experience that he should not talk at all for, if he does talk, he talks of his experience and not of pure experience. If he ontologizes his own experience, he falls into an inescapable solipsism.

Desiring a way out of mind-body dualism, James came close to abolishing anything except the self and its experiences. Because of his rich conception of experience, the resulting solipsism was not as restricting as most varieties are. Even the experience of one person, being replete with relations, insures self-identity and an external world of unlimited scope. In the semantical strangeness of radical empiricism, one moment of experience attains a certain awareness of other, past experiences. The "me" and the world are products of this awareness. But there seemed no sure bridge to other egos or to any world beyond private experience.

James wanted radical empiricism to embrace a transpersonal version of experience. To do this, he seemed, as he so often did in other contexts, to turn pure experience into a vague, substantial ground for individual experiences and thus resort to a virtual unknown to account for the common-sense view of the world. Short of some such ground, he could only use a practically justified version of the pathetic fallacy. Since feelings are unified as a personality by common reference to a physical body, it seems justifiable to attribute such feelings to any other roughly similar body. In this way, we generalize consciousness. Other bodies act as we act and surely feel as we feel. Particularly in the case of talking, these bodies not only behave as we do, but they seem to intend the meanings that we find in their words. Yet, for a stickler, there can be no knowledge of how, or whether, other people feel. There may be only one stream of consciousness in the whole universe. The rigid behaviorist refuses to generalize feelings. He remains at the concrete level of observed behavior and relies on explanatory models that exclude mentalistic terms.

James never seriously doubted a multiplicity of minds. He was thus mainly concerned to show how radical empiricism could account for common experiences. He argued that a given "unit of pure experience" could figure in any number of bisecting fields of consciousness. The common unit of experience could not be identical in all details with the individual percepts, for if James made anything clear it was the almost infinite diversity of perceptual nuances. He believed the individually varying percepts converged at least in their spatial quality (space was thus a universal field) and, by it alone, provided a means of establishing a public world or an objective world. The house I see and you see are the same house because located at the same place. Insofar as we analyze a pure experience into its physical component, there is but one house, however many people perceive it. Insofar as we analyze a pure experience into a moment of consciousness, the perception of a house becomes a quite varied item in many biographies. In terms of the objective reference, the fact that I am color-blind or that you only glimpsed the rear of the house is not important.

But this convergence makes sense only if the "unit of pure experience" is part of an underlying experience stuff or of a broader perceptual field, such as real space. The pure experience, which is the prior reality, cannot be my experience or your experience, for it is the necessary foundation for both of these. It has to be broader than either my experience or your experience; otherwise our perceptions would be identical and our personal separation meaningless. If it is as broad as both our experiences, and more besides, then it has to be a ground of some sort. James hated the idea of an unknown and refused to use loaded terms like nature. Possibly he was cautious out of a justifiable reluctance to let metaphors determine his ontology. Pure experience, as a neutral ground, at least precluded a reduction of the ground either to a material substance or to an overarching mind.

Instead of conceding a ground beyond individual experience, even though one called "pure experience" and virtually similar in quality to one's own experience, James kept returning to a solipsistic position. As a result, he developed two crutches for solipsism and eliminated its more objectionable features. He relied on a credit system to extend the limits of an individually cognized world. Concepts with existential relevance are substitutes for actual or expected perception. Unless false in their claim, they can lead to such perception. But they rarely do so. We live life on credit. In unchallenged areas, we do not seek out the terminal perceptions represented by concepts. We assume the port and go about our long and often circuitous journey. Vast reaches of possible experiences, unified in conceptual constructs, form worlds in which our life inserts itself only rarely and at discrete points. In fact, the nonperceived world, the vast reaches of matter and mind, are often the most orderly and secure worlds we possess. An assumed world, a world of merely possible experiences, plays a major role in our life and is virtually present to us at all times. Not the experienced, but all that can be experienced (a hypothetical quantity) becomes the real world. Reality is the experienceable and not experience. But this also implicates a ground stretching beyond any immediate and personal experience. There still seems a hidden ontology that had best see the light of day.

In some course notes of 1897–98, James struggled with this solipsistic dilemma, seeking some way to retain his experience-is-reality framework. His tentative solution, although never developed or even published by himself, represents the most intriguing tidbit of his whole philosophy. He defined his own field of experience as including immediately present physical things and personal thoughts and feelings, both of which he called "sufficients." These were the directly analyzable contents of his pure experience. But he also professed an experience of "insufficients," of more physical things stretching beyond the margin of direct and discriminate perception, and also other thoughts and feelings, presumably connected with other people. However extensive pure experience, it was all somehow present in personal experience. Then there could be no solipsistic trap and no need to invent some ground back of his own experience. In the same sense that he allowed experienced qualities to account for all the categories, so now he tried the ultimate extension—a quality of "beyondness" or "moreness" accounts for all ontological feelings. He meant nothing mysterious, but tried to describe an actual experience of something beyond the center of a field of awareness, a stretching outward to hazy and indistinct fringes. Thus, all existence, however extensive, was brought onto the same plane. There was no hidden noumenon, no epistemological chasm.

But however he reduced the sting of solipsism, his radical empiricism seemed a covert form of idealism to most materialists and to many realists. However he approached it, existence was still synonymous with a perceptual flow. His critics, like himself, could hardly conceive of a perceptual flow without referring it to a mind. In his own antipathy to materialism, James leaned more toward an idealistic interpretation of radical empiricism. He often sounded very similar to Berkeley, even though his theory gave equal validity to both matter and mind. He also made reality synonymous with experience and had difficulty disassociating experience from its subjectivist meaning. He denied, consistent with radical empiricism, that there was any possible meaning to the term "transexperiential world." Anything not experienceable is existentially meaningless. A material world, existing before any perception, or when there is no perception, or no pure experience, is a meaningless impossibility. The derivative concept cannot usurp the throne of its parent. The inverse is also true, but James did not stress it. Because of the loaded nature of his language (experience, perception), he needed to stress it all the time. A mind existing apart from, and prior to, a realm of matter was likewise meaningless and inconceivable. Any real world, however independent of human perception, is still necessarily tied to experience or to a perceptual continuum. Neither extract—mind or matter —can be exclusive. Both the masculine son and the tender, spiritual daughter must confess their father.

Even as he insisted upon the perceptual nature of ultimate reality, James refused to limit reality to human perception. Even if no person experienced them, James still insisted upon the reality of natural events. In order to uphold this realistic view, he was often tempted to embrace panpsychism. The world beyond human experiencing might rest, not on the experience of lower animals, but on entirely different types of consciousness. The world might be composed of monads, each being a bit of self-contained experience. Possibly atoms were only conceptual abstracts of such bits of experience. Never developed by James, this position would have satisfied most of his motives for developing radical empiricism. It would have provided an objective ground much broader than individual or even human experience, yet by making the ground one with individual experience eliminate any breaks or any temptation toward a materialistic reduction. But it was completely speculative.

An inclusive mind, with a perceptual reach infinitely greater than man's, had been the traditional idealist answer for solipsism. It provided a universe independent of our petty and limited experience, yet a universe of the same nature as our experience. But such a mind violated radical empiricism, for it involved a reductionist position. Here the daughter claimed the throne and the father became her slave. To turn the absolute mind of idealism into a radically empirical postulate, the all-experiencer would be himself a reflective, analytic product of his own pure experience, and thus of something more real than himself, and something that would equally well lead to a materialistic rendering. Yet, such was his softness in this direction that James eventually came back to an idealist position and seemed to repudiate radical empiricism.

As has been frequently intimated, James tried to avoid, but could not always avoid, a substantive ontology, or something in back of individual experience, but by necessity less subjective than individual experience. This position required pure experience to stand for something other than immediate perception, but to be the primal stuff or field into which perception dipped, bringing up its isolated bits and pieces. Even here James would always insist that such a prior realm be *as* perceived, not something qualitatively different or something forever hidden. Thus, it would be a ground of perceptual qualities rather than perception, and a ground always ready to be perceived and in part being perceived. He never developed this position very clearly. To Bergson he suggested that pure experience was something between the old idea of substance and the idealistic view of reality as immediate perception. This intermediate something would always be on the point of becoming conscious; it would be something intermingled with conscious life. It would not be something, like matter or nature, producing or supporting consciousness. James would not have such a vague entity so developed as to lord it over his own experience. He hated dictators even in the ontological realm.

James tried to avoid rather than to develop this vague ontological ground. But this vague position was the one that best anticipated the later development of radical empiricism by both Dewey and Santayana. It is easy to substitute Dewey's "nature" or Santayana's semantically loaded but metaphysically neutral material substance for James's ground of pure experience. Typically, Santayana tried, by his opposite terms, to endear radical empiricism to materialists rather than to idealists, and felt more at home in the materialist tradition. Since radical empiricism would take this line of development in America, it is all too easy to make this James's preferred interpretation. The leading biographer of James, Ralph Barton Perry, so strongly supported such a realistic interpretation that he searched and strained to fit James into it, and even to make him the father of neorealism in America.

Apart from his doctrine of radical empiricism, James usually affirmed a realist position. That is, he believed in a reality apart from any thinker or perceiver, and independent of what anyone thought about it. Very early in his life he defined reality as a "that" which produced human experiences. He occasionally accepted the idea of reality as a "substance" and under Royce's influence defined this substance in spiritualistic terms. But his *Psychology* repudiated substances as useless. The only possible meaning in having phenomena inhere in a substance was a personal protest that phenomena did not make up the total truth. Perhaps this is not an insignificant use. Throughout his life James expressed such a theme. He constantly referred to a world or to nature or to a universe. In the beautiful opening chapter of his *Pluralistic Universe,* he sang a pious song of praise to the great universe whose children we are, or to mother nature as a womb of all existence and the support for all philosophizing. In reprimanding Friedrich Schiller, he confessed his belief in a stubborn givenness in the world, or a grain in subjects that we cannot go against. James was not reluctant to confess such a given world, but only to try and define it. We have no handhold, for we cannot think except in terms of our own experience. The given is an aboriginal presence, dumb and evanescent, glimpsed but never grasped. What we grasp is already some substitute cooked up by human reflection. It is faked when we find it. To Royce he confessed a belief in reality as an undefinable "that" which we encounter and which we roughly predicate in our propositions.

Pluralism, the favorite term in James's vocabulary, had a key metaphysical import. Insofar as he accepted a vague "that," he conceived of it as being of the nature of perceptual experience, with continuities and discontinuities, structure and novelty. The ultimate "that" could not be a neat, orderly thing, clean-shaven, white-chokered, and all buttoned up, but had to be consistent with a vast, slow-breathing cosmos with deep abysses and unknown tides. Any unity had to be actually discovered, or created. His praise of pluralism anticipated the ontological speculation of Dewey, in his masterpiece, *Experience and Nature*. Here, in a systematic way, Dewey showed the traits in nature that would be necessary to sustain both our experiences and our successful action.

Any ontological system involves a conceptual rendering of all existence. The subjective, temperamental bias present in such systems is attested by their variety. Scientific concepts, on the other hand, involve only piecemeal and tentative renderings of existence, but rendering in which there is general agreement. What is the metaphysical import of such concepts? Here James's typical position, and surely his final position, was unequivocal: science has little or no metaphysical import, for its concepts not only do not copy, but in some ways actually distort reality, which is directly present at the perceptual level. From positivistic restraint he easily moved to a romantic distrust. Bergson helped bolster this position.

Yet James was flexible even here. In a course in 1902 he seemed to accept Peirce's hypothesis of an evolving physical order through the survival of the coherent. Thus he hoped for an ever greater harmony of nature and science and for an ever greater convergence of human concepts toward a final unity. Trying to find common ground with C. A. Strong, James admitted that concepts, if they lead invariably to undoubted perception, are absolute in their force. They do not copy, but they fit perfectly and thus insure the possibility of absolute truth. The only limitation is that we cannot verify the fit and thus have to hold tentative views. Absolute truth is a hypothetical possibility, not a sure possession. To Schiller, as late as 1908, he defined objective reality as the product of a social situation, or as the convergence of men's concepts around an unobjectified surd. He was willing to accept, in a common-sense way, the eternality of some concepts that attained a unanimity of opinion, and also willing to concede that these concepts do have ontological reach, or do reveal what things are really like. Thus, in spite of all the contrary testimony, and even as he heeded the vital tones of Bergson, James flirted with a strong, conceptual realism, in which our most carefully acquired knowledge has ontological significance. Our world, however colorful and eccentric in direct encounter, is surely also in some sense similar to our best knowledge.

The metaphysical status of knowledge was always a crucial issue in the development of American pragmatism. James moved back and forth from irrationalism to a near intellectualist position. From the Puritans, in fact from the whole Christian heritage, American philosophers acquired a type of piety, a piety so very evident in Emerson and even in Dewey. The Puritan, in a simple theological context, repudiated the skepticism that denied any knowledge of God and the arrogance of any who claimed to know God. Somehow, in a tension between equally horrible polarities, the Puritan said that puny man obviously cannot know a glorious reality so far beyond, and so much more than, the total of his limited experience or limited imagination. But, at the same time, he also said that man, a rational animal, was obligated to use his senses to drink in the beauty of creation, his understanding to comprehend God's commandments, and his will to obey them. How can it be both ways? Obviously man cannot know reality, at least very much of it. He probably never knows any of it completely. To assume otherwise is presumptuous if not blasphemous. Historically, it is also practically dangerous. Yet, who can deny the practical validity of knowledge and, short of some identity between it and reality, how can it be explained? Is it not possible that man, in small nooks and crannies of reality, does comprehend correctly and possibly even fully? The pragmatists, at their best, tried to maintain a balance of piety and intellectual confidence, of humility and pride. The mediate role of experience seemed to protect both flanks. To Dewey, for example, concepts never copied reality, but symbolized it well enough to guide man unambiguously in his endeavors. To Santayana, concepts revealed not God, but his ways in the world. James could not find this middle way, and vacillated as usual. At times he recognized the validity of rigorous inquiry and the necessity of founding a community on verified knowledge and careful reasoning. At other times he experienced the piety that stands mute before wonders untold.

Always uneasy and baffled when trying to indulge his own ontologic wonder, James was wonderfully tolerant of other people's efforts. He even commended a Spencerian "X" if such an agnostic principle guaranteed a future and spoke in terms of human hopes. Speaking as an avowed pragmatist, he metaphorically pictured a real world as so many beans on a table, spelling nothing but capable of spelling many things when selected and arranged according to human purposes. But any attempt to define the original beans or to chart some external reality seemed of necessity a type of myth-making, subject always to vagueness and vulnerable to deadly criticism. After all, anyone has a license for myth-making. He felt for a while that Royce was so good at it that almost everyone might agree with his version, but his own subsequent defection showed how naïve was this view. Myths often have moral value and contribute purpose and direction to those who believe them. James only asked their adherents to be flexible and tolerant and to acknowledge that the highest goal of philosophy was not agreement about the external reality but moral agreement among the various myth-makers. Trying to be a generous pragmatist, he invited Josiah Royce and Francis Bradley to keep their absolute, for religious and psychological reasons, but to recognize its uselessness in solving day-by-day problems, which had to be approached on humanistic or pragmatic grounds.

James's sympathy was honest, for he eventually joined the myth-makers himself, but with a constant awareness of the tentative and speculative nature of his myth. In his Hibbert lectures (*Pluralistic Universe*), he tried to justify a type of idealism, primarily for religious reasons. Instead of a monistic absolute, he advocated a distributive pantheism—a pluralistic reality composed in part of an indefinite number of suprahuman minds or pooled consciousnesses. He had so often tangled with absolute idealism that he rather apologetically adopted many of its notions. He continued to condemn it for its monistic features and its inability to solve the problem of evil short of denying its reality. But he now granted the necessity of some theory that would unify and dignify human existence. He believed only some higher mind, which somehow and inexplicably embraced our own minds, could do this. But being finite, such a mind was not responsible for evil but only, with man, responsible for combating it.

His final idealistic position seemed to undercut most of his earlier metaphysical probing. It also was based on assumptions diametrically opposed to his own careful criticism of associationism. His higher mind somehow merged individual minds into a larger whole, but without destroying the identity and full autonomy of the parts. This, even though illogical, conformed to a widespread and almost instinctive belief in the possibility of intimate, divine companionship, and was supported by various types of religious experience, by mind-cure doctrines, and by psychic phenomena. He asked skeptics not to discount such a wider self simply because logic refuted it or their own words were inadequate to express it. It was all speculative unless supported by experience. With this support, it was beyond doubt. This affirmation seemed to repudiate his earlier radical empiricism. It also caused all types of dilemmas in James's pragmatism. But no matter. He still believed it.

One effect of all this metaphysical meandering was a tremendous suggestivity. Almost everyone could find sustenance in some of James's metaphysical doctrines. In pragmatic moments, he welcomed any ontology into the field. The best would survive because of their consequences. In religious enthusiasm, he came close to the idealists, or formed temporary alliances with panpsychists. In more scientific moments, he looked to the future unity of concepts and to a world in ever greater conformity to dialectic and law. In moments of sympathy with mystics and mediums, he crucified conceptual thinking and affirmed a version of existential irrationalism. Finally, and more in the mainstream of American thought, he accepted a neutral monism of experience stuff and thus laid the groundwork for a new, presentationalist realism (reality is directly present in perception) and for a purely pragmatic representationalism (concepts represent reality only to the degree required for practical achievement). Rarely has one philosopher drunk at so many metaphysical fountains. Rarely has any philosopher so frequently confessed his own confusion on the most fundamental of issues.

PRAGMATISM

Pragmatism, as first expounded by James, was a publicity success and a logical disaster. Launched in popular lectures, written for mass appeal, and leaning on other of his more precise works for content, pragmatism had all the trappings of a new revelation. Here was the stirring manifesto, addressed to the twentieth century, to young people, and to all the adventuresome and young in heart. Pragmatism was the common content, the core, of a philosophical revolution, finally conscious of a universal mission and ready for a conquering destiny. The absolutist past was dying from irrelevance. Among the apostles of the future, the escapees from dead abstractions, there might be endless disagreement on minor doctrines, but around the banner of pragmatism, of a common method, all could unite, settle all the foggy old arguments, and get on with their moral tasks. This was philosophical Protestantism on the march, scarcely burdened by charges of anarchy or confusion and inevitably headed toward a prosperous future.

Pragmatism added little to James's philosophy. The main boon was an increased clarity on specific issues as a result of an intênse international controversy. The most consistent and enduring parts of his pragmatism had already been introduced in his *Psychology,* although with different terms. The rest was a hodgepodge of James's own dearest causes. He brought in a disturbing amount of his voluntarism, indulged his hatred of a now quite stereotyped intellectualism or rationalism, gave a few new testimonials to the practical benefits of theistic belief, and inserted his temperamental pluralism as an optional benefit. Although full of his personal preferences, his book on pragmatism also breathed tolerance. He deliberately excluded his radical empiricism, for pragmatism allowed but did not require any one technical metaphysical position. It was inclusive, conciliatory, and loose. He asked others, with varied metaphysical theories, to likewise place their doctrines in a handbag and come along on the pragmatic crusade. Pragmatism offered a means of settling any dispute with broad practical bearings and of developing a workable body of at least interim truth. If in the lonely evening hours, after the practical work was all done, the unemancipated absolutist wanted to open his bag and gain consolation, that was perfectly consistent with pragmatism. After all, if their absolute helped them along and did not interfere unduly with their daily work, it was, in some sense of the ambiguous words, pragmatically true. Josiah Royce was not amused.

The noble goal of pragmatism, in James's own terms, was the bridging of fact and value, science and religion. He hoped his new approach to philosophy could justify human hopes and do justice to all the facts. He constantly pleaded that pragmatism had no materialistic bias and was not hostile to religion. To fulfill its goals, James advocated a double-barreled pragmatism: first, as a clarifying device for eliminating purely verbal distinctions or meaningless terms; second, as a new, instrumental conception of truth. The first goal, which he often referred to as a pragmatic test of meaning, seemed to him a metaphysically neutral method of bringing diverse philosophers to agreement on proximate issues and practical concerns. But the new definition of truth implicated a great deal more than a method and pulled James into several complex controversies. In a series of articles (collected and published as *The Meaning of Truth*), James tightened his own arguments but scarcely stilled the debate. The sequel to this controversy came in Dewey's version of instrumentalism, where James's groping matured into a coherent conception of truth.

James added a pragmatic test or method to the test of cognitive relevance already advocated in the *Psychology*. James had first been concerned with one problem—how concepts know reality, reality being the presented content of perception. He showed how certain concepts, as purely mental objects, served as shorthand symbols of discriminated features of experience, and served for all types of mental manipulation. When concepts were related in series, hierarchies, or classes, they correctly claimed to represent large structures of reality, or large, recurrent segments of experience. In each case, cognitive relevance had to be determined by looking behind the concepts to the actual experience they purported to represent. When required to justify their cognitive role, concepts had to guide one to the qualitative experience they represented, even though many intervening steps might ensue. But, as James used the term concept, this was not a test of meaning, but of correct cognitive intent, or of existential truth. By definition, concepts had (or were) clear and distinct meanings. The problem was existential: Could the meaning be had? Was there some cash to back up the very handy check?

But before checks can be cashed they have to be carefully and exactly written. Some checks are unreadable or too confusing to be cashed. They may be imposing in over-all appearance, and even be accepted by gullible clerks, but they still cannot be cashed. To the bank they mean nothing in terms of cognitive cash, even though they are masterpieces of craftsmanship and have given esthetic joy to all who held them. Such meaningless even though beautiful checks are, in moments when cash alone is needed, as frustrating as those checks, perfectly clear and distinct, that have been written on a nonexistent account. In the area of human discourse, and even of that internal discourse called thinking, all our cognitive checks are written in a less than perfect language. As a result, the cash figure has to be most carefully written, or we cheat others and deceive ourselves.

Our negotiable checks, the ones we use in human discourse, are not written in clear concepts or in symbols that unambiguously stand for such concepts. If they were, if we always used a language so precise, then the problem of meaning, even of cognitive meaning, would become insignificant. In most cases meaning could be assumed. In the *Psychology,* where he always thought in terms of very formal or rational concepts, James almost overlooked the problem of meaning and thus jumped on to the problem of correct reference. He assumed clear checks, but worried about the cash. It was Peirce, plus the frustration of trying to communicate with others, and the agony of endless metaphysical wrangling, that turned him to a means of clarifying meaning prior to searching out any cash. In the famous test advocated by Peirce, the key term had been practical consequences, which James now adopted as the keystone of the pragmatic method.

As a strict test of meaning, Peirce meant by practical consequences concrete and public sensations to be experienced. The term house, in the proposition, "there is a house on yon hill," means, if true, whatever actual consequences expected, or even all such consequences that could ensue, in any active dealing with the house. In various active contexts, the focal meaning would vary a great deal, while the full meaning of "house" stretches toward a near infinity of such consequences. Thus, Peirce saw that words are fluid and that their meaning develops or expands in the very midst of our activities. A necessity of successful communication and social intercourse is the translation of terms and propositions into the exact, concrete consequences meant at a given time. This way of arresting the fluidity of verbal meaning, formulated in large part to minimize the confusion of ordinary language, simply bypassed James's earlier concepts, which were, by definition, clear and distinct. In normal discourse, the expected consequences—the expected sensations—of the term "house" vary widely; thus, the word actually stands for many different clear and distinct concepts. The new bride has one concept; the painting contractor another, but both use the same language and talk about the same house, at least if some of their expected consequences overlap. But "house," as a word symbol for the bride's concept, has no fluidity. It has to mean a given and exact group of sensations, no more and no less; otherwise there is no concept present. Thus, to turn words into clear concepts is, in effect, to clarify their contextual meaning. But since words have to communicate concepts, it is the demands of communication, the snares of language, that force us to point to actual sensations in order to make our cognitive meaning clear, or in order to write checks that any bank ought to honor.

Here James had his tool for ending much metaphysical squabbling. Vast belief systems could, by this test, be reduced to concrete meanings. But James, even as did Peirce, easily fell into the habit of talking of the conduct inspired by beliefs. Conduct, in strictest terms, is only a result of the foreseen consequences (or sensations to be experienced) that make up the concrete meanings of a proposition. When we assume the truth of a proposition, we act in light of its meaning. Although the conduct springs from a belief in the truth of the proposition, it is attuned to the meaning of the proposition. If I believe that there is a house at the end of the trail and that it will offer me protection from a blizzard (a concrete consequence), then I may hasten my steps and experience a feeling of great joy. But my quickened pace is not a consequence of a house, but of belief in it. This counterfeit cash is enjoyed even when the bank is empty. But James often made this conduct the *meaning* of a proposition, and the only meaning. Thus, the meaning of a belief was the conduct it inspired. The important practical consequences were none other than the type of conduct that it produced in a person. What does it mean to believe in God? Simply to love one's neighbors.

When meanings are clarified in terms of practical consequences, they determine conduct with great force and precision. This was a good reason for placing emphasis upon the importance of meanings, whether in the restricted context of scientific inquiry or in the larger context of moral endeavor. Here was one of the central themes of pragmatism, from Peirce through Dewey. But the conduct is relevant, not for determining meaning (meaning determines conduct), but for tying meaning to reality, for verifying the truth claim. As I freeze to death, homeless in the blizzard, I possibly never so profoundly understood the meaning of a house at the end of a trail. Also, in a social sense, propositions are very important because of the conduct they inspire, whether justified or not. James never saw that clear and concrete meaning exists as a precondition for confident action and that action in turn may verify the existential relevance of a proposition. He kept reversing the order, letting pleasant conduct establish meanings.

Apart from technical problems, James wanted pragmatism to underwrite religious belief. This seemed to be his principal goal. Thus, he applied his quite unclear test of meaning to his favorite issues—spiritualism, pluralism, God, cosmic design, and free will. He wanted to reduce each position to practical consequences, to what they meant pragmatically. Retrospectively, he found all these concepts meaningless, for opposite positions could equally well account for all the experienced data heretofore accumulated. But in terms of future consequences, he found God, design, and free will meaningful in one respect—they each promised the possibility of a hopeful outcome to man's history. They each affirmed the house at the end of the trail. They assured the victory of good over evil and refuted the idea of a distant death of everything as forecast by deterministic materialism. Vast, verbally different religious formulas all reduced to this one consequence. Men of various persuasions, be they men of hope and good will, could join at this point of pragmatic clarity. Use of this pragmatic solvent should get rid of all morally divisive and dead abstractions, needlessly authoritarian dogmas, purely verbal creeds, artificially fixed principles, closed systems, and pretended absolutes; it should place vitally important issues in the open air among facts, consequences, and action.

Reduced to pragmatic concreteness, these religious and ethical beliefs all looked to a quite concrete consequence—the second law of thermodynamics, which promised a cold and lifeless universe, would be overturned or reversed at some point in the future. But this consequence (the eventual reversal of a general process toward greater entropy) was so far removed from the possible experience of living man as to serve no useful role in verifying belief. If such religious doctrines were to be confidently believed, their meaning had to reside in something closer to the present. Since conduct was always a part of James's conception of meaning, here was his answer. The most crucial meaning of these doctrines was the conduct they inspired. At this point he rejoined his earlier "Will to Believe" and used his pragmatism only to reduce such belief to at least one concrete but distant effect. Thus, he argued that, on pragmatic principles, we cannot reject any hypothesis if consequences useful to life flow from it. If useful, the belief has just that much meaning. When he later confessed the illegitimacy of using the effect of believing as part of pragmatism, James undercut every important application he made, or really wanted to make, of his pragmatic test, for he in effect removed it from almost any religious relevance.

James had even more trouble with pragmatism as a conception of, or a test of, truth. Much of the trouble was verbal, reflecting a horrible looseness of language. Truth, as defined by James in *Pragmatism,* seemed to mean several different things. For example, truth was defined in the following fifteen ways: 1. Ideas that help us get into a satisfactory relationship with other parts of our experience. 2. Ideas that mediate between old truths and new experiences. 3. A name for all sorts of definite working values in experience. 4. Any idea that has a value in concrete life. 5. A name for whatever proves itself good in the way of belief, and good for definite, assignable reasons. 6. That which works best in the way of leading us. 7. An idea that copies sensible things. 8. Ideas that we can assimilate, validate, corroborate, and verify. 9. A means to other vital satisfactions. 10. A name for an idea which launches a verification process. 11. Worthwhile leading. 12. Absolute relations between ideas. 13. A collective name for verification processes. 14. The expedient in the way of our thinking. 15. A growing reality. Obviously, critics had some reason for confusion, although several of the definitions were only verbally different.

The largest number of definitions involved two quite different emphases: the value of propositions, and the way propositions are fitted to reality. Two definitions had no significance for pragmatism: the absolute truth of relationship, and truth as the name for ideas which copy sensible things. James, in order to appease critics, often conceded a rough identification between ideas and the sensible object they represented and in so doing compromised the pragmatic definition. Finally, the last definition—truth as a name for growing reality—was really an awkward way of expressing his philosophical pluralism. Here truth stood for reality itself, with its change and growth, and clearly had nothing to do with true beliefs about reality.

James accepted a central thesis of Dewey's Chicago school—thinking is an adaptive tool. Our ideas may help us to survive and prosper. True ideas are the ones that deceive us least and that help us most in the long run. But this function of truth begs the crucial issue of how we get truth. We certainly cannot work back from present self-satisfaction to truth. Illusion is the very core of ignorance; happiness is often the prelude to disaster. In his many claims that truth is what works best, or best leads us, or has a value in concrete life, James too often confused a social function and a subtle methodological distinction. By so doing he made truth, to some extent, a matter of personal satisfaction.

Dewey preferred to use the term truth only for those propositions about existence that had been carefully fitted to existence in an active, concrete, experimental process. Here he followed James who, in the *Psychology,* insisted that no theory had anything to do with truth unless it could lead to specific experiences, and those exactly when and where the theory required. To Dewey the crucial test, the final criterion, of truth was lodged in the experimental work, which had to be performed under the exact control of the hypothesis. Thus, truth was an end product of a process, which often involved extensive changes in things. He would not assign truth to an untested hypothesis, even though it might be verifiable. The baby could not be christened until he survived the laborious birth process, although he was still in many respects the same baby with the same features. Semantically arbitrary, as are all uses of such a loaded word as truth, this usage at least emphasized Dewey's constant emphasis upon the working role of hypothesis and upon the critical role of experimentation in science. Unfortunately, James was neither as arbitrary nor as precise. He often used "true" to designate a hypothesis that could be, but had not been, verified. In a sense, such a usage refers truth backward in time from a present verification process. Again, James liked to make the verification process itself the meaning of "truth." At other times he assigned truth only to those ideas that led to approved social effects. Thus, truth involved three things: the prior hypothesis, the experimental test, and the moral returns.

At least in some sense of the term, almost everyone agrees that a true proposition about existence agrees with existence. James always confessed that we are not free to choose propositions at will, at least not if we are at all concerned about truth. We have to align our propositions, as well as our purposes, with the world's willingness. But fitting propositions to the world also changes the world. Brilliant, rational hypotheses are born, almost as if mutants, in the minds of individuals. They come almost as if they are gifts. But in order to turn them into truth, in order to establish their fit, the individual has to cooperate with external reality. He has to work. In this sense, truth is additive, or engendered upon reality. In Dewey's terms, the process of inquiry, the experimental testing, amounts to a purposeful redirection of natural events. The new hypothesis is always born and tested in a context of accepted beliefs. James was correct in emphasizing the mediatory role of ideas in harmonizing new experience with past ideas. But unfortunately, James never gave enough attention to the methodological requirements of deliberate inquiry.

James was indicted for grievous sins in allowing feeling or emotion a verifying role. Here he suffered unjust criticism. From the James-Lange theory on, James consistently demanded that concepts find their existential relevance in the area of perception, or of feeling or qualitative experience. Verification, for both James and Dewey, always required some felt quality, some turning to existential experience. There is no other way to tie rational hypotheses to existence. But the verifying quality usually satisfies the cognitive demand by the very fact of its being experienced, and unambiguously recognized, not by any subjective value (any pain or pleasure) of its experience. The two cannot be separated except in function. The shifting red line of mercury, in optics, may cause intense pain to a given observer with eye problems, or it may give a thrill of joy to another who happens to love red with a passion, but its being experienced in a certain place and a certain time alone has cognitive relevance. Here, in the sheer fact of being present, is the most common element of experience, and the element least dependent on purely private sensibility. If anything is public data, this is it. Experience has cognitive value in its very being, in its quantitative occurrence, in its quantifiable intensity, but not for any added value to an individual. The verified or true hypothesis has indeed worked and will continue to work, but only in guiding processes clearly demanded by the hypothesis and in producing the exact experiences demanded by theory. Often these experiences, these called-for qualities, are esthetically rewarding. They may be ugly and painful, but even then they thrill the scientist because they help vindicate his theory and help him procure truth, which he values.

But James would not leave it so. He conceded all this, but said there was more to it. He granted that purely cognitive demands come first and have to be satisfied. The hypothesis has to be internally consistent, externally consistent with other accepted theories, and finally verified as far as possible by the exact experiences it calls for. But when these strict demands are satisfied, other human demands still beg for acceptance. After all, the search for true knowledge is united with other human purposes. As a fact, the truths that we accept will usually be those that also satisfy esthetic and utilitarian demands. Even the scientist seems susceptible to such esthetic demands as elegance and simplicity and such utilitarian demands as theoretical fruitfulness. Esthetic factors incline belief as much as other factors, and anything that inclines belief is part of the truth (possibly a sixteenth definition of truth). Thus, the hypothesis that fits the broadest possible number of human needs, cognitive and otherwise, will be the accepted belief. And rightly so, for our purposes and appreciations are part of the world, and truth is surely not something apart. To segregate truth from other human purposes struck James as a narrow type of positivism and seemed akin to the type of scientism which denied all human values. The implication he drew was quite clear: let other than logical and quantitative factors help determine truth, or truth will remain irrelevant to man's principal concerns.

Here James fell into his greatest logical trap, the one that most vitiated his pragmatism. He mixed the logical and the moral in such a way as to compromise both. He did not see that only the most rigorous and exclusive cognitive demands lead to the type of knowledge that can be trusted, when used to guide events, to produce the required circumstances for our possessing the esthetic and utilitarian values that we crave. The rigorous discipline upon the exact type of experience admitted into the judgment chambers of careful inquiry is not a denial of value, but a concern for it and a fear of the unwanted consequences of illusion. James certainly hoped that his valuative hypotheses—freedom, God, design—did not violate cognitive demands, but he surely realized that they often did not meet these demands at the most critical point of concrete experience, unless indeed he was willing to admit arguments by analogy or mystical evidence available only to a select few. He often inclined toward such an invulnerable mystical refuge, but the bent of his pragmatism was either the justification of beliefs that, reduced to concrete consequences, pointed only to distant and presently unexperienceable events or, even less rigorously, to beliefs that, by the very believing, provided human beings with consolation. To speak of these as true meant that data not clearly implicated by the hypotheses, and not of a cognitive type, had to do the verifying. This does not mean that all hopes are illusions but rather that our hopes should be tied to a more rigorous standard of inquiry and a more critical view of truth. It is fun to dream of a house at the end of the path, so long as we are still on the way. But if the dream is only a hopeful guess, however consistent with other dreams, or even with other facts, we might best be looking for other but cruder shelter, within the purview of our cognitive grasp.

Quite expectedly, James never made a clear separation of, or gave any special priority to, scientific knowledge or to the scientific method. What Dewey and later pragmatists accepted as the best method of inquiry, James often wanted to discount as much as possible. He always had the sense of open possibilities and half-wanted the most entrenched systems of knowledge to give way before some heretofore ignored and ostracized hypothesis. Behind all beliefs are controlling sentiments; in front of all beliefs are compelling hopes. Scientism seemed to him the most intolerable, most suffocating of doctrines. It was a new religion, based on the most sectarian barbarism of all time. The natural sciences contained merely a fragment of truth, broken off of the whole mass for the exclusive sake of practical effectiveness. Even in early lecture notes he described scientific concepts as useful metaphors. While at Stanford he observed the San Francisco earthquake and noted the artificiality of scientific habits of thought when contrasted to his more spontaneous perceivings at a time of crisis.

But James enthusiastically welcomed a growing humility among the best scientists and saw an eventual acceptance of the instrumental conception of scientific laws. He corresponded with a sympathetic Ernst Mach and knew of the works of Jules Henri Poincaré, Wilhelm Ostwald, and Karl Pearson. If science could be divested of its incipient materialism, give up its exclusive claims and its arrogance, and have a truly open mind toward such areas of investigation as psychic research,

James was willing to enlist as an admirer. Then a scientific theory could be viewed as a summary of old facts and a means of discovering new ones. These theories make up the conceptual shorthand by which we write our naïve themes about nature. But rather than seeking an economy of theory or some general agreement among scientists, James often reveled in the luxurious bountifulness of theories. The more the better. Thus, he never worried about reducing the arbitrary elements in scientific theory. He loved them.

PRACTICAL CONCERNS

Since thinking, for James, was a helpmeet of conduct and since a moral theme informed most of his writing, he could never be accused of overvaluing the abstract concerns of philosophy. He often rebelled against overly sterile intellectualism and sought either a strenuous life of action or an appreciative interlude with literature. At times he became deeply involved in political issues. He frequently commented on art and carried on a running dialogue with his brother Henry. He defended unpopular causes, supported eccentric characters, and both sponsored and aided the American Society for Psychical Research. Above all, he talked and wrote about religion, the most inclusive and important concern of man. Yet, to a remarkable extent, James remained aloof from the major theoretical and doctrinal issues that lay behind each practical concern. He hardly began a philosophic consideration of ethics and esthetics, never proposed a political theory of any scope, and was almost completely oblivious of any fine points of theology.

Without any elaborate development, James advocated an experiential theory of value and a utilitarian approach to morality. A pre-eminent position for feeling, or for direct experience, underlay all of his thought. In a moralistic tract of 1899 he argued that all judgments of value depended on the feelings that things aroused in us. To miss the joy of living is to miss all. Ideas only minister to experience. The ultimate goal of life is to have the varied rich feelings that are possible in life. There is no greater gift or grace than to be rapt with satisfied attention and to be able to confess one's sense of unfathomable significance and importance. Too often educated people miss the simple joys and move too far away from the profound and primitive level of perception. Men must not get too far away from seeing, hearing, smelling, tasting, and touching.

This means that values, being experiential and personal, are tied to human preferences. Feelings obviously vary from person to person. There is an almost overwhelming plurality of goods, and these often conflict with each other, even as individuals disagree over what is good. But James did not want to make experienced values purely subjective. He showed that our experience, in its most affectional or valuative moments, refers both inward to self and outward to objects. We either suffer pain or meet with painful objects or situations. Although any feeling is private and can be treated as a purely subjective phenomenon, it usually also has an objective referent. Although human preferences vary widely, they often meet in common objects of experience. At least rough social valuation is possible.

James advocated a humanistic criterion of moral judgment, although he hoped that a God would ensure the success of our moral struggles. In the plurality of feelings, each individual seeks a unity or harmony of purpose. What feels good is good, in itself and in the short run. But a person lives in the long run and wants stability and consistency. Moral harmony is difficult enough at the individual level, but almost impossible at the social level. Some overarching unity, some objective good as a standard, some higher obligation, some moral universe—how attain these? To erect a God, or some higher consciousness, means nothing unless God's claims strike a responsible chord in individual hearts. If they do so, God changes nothing morally. To erect a God on the basis of one's own subjective preferences and then try to enforce these preferences over other people is tyranny of the type that has usually infected established religions. James concluded that a moral universe was an ideal but in no way a present reality. Even if there is a God to aid and console, we live in a moral republic. There is no overarching moral authority.

The result has to be some type of practical accommodation based on the rough similarities in our several preferences. The moral guideline has to be the satisfaction of as many preferences as possible. Trying to disassociate himself from what he conceived as the crudeness of traditional utilitarianism, James insisted that the emphasis be not only upon maximizing satisfaction but also upon minimizing the sacrifice. In an ethical version of the concurrent majority, he wanted to preserve as many individual values as possible and to eliminate no more than absolutely necessary. Even the eliminated preferences should have some representation. Here James expressed his fervent individualism and his constant sympathy with outvoted minorities. The actual determination of conduct in such a moral republic has to depend upon the varying context. Rules are approximate and never absolute. James minimized the role of reason and of philosophy, since theories have little worth in a shifting moral context and have to be revised from day to day. The science of conduct has to be extremely experimental.

James's views on politics, never profound or studied, conformed to his individualistic moralism. In many characteristic attitudes he reflected only contempt for the state and for any type of large social organization. He disliked Spencer's philosophy, but praised his spirit of liberty and his attack on overadministration and great, centralized systems. He felt that classifications and organizations, despite their usually opposite tendency, existed only to aid and protect the creative individual, or the units that are always slipping through the mesh of organization. James hated the herding, branding, licensing, degree-giving, administering, and regulating of a society. He made himself famous, or infamous, for speaking out, as an M.D., against the licensing of physicians in Massachusetts, fearing that it might limit the freedom of faith healers. Even when institutions satisfy individual interests, they inevitably leave other interests unsatisfied, including those residual interests that are purely private and anti-system. The lone and courageous individual, the independent and heroic person, the man of will and even of power, won his greatest plaudits, particularly if he also was or had been an underdog. He once said: "I am against bigness and greatness in all their forms." The larger the unit, the hollower and often the more brutal it was. His most agonizing moments grew out of his futile sympathy with the Filipinos during America's "war of liberation" and with Dreyfus during his ordeal of courage.

Except for the issue of imperialism, James remained largely aloof from national politics. Very much as Emerson had, he held back from espousing political and economic reform and preached his own gospel of individualism. A Victorian gentleman with a soft spot for mystics, he stood high above the battlefield. He hated the "bitch-goddess SUCCESS" and deplored the identification of pragmatism with business success. But he venerated an older, more responsible type of enterprise and believed the desire for private ownership to be deep and primitive. Thus, he cast psychological aspersions on all radical and utopian forms of socialism.

He instinctively condemned cohesive, class-conscious labor organizations and political parties, for they, above all else, ached for solidarity and thus inhibited individualism. The leaders of such movements tended to be crude and vulgar, and James valued breeding and taste, even in radicals. He looked to great men, not to social forces or mass movements, for constructive change. In the manner of an evangelist, or of his favorite minister, Phillips Brooks, he preached to laborers on the value of poverty, on the need to love ideals, and on the importance of manly virtue. He desired a better distribution of wealth, a rectification of economic ills, but, like Emerson, did not think these changes would make very much difference, for "no outward changes of conditions in life can keep the nightingale of its eternal morning from singing in all sorts of different men's hearts." [*Talks to Teachers,* p. 93.] His final hope, it seemed, was for some type of fair socialistic equilibrium in the economic sphere, but with a maximum of individual freedom, and all under the direction of educated and genteel leaders. He somewhat loosely, and perhaps incongruously, combined a near anarchic love of freedom, a class bias in favor of gentility, and a hatred of vulgar and selfish capitalism and of all its abuses.

James was also ambivalent toward war. The Philippine war aroused his political instincts and aligned him with pacifists and peace groups. He thereafter acknowledged a vague pacifism. At the same time, he had long heralded manly virtues and gloried in a strenuous and challenging life. He had a bit of Theodore Roosevelt in him, possibly fanned by his own sickly childhood and his efforts to think himself into health. This ambivalence led him to project a book on the varieties of military experience and to the completion of his famous essay on "The Moral Equivalent of War." In it, he insisted that pacifists recognize the good in war—the escape from mediocrity, boredom, and flatness, the exhilaration and dedication, the manly courage and ideal patriotism, and the daring. These virtues had to be salvaged without the tragedy of actual warfare, which James always believed to be a type of savagery and piracy. War had to be outlawed. But elements of army discipline could be retained and a purely pleasure economy could be avoided through an army conscripted to fight against nature and social injustice. All young men would be conscripted and thus pay their blood tax, get their youth knocked out of them, build health and sober ideas, excite their girl friends, and live on to be more mature parents and workers.

James adamantly refused to develop a theory of esthetics. He professed to love art and beauty too much to indulge in intellectual tampering. The artist, by intuition and analogy, often reached truth of a rational sort, but without reasons or arguments. Esthetic experience was too personal and subjective to be reduced to any general formulations. Appreciation, not criticism, was the proper stance toward beauty, which is always enjoyed at the prerational and primitive level of feeling. No verbal formulas were adequate. No whys and wherefores added anything to art. James's love of beauty and his obvious sensitivity to visual form equaled his love of philosophy. But both were subordinated to moral and religious commitments. Unlike almost every other New England philosopher, he never explored the possible relationship between art and morality or art and religion.

In a nonphilosophic way, James revealed plenty of personal preferences in the fine arts. From his father he received a moralistic attitude, which he retained. Henry, Sr., adopted such an extreme Emersonian attitude that almost no actual artist could meet his standards. To him, existing art was a parlor custom or an artificial, crawling thing, not the gush of God's life into every form of spontaneous speech and act. Too many artists hallowed existing prejudices or consecrated society's censorious moral rules. The true artist, a vehicle of truth, of divine insight and spirituality, had to glorify man's unity with all men, and to unify the spirit with the body, ideas with action. William James was never so critical and demanding. Yet, he hated empty estheticism and freely criticized Henry, Jr., for his temptation to play with language and his tendency to dwell overly much on technique. He wanted the writer to inspire and to dwell on good rather than on evil. Naturalistic amoralism and sensuality horrified him, as did overly romantic or decadent art forms. He hated looseness, formlessness, and shabbiness. Perhaps most revealing, he loved most of the novels of William Dean Howells and the early novels of his brother.

Religion was the one continuous concern of James's adult life. Few philosophers paid it more respect. Every one of James's major books climaxed in a defense of religious belief. Yet, for one who talked so much about religion, James did little to clarify or carefully define it. Religion symbolized the most vivid, concrete experiences of man, particularly those with mystical overtones. It stood for the belief in some supersensible reality, for the hope of some ultimate insurance for our

ideals, and for the present consolation necessary to maintain the good
fight. To James, religion had nothing to do with churches, with theology,
with sacred literature, with sin, with rewards and punishment, or even
with the God of theology (a deliverance of the philosophy shop).
Orthodox Christianity seemed totally irrelevant in any doctrinal or
institutional sense. James almost never mentioned Jesus or a Christ and,
at quite opposite poles from Santayana, never looked for the poetry of
the Christian epic. Sectarian disputes horrified him.

James had a deaf ear for the intricate and often profound concerns of
theology and in this often reflected an extreme and unbecoming naïveté.
He vaguely dismissed his Calvinist past without bothering to find out
about it. Why should any modern person even try to remember a God
who gave so little scope to love, who demanded so much from man, and
who took from endeavor all its zest and fruit? The Roman Catholic
Church, with its extremity of organization and codified doctrines,
seemed to be an enemy of all his deepest commitments. But this hostility
did not include individual Calvinists and Catholics. He gained insight
from Edwards' *A Treatise Concerning Religious Affections* and often
turned to Catholic mystics for the themes of his *Varieties of Religious
Experience.*

James understood religion in its extreme forms of mystical union or
soaring spirituality. He admired the mystic and accepted the reality of
his unexplainable experience. He never embraced or particularly
admired extreme spirituality, as best exemplified by his own father. In a
memorable classification, James contrasted his mild Arminianism, or
healthy-minded moralism, with the antinomian or sick-minded belief of
his father. For the healthy-minded, God is at best a helpful and finite
support. He is not needed very badly. The healthy-minded of the world
are a match for the evils of life and rejoice in the full and successful
exercise of moral energy. They feel no ultimate impotency, no final need
for wrapping up all the enigmas of the world into some overarching
reality, and no inclination to lose themselves in a vaster whole. They see
the world as a pluralism, and they see God, if at all, as a finite portion of
being.

But some people, because of experiences anyone may face, become
"sicklied o'er" with a sense of weakness, helpless failure, and fear. They
reject any sense of vanity, including moral pretensions. All evil is
deemed mere illusion or is resolved into a higher divine purpose. They

are humble and pious. Worldly goodness counts for naught. Man has redemption only in God; glory only in God's glorification. As James perhaps understood, this is at least a vital part, if not the essence, of true religion. The deepest religious thinkers always gravitated toward such soaring spirituality and toward such ontologic resolution of evil. Whatever its moral fruit, religion is neither morality nor morality plus an insurance policy. But James was incurably healthy-minded and had to see religion from that perspective. He preferred naturalistic human-ism to spirituality, even though it promised no sure victory. His religion, in subtlety and depth, hardly went further than that of Benjamin Frank-lin, except for his penetrating psychological insight into varied types of religious experience and for his understanding and pity of all the sickly souls in a world full of sound and fury and, to them, signifying nothing but vanity.

James, in some form or other, and with varying degrees of confidence, always believed in the existence of a God (or gods). Even in his youth-ful spiritual crisis, he kept coming back to the possibility of God. By 1882 he was able to express what remained his most characteristic conception of God: a big boss to insure that goodness wins; a strongest but not omnipotent power; a personage with a definite personality and mental powers; and a struggling instead of a perfect or all-inclusive being. God was an experiencer like man, but of a wider conscious span. His finiteness evaded all problems of evil and foreknowledge. To James, God was never demanding and never so vulgar as to mete out punish-ments. An omnipotent and judgmental God could not be an object of religious devotion. If there were some Absolute such as Royce advo-cated, it would fulfill a cosmic emotion but not be an object of religious adoration. James hated the omnipotent Jehovah of Christian theology, but not the heavenly father of simple, evangelical Christianity; he would not turn God into an ideal, but wanted him to embrace man's ideals. Thus, a real God was on the battlefield, with some victories already won. Evil, as an existential fact, was outside God's domain and was as much an opportunity as a problem. It was part of a larger ground of being that contained both man and God (or gods), and which James never treated in any final ontological way.

In his last religious confession, James viewed God as a broader con-sciousness weaving together into oneness the individual consciousness of many individuals. Even earlier, he suggested that God might be a hidden mind utilizing the human brain to transmit its thoughts into the phenomenal world. In either case, God was hidden and, by ordinary canons of evidence, unknowable. As a larger self, God could know us as individuals, and know all that we know, but it had to be a one-way proposition. As to the numerical question, James was unclear and virtually unconcerned. So long as God was finite, some one God, some complete pooling of all minds, was acceptable. On the other hand he was willing to accept the possibility of many gods. At one point, he even conceded that there might be a higher consciousness for each individual. But some God (or gods) seemed the most rational solution conceivable for man's dilemmas. God at least ought to exist. And in a nonrational, experiential way, well beyond the reach of conceptual thought, or out of its very inadequacy and frustration, some men *knew* such a God.

Although James usually stressed the moral function of God, or of belief in God, he also thirsted after immortality. After the experience of his close family, he wanted to close the circle again. If man were given immortality, he felt all would be solved and justified. He never felt very sure on this issue, but confessed a greater hope with old age. In 1898 he reasoned that the hidden reality behind the veil of phenomena might encompass our own perceptions and memories, add them to its larger self, and thus preserve and perfect them. In *Pluralistic Universe* he speculated that the higher or pooled consciousness knows us completely and thus absorbs our own impressions and feelings and preserves their separate and distinct identity even as they are merged with those of other men. Death is like an eye closed. Past perceptions remain, form new relations, and grow, but no new perceptions come in. God retains all our small efforts and lets them continue to develop. We thus add to the larger whole which is God and have an enduring effectiveness in the realization of his ideals.

But all this was speculative. James was never sure. It all seemed such a "maybe" at times. In any case, he 'had to rely on other people's experiences and not his own. He professed complete tolerance for atheists and only asked them, with their will to disbelief, to respect believers. Defensively, he asked C. A. Strong what harm was done by the little residue or germ of actuality that he left to God. His God demanded nothing but a humanistic commitment and remained so nebulous as to cause hardly a ripple in any doctrinal waters.

To bolster his own insecure affirmations, James constantly turned to other people's religious experiences. Of one thing he was sure: belief was not a matter of logic or arguments, but a matter of need and some type of direct religious experience. Of nonmystical forms of religious experience, he believed the most pervasive was that crisis of identity experienced by his father, or by Martin Luther. After the valley of the shadow of death, the ultimate crucifixion of pride and self, the complete surrender of all conceit, some men seemed to probe a deeper realm and find new possibilities of life out of the very midst of despair. He followed with sympathy both the older types of conversion and the new types of self-transcendence sponsored by mind-cure religions, such as Christian Science. He even had sessions with a mental healer. There was, he always believed, something in it. Some believers reached hidden personal resources never uncovered by naturalism, as if they literally latched onto a higher power, which removed the reality of disease and death. Religion, to these people, was scarcely related to the intellect, but was constantly confirmed by an experience of a wider self. They knew of what they professed with an uncanny certainty, and their faith bore fruit in their spiritual luminosity, in healing and mental health, and in manifest moral effects in their lives. They found their justification for belief in solitude and there discovered the acts and feelings by which one relates himself to the divine. Theirs was a living faith.

Mysticism was only an extension, or a deepening, of more normal types of religious experience. James had some unusual experiences, intense and luminous, but he stopped short of calling them mystical. But these, plus the large body of psychic phenomena that he investigated, convinced him of the authenticity of the mystic's report. In religion, the mystic alone was completely empirical, dealing with a direct and independent sort of evidence. Faith branched off the high road of experience well before reason and retained a primal profundity, pregnant with meaning but quite beyond adequate speech. The religious life, the deepest and widest thing in man, defied our petty phrases. The religious prophets, the most religious of persons, experienced a direct union with what they interpreted as divine. Here, in moments that transcended doubt, they merged with God. In *Varieties,* James explored the elements of mystical union and noted similarities of feeling that cut across religions and cultures. However conceptualized, the experience seemed common. The effects of such vision amounted, at times, to a transformation of character. He only regretted that most mystics, reflecting the inadequacy of language in the temple of faith, interpreted their vision in monistic terms. James happily found one mystic who was a complete pluralist.

James proposed a tentative psychological explanation for the experience of mystics and mind-cure religionists. His search had led him into the bizarre, baffling, but fascinating world of abnormal psychology and psychical research. Even as he wrote his *Psychology,* James began his earliest investigation of such phenomena as hypnosis, divided personality, trance states, telepathy, and automatic writing. These, as well as the phenomena of conversion and mystical union, seemed to vindicate a new theory in psychology, that of a subliminal or hidden consciousness. The idea was first developed, at great speculative lengths, by Frederic Myers, an English poet and early psychologist who helped guide James into the Society for Psychical Research. Later, from a different theoretic stance, it would be given great popularity by Freud. James accepted the basic idea. There was, he believed, a much more extended psychic entity than we ordinarily know. On rare occasions, or under such extraordinary circumstances as hypnosis, this subliminal content burst into conscious life. Here, for example, lay a possible explanation for radical conversions and for all manner of religious phenomena. But, in itself, it left open the question of a larger, transhuman consciousness, and also the question of disembodied spirits. These could be investigated, if at all, only through careful psychic research. At stake in such an investigation was a natural versus a supernatural explanation of mind. Without definitive evidence, without avowed certainty, James eventually accepted a supernatural explanation.

In 1869, in reviewing a book on modern spiritualism, a youthful James asked for a serious scientific investigation of spiritualistic phenomena and rebuked scientists for their suspicion and negative attitude toward such areas of research. In 1910, the year of his death, he was still interested and was even more resentful of a complacent scientific orthodoxy that deliberately ridiculed and ignored all the data. He had experienced ridicule and bitter frustration in his own investigation. Fellow psychologists, including the leaders of the profession in America, refused even to attend sessions with mediums or view any evidence. Stuffy academicians, with narrowed intellects, they helped solidify James's resentment of orthodox science. Their refusal to help in this area of research remains a standing reproach to the young psychological profession in America.

In 1882 several English scholars joined in the formation of a Society for Psychical Research, with James expressing interest from the beginning, and serving as president from 1893 to 1896. He helped found and financially support an American branch of the society. In 1885, after frustrating contacts with many frauds, James first met a Mrs. Piper, a famous Boston medium, and probably the most carefully investigated medium in history. For the rest of his life, almost everything he said about psychic phenomena was at least influenced by his numerous sessions with Mrs. Piper. Although he investigated scores of other mediums and hundreds of other incidents or reports, none were so conclusive. The results of these investigations filled a book and occupied a large proportion of his time. According to the rigorous evidential requirements of the society, every possible precaution was taken to eliminate chicanery. No generalizations were made without conclusive evidence (in effect, none were made). The task of investigation was boring. The evidence was scattered and in some sense almost always suspect. The reports of various controls, via a medium, were often perverse, unconnected, and even playful and teasing. The definitive scrap of evidence—the conclusive proof—always lurked just ahead, but never appeared. In 1905 the secretary of the American Society died and, as he had promised, began to communicate through Mrs. Piper. James followed this case for years and wrote the definitive report for the British society. It was inconclusive.

But the research was not useless. From it James gained some fixed opinions. He could not doubt the existence of inexplicable phenomena. For example, automatic writing and types of telepathy were quite common. Also, he could not doubt that Mrs. Piper communicated information that she could not have known in any natural way. He could not explain the mixed and capricious behavior of the various controls. In fact, as a rule of thumb, any clear and eloquent performances cast doubt on the authenticity of any medium. Yet, he could not rule out some hidden but quite natural explanation. Much of the phenomena could be accounted for by a rich subliminal consciousness. But not all. Thus, in his final judgment, given in 1909, James deliberately went on public record in favor of a supernatural source of knowledge. In good mediums the information was too abundant to discount, and it was otherwise unexplainable. It seemed that mediums were in contact, possibly in very loose and fragmentary contact, with other consciousnesses.

So, here in a never-never land of science, he found evidence for some continuity of consciousness, spreading far beyond the individual and apparently beyond the death of the individual. Our individual minds seem to repress or wall out a larger world, except at rare moments when they may plunge beyond the barriers and into the mother-sea. The fringe is leaky, particularly in some people, and the fitful influences seep in.

Psychical research, so often minimized or apologized for by James's friends and biographers, was one of the three or four major interests of his life. He gave as much time and attention to it as to any other subject save his *Psychology*. The interest was continuous and, if anything, his convictions about it grew stronger with old age. Psychical research, instead of a serious failing or a lamentable aberration, was fully representative of the character of James. It was just one of many luminous facets of his life. All reflected, in brilliant colors, some of the boundless characteristics of human experience. But each reflection was fleeting. Each caught the full sunlight only momentarily and too soon dimmed.

James was less a Puritan than any other American pragmatist. He never quite fitted into the New England setting. He was too swayed by diverse, often European influences, and too immune to Puritan spirituality. His moral zeal and interest in religion did not make him religious in any redemptive sense. He struggled with evil but never overcame it. He cried out for solace and help. He had not the courage, the personal strength, for a completely godless universe. Neither did he have the piety or the intellectual rigor to give his full and gracious consent to the ultimate scheme of things, in the tradition of Edwards, Emerson, and Peirce. He preferred to fight, even curse, existence rather than surrender to the whole of it. The dark valleys of life were not redeemed by the glorious mountaintops. Evil was real. He would have no theodicy. But, apart from confessed and appealingly human weaknesses, from a near sentimental search for a consoling but essentially undemanding divinity, he knew and reflected an unrivaled personal nobility. In his agonizing efforts to bolster his moral commitments, to ward off all the enervating doubts of his age, he developed a larger store of suggestive philosophical tools than any other American. He has taught and inspired us all.

VIII
JOHN DEWEY

THE LONG PATHWAY TO NATURALISM

John Dewey was a climactic figure in American philosophy. He maintained the piety, the confident affirmation, of Puritanism and transcendentalism. He tried, as much as Jonathan Edwards did, to find the unity and wholeness of life. But he had to defend his intensely moral commitments by new intellectual weapons. The various forms of idealism that had been the prime tools of Edwards, Emerson, Peirce, and, intermittently, even James, eventually proved inadequate for Dewey. As a result of his more rigorous and more reasonable philosophic labors and of the influences with which he had to contend, Dewey transformed his youthful idealism into a tremendously broad and humane form of naturalism.

The spiritual affirmations of an Emerson could not rest at ease in the age of Darwin. Peirce proved this. He was able to support an extreme form of logical realism and objective idealism only by radical speculation. James, torn between humane impulses, religious sentiments, and scientific rigor, floundered in metaphysical confusion and brilliant but interim insights. In both Peirce and James there was always a sense of frustrated urgency, of lost motion, of insights not yet ready for the light of day, of a new faith just beyond the horizon. Dewey gathered all the confusing impulses, all the varied but partial insights, and reduced them to a coherent synthesis, to a systematic and well-ordered world view. His naturalism reflected the more recent revelations in biology, logic, and psychology, yet without sacrificing the dominant ethical and esthetic themes of Emerson. In a chaotic and confused age, Dewey displayed the calm and confident reasonableness of an Edwards.

John Dewey's boyhood was as plain, as average, and as middle class as his name. Born in Burlington, Vermont, in 1859, the year *Origin of Species* was published, he attended the local schools and, in later memory, criticized the abstract content of instruction and recalled his own lack of interest. As a youth he was no more precocious than he was sharply brilliant as an adult. He did not become intellectually stimulated until his senior year at the University of Vermont, when he became enthused over courses in physiology and philosophy. Even after this beginning, his intellectual development was slow. He was almost forty years old before he worked out the main doctrines of his mature philosophy. Yet, his growth was steady. He slowly built on his past, constantly revising where necessary but never quite relinquishing anything. For this reason, his youthful Vermont years were of vital importance. He never repudiated most of the values of his childhood. Instead, he correlated them with a new knowledge of man and his environment, a knowledge never possessed by his less sophisticated forebears.

Dewey remained a nominal Christian until his thirties. In Vermont he absorbed the moralistic and evangelistic attitudes of a still vital Congregational church. Even as a young man he reflected more of a social than a doctrinal Christianity. As he developed his own philosophy, he simply dropped, without apparent anguish, the already vague symbols of Christianity, after which he frequently displayed a rather sharp distaste for the supernaturalism which he all too easily and uncritically identified as the central concern of institutional Christianity. Unlike James, he never in later years felt any attraction to any type of personal theism or to any form of immortality. Moreover, he seemed completely oblivious not only of the more profound insights of modern theology but of the many close parallels between some of his thought and that of even traditional Catholic theology. As a philosopher always conversant with growth, with continuities with the past, he was uncharacteristically naïve about the subtle details, the still potent meanings, of his own religious heritage. In this he was the exact opposite of a Santayana, who treasured his religious past but, in basic attitudes, repudiated a great deal more of it than Dewey.

But however much repudiated or ignored, the old Protestant attitudes continued to shape Dewey's beliefs. He always reflected the confident assurance, the doctrinal certitude, and the absolute commitment of his Vermont ancestors. He was ever the Puritan activist and moralist, thinking in order to live and not the reverse. In the flux of existence, Dewey saw man always struggling, aided by knowledge, solaced and rewarded even in the midst of battle by beauty, but never permitted a holiday. And no one had better complain or let on that they tire of the journey. Dewey was ever the critic, the preacher, forcing man to keep on the hard and narrow way, forcing him cooperatively to seek truth, but only to illuminate the dangerous curves that impede human purpose, and begging him to create harmony and beauty, more to inspire and direct the journey than for present consolation.

After completing his undergraduate work at Vermont, Dewey taught for two years in a Pennsylvania high school. Too limited in funds for European graduate study, he yet continued his interest in philosophy and wrote his first two articles, both published by William T. Harris in the pioneer *Journal of Speculative Philosophy*. Encouraged by Harris and by H. A. P. Torrey, his philosophy mentor at Vermont, Dewey enrolled as a graduate student of philosophy at Johns Hopkins in 1882. He was symbolic of a new generation of American scholars who would eschew the German universities in behalf of the growing graduate opportunities in the United States. At Hopkins he was disappointed at the lack of philosophic content in his minor subjects, history and political science, and, ironical in light of his subsequent career, was equally unimpressed by the disappointingly mathematical and scientific type of logic taught by a brilliant young lecturer, Charles S. Peirce. But he relished the psychology courses under G. Stanley Hall and, even more, the philosophy courses under George Sylvester Morris, who left his professorship at the University of Michigan for one semester of work at Hopkins each year. Under his powerful influence, Dewey rejected the intuitionist, common-sense orientation of Torrey and became a convert to German idealism and to Hegel. This commitment, and a concomitant dislike of English empiricism and skepticism, was echoed in four published articles and led him to write a thesis on Kant's psychology.

Dewey was a superior graduate student, completing his doctorate in two years. At the urging of Morris, the University even had him teach an undergraduate course. After finishing his Ph.D. and beginning the almost hopeless search for a secular teaching post in philosophy, Morris invited him to Michigan as an instructor. He remained there for a decade. At Michigan, Dewey's stream of publications soon established him as one of the pre-eminent advocates of the then prevalent idealism, but he was untypical in that he was one much less interested in formal religion than in psychology and science.

Although Dewey slowly emancipated himself from the "traps" of idealism, he departed with a large bag full of useful ideas. He kept the Hegelian emphasis upon process, although he had converted it into a manageable rather than a deterministic, dialectical process. He kept the unifying mind of Hegel, but made it a characteristic of rather than the author of nature. With Hegel, he saw thought as creative, but denied that it was an entity or substance. Whereas Hegel made his absolute Spirit swallow both nature and history, Dewey made mind or Spirit the one, directive, teleological factor in an otherwise purposeless flux of events. Finally, whereas Hegel was radically speculative, building reality out of the magic brick of his own concepts and their logical relations, Dewey was radically empirical, finding man's only vital contact with reality in the existential interaction of organism and environment.

Most important of all, Dewey kept the Hegelian insight that mind is active, dynamic, at work in history. No scientific psychology could treat mind as a passive thing. Thought had to be conceived as functional, not photographic. Mind was always developing. History held the best keys to understanding. Also, for Dewey as much as for Hegel, philosophy had to overcome dualities, embrace all human concerns, and lead to unity. Dewey often had the same recourse to an organic model and looked to a world in process of transformation through reason. Hegel had Spirit realize itself concretely in human history and thus transform and redeem all human struggles. Dewey had intelligence illuminate a process called nature and ever point it toward its highest possible fruition. Finally, Dewey would always retain Hegel's hatred of abstract, static, formal logic.

The most pervasive challenge to objective idealism was a Darwinian interpretation of evolution. The debates over evolution swirled around a youthful Dewey and brought him into contact with such speculative systems as that of Spencer. He slowly worked out for himself the enduring implications of Darwinism and ever after acknowledged its tremendous impact. At the very least, Darwinism reinforced the Hegelian emphasis upon process. But it also seemed to force man fully into nature. This further discredited any dualism of mind and matter, but at the same time suggested, even as the new psychology seemed to prove, the utter uselessness of any spiritualistic or transcendental conception of mind. Chauncey Wright had so early, and so perceptively, worked out just these implications. Dewey would soon follow.

In a more positive vein, the very idea of evolving species, however explained, suggested natural incompleteness, indeterminism, novelty, and the possibility of innovation. Nature seemed open to purposeful direction much more than it had in a former, static view. But any human freedom so justified had to be freedom within nature, not freedom from or without nature. If consciousness or thought had any role, it had to play it in nature. Dewey soon affirmed a continuity of adaptive biological functions, from the lowest to the highest, including even thought. Such terms as mind, if retained at all, had to refer to types of natural, quite recently evolved activity and not to any separate substance. Thinking as activity was securely tied to bodily organs and clearly related to neurophysical activities exhibited by other animals. Thinking was a form of biological adaptation.

The consistent application of these insights, Dewey believed, would end forever the separation of man from his environment, the separation of ends from means and from basic needs and desires, and the separation of science from the realm of action or striving. Dewey also believed the theory of evolution had finally destroyed the old temptation to seek after absolute origins and absolute finalities and had turned thinking away from a priori, wholesale answers and toward present meanings and present needs. It made philosophy relevant to real, solvable problems, thus forcing it to assume responsibility. While all too many Americans tried to salvage freedom and moral responsibility by somehow retrieving mind from the clutch of nature, and thus by inventing evolutionary fantasies of one form or another, Dewey accepted and acclaimed the banishment of separable mind and launched his attack on those who believed in complete determinism within nature. Thus, he threw out the gauntlet to anyone who still believed that the mechanistic concepts of physics represented a full description of reality.

If Darwinism suggested a new, naturalistic conception of mind, a new scientific psychology, based on physiology and behavioral research, seemed to necessitate it. Dewey, still under the Hegelian cloud, wrote a psychology text in 1887 in which he still insecurely and vaguely relied on a substantiative mind. But not again. Only three years later, James's *Principles of Psychology,* despite all its ambivalences, showed the pathway to a rigorous behaviorism which, without any vague entities or spiritual abstractions, yet without any ethical sacrifice, could account for all mental phenomena. As for so many others, the *Principles* marked a landmark in Dewey's development. But he learned only from the incisive, analytical James and easily disregarded and forgave the sentimental lapses and the warm voluntaristic compromises.

In his mature thought Dewey was always a behaviorist in psychology (as were also Peirce and Santayana and, part of the time, James). His behaviorism was a correlate of his belief in an active, involved mind, and his belief that thinking always involved bodily activity. Dewey felt that psychology, if it were to have any scientific status, had to turn to the observation of concrete physical and behavioral changes. It had to enter the laboratory. Dewey did not long remain a working psychologist, but followed closely all the developments in the new field of science, occasionally contributing thoughtful and challenging articles to psychological journals. Essentially, he was the open-minded student, and to a greater degree than any of his philosophic contemporaries, James not excepted, utilized the insight of psychology. Strangely, he was often misunderstood because his philosophic protagonists were completely ignorant of psychologic science; they tried to comprehend Dewey's ideas in terms of some antiquated psychological school or even through the metaphorical nostrums of "depth" psychology. The best case in point, of course, was his futile attempt to get fellow philosophers, particularly in England, to get rid of the spectator or photographic concept of mind, which was almost always rooted in a prebehavioral psychology. On the other hand, he was always considered a "softy" by the more rabid behaviorists, simply because he asked psychology, as well as all other sciences, to heed the experiential, situational point of departure for all inquiry. Here common-sense terms like mind and consciousness were appropriate phenomenological designations of pervasive qualities present in the very situations which prompt any inquiry, including psychological.

As a Hegelian, Dewey had learned to hate the atomistic sensationalism of British empiricism. He welcomed the devastating attack on associationism in James's *Principles*. Even when he had developed a radically empiricist position, he still distrusted the older empiricism and never maintained a close, familiar relationship with English philosophers. The utilitarians had betrayed the full possibilities of empiricism— all because of their false psychology. By ignoring the relatedness, the situational and qualitative wholeness of experience, and by not realizing the active function of thought in nature, they had developed a barren, atomistic sensationalism which opened the door to idealism and invited Hume's nominalistic skepticism. No wonder Kant tried to restore connectivity by a special, synthetic activity in mind. No wonder Mill tried to escape the barren emotional landscape of his own heritage. No wonder an equally warmhearted James had rebelled in behalf of the testimony of his own experience. Even the most speculative of idealists, with their wanton hyperbole in expression, came closer than the older empiricists to the wholeness of experience and more easily embraced a morally acceptable community.

Dewey's years at Michigan paralleled the rapid growth of anthropology as a new and influential academic discipline. For many of the young and often radical intellectuals, such as Oliver W. Holmes, Jr., or Thorstein Veblen, the new intellectual perspectives revealed by cultural anthropology easily rivaled in significance the impact of Darwinism. Dewey was enormously influenced. Eventually he formulated his whole philosophy as a far-reaching criticism of the unexpunged and distorting Greek quest for certainty. Historical in part, his critique was also anthropological. Modern philosophy was interpreted as a vast cultural inheritance, rooted in a more primitive understanding of nature, in a pervasive class system which made contemplation and theorizing a function of a small leisure class, and in an irrelevant, supernatural religion. Like Veblen, he tried to step outside his culture, analyze its institutional development, and point to its inconsistencies. Constantly, Dewey turned to the anthropologist for information on other cultures and incorporated this material into his philosophical criticism.

In 1894 Dewey moved from Michigan to the University of Chicago. He stayed ten years. In this decade he finally completed the outlines of his mature philosophy and cooperatively expressed it in the 1903 manifesto of his Chicago school, *Studies in Logical Theory*. At Chicago Dewey not only headed the philosophy department, but also established and directed an experimental elementary school (the "Laboratory School"), perhaps the most significant educational experiment in American history. Here he also married Alice Chipman, herself an able educator. Their six (four surviving) children increased his psychological and educational interests. At Chicago Dewey formed many of his closest intellectual attachments and gathered his first group of disciples; his influence extended far beyond the campus. Already involved in social reforms at Michigan, he now became a close friend of Jane Addams, and an outspoken advocate of early progressive reforms. His newly developed instrumentalism in philosophy was directed beyond the technical overthrow of idealism and to the needed reconstruction of American society, beginning and ending with education. Of course he was only one of many intellectuals to rise in rebellion against the injustices and inequities of industrial America, but he was certainly the most philosophical.

From his small-town Vermont childhood, from the democratic impulse of Midwestern progressivism, Dewey developed the most equalitarian outlook of any American philosopher. Just as much as he hated the dualities of past philosophy, so he also despised the related dualities created by class, race, occupation, and wealth. He saw, with the same agony as Henry George, whom he greatly esteemed, the injustice of a society which was so bountifully productive but yet so full of poverty and misery. He wanted to make the values of art, of reason, of science available to all. Everyone should be able to exercise critical intelligence and achieve responsible participation in politics. This required a better educational system, greater social justice, and efforts to provide increased opportunities for all. In his social concern, Dewey reflected the revived spirit of enlightenment which pervaded early progressivism. At least until World War I, he and his coreformers displayed a buoyant optimism, a sense of invigoration and hope. A new day seemed to be dawning. Surely the eighteenth-century Enlightenment suffered from an overly naïve rationalism and from an excessive individualism. But for progressives like Dewey, a Jefferson or an Adams could still serve as inspired models, for they too had worked for a humane and free society founded upon the objective authority of a natural order, upon expectations of greater personal growth and fulfillment, and established in opposition to subjective creeds or enslaving superstition.

In one of the few embittered and personal controversies of his life (over educational policy), Dewey resigned his position at Chicago in 1894. The following year he began his long career at Columbia University, remaining a professor until his retirement in 1930, and a revered friend and adviser until his death in 1952. At Columbia, Dewey became the most honored of American philosophers and helped develop a philosophical staff second in strength only to the fabulous one at Harvard during the time of William James. Here Dewey wrote some of his greatest works, including his educational masterpiece, *Democracy and Education* (1916); his major work in moral theory and social psychology, *Human Nature and Conduct* (1922); and the most comprehensive statement of his total philosophy, *Experience and Nature* (1925). He spent three years in Japan and China (1918–20), traveled to Turkey (1924), to Mexico (1926), and to the Soviet Union (1928), and in 1929 gave the Gifford lectures in Edinburgh. After his retirement he wrote his most definitive works in esthetics (*Art as Experience*) and in logic (*Logic: The Theory of Inquiry*). Like Locke and Whitehead, Dewey improved with age. He married a second time at age eighty-six and even adopted two more children. His most intricate book, *Logic*, was published when he was eighty. In his ninety-second and last year (1952) he published two perceptive articles. His letters, even in the last two years, revealed a mind that was still curious and acutely critical.

While at Columbia, Dewey joined his work in ever more technical philosophy with a busy career as an involved citizen. With his great industry and ability, combined with a very long life, he wrote more and did more than, in theory, any one man ever could. He joined innumerable liberal causes, signed his name to hundreds of petitions, and took leadership roles in such organizations as the American Civil Liberties Union, the American Association of University Professors, and even a teachers' union. In politics, he supported Woodrow Wilson's New Freedom, backed America's involvement in World War I (to the horror of many liberal friends), and then repudiated what he considered an unfair and undemocratic peace settlement. For years he fought for a world organization that would represent, not the victorious states, but the people of the world. In the 1920's and 1930's he became even more critical of American society. As a contributing editor for the *New Republic,* he was the philosophical godfather of a group of jurists, institutional economists, journalists, and educators who worked for a melioristic type of socialism and economic planning. He was, in this sense, the pre-eminent American Fabian. During these years he tried to appraise Communist achievements in Russia fairly, even as he repudiated the formal and inflexible doctrines of Marxism, and decried any apocalyptic urge to use violence as the only solution to manifest social ills. Despairing of any significant moves toward a cooperative commonwealth through the two major parties, he helped found a League for Independent Political Action in 1929; throughout the 1930's he voted as a Socialist. He made mistakes in politics. He was often far from wise. He acted as intelligently and as generously as was possible, but in any case acted. He refused to leave the battlefield and even in the midst of failure never gave up hope of some small progress through reason and hard work. He had to modify some of his youthful ambition and expectations and, in his mature years, turned more often to redemptive and esthetic experiences that justify humane ideals and efforts even in the midst of deepest frustration.

In his own perspective, Dewey attempted nothing less than a major reconstruction of Western philosophy. Yet, much more than he ever realized, he remained a part of that tradition in it broadest sweep. In fact, and contrary to his own self-image, he was often a conservative, at least in the sense that he tried to preserve the heart of a great tradition. His naturalism, or at least the terms he used to defend it, often betrayed his real purposes. For example, he was never a materialist, nor even close to being one. He always affirmed that nature had reached its highest development and organization at the level of mind or intelligence. His highest commitment was to nature at this level, to man, and to his fulfillment in society. He believed that man could be fulfilled only by a fruitful interaction of nature in man with nature in the environment of man. When this interaction approached complete harmony and in itself was both delightful and productive of a continuing satisfactory relationship, then man had reached his highest goal. Then he experienced something close to beatitude. But rarely was such harmonious interaction possible, particularly for modern man. He was not at home in his world any more, despite his improved tools, technical and conceptual, for establishing a suitable domicile. Man was divided, lost, and confused. He needed philosophic guidance, a restored sense of unity, and a new and relevant religion. Dewey offered himself as an inadequate guide, as a quiet-spoken evangelist of a redeeming form of humanism and naturalism. Only the terminology separated him from a thousand progenitors.

Dewey, much like Edwards, sought to cure man's alienation from reality, a reality which he called nature instead of God. He did battle with the diverting and dividing devils of his age. He hated the dualism of art and science, of pure versus practical science, of fine versus instrumental arts. He hated the pretentions of myopic esthetes, with their pure and esoteric art, or cultish scientists, with their abstract and occult concepts. But his very concern with reconciliation, with unity and wholeness, with relationships rather than distinctions, with merger rather than division, with overlap rather than outreach, with the social rather than the individual, with the inclusive rather than the part, invited distortion and misunderstanding. Dewey worked so tirelessly at pointing out relationships that he often confused superficial readers. For them, everything seemed to merge, to fall together in some ultimate unity. Everything seemed to be art, or science, or morality, or a theory of education. Dewey, inadvertently, gave an indictment of himself: "Unfortunately, the human mind tends toward fusion rather than discrimination, and the result is confusion." [*Philosophy and Civilization* (New York, 1931), p. 160.]

Dewey always tried to achieve a working synthesis out of diverse impulses. He happily affirmed the incompleteness and the contingency of nature, but saw this as a challenge to human ingenuity and an opportunity for art, or for intelligent ordering. Unlike William James, he never rejoiced in the impulsive, vital, or purely spontaneous; he rejected complete systems because they denied art and excluded man from the valued process of creating system out of partial chaos. The incomplete universe provided a niche for man, but man was most human when he intelligently worked to reduce the areas of indeterminacy. Where Edwards rejoiced in God's order in nature revealed, Dewey rejoiced in a partially disorganized nature in which man could occasionally play the part of an organizer. He could be satisfied with no less a role; he never yearned for a greater one. He shied equally from the security of passive absorption in some grand design and from any illusionary, half-mad search for omnipotence. He had none of the resignation of Santayana and none of the madness of Friedrich Nietzsche.

Dewey tried to relate humane aspirations to the highly successful but seemingly deterministic science of the late nineteenth century. He was, if anything, more concerned to do justice to the richness of human experience than to the rigid rationalism of existing science. He violated neither, but transformed the modern understanding of both. In this he was equally radical and conservative. But any great synthesis is precarious; it suffers the erosive effects of each of its elements. The richness, the qualitative, existential aspect of concrete experience has been

eroded, or at least ignored, in the exclusively formal, abstract, mathematical, and verbal concerns of many contemporary philosophers,
whereas the very possibility of rational control over nature has been
denied by anarchic, irrational, and poetically tragic artists and philosophers of existence. Although Dewey was often aware of the relationship of his thought to idealism, to the whole Greek heritage, or to
varieties of modern realism, today he seems most important as a
reasonable man who, even as the Puritans of old, sought a middle way, a
golden mean, between the polarities of excessive and emotionally cold
conceptualism and the sheer but anarchic intoxication of pure experience. He still fought the Arminians and antinomians. He valued
qualitative experience, but trusted it only when it was focused and fulfilled through the use of intelligence. He venerated science, but trusted
it only when it was regulated and directed by concrete, qualitative
experience.

Dewey was very much a professional philosopher. His letters revealed
how much he was caught up in the crosscurrents of philosophical controversy and how much he enjoyed the dialectical games played so
earnestly in the journals and at the conventions. But, apart from the
innocent delight of the game, he conceived his philosophical labors as
constituting a vital, necessary preparation for conduct that could
effectively deal with personal and social problems. His completed
philosophy was both his total world view and his plan of action. Like
Emerson, whom he so admired, he felt that all truth had to be honored
in act. He was never so much a truth-seeker as a wisdom-seeker, and the
very essence of wisdom is the correct use of knowledge. He was much
less a scientist than a moralist, much less a contemplative philosopher
than a latter-day evangelist.

In the twentieth century the classical view of philosophy as a quest
for a special or higher type of truth has been widely repudiated. In
extreme cases, such as logical positivism, the corollary view of
philosophy as a quest for wisdom, for guidance in the search for the
good, has also been repudiated or relinquished. Then philosophers
became technicians, clarifying the meaning of propositions and contributing directly only to the instrumental facets of life. Dewey early
repudiated the substantiative view that the philosopher was a seeker
after a special type of truth, let alone a particularly favored seeker. But
he made a determined defense of the classical view of the philosopher as

a man of wisdom, in the Socratic tradition. In his definition of the active role of a philosopher in society Dewey was close to the early Plato, although to a strangely equalitarian Plato. But in his thought he was an heir of Aristotle, who also tried to use a comprehensive naturalism to unify form and matter, idealism and materialism, empiricism and rationalism. Yet, Dewey repudiated the contemplative bent in Aristotle and also the substantive role given to metaphysics as a type of superior knowledge.

As viewed by Dewey in his broadest historical perspective, the West inherited from the Greeks both an appetite for certainty and for perfect rationality and an antipathy for the transitory and merely apparent aspects of common experience. This was tied to a class division which separated the thinker from the doer, the philosopher and the mathematician from the artisan, and mind from conduct. Inevitably, the quest for certainty was too often separated from the search for existential truth and found outlet in rational or self-consistent systems that had varied and uncontrolled relationships to experience and existence. The philosopher turned to intellectually pleasing and stable qualities, escaping any obligation to give his ideas any standing in observed existence. This left the insoluble problem of reconciling the rational with the experienced world. These thought systems often became dictatorial in the realm of experience and precluded any self-corrective and experimental features necessary for a growing body of knowledge. But when a few daring innovators finally joined this rational and mathematical bent with experimentation, modern science was born, with each emphasis (rational and empirical) controlled and enhanced by the other. This new approach to inquiry was vastly successful and, to Dewey, represented the only sure path to true knowledge. After the growth of science the philosophers became increasingly pathetic competitors of scientists, building their consistent but often irrelevant metaphysical structures and basking in their own image of lofty and unsullied superiority. Dewey asked for an end to the irrelevance and the false quest. Philosophy no longer had a license to create reality or to delve into any secrets of Being hidden from science and common sense. But divested of its tragic futility in seeking certainty, of its one-sided search for truth, philosophy could regain its status by joining man in his unending struggle for the good life. The philosopher should use knowledge to criticize and improve existing beliefs and institutions in behalf of the good. The very success of science and the transformation of the environment by technology made such a critical and useful philosophy a necessity for modern man.

Dewey could confidently define the role of philosophy but not its content. The task of a philosophy had to be related to an age and place, to existing problems and interests. But in any context the philosopher should struggle to unify life and to restore wholeness in all areas by increasing artfulness and intelligent guidance. This integrative role was too often betrayed by the narrow specializations of contemporary philosophers, by their captivity to one or another highly technical point of view. The philosopher should critically evaluate scientific concepts and try to force the intelligent use of scientific knowledge in all areas of life. He should carry the insight of artists into the moral realm and, in order to focus and make more relevant its inquiry, into science. In other words, the philosopher was to be a complete critic, a sage with both a great breadth of knowledge and great moral and esthetic insight, a Socratic-like gadfly forcing better communication and understanding in his society. He was a liaison man, making provincial voices intelligent to all, rectifying and enlarging meanings in each province. Ultimately, everyone should perform some of the philosophic function, in which case philosophy as a profession could safely disappear. But contemporary man was not so ideally situated; he needed a John Dewey to point out the fullest meaning present in experience. The philosopher could replace the priest and the preacher, with their parochial interests, and with the utmost catholicity of interests and understanding possible to educated man become the teacher of a whole society. To Dewey, to be a philosopher was to be a great teacher.

THE METAPHYSICAL FRAMEWORK

When Aristotle formulated his comprehensive naturalism, he tied it to the science, to the most sure methods and certain knowledge, of his day. But he was not content to stop with knowledge, with physics; instead, he tried to go beyond physics, beyond specialized and accepted knowledge, to clarify as much as possible the ultimate implications of his thought. To do this, he went beyond experience and, by analogy and inference, within the context of Platonic forms, tried to clarify the necessary and ultimate ends in nature. Dewey tried to formulate his own philosophy in the light of modern scientific methods and knowledge and spent a good portion of his writing in defending his instrumental concept of knowledge and his experimental emphasis in the sciences. But, like Aristotle, he later turned increasingly to the elaboration of a metaphysics of nature, to the basis and irreducible elements of existence that are not subsumed in physics. He refused to push beyond experience, to invade ultimate Reality or pure Being, but nonetheless worked out a complex, in part hypothetical, account of the generic traits of existence present in all experiences and common to all scientific inquiry. Although clarified later than his theory of knowledge, Dewey's deepest metaphysical probing eventually provided a framework, a comprehensive philosophy of existence, which incorporated and strengthened his theories of knowledge, of value, and of art.

Nature was the ultimate term in Dewey's thought. It encompasses all reality. Only in the human organism has nature attained some awareness of itself. Thus, any general statement about nature has to be limited to the evidence provided in human experience. On the basis of this evidence, which Dewey always respected, nature is a flux of events in time. All events are temporal, exist in relation or interactivity with other events, and are thus conditioned. But events often exhibit some order and stability as well as spontaneity and novelty. Neither complete anarchy nor complete necessity characterize nature. Change is basic, but varies tremendously in its tempo, permitting enough stability for getting a bearing and thus effecting desired controls and enough uncertainty and instability to allow such guidance and direction. Without some contingency, no prediction and no intelligent control would be possible or needed. Without some uniformity, no science and no intelligent action would be possible or even meaningful. The whole philosophic orientation of Dewey collapses when nature is defined either as a completed or fully rational, deterministic structure, or as complete anarchic flux, for in either case nature is forever excluded from all human manipulation or awareness.

To Dewey, intelligent behavior could only develop and operate in an open universe. The crucial problems of human existence, and thus of philosophy, revolve around the relationship in nature between the assured and the precarious, the necessary and the contingent, the repetitious and the varying, the safe and the hazardous. The interaction of these opposing traits is the fundamental feature of existence. The correct choice and administration of their union is the end of wisdom, the ultimate in art. In these traits of existence are lodged all the joys and perplexities of human life. In them is the source of all desire, all striving, all thought, all feeling. To register these traits is only a prelude to an attempt at managing them, at art. The drama of human struggle revolves around the success in coping with these basic features of nature. In Dewey's words, true wisdom "discovers in thoughtful observation and experience the method of administering the unfinished processes of existence so that frail goods shall be substantiated, secure goods be executed, and the precarious promises of good that haunt experienced things be more liberally fulfilled." [*Experience and Nature* (Chicago, 1925), p. 76.]

Any understanding of Dewey's view of nature must be supplemented by his concept of experience. His profound respect for the importance of knowledge was balanced by a greater allegiance to experience, which precedes any knowing, which is simply had, and which is irreducibly what it is. It is the existence that always precedes essence. The priority of existential, noncognitive experience in all realms—in art, science, value—was the basis of Dewey's version of radical empiricism. Experience involves an interactive or, to use Dewey's choice term, a transactive relationship between a sentient organism and its environment, "an environment that is human as well as physical, that includes the materials of tradition and institutions as well as local surroundings." [*Art as Experience* (Capricorn Edition, New York, 1958), p. 246.] The interaction leads to a continuing modification of organic behavior as well as to a change in the environment, a change which may or may not aid the organism in its adjustment or its survival. In response to interaction the organism expresses, behaviorally, what the human being refers to as feelings or emotions, and which are directed toward the objects encountered. This means that objects in the environment are encountered as good or bad, pleasing or painful, desirable or repulsive. Experience is made up of a succession of such qualitative moments which are had by the organism in the form of primitive feelings or reactions. With a system of language or signs, such as the human being possesses, the qualities are embodied in words, abstractly manipulated, take on multiple meanings, and become the basis of intelligent action. But a word is only a sign which stands, never with complete adequacy, for what was experienced as a quality—terminal, final, and inexpressible.

Dewey not only stressed the qualitative aspect of experience; he also stressed that nature is ordinarily encountered in gross, macroscopic forms, and in large, qualitatively unified situations. The gross subject matter of an experience, delimited by its pervasive quality (i.e., awe-inspiring, fear-producing, interest-inciting), may, by subsequent analysis, be reduced to more elemental simples, either in terms of common-sense objects, sensations, or more elemental constituents (cells, atoms, electrons). It may also be broadly categorized as mental (orders of meaning) or physical (external, concrete). The postexperiential analysis is invaluable both in explaining past experience and in giving man some control over subsequent experience. Yet the analysis must not be taken as fully descriptive, either of what happened in experience or of what was actually experienced. By so taking it, the English empiricists were led into a wild and hopeless game of reconstructing a meaningful universe by associating one set of simples, the sensa or sensations. To Dewey, as to James, the relationships, the multiconnections are part of the basic encounter situation, which is the departure point for all analysis and all knowledge. Thus, the universe is not constructed out of simples, but through analysis the simples are abstracted out of the continuum that is directly encountered.

The burden of a complete naturalism, or of any philosophy, is doing full justice to all types of experience. This is almost impossible for reductionist types of philosophy, such as materialism and idealism. By making existence directly present to man in the encounters of organic life, by a metaphysics based on existential confrontation instead of reason, Dewey made nature as broad as all possible experience. By definition, nothing experienced could be nonnatural. But the burden, at this point, was to fit the various analyzed categories of experience, the prevalent terms of contemporary human understanding, particularly matter and mind, into the naturalistic framework. For Dewey, this meant two things: an attempt to see the prevalent materialistic conception of nature as only an elemental, partial explanation; and an attempt to view language behavior in the human organism as the secret of the traditional concept of mind.

Dewey always emphatically rejected a materialistic interpretation of nature. Yet, after rejecting the Hegelian idea of Absolute Spirit, he always affirmed the pervasive presence of matter in nature. But he also affirmed the equal existential status of life and mind (they are not properties of matter), although they are present in only some natural events. To force a complete materialistic explanation on all experience is to shrink, dwarf, distort, and attenuate nature, which is much more rich and full than any restricted materialistic account. As already suggested, matter is a postexperiential, purely analytical concept referred to certain experience in order to explain certain characteristics of nature. At the most simple and thus most pervasive level of interaction, events in nature, on analysis and investigation, display a relatively stable rhythm of change, of uniform sequential relation, of cause and effect. Here there is also a large degree of uniformity and necessity, of strict quantitative relationships. This is the material realm.

Such an approach to matter, Dewey believed, made all necessary concessions to the physical sciences and to the necessary physical components of biological and social sciences. At the same time, he believed that it sacrificed nothing of moral or esthetic importance; in fact, just the opposite was true. The regularity and order in nature at the level of matter provides the indispensable raw material of more complex organic and mental levels of interactivity. Thus, matter is not an ultimate substance, or even a substance at all, but only a fitting characteristic of nature at one elemental level of activity. As a characteristic of a type of order in nature, it cannot account for other types of organization. Yet, as elemental organization, the material aspect of life and mind can be thoroughly investigated. No part of nature is completely exempt from such physical investigation, but parts of nature exhibit complex interactivity that is not completely explained by the restricted concepts of physics. Although qualitatively diversified in our experience, the distinctive properties of nature at this elemental level are best stated in mathematical, mechanical terms, and are best expressed in the science of physics.

From an evolutionary perspective, Dewey accepted an emergence theory, although a less mystical one than Bergson and a less idealistic one than either Peirce or Samuel Alexander. Both organic life and mind represent evolved and increasingly complex forms of interactivity between natural events. Life and mind, though inclusive of matter, are additive characteristics of nature. Individuality and selectivity are present throughout nature, beginning with the selection exhibited in chemical combinations. But at the level of organic life the selection is in behalf of the maintenance of an organic whole, made up of and included in active parts. Here qualitative distinctions become ever more conspicuous. Bias (valence or tendency) becomes an interest to be fulfilled. By a detailed analysis, Dewey differentiated the levels of increasingly complex organization in nature and stressed the psychophysical mechanism, or brainnervous system, that developed in higher animals. But evolution culminates in mind, in a sphere of interactivity that goes beyond a single organism and embraces a whole community or society of organisms; this interactivity is characterized by the highest and scarcest characteristic of nature, the presence of shared meanings. At this level, where interactivity is most rich, full, and subtle, signs are used to represent objects experienced in abstraction from the object signified; these signs are manipulated and utilized by the organism in behalf of controlled future experience. Selection, through imaginative manipulation of signs for the construction of alternate possibilities, becomes choice. But in a behavioral context, one must not forget that the signs used by men have a material aspect, that the use of such signs is a natural and quite active (eventful) part of nature, and that thinking (use of signs) requires nothing more than the physiological equipment of the human body. Mind is no more than a characteristic of nature, even as matter is such at a simpler level.

All higher animals have feelings (behavioral responses) of great variety, but apparently only man is abstractly aware of his own feelings, for apparently only man has developed a language. In Dewey's estimate, he developed it in the process of interactions with other human beings. The organic prelude, most likely, was the signal type of stimulus, often involving sounds. But the response by another organism was to the signal as a direct stimulus and not to it as a sign of something, or as meaning something beyond itself. At one point, historically unrecoverable, an organism was able to use a sound as a sign of, a stand-in for, something else, and another organism responded, not to the mere sound but to the meaning of the sign. The shout "Here, fire!" was no longer a direct stimulus to a hasty retreat (as is the "caw," of a crow), but words denoting, and inducing in imagination, a familiar complex of experiences (red, hot). The appropriate response was to the meaning of the words. Two people then shared a common meaning, enjoyed the world's first discourse, and, if fortuitously mates, were the figurative Adam and Eve of mankind. The two *people* now possessed something common, could anticipate together, and act with a degree of mutual understanding and cooperation. Intelligence was born. Nature, after a long history, achieved mind and thus the possibility of purpose, of final causation.

Language is man's supreme tool. If a naturalist such as Dewey can be permitted the term, it is of transcendent importance. All other tools, as instruments for effecting purpose, are dependent on language, for without meaning purpose cannot exist. Meanings, or signs, apparently arise spontaneously in social situations (as the "Here, fire!") and in the beginning are always very general in reference. Primitive meanings are usually forced upon many things they do not fit and have to be restricted by long, discriminating experience. Science is just the art of making such careful discriminations. Yet, despite their spontaneous origin, meanings are not completely private, arbitrary, and adventitious, but involve a real interaction between at least two people and generally refer to a common experience of something outside their organic selves. Dewey hated nominalism as fervently as did Peirce, but allowed his realism to come to rest in a nature never fully cognizable. In fact, by his definitions, the assignment of meaning to an experience is the very process of objectifying nature which, as experienced, is the *subject* of knowledge and not the object. All meanings are meanings of something and are tied to some experience, although they may not be correct or true in a disciplined context such as a science.

Meanings are as real as any other aspect of nature and are neither miraculous projections of the organism nor illusionary attributions of psychical properties to physical things. They are additive but never exhaustive. They seem exhaustive and fully identical with reality in a disciplined, logical system such as is any science, but to ascribe all reality to them is to forget their instrumental context and their ultimate dependence on social experience. The experience which can become meaningful by the imputing of meaning and the use of a sign to carry the meaning is not changed by the imputation. It was still what it was in experience. But with meaning, with objectification, something is added to it and to nature. The possible meanings in experience, the possible objects to be defined, are never exhausted. The raw material (nature as experienced) is more than ample for the continuous growth of mind. Moreover, the activity of thinking, of creating and using signs, in addition to being about experience is itself a type of qualitative experience which can be objectified through the use of more signs and definitions (rigorously pursued, this would be the science of psychology).

Dewey stressed both the instrumental and intrinsic value of language. A body of meanings, expressed audibly in discourse with others, or silently in private soliloquy, provides a tool for both private and co-operative transformation of accidental experience of crude events into expected and desired and meaningful experience. Events as experienced are final; events with meanings are also instruments. Every meaning entails some anticipation, some expected consequences. Pleasing experiences, once had by accident, are now seen in relation to other events, and thus take on character, have implications, and become part of demarcated histories. But signs have their own existence apart from what they signify. Language is not a recording. Although instrumental in origin and usually in fact, words become valuable things in themselves apart from their directive power over crude events. They are fun to manipulate and relate and are much more amenable to management than other aspects of nature. Conversation, apart from its larger, practical aspect, is one of the supreme delights of life. In this sense, the use of language is an added experience in life, qualitative and existential. As such an experience, it may be retrospectively objectified by signs, and thus there is a language about language (the above discussion is such).

Dewey, in stressing language and meaning, was trying deliberately to revive the classic Greek concept of essence or form, but in a completely naturalistic setting. Here his naturalism also decisively separated him from Peirce, who tried to do the same thing by means of an objective idealism. Instead of positing prior, Platonic meanings, or some cosmic mind, Dewey insisted that meanings first developed historically and that they develop continually and quite naturally in social intercourse. Instead of essences as immutable forms that exist apart from nature, Dewey stressed the complete continuity of meanings with all the rest of nature. It is proper as a convenience of language to identify essence with the most consummatory consequences of things, and to use the term essence to signify one distinguishable and idealized meaning among many possible meanings, but it is improper to dogmatize this one meaning into a special form of separate existence. The Greeks turned essences into modes of being beyond and above the temporal and made thinking, which deals in essences, a nonnatural activity and even a spiritual force. But the Greek error, with its exaggerated transformation of language terms into reality, was not as fatal as a modern tendency to find, when confronted with language, a strange, private, often embarrassing world totally separate and removed from a real existence which is defined as totally material.

To sever existence and essence is to invite either a dualism or a one-sided idealism or materialism, all wholly abhorrent to Dewey. He wanted his evolutionary, behavioral approach to pull the two together again. But he never denied the importance of Greek-type essences, of consummatory consequences turned into special meanings. They are selective usually toward experienced pleasure (not as in science toward relatedness) and are not exhaustive of existence, but are the root of value and esthetic feeling. They are the real sense a thing makes to us. Often even the quest for truth is motivated by the intrinsic, experienced pleasure that is expected from the inquiry. If we had to rend existence and choose between the qualitative, teleological Greek world of immutable essences, or a modern world of neutral, amoral mechanical determinism, Dewey would have adhered to his Greek opponents.

Dewey was always careful to keep mind securely in nature and tied to bodily organisms. Men, when they employ signs and think, use already existent organic structures, such as the brain. Thinking always involves definite biological behavior, and may be so approached. But owing to the broader interaction made possible with language, both bodily organisms and environmental events are altered, taking on new arrangements and new distinctions. But they are still as "physical" as ever. A stick that, by use, becomes a weapon is still a stick. A brain that evolves to the point of apprehending meanings and using signs is still a brain. To Dewey, a living organism must involve a particular organization of material events (of atoms, if you want); otherwise it would not be relevant to its environment. And unless mind was an organization of physiological and physical events, developed out of more primitive behavior, it would have no pertinence to nature, and nature would not be the scene of its inventions and plans nor the subject matter of its knowledge. A pure, separable mind would be a miracle, purely dialectic in operation, and without any possible relevance to existence or nature. If there is a mystery, if there is room for wonder and awe, if there is justification for sincere piety, it is because nature is as abundant as it is, and not that some mysterious mind bears some mysterious relation to some mysterious universe. If mind evolved in nature, if it denotes the character of complex natural interactivity, then the congeniality and relevances need no explanation.

Dewey, with some loyalty to Hegel, always discriminated between mind as a field of meanings and consciousness as a focal and transitive perception of meaning. When the first two human organisms used the first sign, discovered significance and meaning in one all-important experience, consciousness was as broad as mind, but never again. The history of man is one of the developments of ever more meanings out of experience and of constant revision and clarification of existing meanings. Consciousness, or perceived meaning, operates at the point of development, clarification, or revision—at the point where events are in process of change and meaning is unclear. This agreed with Peirce's idea that consciousness was the feeling that accompanied the breakdown of old mental habits. Qualities of experience, when assigned meaning, point to differences in external things and make sense. As we use meanings to discriminate types of experience and to objectify events in nature, we slowly construct large, organized bodies of meanings. In a social situation, a child learns more and more of these meanings and relates them to qualities of his experience. The child has experience, has immediate qualities (call them feelings if you want) but only slowly learns the names given to the qualities and, even more important, the proper object to which the quality is referred (fear and bear, hunger and food). When he does learn, he perceives meaning, and at the point of such perception is conscious. But from then on perceptual awareness always exists against a background of mind, of a much broader area of meanings which are habitually, behaviorally present and which condition the focal or perceived meaning. In other words, there is a universe of meanings not sharply distinguished from the present idea. In a personal sense, mind represents all the meanings that have accrued to one organism, as it has been involved in the complex interactivity of human society. In a larger sense, mind is the totality of meanings that have developed in the community of man.

Consciousness, as Dewey used it, is not mere feeling, but an awareness of *meanings* in events. This awareness is impossible without *mind,* and thus without language. All consciousness implicates a dictionary. Yet, the act or experience of being aware, like other experiences to Dewey, is existential, and not subject to other than retrospective analysis. It cannot be fully conveyed in speech; a pleasing idea is a pleasing idea and that is all there is to it, experientially. But after the fact, ideas or states of awareness can be compared and classified (as desires, thoughts, emotions, sensations) in reference to conditions, consequences, or over-all context. Being conscious is thus a peculiarly human experience, discontinuous, contextual, temporal.

But consciousness is the *experience* that brings mind as a body of peripheral and often unconscious meanings into the purposeful, active life of the individual. By it our ideas become a controlling aspect of our behavior. Our conscious awareness is constantly focused at points of stress, uncertainty, and need; it "is a comment written by natural events on their own direction and tendency, and a surmise of whither they are leading." It is a response to the need for filling out what is indeterminate, and for filling it out in behalf of desirable qualities of experience. Thus, consciousness exists at the point of natural indeterminacy; ideas are most keen at a time of contingency, of needed but yet absent order. They are "the promise of things hoped for, the symbol of things not seen." Regular repetition does not excite awareness; complete flux cannot hold it. Consciousness is always tentative, problematic, and precarious, unlike the antecedent stock of meanings which we take for granted and often use without awareness. Pure reason, if it existed, would be automatic habit, and is best exhibited by a computer. But consciousness "is a cry for something not given, a request addressed to the future, with the pathos of a plea or the imperiousness of a command." If nature were final and closed, as philosophers have often fancied, then "the flickering candle of consciousness would go out." [*Experience and Nature,* pp. 349–52.]

Dewey realized that consciousness is not always a blessing; instinctive, organically centered qualities are often, in the process of being given significance, perverted and confused. In turn, they become a platform for fixing other meanings and can corrupt all subsequent phases of life. With consciousness, natural needs and adjustments lose the certainty of instinct and become subject to all types of aberration. The unaware level of experience, the vast nonconscious, is, as Freud would have agreed, vastly influenced by meanings acquired in social intercourse. Our meanings exert an influence on nonconscious feelings and often distort sensory appreciation. Vague, in part inexpressible, intuitive feelings are least reliable in man, who has lost many of the structural faculties of animals and must, for the sake of survival, take thought. He does not have the equipment for a safe retreat to nature. To be a human being is a great risk as well as a great opportunity. If Dewey more often saw the opportunity, our contemporaries have thoroughly elaborated the risk.

EPISTEMOLOGY

Taking thought involves more than awareness, more than acquiring and using meanings. It demands discipline and careful discrimination in the use of meanings, for only some meanings correctly refer to existence or make up the objects of science. The primary problem of knowledge, of traditional epistemology, is the justification of the elevated status of certain perceptions (or, more exact, Peirce's perceptual judgments) and of the structured bodies of concepts that are built upon them. These are commonly accepted as the proper or true accounts of existence as contrasted with other perceptions and conceptions, such as those in dreams, in myth, in poetry, in religion, and even in common sense.

Although Dewey tried to skirt almost all traditional and formal epistemological problems, most of which he believed to be rooted in a scientifically antiquated, spectator conception of mind, he spent a philosophic lifetime trying to elaborate a naturalistic, active, functional concept of knowledge, and thus of existential truth and of science. The task was a formidable one; the central insight was usually quite clear, but the details were often confusing. If he was a naturalist in ontology, Dewey was just as fervently an experimentalist in epistemology, but such a label needs extensive elaboration.

Essential to understanding Dewey's theory of knowledge was his precise definition of the subject matter of epistemology. To him, *knowing* was always the issue. He always focused upon the process by which something is securely known, not upon the final, abstracted result of the knowing operation. Most often, man, a creature of habit, simply makes use of, or appreciates, large bodies of accepted knowledge, or what is acclaimed truth. Although logically hypothetical to Dewey, from a practical standpoint most of this "knowledge" will operate in our lives quite successfully, even as if it were sure and certain. He agreed with Peirce's "critical common sensism." Happily, much of it is indeed "truthful"; that is, it has been verified by some type of experimentation and is subsequently only recognized and used. But when this existing body of knowledge, this *reservoir* of unquestioned belief, becomes the subject matter of epistemological inquiry, when questions are directed at its status as true knowledge, the inquiry necessarily focuses upon the procedure by which it was established as knowledge. Any other approach is not properly a function of epistemology. The body of existing knowledge may be studied for its purely formal consistency or contemplated in the beauty of its completed structure, but this is a matter of logic or esthetics. It may be approached purely in terms of its application or use, but then it is a matter of morality and, without some question of its reliability, a rather irresponsible morality.

In his enormous quantity of writing about knowledge, Dewey endlessly moved between two points of reference. On one hand he was concerned with the value of knowledge in effecting human purpose, or in the larger, social significance of valid propositions about nature. Here he emphasized the point of departure for all seeking after knowledge and also the point at which the now better equipped truth-seeker returned to the qualitative, moral realm. But, on the other hand, he was also concerned with the interim process of strictly disciplined and controlled inquiry, and thus in the problem of scientific methodology. Although a problem inviting inquiry is set and delimited by qualitative experience, the interim inquiry involves a single-minded but active search for ordered meaning in nature, and in its separated integrity requires a solitary concern with establishing valid propositions. The absolute integrity, the exclusion of qualitative or purely individual considerations, is in fact necessary for the successful striving back at the less abstract, qualitative realm of life.

In the most natural situation, the quest for knowledge begins with a problematic situation. The organism is disturbed, stymied, and unable to act effectively. In fact, the doubtful situation, with its distinctive quality of feeling, set the bounds for any subsequent inquiry. Both the purpose and the scope of the inquiry is thus established by direct experience and not by reflective conceptualizing. Without this original, experiential tie to natural events, without this nativity in felt perplexity, no concepts, however rational or self-consistent, would have any existential reference. Thus, the experienced situation is both the departure point and a pervasive aspect of all scientific inquiry. If it is unrecognized or denied, the logical force of existential objects and relationships is inexplicable.

Yet, as surely as the qualitative situation contributes the controlling universe of inquiry, just as surely must the qualitative aspect be subsequently denied any verifying role in controlled inquiry. It is usually not so denied in common-sense propositions, which lack the explanatory power of scientific propositions, but which are closer to experience and reflect a first order of meaning in which the quality of a situation is most adequately indicated. Since the very process of inquiry usually generates new, qualitatively disturbing experiences, new problems begging solution, there is, or should be, no ending to inquiry itself. But the isolated inquiry, if successful, issues in or ends with at least a temporary resolution of the situational problem, the doubt, which motivated it, although the form of the resolution may be personally unwelcome. Truth is not always pleasant; ignorance may be bliss. But in any case, inquiry springs from experiential problems and, if successful, issues in resolution.

One of the most crucial aspects of Dewey's view of knowledge was his continuous insistence that cognitive (existentially true or false) propositions are instrumental and not imitative. They are means for guiding processes of change in nature and are adequate or valid (Dewey did not prefer the term true in this context) if they succeed in doing this. From a biological perspective, knowledge helps expand the adequate functioning of the human organism in its environment. The brain is an adaptive mechanism, and brute impulses remain in the background. Right reaction in the organism is the end, and this modifies the total subject-environment relation. That some modification occurs is an ever-present fact; that it occurs by knowing instead of by guess or accident is crucial. Thus, knowing is an active, working aspect of life. Dewey, always the equalitarian, delighted in describing the most comprehensive and best-controlled knowing of science as only an elaboration and extension of the experience of common labor, where things were first used as tools, or cause-effect instruments, to procure distant, valued objects, and not as immediate pleasure possessing qualities in themselves. Instead of a lazy copying of some static reality, knowledge constantly directs and orders the flow of events. But although functional, it is still objective. Knowledge does not create existence; instead the relatedness or continuity of natural events sustains and anchors our knowing even as their indeterminant aspect permits knowing to function, to be effective, to do more than resignedly record events. Of course, this point of view is obvious and necessary if mind is part of nature, as Dewey's psychology always dictated. Inevitably, if mind is viewed behaviorally, knowing does make a difference and copy-knowing (or freezing) is impossible, since the organism necessarily gets in the way and changes the universe in the process of apprehending it. But to reduce (or elevate) knowing to an instrument of human purpose was to ask for a Copernican revolution in epistemology; for Dewey, it was to invoke his most violent condemnation.

To Dewey, the first step in dealing adequately with an environment is to be able to discriminate between various conscious meanings in behalf of those with existential reference. Many concepts, for example, have no cognitive intent; others with the intent are proven false when submitted to a test. Dewey was insistent only that meanings which claim to refer to existence be validated in careful inquiry. He was always aware that many of our most treasured perceptions, particularly in the arts, do not make such claims and are not properly true or false. Actually, for most of mankind, thought is rarely concerned with truth or falseness. The difficult search for truth is an art of advanced civilization; it is less a part of the human bent than imagination, reverie, and fancy. This fact should refute all theories that make cognitive judgments the norm and vainly try to explain away noncognitive concepts. Also, meanings in various ordered relationships, including those in the sciences, may have primarily esthetic value and may be contemplated and enjoyed for themselves; here again the truth claim is virtually irrelevant. Poor science or purely abstract science may be more beautiful to a beholder than the most carefully verified scientific system. But the first, crucial epistemological problem is the separation of the cognitive and the noncognitive (such as dreams). Dewey believed the discrimination was logically impossible within the older, static conception of mind, of truth as *insight*, for cognitive and noncognitive perceptions are similar as perceptions. There are no degrees or varieties of consciousness. But there are different types of action, and these provide the clue for discrimination.

The cognitive claim is additive in perception, not intrinsic. The perception with existential reference implies some belief about extrinsic matters, about interaction between events, about consequences. In fact, the perceived meaning can be clearly stated, as Peirce insisted, only in these extrinsic terms. To discriminate cognitive meanings is to do no more than recognize the implicit reference to practical consequences. These expected consequences can be validated only in an extrinsic way, through acting upon the belief and revealing the consequences. Thus, to Dewey, the old epistemological problems of the relative status of our perceptions is a pseudo- or meaningless problem, for it was predicated upon truth being a correct picture of an external world. In reality, truth is a functionally correct reference to the possibility of certain experiences. Beyond that, in an ontological sense, it is a correct reference to a certain necessary structure or order prevailing in the ongoing processes of nature. And this necessary order in nature is known, tentatively and imperfectly, not by intuitive grasp, but by work, by much doing. The tools of knowing are indispensable if the work is to be done and done well. Without them, myths are rife, and ideas, even though cognitive in intent, remain at the mercy of circumstances and of organic peculiarities. Simple, isolated knowing of limited relationships, of brief causal histories verified by obvious consequences, has always been a tool of man, but a tool used without deliberation or art. Only recently has man developed the methods necessary for more encompassing association of meanings and thus for more extensive control over the course of natural events.

To Dewey, the great fact of modern life was the success of controlled inquiry in all areas of experience, particularly in physical areas. The explanation for this success, he believed, was a method of inquiry that involved, in practice, the constant interaction of formal, mathematical discourse and active experimentation. Just as an artist actively imposes certain predetermined forms (nonmathematical) upon a willing subject matter, so the scientist tries to impose a predetermined structure of meanings (hopefully related to past experience) upon nature. In both cases the forms have to yield to the necessities of the subject matter. In both cases the application of the forms is an existential operation, requiring active manipulation of existential materials through guided experimentation, and often requiring careful revision of the preconceived formal structure. Dewey refused, with absolute tenacity, to sever this interactivity, to give undue attention either to formal discourse or to experimental activity. Both are necessary for assuredly successful inquiry. But Dewey did constantly argue a certain priority for experimentation. Without it there is no science of existence. With it, even without careful theoretical control, there is (historically there *was*) indeed some valid knowledge, although the hit-and-miss, trial-and-error method of discovery is most wasteful and almost never leads to large, related bodies of knowledge.

In the light of this conception of science, Dewey always argued that the formal or theoretical part of science is purely functional although vitally important. The very essence of physical science is mathematical, mechanical laws, experimentally tied to experience and to nature. Apart from experiment, propositions bear a purely formal, abstract relationship to each other. When these relationships are rigorously defined, stated in terms of abstract but exact symbols, and manipulated according to precise rules, they form mathematical or logical systems. Internally considered, all mathematics is purely abstract, without any intrinsic tie to existence. But when a mathematical formulation is hypothetically referred to existence in order to explain it, it becomes a prime tool of inquiry, implicating as well as guiding and controlling subsequent experimentation. At this point, uncontrolled induction and simple enumeration give way to rigorously controlled, rational inquiry. The rational aspect of any science is the formal relationships of its propositions, and not the verifying experience, which is always selective, limited, and conditioned. In light of this analysis, Dewey rejoiced in the belated acceptance by almost all scientists that mathematics is purely abstract and does not by necessity bear any exact correspondence to existence. Abstract mathematics is free mathematics, and thus freer scientific imagination. To Dewey, the more extensive and abstract the mathematical discourse, the greater the tool for guiding physical operations in experimentation.

Although many calculations in science are not directly involved with existence, they are used always in behalf of establishing other relationships that are referred to existence, or they do not function at all in science. Thus, at one point or another, every existentially relevant theoretical structure must bear experimental fruit, must control and direct actual existential operations, must rear its head up out of the ocean of abstraction and bear inspection before the brilliant, multi-colored light of direct, qualitative human experience. This is the inductive aspect of science, in which experiences are sought, in which new, hidden data is searched out, and in which a part of nature is formed in a new, formerly nonexistent pattern (provided, of course, that nature consents). Literally, new objects are *induced* or created (in the sense of bestowing form on an unformed content). If all the data, including the old which guided the formulation, and the new discovered by the application of the formula, is unified by the formulation, then to Dewey the hypothesis has done its work well, is valid (or true), and provides a body of knowledge which, in the limited perspective of science, can be read as an instrument for future inquiry or, in the broader aspects of life, can serve as a tool for more successful endeavor toward humanly meaningful goals.

Knowing, like other creative activities, is possible only because of an area of indeterminacy in nature. The stable structure of some events sets the limits of knowing, but the open possibilities insure the potentiality of fruitful experimentation. Knowing, as it culminates in controlled experiment, takes the accidental relationships of things and transforms them into ever larger associations. Things as normally experienced become only the prior outcroppings, the appearances, that point toward larger, hidden associations and toward longer and more encompassing histories. But with Dewey the emphasis was always upon the experimental activity—the search for new data and the deliberate, concrete relating of data. In knowing, as in other types of deliberate doing, man is free and creative; he is a small god imposing his rationality on a partially formless, but potentially formful nature. The process of verification always leads to concrete, guided changes in nature. The world is different after the knowing operations because natural events have been given a new direction.

Unless this active role of knowing is carefully understood, Dewey can be subject to extreme ridicule. First of all, the original problematic experience that motivated inquiry is not itself changed—it, as experience, was, and will in memory remain, what it qualitatively was. But new experiences are deliberately added by inquiry, and the *meaning* of the original experience (its relation to others or to the parts and elements within it) is steadily developed. Second, the subject matter of inquiry is often, but not always, grossly manipulated in the process of experimentation. When it is deliberately altered or rearranged, it requires organic *activity*. When the subject of inquiry is beyond direct, significant manipulation (i.e., astronomical bodies), other things (measuring instruments, for example) as well as the organism are manipulated in the experiment, and nature is still altered because the verification process was undertaken. At the very least, the organism is altered. The mental processes have their physical aspect. The brain has encompassed and unified a larger area of experience and is in part transformed. Any existential hypothesis is, by nature, predictive. It is a belief about how natural events will be proven to be related to each other, or, more often, how they *can be* related. Always the verification, the controlled induction, follows the theoretical discourse, although in rare cases a concrete experiment is unnecessary. A past, negative experiment, carefully controlled by an unsatisfactory hypothesis and fully recorded, may be vicariously repeated as the only experiment needed to verify a new hypothesis. An excellent example is the Michelson-Morley experiment, which failed to find any effects of an assumed ether, but which later took on new meaning as evidence for the special theory of relativity. Dewey also stressed the thin line between scientific verification and social application. Only purpose varies. The same medical experiment that verifies the efficacy of a new drug will also cure the patient. Every subsequent, careful administration of the drug in medical practice will essentially repeat the experiment.

One final qualification has to be reiterated over and over again, particularly in the light of some of the confusion that plagued William James and even Peirce, and was often unfairly attributed to Dewey. The hypothesis, not subjective desires, determines the experimental operations necessary for verification. If the conditions set by the hypothesis are fulfilled, it is true. Personal considerations of the investigators have no role in scientific verification. Death for the investigator in a medical experiment may, for example, be the crucial datum for successfully validating a hypothesis.

The world of common-sense experience is the world of disconnected appearances. Scientific inquiry relates these appearances by inferring and then exposing to experience (here technical apparatus is all-important) many other, nonapparent objects. The nonapparent objects (the elementary simples) are no more real than the gross objects in the original world of appearance, but they are better instruments for ordering our experience, for developing connected histories. But all inference begins with gross appearances, which are the first signposts of inquiry, some of which give excellent directions and others of which give false ones. The inferred objects, in order to be established as true, must also become apparent and exist at the level of sensation or be necessarily related to another object that is. Yet, while Dewey recognized simple, unambiguous sensations as the ultimate tests of inferences about existence, he denied any historical primacy to sensations. Following James, he argued that they too are selective and artful, involving careful discrimination and analysis, and are neither a blessed form of consciousness, nor some immediate grasp of being, nor even the original data of science. But sensations are a special class of meanings in science, providing the ultimate checks on inquiry. When correctly identified, sensations are irreducible meanings that can be used to check other meanings.

In insisting upon the functional aspect of mathematics and in stressing the active element in experimentation, Dewey was trying to rescue science from its modern temple and secure it for social and moral ends. Here he was at one with Peirce. He feared that the ancient idea of certainty had found a modern refuge in certain static, overly formal theories of science. Too often, even scientists insisted upon turning their concepts into a new metaphysics, a new picture of reality. Conversely, philosophers, theologians, and artists insisted upon derogating science in behalf of another true reality. Correctly understood, science was neither a form of magic nor a type of blasphemy, but it was most dangerous as a new form of magic. Since developed scientific concepts were necessarily (in behalf of functional efficacy) far removed from common sense, they were easily projected as *real* in contradistinction to the merely apparent objects of common sense. The old logic of antecedent truth had been poured into new bottles, and at greater risk to moral man, for the exclusively mechanistic, quantitative aspect of physical science (functionally necessary and justified) was, as a theory of reality, more inhumane and inhibiting than the older, qualitatively oriented metaphysical systems. The very elements of science that insured its *instrumental value* (the deliberate exclusion of quality and of everything distinctively individual) became dangerous when projected as a picture of reality, or as the exclusively real. Then quality, so pervasive an aspect of human experience, was excluded from nature and could be reclaimed, if at all, by a dualism with a separate psychic realm, by supernaturalism, or by the introduction, as by Whitehead, of new *ad hoc* metaphysical constructs by definition beyond science but, essentially, only delightful products of a fertile and brilliant imagination. But there was no problem when quality was left in nature, and science became only a selective, instrumental abstract gaze.

From simple sensations through the most universal concepts, Dewey insisted that knowledge was selective toward ordered, quantitative relationships and away from experienced qualities. Final verification is always at the level of qualitative experience, but apart from setting the situation the quality of experience is excluded from all propositions in behalf of those elements that are quantitative, causal, mechanical, and therefore most *instrumental*. The inferential concepts of science either lead to corresponding experience in the experimental search or remain purely functional abstractions that seem necessarily tied to other experiences (a past example was either). All purely inferential concepts, or numerous concepts that carry a broader explanatory load than justified by direct observation (electrons), are functional and at least one step further away from existence than common-sense objects. Concepts in science do not copy pre-existent entities of existence; rather, existence requires certain explanatory concepts, which are tested and purified in as careful experimentation as is humanly possible. More experience, or broader and more encompassing experience, may constantly force concepts to take on new meanings, or it may even cause them to lose all meaning and be dropped from the vocabulary of science. Purely formal considerations, such as simplicity, are formally significant but not existentially significant. The most simple system *consistent with nature* is best, not the most simple system conceivable. Always nature takes precedence, and Dewey never permitted a dogmatic prejudgment of nature.

Dewey's dislike of a purely formal conception of science was related to his view of logic. As a subject of study, Dewey believed logic to be an inquiry into inquiry, into the operative principles accepted at any one time by anyone engaged in deliberate inquiry. Any person who thinks and has reasons to support his conclusions has a logic. Logical principles become the ingrained habits used in seeking and justifying what is presumed to be true. Good logic is a good tool, not an eternal order subsisting between propositions. The "sacred" first principles of logic (identity, excluded middle) are proven tools that operate as a priori or given points of departure in inquiry. But they became fixed and habitual as a result of a historical process, of successful application over a period of time. They now exist as unconscious habits of inference used to form material in inquiry. That they constantly lead to success, to knowledge, is their justification. Essentially, therefore, logic in any age is the explicated habits of inquiry in the most advanced sciences. Logic is, in other words, an aspect of methodology.

Any formal logic, like that of the classic syllogism, may be useful in setting forth the result of thought but ignores the operation of thought. In law, the syllogism is added after the lawyer reaches a conclusion; it is never the means to the *conclusion.* The same is true in science, where we look for proven logical principles as well as data to establish formerly vague conclusions. If the syllogism, or any formal system of logic, is the sole basis of judgment, we are lazily relaxing in the warm embrace and the sophistry of forms of speech that give an illusion of certainty to all kinds of irresponsible errors. Pure dialectic, in mathematics or classical logic, is only self-consistent, not true or false, for its one central principle is identity. But the logic of active inquiry, of discovery, has changed and grown and will continue to do so. Its use in the existential world is always hazardous; fallibility lurks at every turn when meanings that are truistically what they are, are used to reach ends or make conclusions. This restriction was not, to Dewey, an attempt to derogate logic, but rather to tie it to existential inquiry, where its role is often quite decisive, but where it cannot break free from experience and sail off into a wonderful world of purely fanciful, dreamlike certainty and security. But Dewey's critique of logical formalism, though directed at a real devil, often led him to ignore the full possibilities of mathematical logic as a tool and to exhibit what amounted to a bias against symbolic logic. Also, unlike Peirce, Dewey did not explore in loving detail the logic of inquiry and of creativity.

One final aspect of Dewey's theory of knowledge provided a bridge into the realm of values, which was always to him the final justification for inquiry. Dewey believed that any subject matter could be submitted to controlled inquiry, even though there often may be little reason for doing so. All valid knowledge, in other words, is derived from the same type of inquiry, although the subject matter varies greatly and must be taken into consideration. Yet, he always recognized the more advanced development of the physical sciences and used them most often to illustrate scientific method. But he very much wanted the method to be applied and to become equally fruitful in psychology, the social sciences, and history. As soon as inquiry leaves the material level of nature, it has to encompass new data. In animal behavior, for example, the organic responses and the feelings must be considered. In man, feelings, modes of experiencing and bodies of meaning, all socially influenced, have to be taken into account. Here, in part at least, correspondences and parallels can be established between the numerical or spatial relationships, statistically calculated, and the sensed or felt qualities. This means that the social sciences can be truly scientific, although they are not yet well developed and possibly will always be a bit more hazardous because their problems are complex. Insofar as parallels can be established between quantitative relatedness and qualitative experience, the crucial aspect of life (the experience of quality) is amenable to guidance. Also, the social institutions that determine in large part the measure of life enjoyed by an individual may be placed under the regulation of intelligence and formed in the light of continual inquiry, or in the light of reason and truth.

VALUE

For Dewey, the major problems of modern philosophy were not solvable until quality was once again located in nature and recognized as an integral part of experience. His vast attention to the method of scientific inquiry was in behalf of perfecting a tool for enhancing the qualitative consummations of life. Problems of psychology, epistemology, and methodology occupied a large share of his philosophic labor. Except for education, his work here first established his philosophic reputation. But Dewey was most eloquent, most forceful, most at home in the valuative areas of philosophy, in elaborating his insights about art, religion, morality, democracy, social theory, and education. Those who have criticized Dewey for offering man only a good tool, without any conception of what it should be used for, have read too few of Dewey's writings. He did propose a goal for man. Briefly stated, his *summum bonum* was the use of science (verified knowledge) to create a society in which art is universal. He did more to define art than any other American, save possibly Santayana, and did as much as any other American to indicate techniques for creating a society that would embody such art. But before explaining these highest commitments, his general conception of value has to be clearly understood, and because of his own changing emphases that is not easy.

If human experience, in addition to being cognitively neutral, were also qualitatively neutral, then values would not exist. For Dewey, the source of values was the quality of experience. Things are directly experienced as good or bad, enjoyable or repulsive. Such experience is the immediate occasion for varied feelings or emotions, behaviorally expressed in animals as well as in man. Thus, value is a facet of immediate, existential interactivity between an organism and its environment. Without this experiential grounding, there could be no problem of value and no valid theory of value. The basic, indispensable raw material of axiology, of all reflective examinations of art, ethics, morality, and political theory, is just this qualitative aspect of experience. Without it there is nothing to discuss, evaluate, or criticize. No amount of *thinking,* no theory, can create value, which just *is*—final, terminal. Particularly in art and religion, Dewey focused his attention upon the intrinsic qualities of experience and tried to indicate the features of the highest and most rewarding experiences. But in epistemology, as we have seen, he stressed the disturbing, problematic quality of experience as the springboard of inquiry. In his moral and social philosophy he tried to use the fruits of inquiry to fulfill the vision of good as nourished by esthetic experience.

Although experienced value is the indispensable starting point for any valuative judgment, it was only that to Dewey. When experience is submitted to reflective thought, when meanings are involved, then intrinsic or felt pleasures are transformed in various ways. At the most elemental area, pleasure-giving objects are reflectively savored and become objects of conscious desire. The fulfilling object, whatever it is, becomes an end, a referred value, to be obtained again. Existential value is now accompanied by conscious *valuing* or *liking.* This secondary level (desire) initiates a third level, that of critical judgment. To value something because, in experience, it was good, and to make the re-experiencing of the object an end is to set up a causal history, is to implicate the means that are required to have a certain valued experience and, possibly, the consequences that follow the experience. Then the judgment: In the light of required means, of necessary consequences, does one *really* want to have the experience once again? Or, should he have the experience again? If it were not for the pleasure-giving aspect of the remembered experience, or the pleasure or pain envisioned with the means and consequences, no such questions would be asked, for no desire would exist to motivate the question. But *given* the *intrinsic* quality (and this is crucial), the value judgment itself is completely tied to the realm of fact, to cause and effect, to the quantitative relatedness of natural events. It is, at this point, an objective judgment, established by the same method of inquiry used in all scientific areas.

When value judgment is tied to the rigid but realistic discipline of fact, rather than to either the wayward license of mere liking or the experientially distorting authority of some moral dogma, then intrinsic value is expanded, enhanced, and made as secure as the necessities of existence permit. But it is also drastically changed from its adventitious, primitive status. After critical inquiry into consequences, many valued experiences are condemned and, by the power of habit even in the realm of perception, perhaps ultimately even experienced with horror. Similarly, when inquiry discloses the causes (and hence also the necessary means) of a delightful experience, it may also be condemned. In fact, critical judgment pushes the intrinsic pleasure into a broad perspective, either dissipating it in the sordid whole or enhancing it as it illuminates and harmonizes and unifies the formerly mundane but now meaningful series of events that pertains to it. Dewey was aware that, for humans, there is no real separation of intrinsic or felt value from desiring or liking and from critical judgment. All three are inseparably linked with each other, although the focus may shift from one to the other. Dewey fervently defended value judgments against irrational or positivist denials that they could have objective status or be grounded in existence. But his main plea was simply that valuative judgments be based on verified knowledge when such was available or known, that they always be tentative enough to be amended when such knowledge was forthcoming, and that moral man be honest and concerned enough to seek such knowledge when time permitted.

But such a cursory summary does justice neither to Dewey's theory of value nor to his more astute critics. The most disturbing aspect of his point of view, at least to philosophic critics, was his insistence that value judgments could and should be objective and scientific. In some of his writings, owing to an exaggerated emphasis upon this scientific aspect and a virtual ignoring of the intrinsic aspect, Dewey gave a weapon to his opponents, a weapon not obliterated even by the counteremphasis in two of Dewey's finest books, *Experience and Nature* and, more emphatically, *Art as Experience*. Too often the givenness of intrinsic

value was ignored, and Dewey seemed to push perilously close to Locke
and the idea of a science of values. But he always rescued himself by
insisting that values are experiential and just what they are, and thus
that they are ultimately final and inexpressible. But there is a science of
related events, and this is the sole rightful tool for *valuative judgment*
and for the deliberate achievement of *critically approved values* which,
again, are existential and inexpressible. Since, as a result of the perspective provided by critical judgment, many things lose or acquire value, it
was easy for Dewey to dwell upon the critical aspect, particularly in
light of the dominating influence of culture upon our habits and tastes
and thus upon our conscious experience, our desires, and our judgments.
In human society, that which is experienced as good is inevitably conditioned by the critical apparatus, by the beliefs and institutions (or really,
by the philosophy) that pervade the society. Insofar as these were truly
relevant to the facts, to existence as experienced, Dewey was satisfied.
But he believed, with consuming fervor, that modern beliefs and institutions were neither relevant nor moral. Thus, as a perennial reformer, he
stressed the scientific aspect of his value theory. Make judgments, yes,
but make them in the light of the facts disclosed by careful and
laborious inquiry, not in the light of irrelevant dogmas. When knowledge
is lacking, give your higher commitment to seeking it, for there could in
such circumstances be no higher moral goal.

But finally, Dewey's value theory fell back on the quality of experience and ultimately back on his whole naturalistic philosophy. The
comparisons with science, the stress on knowledge, were indispensable
but not most crucial. Dewey emphasized the normative role of both
scientific and moral hypotheses and, with his active view of mind and his
concept of induction, rightly so. But the scientific hypothesis, in a
restricted sense, regulates behavior in behalf of establishing valid relationships, not primarily in behalf of an enhanced, intrinsically rewarding
experience. Dewey, of course, stressed truth as one of the goods of life,
highly desired by many, and thus a possible intrinsic reward for successful inquiry. Such value is usually present in science, at least in the area
of motivation, but it is not *directly* operative in experimental inquiry, for
the intrinsic value has nothing to do with the verification and cannot
control the inductive activity. In a moral hypothesis (that X should be
acquired) the intrinsic value is all-important, and at one point or
another (either as an accompaniment of X, or as a consequence of X, or

in spite of the means to X) both regulates and verifies. In behalf of a moral quest, many scientific inquiries may have to be carried out and thus become indispensable aspects of morality, as Dewey argued. In fact, few would deny the *role* of knowledge in the moral realm, both in achieving ends and in helping form the moral vision. That moral judgments are, in fact, often based on other factors no one, much less Dewey, ever denied. Trite as it may sound, his whole task was to bring intelligence to bear upon human problems in behalf of a better life for all.

Obviously, for Dewey, criticized values do not emerge directly from the structure of events or from scientific knowledge, even though they cannot exist without some knowledge. They fall back on the experienced quality of events, and these in turn are culturally conditioned. A quick answer for the valuative differences of mankind would be to abolish all culture and start over with only the common sensory apparatus and, presumably, a common reading of experience. Everyone could then agree on values. But such a regression would place man back with the animals and leave him to the vagaries of accidental natural goods. Another course is also illusionary. The scientific method of inquiry, if utilized in social areas, seemingly could rationalize culture and thus nullify the dilemmas based on arbitrary, irrational, and subjective beliefs and institutions. A moral society should make possible a moral man. But even here a circularity is involved, for the social sciences must themselves provide techniques or means in the light of a desired type or quality of living. They can only provide knowledge of limits and of possibilities and then direct human hope into the area of the possible. Ultimately, man is driven back to experience itself, and society is driven back to some common experience as a basis for its values. Man can desire only what he has experienced as good or what others tell him is good. By knowledge, he can dispel prejudice, reappraise events, develop new tastes, broaden his vision, discover new experiences, and change the meaning of experience, but he cannot escape the "isness" of his experience, which precedes all else. If, perchance, humans are so physically different that common, shared experience is impossible, then a real community is impossible and society is at best a coercive compromise. But if human beings are essentially the same, if they are only culturally at odds, then by long effort, particularly in education, the purely arbitrary and factually irrelevant cultural encumbrances can be removed and be replaced by relevant beliefs and institutions, by widely shared experiences, and by common standards of value.

But even this is to fall back on a type of sentiment. It may be called natural piety, or reverence for experience and the conscious life that makes it possible, or something else—in any case Dewey began with a basic affirmation. He was, at the minimum, arguing that our highest goal, in general terms, is to try to expand, enhance, and secure for mortal, living man the highest quality of experience possible. This is not merely a glittering generalization, for Dewey tried to define, in his theory of art, the specific features of this best experience. He also believed that this affirmation was consistent with the generic traits of existence and that it thus was objective. He believed that the subordination or denial of qualitative experience in this world in behalf of a nonnatural world or a "spiritual" immortality was based upon no such objective basis, although it was not logically refutable. But he did not deny that such contrary assumptions exist and can lead to an entirely different valuative orientation.

Dewey asked mankind to share his point of view, believing it a true one, believing that he had read experience correctly. He pointed to the human possibilities that could be fulfilled only when men shared it. He believed that the existence of qualitative experience was as much a fact as anything else and that, despite natural hazards, good experiences could, by the discipline of fact, be made to predominate over bad ones. He knew the role of culture in experience and saw the reality of a divided and chaotic world. He never asked for universal standards in a culturally divided world, but at the same time he believed that cultures, including our own, could be judged by the standard of fact, by existence as experienced. He realized that values are had in context and in the fleeting present have to be judged in context and that contextual judgments, even though relative, alone are objective (alone take into account objective events). He feared purely subjective values just because they are divisive, arbitrary, noncontextual, and usually absolutist. Value, as had in experience, is our own, but not the object experienced or the universe in which it is experienced. All values, potentially, are social and shared. Quality and value are permanent aspects of nature, not full-blown creations of men. A one-sided emphasis on the personal and subjective aspect of value, or on the objective part, is fatal.

Often even empirical philosophers view experience only as an introduction to something else, such as knowledge or correct behavior. Dewey's supreme insight as an empiricist was that ultimately everything should be introductory to, or a tool for, a type of self-rewarding experience that merges and unifies all elements of our being. Such a quality in experience is esthetic. The organism is always interacting with an environment, in part undergoing it and in part changing it. The process is hazardous, full of disharmony, obstacles, and frustrations. But nature has some rhythm and some symmetry. It is the ground of esthetic experience, of experience in which sense, need, intelligence, impulse, and action are all unified, in which fulfillment and harmony are attained, in which our very being is in tune with the conditions of existence. Such an experience, as Dewey exalted it, could seem almost mystical, and his celebration of it revealed his closest ties to an Emerson or, beyond him, to a Jonathan Edwards. But it was, he believed, an experience securely tied to the ordinary facts of natural existence and, except for the all-important broadening and embracing aspect of consciousness, an experience presaged by the activity of lower animals. In line with this approach, Dewey developed the most comprehensive naturalistic conception of art ever devised.

In art, as in all areas, Dewey paid necessary obeisance to his behavioral psychology. The human organism participates in nature by motor activity. His senses are the only means for recording the interaction and should be honored instead of condemned. Finally, by the development of human societies and language behavior, man was able to have and communicate meanings. But even before this last stage, the artistic life was prefigured. In animals internal organic pressures cooperate with external materials, transforming them and providing self-fulfillment. When conscious anticipation and deliberate direction are added, art exists. But always the work of art is nature "formed into esthetic substance." There is no escaping nature. Art is present in any activity skillfully directed toward some ideal which unifies and experientially rewards the total process. Here meanings are immediately enjoyed and the quality of life is enhanced. The experience is esthetic insofar as the art is successful, insofar as the activity produces some unifying pattern, structure, or form.

While "art" specifically denotes the active aspect of experience, the doing, it draws its substance from the esthetic insight, from the rewarding experience of the ideal end that guides the activity. If the artist does not have an esthetic experience, his product will be artificial and not artistic. But as long as the imagined object is present in activity, its consummatory glow infuses the whole process, and the most laborious tasks are made meaningful and rewarding. Conversely, "esthetic" denotes appreciation or the more passive experience of beauty, but such appreciation to Dewey was always in part active. Except for the first, fleeting impression of an art object, appreciation must involve insight into the creative process and is itself a creative mental activity involving acts of re-creation similar in form to the creative acts of the artist. The esthetic element may be present in any experience that is intrinsically rewarding and good in itself, however instrumental or utilitarian it may also be. In the fine arts, however, the esthetic element is completely dominant; few if any instrumental goods are present. But the distinction is always arbitrary and even dangerous if drawn too finely, for it tends to divorce art from everyday life. The qualifying terms most applicable to art objects are good and bad, not pure or fine versus practical or applied. There are artful pans and esthetically empty verses; there is creative mechanics and artificial painting. The most useful or the most intellectual pursuits can be artistic if the activity itself is charged with meanings capable of immediately enjoyed possession.

In his more specialized treatment of the fine arts in *Art as Experience,* Dewey tried to outline a full, naturalistic esthetics. Agreeing with many others that esthetic experience involved a type of perception, he tried to demonstrate the active, dynamic, and developing aspect of such perception and to repudiate an instantaneous, fleeting, or purely impressionistic view. He stressed the role of tension and disharmony in art as necessary for the creative development of harmony, order, and form. He believed that a pervading, emotional quality guided the transformation of the material or medium in art, but at the same time stressed the role of intelligence, or of thinking. In fact, he often stressed a type of nonlinguistic, qualitative thinking expertly used by artists. The creative process, though directed toward a quality of experience, is neither spontaneous nor explosively impulsive, since it always involved the careful, deliberate organization of natural energies and requires knowledge and carefully developed skills. He despised art that tried to calculate the emotional response at the expense of basic integrity and thus condemned moralistic (not moral) art as irritating. He felt that the material of art could not be limited, particularly by convention, and that ever broadening and new experience required new forms and new techniques. He particularly feared the tendency to freeze art by slavish imitation of classic or popular conceptions of orthodoxy. He felt that the artistic imagination had to be free, although it always operated within a body of inherited, imaginatively possessed meanings. But these should be transformed in the very process of forming present experience. Finally, he believed art criticism to be necessary, but he deplored either a judicial attitude that attempted to impose rigid, inherited standards or a radical irrationalism that denied any objective basis for criticism. He felt that the critic was obligated to point to objective criteria, not purely subjective impressions, in order to vindicate his judgments. Thus, without dogmatic prescriptions or absolute and thus stultifying rules, criticism could find a position between rigid objectivity or complete subjectivism. In fact, if Dewey's naturalism and his over-all conception of art as a special type of experience could be accepted, he offered an outline for effective criticism.

But the main emphasis in Dewey's whole treatment of art was a moral one. Here he agreed completely with Emerson. Dewey wanted esthetic experience to pervade all areas of life and saw art as the ultimate vehicle for erasing social gulfs and divisions and for overcoming the frustrations of life. It was his substitute for, or translation of, the Christian idea of salvation. Thus, art had to become a prevailing aspect of all human activities and a possession of all men. In his words, "as long as art is the beauty parlor of civilization, neither art nor civilization is secure." [*Art as Experience,* p. 344.] In past ages, in other societies including even primitive ones, there had been a more pervasive esthetic life than today. Most activities of life were then esthetically rewarding, with symbols and myths enjoyed as arts, and with religion itself rooted more in fulfilling esthetic experience than in doctrinal beliefs. Art had been of the community of man. Even though life was more hazardous it was often more rewarding. But modern art was usually separated from life; it was becoming the exalted and somewhat esoteric property of the few. Thus, in often the very words that Emerson had used before him, he deplored the exaltation of the fine arts at the expense of practical arts, the tendency to find something unworldly and mysterious in art, and the expulsion of art, and of esthetic experience, from vast areas of life. Perhaps influenced by the similar, and more eloquent, preachments of Santayana, he deplored the fact that art, or something claiming to be art, was usually a function of galleries and museums. It should be at the core of the community, pervading work, leisure, education, and worship. Any activity, if it leads to form and harmony and is intrinsically worthwhile in itself, is artistic. Even the scientific quest is such to most scientists, but inquiry as a rewarding art remains the adornment of a few people, of a restricted intellectual class.

Dewey believed modern society was increasingly bereft of esthetic experience because of its failure to integrate old beliefs with the revelations of modern science and, even more, because of political and economic institutions that were destructive of art. His own work in trying to force an acceptance of the scientific method and at the same time in emphasizing the purely instrumental, nonmetaphysical function of science, was an attempt to meet the first problem. He knew, though, that to most people science had disturbed old beliefs and had revealed a new world which could not quickly be integrated into their ordinary experiences. Thus, the modern mind was divided, and art, unable to unify life, had become a side show, an overly idealized but isolated aspect of a disruptive duality of truth and beauty. But Dewey believed, perhaps with unjustified optimism, that the tendency of scientific knowledge to place man in nature would, in the long run, enhance art, which has always been activated by a sense of man's involvement with nature.

But science affected more than beliefs; it made possible a wondrous technology and undreamed-of affluence. It gave man large and impersonal machines and large and impersonal factories controlled by large and impersonal bureaucracies (corporate in most cases, but governmental in some). In the past, work on the farm or in the crafts was often meaningful, directed toward a clear goal, and self-rewarding apart from the purely consumptive results. In the factory it rarely was. The work was not enhanced by any ideal end, was not self-satisfying, and was done out of sheer need or by the bribery of nonesthetic, sensually satisfying luxuries that could be purchased and used to satiate the appetites and make bearable the long hours of leisure, also bereft of esthetic rewards in the mad rush of consumption. To a certain extent, all Dewey's thoughts could be boiled down to a thunderous indictment of modern capitalism, or, in broader context, of a purely acquisitive or consumptive approach to economic life.

With Santayana, Dewey felt that the highest form of art was that which unified and directed the whole life of man, that which encompassed his morals and his institutions. And like Santayana, he found religion within the realm of the esthetic. The imaginative ideals that exist in unity, that give meaning and direction to all our effort, that unite us in harmony with other men and with the larger, all-inclusive whole that is nature, are the source of our supreme experience, of our moments of beatitude. They give form, grace, and proportion to the moral life and, to the extent that they are successfully embodied in the individual and the community, lead to the greatest objects of art—lives well-lived in communities that make such achievement possible. The unity of our common ideals and the near mystical (at least nonintellectual) uniting of ourselves with the whole are the source of attitudes of reverence and worship that Dewey defined as religious.

These redemptive ideals have been present in traditional religions and in part have been directed at man's reconciliation with the whole of existence, but in part they have also been attached to supernatural existence and to ideals already existing in a nonnatural realm. With great hazard of being misunderstood, Dewey applied the term God to the pervading unity, to the form that graces our ideals at a given time (echoes of the Platonic Good), and continually emphasized that his God was not a person or any existing object. But religion, as the supreme work of human imagination, is only an extension, a culmination, of less encompassing artistic vision. Art, in all its forms, is thus educative and moral. It represents, in tangible forms, the fruit of imaginative vision; it displays before man, even though by contrast, the life that can be and the experiences that should be. It points toward fully harmonized experience, which is the end of all religious insight.

PHILOSOPHY IN ACTION

In *Art as Experience,* Dewey asked: "For what ideals can man honestly entertain save the idea of an environment in which all things conspire to the perfecting and sustaining of the values occasionally and partially experienced?" [p. 185.] Thus, beyond the celebration of art and of religious inspiration, there was ever the concrete responsibility of reforming the environment, of transforming the objective world in behalf of human needs. These concrete responsibilities required Dewey to apply his philosophy to existing moral problems. In the practical moral realm, art and science had to merge if human progress was to continue. Scientific knowledge revealed the connection between events and displayed the necessary conditions for the having of any desired experience as well as the necessary consequences of such experiences. Thus, morality, if it was to escape superstition, accident, or personal whims, had to be guided by experimentally verified knowledge of human behavior, or by what Dewey often called a science of human nature. Acknowledging the preliminary research in experimental psychology, he still believed most of this knowledge was lacking and had to be content largely to criticize existing moral theory and indicate general criteria for a more objective morality.

If a person is going to live, he necessarily lives in a society that has certain standards, customs, and habits that claim authority over his conduct. Most of these, in the process of individual maturation, become the habits of the individual. In fact, if we are to live we have to make some adjustment to these customs. But if we are to live better, Dewey believed, we have to use intelligence to change them and the objective circumstances that support them. Lack of individual concern about them reflects an ill society, one in which existing institutions have not fulfilled their educative purpose. But if a minimal concern for betterment is produced by existing institutions and is informed by knowledge, this should lead to the objective changes necessary to improve the institutions and, eventually, to an ever enlarging social concern on the part of individuals. With Dewey, the emphasis always centered upon the changes to be made in society and not upon prior changes in man. He felt that the perennial emphasis upon "corrupt" human nature or upon basic unalterable aspects of human nature, such as instincts, drives, or powers, was largely a matter of myths that explained nothing and, in fact, usually rationalized the existing order. Freud was perfectly correct to emphasize the vast areas of nonconscious behavior, but he was wrong to attribute behavior to psychic forces. Dewey tried to show the almost infinite variety in the expression of such needs as sex and hunger and the multiple objective conditions that were subsumed under such terms as fear. The nature of man is, in reality, most fluid. The institutions, customs, and habits of man are most fixed and impervious. Here is the focal point of moral concern.

Dewey not only emphasized the role of habit in conduct, he glorified it. The substance of the moral life will always be acquired habits; otherwise we would all be futile Hamlets, incapable of action. Habit, as he used it, entailed a basic bent or disposition that is often defined as character or even personality. It embraced ways of thinking as well as other types of doing. By this emphasis, Dewey hoped to do full justice to psychology and also to his reform emphasis, for habits directly implicate the objective conditions which produce them and draw attention away from an overly subjectivist, introspective view of morality. Yet, mere unthoughtful routine is amoral. Morality involves conscious choice. Such choice emerges in the process of altering old habits or developing new ones when existing habits are insufficient, when there is obstruction or interference and an end of equilibrium, or when impulse is blocked or thwarted. Since even habitual conduct points back to conscious decisions, or forward to the need for conscious criticism or revision, all conduct, on reflective analysis, has a moral dimension. But the moral focus has to be on the point of conscious choice, and even here the vast majority of habits are still operative, including habits of thought which in part dictate the decision and the form of an emerging new habit. Of course, to Dewey, the most crucial habit of all was the use of the scientific method of inquiry, not just in select areas but in all the problem situations of life.

Deliberate choice involves responsibility for present causes as they influence the future. Thus morality is always a matter of doing, of conduct. Dewey would not let anyone forget this. Ends, principles, and ideals are involved. But they are *in*-volved, not separate concerns. Moral principles, like logical ones in science, are rules gleaned from past moral choice. If they are good ones, they have support from a broad spectrum of informed moral experiences and, in most moral situations, exist as excellent aids or tools of judgment. But they are not self-evident; they must be subject to revision and expansion as experience necessitates. With the paucity of knowledge concerning human behavior, moral principles have even less claim to certitude than logical propositions or scientific concepts.

The moral judgment occurs in a situational context and is inspired by an imagined quality that, it is believed, will attach to experience in some future situation. The moral choice embraces a series of events, a history, with a beginning (now) and an end (the consummation). But the delimited history is not isolated and final. The moral choice grows out of an infinite past, out of multiple habits; the end achieved is not an end to activity, but only a meaningful, emotionally fulfilling experience that inspires more choice and more histories. If our action is artful, if it is inspired by relevant ends, even the consummation is spread out over the whole history and only in a restricted sense is an end a temporal concept. Thus, ends should permeate all moral endeavor and are inseparably intertwined with what is conventionally referred to as means. In integrated activity, means are not mere instrumentalities, but are colored and infused by the quality of the whole and have experiential value themselves. In fact, contrary to the utilitarians, there is no appropriate pleasure at the end of an endeavor pulling it on to completion. Thus, to Dewey, moral choice cannot be fragmented into separate ends and means. To choose is to take responsibility for both. Ends in abstraction are no more moral than means to no end. The end-in-view (e.g., the security of a high salary) is, after all, only one of many effects, of many consequences, that derive from our deliberate action. It is focal because of selective interest. But any intelligent moral judgment must encompass all indicated consequences. To do so, it must be informed by endless inquiry into the relationships and the structure that exist between events in nature and in the particular human society. In this sense, ends do justify means—that is, all the known effects of present action justify the choice of such action. Nothing else can justify it. But the end-in-view (e.g., security), being only one effect, cannot itself justify action. In fact, only a more searching inquiry into the whole history of events launched in a given direction by present choice, up to and beyond the expected consummation, can fully justify the *end*.

But obviously we never know enough for final moral judgment; there could be a million unforeseen consequences of any act, some fatal to our individual life or even to all human life. Thus, life is never secure. Dewey offered no final solutions and no easy path to virtue. He asked for absolute, unswerving moral commitment, but proffered no absolute end and no perfect ideal. He indicated the quality of experience desired, but could not define all the details of a specific objective society that would produce it. Only a God could. But our frustrating ignorance, and with it the terrible hazards of being free to choose in a universe that has room for choice but no certain guide for choice, was never for Dewey an excuse for despair but rather cause for elation. Our moral success is limited but it is a fact. There is hope; we can progress. In the very effort we relate ourselves to the whole of nature and of life. We become a participating part of the great community and belong to it even as it belongs to us. We are part of the ever struggling church of humanity, and the struggling church is, somehow, alone the church triumphant. It sustains us in our feeble effort by a sense of the whole. It never lulls us into a moral holiday or into the passive celebration of abstract ideals.

In his reaction to the specific problems of American life, and of an increasingly disturbed world, Dewey continually affirmed his faith in the possibility of rational reform, of intelligent reconstruction. He became the leading spokesman for American liberalism and democracy and, despite a shifting emphasis, developed a realistic but hopeful social philosophy. His critical thought cut through many timeworn and meaningless abstractions, such as that of a conflict between the individual and society, and clarified much that should have been obvious. He believed until his death that a truly democratic society, in which all citizens freely and cooperatively participate in the formation of goals and consequent policies, was a realistic goal, and he believed that such a society, to the extent realized, would provide all men access to the goods of life or, in other words, to the quality of experience he celebrated in his discussion of religion and art. All would have a sense of being a distinctive member of a community, understanding and appreciating its beliefs, desires, and methods, and giving their best efforts through it for the enhancement of all experience. He had faith that all normal men are capable not only of such enhanced experience but of responsible participation in the political and economic decisions that make it possible. Abilities vary, but each has some contribution, and each can share in the discovery, the enjoyment, and the use of relevant knowledge. Equality as a moral concept is basic. To Dewey, nothing was more repugnant and more wasteful than the exclusion or the oppression of the less able or less fortunate.

In America, Dewey usually found only the forms of democracy and not the substance, although he developed even greater respect for the forms as he contrasted them with European tyranny in the 1930's. To Dewey, democracy, at the minimum, demanded meaningful involvement and free participation by individuals in all areas of public life, an emphasis best expressed by his constant use of the term "co-operation." Thus, the franchise and majoritarian government were only means to democracy, not the real product. Democracy, as thus defined, implies and demands freedom, particularly intellectual freedom. To Dewey, as to Peirce, the free but at the same time socialized intellect was best exhibited in scientific inquiry. Democracy, even as scientific inquiry, involved a "morale of fair mindedness, intellectual integrity, of will to subordinate personal preference to ascertained facts and to share with others what is found out, instead of using it for personal gain. . . ." [*Freedom and Culture,* Capricorn Edition (New York, 1963), p. 148.] This morale should be present in all associations, in all life. But politics has key importance, since the state provides opportunity and sets the rules for other types of association. This does not mean that the state is the only institution or swallows up others. The state is simply a public working through its representative officers, through its government. Its form varies widely; no set universal model can be invented. Its scope of functions also varies widely and should vary according to needs as experience indicates them. Those who govern, however they gain office, usually reflect the habits and the values of the public or of the average citizen. Thus, an improved society can hardly result from formal changes in government or from a mere change in politicians. A changed public, and behind this changed objective conditions or changed habits and beliefs, is a prerequisite of enduring change in the state. In America, Dewey believed the needed objective changes were primarily economic.

Dewey referred to capitalism as the "serious and fundamental defect" of our civilization and gave much of his time, in practical as well as theoretical endeavors, to the achievement of a "more rational" or a "socialized" economy. Cooperative intelligence led to modern technology and to a new, machine age. To Dewey this was all good, for the machine was a rational tool providing undreamed-of benefits for man. Potentially good also, the new technology produced closer human associations and a corporate society. Yet, because of older, inherited, increasingly irrelevant institutions, such as capitalism or the quest for private profit, the new age was not one of social fulfillment. The old individualism and old liberalism, so relevant in the eighteenth century, were inapplicable now that the objective conditions that supported them were gone. Some lament the passing of this individualism and try to regain it and the past conditions that support it. Others defend it, but give it an exclusive economic interpretation and reflect it in an ignoble, dehumanizing search for pecuniary profit, meantime suppressing free thought and expression and condemning any innovations that threaten the existing order. Others conclude that radical change is imperative, but impossible without violence and revolution, falsely attributing all the material progress, as well as the social evil, to capitalism. Others impede change by denouncing all material things and embracing a separated life of the spirit and thus contribute as much or more than industrial leaders to the divisions and the poverty of American life by monopolizing the spiritual capital, the esthetic and intellectual goods of the country. To Dewey, all these answers to the problems of modern society were wrong because none recognized the role of intelligence in producing such a world or its potential in affecting social changes without destroying the good heritage of the past. He believed that the irrational or the reactionary opponents of science and technology, however clinical their analysis of existing evil, literally wanted to throw the "baby out with the bath water."

The primary evil of capitalism, in Dewey's analysis, was not economic exploitation, but the twisting and warping of human experiences: for the laborer the monotony and the drudgery, the ugliness and the emptiness of most industrial occupations; for the industrial leaders, the spiritual poverty and the lack of moral and social involvements and rewards. It seemed criminal that every person did not have employment and a decent living. But to assure this was no solution. Dogmatic Socialists too often operated within the restricted value system of the capitalist and only desired to broaden the privileges. To Dewey, the solution had to involve the actual, effective participation of labor in the production process, not in behalf of more consumption but in behalf of personal fulfillment. Work had to become an art. Ends, not extrinsic rewards, had to motivate industry. Here again he was the Puritan preaching.

Real reform would require some type of social control over productive property and some type of coordinated management. It would entail economic planning, but not, Dewey hoped, a ruling elite to impose plans on the majority. Ideally, in a democratic country, industrial processes would be cooperatively planned by an informed citizenry, with all men sharing in the process and finding purpose and fulfillment in their work. Not the location of ownership, but the technique of management and control was most crucial. Dewey realized the radical and difficult transformation required to achieve such a society, even as, in the 1930's, he criticized the social tinkering, the palliative measures, and the drifting of the New Deal. He called for a radical liberalism to deal with the radical problems, but hoped that intelligent effort would either eliminate or minimize the amount of coercion or even violence that would be required in the transition to positive, *social* control, which he defined as the central goal of modern American liberalism. But Dewey did not try to evade the problem of coercion; he was far from a pacifist. Force, of one type or another, is a constant accessory of an organized society. In a democracy, it sooner or later is used in behalf of the community, whatever the institution that embodies it. The problem is not the elimination of force, but the responsible discipline of force by verified knowledge used in behalf of the whole community. Even the protection of certain freedoms, which Dewey espoused, involves the positive use of force and coercion.

Freedom presented a crucial problem to Dewey's social theory. He believed his envisioned corporate or Socialist society was not, by necessity, opposed to individual freedom. In fact, it could broaden the range of freedom, particularly in the more creative and intellectual areas. Freedom is freedom in society, not from society. Freedom has meaning only in terms of release from oppression, from inhibition or controls; it thus has a different practical bearing at different times. Always, if a democratic way of life exists in fact as well as form, there will be freedom of inquiry, of thought, and of communication (assembly, press), and thus there will be an intelligently formed public opinion. But freedom of inquiry requires actual inquiry, or the tools and desire to inquire, to seek knowledge and truth; otherwise it is meaningless. Extreme specialization, the prevalence of propaganda, the sensationalism of news reporting, and the subtle conditioning in behalf of the entrenched order all limit freedom. These subtle factors inhibit active inquiry and the experimental method or are reflected in fear of inquiry and of intelligence. In such a society, even democratic forms are means of enslavement.

Conformity, passive or forced, is a danger to any society, indicating a lack of individual autonomy and of conscious involvement in group decision-making. But widespread group action, founded in common experience, a common willingness to seek relevant facts, and a voluntary and intelligent commitment by individuals to rationally established goals, is not conformity but, according to Dewey, freedom realized in effective action. When a group of scientists agree on a problem, conformity is not indicated. When men who have the habit of intelligence agree on solutions to social problems, it is not conformity. The new idea, the insight, always originates in the individual. It is verified and becomes active in the community, but only in a community that refuses to enthrone dogmatic ends, that allows the expression of individual opinion, and that is willing to permit experimental testing of meritorious innovations. Such a community is the crux of the problem, and until it exists change will continue to occur largely through violence or by accident. The best avenue for developing such a society is not revolution, which does not solve the more basic problems, but is certainly the inevitable fruit of oppression. Yet, apart from undue oppression, governmental reform cannot raise a society more than a small degree above the mass mind. But such beginning reform as is possible is also educational and can begin an upward spiral of intelligent demands based on a spiral of institutional changes. The key word, though, was *educational.*

Dewey has been the most influential educator in American history, perhaps even in the modern world. His total philosophy was more frequently focused on education than on any other existing institution. He made it abundantly clear that a philosophy of education is, if pursued far enough, a complete world view, embracing every philosophical specialty. He never desired his ideas in education to be abstracted or separated from his total philosophy, but of course they were. Neither did he wish professional philosophers virtually to ignore his ideas on education, but of course they did. This whole essay on Dewey could have begun with a theory of education, which would have implicated all the other considerations of metaphysics, methodology, and value. In *Democracy and Education,* in 1916, Dewey gave a remarkably complete outline of his subsequent, more detailed, more technical philosophical labors, even as he summarized his existing work in logic and psychology. Thus, a first or a final task, but in any case a climactic one for any student of Dewey, is to point to the implicit educational ideas that both motivated and sprang from his total philosophy, which he often referred to as a general theory of education.

Education is the means of transmitting culture, of continuing a civilization. By it, the habits, the beliefs, the knowledge of a society are continued and transformed in each new generation. Insofar as there is an enduring community, the educative role has to be successfully performed. All areas of social life, all types of communication, and all institutions perform a part of the educative function. If they perform it well, they contribute to the continued enhancement of human experi-

ence. Most social institutions—family, government, church, economic
organizations—are formed for other reasons than education, which
becomes a somewhat incidental aspect of their life. Some distort or
impede real education. But in any complex society, the educative
functions cannot be fully performed by incidental means, although we
always learn the most essential tools in the home and community.

Thus, formal education in schools is an indispensable aspect of a
modern technological society. Dewey stressed the necessity of schools,
but wanted to tie them closely to the more informal educative functions
of the larger community. The school could vastly broaden the scope of
education in time, space, and depth of understanding, but it could only
contribute to an integrated development of character, to an enhanced
quality of experience, when it was clearly related to the more limited,
but always vital and meaningful learning experience found in the
nonschool society. Too often, the schools taught remote, dead, purely
abstract, or irrelevant subjects, and imprisoned the student in a type of
environment that, qualitatively, was stultifying and for some almost
unendurable. Such schools might successfully train for certain tasks,
condition for certain behavior, or inculcate a body of facts, but they
could not educate. They could not reveal an enhanced experience to a
child, could not illumine the possibilities of the whole society, could not
contribute to the formation of personal or group ideals, and could not
provide the crucial tools (habits of correct thinking) for any meaningful
growth, personal or social. Dewey's purpose was to make the school an
integral part of the total educational function and, above that, to make
the schools, as the only planned educational medium, the best educative
tool, one that would be capable of reacting on and improving all other
institutions and thus all of life.

Education in school has to continue the earlier and ever continuous
education outside school. The main character of a person is formed
outside and before school, by the larger environment which sets his
limits and defines his standards. If the school environment is related
enough to the outside to be meaningful, and yet is purified enough to be
better than the outside, then school education can lead to real but
limited growth in language, manners, morals, and taste. To Dewey, the
school environment was the whole key to the quality of education, but
he used the term environment, as always, to encompass the whole range
of interacting objects and persons, including other students and, of

course, the teacher. The school environment should be consciously designed in behalf of an ever growing quality of experience for those who become part of it. As in all his thought, Dewey had no higher goal than a qualitative enhancement of life, a goal applicable to all life and to any aspect of life. The school environment should be simplified and graded to fit the stages of growth in children, should be purified of the gross and unworthy features of the outside, and obviously should extend, in fact or imagination, beyond the confines of the local, usually provincial community. But all such demands imply a degree of superior enlightenment on the part of school officials and teachers.

Those who create a purified or a more esthetic but yet relevant school environment have already, somehow, to be educated and thus have the verified knowledge, the moral insight, and the cultivated taste necessary for forming such schools or teaching in them. Dewey realized that no one can rise too far above society in general (he had no yearning for philosopher-kings, but only for a few more prosaic John Deweys), but if people consciously set about planning their schools, at least in this one social area some critical intelligence and some social inquiry must be at work, which is more than can be said for most politics and most economic organization. Even one man, perhaps, could provoke some such inquiry (ultimately, it is philosophical) and could through it help transform a whole society by the spreading influence. John Dewey did just this. Insofar as the educational revolution was loyal to his ideals, he acclaimed it. If Dewey was all wrong in education, then his philosophy was all wrong, and vice versa. Outside the context of his naturalistic humanism, his educational theories did not make sense. Yet, few educators fully understood the radical import of his total philosophy.

In a planned school, the student, if deeply involved in fulfilling and meaningful (not always easy) experiences, will discipline himself. Dewey believed that the often implicit idea that anything interesting is academically suspect and that purely disciplinary, isolated subject matter is thus necessary, should be relegated to a rubbish heap along with the faculty psychology which supported it. When activities in school have clear meaning in a student's life, then the separation of school and nonschool will disappear; both will then complement each other. Although thinking is an activity in itself, Dewey believed that the most effective learning usually involves other bodily activity as well. Imaginative experience may suffice, but direct experience is often necessary to establish relationships. We learn more efficiently by doing than by reading about what someone else did. The tool to be acquired is the habit of correct thinking, but the tool is developed and appreciated and enjoyed only in the using. The school should offer challenging experience by presenting relevant problems and allowing the student to solve them. The teacher should not give answers; he will often be learning himself. But he should have his subject matter so well in hand that he can concentrate on the individual students. His knowledge is not something to force on the students, but a tool, a resource, that he has to share with the student who is actually involved in learning, in a rewarding process of growth that should never have an ending.

Dewey was probably most radical in suggesting that at least lower education center on group activities, on work and play, and thus in suggesting a complete break from the formal, prestructured curriculum. But he tried to emphasize the need for carefully planned, directed, educationally meaningful activity; he thus simply placed an almost unattainable challenge before good teachers, who have to translate aims into results. As for subject matter, Dewey placed no limits. Any subject that is relevant to a student's need is fit for instruction, although time places limits and forces discrimination. The relevance of the subject matter should be grasped by the student, and at first it should relate to his immediate needs and aspirations. Long-range, remote ends, although almost certain to be accepted later, should not be imposed by the teacher but should enter the picture when the student, as he grows, accepts them for himself. But the planned school environment, including the activities, can contribute to an early awareness. In actuality, almost any traditional subject matter could be justified in a progressive school, but it had to be included with an eye to relevance and to student involvement.

Dewey approached education with a two-pronged objective. On one hand, he wanted education to be a wonderful, self-justifying, unending personal experience. Thus, education is for more education; growth is for ever more growth. Life can be better and better, provided we develop the tools and use them. Education, to him, implied use as well as acquisition, living as well as preparing for life. But, at the same time, he saw and certainly emphasized enough the social aspect of education. Not only is growth personal fulfillment; it is social improvement. The two themes, to Dewey, were inseparable except in emphasis. The individual has his experience in society; he cannot exceed the limits imposed by society, nor can he ignore the customs of society. At the same time, men of intelligence, virtue, and taste are necessary for an improving society. Moral men and moral society not only go together, they grow together. Democracy is both a means and an end in Dewey's educational theory. It is required for his educational ideal to be fully effective, to encompass the teacher as well as students in a situation of mutual respect and equal worth, of mutual learning and growth, and of responsible concern for each other. But it is also the social result of such education, as the attitudes of the school, always hopefully a bit ahead of the community, subsequently become the attitudes of the community. Thus the school is the agency of reform, but not in a hortatory sense. It is an agency for morality, but by revealing ideals, not by preaching or imposing them. It prepares individuals for life, even as it is life at its best. It is free and liberal or it is not education. Even democracy is not a dogma taught but a practice followed. Science is not a predigested body of knowledge but a method to use. Vocational preparation is involved, for work is a major part of life and should be the most rewarding part, but education is not vocational training; it is the broadening of experience of occupations in behalf of discovering capacities and aptitudes. Education, in conclusion, *is experience* raised to the level of art and is ever fruitful in making possible more such experiences for all men.

Dewey's thought was not all of Dewey. But his life was never apart from his thought. More correctly, his thought was a running commentary on his experience. As a result, it lacked perfect structure but had great scope and depth. In a long, active life, Dewey experienced as much of American life as any other person, but unlike an Emerson, he celebrated his experience in careful philosophy instead of poetry, in labored and earnest prose, rendered eloquent on rare occasions only by his deep moral passion. No American, including those more brilliant, more stimulating, and more eloquent, has been quite so perceptive, quite so wise, or nearly so thoughtful. As a result he was both a critic and a fervent defender of our best traditions. Above all, Dewey was a person of deep religious concern, seeking, finding, and celebrating in nature the source of, and the unending support for, man's unending affirmation of worth, freedom, and hope. He was the best of the Puritans.

PART
FOUR
�֍

IN RETREAT

IX
GEORGE SANTAYANA

LIFE

No one human mind can contain and harmonize all the major impulses of Western philosophy and religion. George Santayana sought such a harmony, and in his brilliant failure to attain it suffered a tragic disillusionment. His technical framework was a highly colored naturalism and pragmatism. His sentiments were classical and contemplative. In birth Catholic and Spanish, in education Puritan and American, he remained a stranger in the modern world, without a country, a church, a wife, or a home. Finally, out of a deliberate and honest and cherished disillusion, he tried to erect a disinfected idealism in the realm of spirit, where neither moths nor rust could corrupt.

Santayana loved confession. He turned his own life into a public epic in three volumes of autobiography, in a confessional novel, in dramatic dialogues, and in frequent personal intrusions into even his most technical books. He conceived his philosophy as a lay religion. His own life provided the only revelation. Understanding the meaning of one's life was an obligation and, he believed, was also the correct goal of any philosophy. The richness of Santayana's philosophy rested, in part, on the variety and challenge of his most unusual life.

Santayana was born in Spain, of Spanish parents, and retained his Spanish citizenship until death. He insistently rejected any claim that he was half American. In actuality, he had two ancestral ties to America. Not only were his half-brother and sisters Americans, but his maternal grandparents had moved from Spain by way of Scotland to the United States and had become distinguished citizens of Virginia. Here Santayana's mother spent her girlhood. But after accepting a United States Consul appointment back in Spain under the commission of President Andrew Jackson, the grandfather eventually entered the Spanish civil service and took up duties in the Philippines. He took along his teen-aged daughter. His ailing wife died shortly thereafter in Spain. A disappointed governor of a small island, he suffered from the tropical climate and soon died, leaving an orphaned daughter of twenty, without property and on an island without other Europeans. She bravely remained, bought a ship, and sold hemp in Manila until a new governor, young and unmarried, arrived at the island. Propriety then forced her to move to join friends in Manila. The new governor was, much later, to become her husband and Santayana's father.

In Manila, in 1849, this daughter—Josefina Borras—married a young Boston merchant, George Sturgis. Three children survived from this marriage—Josefina, Susanna, and Robert. A first son, almost neurotically adored by the mother, died at two. A last son was born on the family's one big trip to America, survived a trip back to Manila and the sudden death of the father, only to die back in Boston. The young widow had already died spiritually with her first son and stoically, unfeelingly accepted events with a calm despair. She retained a strange loyalty to the Sturgis family and thus brought her children to Boston for rearing. She received financial help from the Sturgis family, while the children had an inheritance from their Sturgis grandfather. In Boston she lived three years in lonely isolation.

The story should end but for another series of improbable events. In 1861 Mrs. Sturgis took her three children on a visit to Spain, purportedly to visit old Philippine friends. Among these was Augustin Santayana, who had returned home from the small island. Earlier he had been aboard the ship that brought the Sturgis family on their first trip to Boston. Now, apparently without passion or good sense, he married Josefina. Of these elderly parents (the father in his fifties, the mother in her forties) George Santayana was born in Madrid in December 1863. After two years the family moved to Avila, to the west of Madrid and in the province of Castile. Here were the first scenes to be remembered by young George. But after three years the mother and her Sturgis children returned to Boston and to better educational opportunities, permanently dividing the family in both geography and sentiment. George stayed in Avila with his aging father, vaguely sensing the tragedy of his parents, who never lived together again. Then, in 1872, when George was eight, his father brought him to America, perhaps sacrificially providing him with better opportunities. He moved into his mother's home at 302 Beacon Street and into another world. He lived in Boston until 1911. Thereafter he never returned, spending his last forty years in England, France, Italy, and Spain.

In America, Santayana lived not only in a divided family, but with an emotionally ill mother. This permanently warped his life and left him with a terrible, unassuaged longing for a close, cohesive family circle. His mother was dutiful but totally aloof, unaffectionate, and withdrawn. All her love had been spent; all her hopes had been betrayed. In her disillusionment and despair, which Santayana later understood, she found a type of bearable refuge within a total, proud silence. Philosophically she parroted a sterile liberalism or rationalism, without depth or solace. In response to her coldness, Santayana returned a type of respect or filial piety and wanted to give more. Until her death, he was solicitous for his mother. But the lack of affection left visible traces in all of his life. Except for a sister, he never developed an intimate relationship with any woman, while the jealousy-producing figure of Eros hovered only over his relationships with men. In his philosophy he explored to its depths the idea of piety. Toward vital impulse, toward creative power, toward the generative order of nature, he was pious, paying all possible respect, rendering all possible obedience, and refusing to blaspheme by any detraction or denial. Here was the source of everything, good and bad. But he never loved, worshiped, or felt love appropriate for the unfeeling source of life. Instead, he transferred his affection to imaginative ideals that were born out of the generative order but were qualitatively of a totally different kingdom. They were in the purely formal but non-existent realm of eternal qualities. In his cold piety, he knew his mother well and never romanticized her or fooled himself. He wanted no blind, illusionary love. Instead, he idealized love itself and explored as thoroughly as any philosopher its ideal, sublimated, religious aspect.

Santayana's closest personal involvement was with his oldest half-sister, Susanna Sturgis. She filled the role of sister, mother, and even wife. Warm, affectionate, and maternal, she seemed the very opposite of his mother. But she too suffered in the emotionally barren home and in an alien city and found her outlet in the Roman Catholic Church. Without a successful adjustment, she tried to become a nun in a

Baltimore convent. Then, as a lonely spinster, she looked back to Spain as a possible haven. In a near gesture of final surrender, she married a widower in Avila and secured economic security and a sense of belonging. Feminine and impulsive, fervently orthodox, and without Santayana's intellectual prowess, Susanna could not be an intellectual comrade. But both Susanna and her church could seem sensually warm refuges for an overintellectualized philosopher. Her orthodoxy spread a veneer of warmth over her church and gave added impetus to Santayana's lifelong effort to identify and defend the wisdom and poetry of a Latinized Christianity. Santayana was jealous of Susanna's affections and suffered both when she entered the convent and when she married. But in Susanna he had an anchor in a chaotic world. In gossipy letters, and in long evenings of conversation or reminiscing back in Avila, he and an aging sister knew briefly and in part the meaning and comfort of home and family.

Outwardly, Santayana did well in Boston. He mastered English, struggled upward both socially and academically at the Boston Latin School, and entered Harvard with high entrance marks. But inwardly, Boston intimidated and alienated him, leaving loneliness and desperate insecurity. In the late nineteenth century, Boston was insensibly cruel to aliens, particularly to those who were sensitive and intelligent and who needed a community to replace a barren family. Santayana felt excluded, partly because his sensitivity led him to misinterpret other people's intentions. With almost feminine vanity, he yearned for social pre-eminence, for full acceptance by the Boston aristocracy. He retained a sympathy for exclusive clubs, for irrational patriotism, for specific even if narrow commitments. His loyalties were unattached, when, in his words, he craved "home interests" or a clear heritage. He indulged in self-pity when he later condemned the man who represented nothing, wandering from place to place in voluntary exile, querulous, uneasy, alone, without sweetness, fruit, or morality. Almost pathetically, he poured much of this yearning for identity into Harvard institutions, including a club and even the football team. But all this was temporary and false. He could not win the game to his satisfaction; even with a secure home to support him, he probably could not have made the adjustment to Boston. As it was, he grumbled and fought back, often with such brilliant insight as to reverse the terrible odds. Boston felt his satire and ridicule. In reverse snobbery, he decided that the Boston that would not adore Santayana was not worth his devotion. Soon he had his first repertoire of abuse—Puritanism, liberalism, Unitarianism, commercialism, Protestantism, genteel tradition, moral hypocrisy. He did not want to live in a censurious society, without customs and traditions, always emphasizing duty and morality and applying first principles to trifles. He dreamed of Avila, of a sensuous and poetic Mediterranean world, genuine and human, rooted in ancient even if irrational customs.

The dream was better than the reality, but Santayana never stopped trying to make the two match. At the end of his freshman year at Harvard he returned home to visit his father, with thoughts of permanent escape from the moral prison of Boston. He found no opportunities in Spain; even the language was foreign. His father was scarcely more affectionate than his mother; to the young Santayana, his father had seemed to desert him when he brought him to Boston. Now with this aged and almost deaf parent no real friendship was possible. The father—a belated and bitter product of the Enlightenment, narrow, anticlerical, republican, "scientific," an enemy of class and tradition—only helped cement opposite views in his son, who was trying to construct out of Catholicism and aristocracy an intellectually and morally acceptable antidote to all the heresies of the new world. Even his father's liberalism seemed to reflect the shriveled essence of Anglo-Saxon philosophy, while the real Spain lurked in the Cathedral of Avila. Spain was never more than a temporary refuge for Santayana, chosen more because of relatives there than love of country. But Spain was, at times, a vague ideal, standing for all the virtues of Latinity. He assiduously searched for every stone to cast at the brittle glass windows of Boston, but loved and nourished into truth every random illusion reflected from the stained glass of Avila.

Much like Henry Adams, Santayana eventually castigated his slack education. Yet, as a Harvard undergraduate he entered enthusiastically into campus affairs and dutifully sat at the feet of some great teachers, particularly in philosophy. By the time he left the Harvard faculty, he pointed back to spiritual penury and moral confusion and avowed that he had hated it all for forty years. By then he refused to concede the obvious American sources of his own philosophy, while glorifying and exaggerating European and classical sources. Harvard was only an intellectual brothel, an academic grab bag, in which the dissolution of Christendom was forgotten in the service of national wealth and industrial dominance.

In the 1880's Harvard was still strait-laced and Spartan, although New Englanders were already beginning their long and superficial condemnation of their Puritan past. Santayana suffered more than anyone else and thus easily saw through the critical pose. They were all Puritans still. He began a lifelong but ambivalent dissection of Puritan themes, culminating in his novel *The Last Puritan*. Unfortunately, Harvard was a small world to itself, and it was almost the only part of America ever known intimately by Santayana. But he might have liked the rest of America even less. Although a bit diffident and uninvolved, he formed at Harvard almost all of his vital and lasting friendships and developed all his major philosophical doctrines. He ever afterwards returned in memory to his early Harvard years. These were his golden years.

As seniors at Harvard, Santayana and Charles Augustus Strong jointly won the Walker Fellowship, which not only allowed Santayana to study philosophy in Germany but cemented a lifelong friendship with Strong, who became a major philosopher and a fellow expatriate. In his German studies Santayana fell in love with the Greek past and with Spinoza, but developed a growing distaste for German idealism, the Lucifer and Antichrist of his own philosophy. He never lost a distinct bias against Germany and the Germans. He took his Ph.D. at Harvard in 1899 and remained as an instructor, finally ascending the academic ladder to an endowed professorship. Despite some disclaimers, he was a popular lecturer and, with notable publications, quickly became an adornment in the greatest philosophy faculty ever assembled in an American university. He left Harvard in 1911 (he resigned in 1912) at the peak of his professional career (aged forty-eight). In the philosophy department he had been restless for years, spending summers and sabbaticals in England and, in one case, in France. To a large extent his ties to Harvard were financial and personal. But the death of his mother, the move of Susanna back to Spain, a degree of financial independence coming from his mother's estate, and a growing body of new friends in England all contributed to his decision. He now had his chance to study and write in solitude. But his resignation went deeper than this, involving an open repudiation of Harvard, of America, and even of the whole complex of attitudes and values that made up the modern world. It marked a personal crisis, leading to worldly repudiation, permanent moral disintoxication, and an ever increasing emphasis upon spiritual aloofness.

In 1900 Santayana wrote to William James: "I wonder if you realize the years of suppressed irritation which I have past in the midst of an unintelligible sanctimonious and often disingenuous Protestantism, which is thoroughly alien and repulsive to me, and the need I have of joining hands with something far away from it and far above it." [To James, Easter, 1900, in *The Letters of George Santayana,* ed. by Daniel Cory (London, 1955), p. 62.] By then Protestantism had become for Santayana the most comprehensive symbol of all that was grievously wrong in the modern world. It always remained such a symbol, but carried too much weight and was used too loosely to be very specific in reference. With it he identified only a few positive traits, such as sincere feeling, a proper piety, and a rather charming spontaneity, youthfulness, and zest. Overbalancing these were a vapid sentimentality, extremes of irrational romanticism, a barbaric disregard for form, egotism of all types, unthinking optimism, undisciplined will, a lack of respect for authority, hatred of beauty, moral conceit, an unbearable sense of responsibility, awful repression of all kinds, an unendurable practicality, inexpertness, and a vulgar quest for prosperity. Protestantism stood opposed to union with God at God's level, to asceticism, mysticism, pure intelligence, truth, and eternal things. Lost in time, appearance, and fleeting experience, it pointed toward vacuity, toward a nonspecific religion without priests, churches, theology, Scripture, Sabbath, or even a god.

Santayana identified Protestantism with barbarism and with the Teutonic and despised North, with its rarefied but dark and comfortless wintry atmosphere, spiritual yet without any sense of liberation and peace. Rarely have the terms North and South carried such emotional weight. The uncivilized, inexperienced barbarians were incapable of understanding Roman Christianity, either in its pristine, postrational renunciation of the world or in its laughing, paganized Catholic form. To the German invaders it was a fairy story that indoctrinated but never really tamed. Barbarism, free, exuberant, and shallow, inevitably transformed Christianity from its Latin model. The erosion began long before Luther. The German West thus added the misfitting and incongruous dress of Latin Christianity and, through it, of Greek and Roman civilization. The end result was a false, artificial, affected art; an egotistic, sentimental philosophy; and a continuing, undirected inward protest or rebellion among truants from a foreign school of life.

In his early years Santayana identified with the rational, naturalistic, and humane tradition of Greece, which he saw as a leavening element in Roman Catholicism, rendering its myths poetic and acceptable to the intelligent, such as the Renaissance humanists. Later, he moved closer to Christian mystics and to the renunciation, postrational morality, and spirituality of the Hellenistic period and of the early church. But always he sought the best possible interpretation of Catholicism and freely read his own views into its doctrines. The repressive features of Catholicism he also blamed on Protestantism, which triggered a counterrevolution with similar features. Essentially, Catholicism was a religion that found room for the richness of Hellenic and pagan civilization. It was tolerant, particularly of gaiety, splendor, refinement, and poetry, and thus gave full leeway to the free spirit.

Protestantism did its worst work in Germany, where it led to egotistical madness. In America there were a few redeeming factors. England was least affected, since aristocratic feelings and a cult of splendor among the few still hid the commercial ugliness and democratic crudeness. But it was America he had to live with longest; it was the only country he was ever deeply involved with. He loved the authentic, innocent America, the simple kindness and good will, the unaffected joy in possessions, the rough comradeship, the self-trust, even the football games and other truly joyous occasions. Events spun out with vim and vigor, without internal or external frustration. It was easy to view nature and the conditions of life with wonder and love and even in innocence to believe that nature or God loved Americans and worked at their bidding. This egotism, which was arrogance and madness in Europe, was only the healthy exuberance of a newborn will, and not necessarily opposed to the humility and wisdom acquired later when Americans discovered and accepted the tragic contrast between aspiration and destiny. In his disillusioned old age Santayana could congratulate the new, dynamic, all-conquering America. It provided orchestral themes for delight and wonder, but only for one who had escaped the chaos and found peace, quiet, repose, and solitude.

But innocence is barbarism, not wisdom. America confused means and ends and made all functions instrumental. Life was a fantastic game, without humane and liberal goals, without traditions or established roots. No one lived where he was born or believed what he had been taught. Like gluttons, Americans pursued all varieties of experience, but with joyless passion and moral emptiness. They were tolerant without discrimination because they had never seen anything worth seeing or loved anything worth loving. The most basic evils were an artificial veneer of culture, a servitude to demeaning industry, and illiberal social pressures. Santayana hated most the sham culture, the affected love of frivolous art, the growing and always superficial estheticism, the museums and galleries. As the twentieth century advanced these ills grew ever more pervasive. Such infantile sham and false beauty rose above ugly cities and demeaning tasks, above lives lived in the midst of cheap and practical gadgets, above a crudeness in manners and a lack of simple graces. This affectation among the few or the many grew in step with the corrosion of commercialism, the reduction of men to automatons, the prostitution of personality to profit.

Political liberty was no answer to these evils, for most matters of importance had already been settled in the "land of the free." The vaunted freedom, like the art, was a superficial frieze, a freedom to choose among empty ideas and beliefs, none of which were taken seriously or deemed very dangerous. Meanwhile, you had to wave, cheer, and push with the crowd or feel like a traitor. He hated the gospel of work and progress and the many social prohibitions. Life in a monastery could not be as narrow as life in America. All doors opened toward work, growth, enterprise, monogamous marriage, sanctioned reforms, and prosperity, which was good for those who enjoyed them. But a conservative like Santayana, drawn to poetic subtlety and pious retreat, or one drawn toward gay passions, could only fold up his heart and wither in a corner or flee to Oxford or Florence to save or lose his soul. Also, for the orthodox believer who abhorred compromises, America was a burden. Only those with a vague soul, those with great gregariousness and a tendency to be molded by example, could easily find the majority right enough to live with and put their own favorite notions to sleep in the family cradle of convention. These sentiments were at least as old as Tocqueville and were echoed by many another social critic or voluntary exile at the end of the nineteenth century.

As a philosopher, Santayana found modernity bereft of reason, of basic sanity. Subjectivism, conceit of mind, or barren empiricism prevailed everywhere in the Protestant West. In the Harvard philosophy department he reacted passionately against Josiah Royce's idealism, sanctimonious piety, and false optimism. In American literature he found only the irrelevant, feminine sanctity of the genteel tradition or the bracing barbarism of Whitman. In William James's psychology he glimpsed some hardheaded truth and never turned loose of it. But he deplored other aspects of James's thought: the blanket toleration, the voracious appetite for experience, the political liberalism, the softness toward free will and religious sentimentality, the inability to relax, stop preaching, and know the good life. James was the greatest single influence on Santayana, and he tried to be his paternal friend and colleague. But he could never understand Santayana. Much of his concern seemed paternalistic and even condescending. A sensitive Santayana often resented it. Intellectually, James's early versions of pragmatism scandalized Santayana. Pragmatism seemed a particularly vulgar form of romanticism, with no ultimate concept of the good. It either exalted will and power or became a superficial means of correcting whatever in science might disturb religion. Although his own thought incorporated elements of pragmatism, Santayana worked assiduously to obscure all agreement with James. He later branded James's pragmatism the serpent in the garden of pure experience, being belief in the eventual and its nasty fruit—care. This led pragmatists to the terrible illusion that the future could be controlled by wishes and high thoughts. For Santayana, the practical and moral world of James ever seemed more foreign, absent from his better moments, and composed out of human conventions, many variable and foolish. Ironically, his later philosophy led him to a spiritualistic position remarkably similar to that of William James's father and therefore away from what James always believed to be healthy-mindedness.

Thus, in a sense, Santayana *escaped* to Europe, where nature had been purified but not concealed by the hand of men, and where everything had depth and was historical. He spent World War I in England, committed to the Allied cause, disturbed by Susanna's opposite commitment, and absorbed in the intellectual life of Cambridge and Oxford. The war deepened his sense of alienation and detachment, although he never stopped weaving political and moral strictures into his disinterested contemplation. At the end of the war he left England, sharing a Paris apartment with Charles Augustus Strong, but soon began to spend a part of each year in Italy. With the death of Susanna he stopped his trips to Spain. He rejected all entreaties to return to Harvard or to give lectures in other parts of the United States. He also turned down a post at Oxford. By the 1930's Rome had become his favorite retreat. In 1941 he stopped all travels and rented a room in the English-speaking Convent of the Little Company of Mary in Rome; he remained there in solitude during the war and until his death in 1952. The last years were as productive as ever, with no diminution of mind until the last year. He was lonely, ascetic, and above political controversy. In Europe he established few close personal ties (these remained American or English). Paris or Rome, or summer retreats in Switzerland or northern Italy, were only places of comfort, congenial atmosphere, and freedom to write and think. A citizen of the world, he had no binding loyalties. Unlike most expatriate Americans, he carried no grudge and nourished no secret regrets.

But Santayana was not without affectations of his own. He was much given to deliberate poses. Deeply hurt by snobbery, he could be the worst snob in the world. Limited in budget until later years, he yet identified with affluent people as long as they had some taste, intellectual interests, or a love of splendor. He placed great value on simple manners and proper deference. His love of the English upper classes shaped many of his social attitudes in his middle years. Deeply sensitive to other people's praise or blame, he sought status and recognition. In his Harvard years he easily put on a pose of lofty superiority, contemptuous of the vast congregation of deluded souls beneath him. Never ostentatious in personal habits, he yet demanded small comforts and deferential service. As a perennial bachelor, he became habituated to freedom and ease. He could not live in most places all year because of climate. Disrupted routines bothered him. He never enjoyed hard work or any type of compulsion. The maddening details of parenthood would have killed him. Peace and harmony were dominating ideals. But within a protected, refined, even effete environment, among uncarping friends or disciples, he loved conversation, laughter, and beauty. He held on to his friends with all the tenacity of a lover. Half of his autobiography recounted these human relationships, in which he invested more, and risked more regrets, than is normal for most active men.

Santayana was a complete traditionalist—a model conservative. He rejoiced in custom, whatever its form. He could never tolerate the revolutionary urge to overturn entrenched institutions. He loved elegance in a monarchy, in a church, in the traditional luxuries of a leisured or priestly class. He never resented privilege and always condemned those equalitarians who would destroy the small islands of taste and beauty, however dearly purchased. He appreciated the imperfection of all human institutions, including even his beloved Catholic Church. But the imperfections, for those who lived within them, were part of the soil and substance of their only possible lives. If people overturned rather than transmitted values from generation to generation, they would have to live without a heritage, in barbarism. He therefore affirmed as good what he so notably lacked—a clear, unambiguous heritage. He sought this heritage, this citizenship, by seeking the good aspired to or served by ancient customs. He searched for specific traditions, with distinctive flavor and bias, and he hated any resort to some universal sentiment or to some religion-in-general (no Unitarian powderpuff for him). Orthodoxy, any orthodoxy, had unsuspected harmonies, and was beautiful; heresy, any heresy, displayed a vacant iconoclasm or some as yet imperfected future orthodoxy and thus was ugly and fundamentally disloyal.

Unlike so many Americans, and all good Puritans, Santayana did not relish raw, untamed nature. Instead, he loved manmade artifacts and beliefs. How had man dealt with matter? Personal in his philosophy, weakest in areas of social psychology, he became a historian of the human spirit and a connoisseur of its varied poetry. He could find no room for condemnation when the poetry was beautiful.

Santayana was not a generous man, at least not until his last years. Such epithets as ignorant, vulgar, and superficial were attributed to almost everyone else. Like a lofty god, Santayana judged the whole history of Western thought and found almost nothing to praise without serious reservations. He easily drew bogus authorities into his censure, such as "unprejudiced men of letters" or "all original thinkers." Rarely did he give a full and fair statement of opposing views or acknowledge obvious sources of his own beliefs. He often denounced fellow philosophers for what they never believed and occasionally without even reading their works. At times it seemed that only Santayana entirely escaped error.

Even in his later years, when he affected a disinterested and ironic stance toward all human foibles, he was if anything even more irritating to conscientious critics. He then refused to be drawn into debate or to defend what he now acknowledged as personal preference. Yet, his preferences still had about them a veneer of authority and superior insight. He could sound as axiomatic as a Puritan preacher. But all the apparent contempt, all the unfair vignettes, were part of Santayana's defense against misunderstanding and superficial criticism. Displaying some evidence of paranoia, he felt himself all alone, deliberately misunderstood, and insufficiently appreciated. As he treated Boston, so he treated fellow philosophers, and in the process shored up a desperate insecurity. It is hard to stand alone. Santayana did, and in part by his own preference. He was too sensitive and too quick to draw back in hurt and bitterness, to bridge the intellectual gulfs that seemed to separate him from his often more generous but usually less brilliant contemporaries.

Santayana wrote about twenty-five books, all containing at least some of his philosophical tenets. These books were his only children, carefully reared for their career in the world, and each carrying a bit of Santayana into immortality. He loved them, watched their career, and resented criticism. In totality they contained a philosophy as broad in scope as that of John Dewey and as richly speculative as that of Whitehead. Standing outside so many conventions and provincial limitations, Santayana could make old doctrines seem original; with his distinctive and beautiful style, he could make common sense seem oracular. In American thought, only Emerson rivaled him as an essayist. Deliberately personal and opinionated, he could occasionally attain a disinterested honesty and courage never rivaled since Spinoza. At these moments his pose of omnipotence ceased to offend, and willing students stood awestruck before a beauty that was truth and a truth that was always beautiful.

His beauty of style won him criticism as well as praise. He loved images and metaphors and hoped to conquer ambiguity by a many-sided, suggestive presentation. But too many carping critics refused to follow out his dramatic accounts and usually either missed the point or insulted him by narrow textual analysis. Many of his seemingly technical positions were simple and commonplace, as he realized. But his own rhetoric, used to dramatize and reinvigorate these ideas, often seemed to lose them in obscurity or in tedious elaboration. Santayana did not care to pursue many highly technical problems; he never sought exact precision and prided himself on remaining close to the sound philosophy of nonphilosophers. He left many issues without a final solution and was content to stop with suggestive hints or unclear allusions. His philosophy was a luxurious confession of faith, not a sharp analysis of detail or a tight speculative system. The flavor of experience always blended with the more abstract terms of reflection.

For a confessionalist such as Santayana, past philosophers were teachers; their ideas offered points of reference but not the justification of his own beliefs. He always felt that philosophical systems, including his own, were in part accidental, being arbitrary verbal transcripts (rational, ethical, political) of the unique perceptions of an individual. Here his skepticism was as complete as Emerson's; his emphasis upon temperament as great as James's. He wanted to study all philosophies as a part of a liberal education. Each contained a human and thus symbolic conception of reality. He claimed many masters in the art of self-justification and had strong but not invariant preferences. In natural philosophy he always applauded the genius of Democritus and Lucretius; in moral philosophy, of Plato and Spinoza; in contemplative bent and spirituality, of the Indian philosophers and Western mystics. But he had his reservations about all. Appropriately, in his view, the only compelling philosophy was his own, and it could not, in all details, be equated with any other or be completely satisfactory to any other person.

Much as John Dewey had, Santayana viewed philosophy as a type of criticism or interpretation, with no particular body of truth for itself. He was willing to speculate about the main features of existence, but carefully refrained from confusing his verbal pictures with the ultimate structure of things. The purpose of philosophy was moral. It should bring added harmony and joy to life. It began and ended in human experience, in the chance vistas of an individual. Yet he hated the subjectivist strains of existentialism almost as much as idealism and English empiricism. They all tended to solipsism and moved too far from a common-sense acceptance of a substantial realm of matter. On the other side, he despised the narrow scope and the experiential insensitivity of positivism. He wanted, like Dewey, to combine the hardheaded, unsentimental criticism of positivism with the openness to immediate qualitative experience heretofore manifest in poetry and religion. But unlike Dewey, he focused more on the intrinsic joy of philosophic discourse and less on its problem-solving and instrumental value. When purified into detached contemplation, such discourse became the supreme reward of life.

Almost pathetically, Santayana insisted that he was one person and not two. He fought the allegations that his last years were completely inconsistent with his youth. He admitted that he changed some emphases, particularly at the end of the American period and after his first masterpiece, *The Life of Reason*. But except for terms and emphasis, he correctly insisted that all the later themes were present from the beginning. The minor chords became major ones. Nothing was ever repudiated or rejected, although some earlier interests became insignificant. The early, more humanistic works sought a rational and harmonious path for natural impulse, but in order to prepare for the consummation, for free and undistracted spirit, without care or concern. Unlike James and Dewey, he was not content to drink forever from wayside fountains; he wanted to find the one, eternal fountain and drink from it as long as the world would permit. As a moralist he wanted a social order conducive to spirituality, but so long as he was such a moralist he was too distracted to live in the disinterested peace of the spirit. He was in and of the world. But after disillusionment, after his own crucifixion through suffering, he not only celebrated spirituality as a moral goal, but apparently experienced it more often as a possessed good. He then turned from moral philosophy, which lost its urgency and primacy, to ontology, from concern with means to the adoration of the good, from judgment to appreciation.

The early Santayana, despite disclaimers and reservations, was a pious, moralizing, but hardly spiritual Puritan. A philosophical rebel, he set out to criticize irrationality and moral chaos in behalf of reason and moral order. He was then deeply and piously subject to the material order, or to the nature of things, and without any pretensions of omnipotence. Nature rules, not human wishes. But his piety toward existence was not love of existence, as he so often made clear. It was a necessary and wearying obeisance. Even then his joy was in escaping and transcending, at least in quality, the cares of existence. Thus, it was natural for him to turn to a discrimination of the realms of being. He never cut loose from nature, never denied the existential priority (or exclusiveness) of matter, and never repudiated the historical relativity of all claims to truth. But he no longer concerned himself with the genesis of ideas or with their biological sufficiency. Instead, he looked to their essential quality, to their logically eternal aspects. Thus, he turned from an instrumental to an esthetic approach to ideas. That esthetic, consummatory quality, noted even by Dewey, became all-pervasive in Santayana. Nothing else mattered. That this is, in a sense, a fool's paradise, Santayana always admitted. The world will not go away. More than most Western philosophers, he wished it would, or rather wished it could and still leave the spirit free. But honesty rescued him from nirvana. Without the world there is no spirit. He found no consolation in existence, but that is where he found himself.

This is not to deny an ambivalence in Santayana. It was always there. It was personal and moral even more than doctrinal, for with dialectical brilliance and courageous honesty he maintained an internal coherence in his beliefs. He refused to turn his wishes into facts. He was never at home in this world, but there was no other world. His spiritual escape, however much eulogized, was never complete. Salvation remained an aspiration. In his novel, *The Last Puritan,* he loved the laughing sensualist, joyful and free at the level of passion, but his love, his Puritan-like envy, was a confession of his inability to be such a person. He sympathized with the totally spiritual man, out of place and uneasy in the ordinary tasks of the world.

In between there was the latter-day Puritan, Oliver Alden. Without a compelling religious faith, yet with all the inherited attitudes of Puritanism, he was also the last Puritan, the logical end of Puritanism. He had an excess of the Puritan bent for spirituality. Shades of Anne Hutchinson and Emerson lived on in him. Yet, he was caught in the world, and with a Puritan conscience tried to live up to its obligations and duties, but without joy. The inherent tragedy of Puritanism seemed revealed—an uneasy combination of duty and of spiritual thirst, of worldly concern and free intelligence. But Oliver's tragedy may have been only a false parody of Puritanism, and in truth a very dramatic picture of Santayana's own personal tragedy. The real Puritan loved the world and securely tied his ideals to it rather than pushing and tugging to get them apart from it even while, in honesty, always acknowledging their dependence. It may have been naïve, but the good Puritan really loved his mother as well as his dreams.

THE METAPHYSICAL FOUNDATION

Although he disliked the term, Santayana's ontology was a variant form of radical empiricism. As such, it was comparable to the mature position of William James and, even more, to that of John Dewey. Santayana clearly and decisively rejected the voluntarism and incipient idealism of James's middle period and of his essays on pragmatism. Yet, pragmatism, as a loose term for the philosophical movement encompassing both the unities and some of the divergencies of Peirce, James, and Dewey, surely also encompasses the doctrines of Santayana.

Even Santayana's one major deviation from James's and Dewey's view of consciousness still drew directly from James's psychology. It was also supported by a close friend of James, the erratic and brilliant English experimentalist philosopher, Shadworth Hodgson. This was Santayana's epiphenomenalism, or his view that consciousness was an inefficacious offspring of matter, which seemed to involve a less complete integration of mind and matter and a more radical cleavage between the physical and phenomenological aspects of thinking than Dewey's naturalism. This doctrine abetted, or possibly sprang from, Santayana's increasingly conservative social and political attitudes, and from a marked contemplative stance. These differences helped conceal his many doctrinal affinities with James and Dewey and quite falsely let even Santayana suffer the illusion that he betrayed no typical American presuppositions.

Radical empiricism is an ultimate position, an irreducible starting point for all other beliefs. As an ontological perspective, it expresses a cognitively neutral form of monism, or an existential type of realism. By making both matter and mind eventual conceptual renditions of experience, and not the content of experience, radical empiricists repudiate both classic materialism and idealism. But in doing this, as James's ontological explorations so well illustrated, the radical empiricist flirts with solipsism or else embraces a reality that is more nearly affirmed as an act of faith than known as an object of knowledge. At least the reality or ground behind human knowing is so transformed in the process of knowing as to remain in part hidden from our cognitive efforts. Reality is had, is felt, but only roughly or abstractly known. Knowledge is a practical or instrumental tool for successful adaptation, not a metaphysical peephole. Yet, the universal features of the knowing process gave Dewey an ontological weapon. He used it to develop his concept of Nature and, speculatively, to adorn it with many beloved traits.

But such ontological speculation has to remain tentative and, as Santayana used the term, poetical, meaning symbolic and nonliteral. The terms of ontological speculation are variable, suggestive, and pictorial, but never photographic or in exact correspondence with reality. Our best metaphors have always been mediated by the limited human senses and organized by a limited human imagination. Accepting this position, Santayana always denied that he had any metaphysics, any "love affairs of the understanding."

To Santayana, all the terms of human thought and all the concepts of any philosophy fall back on and are projections from "one rolling experience, which shows up one aspect or the other as it develops various functions and dominates itself to various ends." [*Life Of Reason* (New York, 1903–6), I, 122.] As early as a letter of 1887 he stated his starting point. Philosophy, he said, was a "late and rather ineffective activity of reflecting man. It is not the business of philosophy to show that things exist. You must bring your bullion to the mind, then reason can put its stamp upon it and make it legal tender. But if you don't bring your material, if you don't give reason your rough and precious experience, you can get nothing from her but counterfeit bills—nostrums and formulas and revelations." [To Henry Ward Abbot, Feb. 5, 1887, *Letters,* p. 18.] Ideas are acquired in action. They are given facts. We can not get rid of them. But they are always derivative, never exhaustive, and they are not the center of things. Beyond the most comprehensive idea there is still an infinite plus untouched by any thought. All the categories by which an accidental reason catalogues experience are symbolic abstractions. Such are terms like matter and mind.

Experience, to a radical empiricist, is prior to knowledge. It is the *given*, that which is at the level of feeling and animal action. But it is not, at least of necessity, prior in the order of existence. Santayana accepted the primitive, organic roots of reflective thought. Self-consciousness was only a step beyond pure, undiscriminated feelings or animal reactions. But he feared that a radical empiricist would grovel in experience, in any and all experience and in its irrational immediacy. He thought he detected such a tendency, such an omnivorous appetite for any new experience, in William James, and abhorred it. In fact, he usually so interpreted the label "radical empiricism" and thus did not use it for himself. Such undivided attention to experience, to feeling, could lead to a solipsism more irrational and more mad than that of idealism—to a solipsism of will instead of intellect, of power instead of idle discrimination. Instead of simply viewing experience as the given in knowledge, an empiricist might view experience as the only reality, a reality vague and sensuous, undefined and amorphous. On one hand, this severed man from a generative order, or from nature. On the other, it prevented the rightful appreciation and love due to abstract but self-fulfilling ideas which emerge from the experiential seedbed. It placed undue love upon a lower, enslaving level of animal passion and thus was neither properly pious, for it ignored the realm of matter, nor spiritual, for it discounted contemplation. The road to personal sanity and peace is a road to an ideal permanence that rises above the chaos of the moment.

Santayana was always a determined realist. He never *practically* doubted an existing substance underlying his own experiences, feelings, and ideas. Yet his radical empiricism precluded any full or exact knowledge of this substance. With greater insight than Dewey, and with acknowledged indebtedness to Spinoza, Santayana saw that this encountered substance, the source of life and mind, had many of the traits attributed to the Hebraic God, or to the Father of the Christian Trinity. Due respect to it was not only evidence of sanity but of humility and piety. To ignore it was blasphemous. But to love it unduly was a mark of youthful impetuosity. In one of many instances of an arbitrary and exceedingly subjective terminology, Santayana named this ultimate substance "matter" or the "realm of matter." This obviously invited all manner of semantic confusion.

For a radical empiricist, any existent substance is encountered at an existential level, not at the intellectual level of essence and determinant relations. It is had, not known. The known world—the objective universe of human science—is only an intellectual abstract of experience, however universal in its terms, however well justified by its instrumental efficacy, however rational or consistent in its form. No such abstract can be complete or fully exclusive, for no such abstract can possibly encompass substance. How, then, can a radical empiricist be a materialist? He cannot if the term matter has any metaphysical import. For Santayana, it did not, but he used it so often and so loosely that this all-important qualification too easily slipped from view. Instead of any number of variant terms, such as God or Nature, he preferred matter as a term standing for a single, existentially encountered substance. It was the principle of existence and fertility, of a contingent world of flux, without logical necessity or teleology. His materialism committed him to no one view of matter, to no one system of physics. In fact, he even argued that "if matter does not exist, a combination of other things exists which is just as material." [*Character and Opinion in the United States* (London, 1920), p. 184.] He suggested that any substance that existed, whatever its qualities, would be matter. In verbal gymnastics, he loved to goad idealists by pointing out that they also believed in substance, and thus were materialists.

Santayana's lifelong insistence upon his "materialism" was not a verbal trick, but somehow a deeply personal claim with great symbolic value. It had almost a prayerful aspect, comparable to that of a highly religious person who insists upon paying frequent verbal respects to his God. Santayana even suggested that it would be treason to avoid the term. In part, he wanted to be different, to disassociate himself from other naturalists (a more fitting but less often used term). He also wanted to identify himself with Democritus, one good philosopher who lived before any idealist. He clearly wanted to use it to disassociate himself from both James and Dewey—from all of American thought. It always seemed to him to be a sharp and shocking term to throw at idealists. Early in life it possibly symbolized his friendliness to modern science. Later, it set off by honest contrast his emphasis upon ideals and upon spirituality. Santayana loved to stand all alone against the world. He invited philosophic conflicts where none really existed. With a bit of arrogance and a bit of paranoid delusion, he pictured his materialism as a courageous commitment. In fact, in *Skepticism and Animal Faith,* he avowed he was the only living materialist. He enjoyed making the distinction, even though it was virtually meaningless.

Since Santayana's matter was a surd, a brute existent, he was reduced to a type of skepticism, a second of his favorite but misleading terms. The net import of his skepticism, or of man's inability to know substance either exactly or in totality, was simply that man's experience is limited and that he is not omniscient. Surely this was no great revelation, although it was one still worth making in the late nineteenth century. But his skepticism was a prefatory qualification for his speculative commentary about the realm of matter, for some enjoyable extrapolations from the physical sciences and from common sense. In other words, despite all the clarified limitations, Santayana freely speculated about the nature of matter, periodically noting that the essence of matter, or its intrinsic character, is unknowable. In this ontological speculation he joined John Dewey, although in an even more loose way. His heart was not in the task. Spencer and Peirce were the last philosophers, save possibly Whitehead, who confidently constructed speculative cosmologies and promoted them as if they were scientific.

Santayana saw matter as a flux of natural moments or events in time. The flux had some enduring structures, some varying degrees of permanency, although as a whole it was irrational and full of contradictions. He believed the natural moments had a type of forward tension, or a type of momentum. Nature falls into a rhythm in the flux and often maintains the rhythm. This permits organized structures and even life to develop. He found no overarching scheme, no ultimate cause, no teleology in nature. Matter as a whole, or in each moment, is ultimately contingent, although events form causal series that are internally determinant. Any order, any form, is precarious and insecure. Contingency is the more enveloping concept; mechanism, the more limited one. Finally, and most crucially, he saw consciousness as a climactic issue from matter, its highest achievement, but one essentially or qualitatively so different from matter as to introduce an entirely different realm of being (but not of existence). This outline was never carefully developed, but contained the basic presuppositions back of Santayana's philosophy. It did not contain a careful survey of natural or biological evolution (such was implicit) and had no concept of emergence. Neither did it carefully distinguish orders in nature, such as inanimate, animate, and mental, although his great emphasis upon consciousness implied an exceptionally rigid break between two orders, the physical and the spiritual.

If nothing else, Santayana hoped his materialism could batter romantic idealism into surrendering its dominant position in philosophy. Before G. E. Moore, before any of the organized realist movements, Santayana engaged in a lonely battle against the entrenched orthodoxy of late nineteenth-century thought. Many philosophers would soon join him, but none hated idealism with quite as much passion. None turned it, as he did, into the eternal Lucifer of human history, born in a blind and egotistical rebellion against God, matter, and fate. Not that he totally lacked sympathy for the old devil. Much of the idealist position went into his own.

The idealistic heresy began with Plato, but it was not too uncomely in its beginnings. The materialism of Democritus was too positivistic, too inclined to ignore the spirit and to evade moral and political issues. This deficiency Plato remedied with a vengeance. He saw correctly what, in one of his appeals to bogus authorities, Santayana said no sane person would ever doubt, that the dynamic source of sensation was a material thing and that the logical theme of definition was an essence. But Plato inverted the natural order. Instead of mind acknowledging its natural origin and dependence, it became a self-sufficient substance, existing apart from matter and even, in Plato's cosmological myths, possibly accounting for its origin. Thus the son first turned on the mother; the derivative angel first rebelled against his creator. Spirit, the supreme achievement of matter, in fact its very consummation, became a cosmological force. Even worse, Plato, the politician and moralist, conceived the universe in moral and teleological terms. The limited preferences of Greek moralists were read into the universe. A corrupted physics was rendered even more blasphemous. But in Plato the moral vision was sublime, the false physics muted and possibly never taken very seriously, and the cosmology always presented as mythical and poetical. In the modern world only Emerson used idealistic themes in such a poetic and inoffensive manner.

Santayana had two reasons to love Aristotle—he was a naturalist and he glorified contemplation. Thus, he canceled some of the errors of his mentor. But he kept some of the worst errors, including a nonderivative spirit or mind, although one no longer mythically implicated in creation. Instead of eternalizing the logical themes of discourse, Aristotle and his scholastic imitators eternalized the apprehending intellect and thus severed it from its dependence on matter. A fatal dualism of mind and matter resulted. At the same time, the object of sensation was assumed to be not just an intuited essence, but the essence of a material object. A correspondence theory of truth replaced the intuition or mythical memory of Plato. The whole universe was encapsuled in the formal categories of human thought. Nature (or God) was shriveled to fit human perceptions. Even the adored Spinoza was infected with some of this formalism and rationalism, despite his wonderful insight into the relation of matter and spirit. To Santayana, rationalism was a builder's bias. The logical outlines of our most soaring thoughts are only a method and style of architecture, which neither absorbs the material of life nor monopolizes its values. But in Aristotle, in St. Thomas, in Spinoza, despite all the rationalistic presumption, there was still an admirable sanity, a balance and harmony so totally lacking in the modern world. The worst impiety was absent. Even in the Roman Catholic Church, where true history and physics were blatantly mythologized, the result was obtained by frank supernaturalism and not by philosophical sophistry. He always preferred transparent myths to the covert idealism of Protestant philosophers.

The awkward but integrated dualism of scholasticism broke down in the modern West. It cleaved into Descartes' ghost in a machine, was imperfectly merged in Spinoza's rationalized substance, and was fragmented into a panpsychical eclecticism by a brilliant Leibnitz. All these early trends were arrested and soon terminated by the erosion of English skepticism and were transcended by the new systems of the German idealists. By the seventeenth century philosophers were beginning a 300-year-long investigation of the thinking process. The emphasis shifted from logic and physics to an ersatz type of psychology, or psychologism. The subjective side of thought absorbed all interest in a Protestant age. In Britain this subjective interest led to Hume and to psychological atoms. The whole world had driven inward until only discrete sensations remained. They were falsely identified as the irreducible ground of experience, although in reality were themselves products of reflection and once removed from the rich and undifferentiated level of primitive experience (here he followed James in all details). But Santayana had some respect for the English empiricists. Their inward excursions, inexcusable perhaps in forgetting the point of departure, nonetheless clarified, almost to literary perfection, the phenomenalistic aspects of thought. Besides, the cautious British never took their skepticism too seriously and remained in practice good materialists and good scientists. Their philosophical nearsightedness was never damning, although it could blight the imagination and deny the spirit.

The Germans had no such practical discipline. They subjectified knowledge, turning it into the intuition of terms rather than the discovery of objects. Soon the thinking subject, the human spirit, was absolutized into the only form of existence. This blindness and pretension Santayana called egotism. The Germans substituted a dialectical and poetic history of the world for good physics and then adored their false product. At its best, this idealism was an engaging phenomenon, full of afflatus, sweep, and deep romantic searchings of heart. It reflected a worthy if too exclusive interest in the inner life. But when accepted by unromantic people, such as professors (Royce?), and sponsored as the rational foundation of science and religion, for neither of which it had any honest sympathy, it became odious. To Santayana, it was the worst imposture and blight to which a youthful imagination could be subjected, and he clearly spoke from bitter experience. Constantly he reiterated the sour fruits of idealism: willfulness in morals, subjectivity in thought, arrogant self-assertion, hatred of true reason, incipient solipsism, loss of respect for truth, contempt for happiness, tolerance of all passions, and extremes of personal and national egotism.

EPISTEMOLOGY

To tangle with the idealists, whether of the British empirical or the German romantic tradition, was to enter the labyrinth of epistemology. Technically, this was the most difficult area of Santayana's thought. As a radical empiricist he supported a type of instrumentalism. He added little of importance to the pragmatic conception of knowledge, save a new rhetoric and a few subtle distinctions. With Dewey, he denied a "problem" of knowledge and thus circumvented most epistemological issues of his day, even as James spent years struggling with them. For those who remained absorbed in the old puzzle—how do our ideas, being only ideas, reveal an external or objective world?—Santayana's answer could not satisfy. Even when dressed in the verbal guise of animal faith or paraded as a variety of the new realism, it still represented a complete rejection of the conventional ground rules of epistemology.

To Santayana, knowledge correctly represented the relation of a knowing animal to other things, not the internal nature of things. Absolute knowledge is a meaningless ideal, unless immediate, qualitative experience is called a form of knowledge. To refer to things, to objects, is to implicate existence; thus, knowledge presupposes substance, but it neither creates nor proves nor perfectly reveals the existent substance. The terms of human knowledge are symbolic and will never be fully adequate as long as men are finite, bereft of miraculous illumination. In symbols now rich and poetic, now disciplined and precise, some of our ideas accurately but selectively transcribe the effects of a substantial world upon our own bodies. A few months before his death, Santayana eloquently summarized his position: "But I do believe in the incapacity of images or concepts to fathom or 'explain' reality. Matter, or if you prefer, Wind, is not exhaustively representable in Spirit (which is an *original music* made by the Wind) but Spirit being secondary and an approximate index to the way the Wind is blowing in one place at a certain time, Spirit knows a lot about the ways of the Wind. The Hebrews were wise and prudent in speaking about the 'ways' of the Lord, rather than of his nature." [To Richard C. Lyon, Mar. 16, 1952, *Letters*, p. 433.]

But how do we know the Wind exists? How can we escape illusion? Santayana's answer is clear. If illusion is anything less than exact knowledge of substance, we cannot escape some type of illusion. We always dwell in the nonliteral and imaginative realm of poetry, unless we take the images of discourse as the only reality, thus capitulating to idealism and obvious egotism. Certainty can be found (or developed) quickly within the abstracted terms of discourse, but this certainty has no tale to tell about existence. Those who want knowledge to possess the same certainty simply misconstrue the very nature of knowledge. They are dissatisfied with poetic images or mere appearances and thus are really dissatisfied with knowledge itself. They want a different commodity. Knowledge, properly conceived, is nothing more than the acceptance of certain discriminated symbols as rough appearances of something beyond us. If at least some refined products of our experience are not conceived as appearances, then knowledge is impossible. What better medium of knowledge could be conceived than appearances?

But one can still doubt. In fact, a critical mind cannot escape it. Santayana explored to the quick this doubt and drove it relentlessly to its bitter end of complete solipsism. Yet, he conceived such complete skepticism as *practical* foolishness, as a feigned, abstract product of reflection torn asunder from the active life of an animal. Consciousness arises out of the harmonies attained by matter in the animal body. It rises above a prereflective level of interaction, which is marked only by

feeling. When carefully disciplined, human thought reflects the successful strivings of the animal. Then our language of sense data correctly
defines the action of matter upon our body, or of our body upon other
things. Born in the primitive mold of brute experience, reflection reaches
the height of practical (not logical) absurdity when it feeds upon itself
and denies the existence of matter or, in interpreting its inability to
mirror perfectly the whole universe, as license for complete doubt.
Thought cannot validate itself, nor should it be expected to, since it is
derivative from something more fundamental. At the level of an animal,
or of an unsophisticated man, skepticism is unknown. The sense of
existence is rooted in the strains of life; it is prior to all intuition or
thought. Here a type of trust, or simple faith, exists unspoken and
unremarked—a faith rooted in the vital physical compulsions of the
organism. This faith is far wiser than any skepticism. It is a trust in an
unfathomable power, whose workings are sufficiently clear for human
art—for adequate biological adaptation. It is validated, if at all, in
successful activity. Santayana called this animal faith and drew the
parallel with Protestant piety. It is the Puritan and Hebraic strain again,
the trust that is given without an egotistic concern for total comprehension or complete certainty. Here, at least, Santayana drew closer to the
Protestant than to the Greek, to an existential level where real doubt is
irrelevant and impossible.

In order to defend his idea of animal faith, Santayana first developed
his concept of nonexistential essences. He believed his concept of
essence was the most important doctrine in his philosophy. He used it to
segregate all the attributes of existence from the formal qualities of
thought. Yet, in generous moments, he admitted that his essences were
arbitrary distinctions, or a language he found necessary if he were to
express the full nature of things. Matter is a flux of existent things.
Consciousness is an accidental, fleeting climax in matter, yet it is
adequate for a pragmatic representation of matter. But how can spirit
(consciousness) adequately explain its own distinctive quality? How can
we really express the essence of being conscious? Only, it seemed to
Santayana, by isolating and describing the moments of consciousness, or
the quality of such moments. This is an elusive undertaking. Santayana,
very much like Peirce, attempted to attain a radical phenomenology, a
discrimination of pure, irreducible moments of consciousness. The unitary content of such a moment—the pure datum—however simple or

complex, is what he called an essence. Later, he ontologized this phenomenology by positing a logical or implicatory realm of essences, or of pure Being, which included all possible data of all possible moments of intuition. But this nonexistent realm, as he occasionally felt, is so indiscriminate and so lost in pure possibility as to be tenuous and hopelessly abstract. However, in his contemplative moments it became the sole focus of his interest, a realm of pure delight.

His doctrine of essence created confusion among fellow philosophers. No one ever understood it well enough to please Santayana. He believed essences were so obvious that they scarcely needed to be pointed out before everyone jumped in recognition. Possibly his extensive, mostly negative delineation, only helped confuse his audience. He was influenced by mathematicians in his first formulation (he acknowledged both Russell and Whitehead) and believed that the terms intuited in mathematical discourse were excellent illustrations of essences. But the Platonic ideas, the real source of his own concept, came even earlier. Unfortunately, Plato gave existence to his essences and threw all of Western philosophy off on a false tack, which Santayana finally remedied by denying their existence (actually Peirce did it first). The problem of most Western philosophy had been a confusion of existence with the perfect Being of pure dialectic. Being does not exist; it is a formal and logical category, the most complex of all essences. It is a realm of potentiality, in which every existent thing partakes, since everything is some thing. When Santayana referred to the eternality of an essence, he really denoted its nontemporal, nonexistential quality, not any permanence. An essence is and always remains just what it is. Things change; essences cannot. Yet, language becomes treacherous when Being does not exist and when eternal essences are only logical potentialities.

In Santayana's epistemology, essences had a distinct but limited function. In summary, he used the idea of nonexistent, purely formal entities to prove that existence is never given or a priori. Much as John Dewey pointed to the cognitive neutrality of perceptions as perceptions, so Santayana showed that thought itself had no intrinsic guarantee of existential relevance. The cognitive claim is external to the nature of thought, being an aspect of an active animal's watchfulness or intent. In his private nomenclature, Santayana usually limited the term perception to cognitive or objective ideas—that is, to ideas intended to picture

some part of existence. Sensations were the atomic raw material of
perceptions. Dreams and fantasy were made up of images. Thus, his
blanket term, embracing the distinctive content of all types of thought,
cognitive or fanciful, literal or highly poetical, was essence. As the
purely formal content of thinking (as distinguished from the physical
organs), essences could not exist. Their nonexistence precluded any
objective idealism and helped distinguish the possible confusion between
purely formal thought and cognitive claims.

For Santayana the only cognitive problem was the practical one—
how to act correctly. Skepticism is a healthy chastity of the intellect,
warding off many frivolous suitors, but it should eventuate in a happy
marriage with nature and science. Of course, a type of solipsism, a pure
contemplative enjoyment of essences with no regard for their usefulness
in explaining existence, is a possible mode of life and is exemplified by
some mystics. Everything is thinkable and, as pure thought, immune to
error. But such contemplation of essence, increasingly inviting to
Santayana, leaves man helpless in the practical affairs of life. To leave
the realm of pure essence and tangle with existence is risky and requires
faith, even as it involves choice, reflects preference, and invites anxiety.
But if the struggling animal tries to live rationally (or at times even to
live at all), it will discriminate between essences, using some to define a
world not present in consciousness, but posited in the very act of referring certain formal qualities outward to it. The only test of the essences
chosen is a practical one. Do they accurately reflect the type of activity
which enhances human art and harmonizes vital impulses? Here Santayana was a pragmatist. The ultimate test of the validity of propositions
about existence is experimental. There is no other way to separate fact
from fancy or to make a practical distinction among essences. The test
is never intrinsic; it is always extrinsic, applied in the realm of animal
action, of satisfactions procured, dangers avoided, desires achieved.

There is one important distinction between Santayana's epistemology
and that of the instrumentalists, one so subtle that it almost dissolves on
careful analysis. Santayana believed that valid propositions (good
science) mirror successful action rather than directing or guiding it.
The animal makes the correct adjustment. Consciousness may follow
and may correctly interpret the action. Even when prophetic or anticipa-
tory, consciousness only reads correctly natural processes already
directed to the predicted end. Thus, consciousness is never a power.

Obviously, nonexistential essences do not have causal efficacy. But sustaining consciousness and preceding it is bodily activity, including brain activity, which does involve redirected energies. Thus, in a sense, consciousness is a gauge that shows what the brain is about but in no way controls it. Knowledge, being made up of chosen essences directed by animal intent upon an unknown reality, has no efficacy. In no way can it influence the course taken by natural events. But the very behavioral process that led to the consciousness is redirecting the body in a certain direction. Animal faith, the behavioral affirmation, is prior to, and not a product of, consciousness. Skepticism at other than a formal and purely intellectual level reflects indecision, a failure of faith, and a breakdown of effective activity. In alarm, any healthy animal will desperately try to rectify this situation.

This epiphenomenalism altered the usual view of scientific hypotheses. The experimental activity, by which a hypothesis is verified, is simply the continued and prefigured activity that produced the tentative conceptualization. The essences that make up the hypothesis have no causal role, even though they seem to control the experimental activity. The physical mechanism of thought does play a causal role. The brain activity involved in framing a hypothesis has already reoriented the body and, through it, external objects toward a type of activity, which will actually take place if opportunities allow (if they do allow as intended, then the hypothesis is a true or valid one). If all ends in frustration, it simply shows the bodily futility of an organism unable to make a satisfactory adjustment. It is only a confusion in thinking, or a grievous egotism, that concludes that our ideas were at fault, as if they controlled the material world. The machine does the work, not the gauge.

The problems involved with this view are many and quite complex. Most were not adequately developed by Santayana. But possibly the real difficulty is semantic. His seeming rejection of an instrumentalist conception of intelligence resolves into a rather abstract distinction between the formal and physical aspects of one human activity. His separation of essence and existence required this awkward distinction, a distinction that Santayana easily acquired from William James's intricate psychological probes into cognition and from a quite warranted interpretation of the James-Lange theory of emotion. In his desire to render idealism absurd, and in his later desire to escape the anxiety of practical life, Santayana isolated essences from matter, form from substance, and made essences so purely logical and formal that they could not exist. Indeed, this pushed absolute idealism into a narrow, impossible solipsistic corner, but at the same time introduced quite arbitrary, verbally unmanageable concepts into what purported to be a common-sense view of knowledge.

The universe of the physicists (any one will do) is always a vast, hopefully expedient hypostatization, without metaphysical value. The universe is always "more than human, less than moral, other than dialectical." The objects that make up any universe are intuited essences, or ideas, which are taken by the animal in some way to symbolize how an external environment affects him. By means of this expedient symbolization, human experience is objectified and brought into complex patterns of relationship. The discipline for the picture we select is both logical and experimental. Primitive man attained consciousness without this discipline. His mind was flooded with images, with random essences, many inexpediently referred to existence. His action was free, but all too often accidental and helpless. With an ever more complex bodily adaptation, with better habits, came more disciplined and discriminating symbols, although their adaptative adequacy often lessened their suggestive and enjoyable aspect even as it destroyed all playful and irresponsible freedom. Mind had to go to school; fancy became docile. The end product—modern science—was a masterpiece, even as the life fully harmonized with the environment according to the best scientific knowledge has achieved unbelievable biological mastery.

Knowledge expresses in language the modified habits of an animal plastic to experience and capable of readjusting its organic impulses. Santayana, as much as Dewey, tied all inquiry to the qualitative level of bodily interaction. The subject matter of cognitive thought is first a bodily effect, a relationship between an organism and something outside or within the body. This situation, at the level of purely physical behavior, delimits the sphere of any subsequent reflection and marks off its vital intent. As the animal copes with new situations, it may, if it has developed consciousness and the complex neurological equipment supporting a symbolic language, turn certain fleeting essences into descriptive terms, or into perceptions. The very fact of consciousness indicates a much more complex and plastic organism, one with great adaptative assets and a superior brain. Thus, in man the painful moment is known as painful. The sharp point of pain, if carefully reflected upon, is identified as a sensation. The cause of the pain, when located, is objectified and, if new to experience, given a name. Then the triumphant and egotistic man will report that a pin caused a particularly irksome sensation of pain. When, in the future, he is able to avoid all pins, he will falsely attribute it to consciousness. But actually, this conscious side of behavior is only the inefficacious esthetic or moral side of a physical process. If the active response to the pin was correct and led to a new and fruitful habit in the body (most emphatically including the brain), then the animal learned from the experience. The subtended terms or essences of consciousness constitute true knowledge, being the counterpart of a successful physical adjustment in which they played no physical role.

In the above case, the conscious formulation of the causal relationship of events represents a hypothesis. It may be very crude and should be very tentative, just as the active response was crude and tentative. Subsequent, refined, and less tentative hypotheses may accompany more successful and less tentative responses. Hypotheses are born, live, and die in the context of animal behavior. But behavior does not depend on consciousness. Learning usually occurs without a conscious counterpart, by what is often set apart and distinguished as sheer conditioning. Instrumentally, such conditioning is just as efficacious as conscious learning; physically, it is indistinguishable.

Since consciousness apparently occurs only in animals capable of very complex cerebral modifications, there would indeed be a physically discernible difference between such learning and that of a lower animal presumably (it is only a guess) without consciousness. But, obviously, the essences of conscious awareness do not constitute the physical difference; at best, they only testify to it. Santayana frequently acknowledged that human adaptation and that advanced human arts were possible only because man was conscious. But here, to be consistent, he had to qualify very carefully. It is not consciousness that enables man to master parts of nature, since ideas cannot direct or propel anything. But when ideas exist, small, subtle brain tissues are redirecting energies, and whenever this redirection is biologically or esthetically successful, we poetically say that we have the knowledge that will change the world. In fact, we only have new habits that are changing the world.

Santayana emphasized the moral aspect of consciousness (this is its only importance), again with great subtlety. Few critics ever understood

his point, for they understood "moral" as instrumental, and Santayana
clearly ascribed instrumentality only to matter. Thus the seeming
paradox. How could Santayana write five volumes in behalf of rationality and art, yet deny the efficacy of reason and knowledge? And, in
the very denial, how could he urge that nature becomes moral only in
attaining consciousness? It seemed a puzzle to unimaginative critics,
who were only philosophers, often given to a stultifying analytical turn
of mind. His meaning was quite simple and was crucial to his whole
thought. He believed consciousness added a moral dimension to the
nonmoral flux of matter. The distinction between nonconscious conditioning and conscious learning was not instrumental but esthetic. In
conscious learning, essences are entertained, contemplated, possibly
appreciated. Through them, an experience means something to the
individual. When the learning is successful, when animal impulses are
satiated, when art is enhanced, when a disturbed situation gives way to a
new harmony in action, it means also a blessed harmony in ideas and
joy for the conscious animal. At a low level of consciousness, the
harmony is quite physical, for example in the lessening of physical pain.
In art and in advanced science, the harmony is more formal and intellectual. In all cases it is relative or contextual, tied to the varied preferences of a unique individual. But at either level life acquires value and is
enjoyed. Nonconscious instinct might have as much biological efficacy,
but it has none of the moral consummation. Imaginative contemplation
of essences might be even more rewarding esthetically, but would be
biologically useless. Insofar as man has to be an animal, he should be
rational, and *maybe* (Santayana had increasing doubts) the conscious
joy could outweigh the anxiety and pain; if not, death or imaginative
escape would be preferable (as he sometimes believed). Here, of course,
is the bridge from Santayana's epistemology to his moral philosophy, a
bridge too seldom appreciated by his critics.

For Santayana there was no substantive distinction between knowledge and science. The term "scientific," if it has any epistemological
meaning, simply denotes the careful distinctions and consistent relations
present in the most disciplined products of human thought. Science may
be thus distinguished from the more loose and colorful content of
common sense. Instrumentally, science is more reliable than common
sense. Scientific propositions are as true to existence as any human
propositions can be. They represent the best art of inquiry in any age.

But they are still limited to the human organs employed. Practically, rigorous scientific knowledge provides us the best possible index to adjustments necessary for successful animal life. In a pragmatic use of the word, science is the only truth we may have. Biologically, no other type of truth matters to us.

But scientific hypotheses are selective and narrowed abstractions and are thus ever tentative. Even when called laws, these abstractions have no metaphysical status. From Democritus to Newton a false sense of certainty was read into physics. But the skeptical reservation should not be driven too far, as voluntarists like William James tended to do. The best established scientific laws are *virtually* true. They arise out of nature and reflect the harmony of an organism in nature. As far as they go, and on a limited plane of relevance, they must reveal to a very great extent the actual habits present, or developing, in the flux of matter. Thus, a virtual correspondence was assumed by Santayana, but all arrogant pretension was excluded. Even if a trope or enduring pattern were perfectly pictured by a scientific concept, man would have no ulterior insight to prove the perfect relationship.

In every sense applicable to epistemology or scientific method, Santayana believed that the only truth was a type of experimental validity in belief. But he never relished this pragmatism and refused to relinquish an older concept of Truth, absolute and eternal. Our propositions are only true pragmatically. But if there were an omniscient mind (there is not to Santayana) it would know the Truth. It would know all events in all history in their essence. This concept of Truth, close at times to the Logos of Neoplatonism, and related to the impartial and absolute mind affirmed by Royce, had no operative function for Santayana, except possibly as a way of reiterating his realism. But it solaced him to acknowledge such an unknowable Truth and to hope that our ideas often came close to a part of it. In any case it seemed a quite dignified and elegant backstop to vulgar pragmatism. He frequently referred to it, and with all the emotional force of a Christian referring to Christ. The concept of Truth could be elevated into a blurred vision, a sublime ideal, and operate in a moral context. Man could respect pragmatic truth but not worship it. But the eternal Truth of things, held as an unrealizable but conceivable ideal, could command our ultimate loyalty.

Always commending Democritus, Santayana argued that all physical science is atomic and mechanistic in form. Atomicity points to dispersion in centers, to a corpuscular arrangement of matter, and not to the tiny and complicated atoms or universes of modern physics. To try to define atoms (or discrete units) is to transgress the metaphysical modesty appropriate to science. Likewise, the mechanistic form of scientific explanation does not entail a determinant universe; otherwise, once again science sponsors a particular metaphysical view. Mechanism does mean that whatever aspects of nature encompassed by scientific laws (some very abstract and quite fictitious) are, at present, affecting man in a regular, ordered, determinant way. The whole vast trope encompassed by a physical law is part of the even larger flux that is existence, and therefore it shares in the contingency of the whole. Also, causal determinism itself leads to constant novelty, for the complex of elements entering a given situation may never have entered such a situation before, and something new is thereby formed. In this sense, the flux is ever pregnant with new events even in the midst of determinant series. Physical laws are only the form, the habit or path, followed by the ever changing river of events.

The uniform laws of science, however poorly integrated and harmonized with each other, are still the very skeleton or framework by which men organize all their experience. Santayana insisted upon the full scope of such explanatory laws. That is, no part of nature, including man, is exempt from mechanistic explanation. But all such laws are selective and abstract. They underlie and participate in all experience but do not exhaust it nor fully represent it. To say that scientific laws are constant and determinant is truistic, for constancy is the very essence of such laws. Without a pervasive mechanistic framework, without enduring structures in nature, knowledge and art would be impossible, and a contingent existence would become a complete anarchy without any continuity, without any handhold for organization (and thus for life and mind). Scientific law is a growing, always tentative blueprint of nature's more orderly habits as encountered by man. In a contingent world, there is no absolute assurance that these laws, so essential and so reliable, will continue to operate. All tropes may be temporary. We have no ultimate secrets. The sun may not rise tomorrow.

Almost as much as Dewey, Santayana emphasized the role of formal thought (logic or dialectic) in scientific inquiry. In fact, he actually used the term science to encompass dialectics as well as physics, since animal faith is involved in both. In mathematical reasoning, for example, intent is not directed to an unknown substance impinging upon the body, but to a term of discourse entertained in the past. Thus, mathematical reasoning relates an essence present in intuition with one absent and involves both faith and a risk of error. As much as cognitive thought, dialectic originates at the level of experience and here finds its first terms, however far it later travels away from this experience. Dialectic, truistic in itself, free to take any deductive pattern it prefers, provides the form or the rational part of all scientific theory. It is the indispensable tool for any broad explanation and also suggests such guiding ideals in science as unity and simplicity. Inspired by a perfect logical universe, man tries to find an existent one. The most essential unifying concepts in science, such as space and time, are logical entities that work in practice. The goal of science is to apply as much dialectic to nature as can be made to fit in experiment.

Suprisingly, for one who later gloried in contemplation, Santayana did not always relish mathematics. Possibly the pure and rarefied content repelled him as much as northern winters. He insisted on mathematics as a tool for science, on science as the very essential of art, and on art as a road to spiritual peace, but he wanted no mathematics for mathematics' sake. He acknowledged that pure dialectic had a sense of profundity absent in empirical science, but feared the impiety so easily provoked by dialectical intoxication. Pure dialecticians are too prone to deny the place of pure thought in the world, its source and parentage. They may become as mad as esthetes. Extreme rationalism is always a bastard. Pure dialectic, totally severed from its moral function in science, loses its dignity and becomes the ballet of science. It is a method without application, delightful to some but not useful. He believed it antithetical to the best spirituality, which involves not a limbo of pure rationality but a type of salvation gained out of the disillusion and suffering of a life in the world. It is the wrong type of escape; it is not even a redeeming escape, since it involves faith and a type of anxiety. But as a liberalizing subject, not as a vocation, mathematics is emancipating, showing the possibilities of other, less contingent worlds, and revealing a congenial and perfectly secure and free realm of internal accuracy and ideal truth.

Except for dialectics, Santayana made physics the only science. By physics he meant the laws governing the whole realm of matter. Mechanistic tropes pervade all existence; they are equally physical in a man or a stone. Admittedly, certain tropes in the organic world are not encompassed by known causal laws, probably because of their greater complexity. These are dealt with at a level of classification or measured regularity in behavior. But this also has to be the method of explanation in inanimate science in specified cases. Santayana felt that mechanistic explanation, potentially, encompassed all nature and that the distinctions between different sciences were always arbitrary.

From William James, Santayana acquired a great interest in psychology, which he always defined as a somewhat narrow field of physics. Santayana found in James's psychology courses two quite distinct subjects, illogically combined as if they were one. On one hand, and presented with great technical skill, there was a science of psychology, being a limited speciality of physiology. On the other hand, and with equal skill, there was an unscientific and unverifiable but suggestive literary picture of consciousness, drawn in large part from idealistic and transcendental sources. Santayana, with typical rigor, would have none of the mixture. He deplored the confusion, the false assumptions, but loved both of the two subjects when properly distinguished.

To separate the two, Santayana used the same type of trick involved in separating essence and existence. He distinguished the psyche and consciousness. The psyche was a term standing for a mode of substance or matter or for the animating form of an animal. It included all the physical processes of thought and all the animal impulses and instincts. As a material trope, the psyche could be investigated by scientific methods, leading to subtle developments in physiology and to the discovery of revealing uniformities in behavior. Thus, physiology and behavioral studies exhausted psychology as a science. In this sense Santayana was always a vociferous behaviorist. The psyche, which looks out for the bodily needs, is terribly practical. In man, the psyche includes all so-called mental attributes but consciousness and, in a sense, also has this. For consciousness arises out of the psyche, uses the same physical organs, and generally remains captive to psychic goals—sex for example. Behaviorism explains all there is to explain scientifically—the mechanisms involved. Thus, Santayana again draws a subtle distinction in what is generally taken to be one mental life.

Past psychologists too often interpreted consciousness as a physical substance or force. Poetically, they were correct, for common-sense experience easily interprets it this way. The ghost directing the bodily machine is a metaphor sufficient for expressing the way we actually experience life, but it is totally inadequate as a scientific explanation. But these psychologists were correct in insisting that the felt quality of conscious experience could not be defined by a mere enumeration of its underlying material base. Even a behaviorist knows how it feels to be conscious, but except for an analogy of similar structure or behavior, by a practically justified use of the pathetic fallacy, he has no way of discovering the existence of consciousness in another, let alone the exact feelings and thoughts of another person. In strictest scientific discipline, he cannot attribute consciousness at all. Even if he did assume its existence, his assumption is operationally meaningless, for consciousness plays no efficacious role anyway. Even such a term as pain has to stand for a type of behavior, not a type of feeling. But neural complexity and behavioral subtlety (such as a complex language) are proper and observable subject matter for a behavioral science. A better understanding of those would help explain the material foundation of an assumed consciousness in an organism. But consciousness, a qualitative, phenomenological function, cannot be investigated or even explained except in the most metaphorical way. By failing to make these simple distinctions, psychology (or philosophy) becomes a type of sophistry, half-poetry but claiming explanatory authority; half-scientific but corrupted by poor poetry.

When divested of false scientific claims, literary psychology, or the art of imagining how animals feel rather than the task of observing how they act, can be extremely valuable in a humane, suggestive way, just as biography and history are valuable. Even in its illusions it expands one's own mind. Literary psychology appeals to what another man says to himself when he surveys his adventures. There is, at best, only circumstantial evidence to verify such judgments. Yet, in a person of broad experience, with a dramatic and imaginative flair, such speculation may be honest, appealing, and close to the mark. Good novels attain this successful mind reading. So does good history. But neither good novels, conventional epistemology, nor good history has anything to do with the validity of knowledge, for they are not knowledge. English empiricism, with its imagined sensations in a void without material organs or occasions, was a type of literary psychology, in which knowing became either impossible or a miracle. Insofar as literary psychology is true, it happens to correspond with underlying material facts. In Freud, this literary psychology was deliberately grafted onto natural substance and animal life, a commendable effort. But it was done in comparative ignorance of any exact correspondence between conscious states and subtending physical substance, a knowledge still sadly lacking. Thus, Freudianism was not literary psychology turned into a science, but rather encased in a deceitful mythology. The mythology not only included impious assumptions about nature, but tried to destroy the distinctive phenomenological elements of consciousness by unraveling it into a labyrinth of dreams and chaos. On the other hand, the Freudian metaphors often expressed a needed wisdom. Never one to deprecate myth, Santayana found many congenial ideas in Freud.

History is a form of literary psychology mixed with a small amount of authentic science. It builds from a skeleton of verifiable evidence, a skeleton properly a part of natural history or physics. It fills in the skeleton with moral prejudice and dramatic art, pretending to rehearse the ideas and feelings of dead men. Even the more positivistic historians try to explain how men felt or why they chose as they did; more dramatic historians indulge in such poetic nonsense as the spirit of an age or such vague concepts as public opinion, as if these were causal forces. This concealed literature has no scientific value, but may provide incidental information and reveal the skill and wisdom of the historian. With age and disillusionment, Santayana turned more often to history and particularly enjoyed Arnold Toynbee. As in psychology, he only ridiculed false claims and methodological pretense.

In his early life Santayana seemed to be an avid fan of modern science. In his later years he seemed more dubious about its merits and often said harsh things about it. There was no shift in his conception of science, but there was a large shift in his allocation of preferences. From the beginning he tried to discipline science in range and import. Besides, he always knew that man lives on more than knowledge. Science provides a perspective on experience that is instrumentally unimpeachable but morally abstract and cold. Other perspectives coexist without equal explanatory power but with great beauty and suggestivity. Some of these contain limited amounts of correct knowledge and thus are practically adequate for restricted problems. The farmer does quite well with a flat earth. Besides, all human knowledge is symbolic, and to that extent poetic. The choice between one poetry and another is contextual—for what are you choosing? The Christian epic may be a better choice than modern physics in a limited and appreciative context. Both arose out of the same level of direct experience and animal faith, but responded to different criteria in their development. The religious symbol does greater justice to the sensuous richness of this original experience; physical symbols do greater justice to the quantitative aspects and to causal relationships. But the two must be clearly distinguished; otherwise, we have a theology that believes in causal myths or a science that tries to shrivel all experience into the narrow terms of its abstract symbolism. Then we have literal Christians and narrow positivists.

Scientific systems are not only rational but, to many people, quite beautiful. In an esthetic context, science is a liberal discipline, as much so as philosophy or the fine arts. Here is a great imaginative structure created by man. As Santayana lost some of his moral earnestness, his youthful desire to rationalize the modern world, he loved science only in these moral or esthetic terms, as an immediate object of value. But he never preferred it as an appreciative object, just as he never preferred mathematics as a form of contemplative amusement. In its earliest development, our knowledge may not have been pure or perfectly efficacious, but it remained close to our sense images. Stars were all visible and twinkling. Science always has to keep its tie to the twinkles of sense, but today these are only departure points for a vast realm of nonsensuous conceptualization, of nonexperiential but necessary entities. Here Santayana admitted an old-fashioned and purely emotional aversion to science. He never tried to keep abreast of the latest scientific theory and, in humorous detachment, tended to smile at much of it. The scientists seemed to be doing well enough without his help. But could it be that the speculative physicists knew their theories perfectly, but that these same theories only helped them know more theories? If so, they were in the same trap as the mathematicians.

To Santayana, causal explanation never had the beauty of more playful types of imagination, and it had ever less so as it became more abstract, scientifically more exact, and technologically more useful. He preferred to remain as often as possible at the level of colorful experience, where a restricted practicality in thought hardly limited, but often enhanced, its intrinsic value. Also, with his deep aversion to the prevalent forms of modern industry, he believed that much of modern science was simply a buttress to technology, that it was not pursued as a liberal discipline. It gave men domination over nature but no sense of liberation and joy. At times it seemed to be degenerating into a barren operationalism. He may have been wrong and simply expressing a bias against an art form whose technical demands outgrew his appreciative equipment. Also, he may have expressed an arbitrary, personal preference in dismissing the language of modern science as pictorially blind and morally (or esthetically) deficient.

His reservations about science were even more basic. Man, he believed, was at his best when he loved and nourished imaginative ideals. These sprang from his animal life, which depended for its existence upon a degree of social order and economic adequacy. Until he could procure these animal needs, man could hardly avoid devoting much of his time and attention to them. Science as an instrumentality thus lay in back of all successful human aspiration. But he hoped that science, like all practical concerns, could be as habitual and unobtrusive as possible, particularly when intrinsically boring or limiting. But in the modern world it was most explicit and obvious, while moral knowledge, knowledge of what things bring joy and laughter and peace and beatitude, was sadly missing. To turn knowledge of existence, a poetically attenuated type of truth, into an ideal, even into a religion, was the worst form of idolatry. For the truest God is not nature but an imaginative product of nature—an ideal of excellence and beauty and truth, loved and enjoyed (not pursued) by man. Man should square his accounts with matter as quickly as possible and get on with being human. This shifts the focus to what Santayana most prized, from his doctrines to his preferences.

AXIOLOGY

Santayana's thought was a nightmare of subjective definitions. He was an avowed materialist, but was not really a materialist at all; he was a type of skeptic, but was violently opposed to skepticism. In his literary playfulness, almost every label took on a personal and idiosyncratic meaning. This was most true in the broad reaches of his axiology. He posed as a moral philosopher, yet rarely used the word "moral" in a conventional sense. He affected a Platonic emphasis upon politics, yet in many ways remained aloof from politics. In art and religion his thought was richest and most suggestive, yet even here was full of semantic pitfalls. At times his distinctions were too subtle to be understood, or involved complete contradictions.

In his conception of value, Santayana was again very close to the instrumentalists. He located value (both negative and positive) in conscious experience, in existential appreciation. Like Dewey, he saw experience as qualitatively colored. Value is something felt or possessed and is in no way a product of reason. But much more than Dewey he made consciousness the key to value. Even though values are established by vital impulses in the animal, consciousness is the esthetic counter, the gauge. Without the gauge, Santayana believed it would be as meaningless to talk about values, as about ideals and purposes. Value and consciousness go together. In registering or even creating value, consciousness adds a moral dimension to an otherwise amoral nature. In a sense, consciousness is itself the overarching value, for it contains within itself the value of everything else.

Santayana always argued for an honest but broad hedonism or utilitarianism. Pain and pleasure are good terms to distinguish the two qualitative poles of experience. Happiness is the traditional term denoting a state of preponderant satisfaction, or the prevalence of pleasure over pain. Santayana could conceive of no real alternative to an ethic based on the most happiness for the most people. He believed such a general and sane prescription ruled out no type of pleasure and later developed his own defense of spirituality within a utilitarian context.

At the lowest level of consciousness a frustrated animal impulse is registered as undifferentiated pain. Here value is born, for here a quality is first distinguished, an essence is first intuited. Even the subsequent discrimination of sensations is a great deal more analytical, more reflective, more related to instrumental action, and more removed from the actual painful situation. In memory the intrinsic or felt value of an experience is spread over a longer time span, but memory may be highly selective and thus unjust to the original experience. Memory provides the value context of anticipation and conscious desire, which may in imagination completely distort the actual feeling to be had in the subsequent situation. Despite the hazards, in memory and in anticipation, man is at the threshold of an always precarious rationality. He can order his affections and live in the perspective of ideals. This moral reasonableness requires self-understanding, harmonious purposes, and efficacious art.

Reason does not discover or create value or manufacture impulse. These are, and always remain, at the bodily level. But reason, meaning both logical consistency and scientific knowledge, can criticize irrational, conflicting, or impossible aspirations. The criticism can result in a harmonious set of desires, or in a unified ethical ideal. This ideal cannot incorporate all random desires, nor can it do justice to all types of pleasant experience. Some impulses will have to be rejected in behalf of others. But impulse is not destroyed in the process. Value remains in the fulfillment of organic impulse. The impulses rejected by criticism were already fated to be frustrated by contradictory impulses or natural impediments. Desire is the mainspring of all value-seeking endeavor and should be even more profound and voluminous after rational criticism. Santayana admired the sheer force of Hebraic zeal as much as the intellectual harmony of the Greeks and believed that both had to merge in a rational utilitarianism. One effect of his emphasis upon harmonized impulse was a willing acceptance of moral relativity. Each individual must harmonize his own impulses, discipline his own preferences, and in his dealings with other men take into consideration their varying preferences. Thus, self-knowledge is the launching platform of moral judgment.

As he grew older, Santayana steadily lost faith in the possibilities of more than a strictly individual moral science. The emphasis upon relativity increased. In the *Life of Reason* he analyzed the constant elements in man—the old idea of human nature. He found no essential human type and no sure area of constancy. There seemed no basis for ethical universals or for any final or supreme good that was applicable to all men. A fully rational ethic had to be restricted to the harmonized impulses of a single person. But this limited context did not preclude rationality and perhaps made it even more imperative for the individual. Beyond this, he believed common experiences, traditions, institutions, and bodily structure provided a large area for rational agreement, and thus for cooperative ideals, although less than wholly rational or comprehensive ones. But even this could form the basis for a rational polity. Within a nation or race, the steady accumulation of knowledge and art might broaden the area of common experience and thus increase public rationality. Progress would be possible at the corporate as well as at the individual level. Such progress seemed a fact in the past. He tried to help it along by indicting the evident stupidities still present. But political and personal changes slowly eroded his optimism. Whatever the logical possibility, he lost most hope for a rational politics. At the same time, he slowly retreated from his personal desire to harmonize impulses, to be a rational animal; he replaced it with a desire to escape animal impulse, to sublimate desire, and to live for the few undisturbed moments of spiritual peace.

In all his moral philosophy, Santayana stressed the natural status of value and, derivatively, of all human ideals. He hated popular notions that ideals rested in some indeterminant realm of fancy, separated from ordinary experience and art. A rational ideal, a personal conception of good, is meaningless outside a natural context. But with a classical bent, he always stressed the supreme good, the authoritative ethical ideal. Hating romanticism, he wanted this ideal to possess order and harmony. With the pragmatists, he desired wholehearted commitment to it, even though it had to be founded upon accidental impulse, deceptive memory, incomplete self-knowledge, and inadequate understanding. Although he believed that an ethical ideal could, in form, be consistent and harmonious, he knew that the moral life could never attain this perfection. In fact, most rational morality, in terms of results, was supported by irrational traditions and codes, just as consistent ideals often proved inadequate to the flux of events. Morality, after all, is habit, whereas moral philosophy is imaginative construction. But in such construction lies all rational change or adaptation. Even when unrealizable, ideals have a value in themselves. Early in life, Santayana exalted rational ideals and tended to minimize the circumstances upon which the practical fruit of such ideals depended. Not that he ever completely severed the ideal from its practical locus, but he surely emphasized the formal aspect at the expense of the instrumental. The immediate and intrinsic reward was in the ideal appreciated, not in the frustrating, anxiety-ridden effort to embody it in practice; in its immediate esthetic value, not its artistic guidelines.

In addition to a rational ethics, Santayana distinguished two other types of morality. The earliest, the prerational, remained at the level of emotion, sheer impulse, and chance reflection. It was nonrational and haphazard, with no developed art and limited knowledge. Yet, by accident, it might lead to sustained value. Even the irrational fanatic may behave rationally in some situation, but by chance and not by art. Prerational morality may be sacrificial, even sublime, but yet blind. Or it may take the form of open sensuality, pursuing free and concrete but momentary values. Innocent sensuality appealed to Santayana. Eventually it reaped its harvest of unforeseen tortures and death but, carefree and without agony, it liberated for the moment and thus bestowed its appropriate good. Like Santayana, children of Puritan New England often envied voluptuousness but from afar or, also like him, contrasted it with the commercial and worldly types of pseudo-rational morality so evident in America. In them, rationality applied only to instrumentalities, not to ends. Worldly babels might endure longer than the fleshpots of the profligate, but, enslaving and hypocritical, they were equally vain and much less natural and spontaneous. Santayana always preferred Don Juans to Babbits.

At the other end of life, after an excess of experience and suffering, a postrational morality usually developed, particularly at the end of an epoch and in a declining civilization. Postrational morality is full of disillusion, pessimism, and disenchantment. It rejects a life of reason in the world and instead seeks a redemptive escape. Founded in despair and renunciation, it often falls into narrow, one-sided, escapist nostrums, such as Epicureanism or early Christianity. It struggles not to harmonize and realize human passions, but to suppress them, possibly in some mystical insight, or in prayer and detachment and peace. Santayana's own one-sided emphasis upon spiritual peace was a perfect, self-conscious example of a postrational morality, his own form of desperate wager made at low fortune. In early Christianity Santayana found the archetypal example of this attitude and found in it a beautiful and one-sided achievement. It sponsored ideals that, when adopted with prerational passion by German barbarians, had some civilizing force, at least until the Protestants converted renunciation into worldliness. In Latin Christianity the postrational ethics remained as a thinly veiled, poetic conceptualization under which a natural and rational morality was reinstated and recommended to (or forced upon) the nonrational majority of mankind.

The foregoing seemed a consistent and, to many Americans at least, a commendably reasonable conception of value and morality. John Dewey, in many ways, took his departure from Santayana's *Life of Reason*. But a devil seemed to lurk behind the scenes. Over and over again throughout his life, Santayana tried to prove the devil a false caricature of critics, but he could never successfully dispose of the problem. Here again, the epiphenomenal conception of consciousness was the culprit, or possibly the glory of Santayana's axiology. It must again be elaborated, or his practical commitments, his views on politics, art, and religion, will not make sense.

Since a nonexistent essence is the unit of consciousness, all value has to involve the intuition of essences. Some nonexistent essences (that is, some feelings, images, perceptions) are pleasing and some are not, according to the animal impulses involved. Thus, what makes some essences enjoyable is animal and material, but the essence, the real value, is immaterial. Value is created by mechanistic process, but transcends that process. Matter and essence are both involved. In all conscious experience, motor activities are present (his behaviorism again). Cerebral events underwrite all ideas. The control lies beneath. There are not two parallel streams, but only one stream. But it, "in slipping over certain rocks or dropping into certain pools, begins to babble a wanton music, not thereby losing any part of its substance nor changing its course. . . ." [*Realms of Being,* I (*The Realm of Essence*), Combined Edition (New York, 1942), p. 134.]

The startling result of this position is that moral standards, ethical ideals, have no controlling effect upon conduct, but only upon appreciation. Morality is properly concerned with the modification of human affections, not with the control of physical events. In a human sense, consciousness is most practical, for it alone brings a type of consummation or fulfillment to events. It even judges the world. It is a rare and precious gift when it brings beauty. It can be a curse when it (like most Bostonians) finds only what calls forth censure. Consciousness even prophesies future events but does not produce them. If events fulfill our dearest plans, we feel freedom and joy, but nonetheless remain playthings of nature. If our fondest ideals never come true, we are simply not at home in this world. We can either learn to love it, suffer it in helpless futility, or escape from it.

By severing consciousness from the human psyche and its complex cerebral operations, Santayana gave it a type of freedom which he felt could not exist if it were an integral part of the physical organism. Nonetheless, the psyche always tries to draw the spirit into its own orbit and infuse it with its own preferences. When the psyche is not frustrated, this captivity is innocuous. But when thwarted, the spirit suffers a type of hell. The spirit can never be completely free of psychic impulses and thus can never be completely free of care and anxiety. Santayana wanted to minimize the dependence.

Santayana carefully analyzed the idea of freedom, and with a great deal more rigor than he defined such loaded terms as consciousness and thinking. He believed in a type of human freedom and always rejected critic's complaints that he was a fatalist. The human organism is a trope, a highly organized and self-perpetuating focus of energy. Consciousness does nothing, but men have changed the world. They have been agents in massive transformations, some of which flowed directly from their own impulses. When men act consistently with their own natural impulses, and when these impulses are registered as conscious preferences, they experience a type of freedom, or what he called moral freedom. But this sense of freedom depends on a happy correspondence between human ideals and natural necessities. It also requires a type of natural piety, or the ability to give full and gracious consent to the inscrutable power behind all events (Edwards, Spinoza). Man is then in harmony with nature; its laws are also his laws. He may even, like the sensualist, be an abject slave to animal needs, yet have the joy and zest of perfect freedom. Although incapable of changing the world, a free person feels no repression, for he is an active part of it, identifies with it, loves it, and shares in its glory. He is a participating citizen and gladly casts his small but necessary vote. When this view becomes a bit forced, as it so often was in Puritanism, he even loved what was evil in the world and willed his own potential damnation. It takes brave men to endure such a freedom and not yearn for more. The yearning for more freedom, even absolute freedom (a God-wish), lay in back of such irrational and impossible ideas as free will. It also lay in back of the idealist concern to turn the cosmos into a creation of human reason or a support and ally of his provincial preferences.

Moral freedom involves a sense of moral responsibility. Morally free men take responsibility for their chosen actions and for the world. Conscious acts are not blind compulsions, even though they are similar in material effect. Here Santayana agreed completely with Jonathan Edwards' concept of predestination and with Emerson's similar concept of fate, both of which affirmed responsibility and denied fatalism. Again, consciousness is the difference. It allows wisdom in choice, in affection. In figurative terms, it allows men to love God and gladly suffer his commandments. By grace, some do love and are free. This is a fact. For those happy few, their acts fulfill their wishes, for their wishes are consistent with the whole, in which destiny resides. If future events are by them preconceived and desired, they may even enter the kingdom of heaven. But their desires do not build it, or even get the building under way. Their bodies do it and were materially disposed to do it even before they willed it. Thus, responsibility is a product of conscious commitment, or a feeling or attitude that accompanies it. We take responsibility and also ascribe it to others. Yet, on close analysis, it dissipates into the vast whole, which contains all existence. As Edwards conceded, God alone is responsible, for in Him resides all power. But this God, to Santayana, was unconscious, impersonal matter. He could love Edwards' spiritual deity, but had to deny any material efficacy to pure spirit. God as a spirit would have to be a moral outcome of material processes, and in no way a cause of them, or responsible for them. To love this God would be to love pure spirit or consciousness, not existence, to love a product of nature, not nature itself.

This path Santayana explored. He could not be satisfied with moral freedom; he could not love the world, and as time passed he loved less and less. Gracious consent to an unlovely existence seemed demeaning and barbaric. This was his ultimate but uneasy criticism of Puritanism. They had no right to love the world and the God that created or sustained such a world. Surely behind it was some vast confusion or some hopeless naïveté. But he loved his own ideals and, with increasing detachment, all the nonexistent themes of consciousness. In the realm of essence, of pure quality, there was beauty and peace. He could not, as an embodied spirit, totally divest himself of some care and concern for his bodily fortunes in the world. But he tried to subordinate this worldly care and to escape it as much as possible. Unlike the Puritan, who gladly accepted responsibility, who willingly identified his creative activity with that of God (or Nature), and found his joy and peace along the way, Santayana separated existence, the source of all passion, care, and concern, from essence, the content of all joy and consummation. In this cleavage, he naturally turned toward consummation, toward the appreciative side of life. In doing this, he denied responsibility for his bodily self and for the world. He took the path that many people always thought the Puritan should take—he left responsibility to God. Thus morality could assume its proper stance—appreciative enjoyment and spiritual peace, not worldly judgment and moral censure. When the cares of the psyche are transcended, the world loses all its appeal, and necessary bodily needs and animal doings are satisfied and performed without passion or significance. Moral freedom is replaced by spiritual freedom, in which consciousness is no longer burdened by anything in the world and is free to rejoice in the eternal qualities of Truth and pure essence. The mystic replaces the Puritan.

Thus, epiphenomenalism was Santayana's entree into a morality of nonresponsibility and escape. Here, rather than in the technicalities of epistemology, it justified a complete break with the Puritan-pragmatist tradition. John Dewey tried to conjoin, in a more rigorous naturalism, the twin themes of Santayana—existence and essence. He conceived of nature in such a way as to encompass both material processes and experiential consummation. In order to do this, he refused to intellectualize value in the same way as Santayana. He believed that existential quality or feeling was not only prior to, but essentially different from thinking, whereas Santayana used his concept of essence to conjoin both passive feeling and what most people assume to be constructive reflection. Since both are conscious, both share the noncausal role assigned to intuition, and both are equally reduced to an impotent, phenomenological level. Dewey, fully as much as Santayana, stressed the esthetic nature of feeling, but unlike Santayana did not reduce thinking to an esthetic level. But in making thought instrumental, Dewey did not imply any doctrine of free will or suggest that the qualitative side of ideas had causal efficacy. In cognitive thinking, Dewey acknowledged an appreciative side, a possible quality of pleasure that could accompany the most instrumental science. But more pertinent to this one type of thought were the physical processes being redirected by a quite natural and quite bodily function.

The Puritan and pragmatist refused to sever the arena of action from the site of experienced pleasure. Acting and enjoying are formally distinguishable, but in fact are always conjoined. Esthetics (appreciation) and art (instrumentality) cannot be cleaved; if they are, man becomes divided and tormented within. Nature is one. God (existence) is the sustaining father and, in at least some of his random moods, also the beloved comforter. Why separate the two?

The crux of the difference lay in Santayana's rejection of the world and of worldly care. No logic, no philosophic formulas, caused his

despair, and none could suffice to "cure" it. But the divergence in doctrine lay more in problems of definition. Santayana was surely quite
correct in denying physical existence to the experienced quality of
thought. In this sense, ideas do not exist, and they do not have causal
efficacy. But is it proper to say a quality does not exist without assuming
that every quality is a quality of something that does exist? Santayana
insistently pointed to the physical source of spirit, but he just as insistently argued that spirit was ontologically distinct from existence and,
so to speak, could forget (not deny) its parentage. This clever dualism
justified Santayana's spirituality, but mystified even his most sympathetic critics. How could it be that nature, the source of value, is not
valued? Is it sophistry to talk of value as being alone valued and to say
no more? Santayana was too sophisticated and too much a radical
empiricist to accept a true materialism. Besides, he seemed to feel that
any materialism or naturalism threatened the legitimacy of experienced
value. The locus of value had to transcend ordinary existence and
partake of another realm which, again because of his rigorous honesty,
could not really exist except as a logical concept. He could find no way
of bridging his two worlds, of merging essence and existence. His single
substance, matter, could not include mind. He never tried what he
believed impossible—a resurrection of scholasticism, of a substantial
duality of matter and essence that could be related in such a way as to
do no injustice to either.

Santayana was afraid of Dewey's instrumentalism. To make consciousness, or any form of consciousness, in any way efficacious was to
plunge it into nature and turn it into another material cause. Would this
not destroy its real function as consummation, as the end and reward of
causal forces? He feared that placing mind in the middle of working
nature would mean a capitulation to a narrow positivism, and thus a
denial of value, or to a type of idealistic magic, in which ideas create the
world. Consciousness as a cause would be without value, that is, without
any intrinsic reward. It might contribute to some future value, to a good
experience. But what would be the nature of such experience? Exactly
the type of qualitative consummation that Santayana defined as consciousness. Obviously, one cannot have it both ways. Instrumental
thought would not be worth having, and if all thought were instrumental, life would not be worth living. Since consciousness involves only
intuited qualities, it cannot be efficacious. Since all thought is a form of

consciousness, thought cannot possibly be efficacious. So painted into a corner, Santayana had to struggle to maintain his own distinctions. He had, for example, to distinguish language behavior from consciousness, and he defined it as a physical appending of signs to intuited ideas. Perhaps fortunately for his literary reputation, he never tried to maintain his epiphenomenal distinctions in talking of art or politics. Then loose terms like rationality were used in conventional ways to designate what he separated into quality and material processes. Then he sounded like a humanist with a soft spot for mystics and escapists.

POLITICS AND ART

In his early career, Santayana tried to measure human progress, assess its prospects, and help attain a republic of virtue, beauty, and truth. He wanted mankind to break free from the false values, dogmatic myths, genteel clichés, egotistic presumptions, and pervasive vulgarities of nineteenth-century liberalism. He not only desired to be a rational animal but to live in a rational society. Often he identified his primary concern as moral and political, correctly seeing the identity of the two. He never achieved very much, and at times renounced the whole endeavor. Then, in spiritual detachment, he stopped criticizing the world and laughed at its insanity. His spiritual retreat was an almost desperate attempt to attain salvation beyond a world that seemed headed for disaster. As an old man he assumed the imminent destruction of Western civilization under an eruption of brute humanity, of democratic majorities, armed with the material equipment of modern industry, but already dehumanized by it. All the polite adornments and luxuries and all the aristocratic beauty would be crushed. There would be no honor, no sense of right, no chivalry, and no cultivated taste. Politics, in possibility a rational tool, would become the coercive arm of a barbaric proletariat.

Santayana saw all government as resting at least in part on custom or group habits. These habits vary immensely and are more sacred and unbreakable than any laws. In a primitive tribe, a chief may exercise the only political control and require few laws. Except for aliens and a few poorly indoctrinated rebels, he scarcely exercises coercive authority. Here government is tied to the generative order and easily reflects it. The minimal political institutions register group customs, apply and enforce them, and adjudicate debatable situations. But in the modern state, where perfect homogeneity is lacking, governments have to compromise contending interests and use a great deal more overt coercion, often to suppress dearly held group customs. In this case, government is force or the threat of force. Abolish this threat and only moral philosophy remains. Government is a modified type of war; a coercion that works without extensive bloodshed. Each government maintains a perpetual campaign in its own country against factions and unacceptable habits. Thus, government involves a militant order and some degree of suppression. In a sense it is an evil, but necessary to provide some freedom from strife and from enslaving practical needs. It is rationally justified when it secures a degree of cooperative action otherwise impossible. However broad the power it exercises, a poor government is better than no government, for then war would be constant and bloody and life would be insecure and brief. In this analysis, Santayana was close to Hobbes and Spinoza.

In politics as in morality, Santayana argued for a necessary relativity, only to follow this by making his own preferences at times sound like the voice of God. Since customs, climates, and races vary immensely, governments must take varied forms and assume varied functions. The best government will always serve the needs of the largest possible number of citizens. In practice, governments too often establish the irrational prejudices of a majority and force them on everyone. He believed that the rational authority for government was factual—the actual and varying needs or desires of people, and the conditioning circumstances. The old Christian idea of respect for God's will adequately symbolized this mandate, for God was conceived as the power governing circumstances and as the source of all virtue and joy in the soul. To replace the authority of fact with the authority of conscience was to moralize blind will and, quite often, to ignore circumstance. Conscience is simply the end product of social coercion and pressure, by which a child has been forced to absorb the beliefs of others. These may ill represent his real interests, although he feels they are his interests. Thus a good government, as Santayana conceived it, might go against the beliefs and customs of a majority and do it in their interest. Coercion, in this case, would enhance the true interests of the subject.

An aristocrat and paternalist, Santayana praised good government, not popular government. He argued either for patient subjection to existing institutions or, at most, patient reform. It did not matter if government were maintained by a few able men or by a single monarch; as long as it was beneficent and rational, it truly represented, not the person, but the interest of the person. The monarch who divines the true needs of a nation is the most rightful authority. Jealousy, in such a case, is irrational and blind. Why not let a good man rule? He is the instrument of our own purposes.

Santayana would not admit the right of equal participation. He always saw government as an external force. Always authority in the state is unequally distributed, as are talents among men. All particular stations are in part accidental. Only an egotist or snob is bothered by not sharing in one function, or by not having the same privileges as other men. Santayana appreciated rather than deplored diverse classes and orders and saw no injustice in forcing exceptional and superior individuals to share the station of their class or race. He saw an ultimate injustice in denying honor and dignity to all tasks and all classes. Very interested in freedom, he simply believed that the most important freedom was not the freedom to govern but was a product of good government. He did not believe the people the best protectors of their freedom, unless, as in England and America, they were indoctrinated with authoritative constitutional principles and with habits of political tolerance and compromise. In cases where governments exercised broad authority (totalitarianism) he preferred the grandeur of Catholic Spain to the colorless conformity of socialism. He found much that was admirable in Italian fascism, despite its evil and vulgar architect. Italy needed a dictator, not a reckless adventurer. For more equalitarian societies, he preferred a timocracy, without hereditary classes but in which an aristocracy of talented men, drawn from the people, actually ruled, and in which public zeal and patriotism created an organic state, without strife and jealousy, and with a shared glory in the corporate achievement. His model reflected the organic emphasis of medieval theory or of the early Puritan commonwealth, and the natural aristocracy of Jefferson's America. In the post-World War II years he proposed without careful elaboration a world economic government, with almost unlimited powers in the area of production and distribution, but with all cultural and religious enterprises left to many local, voluntary societies or churches.

Santayana was contemptuous of most reformers. Most rebels are ignorant and seek not a rational society but some vacant and anarchical liberty or some utopian chimera. Although a constant critic of virtually every modern political order, Santayana still believed there was more reason in old and corrupt institutions than in the slogans of demagogic revolutionaries. Blind force inspired by hate and petty jealously could destroy all good as well as all evil. Reform in the twentieth century seemed fated to fall into the hands of the proletariat, the stupid, ill-bred, pathetic products of a dehumanizing commercialism and liberalism. In communism, the leaders of the poverty-hating masses militantly condemn most human institutions and affections. Communism, which Santayana often identified as the wave of the future, had a moral inspiration—brotherly, pacificist, ascetic, even saintly. But in fact it became ferociously egotistic, led by a small group of conspirators hardly above bandits and conquerors, and devoted to a fantasy future that would somehow survive a present apocalypse of inhumanity and cruelty.

The ignorant dissident never realizes that his disaffection is most likely not a fault of existing institutions but of an accidental and whimsical newness in his demands. The reformer thus blames the world for his own incapacity to live in it. Santayana cherished the freedom to be constant, to maintain and preserve, even more than the freedom to innovate. Twentieth-century innovators usually lacked intellectual discipline, possessed bad manners, had no humor, and tended to become dictatorial and tyrannical. Truly enlightened reformers hated fanaticism and revolution, understood the real needs of people, correctly estimated possibilities and prospects, recognized the relativity of political forms, and comprehended the relative rightness and justification of traditional institutions. As he grew older, Santayana joined Emerson in pointing out that no real reform is possible when individuals are enslaved. Conversely, happiness and perfection are possible for the soul in any society and in any station. All kingdoms of the world are ephemeral, but the kingdom of the spirit is eternal.

From his earliest writings, Santayana was an avowed enemy of democracy and liberalism, although he was often a bit ambiguous in defining either. Often, he used the term democracy to mean a rampant equalitarianism and socialism, with a government directly responsible to majority will. In a simple pastoral society, as on the American frontier, this type of government was natural and inevitable. But in a modern industrial society such equalitarian democracy would level all men down to the crude level of the laborer (the slave of modernity) and abolish all emulative centers of culture and deserved privilege. This would cut off the source of beauty and intelligence and leave only a dull vulgarity. In government this would promote a blind majoritarian tyranny and eventually enthrone a vulgarian as a representative dictator.

But political democracy, particularly in England and America, was not equalitarian, and thus was admired by Santayana. In England a social aristocracy leavened the democratic forms. The mass franchise, a late and artificial product, was reared onto vast, inherited, self-perpetuating institutions. The major decisions had long since been made, or were still made by a few. The suspicions and jealousies of the people were quieted by allowing them a vote that, at best, modified administrative policies, allowed minor amendments, or expressed confidence in a party leader. Democracy was a tool, an expedient, not a political philosophy. The political parties served the same vested interests, and by electoral games secured one-party results without compulsion. Men of true eminence continued to rule, usually in the public interest. In America the same traditional institutions provided restraints and safely guided electoral processes. But here, with fewer aristocratic traditions, politicians were usually more vulgar and followed public feeling all too well. Popular pressures for conformity were greater. Politicians too often used propaganda to stimulate innocent greed or to enlist enthusiasm for impossible promises.

Liberalism sponsored the idea of political and religious liberty. It paralleled the spread of Protestantism. Naturally, Santayana emphasized all its covert weaknesses. To him, liberalism was never as freeing as it claimed. It opened a seemingly broad margin of intellectual freedom even as it supported economic institutions which narrowed the margin of action. When an economy is organized on a capitalist basis, and abetted by compulsory education, severe laws against libel and slander, rigid laws governing personal morality, and a practical science, it inevitably creates an official mentality and morality. American authorities arrest people for vagrancy or idleness, not for religious blasphemy, and somehow consider it a vast improvement. Sanctified private property means a sanctified set of corresponding virtues. In this context, intellectual freedom is a chimera. What does it mean to leave thought and religion free? Is not an official, largely irrelevant, genteel type of

freedom about as meaningless as a woman's freedom to change her
dress styles? True intellectual freedom means, first of all, the freedom to
rearrange material conditions, not to manipulate idle concepts. Thus,
liberalism, instead of freeing man, established the most militant domination in history. The private and poetic soul was only free to make his
way through the uncoercive space of vacant responsibility, drinking in its
wind. In America this vaunted freedom moved toward a universal
hygienic hypnotization by behavioral manipulators and advertisers, none
of which had the slightest conception of any worthy end for all the
manipulation. Even in its compulsory good will, social life was artificial
and compulsory.

As long as he remained an active citizen of the world, decrying its
manifold sins, Santayana never relented in his merciless condemnation
of the commercial spirit and of modern industrialism. Here he was as
insistent as Emerson. He spoke with deep feeling, as if the dirty factories
of New England forever haunted his dreams. In his last major book he
despairingly recited the end of it all: a nightmare of machines, a plague
of omnipresent advertisements, a pathetic proletarian quicksand beneath
the feet of wealth, and a new serfdom of hierarchical and dehumanizing
occupations. And there was no end, seemingly, to further expansion.
There seemed to be no prospect of labor again merging with self-
rewarding arts or of imagination breaking loose from the machine and
cultivating liberal arts and moral freedom. In the past all ultimate
objects of life were close at hand, visible and obvious, but now man was
"lost in a spider's web of machinery, material and social, and don't
know what we are living for or how we mange to live at all." [To
George Sturgis, Oct. 4, 1931, *Letters,* p. 260.] If business could mean
once again the exercise of a needful profession, with moderate compensation, Santayana applauded it. But in a producer's economy, it meant a
type of private adventuring without any conception of any social good
beyond more and more consumption.

There were no panaceas. Santayana hardly expected a return to the
guild system. More likely, the proletariat would soon rise up and begin
such awful and hopeless convulsions that it was depressing even to
contemplate the future. The very fact of a proletariat was the overarching condemnation of a commercial age, but a fact concealed by
remaining echoes of effete culture, by the narcotic effect of an excessively spiritual and transcendental religion, and by the empty forms of

political democracy. He pitied, but did not identify with, the proletariat any more than with the equally repugnant capitalist. He suffered a moral twinge in having his own inheritance invested and managed by his capitalist half-brother, George Sturgis. His largest constructive role was to expose the artificiality and pretense in what purported to be high culture. At least the effete superstructure could be revealed in all its superficiality.

Santayana celebrated art as much as any other American philosopher. In esthetics his contribution matched that of Dewey. His interest was lifelong, including his first book, a major share of his *Life of Reason,* several critical works, and in a modified sense his *Realms of Being.* He was a significant poet, a minor novelist and dramatist, and in all his writing a literary artist. Yet, almost every one of his ideas on art were in conflict with prevalent critical fads. He hated a dying romanticism, rejected realism in its heyday, and, with every passion he could command, condemned all the types of expressionism, estheticism, symbolism, and irrationalism that often went under the blanket term, modern art. He shared his classical preferences with the new humanists, but came closest to the ideas of Emerson and John Dewey. In fact, in most ways, Santayana was part of the Puritan (and Platonic) tradition in esthetics, although his later contemplative stance represented a retreat from the Puritan and from his own earlier emphasis upon the necessary tie between art and all other moral concerns.

Santayana clearly distinguished art and esthetics, yet usually restricted art to activities with esthetic content. By art, in its broadest sense, he meant either an activity, a type of purposeful or skillful doing, or else the developed habits or techniques that underlay such activity. But generally he used the term to denote such a deliberate and intelligent transformation of materials as to provide some conscious enjoyment or, in other terms, some beauty. He paid obeisance to his epiphenomenalism by insisting that preconscious and spontaneous action preceded art. Man's first creations were automatic and blind. But some of these rose to the level of consciousness and assumed a rational, deliberate aspect, at which point they became artful and were treasured for the beauty they bestowed. For this reason, Santayana always stressed the playful and spontaneous background of art and its experimental nature. Ideas and images are not sought; they come. The conscious side of art, like all spiritual things, is not a product of reason, but part of reason and a gratuitous product of matter and of external forces. It is the moral (consummatory) aspect of well-adjusted and fruitful manipulative habits, which provide man with a sense of pleasure and liberation. Thus, art is in all ways natural; it is tied intimately to the structure of things (to their plasticity) and to the bodily structure of the artist (to his skills). By his stress upon the intrinsic joy of art, Santayana excluded any activity that was forced and slavish or without self-rewarding goals. But by his insistence upon its rational, deliberate aspect, he also demanded that it be more than spontaneous expression. Artful habits begin in spontaneous play, but they reach the level of art only when they are maintained and developed with consciousness of purpose and function.

Always ready to glorify art, Santayana was jealous to refute any esoteric or romantic conception of the artist. Every man except an unrelieved slave is an artist, although some remain very poor ones. He ridiculed unmercifully the esthetic drivel of modern critics and the pretentious nonsense of some professed artists. The best artists never profess and never have the time or interest to absorb all the idle chatter about art. The artist, whatever his field, is an artisan or craftsman, a professional, usually working with tools and skills that have developed over the centuries, perhaps in his own family. The material, the skillful habit, and the ideas totally encompass art. The good artist is sensitive and imaginative, just as is the good craftsman. Shakespeare was a working playwright. As Santayana concluded in *Reason in Art*, "an artist's business is not really to cut fantastical capers or be licensed to play the fool. His business is simply that of every keen soul to build well when it builds, and to speak well when it speaks, giving practice everywhere the greatest possible affinity to the situation, the most delicate adjustment to every faculty it effects." [*Life of Reason*, IV, 228.]

Likewise, Santayana made short shrift of any convoluted or obscure talk about the purpose of art. Simply stated, its purpose is to make men happy. In its intrinsic rewards, artistic activity brings beauty, peace, and consolation to life. At best, it may bring man to a sense of perfect unity and harmony, to enlarged vision, intense contemplation, and even virtual ecstasy. Art may add beauty even to painful experiences, but must not itself increase the pain. It cannot abolish pain, as illustrated in tragic drama, but it may enable the participant to endure extreme suffering and even, in a sense, reap happiness from the experience. But whatever the subject matter, an artist is obligated to enhance life and should be held to this responsibility. He is in no way exceptional or exempt from moral criticism. As Emerson also insisted, the artist must bring a kindly voice, inspire cheer, and increase vision. In art, man is free in the best sense save possibly in pure contemplation. He is master of his material, unlike the servile industrial worker. He is not cowed by an ugly world, for he is successfully remaking it. He is not the disinterested observer of science, only getting ready to live, but is in the most vital way already living. In art, man becomes one with nature. Here Santayana, the rational animal, the citizen of the world, found the pinnacle of human experience. Later, he felt that he had to transcend the world in a type of esthetic reverie not clearly connected with art.

In contrast to art, esthetics concerns beauty and the experience of beauty, whether in nature, in contemplation, or in objects of human art. Esthetics was the most unifying theme in Santayana's life, for it equally embraced his rational and spiritual phases. In the broadest sense, Santayana identified esthetics and value. All experienced value is rooted in the immediate, in the sheer pleasure of possession. But he believed it was possible to discriminate beauty as one type of value and thus isolate it from other types. The purpose of his first book, *Sense of Beauty,* was to discriminate psychologically the special qualities experienced as beautiful. In a somewhat arbitrary analysis, he found that in the case of identified beauty the quality was objectified, unlike other pleasant experiences which were always internalized or subjectified. Thus, the sunset is beautiful, but good food only pleases us. The attribution was psychological only. Later, with his doctrine of essences, he made clear that all beauty is in the eternal quality of an intuited essence, which only by animal faith is projected outward as a description of existence.

In *Sense of Beauty* Santayana analyzed the material foundations of esthetic experience, with particular emphasis upon sex and sexual sublimation as a source of sensitivity. In beauty itself he found three elements: sensuous pleasure, form, and expression. Sensibility was fundamental but primitive. Form, a difficult concept, seemed most important to Santayana, although more intellectually demanding than the other two elements. He particularly deplored vague and indeterminant forms, often rich in suggestivity, with a sense of profundity, but always deficient in art. Expression, especially pertinent in literary arts, transfers beauty from sensuality or form to associated objects. Without sensual or formal appeal, a novel may nonetheless evoke all types of beautiful images.

In exact agreement with Emerson and Dewey, Santayana refused to sanction any qualitative distinction between fine and useful arts. He hated an ascetic suppression of beauty, but not so much as he hated the empty estheticism that seemed to infect all the modern fine arts. Harmony was being sought in appearances; life was lost in imaginary passions and histrionic woes. Lovely dreams, excellent in themselves, left the world no less a chaos. Fine arts have a certain dignity if they express or enhance moral and political greatness. They are butter to man's daily bread; a temple of beauty in his midst. But this is only to say that fine arts should indeed be practical and functional, which Santayana desired. Without this moral demand, artists become abstracted triflers, "and the public is divided into two camps: the dilettanti, who dote on the artist's affectations, and the rabble, who pay him to grow coarse." [*Life of Reason,* IV, 217.] A few naïve souls, particularly in capitalist countries, make art a byplay to the sober business of life, and the more functionless and gratuitous the byplay the more those who indulge it think they are idealists. These genteel souls feel that "they are champions of what is most precious in the world, as a sentimental lady might fancy herself a lover of flowers when she pressed them in a book instead of planting their seeds in the garden." [*Ibid.,* p. 226.] This madness degrades art and leads to an atmosphere of dependence and charlatanry. Soon religion, philosophy, and manners are infected with a false esthetic spirit and are reduced to voluntary hallucinations or petty flattery. Then, that "beauty which should have been an inevitable smile on the face of society, an overflow of genuine happiness and power, has to be imported, stimulated artificially, and applied from without; so that art becomes a sickly ornament for an ugly existence." [*Ibid.,* pp. 217–18.] Estheticism alienates man from the world and does not create a better one. It is not a joy added to labor to escape slavery, but an interruption of necessary labor. Emerson called it decadence. Dewey called it a side show.

Santayana equally ridiculed the cultivation of dead art and the frivolity of modern art. He hated museums and all esthetic pretense. In all great ages of art, no one talked about it, or collected it, or built careers around their meaningless verbosity. Then the arts were skilled ways of making pots, clothes, houses, of speaking, praying, and dancing.

When some began to collect paintings and statues—almost as an aim in itself—it was an omen of the end. Works of art became curiosities and prizes, detachable and detached. Soon the experts came with their knowing smiles, anecdotes about artists, and their elaborate comparisons. Artists became adored, superior persons, contemptuous of a stupid public and of traditional craftsmen. They struggled for originality (rarely important in esthetics), called themselves creative, and kept themselves before the public by extravagant self-praise and by outraging good sense in their lives and work. Art became bohemian, irresponsible, and sloppy, while democratic societies took self-adulating artists seriously and gave them free reign even as they ignored the pervasive ugliness of their environment and lost all respect for the responsible artisans who might have remedied it.

The connoisseurs of past and legitimate art were no better. Santayana pitied a fellow expatriate and frequent companion, Bernard Berenson. Lost in his concern with who painted best, he saw no real harmonies. His flame was kept going by a forced draft, by social and intellectual ambition, or by professional pedantry. He turned from the evening sky to see, by electric lights, how Veronese painted it. In the same way, in an age when most good art was dead and interred, and all the rest was frivolous and detached, almost everything connected with what is called "art" was a pose.

Not that Santayana condemned all criticism. He was a critic himself. To him, criticism was simply moral judgment; it was a branch of moral philosophy. What is a work of art good for? If fine art is involved, one's judgment may be quite restricted, and in essence one may ask, "does it please me?" This has nothing to do with either the artist or what he intended. It has a great deal to do with what he achieved and with the varied preferences and developed tastes of the critic. While demanding discipline in skill and reason in purpose, Santayana precluded a rigid science of criticism. Men of acquired taste could set up standards of execution and judge accordingly. Above this limited esthetic judgment, there was always the other interests of a society, and the need to harmonize all of those with the arts. Santayana sympathized with a type of social discipline exerted upon an artist, although he preferred the discipline to take the form of public disapproval rather than legal censorship. The artist, like everyone else, must accept his broader political and religious responsibilities and govern his artistry accordingly.

Often the critics of existing art, such as Plato, were simply asking for nobler art, for art on a broader scale, such as a beautiful social order or a harmonious and beautiful life. In the same sense, the moralistic Puritan saw extant art as frivolous, divisive, and scandalous. In like manner, Santayana condemned almost all modern art.

As a young man, Santayana lived in an atmosphere in which poetry was serious. He rejoiced in the tradition of Lucretius, Dante, Goethe, and even Emerson, all philosophical if not inspirational. As he later lamented, poetry was then written as a memorial, a revelation of what the soul had lived in her better days. Like Matthew Arnold's, much of Santayana's poetry dwelt on religious themes, and on the passing of the old faith. In technique, Santayana had striven for discipline, eloquence, and classic form. In content, he had sought wisdom. But poetry, like other fine arts, was moving away from Santayana's conception, and he believed for the worse. Standards, order, reason seemed to evaporate. Art went the way of Christendom during the Reformation and became equally barbaric. Artists, like truant children, ran away to play and forgot all ideal passion, all moral intent. Like revolutionaries everywhere, they were mighty in independence, vile in manners, feeble in execution, foolish in their lives, and without a total vision or the capacity for sane and steady idealization. Like one of his prime examples, William Faulkner, they were lazy and self-indulgent, leaving assorted droppings of the mind. Santayana insisted that he was no psychological dog and required his "dog biscuit to be cleanly set down for me in a decent plate with proper ceremony." [To Robert Shaw Barlow, June 22, 1936, *Letters,* p. 313.] But in the end, those who played with images would lose their labors and, "pregnant as they feel themselves to be with new and wonderful universes, they cannot humanize the one in which they live and rather banish themselves from it by their persistent egotism and irrelevance." [*Life of Reason,* IV, 86.]

He suggested that the person who "would emancipate art from discipline and reason is trying to elude rationality, not merely in art, but in all existence." The way such "foolishness had of revenging itself" was to excommunicate the world. [*Ibid.,* pp. 3–4.] Fine art, itself without any but immediate utility, should at least be a rehearsal of rational living, a forecast of ideal possibilities. Anything less, particularly an indulgent art for art's sake, was an idolatry, an irresponsible luxury, which a militant state might well suppress in behalf of an ideal social order. But such art,

in the modern world, was never taken so seriously. Men of vital importance could pass it over with a smile, thereby proving its insignificance.
In a rational society, with a real artistic tradition, questions of art would
be the most urgent of issues, even as art was the most important of
blessings.

Santayana's constant goal was the reintegration of art with other
vital concerns of life. His message here was even more eloquently
expressed than by Emerson and Dewey: "If the passions arose in sea-
son, if perception fed only on those things which action should be
adjusted to, turning them, while action proceeded, into the substance of
ideas—then all conduct would be voluntary and enlightened, all speculation would be practical, all perceptions beautiful, and all operations
arts." [*Ibid.*, p. 208.] Then no man would be a natural slave, confined
to the purely instrumental, without joy or satisfaction. The economic
arts would liberate, not enslave. All industry would contain an element
of fine art, as all fine art inevitably has an element of industry. "There
then would need be no division of mankind into mechanical blind
workers and half-demented poets, and no separation of useful from fine
art, such as people make who have understood neither the nature nor
the ultimate reward of human action. All arts would be practical together and merged in the art of life, the only one wholly useful or fine
among them." [*Ibid.*, p. 215.]

This would mean a laudable diffusion of art, with no further confinement to dead and unproductive objects called works of art, or abstract
monuments to lost intuitions. It would rid the world of museums in
which fossils remain. In such a world there would be an uninterrupted
flow of music and ornaments, furnished by its citizens in the same
modest and cheerful way they furnish other commodities. Every craft
would have its dignity. There would be no arts separated from the
context of things, no narcotics or stimulants to sweeten the evils experienced at home, or to liberate a part of the mind while leaving the rest in
slavery. In direct paraphrase of Emerson, he pronounced the only precious materials to be flesh and blood and condemned abstract words and
marble as cheap materials. If fine art could be knitted to other functions,
it would beautify and render things more useful, allowing imagination to
see things in their fullest truth. The one human imaginative undertaking
that came closest to this goal, to an art encompassing and unifying all

areas of life, was religion. In recognizing this, Santayana was neither the least nor last Puritan, but the best.

RELIGION

Always fascinated with religion, Santayana finally pulled all the threads of his life into a religious synthesis. Until the end of his Harvard period, his religious interest was more that of a scholar and sympathetic critic. He was outside, with only vague yearnings to be somehow a part of Catholicism. Later, with his professed moral disintoxication, his turning from the world, he spoke as a religious seer vainly trying to communicate the reality of his own redemption.

All Santayana's views on religion departed from a rigorous and militant atheism, just as his epistemology built on a complete skepticism, his value system on complete hedonism, his metaphysics on an avowed materialism. He rejected all "superstitions"—any personal creator, cosmic purpose, unembodied spirits, immortality, or divine revelation. He believed this iconoclasm necessary for a purified religion of piety and spirituality, built on nature as it is and on the hard rock of truth. Reared as a nominal Catholic, he apparently rejected any literal belief in Catholic doctrines while a boy, but not without some guilt and regret. Later he had the task of rediscovering the origins of the mythical gods, which always remain haunting ghosts for religiously reared naturalists. Catholic piety he translated into natural meanings; Catholic imagery into poetry; Catholic eschatology into purified spirituality. He saw the foolishness of much Church doctrine, the inhumanity of much of its practice, yet always loved the idealism, freedom, and imagination of religious myth.

Santayana, the atheist and materialist, used much of his early writing to defend the legitimacy of religion and the relevancy of myth. The superstition present in Western religion, the mistaken ascription of material efficacy to ideals, never seemed to him the central motif of religion. At best, the foolish cosmology was taken metaphorically. It was only an error in science and correctable by science. Behind the myth, behind the nonliteral poetry of the Christian epic there was a sublime moral truth, a recognition of the good attainable, of the value and purpose of life. His ire, therefore, rarely fell on the superstition of believers (a pardonable error of fact), but on the enemies of religion (an unpardonable error of value). Those who followed his parents in a flimsy criticism of religion were despising truth and all sublimity, perhaps in behalf of ambition and the worship of material comfort. He decried religious fanaticism, but attributed this to political rather than truly religious motives. The same was true of the fanatical hatred of religion by shallow naturalists. A true materialist had to be sensitive to the human plight and to what man most loves. He will love, not hate religion. He too recognizes the Powers on which his destiny depends, and, although he may use less poetic terms, tries to live in devout harmony with them. Various historical religions are then perceived as imaginative echoes of things material and moral. In fact, with their vast poetic renderings of experience, traditional religions are the most beautiful products of human art.

In endlessly dissecting the themes of piety and spirituality, Santayana rejected the deviant extremes on both sides. A superficial spirituality, a mad apotheosis of consciousness, breaks free from its source in nature and assumes it own omnipotence. But piety alone, without the moral leaven of spirit, tends toward a natural religion in which forces and events are its sole object of reverence and ideals are ignored. This is the positivistic fate of Protestantism: the reduction of myth to fact, salvation to prosperity, eternity to survival, God to nature, divine commandments to discoverable conditions of well-being, divine omniscience to the practical truth of things, and divine love to human friendliness. In his early reaction to idealism, Santayana almost assumed this very position, but found it terribly inadequate. It was death to spirit, a religion of the irreligious, although an inevitable but barren alternative to the mad egotism of German idealism. Piety should foster the life of the spirit, not inhibit it. It should liberate, not enslave. An acceptance of the world does not mean subjection to it or undue love of it. His own conversion and redemption, in his terms, was an attainment of spiritual insight and peace in the very midst of a cruel world. Spirituality was Santayana's ultimate term and one that drove him toward a one-sided emphasis, but, he hoped, without impiety.

Spirit was Santayana's favorite term for consciousness, or for the pure light of awareness in man. As an atheist he certainly never believed in disembodied spirit. Spirit exists only when an animal psyche attains awareness. When conscious, every person is a spirit. But this spirit in man normally lives in captivity. A product of the psyche, it can scarce break free from psychic entanglements, such as the inclusive will to live. It must suffer undeservingly, and possibly use its suffering as a means to insight and eventual detachment, which is redemptive. Sin is this cosmic affliction of Spirit, not the transgression of some code.

Spirit, as a further extension of the psyche, a fuller organization in life, brings the risk of confusion and disaster. So far, consciousness has brought man domination over matter, but at the price of terrible inner conflict. The soul of man is the most distracted in the animal world. Against its own nature, the spirit joins the psyche in its local career, and both furthers and complicates it in its simple aims. It destroys all vegetative peace and cannot achieve spiritual peace in its captivity. Thus, spirit is born of woman, becomes incarnate in the flesh, but is never at home in the world, a world that, at best, wants a helpful slave and not some detached and contemplative vision. The spirit has its own kingdom not of this world. It loves truth for truth's sake, essence for essence's sake. It desires only ideal possessions and perfect love and understanding of all things. For the psyche, with its particular goals and commitments, its animal needs and cravings, its inevitable frustrations and enmities, this spiritual kingdom is irrelevant and unsought. But for an emancipated spirit, living in perfect charity, the psychic commitments are bothersome distractions.

Santayana carefully elaborated the distractions that beset spirit in its quest for freedom. The flesh, the world, and the devil each make their claim. The innocent claims of flesh are least bothersome. From the viewpoint of spirit, conventional morality is meaningless, for it is rooted in respect for life, for psychic goals, and not in respect for spiritual freedom. The sensual man only violates these worldly codes. He may be a criminal, callously but innocently abusing other people in behalf of his passions, but at the same time he may have the detached spirit of a saint. In such simple sensuality the psyche and the world move in perfect harmony, without care or anxiety. This is a cruelly brief taste of spiritual detachment. The kingdom of heaven opens to the vilest sinner.

The claims of the world are more serious. Not that Santayana wanted to go back to animality; rather, he wanted to overcome worldly distractions by understanding their tragic and comic character. As the Preacher, he found wisdom in the realization of life's vanity as experience and its richness as truth. The adornments of material existence may be enjoyed along the way, but they usually set up artificial wants and compulsions and lead to a hard slavery to labor, war, politics, morality, or even an imposed religion. Worldly concerns misplace our spiritual affinities, although spirit will still soar free in odd but temporary moments of sensual transport, heroic self-forgetfulness, philosophic or scientific detachment, or most often in the free labor that is art.

There is still the devil, or old Lucifer. He is the worst rebel, a spiritual transgressor. For the spirit may lose all piety and claim domination over fact and circumstance. In this fatal egotism (our original sin) the spirit tries to give orders to the universe, indulges in magic and in vain prayers, and turns religion into a pseudo-mechanical art. A vain and mad idealist is worse than a sadist. Pride is the worst sin. Spiritual pride leads to vain efforts at domination and distracts spirit from its true aim of contemplation and disinterested truth. Spirit has to transform its natural piety, not abolish it. Spirit is of the image of Christ, not the Devil. It is divine, but born in swaddling clothes, helpless and despised, and fated to suffer in all who suffer and rejoice in all who rejoice.

Santayana's celebration of spiritualism accompanied his despair of the world. Instead of death, he sought a type of release through renunciation. Existence seemed, on better acquaintance, and after all illusion was banished, to be a constant torment, with a thousand passions and desires. The world was mortal, tormented, confused, and forever deluded. Although the world was also an occasional source of beauty, love, and laughter, in whose odd moments man has a fleeting sense of peace, he has no permanent peace. Any real peace has to transcend the war and suffering endemic to existence rather than try to remove them. He lost all faith in what he called the Protestant illusion—that the world can be washed white and clean and set up as respectable. Instead, it was a place of exile, and of possible deliverance. The distractions and trivialities of Santayana's life became more oppressive with age, even as he lost most of the assurance that had bolstered his own moral but pathetic preferences. His own dearest commitments of youth now seemed like flowers in the field, blooming today but withering tomorrow. A stranger in the world, impartial in interests, but caught up in a world of trouble not his own, Santayana yearned for salvation. The vale of tears, when honestly confronted, was the crucifixion needed for deliverance. Then the failure of his own overexact hopes would not prevent his spirit from turning "the passing virtues and sorrows of nature into glimpses of eternal truth." [*Persons and Places,* III, *My Host the World* (New York, 1953), p. 144.]

Santayana's metaphorical celebration of spirituality drew from both Christian and Indian sources. He described something close to nirvana, but preferred to clothe it in his own version of Christian truth. For worldly men, spiritual fulfillment could only seem a form of madness, or what William James described as sick-mindedness. But it was a joyful madness. In moments of pure intuition, of undistracted contemplation of essences, the whole vain world became as nothing. Truth, beauty, and the good all exist in this world of Being, of eternal essences. Here all desires are forgotten. Belief, expectation, and hope are transcended. There is no will left, but only compassion, charity, and full understanding. In perfect peace, all moralities, all politics, all concern with scientific truth, all passions, even all art seem as naught. Care, the old devil of Boston, of Protestantism, of America, is finally replaced by a soothing peace that approaches the peace of death. Spirit has no causes to further, no wishes to fulfill, no hopes to be achieved. In contemplative beatitude, it does not castigate or deny anything, but sees everything in truth and with compassion. Only a psyche raises essences into obsessions. Evil, a function of special wills which inevitably face some frustration, is replaced by a complete and equal charity to all wills and to every aspiration. Death has no sting, for life has no ultimate value. Spirit dwells with eternal qualities; it is reborn continuously, in each person and in each new person.

Santayana paralleled this conception of spirituality with Christ, a truly spiritual man. Jesus came into the world (not, as an egotistic idealist, by creating his world) and acknowledged his Father (matter) in prayerful submission to his (or its) will, but held these bonds to be as nothing. He was detached from family, religion, and race. He had a detached charity for the world, but he had no involvement in or care for it. His spirit (the Holy Spirit) was uncontaminated by the world, yet was humble and willing to suffer for it. Toward worldly suffering Jesus was merciful, seeing that no suffering is deserved and that all sins are forgiven. The cross symbolized the liberation of spirit from psyche. In Christ's postmortal sojourn, he illustrated the final joy of liberation, the upward rise into heaven possible for spirit at any moment.

At rare moments of spiritual peace, man attains a type of union and loses himself in Being. Understanding completes itself and weaves all into a many-colored garment. In a single complex essence, all life is summed up in a single image of the Good. Spirit, in transport, flees to essence and truth, leaving the body behind, which possibly breaks out into irrelevant action. In this full and perfect intuition, every earthly evil is transformed into an aspect of the good, and is thus purified. Even spirit in ideal becomes one with essence and thus loses all separate identity. Resignation is complete. Prayer is then the only possible attitude—prayer not as petition but as confession, reflection, contemplation. "Then to the spirit that has renounced all things, all things are restored: and having renounced itself also, it cannot resist any inspiration or think evil of any good, but embraces them all in the external object of its worship, not as they may have existed in the world in passing and in conflict, but as they lie ideally reconciled in the bosom of the Good, at peace at last with themselves and with one another." [*Realms of Being,* IV, *Spirit,* Combined Edition (New York, 1942), p. 825.]

How does an ordinary, entrapped, passionate mortal attain such renunciation? Santayana had no handbook. He found anything that reduced the pressure of circumstances an aid. Christianity could be either a worldly care or such a screening device. At least it often seemed to create the necessary ache for salvation, or possibly reflect it. He believed intelligent persons more likely to be spiritually inclined, more likely to use a force of intellect to reduce experience to its pure essence. Oliver Alden, *The Last Puritan,* was unable to take the last step, and, a Christlike figure, suffered the world as a tragic misfit. Ultimately, Santayana believed that spiritual people are born. No work or circumstances avails spirituality. It is a gift, a special grace, even though it flowers only after long discipline or a Puritan-like weaning of the affections. Odd moments or spiritual peace are present to everyone, beginning with the laughing child. But only in rare individuals, in mystics and saints, does it become a secure gift. Certainly it is not something worked for or sought, for it then becomes infected with passion and care and is thereby counterfeit. The type of morality present in the world, with its codes and rules and prohibitions and admonitions, is the very antithesis of spirituality. Moral men, like the Pharisees, may never enter the kingdom of heaven. Sinners may.

How serious or complete was Santayana's rhapsodic apotheosis of spiritual peace? No one can say for sure. For over thirty years he gave his highest praise to a type of escape from worldly cares. Yet, he occasionally insisted that he remained a rational animal and backed this up by a continued involvement in what could only be called psychic interests. His seemed more the fate of Oliver—born with a spiritual nature but forever cursed with a worldly conscience. Perhaps a Puritan could never become a saint. Thus, he suggested that his spiritual interests only supplemented his life of reason, somewhat as a moral holiday, or as necessary moments of esthetic appreciation. He thus only selectively emphasized immediate appreciation, or the free and spontaneous value present in experience, and tried to give a detailed and dramatic account of this value at its experiential best. He thereby eulogized the moral sanction for life and showed the foolishness of care for care's sake, or of morality for morality's sake. Morality is not the end of life, but at best a means, at least when morality is conceived as a type of discipline. In Puritan thought from Edwards to Dewey there was always a recognition of a type of beatitude, of experiential exaltation that redeemed all struggle and care and redeemed it in the present and not in a far-off future Zion.

Even in his most soaring flights, Santayana insisted upon his naturalism. Spirit is a part of natural life, and even when it attains beatitude is still reflecting a destiny determined in the realm of matter. Spirit, as spirit, is no reformer, but a reformed world would help liberate spirit. In this sense, he always desired a rational society. But he did not expect it. Spiritual men continue to live in the world and perform their natural functions. They do it, like some Stoics, without passion or vital concern. The world goes on, scarcely aware of its saints. In certain political orders, such saints may be adjudged dangerous and be justifiably exiled. The saint does not suffer. If concern for the world could not be forgotten at times of spiritual peace, then there could be no peace, and all would be anxiety and distraction. Santayana would not wager his salvation on a better world tomorrow. Neither will any sane person. But unlike the Puritan, he did not see these spiritual moments as vistas on the rocky road to Zion, but as secluded nooks which awaited those who, like himself, found the tortuous road headed toward illusion. Here, in reflection, poetry, and prayer he watched the busy pilgrims on their vain journey, and in deepest compassion wished they too could stop and see that heaven was all around if they only had the eyes to see and the spirit to comprehend.

This disillusion, this moral disintoxication, left no leverage for political judgment. Empires rose and fell, nations rushed toward annihilation, injustices multiplied, and Santayana only seemed to smile at the chaos. He had no word of encouragement, only pessimistic words of consolation, for those who were still striving to make the world more sane, to follow his own earlier life of reason. In the engaged 1930's, in the crusade of the 1940's, his fellow philosophers believed that Santayana had betrayed them. He abandoned moral idealism, sought refuge in abstract essences, minimized the work of busy scientists, and took no responsibility for the world's manifest and, to them, eradicable evils. Surely his escape, his postrational detour, was the epitome of selfishness. When the world needed a higher courage, he took the easy way out. Instead of universal sympathy, the world needed philosophic guidance. Santayana only offered a contemplative narcotic. But, he vainly insisted, his critics could not understand, for they had not tasted the dregs, had not suffered the crucifixion of reason and the loss of hope. They awaited his disillusionment. Then they would understand his salvation.

In Puritan Boston Santayana learned well. He absorbed and critically accepted a Puritan piety, with its hardened reasonableness and humaneness. He also learned of its rapturous but disciplined spirituality. He rejected its abuses—its hypocrisy, self-righteousness, and superficial worldliness. These he excoriated and half-believed to be the essence of Americanism. But at first he fought back in Puritan terms, in the vein of the greatest Puritan intellects, such as Edwards and Emerson. He was unable to prevail or to maintain the struggle, a desperate and seemingly hopeless struggle at the turn of the century. The perversions of Puritanism were too much in the saddle. He did not let his frustration destroy him. Without consuming bitterness or ultimate despair, he resigned himself to a mad world and sought inner consolation; he sought the wisdom of age and disillusionment, of dying civilizations, of primitive Christianity. In a kingdom not of this world, he found peace. As a young man he weeped for the world. As an old man he laughed at it and thus endured it. A sensitive Spanish lad, imprisoned in a cold home in a cold and alien city could surely be excused his belated laughter. It contained more sanity than the thoughtless cheers of those who still applauded a society in which there was no end of caring, and which spread a veil of false sanctity around all its meaningless weeping.

A READING GUIDE

The preceding essays are only introductions. They involve highly compact summaries of often very intricate and complex world views. But by briefly presenting the total beliefs and interests of each individual, and by placing each in a larger intellectual tradition, I have tried to provide a reader with a sympathetic overview, without oversimplification, and with as little sacrifice of scope and depth as possible in a limited space. The essays are in no case a substitute for the original writings from which they were abstracted. I hope that these essays will inspire reading in the sources and that they will provide even beginning students with the over-all understanding so necessary for an immediate enjoyment and full understanding of specialized books and articles.

The following recommendations are based on my own experience. They may help some students get maximum benefit from limited reading programs. In most cases, I will ignore secondary materials. If these essays have served their purpose, the student is prepared for the originals. Also, I am not presenting full bibliographies. Relatively complete bibliographies have already been prepared and published for Edwards, Emerson, Peirce, James, Dewey, and Santayana. Elaborate editions of the complete works of Edwards, Franklin, and Adams are underway. Guidance, not lists, is most needed.

I. The Puritans

There is a vast literature on Puritanism, but few sources are easily acquired. The most important ideological backdrop is John Calvin's *Institutes of the Christian Religion,* ed. by John T. McNeill (Philadelphia: Westminister Press, 1960), 2 vols. There are also several anthologies of Calvin's writings. The best collection of American Puritan literature is Perry Miller and Thomas H. Johnson, *The Puritans, a Sourcebook of Their Writings,* rev. ed. (New York: Harper and Row, 1963). An excellent source on Puritan political thought is Edmund S. Morgan's *Puritan Political Ideas* (Indianapolis: Bobbs-Merrill, 1965).

On the vast subject of Puritanism in America, the student should read some secondary material. No aspect of our past has been so thoroughly explored; none has bequeathed such difficult questions of interpretation. I believe that almost all Puritan historiography until the late nineteenth century was distorted by a false evangelical glow or by misleading national myths. The reaction went too far the other way. From 1890 into the New Deal period, our view of the Puritans was warped by a self-conscious rebellion against Victorian repressions, against Protestant orthodoxy, and against an economic system that, on superficial examination, seemed rooted in Puritan thought. Thus, the contemporary student should start his secondary reading with Perry Miller, our greatest Puritan scholar and the one person most responsible for a fresh and sympathetic re-evaluation of our Puritan heritage.

Miller's masterpiece is *The New England Mind* [I. *The Seventeenth Century* (Cambridge: Harvard University Press, 1939) and II. *From Colony to Province* (Cambridge: Harvard University Press, 1953)]. But this work is involved, subtle, and often technical. Many students will prefer his *Orthodoxy in Massachusetts* (Cambridge: Harvard University Press, 1933) or *Errand into the Wilderness* (Cambridge: Harvard University Press, 1956). Our greatest living Puritan scholar, Edmund S. Morgan, is more direct, more sympathetic, and more readable than Miller. His key books are *The Puritan Family* (Boston: Trustees of the Public Library, 1944), *Puritan Dilemma* (Boston: Little, Brown and Co., 1958), and *Visible Saints, the History of a Puritan Idea* (New York: New York University Press, 1963). Too often the Puritans are viewed as complete ideologues. As a perfect corrective, read Sumner Chilton Powell's delightful classic, *Puritan Village; the Formation of a New England Town* (Middletown, Connecticut: Wesleyan University Press, 1963).

II. Jonathan Edwards

The best works of Edwards are all available in modern editions. I recommend, far above all others, his small but beautiful little book, *The Nature of True Virtue* (Ann Arbor: University of Michigan Press, 1960). This little volume combines his youthful metaphysics and his ever pervasive Christian commitment. It elaborates his Neoplatonic estheticism, is an excellent prelude to transcendentalism, and expresses themes prevalent all the way to Santayana.

The two completed volumes in a strangely laggard series, *Jonathan Edwards, His Works* [I. *Freedom of the Will,* ed. by Paul Ramsey (New Haven: Yale University Press, 1957), and II. *Religious Affections,* ed. by John E. Smith (New Haven: Yale University Press, 1959)], represent Edward's two most influential books. The polemical *Freedom of the Will* reflected his most compelling logical defense of moral determinism and human responsibility. The *Religious Affections* was a manual of devotion, a defense of the Great Awakening, and a definition of affectionate and experiential religion. For those who want to read further, Edward's pure philosophy is best illustrated in *The Mind*, as reconstructed by Leon Howard (Berkeley: University of California Press, 1963) and in *Jonathan Edwards from His Private Notebooks*, ed. by Harvey G. Townsend (Eugene, Oregon: University of Oregon Press, 1955). Two competent anthologies provide samples of his sermons, his early accounts of the Great Awakening, and his work on original sin: *Representative Selections*, ed. by Clarence H. Faust and Thomas H. Johnson (New York: American Book Co., 1935), and *Puritan Sage; Collected Writings of Jonathan Edwards*, ed. by Vergilius Ferm (New York: Library Publishers, 1953).

III. Benjamin Franklin

Benjamin Franklin never completed a single book. His famous *Autobiography* (in numerous paperback editions) was compiled after his death. His book on electricity [see *Benjamin Franklin's Experiments*, a new edition of Franklin's *Experiments and Observations on Electricity*, ed. by I. Bernard Cohen (Cambridge: Harvard University Press, 1941)] was compiled from his letters to English friends. His numerous letters, essays, jokes, and almanacs have been variously mined for anthologies on subjects as varying as chess, masonry, politics, and wit.

But I very much recommend selective reading in the almost perfect new edition of the *Papers of Benjamin Franklin*, ed. by Leonard W. Labaree and Whitfield J. Bell (New Haven: Yale University Press, 1959–   ). As I write, only ten volumes have been published, but these early volumes contain *Poor Richard*, almost all the important scientific papers, and many of his most revealing letters. For his later career, the best available source is still an older, selective ten-volume edition of *The Writings of Benjamin Franklin*, ed. by Albert H. Smyth (New York: Macmillan Co., 1907). There is a plethora of secondary material. Do not be tempted. Read Franklin.

IV. John Adams

For John Adams I recommend above all else the brief anthology: *The Political Writings of John Adams, Representative Selections*, ed. by George A. Peek, Jr. (Indianapolis: Bobbs-Merrill Co., 1954). It includes much of Adams' own contribution to his long, largely quoted three-volume *Defense of the Constitutions of the United States of America* and his shorter *Discources on Davila*. These, in all their original redundancy, plus most of his correspondence, diary, and public papers, are available in the twelve-volume, all too carefully selected *The Works of John Adams*, ed. by Charles Francis Adams (Boston: Little, Brown and Co., 1850–56). One of the most stimulating correspondences of all times is faithfully recorded in Lester J. Cappon's two-volume edition of the *Adams-Jefferson Letters* (Chapel Hill, North Carolina: University of North Carolina Press, 1959). Finally, the early returns from one of the great publishing ventures of all time, *The Adams Papers*, under the editorial supervision of Charles H. Butterfield (Cambridge:

Harvard University Press, 1961–   ), already provide definitive editions of Adams' early diary, autobiography, legal papers, and correspondence.

V. Ralph Waldo Emerson

Almost no one can profitably read all of Emerson's major writings, nor should they try. He has to be tasted in small bits, chewed over, and finally digested. Possibly students should read selected essays and poems and even sample his *Journals* and *Letters*. Fortunately, there are innumerable anthologies. I prefer the selection and balance of *Selections from Ralph Waldo Emerson,* ed. by Stephen E. Whicher (New York: Houghton Mifflin Co., 1963).

All his major essays and poems are contained in *Emerson's Complete Works,* Riverside Edition (Boston: Houghton Mifflin Co., 1889–90). The older, ten-volume edition of the *Journals of Ralph Waldo Emerson,* ed. by Edward W. Emerson and Waldo E. Forbes (Boston: Houghton Mifflin Co., 1909–14), is being superseded by the *Journals and Miscellaneous Notebooks,* ed. by William H. Gilman *et al.* (Cambridge: Harvard University Press, 1960–   ). *The Letters of Ralph Waldo Emerson* are excellently edited by Ralph L. Rust (New York: Columbia University Press, 1939), 6 vols.

VI. Charles S. Peirce

Pierce is a problem for all but technical philosophers. *The Collected Papers of Charles Sanders Peirce,* ed. by Charles Hartshorne, Paul Weiss, and Arthur Burks (Cambridge: Harvard University Press, 1958–60), 8 vols., is the one main source. But the *Papers* are organized around quite arbitrary topics and are totally lacking in any sense of chronological development. The beginning student has to seek elsewhere. He has no alternative save anthologies. The most balanced is the *Philosophical Writings of Peirce,* ed. by Justus Buchler (New York: Dover Publications, 1955). There are also three more selective anthologies: *Values in a Universe of Chance; Selected Writings of Charles S. Peirce,* ed. by Philip Wiener (Garden City: Doubleday, 1958); *Chance, Love, and Logic; Philosophical Essays by the late Charles S. Peirce,* ed. by Morris R. Cohen (New York: Harcourt, Brace and Co., 1923); and *Essays in the Philosophy of Science,* ed. by Vincent Tomas (New York: Liberal Arts Press, 1957).

More than any other major American philosopher, the life of Peirce is hidden from the lay reader. There have been no full biographies, nor even very helpful intellectual portraits. Thus, of greatest assistance to me, was Joseph Lancaster Brent, III's unpublished Ph.D. dissertation, "A Study of the Life of Charles Sanders Peirce" (University of California at Los Angeles, May 1960).

VII. William James

Every student should read James's great masterpiece, *The Principles of Psychology* (New York: Henry Holt and Co., 1890), 2 vols., or at least the abridged *Psychology: The Briefer Course* (New York: Henry Holt and Co., 1892). Next to this I recommend the part biography, part published sources that make up Ralph Barton Perry's *The Thought and Character of William James* (Boston: Little, Brown and Co., 1935–36), 2 vols.

Today James is best known for an unending series of philosophical essays, some delivered as lectures and all published in the following books: *The Will to Believe, and Other Essays in Popular Philosophy* (New York: Longmans, Green and Co., 1897), *The Varieties of Religious Experience* (New York: Longmans, Green and Co., 1902), *Pragmatism* (New York: Longmans, Green and Co., 1907), *The Meaning of Truth* (New York: Longmans, Green and Co., 1909), and *A Pluralistic Universe* (New York: Longmans, Green and Co., 1909). Ralph Barton Perry published a group of more technical and influential essays just after James's death. These *Essays in Radical Empiricism* (New York: Longmans, Green and Co., 1912) were not composed for popular audiences. The best of all these essays have been variously combined in three anthologies.

In addition to these major works, some curious students will want to sample James's work in psychic phenomena and can do so in *William James on Psychical Research,* ed. by Gardner Murphy and Robert O. Ballou (New York: The Viking Press, 1960). Some of James's latest and most cautious beliefs illuminated an uncompleted textbook, *Some Problems of Philosophy* (New York: Longmans, Green and Co., 1911). Nice tidbits appear in *Collected Essays and Reviews,* ed. by Ralph B. Perry (New York: Longmans, Green and Co., 1920), and *Memories and Studies* (New York: Longmans, Green and Co., 1911).

VIII. John Dewey

Dewey awes everyone with the sheer volume of his writing and often with the awkwardness and imprecision of his style. He published over twenty-five important books, many minor ones, and hundreds of articles. Personally, I believe a student can get a fairly comprehensive account of his total philosophy by reading what I believe to be his five greatest books: *The Quest for Certainty* (New York: Mouton, Balch and Co., 1929) presents the vast historical and anthropological backdrop; *Experience and Nature* (Chicago: Open Court, 1925) contains his most lofty metaphysical insights and includes the most comprehensive overview of his mature system; *Democracy and Education* (New York: Macmillan Co., 1916) is a preface to his whole philosophy and presents his most influential views on education; *Logic: The Theory of Inquiry* (New York: Henry Holt and Co., 1938) summarizes his best thought on epistemology and methodology; *Art as Experience* (New York: Mouton, Balch and Co., 1934) illustrates his value theory and demonstrates the esthetic climax of his whole philosophy.

Beyond these foundational books, any guide tends to degenerate into mere listing. But a warning is in order. Two of Dewey's most popular books [*Reconstruction in Philosophy* (New York: Henry Holt and Co., 1937) and

A Common Faith (New Haven: Yale University Press, 1934)] easily mis-lead. Even more than his technical works, they need to be supplemented and supported by other books. In no case should they be read first.

At the near great level are *Human Nature and Conduct* (New York: Henry Holt and Co., 1922), which contains Dewey's best work in social psychology and moral theory, and *Philosophy and Civilization* (New York: Mouton, Balch and Co., 1931), which combines some of his best articles. Dewey's running commentary on politics and society climaxed in *Liberalism and Social Action* (New York: G. P. Putnam's Sons, 1935) and *Freedom and Culture* (New York: G. P. Putnam's Sons, 1939).

There are three anthologies of Dewey's thought. I prefer the brief but well-balanced *On Experience, Nature, and Freedom; Representative Selections,* ed. by Richard J. Blumstein (New York: Liberal Arts Press, 1960). The others are *The Philosophy of John Dewey,* ed. by Paul A. Schilpp (Evanston, Illinois: Northwestern University Press, 1939), and *Intelligence in the Modern World; John Dewey's Philosophy,* ed. by Joseph Ratner (New York: Modern Library, 1939). The only collection of letters is *John Dewey and Arthur Bentley; a Philosophic Correspondence, 1932–1951,* ed. by Sidney Ratner and Jules Altman (New Brunswick, New Jersey: Rutgers University Press, 1964).

IX. George Santayana

Santayana is much like Emerson. He must be savored rather than quickly consumed. Since he always combined autobiography and philosophy, his three-part memoirs, *Persons and Places* (New York: Charles Scribner's Sons, 1944–53), reveal very well his final philosophical stance. Complementing this is his delightful but treacherous novel, *The Last Puritan* (New York: Charles Scribner's Sons, 1936), which projects his own views onto several different characters. Even more intimate and personal are his *The Letters of George Santayana,* ed. by Daniel Cory (London: Constable, 1955).

Santayana wrote two philosophical masterpieces. His early five-volume *Life of Reason* (New York: Charles Scribner's Sons, 1903–6) climaxed his American and moralistic early years and remains his most eloquent and coherent philosophical contribution. His later, more detached and spiritual stance was celebrated in his four-volume *Realms of Being* (New York: Charles Scribner's Sons, 1927–40), which was introduced by his epistemo-logical classic, *Skepticism and Animal Faith* (New York: Charles Scribner's Sons, 1923). These difficult books are supported by his delightful *Dialogues in Limbo* (New York: Charles Scribner's Sons, 1926 and 1948), *Platonism and the Spiritual Life* (New York: Charles Scribner's Sons, 1927), and *The Idea of Christ in the Gospels* (New York: Charles Scribner's Sons, 1946).

Santayana mixed a bit of social criticism in all his books. His belated commentary on America and Americans, *Character and Opinion in the United States* (London: Constable, 1920), and his earlier *Winds of Doctrine* (New York: Charles Scribner's Sons, 1913) were largely critical. His confused and difficult political treatise, *Dominations and Powers: Reflections on Liberty, Society and Government* (New York: Charles Scribner's Sons, 1951), reflected ideas from three decades. Since almost everything he wrote had an esthetic flavor, his earliest book, *Sense of Beauty* (New York: Charles Scribner's Sons, 1896), is today largely biographical in significance. His later estheticism dominates in *Obiter Scripta* (New York: Charles Scribner's Sons, 1936).

Out of all this, what should a student read? Actually, almost anything. There is a flavor, a syndrome of attitudes, that characterizes all that Santayana wrote. These outweigh specific doctrines. For an excellent sample, I recommend *The Philosophy of Santayana,* ed. by Irwin Edman (New York: Charles Scribner's Sons, 1953).

INDEX

First Class
Permit No. 122
Bloomington, Ind.

BUSINESS REPLY MAIL
No Postage Stamp Necessary If Mailed In The United States

POSTAGE WILL BE PAID BY

INDIANA UNIVERSITY PRESS
TENTH & MORTON STREETS
BLOOMINGTON, INDIANA 47401

ATT: R. GRANICH

INDIANA UNIVERSITY PRESS

TITLE: _____ AUTHOR: _____

Comments: ☐ You May Quote Me.

I Plan To: ☐ Adopt This Book, ☐ Recommend This Book, ☐ Not Applicable For My Course.

COURSE: _____ PROBABLE ENROLLMENT: _____

TEXT NOW USED: _____

Name _____ Dept. _____ Office Phone No. _____

School _____ Address _____

City _____ State _____ Zip _____